HOPE
&
GLORY

For Fancy, Jeff and Alexa. –

Kathryn – Greenthal
May 17, 2001

HOPE

& GLORY

ESSAYS ON THE LEGACY OF THE FIFTY-FOURTH MASSACHUSETTS REGIMENT

Edited by

MARTIN H. BLATT,
THOMAS J. BROWN, AND
DONALD YACOVONE

University of Massachusetts Press
AMHERST
in association with
Massachusetts Historical Society
BOSTON

Designed by Dennis Anderson
Set in Trump Mediaevel by Graphic Composition, Inc.
Printed and bound by Sheridan Books, Inc.

This book is published with the support and cooperation of the Massachusetts
Historical Society and the University of Massachusetts Boston.

Library of Congress Cataloging-in-Publication Data

Hope & Glory : essays on the legacy of the Fifty-fourth Massachusetts Regiment /
edited by Martin H. Blatt, Thomas J.Brown,and Donald Yacovone.
    p. cm.
Includes bibliographical references and index.
ISBN 1-55849-277-1 (cloth : alk. paper)
    1. United States.Army.Massachusetts Infantry Regiment, 54th (1863–1865)—
Influence.   2. United States—History—Civil War, 1861–1865—Participation,
Afro-American.   3. United States —History —Civil War,1861–1865—Regimental
histories.   4. Massachusetts—History War, 1861–1865—Regimental
histories.   5. Afro-American soldiers—Massachusetts—History—19th century.
6. United States —Civilization —Afro-American influences.   7. Memory—Social
aspects—United States.   I. Blatt, Martin Henry, 1951– II. Brown, Thomas J.
III.Yacovone, Donald.
E 513.5 54th .H 66 2001
973.7´444—dc21   00-042312

British Library Catologuing in Publication data are available.

Frontispiece:Augustus Saint-Gaudens and Charles F.McKim,The Shaw Memorial,
1897, Boston Common. Courtesy Library of Congress.
Foreword frontispiece:General Colin L. Powell delivering the keynote address
at the Centennial Celebration of the Augustus Saint-Gaudens Monument to
Robert Gould Shaw and the Fifty-fourth Massachusetts Regiment, May 31, 1997.
Courtesy National Park Service.

For

Emma Zula Munson Blatt,

Rosa Jean Munson Blatt,

the memory of Jean Blatt Flores,

Lucian and Veronica Brown,

Natasha Nicole Mary Logan Burke Yacovone

I know not, Mr. Commander, where in all human history, to any given thousand men in arms there has been committed a work at once so proud, so precious, so full of hope and glory as the work committed to you.

GOVERNOR JOHN A. ANDREW

CONTENTS

ILLUSTRATIONS

FOREWORD

Hope and Glory: The Monument to Colonel Robert Gould
Shaw and the Fifty-fourth Massachusetts Regiment

I DOUBT THAT bronze has ever spoken more eloquently than in this celebrated work by Augustus Saint-Gaudens. What a powerful image—the proud, young, fatalistic Colonel Robert Gould Shaw and his black soldiers, heads high, rifles on their shoulders, resolution in their every step, marching southward with fortitude, looking just as they did when they marched past the site of this statue on May 28, 1863, on their way to hope, on their way to glory, and for many of them, on their way to death.

To more than one of the thousands of onlookers on that fateful day, Colonel Shaw appeared as an avenging angel, a being who was at once beautiful and terrible, sent from God to lead the oppressed to freedom. It was an occasion of apocalyptic imagery worthy to be forever remembered in bronze. And we give thanks to the artistry of Saint-Gaudens, which has well stood the test of time. But to understand this memorial and to understand the events of 1863 that it captures, we must put them in perspective. And to find that perspective we must go back to an earlier time.

We must go back to the birth of our nation in 1776, the birth proclaimed by a ringing Declaration of Independence that said, "We hold these truths to be self-evident, that all men are created equal, that they are endowed by their Creator with certain unalienable Rights, that among these, are Life, Liberty, and the pursuit of Happiness." Some of my friends often forget that the Declaration of Independence also says that governments are instituted to secure these God-given rights. At that time it was just as self-evident that these God-given rights intended to be secured by government were being withheld from black Americans.

The institution of slavery justified the tragic denial of these God-given rights by treating slaves—black men and women—as property, not as human beings. Black slaves were seen to be the tools of their owners to be used as the owners saw fit. And, of course, tools did not need education; tools did not own property or vote; they did not need religion or a culture or a history. They did not even need their own names. They did not need pride or ambition or aspirations. They did not need families, it was thought, and they had no more right to their own children than had any other domestic animal to its offspring. The true horror and mortal sin of slavery lay in this attempt to dehumanize and degrade a group of Americans who were defined by their color. Later, our Constitution condoned slavery but offered a ray of hope that somehow, someday, things would change. Somehow, someday, we could achieve a different kind of union, a union that would redeem for all Americans the original promise of the Declaration of Independence.

There was the hope that the fundamental contradiction between promise and reality would eventually be resolved. It was also clear, however, that equal rights were not going to be given to blacks—free or slave. Those rights had to be won. Blacks would have to prove that they were men and women and not property. They would have to prove that when they were given the opportunity they could be equal to their white fellow citizens. And in those days there was only one field of endeavor, only one place in this society where blacks could demonstrate their worthiness as full citizens of this country: that was as soldiers, by their willingness to shed the same color blood as their white brothers on the field of battle. It was a path that blacks had taken as early as 1652 in Massachusetts, when they served in the militia, though they eventually lost that right as well.[1] We all know the story of Crispus Attucks, who fell at the time of the Boston Massacre in 1770, and we cannot forget that six thousand blacks fought in the Revolutionary War to help secure our freedom and liberty.

Blacks fought and died again in the War of 1812, serving valiantly with Oliver H. Perry on Lake Erie and with Andrew Jackson at the Battle of New Orleans. Yet each time the country called on black Americans to bear arms, they served a nation that would not serve them. And each time they did, it became harder and harder for the nation to assert that blacks were somehow less equal, less capable than their white fellow citizens. Ultimately, the horrible inconsistencies between the promises of the Declaration of Independence and the Constitution and the reality of life for millions of black Americans led us to the Civil War. Because the truth was that no nation so conceived in liberty as ours could long endure without ridding itself of the sin and crime and degradation of slavery.

So, in 1861 when Fort Sumter was fired on, black Americans again rushed to aid their country and pleaded to serve. They knew they had to fight to enjoy the fruits of a just victory that they knew would soon follow. President Abraham Lincoln initially rejected their demands, but in time the need to fill the Union ranks and the moral imperative to allow blacks to fight overcame the president's resistance. As the South's hopes for independence began to fade, Confederate president Jefferson Davis also came under pressure to use blacks as soldiers. Confederate general Howell Cobb wrote to President Davis and urged him not to recruit slaves. Yes, use all the Negroes you can get; use them for cooking, digging, and chopping. But don't arm them. Because, he warned Davis, if slaves can make good soldiers, if slaves can fight, if slaves can die alongside white men, if that is true, then our whole theory of slavery is wrong and the Confederacy is doomed.[2]

Frederick Douglass knew how right General Cobb was, so he kept pressing President Lincoln. "Once let the black man get upon his person the brass letters, U. S.," Douglass proclaimed, "let him get an eagle on his button and a musket on his shoulder and bullets in his pocket," let him stand tall and proud as soldiers of the nation, and when that happens, when that is allowed to happen, then "there is no power on the earth . . . which can deny that he has earned the right to citizenship in the United States."[3] The simple message was, give him the opportunity, the training, and the weapons, and watch him succeed.

It was in this spirit that the Fifty-fourth Regiment of Massachusetts Voluntary Infantry came to life. Free blacks from Massachusetts and from across the North raced to the sound of the drums. The ranks of the Fifty-fourth filled so quickly that a second Massachusetts black regiment—the Fifty-fifth—was formed, and the Fifth Massachusetts Cavalry after that. The Fifty-fourth was not the first of all the black regiments to be raised throughout the United States, but it was the first official regiment raised in the North. It was the cherished project of Massachusetts's abolitionist governor John A. Andrew and of Frederick Douglass, whose two sons joined the unit.[4]

The regiment was to be led by a young man of privilege, Robert Gould Shaw, who volunteered to leave a regiment of his own kind in order to lead this noble venture. Robert Gould Shaw believed in the cause, believed in his men, and insisted on the highest standards for them. He ensured that his men were properly outfitted and trained. He fought for equal pay and overall was decent and fair to the Americans who were entrusted to his command. It must have been quite a sight on that May day in 1863 when the fair-skinned Robert Shaw and his dark soldiers marched by the corner of Beacon and Park Streets in Boston, where the Saint-Gaudens monument stands today. As they marched by, they saluted their governor. No wonder that "angels of light" was the appellation given to them by the onlookers.

Seven weeks after they left Boston, Robert Gould Shaw would be dead, killed leading his soldiers into battle. On the evening of July 18, 1863, the Fifty-fourth led the assault against Battery Wagner outside of

Charleston, South Carolina. It was a bayonet assault across three-quarters of a mile of open beach. It was a race to death. Colonel Shaw knew it and his men knew it, and yet they surged forward with a courage we wish that all of us possessed. It was a race fueled by hope, with glory the prize. We can only guess what went through their minds as they fell like wheat before hail. Did Bob Shaw think of the young wife he had married just three months earlier? Did Lewis Douglass draw strength from thinking about his illustrious father? What were the others thinking as they charged into that terrible twilight of fire from which many would never return? We will never know what their thoughts were, and I do not think we can ever conceive of the horror that moment held for them.

The rebel fort was breached briefly but at a terrible cost. Hundreds of proud black men became casualties alongside Colonel Shaw and their other white officers. As a gesture of contempt, the Confederates tossed Shaw's body into a common grave "with the Negroes that fell with him."[5] They thought they were disgracing his memory, but instead, by so doing they covered him in glory everlasting. His father later insisted that his son's body not be exhumed. He said that there could be "no holier place" for his son to rest than with his fellow soldiers.[6]

The Fifty-fourth's colors never fell. Soldiers returned from the doomed assault bearing the flag that they believed in, and Sergeant William H. Carney, although severely wounded, carried that flag back. Sergeant Carney became the first black soldier to earn the new Congressional Medal of Honor.

Battery Wagner was not the first battle for black troops, and it certainly would not be the last. But it served as a gleaming example of their courage and their fortitude. It was a tremendous moral victory. Black troops had proved every bit the equal of their white brothers. They had earned in blood the blessings of liberty. Two more deadly years would pass before the war and slavery came to an end. The Reconstruction period that followed the Civil War brought hope to black Americans. Now that they had earned in blood the blessings of life, liberty, and the pursuit of happiness, that was what they would receive. Surely, *surely*, after what we had been through, equal opportunity and equal preparation would lead to equal performance and equal reward. Certainly, we had proved that skin color was not the measure of a man or a woman. But it was not to be.

Reconstruction came to an end as the political consensus for it collapsed. After the Civil War, we entered a new dark period of American history: the period of Jim Crow and segregation, poll taxes, repression, and the denial of justice. All of this was codified in a terrible doctrine known as "separate but equal," enshrined by the U.S. Supreme Court in *Plessy vs. Ferguson* in 1896 just as the Saint-Gaudens memorial was being completed.

And so the struggle continued. One hundred summers after Battery Wagner, Martin Luther King Jr. would stand in front of the Lincoln Memorial and give his famous "I Have a Dream" speech, praying for the day once again when the content of a person's character would be the sole measure of that person's worth. It was the same prayer that had inspired the soldiers of the Fifty-fourth Massachusetts. It is a prayer that still must inspire us today.

Despite the obstacles that are before us, remarkable progress has been made, of course, since 1863 and since 1963. In my profession, the profession of arms, the Fifty-fourth was followed by the Buffalo Soldiers and the Tuskegee Airmen. President Harry S. Truman desegregated the armed forces, and blacks rose in the ranks. I was privileged to become the first black person to be appointed chairman of the Joint Chiefs of Staff of the armed forces of the United States, but I was not the first one qualified. I was not the first person who had the potential. I was the first one who came along at a time when our nation's government secured our rights through affirmative action and equal opportunity so that I would be measured by performance and not by the color of my skin.

To my dying day, I will also never forget that I became chairman because there were men of the Fifty-fourth, Buffalo Soldiers, Tuskegee Airmen, and others who were willing to serve and shed their blood for this country. They served this country knowing full well that their country would not serve them. I am very proud to be an American. I love this country with a depth and a passion that has no limits, but I am just as proud to call myself a black American. I have to do this. I do this in order to be faithful to the legacy of those who went before me and to the history of those who suffered and did not have the opportunities that would be given to me. And I do it so that those who now come after me, the young men and women of America, black and white, who are now trying to serve in a new way, will understand the history and tradition that they are inheriting from us. There are so many more opportunities now than when I started out forty years ago as a black person entering the only integrated institution in America that would allow you to go all the way to the top. So many more opportunities are available now.

But we dare not believe that our work is done. There are still barriers to the dreams that the men of the Fifty-fourth marched for and died for. Let us not pretend otherwise; let us keep faith with them; let us keep faith with Colonel Shaw and all Americans who are dedicated to seeing that we become the perfect Union that God has destined for us.

The Saint-Gaudens memorial speaks to us of our past, speaks to us of our present, and reminds us of the continuing challenges that will face us in the future. A private in Company A of the Fifty-fourth, whose name is unknown, wrote a marching song that summed up the spirit of his regiment. It was not written by a professional songwriter or poet, just an average soldier, and like so many barracks-room ditties, it was ragged, it was cocky, it was irreverent, but it was heartfelt. Perhaps it was the song that the soldiers of the Fifty-fourth sang on that fateful evening in July of 1863. The little marching song ends like this:

> So rally, boys, rally, let us never mind the past,
> We had a hard road to travel but our day is coming fast,
> For God is for the right and we have no need to fear,
> The Union must be saved by the colored volunteer.[7]

That soldier believed in the Union. That soldier believed in America. The Union was saved by the "colored volunteer" and by hundreds of thousands of his white brothers, all of whom believed in freedom, all of whom came together to preserve a dream of hope and a dream of glory. That is the enduring message that this memorial has for us today. Be as proud of America as that soldier was. Believe in America as that soldier did.

When we look at this great memorial, we see soldiers looking to the front, marching solidly and straight ahead on a perpetual campaign for righteousness led by their brave colonel. So let us too follow these heroes. Let us carry on the work to make this God-given, beloved country of ours an even more perfect Union, a land of liberty and justice for all. And in our ongoing struggle we owe a great debt of gratitude to the artist Augustus Saint-Gaudens, to Colonel Robert Gould Shaw, and to the colored volunteers of the Fifty-fourth Massachusetts Regiment.

ACKNOWLEDGMENTS

T HE EDITORS have benefited enormously from the assistance of many people in the course of organizing and producing this book. Our greatest debt of gratitude is to the contributors. We have had the good fortune of working with an outstanding group of scholars dedicated to a common cause, and their hard work has made our efforts easier. We cannot thank them enough. Paul Wright, editor at the University of Massachusetts Press, lavished us with attention from the project's inception. He showed us all the patience one could ask for and offered all the wisdom that one might need in undertaking such a project. Without Paul it is hard to imagine how we would have completed this book.

We feel grateful to all the scholars and historical reenactors who, beginning in 1997, influenced us and helped shape the contents of this book. We also wish to thank Nina Silber, Ken Greenberg, Ed Linenthal, Bill Gwaltney, and Jim Cullen for their support. Rodney Armstrong, the former director of the Boston Athenæum, offered the full cooperation of his staff during the earliest stages of this project and allowed us to enjoy his graciousness. Louis L. Tucker, the former director of the Massachusetts Historical Society, William M. Fowler Jr., the current director, and Henry Lee, the society's president, provided support without which there would be no book. The same is true for the National Park Service, especially Boston National Historical Park, which played a central role in the creation of this collection. The Massachusetts Foundation for the Humanities provided a timely grant that got this effort off the ground, and we also want to acknowledge the generosity of the Houghton Library at Harvard University and Farrar, Straus, and Giroux. The spirit of the late Edwin Gittleman, scholar and teacher, contributed to our work. We owe special thanks (and apologies) to our wives—Betty Munson, Josie Brown, and Cory Burke Yacovone—who shared our vision and supported our efforts from the start.

This book originated in the 1997 Centennial Celebration of the Augustus Saint-Gaudens Monument to Robert Gould Shaw and the Fifty-fourth Massachusetts Regiment. Not since the Civil War has Boston or any other city in the United States witnessed such an outpouring of admiration for the African American soldiers and their white brethren who together risked their lives so that others might be free. The Centennial Celebration, planned by blacks and whites, men and women, public servants and private professionals, reflected the highest ideals of the men the organizers sought to honor and touched the hearts of the thousands who came to Boston that May from across the state and the nation. For us at least, the world stood still for two days to recognize genuine, unalloyed heroism. This book is one way to help preserve the legacy of the Fifty-fourth Massachusetts Regiment for future generations and to further recognize those individuals who sacrificed so much to fulfill the promise of American freedom and democracy.

M. H. B.

T. J. B.

D. Y.

HOPE
&
GLORY

INTRODUCTION

T HE FIFTY-FOURTH MASSACHUSETTS Regiment is central to the
meaning of the American Civil War and has inspired a remarkable series of efforts to represent its experience. Frederick Douglass wishfully foretold the story in calling for volunteers to join the first
unit of African Americans organized in the North after the Emancipation Proclamation. "One gallant rush," Douglass predicted, would fling
open "the Iron gate of our prison."[1] That gallant rush took place only six
weeks after the regiment left Boston in an emotionally charged procession on May 28, 1863. The death of Colonel Robert Gould Shaw and so
many of his soldiers in a frontal assault on the Confederate stronghold
of Battery Wagner outside of Charleston, South Carolina, on the night
of July 18, quickly became one of the most famous episodes of the war.
Sculptures, paintings, prints, prose, and almost twenty poems honored
the Fifty-fourth Massachusetts during the next two years, an outpouring of remembrance that continued after the war, though shifting in
significant ways. The dedication of Augustus Saint-Gaudens's so-called
Shaw Memorial in Boston on May 31, 1897, prompted a new wave of
literary reflections, and during the twentieth century the monument
served as a touchstone for powerful reconsiderations of the regiment in
music, poetry, and film. A rededication in 1983, designed to signal civic
recovery from a bitter dispute over racial segregation in Boston public
schools, adjusted the representation offered upon the monument itself
by adding to the names of the white officers who died at Battery Wagner
a list of the African Americans who fell alongside them.

This book brings together fifteen previously unpublished essays on
the Fifty-fourth Massachusetts in history and memory. The collection
surveys the major facets of the subject and does not claim to provide an
exhaustive treatment of any aspect. It offers an opportunity to explore
what T. S. Eliot called the shadow that falls "between the idea / And
the reality."[2] The arrangement of the book separates experience and
remembrance. The first set of contributions focuses on the background
and wartime career of the regiment. The second addresses the commemoration of Shaw and the soldiers from the reports of the attack on
Battery Wagner through the dedication of the monument on Boston
Common. The third section takes up meditations on the regiment in

twentieth-century American culture. Although thus divided chrono-
logically, the essays are linked thematically in different ways.

Most obviously, the story of the Fifty-fourth Massachusetts provides
a prism for analysis of race relations from the Civil War era to the
present. The integration of the Union army epitomized the citizenship
of African Americans and underscored a more fundamental human
equality starkly dramatized by the burial of Shaw and his black comrades together in the same rude ditch. The uneven recognition of that
entitlement might be traced forward in politics, society, and culture
from the earliest phases in the organization of the regiment. The following pages describe the continuing march of the Fifty-fourth Massachusetts to a cadence marked by shameful betrayals of the national obliga-
tions and sublime moments of renewal. Black and white approaches to
the story have sometimes converged and sometimes conflicted, and
racial attitudes have blended in complex, sometimes ironic ways with
the other lenses through which individual observers have looked at
the regiment.

In addition to measuring the commitment to equality, the story of
the Fifty-fourth Massachusetts has figured significantly in the expression of American ideas about heroism. Like the British charge of the
Light Brigade at Balaclava and the Australian charge at Gallipoli, the
assault of the Fifty-fourth Massachusetts on Battery Wagner became a
horrific defeat celebrated as a national victory, singled out from countless battles as an example of glory achieved by accepting death. As
William James remarked to his brother Henry, "poor Robert Shaw [was]
erected into a great symbol of deeper things than he ever realized himself."[3] Beginning with the wartime poets and artists who interpreted
his sacrifices in Christian terms of martyrdom, the image of Shaw has
stimulated reflections on the value of a surrendered life; the example of
Sergeant William H. Carney, who kept the national flag aloft amid the
storm of gunfire, has served as a model of patriotism and African American achievement. The essays in this volume examine the theme of heroism from many different perspectives, including not only the cultural
mirror that American society has made of the Fifty-fourth Massachusetts, but also the gender constructions that prepared black and white
men to fight and die in the Civil War and the courageous struggles of the
African American soldiers for fair treatment that have been obscured by
their record of valor on the battlefield.

From the outset, remembrance of the Fifty-fourth Massachusetts has
been remarkably self-conscious, extending beyond the preservation of
a specific story to address directly the underlying process of collective
memory. Shaw's burial in an unmarked grave played an important part

in impressing this topic upon contemporaries, as did the well-publicized refusal of his parents to permit the army to retrieve his body and separate their son from his fellow soldiers. Early eulogies of Shaw often veered into discussion of the purposes and forms of commemoration, invariably concluding that the Confederates had unintentionally provided him with the grandest possible monument. The enthusiastic acclaim for Augustus Saint-Gaudens's sculpture on the Boston Common deepened and shifted this self-consciousness, for seldom has an American work of art so persuasively refracted the memory of an event. As subsequent poetry, music, and film responded not only to the experience of the regiment but to the challenge and inspiration of Saint-Gaudens, the transformation of history into art became an essential part of the story of the Fifty-fourth Massachusetts. While writing his masterpiece *Invisible Man,* novelist Ralph Ellison found that a sudden recollection of Saint-Gaudens's monument evoked "images of black and white fraternity" and also the hope "that war could, with art, be transformed into something deeper and more meaningful than its surface violence."[4]

Beyond the explorations of form invited by the self-consciousness of this commemoration and its impressive record of artistic achievement, the creative talent energized by the Fifty-fourth Massachusetts has helped to make the story a window into the relationship between intellectuals and society in the United States. Shaw's close connections to the educated elite certainly brought extraordinary literary and artistic attention to him. Even before the assault on Battery Wagner, his brother-in-law George William Curtis published a poem in the widely circulated *Harper's Weekly* honoring the colonel and the regiment. After his death, the family friends who presented literary tributes included Ralph Waldo Emerson, Lydia Maria Child, James Russell Lowell, and Francis Parkman.[5] But as several essays in this volume demonstrate, the memory of the Fifty-fourth Massachusetts also illuminates the challenges to the authority of this narrow circle, including its waning influence in public affairs and the rise of rival factions in the arts. Recently, the reinvigoration of the story of the Fifty-fourth Massachusetts through the movie *Glory* and the reenactment of the Civil War has demonstrated the complicated and sometimes tense relations between academic historians and other Americans interested in the national past.

This collection of essays grows directly from an attempt to bridge the divide between scholars and the general public, the celebration of the centennial anniversary of the dedication of the Shaw Memorial. The event featured the largest encampment yet held by African Americans who reenact the Civil War, a screening of *Glory* on the Charles River

Esplanade, and a widely attended two-day symposium featuring reen-actors, film critics, and scholars specializing in history, literature, art, and music. Many of these essays originated as presentations in the symposium. General Colin Powell, the first African American to hold the highest-ranking position in the armed forces of the United States, delivered the principal oration at the ceremonies held on the anniversary of the dedication, and his reflections on the African Americans who preceded him in the service of the country are included here in revised form. As the commemoration of a commemoration, the centennial celebration testified to the continuing power of thoughtful remembrance and aspired to act upon the awareness that "it's a poor sort of memory that only works backwards."[6] The participants in the enterprise can only hope that this effort has earned a place in the distinguished tradition of representing the glorious story of the Fifty-fourth Massachusetts.

I

The Soldiers and
Their World

JAMES OLIVER HORTON

DEFENDING THE MANHOOD
OF THE RACE

The Crisis of Citizenship in Black Boston at Midcentury

I T WAS ON the third of April in 1857 when Charles Lenox Remond of Salem, Massachusetts, stood before a meeting of free people of color in Philadelphia to express the outrage that black people felt so intensely at that moment. "We owe no allegiance to a country which grinds us under its iron heel and treats us like dogs," he said. "The time has gone by for the colored people to talk of patriotism."[1]

Remond was reacting to the most recent federal assault on African American civil rights. Just one month earlier, Roger B. Taney, chief justice of the U.S. Supreme Court, had issued an opinion that wrote black Americans out of the Constitution. The case concerned Dred Scott, a Missouri slave who had lived with his master in the free states for several years. Scott had brought suit claiming his right to freedom based on his long absence from the legal hold of slavery. Begun in Saint Louis, the case worked its way through the justice system to the high Court, which, on March 6, 1857, finally ruled against Scott's claim. But the opinion of Chief Justice Taney went further and dismissed all assertions of black citizenship. The Constitution did not apply to African Americans, slave or free, he said, and black people had "no rights which white men were bound to respect." They had never been, were not, and could never be citizens of the United States.[2]

Boston's black community was horrified and infuriated by the Court's decision making them constitutional nonpersons. They had fought to bring the United States into existence during the Revolution; they had fought to defend it again in the War of 1812; and they had treasured its principles of liberty and justice as few others had done throughout the pre–Civil War decades. Yet they had never felt completely at peace with their American identity, largely because America had never completely accepted the concept of African American citizenship. From the earliest years of nationhood, racial restrictions had placed such citizenship in serious doubt. For most white Americans, the phrase "all men are created equal" never included people of color, and most believed that,

7

as one observed, "Negroes [were] not men" for the purpose of the Declaration.[3]

The term "men" was not used idly, for during the late eighteenth and early nineteenth centuries, citizenship was defined in gender-laden language. The language of independence, civil rights, and citizenship was the language of masculinity. When the Supreme Court sanctioned the denial of African American citizenship, blacks—women as well as men—saw it as a strike at the basic manhood of their race. When the black abolitionist and civil rights leader John Mercer Langston spoke before a convention of Ohio blacks, he used the language of the American Revolution, which espoused a claim to natural rights that he too claimed, "in the name of the manhood of black and mulatto persons." Contrary to Taney's opinion, Langston argued that the basic manhood rights of a race of people "are not created by constitution, nor are they uncreated by constitution."[4]

For Langston, the manhood of the race required access to the basic rights of citizenship, what many blacks called "manhood rights." In the gendered language of the day, the ideal of a strong, autonomous, male citizen was counterpoised to the supposedly frail and dependent women and children who fell under his guardianship. As historian Linda Kerber described it, "Women's weakness became a rhetorical foil for republican manliness."[5] Only those who could fully demonstrate republican manliness could assume a broad range of citizenship rights. This association of manhood with citizenship encouraged references to manhood rights. Women's limited citizenship and legal dependence were included in the laws of coverture, which transferred the control of a wife's property to her husband at marriage. Coverture granted a wife representation and political communication through her husband's civic standing and legally placed her under his control. Although a woman might sue in the courts, petition her government, and even play significant nonvoting roles in the political process, because she could not vote she did not possess the central right of citizenship. She had little civic independence, and in most public matters, coverture invested her public identity in her husband.[6] The language of the period reflected this gender inequality, and the discourse of coverture was a feminine discourse of dependency. Therefore, to refer to black people in terms of dependence and weakness was to feminize the race.

From this standpoint, the institution of slavery sought to "feminize" all black people, denying male and female alike independence, self-assertion, self-protection, and a voice in political formation and representation, assumed as primary rights of citizenship. To demand the manhood of the race was to demand racial independence and respect.

In the most narrow sense, these demands seemed to benefit only men, but because manhood rights enabled the freedom of all blacks—including women—they became a benefit to the race as a whole. When applied to direct citizenship rights, such as the right to vote, black women could be included under the principle of coverture only if black men could exercise the franchise. The Dred Scott ruling struck at the manhood of all African Americans in that it removed from the African American family and community access to the basic protection that its male representatives could have provided.

Although the racial bluntness with which Taney hammered home the federal government's contempt for the manhood of black people was particularly maddening, the sentiment was nothing new. It did, however, clearly define the enemy against which blacks had constantly struggled. The Northern states offered better conditions for African Americans than the slaveholding South, but even in the North and before the Dred Scott decision, life was hard. Opportunities were severely limited, freedom was precarious, and the defense of racial manhood was difficult. New England, in part because its black population was tiny, offered some of the best possibilities for African American freedom. Massachusetts had abolished slavery in 1783 and, compared to other Northern states, seemed extraordinary in its racial tolerance. African Americans had voted in the Bay State since before the turn of the nineteenth century when state courts had agreed that denying black taxpayers the right to vote was "taxation without representation." Massachusetts blacks could also testify against whites in the courts, migrate to and settle in the state without legal restriction, and obtain passports and legal documents affirming their American citizenship.[7]

Vermont, in 1777, was the first state to abolish slavery outright. Connecticut adopted a gradual emancipation law in 1784, which provided for slave children born after March 1 of that year to be freed after serving for twenty-five years as indentured servants. Rhode Island's emancipation law was similar, and Pennsylvania, New York, and New Jersey all abolished slavery through acts of gradual emancipation. Nevertheless, by the time of the Civil War, in most Northern states African Americans either had been denied the right to vote or found that right severely restricted. Ironically, as property requirements were removed for white male voters during the first third of the nineteenth century, black men found prohibitions against their voting imposed, maintained, or increased. The New Jersey constitution limited voting only with property requirements until an 1807 state law added racial restrictions. African Americans were allowed to vote in Connecticut until an 1814 law, incorporated into the state constitution four years later, denied the vote to all blacks who had not voted up to that time. In 1822 Rhode Island's legislature disfranchised blacks for the first time.[8]

In New York, the constitution of 1777 had guaranteed all men who could meet the property requirements, including free blacks, the right to vote. New York Republicans tried repeatedly through the early years of the nineteenth century to disfranchise black voters, but Federalists defended black voting rights and foiled several attempts to institute racial restrictions. The War of 1812 was a turning point for Federalist political power in New York as elsewhere. Discredited by their opposition to the war, the Federalists lost control of state politics and were unable to stop Republicans from limiting the black vote in New York City in 1814 and, in 1821, from changing the state constitution. The revised constitution removed property qualifications for white males but required black males to have lived in the state for three years and have more than $250 in property in order to vote. This so limited the number of qualified black voters that by 1825 only 298 of a total state black population of almost 30,000 and only 16 of New York City's more than 12,000 blacks possessed sufficient property to vote.[9]

In the states farther west, blacks found conditions even worse. Ohio not only denied blacks the vote, full protection of the courts, and the right to sit on juries, but even demanded that free blacks post a $500 bond to settle in the state. Indiana and Oregon denied black settlement within their borders entirely, and other Northern states west of the Mississippi River also limited African American rights. Thus, Taney's opinion denying black citizenship was entirely consistent with most state laws and regulations. It also gave the sanction of federal law to discriminatory social customs that narrowed the economic opportunities available to African Americans. Racial discrimination was omnipresent, even in the most tolerant of communities. In relatively liberal Boston, for example, blacks suffered galling limitations on their occupational opportunities and on access to public accommodations, public education, and legal protection. They were openly despised and denied the common courtesies of a decent society.[10]

African Americans waged a continual struggle against these assaults on their racial manhood. Throughout the Northern states they had spent the better part of the century organizing for their own protection and social welfare. In their churches, fraternal associations, mutual aid societies, and political and social protest organizations, African Americans, male and female, struggled for the recognition of their rights as Americans. No matter their ostensible purpose, through these groups blacks sought not only the basic needs of daily life, but also to continue their fight for the manhood rights of their race. In Boston especially, their organization toward this end, often with the cooperation of supportive white allies, was impressive. But it faced a continuing assault from the highest levels of the federal government.

The Dred Scott decision came near the close of a particularly discouraging period for black Americans. The new Fugitive Slave Law passed by Congress in 1850 was the decade's opening shot in the federal war on black manhood rights. It allowed accused fugitive slaves no right of legal self-defense or the opportunity to challenge the allegation that they were runaways. Under it all black people, even free blacks in Boston, were vulnerable; no African American was safe from enslavement in the decade before the Civil War.[11]

Although slavery might represent the ultimate denial of human dignity, freedom did not insulate black people from regular affronts to their racial manhood. Even the most seemingly innocuous aspects of a highly racialized American culture might threaten black civil rights. The argument used to justify slavery included language that stereotyped all black people, creating caricatures that confirmed what one historian has called the "black image in the white mind."[12] The less aggressive proslavery argument, defined by Jeffersonian assumptions of the early nineteenth century about racial inferiority and natural dependence, held slavery to be a necessary evil. According to proponents of this notion, slavery had a detrimental impact on the morals and the industry of white people, and it had been forced on Americans by British colonial slave traders. By the 1830s, however, a more aggressive Deep South argument, once overshadowed by that of politically dominant Virginia, rose to public prominence with its more contentious, unapologetic justification of slavery.[13] It maintained that slavery was the best and most natural condition for black people. The South's peculiar institution, it asserted, was in fact a "positive good," in part because it supposedly protected slaves from the harsh realities of the competitive world, providing for their care and support and structuring their lives in beneficial ways. In the nineteenth century, white Americans accepted the notion of black inferiority and accounted for it in several different ways. Whether they attributed it to presumed irreversible environmental conditions, to biological limitations that were part of the genetics of the race and were, thus, immutable, or to a spiritually determined condition fully understood only by God, most proslavery advocates accepted black inferiority as a natural, permanent state.[14]

These justifications, then, rationalized the notion that black people, like women, were naturally dependent. Assuming the natural inferiority of blacks and asserting their vulnerability to the inhumanities of capitalist competition, proslavery advocate and anticapitalist George

Fitzhugh defended bondage as a benign, even beneficial shelter for the weak. Slavery, he argued, fostered love between master and slave just as marriage fostered love between husband and wife. Whereas "a state of independence always begets . . . jealous rivalry and hostility," this state did not exist between a ruler and his dependent.[15] A father loves his children until they grow to independence, and then he transfers his affection to his grandchildren. A good slave, like a good wife, is one who does not become "masculine or rebellious," will never outgrow dependence, and thus will retain his master's fondness. Fitzhugh's writings repeatedly invoked the analogy of the good slave and the good wife. Just as a wife takes pride in what her husband is able to provide for her comfort, so the slave on a thriving plantation "boasts of 'our crops, horses, fields and cattle,'" while looking down on the less fortunate slave as "a poor man's negro."[16]

Fitzhugh compared master and husband again when he argued that abolition would be analogous to "set[ting] children and women free" to be consumed by the "constant struggle of society," which they were not competent to deal with. The denial that blacks could be "men" and the comparison of black men to women and children helped form a general pattern that defined "black inferiority" as the absence of the essential qualities of manhood. The social and legal status of women provides a revealing comparison because, unlike the temporary dependence of male children, in nineteenth-century America to be female was to be permanently dependent and inferior.[17]

This description of African Americans, slave and free, male and female, relegated them in language, as in fact, to a permanently degraded position in society. The Sambo stereotype of the slave came to embody the gendered definitions that whites imposed on African Americans, emphasizing the supposedly childlike quality of blacks and the notion that slavery had "domesticated" the African savage. This image feminized all blacks, and its noxious presumptions were not limited to pro-slavery advocates. Even many white social reformers and abolitionists, who saw themselves as friends of the "unfortunate Colored People," employed similar linguistic devices. Harriet Beecher Stowe's *Uncle Tom's Cabin*, the best-selling novel of its time, best exemplified the central role romanticized racialism played in the North.

Serialized in 1851 and published in 1852, the book sold three hundred thousand copies in its first nine months, and by mid-1853 its sales topped one million. The novel spawned a small industry of similar novels, magazine articles, and celebrated dramatic productions. Stowe used a plantation in Kentucky as the novel's setting and portrayed its central character, the slave Uncle Tom, as a model Christian, even a Christ figure. The lovable Uncle Tom was kind and loyal, even to those who mistreated him, and nonviolent even in the face of unrelenting brutality. Stowe portrayed Uncle Tom as representative of Africans—characterized by "their gentleness, their lowly docility of heart, their aptitude to repose on a superior mind and rest on a higher power, their childlike simplicity of affection, and facility of forgiveness." In her treatment, Uncle Tom became the embodiment of the romantic racist construction of the black character. Although he was presented as a physically powerful worker, Stowe emphasized his strength of character, a stoic, selfless, religious strength of the type often reserved for nineteenth-century female stereotypes. Uncle Tom's image as a pure and nonresistant victim justified the abolitionist zeal of many Northern whites who felt that slavery's greatest wrong was its brutal treatment of this meek race.[18]

By contrast, Stowe pictured slaves who were not "pure black" very differently. George Harris, the most rebellious slave on Tom's plantation, was related to "one of the proudest [white] families in Kentucky." He was a mulatto, having "inherited a set of fine European features and a high indomitable spirit." Unlike Uncle Tom, who resisted slavery passively, George refused to accept slavery in any form and was prepared to use any means necessary to secure his freedom. Significantly, the mulattoes of Stowe's fictional plantation were those most likely to run away. Stowe's story line reflected her belief and the popular stereotype of the era that mixed-race slaves were the most intelligent and the most dangerous. Should a general slave rebellion overtake the South, Stowe believed, "Anglo-Saxon blood will lead on the day." She harbored no doubts about the manliness of her own race. The "sons of white fathers, with all our haughty feelings burning in their veins," she was sure, would not "be bought and sold and traded."[19]

Stowe's romanticization of African Americans was not limited to black male characters in novels. In 1853 the abolitionist, women's rights reformer, and former New York slave Sojourner Truth visited Stowe's home in Andover, Massachusetts. Although Truth's visit was totally unexpected, the two women got on very well, so well that Stowe asked her guest to remain for several days. A decade later, Stowe published an account of that visit entitled "Sojourner Truth, the Libyan Sibyl," in the *Atlantic Monthly*. The Truth of Stowe's article was much changed from the rough-edged reformer who had barged into the Stowe home unannounced ten years before. More minister than reformer, more passive than the confrontational speaker who had once while on the stump bared her breast to silence a heckler who expressed doubts about her womanhood, this Truth had a gentle spiritual quality that Stowe stereotypically assigned to all African people. She even insinuated that Truth was African-born and that when they met, Truth stood "calm and erect as one [of] her own native palm-trees waving alone in the desert."[20]

Sojourner Truth was in fact born near the Hudson River in Ulster County, New York, and it is very unlikely that she ever saw a palm tree, waving or otherwise, except in Stowe's imagination. Just as she had given Uncle Tom feminine traits, the novelist attributed to Sojourner Truth a more culturally feminized character than was true of this six-foot-tall woman of unusual strength and biting wit. The real Truth was a person of singular, aggressive intelligence, sometimes defiant, with a sense of calculation hardened by the brutality of slavery. She was proud to bare "her right arm to the shoulder, showing its tremendous muscular power," and proclaim, "I could work as much and eat as much as a man (when I could get it)." Truth displayed the strength of character, the aggressive power and determination, and the physical strength reserved for nineteenth-century male stereotypes. "I am as strong as any man," she told an Ohio audience in 1851. She was hardly the passive creature that Stowe helped to create and that many whites found comfort in.[21]

The belief that blacks were less manly than whites was widespread among white reformers. Theodore Parker, a militant white abolitionist who supported John Brown and his raid on Harpers Ferry, believed blacks to be more "feeble" and less vengeful than whites. He argued that it might benefit whites to mix with Africans "just enough to temper" the natural aggression of Anglo-Saxons.[22] Thomas Wentworth Higginson, a radical white Boston abolitionist, speculated that "the Anglo-Saxon despises the Negro because he is not an insurgent, for the Anglo-Saxon would certainly be one in his place." Higginson's experience leading black troops in combat during the Civil War changed his attitude about African American bravery and aggressiveness, but at the beginning of the war he shared many of Stowe's beliefs about blacks and described them with the feminine language of passivity and dependence.[23]

Northern reformers commonly stereotyped African Americans with distinctly feminine characteristics to mold a less frightening racial image designed to fit their preferences, just as slaveholders had done to fit their conscience. Theodore Tilton, one of the most important male figures in the women's rights movement of the mid–nineteenth century, insisted that blacks were, in fact, a "feminine people." "In all the intellectual activities which take their strange quickening from the moral faculties—which we call instincts, intuitions—the negro is superior to the white man—equal to the white woman." He believed, as "it is sometimes said . . . that the negro race is the feminine race of the world.

That is not only because of *his* social and affectionate nature, but because *he* possesses that strange moral, instinctive insight that belongs more to women than to men."[24]

That Stowe and other leading Northern reformers, who saw themselves as friends of African Americans and who were held in high regard by many blacks, could hold such beliefs emphasized the need for blacks to assert their masculinity. Is it any wonder, then, that Maria Stewart of Boston insisted that black men stand up for their manhood to gain respect for themselves and the race? She challenged the "sons of Africa" to show that they possessed the "spirit of men" by confronting white society and demanding their full "manhood rights." If the measure of the race was its manliness, Stewart's challenge seems a rational one. Black men must stand for the race, she charged, "African rights and liberty is a subject that ought to fire the breast of every free man of color in these United States."[25]

Slavery's attempted emasculation of black men and the highly gendered rhetoric of its defenders—and of many white reformers—complemented the general denial of African American civil rights and freedom. Securing the manhood of the race was a joint venture, difficult at best, impossible without the cooperation of black men and women. The structure of American society, its politics, its economy, and even its language formed nearly insurmountable hurdles.

Hopes for change demanded action from nearly every African American. They, and they alone, were required to take steps to secure and ensure the preservation of the basic human dignity and respect that most white Americans assumed as their birthright. But in America, both law and racial tradition guaranteed that blacks could never assume the recognition of their racial manhood. Neither could African Americans count on living out the expectation of nineteenth-century gender roles. As slavery sought to emasculate black men by denying them the right to defend and protect their families, it also attempted to defeminize black women. Basic gender expectations for slave women were almost always subordinated to economic and social needs and, often, the whim of the master. No job was too hard or too "unladylike" for a slave woman to do, if need be, and rarely could a male family member provide her with protection from the desires of white men. The "female instincts" of a slave woman meant little or nothing to slave owners, who routinely made business decisions that could dictate every aspect of her motherhood from impregnation to the sale of her children.[26]

Slave women, then, filled critical economic roles in slavery and were permitted few of the feminine protections available, in theory at least, to white women. Free black women experienced better conditions than those in chains, but they too enjoyed few of the advantages reserved for white women. They could seldom adopt the middle-class gender ideals that imagined white women as homemakers and child raisers, not laborers. Generally, black women, forced by the constant precariousness of black male employment and continual economic need, sought paid work as a matter of course. The vast majority of black men in Boston could find only irregular, unskilled employment, regardless of their skill levels. The largest number worked as laborers, some of whom found jobs only on a day-to-day basis. Boston's port offered opportunities for black men as maritime workers, providing more stable employment than day labor, but such work forced long absences from home and was extremely dangerous. All this made the labor of black women even more critical. Although their wages were lower, they often worked more regularly than black men. Almost never could black families conform to the middle-class expectation of a single male breadwinner with a wife who remained at home with the children. Women filled essential roles in the economies of Boston's black families and in black communities across the North.[27]

The largest number of working black women found employment as domestics in the households of affluent white families. Many became live-in servants, a situation that often limited the possibility of normal family life. Black women commonly took in washing, a terribly laborious and dangerous job that required lifting heavy cauldrons of boiling water. But such employment often allowed a woman to work at home and spend more time with her family. For those lucky enough to have a home large enough, taking in boarders could be a more pleasant alternative to laundry work and provide many of the same advantages. Other women took in sewing, and a fortunate few served as teachers in private schools or the segregated public schools; some operated their own businesses. Nancy Ruffin and her children ran a market from their home, selling fish and fruits.[28] Yet, the urgency of economic necessity gave most black women few choices, compelling many to labor at a variety of jobs simultaneously. Chloe Spears, for instance, worked in the household of a prominent Boston white family during the day, saw to the needs of her boarders in the evening, and took in laundry at night. This last job required that she interrupt her sleep several times during the night to transfer clothing to and from drying lines.[29]

The significance of African American women's economic role reflected their broad participation in the political life of the black community. They shared in every phase of the struggle for racial manhood. Although in practical terms only men enjoyed full political rights in nineteenth-century America, black women looked upon the right to vote and to stand as full citizens before governmental authority as important rights to be conveyed upon *them* and their community. The quest for full citizenship demanded action in defense of individuals oppressed by the racism that threatened all black people. Resistance to slavery and assistance to and protection of those who fled from it became one of the most significant means to defend racial manhood, and black women played key roles. They served as the chief fund-raisers for resistance movements, and they organized much of the underground railroad activity, providing shelter, clothing, and medical attention to fugitives in need. They even took to the platform, speaking out against the prejudice and injustice that all African Americans experienced. Without the work of women there could have been no effective black resistance movement.[30]

Boston's black women as well as men took active roles in these efforts to free fugitives and fend off attack from racist sources. In the summer of 1836, Eliza Small and Polly Ann Bates, fugitives from Baltimore, were arrested in Boston and brought before the court to be returned to their master. A group of Boston women rushed the courtroom and rescued the captives; a black cleaning women of "great size" immobilized court officers while the escape was effected.[31] During the late 1840s, Boston's black historian and abolitionist William Cooper Nell, in the company of two black female social activists, Sarah Parker and Caroline E. Putnam, challenged the local custom of segregated seating in the Howard Theater, the only establishment of its kind in Boston that "observed the color line." They fought with the police officer who attempted to evict them from their reserved seats and later brought charges against the theater. Like the slave rescues, this aggressive protest was, at base, about establishing and protecting racial dignity and citizenship rights.[32] Many black women in Boston sought to directly advance the manhood of the race, and with their men, they established underground resistance groups like Boston's Freedom Association, formed in 1842.

After the passage of the Fugitive Slave Law in 1850, Boston's underground became even more active. Weighted heavily in favor of slaveholders, this was the strongest such measure ever enacted by the federal government to facilitate the recovery of runaway slaves. If slavery was the nearly complete deprivation of individual freedom and the nullification of all human rights, this law posed the greatest threat to the manhood rights of every African American. It also directly challenged Boston's reputation as a safe haven for fugitives. As one historian suggested, "Perhaps in no community in the North did fugitive settlers feel themselves more secure than in Boston," and black Bostonians were determined that the reputation of their city would be justified.[33] In

October 1850 a large gathering of blacks at the Belknap Street Church heard Nell, Remond, Benjamin Roberts, and others denounce the new law. The meeting then resolved to resist "unto death" any assault on their freedom. "No man will be taken from Massachusetts," they vowed, and when informed of President Millard Fillmore's determination to enforce the law at all costs, they replied, "Let him try!"[34]

This defiance expressed African Americans' intentions to protect fugitives and illustrated their determination to defend their basic rights as Americans. Although hundreds of fugitives and some free blacks fled Northern cities for the safety of Canada after the passage of the Fugitive Slave Law, Nell and other black activists urged them to stay and resist. If they remained, they could count on the assistance of free black resistance groups, which were growing ever more militant during the 1850s. The attack on the black community's ability to aid and protect fugitives represented an attack on the racial dignity of all black people; the greater their resistance, African Americans believed, the more they strengthened their claims to full citizenship. One way to nullify the Fugitive Slave Law and to establish the manhood of the "colored race" before the nation, many blacks agreed, was "to make a few dead slave catchers."[35] Black Bostonians agreed with Frederick Douglass that every "slavehunter who meets a bloody death in his infernal business is an argument in favor of the manhood of our race."[36]

During the 1850s Frederick Douglass's prediction that if authorities attempted to enforce the law, "the streets of Boston . . . would be running with blood" was nearly fulfilled. Not all attempts to protect fugitives were successful. William and Ellen Craft and Shadrach Minkins were saved, but others, most notably Thomas Sims and Anthony Burns, could not be protected. Yet each attempt bolstered black resolve.[37] By 1857, when Chief Justice Taney penned his infamous legal opinion, black Bostonians were steeled with the determination to protect fugitives, to assert their constitutional rights, and to defend the manhood of their race, no matter the cost. Some pressed for the establishment of an independent black military company, an official black militia sanctioned by the state. In the early 1850s, many African Americans in Boston and elsewhere anticipated a violent conflict to free the slaves and believed that their participation might bring an end to slavery and be a major step toward securing their own civil rights. In 1852 Remond and black lawyer Robert Morris led a campaign to petition the Massachusetts legislature to establish a black militia, but the effort failed. The next year they tried again. This time, Morris cited an old Massachusetts law that, during colonial days, had required blacks sixteen years and older to enroll in a militia company under pain of a twenty-shilling fine. It was an eloquent plea, but again the legislature rejected the request.

Boston's blacks would not be deterred, however, and they received support from a broad spectrum of the community. Finally, in 1854, blacks organized a military company without state sponsorship under the name Massasoit Guards. With no assistance from the state, the company depended on private donations for its equipment. Its existence swelled community pride, and during the turbulent 1850s, many blacks viewed it as a necessary defense against kidnappers and slave catchers. African Americans and their white allies continued to push for official recognition from the state government, but with limited success. In 1859 Governor Nathaniel P. Banks vetoed a bill that would have authorized blacks to join the Massachusetts militia, calling it unconstitutional in light of the Dred Scott ruling. Yet, the drive for a black military company expressed community solidarity that only increased with time. The Massasoit Guards reflected, in part, the black expectations that an "impending conflict" would soon bring a violent end to the institution of slavery. It encouraged Boston blacks to stand with stiffened resistance against those who, with the support of the federal government, threatened the security and freedom of fugitive and freeborn alike.[38]

Within three years, Southern secession brought on a war that would lead to the extinction of slavery that African Americans had demanded for generations. Although offers of military service that black Bostonians tendered in 1861 were not accepted by the federal government until after President Abraham Lincoln issued the Emancipation Proclamation in 1863, black militia units stood ready to strike a blow for freedom from the first. When the word came that Governor John A. Andrew would organize a black infantry regiment, the Fifty-fourth Massachusetts, Boston blacks took the lead. They recruited African Americans from across the North, who flocked to the city to offer their service. Black Bostonians viewed the regiment with special regard, seeing its organization as a community effort; black women served as recruiters, participated in community meetings, and supported it with their scant financial resources.

Because the War Department rejected the idea of commissions for black officers, the Fifty-fourth Massachusetts received a mixed response from some black Bostonians at first. But Governor Andrew's assurances that he would guarantee equal treatment for black troops and, ultimately, commissions for meritorious blacks, overcame the initial reluctance. Threats from Jefferson Davis and the Confederate Congress that black troops would receive no quarter from Confederate soldiers and would be enslaved or killed if captured, failed to destroy black enthusiasm for the unit or its mission. Recruiters argued that the success or failure of the Fifty-fourth would "go far to elevate or to depress the estimation in which the character of the Colored American will be held throughout the world," but some blacks argued that accepting these discriminatory restrictions was no way to defend racial manhood.[39] Nevertheless, most black Bostonians agreed with John S. Rock, one of their community's most respected activists, that black men under arms could strike not only a blow for freedom but also one that would demand dignity and respect for the race as a whole. Paraphrasing the words of the Taney decision, he advised that 150,000 free blacks across the North and millions of slaves armed and trained would be a power "which white men will be bound to respect."[40]

And so it was that on a warm spring day in May of 1863, the Fifty-fourth Massachusetts Regiment, in full dress uniform, displaying flags presented to them by groups of black women, marched to the Boston Common. Crowds of black people cheered as the troops passed in review before the governor and a host of dignitaries. Many whites saw the regiment as a great experiment, but most African Americans understood that it was simply the latest example of a long tradition of blacks fighting for the nation. This time, black men and women hoped that their offerings of young men would be rewarded with respect for their humanity and recognition of their citizenship and the manhood of their race.

EDWIN S. REDKEY

BRAVE BLACK VOLUNTEERS

A Profile of the Fifty-fourth Massachusetts Regiment

IN HIS MASTERPIECE sculpture on the Boston Common, Augustus Saint-Gaudens carefully portrayed Colonel Robert Gould Shaw. He painstakingly displayed the faces of a few young African American models, men born long after the Civil War. Behind them he paraded the rifles of many more men—the thousand black volunteers of the Fifty-fourth Regiment of Massachusetts Volunteer Infantry. For most of those soldiers, their bronze rifles offer the only evidence that they served. In the film *Glory, every* black character, however well written and acted, is fictional—a make-believe soldier. These two fine works of art only *represent* the troops; the men themselves are missing—the unknown soldiers of the Fifty-fourth.

RATHER THAN discussing the regiment's battles, military or social, this essay describes those unknown soldiers, suggesting a profile of the unit and recalling details of the lives of several who served to give the group some individuality and identity. The superb history of the regiment by Captain Luis F. Emilio has guided my research.[1] But this profile is based mainly on a reading of the military service records of every man in the Fifty-fourth and on information from the files of all who applied for government pensions. Of course, many records are inaccurate or incomplete; some were never written because of wartime conditions, and others have been lost or misfiled since the war. Nevertheless, they provide the best available biographical information on the regiment.[2]

ORIGINS

A Civil War infantry regiment theoretically held a thousand enlisted men and forty officers. The Fifty-fourth left Boston with 1,007 black enlisted men and 37 white officers on its rolls. During the following two years, as battle casualties and diseases took their toll, 286 additional enlisted men and 27 officers reinforced the regiment. Altogether, from February 9, 1863, through August 20, 1865, 1,357 men—white and black—served in the Fifty-fourth.

When the War Department, early in 1863, authorized Governor John A. Andrew to raise an infantry regiment of African Americans, the Census Bureau estimated that 1,973 black men of military age (eighteen to forty-five) lived in Massachusetts. If they volunteered at the same rate as the white men who had enlisted up to that time, the governor could count on only 394 Massachusetts men for the regiment.[3] But after four months of intensive recruiting for its thousand men, only a few recruits hailed from Massachusetts. One might expect that most of them came from Boston, the largest city in New England; but that is not the case. Boston provided 27 men, but New Bedford sent 39. More surprising, rural Berkshire County in the western part of the state sent 33 men. This success largely resulted from the recruiting efforts of Reverend Samuel Harrison, a black Congregationalist minister from Pittsfield. He later became the chaplain of the Fifty-fourth and a major figure in the dispute over pay for black soldiers. But when it left training camp and marched through Boston on its way to the war front, the Fifty-fourth Massachusetts contained only 133 men (13%) from the Bay State.

Individual states recruited and trained most Civil War soldiers before sending them to the federal army. This meant that most of the thousand men in any regiment came from the same state, even from the same town. But the Fifty-fourth Massachusetts was unique at the time because its men came from many states. Thus, the original Fifty-fourth Regiment formed a broad sample of the black men who made up the African American population. They came from fifteen Northern states, all four border states, five Confederate states, Canada, and the West Indies. The largest delegation hailed from Pennsylvania, 294 men. New York sent 183, and Ohio sent 155 to join the 133 from Massachusetts. Michigan sent 64, Illinois 33, and Indiana 22. Thirty-seven men listed their residences in states with slavery.

The energetic Boston industrialist George L. Stearns, one of the "Secret Six" abolitionists who had financed John Brown's raid at Harpers Ferry, led this nationwide recruiting. Stearns raised most of the Fifty-fourth in the spring of 1863 by building a network of prominent African Americans who did much of the actual recruiting—traveling, speaking, signing up the men, and putting them on trains for Boston. These included such men as Frederick Douglass in upstate New York, Henry Highland Garnet in New York City, John Mercer Langston in Ohio, Martin R. Delany in Chicago, and T. Morris Chester in Harrisburg, Pennsylvania.[4]

The original recruits joined the Fifty-fourth before May 28, 1863, the day when the regiment sailed from Boston for the South. Replacements began appearing that summer, after the devastating fight at Fort Wagner on July 18.[5] The 286 new men came from places quite different from those of the original recruits. One hundred sixty-one (56%) came from Massachusetts, and 68 (24%) came from Vermont. The change was due to five factors. First, the heroic reputation of the regiment after the charge at Fort Wagner attracted Massachusetts men eager to share its glory. Second, a national draft took effect that summer, influencing some men to enlist before the draft got them. Third, the states and local communities, in order to meet their quotas, competed with one another for soldiers by raising the dollar value of the enlistment bounty to extraordinary levels. Fourth, other states, including Pennsylvania, Ohio, and New York, started recruiting black soldiers to fill their own quotas. And fifth, Vermont had no other place to send its black volunteers.

DESCRIPTIONS

Governor Andrew and Colonel Shaw wanted the Fifty-fourth to be not only a black regiment but also an excellent regiment, a model regiment that would overcome the national prejudice against colored troops. Army doctors carefully examined the recruits, rejecting perhaps a third of the men who volunteered. The result was a regiment of healthy, sturdy, eager black warriors, one of the best in the Union army, regardless of color.[6]

The recruiting officers filled out enlistment papers in triplicate (this was the army, after all!), recording the age; height; color of skin, hair, and eyes; place of residence; place of birth; marital status; and civilian occupation of the volunteer. The enlistee then signed all the copies, attesting that the information he gave was true. These documents give important information about the men, but their complete accuracy cannot be guaranteed.

How old were the men of the Fifty-fourth? The Union army accepted men between 18 and 45 years of age. Some recruits, however, did not know their ages. Some youngsters and some grandfathers lied so they could get in on the action. Twenty men aged 16 or 17 joined; most were assigned as musicians or drummers. (Underage "drummer boys" were common in the Civil War.) Among the first to enlist in Boston in February 1863 were Eli G. Biddle, 17, and America C. Tabb, 57. Tabb, who had been allowed to enlist to get some momentum for recruiting among Boston men, had to be discharged in October as "unfit for duty ever since his arrival in the South." Biddle, however, served throughout the war despite wounds received at Fort Wagner; he lived until 1940.

Although most were between 18 and 23 years old, the average age of the men of the Fifty-fourth was 24.3 years, eighteen months younger than that of the average Union soldier.[7] Later draftees and replacements were slightly older. The average age of the white officers who led the regiment was 24.1 years, slightly younger than the black enlisted men. Lieutenant Edward Emerson was barely 17. Captain Luis F. Emilio was not yet 19 years old. Captain Cabot Russel died at Fort Wagner three days before his 19th birthday. And Colonel Shaw was only 25. Although young, Shaw and many of the other officers had previously served in battle and proved their leadership abilities.

The Fifty-fourth provides a sample of the African American population across the country in the 1860s. In the Union army as a whole, white and black, about half of the enlisted men described themselves as farmers, and another 10 percent said they were laborers. But the occupations of the men in the Fifty-fourth were significantly different. Only about a quarter enlisted as farmers, and a third called themselves laborers. These job categories, though not precise, give us some clues to the social background of the men: many more Northern blacks than whites worked as laborers, men hired to work for other people, increasingly in nonagricultural jobs.

The other occupations in the Fifty-fourth ranged from artist to yeoman. There were 51 barbers, 38 seamen, 34 waiters, 27 boatmen, and 24 teamsters. George E. Stephens of Philadelphia was a cabinetmaker; Joseph Sulsey of Mount Holly, New Jersey, age twenty-one, was a dentist; Bill Underwood of Mason County, Kentucky, was a druggist. Five men were students, but there were no teachers. Six men were clerks, but only one was a preacher. There were two peddlers but no merchants. There is much we still do not know about the free black community, but these occupations confirm expectations that, aside from a small elite, it was a working-class society.[8]

The enlistment papers also listed skin color. There was no official color code—the one-word description depended on the judgment of the white army officer who filled out the form. This very unscientific description might hinge on such factors as how many African Americans the officer had met before, the size of his vocabulary, and the time of day. For the Fifty-fourth the color descriptions ranged from black, dark, and brown to dusky, medium, mulatto, colored, light, yellow, and even white.

Of the original 1,007 men in the Fifty-fourth, the papers described 450 (44.6%) as black or dark, 250 (24.8%) as brown, and 302 (30.0%) as lighter-colored. Five men (0.5%) were described as white (including one with blue eyes and brown hair), and six men (0.6%) were not identified by color. This profile changed significantly for the 286 men who joined the regiment as replacements. For those men, 200 (69.9%) were labeled black or dark, 18 (6.3%) as brown, and only 64 (22.4%) as lighter. Four men (1.4%) were not described by color. Why were the reinforcements so much darker (69.9% to 44.6%)? Geography does not seem to have made much difference—men from the Northeast had about the same color distribution as men from the Midwest. Slave background also made little difference.

What explains this color difference? The original recruits of the Fifty-fourth went through a more rigorous examination and selection process than most army units, including later black regiments. If recruiters and doctors rejected one out of every three men, skin color might have been a contributing reason for rejection. Later in the war, after the Fifty-fourth had shown that African Americans could fight well, the selection standards relaxed. In other words, subtle white prejudice, rather than the general makeup of the population, could have led to an original regiment of lighter color overall.

What of the five men described as white? They did not enlist to be drill sergeants for the new recruits. None had previous military experience, all started out as privates, and none particularly distinguished themselves as soldiers. So these white men remain an enigma, a riddle in a black regiment.

Did the Fifty-fourth have men with no African heritage? Apparently so. At least one man, Alex Johnson of New Bedford, claimed to be a full-blooded Narraganset Indian. And probably many men in the Fifty-fourth had some Native American ancestors. But the records give little evidence of that connection. Prejudices and laws being what they were, white Americans considered anyone with African ancestors, regardless of color or ethnicity, to be black. There is little evidence of Hispanic men in the Fifty-fourth: two men were born in Mexico, and five came from the West Indies, but none had Spanish names.

EX-SLAVES

The Fifty-fourth became deeply involved in the campaign for equal pay for white and black soldiers. Although Governor John A. Andrew had promised that black soldiers would be treated the same as whites, the federal government refused to pay them equally. White privates received thirteen dollars each month, plus their clothing; blacks received only ten dollars monthly, from which they had to deduct three dollars for their clothing. Most of the soldiers of the Fifty-fourth refused to accept any money until Congress authorized full equality. They went for eighteen months before being paid in full.

At one stage in that struggle, if blacks were to get their pay, Congress required them to swear that they had been free on or before April 19, 1861. Those who had been slaves on that date would not get full pay. To avoid "class differences" among the men, Colonel Ned Hallowell, an abolitionist and Shaw's successor as commander of the Fifty-fourth, devised a "Quaker Oath" that every man in the regiment could affirm: that he "owed no man unrequited labor" on April 19.

How many men in the regiment had indeed been slaves? After the war, with slavery ended and the Fugitive Slave Law just a harsh memory, the men could talk more freely about their slave origins. Direct, written evidence shows that at least thirty men of the Fifty-fourth had been slaves. How they got to the North illustrates some of the complexities of slavery. For example, the owner of the teenage Hewett brothers, James and Thomas, of Texas, sent them to Xenia, Ohio, and set them free in 1855. A prominent politician who later served as Lincoln's secretary of the navy, Gideon Welles, bought the infant Joseph Hall, with his mother and sisters, in Washington, D.C., took the family north, and freed them in Connecticut. Yankee troops persuaded Charles Bell of New Orleans to join the Navy; his ship went to Brooklyn, where Bell deserted and went on to Boston to join the army. And the master of Thomas Betts of Arkansas sent him with a Confederate work crew to help build Fort Donelson in Tennessee. He ran away while gathering firewood and served for a time as a cook for an Ohio regiment. He ended up in Columbus, where he met the recruiters for the Fifty-fourth and enlisted.

In addition to this direct evidence, indirect clues about slave backgrounds lie in the records that show each man's state of birth. One-fourth of all the men who served in the regiment were born in one of the slave states—322 soldiers. Most came from Virginia or the border states, but natives of every state in the Confederacy except Florida joined the Fifty-fourth. How many of these men had actually been slaves? It seems reasonable to assume that perhaps half of these Southern men, at least 160, had been born into slavery and had somehow made their way north to freedom. The fact that so many of them had been born in slave states, combined with the details of some of the men's lives, indicates that ex-slaves formed a significant part of the Massachusetts regiment, just as they did in the larger African American community across the North.

NEIGHBORS AND RELATIVES

The typical Civil War regiment was drawn from a single state; most of its men were neighbors from the same town or region. When disaster or defeat hit a regiment, a whole county might be affected. Although the Fifty-fourth was drawn from all across the North, some African American communities sent large groups to serve as soldiers. New Bedford, for example, sent thirty-nine men. But the little town of Mercersburg, Pennsylvania, with fewer than five thousand people even today, sent thirty-three men. Twenty-one of them were killed or wounded in action. Among these were the two Burgess brothers, Thomas and William, and their cousin Bill—all wounded in the charge at Fort Wagner; the four Christy boys, Samuel, William, Jacob, and Joseph, three of whom were killed or wounded; and the four Krunkletons, Wesley, William, Cyrus, and James, one killed and three wounded all on the same day, July 16, 1863, at James Island. The Fifty-fourth and its war had a powerful impact on that small place.

Mercersburg, of course, was not the only town to send brothers to the regiment. Although the records are not explicit, it seems that at least seventy-seven families of brothers served in the Fifty-fourth. Lewis and Charles, the sons of Frederick Douglass, attracted the most publicity. The Jennings brothers from Amherst, Massachusetts, and the Wentworths from Woodstock, Vermont, enlisted along with their fathers. Altogether, seven fathers seem to have enlisted with their sons to defend the Union, giving the Fifty-fourth a sense of family.

SERGEANTS

The noncommissioned officers—the sergeants and the corporals—played important roles in an army regiment. The white officers of the Fifty-fourth selected them from among the enlistees to serve as a bridge between the other men and their commanders. An infantry regiment contained fifty-four sergeants and eighty corporals.[9] The duties of these men included leading and reading. The sergeants did much of the vast amount of paperwork required by army regulations, a task that required good literacy. But their primary function was to lead: to inspire their men, to help direct them in battle, and to ensure that the privates did their work properly. According to an official army manual, they were to instruct privates; therefore, "they should be taught not only to execute, but to explain intelligently" how to be good soldiers.[10] All the sergeants and corporals in the Fifty-fourth were African Americans.

The senior enlisted man in the Fifty-fourth was the sergeant major. In April 1863 Colonel Shaw appointed to this rank Lewis Douglass, son of Frederick Douglass. He helped recruit new men, set a good example for the privates, informed the colonel about the concerns of the men, and marched prominently at the head of the regiment on parade. After

Douglass was discharged for health reasons, John H. Wilson of Cincinnati succeeded him.

Several of the men who served as sergeants in the Fifty-fourth are noteworthy: William H. Carney of New Bedford won the Congressional Medal of Honor for rescuing the regiment's flag from the walls of Fort Wagner on July 18, 1863. Sergeant Robert J. Simmons of New York won high praise for his bravery at Fort Wagner. He had served with the British army in his native Bermuda before migrating to New York. Had he not been wounded, captured, and allowed to die in a Charleston prison, Simmons too would probably have won the Medal of Honor.[11] Stephen A. Swails of Elmira, New York, was the first African American to rise from the ranks and serve as an officer. Sergeants Peter Vogelsang of Brooklyn, New York, and Frank Welch of Bridgeport, Connecticut, despite the protests of some of the white officers, both earned commissions at the end of the war. Albert Thompson of Buffalo and George E. Stephens of Philadelphia also earned commissions but did not receive them before their discharge at war's end.

CASUALTIES

The Dead

When the Fifty-fourth returned to Boston on September 2, 1865, only 598 of the original 1,007 men marched to the final ceremonies on the Common. The war had taken a heavy toll on the regiment. It had fought in four battles and several skirmishes. Death paid its first call on July 16, 1863, when the Fifty-fourth fought a brief but bloody battle on James Island, near Charleston. The men showed good discipline and courage in the regiment's first combat action. But they paid a price for the honor of proving that African American troops could and would fight well. One man in particular, Sergeant Joseph D. Wilson of Chicago, had vowed he would never be captured by the rebels, but he found himself surrounded by Confederate troops. With his musket and bayonet he single-handedly killed or wounded several of the enemy before receiving a fatal pistol shot to the head. That day, nine men of the Fifty-fourth died in action.

Two days later, on July 18, 1863, the regiment fought its most famous and costly battle, the nighttime charge across Morris Island to Fort Wagner. There Confederate defenders killed Colonel Shaw and buried him in a mass grave with his black soldiers. Thirty-eight enlisted men of the Fifty-fourth were killed outright that night. Of the men missing in action, 36 were "supposed dead" and were never again seen alive. Altogether, 74 enlisted men and 3 officers of the regiment can be confirmed as having died in the battle. The exact fate of some of the men will never be known.[12]

The Fifty-fourth moved to Florida early in 1864, and on February 20 it participated in the Battle of Olustee. Union forces planned to cut a railway and interrupt the flow of supplies northward. Poor judgment by the commanding general led the Union force into a disastrous ambush. The Fifty-fourth fought a valiant and steady rearguard action that enabled many other units to escape the trap, saving them from sure annihilation. Eight men of the Fifty-fourth died in the fight. One of them was Private Bill Thomas of Boston, accidentally shot by one of his own comrades.

The regiment soon returned to South Carolina, where it helped keep pressure on the defenses of Charleston. On November 30, 1864, it fought again at Honey Hill, near Grahamville. It tried to cut the railway between Charleston and Savannah in order to keep the Confederates from reinforcing their troops as General W. T. Sherman "marched through Georgia." The fight at Honey Hill failed to cut the railway, and one man from the Fifty-fourth, Richard Foster of Troy, New York, died in action.

Counting these men killed in battles, the ones "missing and supposed dead," and those killed in other actions, 104 of the original 1,007 men died in action with the enemy. Although hospital records did not always clearly state the cause of death, at least 37 additional soldiers died of their combat wounds. Furthermore, many of the men captured by the Confederates had suffered wounds in battle; at least 9 of them died of their wounds while in rebel prisons. Counting the men killed in action and those who died of their wounds, 150 men died as a result of combat. Of the 286 reinforcements who joined the regiment later, 1 died in action and 1 died of wounds, bringing the total to 152 fatalities.

The Wounded

Whether from musket or cannon fire, bayonets, or torpedoes (land mines), the men of the Fifty-fourth suffered wounds of every description. At James Island 27 were wounded. Sergeant Joseph Palmer of Dayton, Ohio, was one of those who received a rebel bullet there. But he stayed with the regiment for its attack two days later on Fort Wagner. There he caught a second rebel shot, this one in his arm and chest. He spent weeks in the hospital and never completely regained his health. At Fort Wagner the wounded lay scattered across the sand dunes and along the shore of Morris Island. Some, like Sergeant William H. Carney, struggled back half a mile from the fort with severe injuries. Bravely, Carney continued to carry the regiment's flag even though there was a bullet in his hip. He was hit a second time before he reached safety, this time in the head by a shell fragment. Comrades dragged some of the wounded to safety; others crawled through the rising tide on the beach in the darkness. That night 175 men of the Fifty-fourth were wounded.

Much of the Battle of Olustee was fought in the piney woods of northern Florida. Artillery shells frequently tore off branches that crashed onto the soldiers below. Private Joseph T. Wilson of New Bedford had already been hit by a musket ball when a falling tree crushed his spine and left him permanently crippled. The rebels wounded 72 men of the Fifty-fourth at Olustee. Thirteen of them also had been wounded seven months earlier at Fort Wagner. They were among the casualties loaded onto a flatbed rail car to be sent to hospitals in Jacksonville. But the locomotive broke down. So on foot, soldiers of the Fifty-fourth pushed the car full of wounded men to safety.

The Fifty-fourth played a smaller role at the Battle of Honey Hill. Nevertheless, 41 men were wounded there. Sergeant John Barker of Oberlin, Ohio, Corporal Sam Stevenson from Washington, D.C., and Private Bill Stevenson of Fayetteville, Pennsylvania, each received his third combat wound, having been hit earlier at Fort Wagner and Olustee. Ten other men suffered their second wounds in action. These men showed in combat that black troops could be as courageous as any other soldiers. Altogether, throughout the war, 326 men of the Fifty-fourth received combat wounds. For at least 46 of them, their wounds were eventually fatal.

The quality and efficiency of care for the wounded soldiers varied, depending on combat conditions, the severity of their injuries, and luck. Surgeons attached to the Fifty-fourth set up field hospitals behind the battle lines, especially on Morris Island, the main base of the regiment. For the severely injured or sick, hospital ships took the casualties to the federal hospitals at nearby Beaufort. The most serious cases were sent to hospitals in New York or Worcester, Massachusetts. Three men had mental breakdowns and were sent to Washington, D.C., to the Government Hospital for the Insane. One of them, Private Thomas Jackson of Lenox, Massachusetts, broke down after the fight at Olustee. His tentmates recalled that he was "taken crazy and was often thereafter . . . out of his mind and senses until he was removed to Washington." They said the whole company believed that Jackson "was crazed by the excitement of the battle . . . and the concussion of cannon." He died after a year in the hospital for the insane, a victim of what today would be called "post-traumatic stress."[13]

The Sick

Diseases also took a heavy toll on the Fifty-fourth, as they did on both armies throughout the war. At one time or another, for shorter or longer periods, almost every man in the regiment became too sick to work or fight. One hundred eight men died of disease. Their medical records are sketchy and cryptic, but clearly fevers caused most of those deaths—typhoid, malaria, or just "fever." Diarrhea and dysentery were common. Diseases of the lungs, such as tuberculosis and pneumonia, killed others. Heart disease and smallpox claimed a few. Some records simply said, "Died of disease."

Theodore Becker had been a physician in Framingham, Massachusetts, before joining the army. Had he not been "colored," he might well have won a commission as surgeon. Instead, he enlisted as a hospital steward, an assistant to the white doctors of the Fifty-fourth. Many of the enlisted men praised Becker for his effective care when they were sick and his willingness to visit them in their tents when the surgeons would not do so.

There is no way to measure how much disease reduced the ability of the Fifty-fourth to carry out its work. When the regiment fought at Olustee, for example, a significant number of its men remained in South Carolina because of sickness. Most stayed on the active rolls of the regiment and did light duty, such as cooking or doing laundry, instead of marching or digging trenches. Toward the end of the war, many of the light-duty soldiers were finally discharged from the army. Of the original 1,007 men, the army discharged 127 early for reasons of health. Of the reinforcements, 37 went home early.

The Prisoners

Black prisoners of war faced a severe fate at the hands of the rebels. Southern troops sometimes massacred colored prisoners, as they did at Fort Pillow, Tennessee. The Confederates threatened to return them to slavery or to try them as war criminals. The men of the Fifty-fourth knew this when they enlisted, and when they were captured they expected to be hanged or shot. The Confederates changed their official policy after President Abraham Lincoln threatened to shoot a rebel prisoner for every African American prisoner executed, though on the battlefield black prisoners often faced summary execution. But even if he did not face imminent death, becoming a prisoner of war was a difficult fate for a black soldier.

In each of its battles, the Fifty-fourth had men "missing in action."

Many of them had actually died in the fighting, but others, especially wounded men, were captured by the enemy. At James Island the rebels captured 13 men of the Fifty-fourth. Two days later at Fort Wagner, 35 men became prisoners. In the Battle of Olustee another 13 were captured. And at Honey Hill, the Confederates captured another wounded man, Private Hill Harris of Louisiana. They took him first to Charleston for medical care, then sent him to the notorious prison camp at Andersonville, Georgia. At Andersonville he found the men captured at Olustee and one of the men taken at Fort Wagner. Of these 15 men, 5 died of malnutrition and exposure; their graves are among the thousands of Union graves at Andersonville.

South Carolina authorities held most of the regiment's prisoners of war in the jail at Charleston. They had to do the most degrading tasks around the prison, but they kept up their spirits by nursing the sick and wounded, by singing spiritual and patriotic songs every evening, and by cheering whenever shells from the Union guns on Morris Island landed nearby. Their jailers usually fed them a cup of cornmeal each day— little wonder that 4 of them died of malnutrition in that jail.

Toward the end of 1864, as Union forces took more territory in the South, the Confederates moved prisoners from both Andersonville and Charleston to a prison camp near Florence, South Carolina. The conditions in the new prison proved to be more harsh than at Charleston Jail and even worse than those at Andersonville. At Florence, epidemics of smallpox and typhoid fever broke out in January and February 1865. As a result, 10 men of the Fifty-fourth died there after having survived as much as a year and a half in captivity.

By March 1865, when the war was drawing to a close and General Sherman was marching through the Carolinas, both sides began exchanging prisoners of war. The Confederates released most of the surviving prisoners from the Fifty-fourth at Goldsboro, North Carolina, on March 4. Two of them died of disease shortly after their release. The others, after short furloughs or stays in the hospital, returned to the regiment for the final days of the war.

THE VETERANS

After the war ended, most of the African American soldiers of the Fifty-fourth, like white soldiers, returned to civilian life. A few stayed on in the army as "Buffalo Soldiers" on the frontier. But most had started as laborers or farmers, and they lived out their lives as working-class men. Some belonged to local posts of the Grand Army of the Republic, the Union veterans' organization. They applied for government pensions, and most of them voted Republican. For all of them, the war was *the* great event to be remembered and celebrated during the succeeding years of hard work, hope, and discouragement about the persistence of racism and their failure to receive the equal rights they had fought and suffered for.

A few veterans of the Fifty-fourth achieved public notice. Sergeant Carney told and retold the story of his bravery at Fort Wagner; he worked as an elevator operator in the Massachusetts State House. Sergeant Major Lewis Douglass edited the *New National Era,* urging political reform and rights for African Americans. Sergeant George E. Stephens taught school in Virginia, and Lieutenant Frank Welch became a letter carrier in Bridgeport and a major in the Connecticut National Guard. Lieutenant Stephen A. Swails advanced the furthest in public life. He became an agent of the Freedmen's Bureau and returned to South Carolina, where he entered vigorously into Republican politics. He attended that state's constitutional convention in 1867 and won election four times to the state senate, where he served throughout Reconstruction as its president. But most of the men of the Fifty-fourth never attracted notice by the American public.

On Memorial Day 1897, thirty-two years after their discharge from the army, about sixty surviving veterans of the Fifty-fourth marched in the parade and watched the unveiling of the Saint-Gaudens memorial on the Boston Common. They then proceeded through the rain to the Music Hall to hear speeches by William James and Booker T. Washington. That evening, joined by the colored veterans of the Fifty-fifth Massachusetts Infantry and the Fifth Massachusetts Cavalry, they enjoyed a splendid dinner at Faneuil Hall. It was a triumphant day for the old soldiers, a celebration of all the African Americans who, despite slavery and racism, had defended the Union. The sculpture on the Common has now stood for a century to remind us of their heroism.

By 1897 perhaps half of the regiment still survived. As more years passed, their numbers thinned rapidly. Eli Biddle, who had enlisted in Boston at age seventeen and survived serious gunshot wounds at Fort Wagner, went on to a long career as a Methodist preacher. When he died in Boston in 1940 at age ninety-four, his daughter wrote to the pension office insisting that he be given a burial befitting the last survivor of the "old 54th." But he was *not* the last old soldier to fade away. Ira Waterman, who worked as a laborer for almost seventy-five years after the war, died in Springfield, Massachusetts, in August 1941.

The bronze men with their muskets marching with Colonel Shaw across the Boston Common, and the make-believe soldiers in *Glory,* represent 1,293 flesh-and-blood African Americans of the Fifty-fourth

Regiment of Massachusetts Volunteer Infantry. It must be remembered, though, that the real soldiers of the Fifty-fourth each had a name and a story. They came from all over the nation, from all walks of life, many as escaped slaves. Containing the history of their race in America, black, brown, and lighter hues, they proudly fought not only to save the Union but also to destroy slavery and earn their long-denied equality and their right to citizenship. Many died, more were wounded or endured disease in the struggle, and some fought their war in rebel prisons. Their honorable sacrifices and ultimate victory became a major chapter in the struggle for a just society in America. They deserve to be remembered.

DONALD YACOVONE

THE FIFTY-FOURTH MASSACHUSETTS REGIMENT, THE PAY CRISIS, AND THE "LINCOLN DESPOTISM"

W HY DO WE remember the Fifty-fourth Massachusetts Regiment? The regiment's success in helping to win the right for black men to serve in the Union army and the recognition of citizenship that service implied are crucial to understanding the full meaning of the Civil War. The Fifty-fourth's valiant combat record led to the general recruitment of African American soldiers, who eventually accounted for about 10 percent of the Union army, and to the Confederacy's defeat. But the regiment's successful eighteen-month campaign for equal pay and the recognition of racial equality that victory implied represented the unit's most important achievement. Combined, these elements constitute the Fifty-fourth's central historical legacy.[1]

But in the popular imagination, the sacrifice of the Fifty-fourth's youthful commander and so many black soldiers in a heroic, if impossible, mission on July 18, 1863, understandably has overwhelmed all other aspects of the regiment's history. The evocation of Christ's death and resurrection in the story of Robert Gould Shaw and his men has become, through poetry, art, and film, part of the nation's identity. The arresting artistry of Augustus Saint-Gaudens captured the mythology in a moment and wrapped it forever in bronze.

Saint-Gaudens's work stands as a perpetual reminder of the Civil War and the struggle over slavery. It has resisted efforts to expunge the African American role in the war from the historical record and fills a place in the nation's culture occupied by no other piece of art or literature. To borrow from Robert Lowell's great poem, the Saint-Gaudens monument and the Fifty-fourth's heroism at Battery Wagner sticks like a fish bone in the nation's throat and cannot be dislodged. And that is precisely the problem.

The drama, daring, and romance that envelop the Fifty-fourth Massachusetts Regiment and Saint-Gaudens's work have become an impenetrable shield, a bronze capsule, preserving the unit's mythology but excluding much of its history. Although the heroism of Shaw and the

Fifty-fourth at Battery Wagner must not be denied, it has overwhelmed an equally heroic struggle the regiment's men waged against the racism of their own government. The Fifty-fourth's campaign for equal pay represented a triumph as important as anything captured by myth, and it is critical to understanding African American wartime aspirations.

Massachusetts governor John A. Andrew received the War Department's consent at the beginning of 1863 to recruit a regiment of free Northern blacks on the same basis as all the other state units that served in the Union army.[2] The Fifty-fourth would, Andrew promised every recruit, have the same equipment, be eligible for the same bounties and federal benefits, and receive the same pay as white Union soldiers. As an abolitionist and a defender of black rights, Andrew fully understood the importance of the unit to African Americans, to the struggle against slavery and racism, and to the course of the war. He intended the Fifty-fourth to be the model for all subsequent black regiments raised by the North. Federal authorities would not permit him to commission black officers, but the War Department had not entirely closed the door to promoting blacks in the future. Clearly, everything depended upon how the men acted under fire.

Black leaders across the North understood the magnitude of the opportunity facing them, and its burdens. Although Union regiments of former slaves already on the battlefield had proved their valor under fire, Northern resistance to the widespread use of black troops remained firm. The very idea of armed blacks left many white Union soldiers with "a chilling sensation" and provoked, as in one Pennsylvania unit, feelings "akin to disgust." As the volunteers of the Fifty-fourth Massachusetts Regiment assumed responsibility to refute racist accusations that blacks could not or would not fight, black men and women from across the North felt the "eyes of the whole world" upon them. The *New York Weekly Anglo-African,* the era's most influential black newspaper, best summarized the challenge: "Civilized man everywhere waits to see if you will prove yourselves. . . . *Will you vindicate your manhood?*" African Americans understood that if the regiment should fail, "it will be a blow from which we Northern men would never recover."[3] The regiment's success would constitute a fatal blow against slavery and racism; failure would mean disaster.

The Fifty-fourth's heroism at Battery Wagner ended the debate over the recruitment of black troops, but it did little to alter the racial prejudice of whites in the North. Even those blacks who had long experienced the reality of American racism were shocked by the depth of white treachery. The Lincoln administration, first promising equal pay, belatedly determined that the Fifty-fourth and all other black units had been enrolled under the Militia Act of July 1862, which mandated that blacks could be paid only $10 a month, minus a $3 clothing allowance. All "persons of African descent," regardless of rank, according to the Lincoln administration's interpretation of the act, could receive only $7 a month, rather than the $13 a month accorded to white soldiers. Black noncommissioned officers, the backbone of any unit, should have received the $17 to $21 per month paid to white sergeants; blacks serving

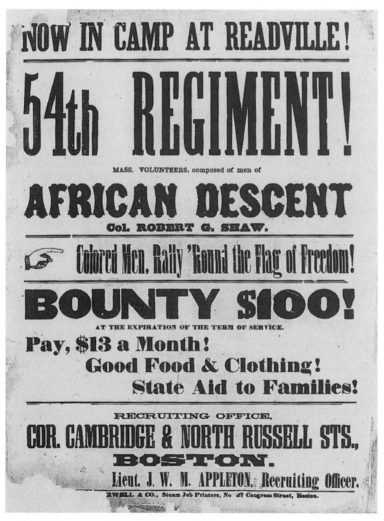

Recruitment poster, 1863. Courtesy Massachusetts Historical Society.

as army surgeons or regimental chaplains were due an officer's pay, but all would receive the same amount. Thus, the highest ranking black soldier received about half the pay of the lowest ranking white.[4]

The men of the Fifty-fourth Massachusetts fought one war against the slave-owning South and another against their own government's galling racism. Unequal pay struck at the heart of black motivation to serve, undermined their claims to equality, threatened the safety and lives of the soldiers' families, and imperiled black hopes for the postwar world. It brought black troops in the Department of the South to the brink of mutiny and nearly destroyed Massachusetts's prized black regiment. For eighteen months the Fifty-fourth refused to accept any pay rather than submit to the federal government's demeaning offer. The Lincoln administration not only betrayed the men but seemed determined to prevent blacks from grounding their claims for full citizenship on their military service. As Sergeant George E. Stephens, a Philadelphia cabinetmaker, a correspondent for the *Anglo-African*, and the spokesman for the men of the Fifty-fourth, exclaimed, "Because I am black, they tamper with my rights."[5]

For readers of the *Anglo-African*, widely considered the black soldiers' newspaper, Stephens chronicled the regiment's principled stand against federal policy. He denounced the "Lincoln despotism" for its attempt to reduce free men to slaves and keep its foot on the necks of African Americans, compelling them to accept a position of inferiority. "Thus free men were reduced to servitude," Stephens bitterly concluded. "No matter what services [the black soldier] might render—no matter how nobly he might acquit himself—he must carry with him the degradation of not being considered a man, but a thing." But Stephens, the Fifty-fourth Massachusetts, and the other black soldiers in the Department of the South refused to submit. "Does the Lincoln despotism think it can succeed?" Stephens cried. The black troops would resist the government's injustice; "Do you think that we will tamely submit like spaniels to every indignity?" he warned. "Suppose we had been white," Stephens asked, "Massachusetts would have inaugurated a rebellion in the East, and we would have been paid." Horace Greeley's *New York Tribune* considered the government's conduct to be a swindle and a scandal so outrageous that it seemed "intended to provoke a mutiny." In defending their rights, the Fifty-fourth came perilously close to that end.[6]

As early as March 1863, when the unit was still forming, Colonel Shaw warned Governor Andrew that the matter of pay already had become a damaging threat. Rightly suspicious of the government's intentions, the soldiers quickly demanded their state bounties. Shaw hoped to head off a confrontation by requesting advance payment, which would, he informed the governor, "relieve the officers from constant fear of a row." Shortly after arriving in South Carolina, Shaw learned that the War Department had considered substituting pikes for the soldiers' rifles and providing uniforms different from those worn by white soldiers. Those moves were rejected, but it did decide to give black soldiers the inferior pay provided to noncombatant "contraband" laborers. He advised Andrew that the men would accept nothing less than full pay.[7]

Shaw's death at Wagner did not affect the brewing confrontation with the Lincoln administration over unequal pay. The Fifty-fourth, almost to a man—including the officers—rejected the government's unjust offer. Sergeant Frederick Johnson, a Boston hairdresser in Company C, informed Governor Andrew late in the summer of 1863 that the men felt "they have been duped." If the regiment would not receive its full pay, he insisted that it be called back for home defense or discharged. Andrew replied to Johnson's letter, which the sergeant shared with the unit's other noncommissioned officers, guaranteeing Massachusetts's full support on the pay issue. Andrew also contacted black community leaders in Boston and across the North to assure them that the regiment had his personal support. Ohio's John Mercer Langston responded to Andrew with a warning that a broken promise on equal pay made blacks doubt that justice would be forthcoming on all other issues.[8]

Parents, spouses, and champions of the Fifty-fourth sent protest letters to Andrew and his recruitment committee. They communicated the disillusionment and sense of "real sadness, and disappointment" that permeated the regiment. Committee members in particular felt deeply ashamed since they had promised the men the same pay and treatment as all other Union troops. "It is true," committee members admitted, "they *have been deceived,* they cannot even be permitted to die for their country on an equality with other soldiers, they have been made to feel that they still are only *niggars* not men."[9]

At noon on September 30, 1863, the U.S. paymaster visited the Fifty-fourth and presented the government's offer of $7 a month. He explained to the men that the law offered him no alternative. He suggested that they might accept the pay under protest, which would still sustain their principle and relieve their families' suffering. "The regiment to a man," one officer recorded in his journal, "refuses the insolent $10.00 or rather $7.00." Some officers expressed astonishment at the soldiers' fierce determination to reject the offensive policy. Reflecting the increased level of racism among the unit's officers who replaced those killed or disabled during the Wagner assault, they found the men's resolute stand "inconsistent with many traits of character that have been ascribed to their race."[10]

Not long after the paymaster's futile visit, the Fifty-fourth received a shocking dose of army racism, sadly reflecting Northern racial opinions. Colonel James Montgomery of the Second South Carolina Volunteers, the Fifty-fourth's former brigade commander, had been one of the earliest advocates of black recruitment. Because of his reputation as a fierce abolitionist, Montgomery enjoyed the confidence of most of the black soldiers under his command despite his sometimes harsh and capricious discipline. Thus, his words struck with even greater force.

"You ought to be glad to pay for the privilege to fight, instead of squabbling about money," Montgomery exclaimed. He warned that the soldiers' refusal to accept what the government offered amounted to mutiny, "and mutiny is punishable with death." Ignoring the regiment's enviable reputation, Montgomery declared that the Fifty-fourth still had not proved that blacks could fight as well as whites. He confessed that black soldiers' "inherent" disadvantages left them with much to overcome. With words that enraged all who heard them, Montgomery declared, "You are a race of slaves. A few years ago your fathers worshipped snakes and crocodiles in Africa." The men of the Fifty-fourth listened to Montgomery berate their very appearance: "Your features partake of a beastly character. . . . Your features can be improved. Your beauty cannot recommend you. Your yellow faces are evidences of rascality. You should get rid of this bad blood," he recommended. "My advice to you is the lightest of you must marry the blackest women."[11]

Montgomery's outrageous remarks "fell with crushing effect on the regiment"; no one had even suspected that he harbored such repulsive attitudes. The entire regiment, including white officers, refused to acknowledge Montgomery and turned away when he appeared in camp. Blacks should be grateful for the privilege to fight? Stephens asked in astonishment. "For what are we to be grateful? Here the white man has grown rich on our unpaid labor—has sold our children—insulted our wives—shut us out from the light of education, and even kept the Bible from us." "I think," Stephens thundered, "it [is] a question of repentance on his part instead of gratitude on ours."[12]

When the paymaster returned on October 31, the Fifty-fourth's new commander, Colonel Edward N. Hallowell, who had served under Shaw and had been severely wounded in the July 18 attack, backed the regiment's refusal to accept the $7 offer. "My honor as a soldier & a gentleman, the honor of Massachusetts & the honor of the government of the United States," Hallowell informed officials back in Massachusetts, "was pledged to the officers & men of the Fifty-fourth that they should in all respects be treated as other soldiers of the U.S. Army." In the strongest language he could muster, Hallowell urged the state to honor its pledge to give the men equal pay.[13]

On December 12, Major James Sturgis and the wealthy Republican merchant Edward W. Kinsley, Governor Andrew's personal representatives, addressed the Fifty-fourth and presented the state's compromise measure. Though they assured the men that Andrew was working to change federal policy, for the present the state legislature had adopted legislation to pay the men the difference between black and white pay rates. Sturgis and Kinsley stood ready, cash in hand, for the soldiers' answer. The officers, noncommissioned officers, and enlisted men met in separate groups to discuss the proposal. Stephens and his fellow sergeants, representing the unit, met with Sturgis and Kinsley to advise them that, though they appreciated the state's generosity, they could not accept the plan without compromising their principles. Colonel Hallowell informed Andrew that nothing short of full pay from the federal government would satisfy the men. Any distinction made between themselves and other federal troops raised in Massachusetts, Hallowell wrote, "would compromise their self respect." The men would fight for the rest of the war without any pay before they would submit to any act that appeared to even hint "that because they have African blood in their veins, they are less men."[14]

The pay crisis quickly spread beyond the confines of the Fifty-fourth. General Quincy A. Gillmore, commander of the Department of the South, cautioned the army's general-in-chief Henry W. Halleck that "the pay of the white soldiers and of the colored soldier should be the same. All distinctions calculated to raise in the mind of the colored man a suspicion that he is regarded as an inferior being, should be scrupulously avoided." George L. Stearns, who had assumed control over the federal government's black recruitment campaign, resigned in protest over the War Department's policy.[15]

The Fifty-fifth Massachusetts Regiment, organized before its more famous sister unit first left the state for South Carolina, also served in the Department of the South. Word of the government's offer of unequal pay quickly rippled through the regiment. The enlisted men assembled at their camp on Folly Island, south of Charleston Harbor, to plan action. Nearly all determined to follow the Fifty-fourth's lead and take nothing until given full pay. Sergeant James Monroe Trotter, father of William M. Trotter, the well-known Boston civil rights crusader, urged the men to stand firm on principle. All pledged to die before they would accept unequal pay and the "position of menials in the Union army."[16]

By the close of the year, morale in the Fifty-fourth had plummeted.

Away from his family, risking his life to save the Union, the average soldier felt betrayed and mocked by his own government. Despite repeated assurances from Andrew and other state political leaders that justice would be forthcoming, the men doubted it. Soldiers like Stephens became desperate. Other than the $50 bonus awarded to enlisted men upon joining the unit, he had not received any pay since the Fifty-fourth had arrived in South Carolina. Unable to send any money home, he applied for state aid. But Stephens and men in the Fifty-fourth and Fifty-fifth regiments who had legal residences in other states—the vast majority of both units—discovered that their home states considered them ineligible for assistance. Andrew and the state of Massachusetts sought to arrange assistance for those soldiers' families who verged on destitution. Black families in Republic, Ohio, for instance, received some state allocations, and in the case of men like Stephens, Massachusetts agents arranged for private charitable donations for their families. But the families of many men suffered grievously.[17]

By January Governor Andrew had received so many disturbing reports of conditions in the state's black units that he advised Edward W. Kinsley to investigate. Had he begun his investigation only a few weeks later, his report would have been explosive. Trust between the Fifty-fourth's men and their officers was crumbling. Though relations remained good in some companies, dissension grew between black soldiers and officers who had joined the unit after July 18, 1863, promoted in place of worthy black soldiers in the Fifty-fourth. The black troops distrusted whites "whose antecedents or sentiments we know nothing of." One new officer insulted Stephens when he "told me to my face that noncommissioned officers were not as good as they are in white regiments." Though the remaining original officers supported the soldiers' demand for equal pay and for commissions, the newer ones lacked antislavery zeal or, worse yet, were unabashed racists. When enlisted men in the Fifty-fourth petitioned their superiors seeking a commission for the regimental hospital steward Theodore Becker, three white officers protested. "They did not want a negro Doctor," an anonymous soldier reported to the *Christian Recorder*, and "neither did they want negro officers." A few openly disparaged the men they commanded, declaring that "a negro stunk under their noses."[18]

After the February 1864 Union defeat at Olustee, Florida, morale in the Fifty-fourth and the Fifty-fifth sank precipitously. Strife surged throughout the Department of the South over unequal pay and the War Department's continued refusal to commission blacks as officers. Charles Sumner, the powerful antislavery senator from Massachusetts, admitted that the prospects for legislation to resolve the pay crisis seemed "doubtful." Though the state's influential politicians lobbied hard for equal pay, mulish opposition in Congress and in the War Department frustrated their efforts. Stephens became despondent. His own government treated him as a "thing and not a person," and the army executed black troops with unseemly swiftness if not outright illegality. "We are unprotected and there is no refuge—no appeal." Freedom became a false hope, and the nation, he mourned, remained determined "to maintain a line of demarkation between the white and black race, and to deny to the black equal rights and justice as enjoyed by the white." A year of service in the army, Stephens lamented, had "purged me of the major part of my patriotism."[19]

"Our debasement is most complete," a soldier from the Fifty-fifth Massachusetts asserted in April. "No chances for promotion, no money for our families, and we [are] little better than an armed band of laborers with rusty muskets and bright spades." Contrary to orders, white officers in the Fifty-fifth ordered enlisted men to do degrading work as personal servants and cooks. Other officers in the Fifty-fifth, recently arrived in the South, openly boasted of their participation in the horrid New York City draft riots. Before the end of the year, even the Fifty-fourth's abolitionist colonel, Edward N. Hallowell, had nearly given up on the Department of the South. "I'm disgusted with it," he wrote home, "& I wish I could get to the Army of the Potomac."[20]

Mutinous discontent in the Fifty-fourth began early in 1864. Anonymous letters appeared in Colonel Hallowell's tent prior to the Battle of Olustee, threatening that the men would refuse to fight if not immediately awarded equal pay. Word spread to the other black regiments in the department that the Fifty-fourth had gone into battle with provocative cries of "seven dollars a month." About half the men talked openly of refusing duty until given their full pay. Hallowell tried to quiet the growing unrest by reading Senator Henry Wilson's March 2, 1864, bill equalizing pay rates to the men. Few were satisfied, especially as word filtered throughout the army that blacks in other regiments had stacked arms in response to the pay crisis and had been shot for it.[21]

The first and most notorious case of mutiny occurred on February 29, 1864, when Sergeant William Walker of the Third South Carolina Volunteers (Twenty-first U.S. Colored Troops [U.S.C.T.]) faced a firing squad for protesting unequal pay. On November 19, 1863, Walker had ordered his company to stack arms in front of their colonel's tent. Warned that he would be shot for mutiny if the protest continued, Walker refused to "do duty any longer for seven dollars a month." The Walker case provoked outrage in the North. Governor Andrew directed Senator Sumner to deliver a letter of protest directly to President Lincoln. "The Government which found no law to *pay* him except as *a nondescript or a contraband,*" Andrew fumed, "nevertheless found enough law to *shoot* him as a *soldier.*" The army intended Walker's execution to show black soldiers what they could expect if protests over pay continued. But the men of the Fifty-fourth and the Fifty-fifth regiments would not be cowed or agree, as Stephens wrote, to live "under a tyranny [as] inexorable as slavery itself."[22]

When the Fifty-fourth camped outside of Jacksonville in April 1864, discipline disintegrated. Captain Luis F. Emilio, who became the regiment's historian, worried that solidarity among the men over the pay crisis was destroying the unit. On April 12 Colonel Hallowell assembled the men and informed them that he planned to visit Washington to plead their case for equal pay. He warned against insubordination and advised the men that he had given Major John W. M. Appleton authority to shoot the first man who refused duty. The men grumbled after Hallowell dismissed them. When Appleton returned to his tent, he found an anonymous note declaring that without equal pay he had no right to take the regiment into action. Carrying out Hallowell's orders, the note warned, would cost him his life. Appleton reassembled the regiment. He assured the men of his commitment to their cause but warned that if ordered into battle he would obey, threats to shoot him notwithstanding.[23]

When the regiment left Florida on April 17, discontent erupted. Several soldiers on the troop transport *Cosmopolitan* planned to seize the ship and steam to New York, but they failed to persuade their comrades to join them. When the transport moored at Folly Island, the regiment's commanding officers waited on the dock in a driving rain for the men to disembark. The soldiers refused to leave and paced back and forth on deck unsure of exactly what to do. Hallowell, who had not yet left for Washington, ordered Appleton to reboard the ship and pull the men off. He grabbed one soldier by his pack and shoved him down the gangplank. Others followed, grumbling in the miserable weather, "money or blood!" and "muster us out or pay us!"[24]

The immediate crisis passed, but discontent continued. The men had not received any pay for over a year. They showed their tear-stained letters from home to sympathetic officers who felt both powerless and vexed by the politicians who stood in the way of legislation equalizing pay. One man in the Fifty-fourth, who had lost his home in the 1851 Christiana, Pennsylvania, fugitive slave uprising but had reestablished himself in Canada, was thrown back into destitution because of the pay strike. Sergeant Stephen A. Swails, who returned from Olustee with a bullet through the neck, received a letter informing him, inaccurately, that his family had been sent to the poorhouse. The news tore through the regiment. Other soldiers' families did lose their homes, and some soldiers learned that town officials had bound out their children for support. The government's refusal to uphold its promise to award black soldiers equal pay destroyed the regiment's will to fight and undermined its loyalty. One soldier in Company H wrote home, "We have not our Pay yet and I never think we will[.] Oh for shame on Such Equality[.] Such A Government as this don't suit me[.]"[25]

Conditions in the Fifty-fifth Massachusetts, with fewer antislavery officers, descended into open mutiny. Desperate letters from home poured into the regiment. One poor woman begged her husband to send her just fifty cents. "Was it any wonder," one soldier wrote to the *Anglo-African*, "that the tears rolled in floods from that stout-hearted man's eyes?" Mutinous letters began appearing in the black press from anonymous soldiers in both units who could not endure the stress of the strike and the reprimands of their officers for complaining about pay. Colonel Alfred S. Hartwell, the Fifty-fifth's new commander, found anonymous and threatening letters in his tent. Then, 120 soldiers refused orders to man picket lines. He assembled the men and informed each company commander, loud enough for all to hear, that anyone who refused orders would be court-martialed and shot. All but one complied. Hartwell ordered the protesting soldier bucked and gagged "until the doctor said that he could stand it no longer."[26]

President Lincoln came under increasing pressure from Charles Sumner, Henry Wilson, and other friends of the black regiments to resolve the pay crisis and act with charity, dispatch, and justice toward his black soldiers. But Lincoln, as late as May 1864, knew relatively little about the controversy over unequal pay and declined to "interfere" in a matter that he believed should be settled by Congress. When Frederick Douglass met with the president in the White House, Lincoln listened attentively to the case for equal pay. He then advised Douglass that blacks should view military service as a great benefit and be "willing to enter the service upon any condition." Unequal pay, Lincoln thought, was a reasonable concession to the prejudices of white troops who preferred that blacks not serve at all. Whatever Congress could have done about unequal pay, Governor Andrew was right to lay blame for the crisis "at the door of the executive."[27]

Black leaders like William Wells Brown assailed Lincoln. "We have an imbecile administration, and the most imbecile management that is possible to conceive of." Discouraged by the treatment of black soldiers, John S. Rock, the first black lawyer to win the right to argue cases before the U.S. Supreme Court, wondered what African Americans could expect once the war concluded and the government no longer needed their services. The resurgence of the racist Democratic Party, the faltering war effort, and the government's timid, initial reconstruction policies—especially in Louisiana—convinced many blacks that a Northern victory would not end oppression or even slavery. "The President of the United States," one black leader decried, had "pronounced a death-knell to our peaceful hopes."[28]

Seventy-five men from the Fifty-fifth wrote President Lincoln—who likely never saw the letter—demanding equal pay. In clear language bordering on insubordination, if not mutiny, the men demanded Lincoln's immediate action, the absence of which would result in "more stringent measures" by the regiment. The men of the Fifty-fifth refused to accept any further insults from the federal government. For anyone who missed the point of the protests or doubted the soldiers' resolve, "Bay State" set them straight. Writing in the *Anglo-African*, he promised that "We, by God's help, will settle it for ourselves before this war is over, *and settle it right too, or die in the attempt.*"[29]

One man did die. Private Wallace Baker, a twenty-year-old farmer from Hopkinsville, Tennessee, was, according to his fellow soldiers, awkward and quarrelsome. He felt especially recalcitrant on the afternoon of May 1, 1864, when Lieutenant Thomas F. Ellsworth ordered a company inspection at the Fifty-fifth's camp on Folly Island. Baker was the last man to assemble and fell in without his weapon and equipment. Given that he had had all day to prepare, Ellsworth asked Baker why he was not ready. "I'm not going to hurry," he snapped.[30]

The confrontation quickly escalated. Baker refused to be silent and mocked the lieutenant, causing a roar of laughter in the ranks. Ellsworth then ordered Baker to his tent. Baker responded, "I won't do it, I'll be damned if I will" and then brayed his refusal to obey any "damned white officer." Ellsworth grabbed the private by the collar and shoved him toward his tent. Baker knocked Ellsworth's hands away and struck him twice in the face. "You damned white officer," he shrieked, "do you think that you can strike me, and I not strike you back again? I will do it. I'm damned if I don't." Ellsworth drew his sword, but Baker seized it and struck the officer several more times. While the two men grappled, Ellsworth called out to the sergeants for help. No one budged. The company commander, Captain John Gordon, rushed to assist, but the two men still struggled for the sword. Ellsworth called for a guard to remove Baker, but the hundred or so men standing aside refused to move. Corporal Henry Way—later court-martialed for his role in the affray—also refused Ellsworth's calls and told him, "If you or any other officer strikes me, I shall strike you back, and do my best to defend myself." Ellsworth and Gordon finally subdued Baker and confined him in the guard house.

Originally scheduled for May 17, Baker's trial did not commence until June 16. It moved swiftly, though with procedural fairness. Lieutenant Colonel Henry N. Hooper of the Fifty-fourth Massachusetts presided, and the trial records and regimental books make it clear that the presiding officers searched for mitigating grounds to prevent the inevitable. There could be no denying, however, that Baker had committed mutiny and struck an officer; in the military code the penalty was death. They also knew that the crisis over unequal pay lay behind the confrontation. With discipline breaking down and no resolution of the pay issue in sight, the court ordered what military justice mandated. Baker was "to be shot to death with musketry."[31]

"It is by such stern and sad examples that the great arm of military law asserts its power," Colonel Hartwell wrote when he ordered Baker's execution on June 18. The Fifty-fifth had come to South Carolina "in defence of the rights and civil and military equality of a race so long held in bondage." Baker, Hartwell explained, brought "reproach upon our regiment and cause." Every black soldier on Folly Island assembled at 10:30 A.M., in the muggy and mosquito-choked air. Baker stood before his yawning grave "with unflinching courage," one enlisted man observed, denouncing his execution as an injustice. One of the Fifty-fifth's officers simply noted that Baker died "cursing to the last." Stephens witnessed the execution and remarked that Baker remained firm throughout, "and when he spoke no tremor could be detected in his voice." Three bullets to the head and four in his chest finally silenced Baker's protest.[32]

The commanders of the Fifty-fourth and the Fifty-fifth deplored the execution. "For God's sake," Hartwell wrote Governor Andrew, "how long is the injustice of the government to be continued toward these men?" He wondered if the government intended to "goad them into mutiny and [then] quench the mutiny with blood." The lieutenant colonel of the Fifty-fifth, Charles B. Fox, placed responsibility for Baker's death squarely on the federal government. The Massachusetts adjutant general agreed, blaming the government's mishandling of the pay crisis for the execution. If the army believed that it could shoot its way out of the controversy, subsequent events proved it wrong. Members of the regiment again refused picket duty, and officers began to resign in disgust. Baker's company remained strife-torn; at the end of June another soldier was court-martialed for clashing with an officer.[33]

Stephens voiced the fury that swept through the Fifty-fourth over the pay crisis and Baker's execution. "Nearly eighteen months of service—

of labor—of humiliation—of danger, and not one dollar." He denounced the government for reducing his wife to beggary. "What can wipe the wrong and insult this Lincoln despotism has put upon us?" he exclaimed. He remained determined to speak out, "and nothing shall prevent me but double irons or a pistol-ball that shall take me out of the hell I am now suffering."[34]

Colonel Hallowell had good reason to worry that he was losing control of his own regiment. The "men [are] in a state of extreme dissatisfaction bordering on mutiny," he advised Andrew. The pay crisis drove everyone to desperation, and, he wrote, the only way he could prevent anarchy was to shoot the regiment's troublemakers, "a catastrophe we should always deplore."[35] While Baker awaited his court-martial, the "catastrophe" Hallowell feared occurred. On May 12, 1864, Lieutenant Robert R. Newell of Company B ordered six of his men to fall in. Each refused. Newell struck one with his sword and repeated his order. When the men still ignored his orders, Newell sent for his revolver. He repeated his command, and when the soldiers balked, Newell shot one in the chest. The others scampered into line. Newell, who had a reputation for being easy-going, turned "white as a sheet" and took the man to the hospital. The incident shocked the company. If Newell would not hesitate to shoot them, the men thought, "what won't the others do?"[36]

A week later, Captain Charles E. Tucker of Company H shot another man for disobeying orders. Then a detachment from Company A refused guard duty and, as one officer noted, "great turmoil" roiled the regiment. Hallowell ordered his captains to get their pistols and commanded the men to fall in. Instead, the soldiers loitered in company streets and drew spectators from other companies who pressed between the tents to witness the confrontation. When some of Stephens's men in Company B approached the officers, muskets in hand, Hallowell ordered his major to beat them back. Those who refused to move felt the butt end of a pistol against their skulls. Both Hallowell and Major Appleton turned to the protesting soldiers, pointed their revolvers at each man's head, and gave them a count of three. "Do you refuse to go on guard? One, two." "No Sir!" came the reply. Hallowell passed down the line pointing his pistol at each head and asking the same question. All the men fell in, and the crisis passed.[37]

Hallowell, caught between his sympathy for his men and his duty as commanding officer, pleaded with Governor Andrew to force the War Department to pay the men or muster them out of service. He warned that several men had been shot in a "small mutiny" and that without action a general mutiny would soon destroy the state's, if not the country's, most important black regiment.[38] Letters from Stephens and others in the unit swamped the black press, renewing their demand for action and holding the state accountable for the crisis. "If we fight to maintain a Republican Government," another man in Company B insisted, "we want Republican privileges." The men maintained that they would no longer fight "for anything less than the white man fights for. . . . Give me my rights, the rights that this government owes me, the same rights that the white man has." More letters poured into Andrew's office, this time from men who attached their names to the letters, demanding full pay or their discharge.[39]

Officers from the Fifty-fourth and their antislavery allies at home, even the governor of Vermont and the Union League of New York, increased the pressure on Andrew to compel federal authorities to pay the men. Abolitionists and the state's politicians descended on Lincoln's attorney general and the secretary of war to lobby for equal pay. As late as June 27, Attorney General Edward Bates still asserted that, because of the Militia Act of 1862, black and white pay rates could not be equalized.[40] Andrew filled with disgust. The federal government seemed intent on disgracing and degrading blacks, making them "in the eyes of all men 'only a nigger.'" Hot with impatience, he wrote Charles Sumner, exclaiming, "I *demand* their rights as Massachusetts Volunteers according to the law." Near the end of May, he sent George S. Hale, president of Boston's common council, to ask President Lincoln to order full payment to the state's black regiments.[41]

Sumner lobbied other senators and congressmen who served on committees that oversaw military legislation. Most claimed that until Bates changed his ruling on the Militia Act of 1862, nothing could be done. "I lost no time in calling on the Sec. of War & the Atty Gen.," Sumner advised Governor Andrew, "& have pressed upon each the duty of an early settlement of the case of the colored regts." Both men resisted Sumner's efforts, and Bates refused to read any more letters from Andrew concerning black troops. Sumner had argued with Stanton so many times over the issue of equal pay that the secretary of war "has lost his temper" and refused to meet with him again.[42]

To head off further mutiny, Andrew orchestrated an effort by friends of the state's black regiments to assure the soldiers of his support. One soldier's letter he received may have been especially worrisome. It questioned Andrew's antislavery commitment and charged that "all he cared for was to get them [black soldiers] into the service." Andrew turned to Lewis Hayden for help. Hayden, an influential Boston black abolitionist, served as an unofficial liaison between Andrew and both of the state's black regiments in South Carolina. Because of his standing as a trusted black leader, Hayden's assurances went far to quell unrest. He

passed along copies of Andrew's correspondence with the War Department to the units to prove the governor's fidelity and to show how
hard he labored in their behalf. Other blacks, especially Boston's black
women, staged fairs to raise funds and collect goods for soldiers' families. White abolitionists and political leaders wrote to both regiments,
professing their complete support for equal pay and condemning the
"criminal neglect of the government to do justice to the colored troops."
Edward W. Kinsley contacted enlisted men in the Fifty-fourth and the
Fifty-fifth, pledging the state's support and keeping them apprised of
moves in Congress to equalize pay. "All you Boys have to do is to *hold
on*," he assured one sergeant in the Fifty-fifth Massachusetts. "You will
yet come out all right, and get all that is due you both in money &
honor."[43]

The pressure from antislavery congressmen and the black troops in
the field finally persuaded the government to act. Within days of Wallace Baker's execution in June, Congress adopted legislation authorizing
equal pay retroactive to January 1, 1864. Unsatisfied with anything
short of full reimbursement from the beginning of enlistment, Andrew,
Sumner, Wilson, and a host of others pressed further. Finally, in July,
Attorney General Bates reversed his opinion and ruled that the Militia
Act of 1862 did not apply to black soldiers who had been free at the
start of the war. This meant that Stephens and most other blacks in the
Massachusetts units would receive equal pay from the first day of their
service. But the law excluded regiments like the First South Carolina
Volunteers and all soldiers who had been slaves at the start of the war,
although, as Sumner asserted, even the Militia Act of 1862 made "no
distinction" between "free black & slave black in the military service."[44]

For Massachusetts's black soldiers, Colonel Hallowell devised an in-
genious "Quaker oath" that permitted soldiers who had been slaves to
swear that before April 19, 1861, "no man had the right to demand
unrequited labor of you, so help you God." By the end of August, most
officers had employed Hallowell's handiwork, and with few exceptions
the men complied. The Fifty-fifth, with a higher percentage of former
slaves than the Fifty-fourth, found it more difficult to resolve the problem, and several men refused to take any oath. The South Carolina
regiments, excluded from the law, continued their protest for another
nine months until Congress agreed to full equal pay in March 1865.[45]

Between September 28 and October 5, the Fifty-fourth and the Fifty-
fifth received their full pay. Jubilation swept through the department.
Time after time soldiers exclaimed that they could "send money home
at last to my wife, my child!" Dancing, shouts, and singing replaced the

thunder of cannon throughout the day and into the night. To commemorate their victory, soldiers sang:

> Fight we like *men* our conflict,
> Renew our vows to-night,
> For God and for our Country,
> For Freedom and the Right.

As one officer observed of the celebrations: "It was like the apparition of a man's self in a more perfect state." Official ceremonies on October 10 left the men in raptures. Equality had been won; a *black* victory had been achieved. Not money, but rights, had been gained, proclaimed Sergeant James Monroe Trotter. A "great principle of equal rights as men and soldiers had been decided in their favor."[46]

The African American soldiers had, indeed, won a great victory, and their efforts, as they had hoped, supported their postwar claims to the vote and full citizenship embodied by the Thirteenth, Fourteenth, and Fifteenth amendments to the U.S. Constitution. But as the Reconstruction amendments and civil rights legislation gained approval, white interest in social and political reform for African Americans dissolved, and black hopes for full equality faded further from view.

By the time Saint-Gaudens completed his memorial to Shaw and the Fifty-fourth Massachusetts, histories of the Civil War were neglecting the black role in the conflict, and many eloquent veterans of the black regiments, like Stephens, had already died. Much responsibility for preserving the memory of the Fifty-fourth in the popular mind, then, rested on what stood on Boston Common across from the State House. Certainly, no single monument can be expected to capture the full meaning of so complex an experience as the black role in the Civil War. It must fall to the written word to record the full heroic story of the Fifty-fourth Massachusetts and how African Americans fought against the institution of slavery and the tyranny of their own government.

JOAN WAUGH

"IT WAS A SACRIFICE WE OWED"

The Shaw Family and the Fifty-fourth Massachusetts Regiment

O N JULY 27, 1863, Charles Russell Lowell of the Second Massachusetts Cavalry wrote his fiancée, Josephine Shaw, a letter of condolence upon hearing of the death of her brother, Colonel Robert Gould Shaw, while leading his African American troops in battle. "I see now," he said, "that the best Colonel of the best black regiment had to die, *it was a sacrifice we owed,*—and how could it have been paid more gloriously?"[1] The words from Lowell, who would himself die courageously at the battle of Cedar Creek in October 1864, perfectly summed up how Rob Shaw's parents, Sarah Blake and Francis George Shaw, wished their son's heroic actions to be remembered. The phrase powerfully evokes an image of Christian sacrifice, placed in the service of erasing the sin of slavery.

This essay explores the social, psychological, religious, and gendered contexts of the Shaw family, illuminating our understanding of how and why Robert Gould Shaw achieved wartime abolitionist martyrdom. Moreover, it demonstrates how the very concept of sacrifice infused with meaning the lives and careers of the surviving Shaws long after the guns of war fell silent. For a historian of the Shaw family, the phrase serves as a motif linking the Shaws' private and public lives as they unfolded before, during, and after the Civil War. Indeed, any personal and psychologically driven analysis of the family would be inexplicable without a public context. My purpose is not to romanticize the familiar story of Robert Gould Shaw, nor is it to diminish the accomplishments of this truly remarkable family circle, but to provide a balanced and nuanced account of their impact on the Civil War era.

HISTORIANS AND THE SHAWS

The Shaw family of Boston and Staten Island is forever united with the cause of black liberation in the Civil War. As radical abolitionists and activist Unitarians in the 1840s and 1850s, Sarah and Francis Shaw agitated for the ideals of immediate freedom and equality for African

Americans, ideals that their son, Colonel Robert Gould Shaw, died for when he led the Fifty-fourth Massachusetts Regiment in the assault against Battery Wagner, South Carolina, on July 18, 1863. The heroic sacrifice of Rob Shaw and the soldiers of the Fifty-fourth Massachusetts was quickly transmuted into a symbol for black manhood and citizenship.

The essence of the ideals of freedom and equality that animated the history of the Fifty-fourth Massachusetts was embodied in Augustus Saint-Gaudens's beautiful bronze bas-relief in Boston. Attending the unveiling ceremony on Decoration Day, May 31, 1897, Robert Gould Shaw's family—his mother, Sarah Shaw, and his sisters, Anna Shaw Curtis, Susanna Shaw Minturn, Josephine Shaw Lowell, and Ellen Shaw Barlow—basked in the reflective glory of the sculptor's achievement. William James, a principal speaker at the unveiling, proclaimed to his brother Henry: "The monument is really superb, certainly one of the finest things of this century." Modern art critics have agreed, and art historian Robert Hughes described it as "the most intensely felt image of military commemoration ever made by an American." But no one could ever match Sarah Shaw's heartfelt tribute: upon viewing the monument for the first time, she turned to Saint-Gaudens and said, "You have immortalized my native city, you have immortalized my dear son, you have immortalized yourself."[2]

And so he had. From the beginning of the project, the Shaw family had definite ideas about how they wanted Rob's story, and hence theirs, to be commemorated. They naturally preferred to emphasize the sacrifice and idealism of Colonel Shaw and the courage and worthiness of the ordinary black soldiers of the regiment. The family preserved Rob's letters and saved every condolence missive received after his death. They made sure that their version of history would be written so that Rob and his regiment would be honored respectfully, not just in bronze, but in songs, poems, and stories. There is no question that the Shaws' idealistic version of the Fifty-fourth's achievements in the Civil War prevailed, a version perfectly epitomized in this sentimental poem written to commemorate Sarah's own death in 1902:

> Mother of heroes, she of them who gave
> Their lives to lift the lowly, free the slave
> Through lengthened years two master loves she found:
> Love of our free land; and of all sweet
>   Found
> 'Twas praising her to praise this land of grace
> and when I think on music—lo! her face.[3]

Inevitably, the Shaws and their story have been subjected to the prob-ing analysis of modern scholars trained to view history through the lens of gender, race, class, and psychology and trained to be suspicious of heroic figures. Recent scholarship has significantly revised the earlier celebratory versions of Shaw and his leadership of the Fifty-fourth Mas-sachusetts. Historians have downplayed Robert Gould Shaw's role (and the Shaw family's) in the formation and performance of the storied unit. The black soldiers themselves have become the focus of attention as interest in the role of African Americans in the Civil War has increased dramatically in the last three decades. Scholars such as George Fred-rickson, Peter Burchard, Lewis Simpson, and Russell Duncan have deftly exposed the racist and class themes that belie much of the older, unrealistically rosy depiction of Robert Gould Shaw. The previous im-age of Colonel Shaw as the exemplar of his class and generation man-fully sacrificing his life so that black men could gain respect as soldiers has been described as paternalistic and condescending. In fact, Rob was not at all the idealistic abolitionist his parents wished him to be: "I don't talk and think of Slavery all the time," he complained to his ever more stalwart mother.[4]

Indeed, Rob's behavior as a teenager and a young man caused both his mother and his father great concern. While in school in Europe, he spent too much money, drank and partied with abandon, and in general behaved with extreme irresponsibility. We doubt Sarah's words describ-ing herself as Rob's "most intimate friend from his earliest boyhood, he loved me with a devotion of which I was unworthy. . . . Our whole intercourse is without a shadow." Instead, Russell Duncan's examina-tion of the letters lovingly saved for posterity by Frank and Sarah Shaw demonstrate that she was so pained by his racist and condescending language toward blacks that she deleted some of the more offensive passages. Moreover, several of his wartime letters reveal that Shaw singled out the Irish as objects of derision, hardly surprising for a mem-ber of the New England upper class.[5]

Like many a Civil War hero, Shaw has fallen in our estimation. His fall is more notable because of his allegedly undeserved iconographic status as one of the few white martyrs for black freedom. Now, Rob's well-documented lukewarm commitment to abolitionism clearly ex-plains his initial refusal of the colonelcy of the Fifty-fourth, glossed over in earlier versions of his life. It seems as if the whole of idea of black soldiers fighting for the Union was much more important to his parents, and especially his mother, Sarah, then it ever was to Rob. Both Burchard and Duncan argue that far from being "a beautiful, sunny-haired, blue-eyed boy, gay and droll, and winning in his ways," as described by friends, Rob's youth was marked by rebellion and fueled by feelings of unexpressed rage at his "female-dominated" family.[6]

A most unflattering portrait of Sarah Shaw has emerged. "Dying in obedience to the New England moral absolute," argued Lewis Simpson, "Colonel Shaw had done—in accordance with the American cult of matriarchal motherhood that first strongly manifested itself in the age of the Civil War—what every American boy must ideally do: he had fulfilled the expectation of his mother." Here we have Sarah portrayed as a strong-willed and selfish woman who dominated her weak husband Frank. According to current views, she forced Rob into being the unwilling instrument of her ambition—thus ensuring his death in the war—and reveled in his apotheosis afterward. "I never could see why mothers made such a fuss about their children dying," Sarah is reputed to have said. Russell Duncan has argued that Robert Gould Shaw was a hapless young man who was never "able to break free of his mother's dominance." Moreover, Duncan asserted (in agreement with Simpson) that even after his death, Sarah controlled Rob's legacy to the point where "the monument on Boston Common is much more representative of her ambition than of his."[7]

The psychological dynamics of the family were profoundly unsettling for the son. A strong mother who made reform her life's work, four intelligent, lively, passionately reformist sisters, and a father who seemed to bow to his wife's wishes in all matters made achieving his own identity problematic for the young Robert Gould Shaw. Historians, then, have recovered a decidedly troubled aspect to the Shaws' family relations. The blame has been placed upon Sarah's shoulders. But there are good reasons to challenge the revisionists' depiction of Sarah and of the private life of the Shaws.[8]

Sarah Shaw's lifework was reform, and particularly abolitionist reform; it was work she shared with her husband and a cause she wanted her children to embrace. Thus, Duncan's keen observation that "the monument on Boston Common is much more representative of her ambition than of his" is richer and more understandable if we situate Sarah, Frank, and their children within a nineteenth-century *gendered* religious and social context. In this way Sarah's evident willingness to sacrifice her son's life and claim it as a vindication of her own makes more sense. When Sarah wrote to Rob, "Now I feel willing to die, for I see you willing to give your support to the cause of truth that is lying crushed and bleeding," she was not being a monster mother but rather reflecting the Christian abolitionist belief that the Civil War was Armageddon, an all-encompassing struggle between good and evil, in which evil would be vanquished through a terrible sacrifice.[9]

Frank Shaw's role should also be revisited. Every bit as dedicated as Sarah was to the ideals of Christian responsibility, Frank was a powerful emotional and spiritual presence within his family and in Rob's life. The war strengthened the father-son bond. "I could not think of any higher work for him," declared Frank of his son's sacrifice at Battery Wagner, "but he had one wish, which he expressed to me as we parted: to fight his regiment alongside of a white one and prove its equality . . . he died in what was to him a moment of triumph—could we wish for him a nobler death." In another letter to William Lloyd Garrison, Frank revealed that although he and Sarah felt deeply the bitter loss of their son, they had come "even to thank God for it," because Rob was now "the martyred hero of the down trodden of our land." Neither Frank nor Sarah thought to shield the children from bearing their share of the burden of ending slavery.[10]

THE SHAWS BEFORE THE CIVIL WAR

In 1842 Francis George Shaw (1809–82) and Sarah Blake (née Sturgis) Shaw (1815–1902) moved from Boston, where their forebears had distinguished themselves in the worlds of finance, politics, and culture, to a large estate in the beautiful and still rural suburb of West Roxbury, Massachusetts. At the age of thirty-two, the handsome and elegant Frank had retired from the mercantile business owned by his father, Robert Gould Shaw, to try his hand at being a gentleman farmer and to pursue his and his young wife's interest in reform. Not coincidentally, their place adjoined Brook Farm, an experiment in communal living and radical politics that briefly attracted some of the most brilliant and talented people in America. The larger and lesser lights of the transcendentalist movement, of which Brook Farm was a part, flocked to the commune during its brief existence—to visit, to observe, to attend lectures and concerts, or simply to join ongoing conversations about the nature of society and how it could be positively altered.[11]

Frank Shaw was more than a good neighbor to the Brook Farmers. He too wanted to provide the world with a model of communitarian life. Shaw believed such a model would offer alternatives to the greedy materialism that seemed to poison relations among rich and poor Americans in the 1840s. And he, along with two brothers-in-law, George R. Russell and Henry P. Sturgis, provided the major financial backing of the corporation from its inception in 1841 to its demise in 1849. The move proved to be an excellent one for Frank. He truly blossomed during his stay in West Roxbury, becoming an intimate and colleague of the inhabitants of Brook Farm. He participated as a writer, critic, and translator for the *Harbinger,* the famous journal of the community.

Sarah Shaw also took eager advantage of the educational and cultural activities that were available at Brook Farm. She attended many classes there with her close friend Lydia Maria Child, the writer and reformer. When the feminist intellectual Margaret Fuller began her series of "Conversations," providing an opportunity for women (only) to study and discuss serious subjects in a comfortable atmosphere, Sarah was an avid participant, along with many of her friends and relatives, including two of her cousins, Ellen Sturgis Hooper and Caroline Sturgis Tappan. Later, Sarah and Frank together attended the meetings Fuller held at which both men and women were present.[12]

And so it was that the five Shaw children (Anna, 1836–1923; Robert Gould, 1837–63; Susanna, 1839–1927; Josephine, 1843–1905; and Ellen, 1845–1936) spent their formative years in a dynamic environment of social experimentation and lively sociability. Visitors flowed easily between Brook Farm and the Shaw home, which became a center of hospitality for Ralph Waldo Emerson, Margaret Fuller, Orestes Brownson, Amos Bronson Alcott, James Russell Lowell, Theodore Parker, William Lloyd Garrison, and Harriet Beecher Stowe. Members of the Shaw family were in constant attendance at Brook Farm lectures, costume parties, picnics, and the formal and informal debates that played so large a part in attracting the legion of friendly visitors and curiosity seekers to West Roxbury. Dr. John T. Codman, a boarder at the farm, remembered with pleasure the sight of "Mr. Shaw, on his horse, with his young son, a tiny little fellow, on a pony by his side," making one of his frequent visits. The Shaw children benefited from the progressive educational system set up by the utopian community.[13] They attended its infant school, although Rob was sent to Mary Peabody's grade school in Boston. Anna, Robert, and Susanna also joined the West Roxbury Sunday school of their parents' friend and neighbor Reverend Theodore Parker. There they received basic Bible lessons, and Sarah and Frank listened intently to Parker's eloquent sermons advocating Christian activism.

Frank and Sarah openly declared their abolitionism when they joined the American Anti-Slavery Society in 1838. Although far removed from the slave system of the South, the Shaws, devout Unitarians, deeply felt the sin of slavery as their own and determined to erase it from the country. "My mother and father were among the earliest abolitionists in Massachusetts," one of their daughters later proudly recalled. Throughout the 1840s, Frank supported legislative measures to abolish the slave trade in Washington, D.C., and contributed money to assist runaway slaves.[14]

Sarah participated in the abolition crusade on her own and with Frank. Indeed, women both married and single played important roles in shaping the movement from its beginnings. Shortly after William

Robert Gould Shaw, 1863. Courtesy Staten Island Institute of Arts and Sciences.

Lloyd Garrison founded the New England Anti-Slavery Society, Maria Weston Chapman created a women's auxiliary to the men's organization. Sarah became an active member, not only working in the antislavery fairs and writing the society's annual reports, but also contributing her friendship and finances to one of the great female luminaries of abolitionism, Lydia Maria Child. "I love Frank and Sarah Shaw," declared the fierce democrat Child, "partly because they are very good-looking, partly because they always dress in beautiful colors, and partly because they have many fine qualities." Even better than that, mused Child, "they are very free from sham; for which they deserve the more credit; considering they are Bostonians and are rich."[15]

Sarah Shaw advocated immediate freedom and equality for black slaves. The truth is that female abolitionists played an important part in promoting the antislavery crusade and hence heightening the sectional tensions that led to the Civil War. In their speeches, petitions, and written work, women such as Lydia Maria Child and Harriet Beecher Stowe painted a stark and terrible picture of slavery and condemned a nation content to tolerate this unmitigated evil. They emphasized the denial of basic Christian humanity to slave families, particularly to the women and children of those families. Drawing upon deeply held convictions about the sanctity of the family, abolitionists stressed the vulnerability of slave women to sexual exploitation and the constant fear that their children would be sold away from them. Antislavery women helped shape the negative images that Northerners increasingly held about the Southern system of slavery.[16]

The strong-minded Sarah Shaw shared, and to some extent directed, many of the couple's cultural, intellectual, and social reform activities. Her interest in transcendentalism, for example, began in early youth. Sarah declared that Ralph Waldo Emerson captured "my heart and *my soul*" at age fourteen, when she heard him preach at her church. She added, "As I grew older I went to all his Boston lectures and my reverence for him grew with my growth and strengthened with my strength." Frank's decision to "retire" at thirty-two from the world of business not only had Sarah's full agreement but also ensured for her a more compatible and equal place for her own work within their marriage. In other words, they enjoyed a "shared career" that challenges our prevailing notions of Victorian womanhood, with its alleged strict dichotomy of public (male) and private (female) spheres. The truth is more complex. The marriages of many American reformers demonstrated that when women acted in public ways, they often did so with their husbands' enthusiastic approval.[17]

Even though Sarah was understandably bound to home and family, especially during her childbearing years, she was an intelligent and thoughtful woman who again and again demonstrated her eagerness to participate—with her husband and on her own—in reform activities that took her outside of the immediate family circle. One admirer described Sarah as "a woman of exceptional charm and force of character, beloved by many gifted friends, and inspiring through a long life the

utmost devotion of every member of her family." She was highly knowledgeable about literature, music, art, politics, and religion and supported any person or cause she thought worthwhile. Her social commitment sent an important message to her four daughters, all of whom, to
a greater or lesser degree, participated in the public sphere as adults.
The fact that Sarah took such a prominent role in family affairs demon-

Sarah Blake Sturgis Shaw with grandson, 1863.
Courtesy Staten Island Institute of Arts and Sciences.

strates that Frank's public championing of women's rights was one that he honored in his private relations with his wife, his daughters, and with his many women friends.[18]

Sarah Shaw's delicate health precipitated another family move to the still more rural environment of Staten Island, New York. This move had been preceded by many visits by the ailing Sarah to Dr. Samuel MacKenzie Elliot, one of the foremost eye specialists of the time. Dr. Elliot, a native of Scotland, had come to the North Shore of Staten Island in 1836, where he not only established a thriving practice but also founded a small settlement called Elliotsville, overlooking the beautiful Kill Van Kull River. There his more affluent invalids could reside in comfortable proximity to his ministrations. In 1847 Sarah, nearly blind, was admitted to a New York City hospital under Elliot's care, while Frank tended to the children in a rented house on the island. Sarah's eyesight improved dramatically, and her overall health responded well to the bracing climate of Staten Island. That year the Shaws decided to settle in Elliotsville, renting for three years before a European sojourn in 1851 and then moving into a newly built house upon their return from Europe in 1855.

The Shaws' four-year stay in Europe (and a brief trip to Northern Africa) included extended visits to Switzerland, Italy, France, and Germany, where the various Shaw daughters and son attended schools and immersed themselves in European language and culture. Even though physically distant from the growing controversy over slavery in their homeland, Frank and Sarah kept up their active interest in political events through newspapers and correspondence. In 1854, while sixteen-year-old Rob finished his education in Hanover, Germany, and Frank was in New York overseeing the construction of their new house, Sarah and her young daughters surveyed the delights of Paris from a spacious apartment overlooking the Tuileries Gardens.

A glimpse of the Shaw women *en famille,* and an insight into Sarah's character, came from the pen of the British novelist Elizabeth Gaskell, who met the Shaws in the winter of 1854. Gaskell, also a Unitarian and an abolitionist, enjoyed long conversations with Sarah about the politics of antislavery, religion, and the state of morality in America. Gaskell was struck by the Shaws' implacable stance against human bondage. They were not "fanatical" she recalled; rather, they were "deeply impressed with the sense of a great national sin, in which they themselves were, to a certain degree, implicated . . . they spoke of slavery as a crime which must be done away with, and for the doing away of which they were not merely willing, but desirous, to make their own personal sacrifices."[19]

According to Gaskell, Sarah often voiced concerns for the future of her children. Affectionately called "the Four" within the family circle, Anna (Nan), Susanna (Susie), Josephine (Effie), and Ellen (Nellie) were described by Gaskell as "pretty, thoughtful, original girls." She also claimed they were indulged by their "sweet, loving, mother." Sarah, however, worried that her daughters might be led astray by the temptations of great wealth. American girls, she declared, were too apt to marry for financial reasons, and not for "true love." During their European sojourn, Sarah exposed "the Four" to the highest cultural and educational opportunities that Europe had to offer—lessons in painting, languages, deportment, music—but she feared that they would be drawn toward a life of ease and materialism and away from the high moral standards of their New England reform heritage. She particularly stressed to Gaskell her admiration of Frank for resigning from the power and privilege of his father's world of business for the less prestigious, unpopular role of an intellectual and a reformer. To Sarah, her husband set a shining example of a life lived according to principle rather than expediency. This is what she wished for their children as well. A notable theme of Sarah and Elizabeth's conversations was the social responsibility that wealthy people owed to the larger society.[20]

A primary function of the Christian Victorian family was to inculcate in children the moral and cultural values necessary to "do the right thing" in both private and public spheres. Thus, Sarah and Frank sought, through punishment and rewards, to shape the personal identities of their children. They urged them through earnest instruction, and by example, to connect their individual concerns with the larger economic and political injustices that confronted the society as a whole. They took particular care to make an explicit link between private morality and public activism in the service of the community. One would be useless without the other; and both were necessary to living a useful life. The Shaws would be disappointed if their children failed to live up to this expectation.

Sarah's motherly concerns with her daughters' moral development extended to her son's growth as well. Unlike his sisters, however, Rob's education occurred away from home, at boarding schools in New York, Switzerland, and Germany. At these schools he engaged in a pattern of misbehavior, for which his parents held him accountable. Yet they were indulgent with him as they never were with their daughters. A question persists about this deeply religious and serious couple: why tolerate Rob's frequent lapses into riotous living if they were so concerned about his moral health? One answer is found in the different expectations for male and female adolescents in the 1850s. To say that a young middle- or upper-class woman's reputation would be seriously damaged by "bad" behavior is a dramatic understatement. She would be, quite literally, "ruined" for her one likely occupation: marriage and raising a family. Not so for a young man of the same class. Although his parents' expectations and training would be equally high, they would be much more forgiving if, as a college student, he gave in to what were still understood as traditional sins of male indulgence such as occasional bouts with alcohol. If, in the end, a responsible, independent young man emerged to take his place in society, the moral testing was well worth the effort.[21]

The young Robert Gould Shaw committed many sins of indulgence. Placed in boarding schools in Switzerland and Germany while the rest of his family moved through the capitals of Europe, Rob alternately rejected, defied, and yearned for his family. Dismayed by their son's excesses, Sarah and Frank evidently never considered taking him out of school, sending him back to America, or inviting him back into the family fold in Europe for more than a few months at a time. And when they sailed for home in the summer of 1855, Rob was left to finish his schooling in Hanover. In short, he was on his own and expected to take care of himself. Of course, his independence was circumscribed by school rules and regulations, as well as understood boundaries of proper moral behavior, boundaries that he transgressed time and time again.[22]

Rob's attention-getting activities severely bent, but did not break, the powerful and loving bonds that tied the family together. Missives flew between the son and both Frank and Sarah. They did not take his irresponsible behavior lightly. They repeatedly asked him to account for his high expenses, and they pointed out to him the benefits of upright living and dedication to the Christian ideals of their family. Their moral instructions had little effect: "All I can say," wrote this occasionally alienated and sullen son of passionate do-gooders, "is that I have no taste for anything excepting amusing myself." He excelled in that activity, as he never would as a scholar or, later, a businessman. The elder Shaws constantly heard rumors of Robert's attendance at various balls, his gambling losses, his bohemian friends, and his drunken escapades. As if confirming their worst fears, he declared, "I don't want to become reformer, Apostle, or anything of that kind, there is no use in doing disagreeable things for nothing."[23]

Rob did not always write letters so repellent to his parents. Another side can be seen as well, especially in his correspondence with his mother and sisters. "Everyone must have a lark now and then," he pleaded in one of his frequent attempts to appease his mother. He was genuinely interested in the progress and growth of the antislavery movement, and he commented intelligently on many other newsworthy items. Few can read the Shaw family letters without coming away impressed by the closeness and respect they all shared for each other. Many letters reveal a tradition of family humor. "I am very glad indeed to hear that Mother is so well," Rob teased his favorite sister, Josephine. "It is very fortunate you mentioned the quarter orange mark on her ankle, as I may stay away so long that on my [return] I shan't recognize her, and in that case she will only have to take off her stocking to prove her identity—'Then you are my long lost Mother!'"[24]

It is worth noting that Rob felt free to express his feelings to his parents, feelings that were obviously going to displease them. In doing so, he not only engaged their attention, which was his goal, but also sustained a dialogue with them regarding the proper course of his life. He clearly wanted their approval, even as he acted out his rebellion. Most of his letters included pleas to be allowed to join the family whenever possible. Rob hoped, for example, to derail his parents' plans to enroll him at Harvard in the class of 1860; he angled for permission to live nearer to Staten Island: "I have only been one year with you since I first went to Fordham. Don't you think I had better enter Columbia College?" His wistful request was turned down as Frank and Sarah insisted that only Harvard would do, thus ensuring his continued absence from his family.[25]

Rob's stay at Harvard was brief and undistinguished; he dropped out after only two years to accept, in 1858, a position in his Uncle Henry P. Sturgis's mercantile firm in New York City. Although happy to be closer to his parents and sisters, Rob did not relish the life of a businessman. Restless and miserable in a boring position, he wrote that he would "rather be a chimney sweep" than engage in a business career.[26] His evident immaturity and restlessness continued to be a source of anxiety to Frank and Sarah, who longed for the awakening of their son's moral consciousness and the settling of his practical future.

THE SHAWS' CIVIL WAR

When the Shaw family returned from Europe in 1855 with their daughters (eighteen-year-old, Harvard-bound Rob would follow them early the next year), they came back to a beautiful, newly built house in Staten Island and a nation in the throes of sectional conflict that would eventually erupt in war. They also reestablished themselves within a community of like-minded people from New England. Their neighbor Sydney Howard Gay, editor of the *National Anti-Slavery Standard* from 1843 to 1857 and later editor of the *New York Daily Tribune*, was just one of many abolitionists residing in Staten Island. The Gay house was a refuge for runaway slaves, and Gay's frequent guests included William Lloyd Garrison, Angelina and Sarah Grimké, and Lucretia Mott. Frank and Sarah often attended meetings at the house, where they expressed their growing concern about the moral and political problems engendered by slavery. The abolitionist community of Staten Island would stand together in the 1863 Staten Island Draft Riots (a smaller offshoot of the New York City Draft Riots) when roving bands of Irish youth terrified the local neighborhoods from July 14 to July 20, just two days after Rob's death.[27]

In the fall of 1856, Frank and Sarah's eldest daughter, Anna, married George William Curtis, who was the editor of *Harper's Weekly*, a popular novelist, and an antislavery lecturer. "Human slavery annihilates the conditions of human progress," cried Curtis in one of his many speeches on the subject. "Its necessary result is the destruction of humanity." The Shaws and all abolitionists had long agreed with his statement, but events in Kansas and Washington, D.C., moved the nation toward a much anticipated breakup. Both Frank and his son supported Lincoln in the frenzied 1860 election, which split the Union. It was twenty-three-year-old Robert's first voting experience, and from his home in New York City he relished the excitement of the campaign. His biographer wrote that "Shaw, the young man in the street, his straw hat worn at a slight angle, a thin cigar in his teeth, listened to the speeches and in the evenings, with his friends, watched the torchlight parades."[28]

Like other young Northern men, Rob Shaw dropped everything when the war began and enlisted as a private in New York's elite Seventh Regiment. As luck would have it, the rest of his family (except for Anna) was vacationing in the Bahamas, and Rob departed with his regiment for Washington, D.C., without their knowledge. "It is very hard to go off without bidding you goodbye, and the only thing that upsets me, in the least, is the thought of how you will feel when you find me so unexpectedly gone," Rob confessed. "But I know, dearest Mother, that you wouldn't have me stay, when it is so clearly my duty to go."[29] While still a private in the Seventh, he applied for and received a commission in the Second Massachusetts Volunteer Regiment, where he saw duty on the bloody battlefields of Cedar Mountain and Antietam.

The entire Shaw family supported the war effort; Sarah and her daughters volunteered as workers in their local ladies aid society, sending food, clothing, and medicine to Union soldiers. Sarah and Frank joined with other abolitionists to press the Lincoln administration to emancipate the slaves, enroll black soldiers, and acknowledge black freedom and citizenship as war aims. They rejoiced at the issuance of the Emancipation Proclamation on January 1, 1863, for it meant that the government fought the war for the Union *and* freedom; now it was a true revolution; now black men could wear blue.

Massachusetts governor John A. Andrew's plan for an African American regiment was approved of by Secretary of War Edwin Stanton on January 26, 1863. Andrew quickly set in motion his well-laid strategy for the recruitment of officers and men for the Fifty-fourth. He formed a committee of concerned citizens, led by the manufacturer George L. Stearns and including Frank Shaw, who helped to raise money and recruit black volunteers from a New York office. President Lincoln and Secretary of War Stanton refused Andrew's request to commission black officers, fearing that Northern public opinion would not support that advancement. Although disappointed by the decision, Andrew recruited the officers of the Fifty-fourth from the cream of abolitionist white society. They must be, he wrote, "young men of military experience, of firm Anti-Slavery principles, ambitious, superior to a vulgar contempt for color; and having faith in the capacity of Colored men for military service. These officers must necessarily be gentlemen of the highest tone and honor."[30] Andrew then offered the colonelcy of the regiment to Shaw and the lieutenant colonelcy to Norwood P. Hallowell, the captain of the Twentieth Massachusetts and the son of prominent Philadelphia abolitionists.

The governor asked Frank Shaw to deliver a letter in person to Rob (who was in camp near Stafford Courthouse, Virginia), asking him to accept the commission. Frank and Sarah were thrilled. They knew that this was an undertaking of great importance, one whose "success or . . . failure" would, in Andrew's words, "go far to elevate or depress the estimation in which the character of the Colored Americans will be held throughout the World." Indeed, by the time Frank left Staten Island with Rob's letter in hand, the governor was assured that the Shaws had given their heartfelt "consent and sympathy and support" to the planned project.[31]

But one Shaw had not given his "consent and sympathy and support." As he traveled to Washington by train on February 3, 1863, Frank feared that Rob's innate modesty might hold him back from accepting the colonelcy. Frank's misgivings were well founded. Father and son spoke at length, after which Rob refused, officially maintaining that he was not worthy. The official version must be expanded. Rob had other reasons for declining. He was a good officer, popular with both officers and men, and had achieved an honorable military record. Further advancement seemed guaranteed. It might be too risky to abandon his Massachusetts comrades for an unpopular cause and unknown dangers.

Clearly, Frank Shaw was disappointed, but he sympathized with Rob's dilemma. Rob, however, experienced immediate misgivings about his decision. He communicated those misgivings to his fiancée, Annie Haggerty of New York. "If I had taken it [the Fifty-fourth colonelcy], it would only have been from a sense of duty. I am afraid Mother will think I am shirking my duty."[32] How well he knew his mother. Sarah dashed off an extraordinary letter to Governor Andrew: "I have just received a telegram from Mr. Shaw saying, 'Rob declines, I think rightly.' This decision has caused me the bitterest disappointment I have ever experienced. . . . It would have been the proudest moment of my life and I could have died satisfied that I had not lived in vain. This being the truth, you will believe that I have shed bitter tears over his refusal."[33]

Sarah's words and the emotions behind her words warrant careful examination. At first reading, a harsh interpretation of Sarah's letter appears justified. It is *her* "ambition" to which she referred when she wrote "the proudest moment of my life" and "I could have died satisfied that I had not lived in vain." Preoccupied with her own feelings and her own disappointment, she seemed perversely blind to the real hazards Rob faced in accepting command of a black regiment. We stand back and wonder at her willingness to risk her son's life to satisfy her own ambitions. It is truly a chilling letter.

Two observations can be made in Sarah's defense. One has to do with Rob's personal development in wartime. The second has to do with the social and religious underpinnings of Victorian culture. As is well known, Frank and Sarah's despair at Rob's evident lack of courage to seize this historical moment for the abolitionist cause was bitterly felt but short-lived. Rob sent this telegraph message to his father on February 5, 1863: "Please Destroy My Letter and Telegraph to the Governor that I Accept." Why did Rob change his mind? Surely he wanted his parents' approval; a lifetime of Christian abolitionist influence could not be lightly dismissed, even by a rebellious son. There were other reasons as well. Captain Shaw of the Second Massachusetts was not the callow youth he had been before the war. Like many of the young men who volunteered for the war, he matured in the heat and blood of battle, developed an intense loyalty to his comrades, and acted with a self-confident independence he did not possess before 1861.[34]

In nineteenth-century parlance, Rob had successfully achieved his "manhood" in circumstances that demonstrated his courage and leadership qualities. His new strength of character extended to the political realm as well. Rob was immersed in wartime politics and went on record several times as recommending the use of black troops in battle. "Isn't it extraordinary," he opined to Sydney Howard Gay in August of

1861, "that the Government won't make use of the instrument that would finish the war sooner than anything else—viz. the slaves?"[35] In other words, his decision to accept the leadership of the Fifty-fourth Massachusetts was no abject bowing to his parents wishes. He knew what he was doing and why he was doing it. Shortly after accepting the command of the Fifty-fourth, he wrote to Annie:

> The first thing I thought of, in connection with it [the Fifty-fourth], was how you would feel, and I trust, now I have taken hold of it, I shall find you agree with me and all of our family, in thinking I was right. You know how many eminent men consider a negro army of the greatest importance to our country at this time. If it turns out to be so, how fully repaid the pioneers in the movement will be, for what they may have to go through! And at any rate I feel convinced I shall never regret having taken this step, as far as I myself am concerned.[36]

The war's emphasis on the masculine ideals of courage and duty drew father and son even closer together in an effort to bring the bright potential of the Fifty-fourth to fruition. Letters between the two demonstrate the resolve on Frank's part to match his son's contribution to the war effort. He not only opened his purse to the Fifty-fourth but opened a recruiting office in New York City as well. "Dear Father," instructed the younger Shaw, "The regimental committee here have engaged a coloured man, named W. Wells Brown, to go to New York and help along the enlistments there. He will call at your office immediately after his arrival . . . you had better buy tickets in New York for their transportation."[37] Rob's tone with his father was distinctly less affectionate and more businesslike than with his mother and sisters. Rob expected his father to take care of his financial matters, visit him in camp when called, send him any necessary articles of war unobtainable at the front, and, after he was colonel of the Fifty-fourth, champion his unit's cause to political and military leaders. All these duties Frank performed with alacrity. For that, Rob was deeply appreciative and usually signed his letters "Your loving Son."[38]

The second point in defense of Sarah's attitude is almost too obvious to make. Sarah was only one of many mothers who willingly and enthusiastically sent their sons off to war, yes, to be killed for a cause. Women played critical roles in the Civil War. They not only contributed to the military effort through ladies aid societies, fund-raising, and nursing, but also in keeping the personal morale of the soldiers high. Letters expressing women's love and support were treasured by the homesick soldiers. Rob received many such letters from Sarah and all of his sisters. Indeed, when women, North or South, withdrew their support of the war, when they wrote sad and frightened and angry letters to their men, letters of protest against the sacrifice and the violence of the war, the desertion rates rose notably. In the gendered world of mid-Victorian America, men were expected to be courageous on the battlefield and women were expected to be brave on the home front. And the home

Francis George Shaw, 1863. Courtesy Massachusetts Historical Society.

front—lovingly portrayed in sentimental songs, books, and magazine and newspaper articles widely sung and read by soldiers—was symbolized by that bastion of domesticity and security presided over by women: the home. Lonely men missed the idealized warmth and safety of the home, especially when confronting the realities of the battlefield.

Rob was no different. In a letter to his sister, he described a conversation with a friend in which "we both think more and oftener of the time when we shall see our Mothers and sisters again than of anything else, and pray that we shall find you all well and happy as when we came away." Mothers, sisters, sweethearts, and daughters embodied this home for which the soldier fought: "For finally," wrote one historian, "wasn't the Civil War a war over the meaning of the home?"[39] So it was that many women, like Sarah Shaw and her daughters, along with politicians, generals, and ministers, provided the emotional and ideological as well as material support in the war.

Moreover, the Christian abolitionist depiction of the war as a holy crusade to erase the sin of slavery from the land gathered momentum as its horrors increased. Sarah vividly expressed this sentiment in a letter (written before Rob's death) to a wartime correspondent: "That dreadful curse of slavery has so permeated the people, and . . . has caused such a rot in society, that it still holds many in its horrid grasp. You must not think me superstitious, if I say that I still see the hand of Divine Providence even in that. Every defeat opens hundreds of blind eyes to the fact that slavery is at the bottom of all . . . I have great faith that our land is to be rid of slavery. Would God have inspired now again thousands of mothers and young wives to look upon it with resignation, but for some great end?"[40] We can surmise that she prepared herself for the distinct possibility of her son's death in this divinely ordained conflict. The last line, however, demonstrates the power of redemption. Sarah believed that out of the pain, the terror, and the death, there would emerge a new people and a new nation that, from the abolitionist point of view, would be finally cleansed and purified from the "curse of slavery." The sacrifice of those near and dear to her would be worth the price for achieving this "great end."

Sarah's prose reached a poetic and spiritual epiphany in her famous letter to Rob just before he was to take command of his black regiment:

> My Darling Son,
>
> No words written or spoken can ever make you understand the deep and holy joy that your acceptance of this call has given to me. I see you 25 years ago, a little white baby lying in my arms, and now I see you willing to take up the Cross.

God rewards a hundred fold every good aspiration of his children; and this is my reward for asking for my children not earthly honors, but souls to see the right and courage to follow it. Now I feel ready to die, for I see you willing to give your support to the cause of truth that is lying crushed and bleeding.

I believe this time to be the fulfillment of the Prophecies, and that we are beholding the second advent of Christ, and I know now how those Jewish mothers felt when their only sons were willing to give up the praise of men, to follow Christ. . . .

You have done just what we are commanded to do . . . and you have made me the happiest Mother in the world.[41]

Simply put, Sarah gloried in her son's dedication to duty. The arming and training of black soldiers to fight for their own freedom had long been an abolitionist goal. Rob was a major instrument in fulfilling that goal, because of what his parents stood for in their lives. Both Frank and Sarah had taught their children to be warriors in a holy cause, and now their son fulfilled his and their destiny by assuming command of the country's most important black regiment.

Surely, then, one must think, the Shaws were ready for Rob's death on July 18, 1863. It appears not. No matter how prepared they thought they were, no parent can easily accept the loss of a child. In the meantime, the Northern press and public celebrated the sacrifice of the Fifty-fourth, and overnight the regiment became a powerful symbol of African American manliness. Now the path was cleared for the full-scale recruitment of black regiments, eventually amounting to 10 percent of the Union Army. And Rob was already being celebrated as an abolitionist hero. This offered cold comfort in the Shaw house, where many tears fell. The strength of their convictions and the fact that they had expected Rob to accept the command could not cushion his family from the sorrow they felt upon his death. An inconsolable Sarah described her "almost Pagan grief" and explained to a friend: "He and I . . . often talked over this possible end, and we thought we were ready, if it should come. It found him ready, but not so, his Mother."[42]

AFTER THE WAR

Frank and Sarah continued to live on Staten Island surrounded by their children and grandchildren. In 1869 they sold their large homestead on Bard Avenue to their daughter and son-in-law, Susanna and Robert Minturn. The elder Shaws then purchased a more modest residence on the shores of the Kill Van Kull, where they lived with their widowed daughter Josephine and her small daughter. During the 1870s all four daughters lived on Staten Island. Every member of the Shaw family contributed to the Northern effort during the war and, characteristically, remained socially and politically active citizens. Their challenge was to do justice to Rob's legacy, as they perceived it, as well as the legacy of abolitionism. This meant more than just memorializing Rob in pictures, or poetry, or bronze; it meant in their actual, daily existence uniting thought and action, prayer and ideals, with a practical program for the country.

Always, for the Shaws, as for so many others of the era, American citizenship was defined by the willingness of a large number of virtuous Christian people to assume public responsibility no matter what the cost. The "Union" had been saved at a dear price, but it was a price worth paying because it cleansed the nation, as Sarah phrased it, of the "sins of a pro-slavery democracy." The Shaw family would emerge from the Civil War years with a firm belief that the American nation had redefined itself by producing a second birth of freedom for black people. This moral achievement had to be built upon for the generations to follow. George William Curtis spoke for the family when he said that the war showed that "national greatness is a moral, not a financial fact."[43]

From the late 1860s to the early 1900s, the Shaws devoted their energies to the education of the freed people, the labor question, civil service reform, charity organizations, and the anti-imperialist movement. At the war's end, Francis George Shaw served as president of the New England Freedmen's Aid Society, which, along with numerous other local societies, both secular and religious, sought to provide the former slaves with food, medicine, clothes, and other necessities. Frank Shaw made frequent trips to Washington, D.C., during the winter of 1864–65 lobbying for the passage of a bill authorizing a national Freedmen's Bureau (the Bureau of Refugees, Freedmen, and Abandoned Lands). Frank and Sarah and two of their daughters, Ellen and Josephine, supported the establishment of black colleges and schools in the South during the 1880s and 1890s and made substantial financial contributions to that cause. Frank Shaw retired from reform and public life after his work for the Freedman's Aid Society and lived out his remaining years quietly but purposefully. Just before his death in 1882 at the age of seventy-three, he helped spread the message of the radical economic reformer Henry George by funding the initial printing of George's manifesto *Progress and Poverty*.[44]

Two sons-in-law of Frank and Sarah played prominent roles in Gilded Age public life. George William Curtis condemned the political corruption of the Grant administration and worked mightily to implement an "honest" government through Civil Service Reform. A prominent figure in the Republican party until he could no longer bear its unsavory political practices, he led a new movement to promote independent political action. Known as one of the foremost "genteel reformers" or "Mugwumps," Curtis wielded considerable authority as an editor of *Harper's* until his death in 1892. Yet another son-in-law made the goal of "clean and efficient" government his career. Francis Channing Barlow, dubbed the "Boy General" by Civil War journalists, married Ellen Shaw in 1867. As New York state attorney general, Barlow initiated the legal proceedings that brought down the infamous William Marcy Tweed, the Tammany Hall boss whose $13 million courthouse still stands as the symbol of Gilded Age corruption.[45]

Three of the Shaw sisters—Anna Shaw Curtis, Susanna Shaw Minturn, and Ellen Shaw Barlow—were married and raising families during this period; their public and charitable activities were muted at first but became more evident with maturity. Anna Shaw Curtis, her husband's indispensable helpmeet for many years, worked with him to support woman's suffrage and political reform. After Curtis's death in 1892, she served as vice president for the Society for the Prevention of Cruelty to Children and was a member of the Staten Island Board of Education. Susanna Minturn, mother of seven children, also found time for public service and among other duties helped her sister Josephine in her charitable work. The youngest Shaw, Ellen Barlow, was an indefatigable worker for black education and prison reform and also served as a vice president of the Civil Service Reform Association. Ellen, a charming, outgoing woman who lived to the age of 90, corresponded with many prominent figures, engaging them in lively debate over controversial issues.[46] Rob's widow, Annie Haggerty Shaw, never remarried. An invalid, she resided in Paris, returning often to stay in Lenox, Massachusetts, where she had a country home. Annie devoted herself to various local charities and helped to found the local public library. The Barlows also had a home in Lenox, and so geographical proximity facilitated Annie's continuing close relations with her husband's family.[47]

After Colonel Charles R. Lowell's death, Josephine Shaw Lowell plunged into charity work and became one of the best-known reformers of the era. She was well prepared for the role. During the war she worked long hours for the United States Sanitary Commission, the era's premier philanthropic organization, which proved to be a model for postwar charitable endeavors. In the early 1870s, Josephine volunteered to lead the New York State Charities Aid Association's study of "pauperism," a social problem comparable to today's homeless population. In 1876 the governor of New York appointed her the first woman commissioner to the State Board of Charities, which established state regulation of both private and public social welfare. In 1882, amid rising concerns that city charities were being tainted by association with politics and corruption, she founded the Charity Organization Society of the City of New York. Her organization shortly became a powerful and influential force for charity reform.

By the mid-1890s Josephine Shaw Lowell was an acknowledged national expert on charity and social welfare. Building on her family's record of social activism, Josephine also vigorously advocated civil service reform and labor reform. In doing so, she carved out an important public role for women at the close of the nineteenth century. In 1892 she founded the New York City Consumers' League, an organization dedicated to improving working conditions for the city's burgeoning population of female sales clerks. Lowell's and the league's drive for better labor conditions led them to the state legislature to demand substantial reform. Josephine, like her male relatives, became a powerful and vocal opponent of traditional machine politics, embodied by Tammany's rule in New York City.

After Frank's death, Josephine, her daughter, Carlotta, and Sarah lived in adjoining brownstones on East Thirtieth Street between Park Avenue and Lexington in New York City. Sarah remained a formidable presence in her children's life, but her influence on Josephine proved especially powerful. Together, they relished the victories and mourned the defeats of Josephine's career. At the end of Sarah's life, she joined with her daughter, a leader in the anti-imperialist movement, to oppose American expansionism in the Philippines. The movement's leadership was studded with familiar abolitionist names like Storey, Garrison, and Higginson, and its geographical center was New England. The movement's moral center, with its emphasis on freedom for an oppressed people of color, echoed the earlier protest movement as well. "We want an agitation like the Abolitionist movement," declared Josephine in 1901, in one of her many comments linking the two reform traditions.[48]

When the eighty-seven-year-old Sarah died on New Year's Eve in 1902, Josephine was in the midst of a heated campaign to force the political parties to acknowledge the Philippine independence movement. Propriety demanded a mourning period, but she brushed aside the social conventions, explaining to a friend whom she invited to a strategy meeting, "We should not ask any one to dine here so soon after my mother's death, unless in a cause so vital in its importance and so dear to her."[49] Another friend received a more personal view of her mother's passing: "She died very peacefully Monday morning, just as she had hoped to, without any pain. . . . That evening her nurse heard her talking to my brother's picture—saying: "Rob, Rob, where are you? Why don't you come and get Me?"[50]

A few years earlier at a ceremony honoring the unveiling of the Saint-Gaudens Memorial, Sarah and her daughters heard one speaker describe their family this way: "Our land is to-day the richer for the work and the lives of this family circle,—of brilliant soldiers, scholars, public citizens."[51] The women of the Shaw family were proud of Colonel Shaw's and the Fifty-fourth's bronze commemoration, but they were proud in another way as well. *They* had fulfilled the duty of their generation to honor those who died in the Civil War and to live out the statement "It was a sacrifice we owed" in its fullest and most positive sense.

II

A Saintly Shape
of Fame

DAVID W. BLIGHT

THE SHAW MEMORIAL IN THE
LANDSCAPE OF CIVIL WAR MEMORY

> What, was it all for naught, those awful years
> That drenched a groaning land with blood and tears?
> Was it to leave this sly convenient hell,
> That brother fighting his own brother fell?"
>
> Paul Lawrence Dunbar, "To the South, on Its New Slavery," 1901

L IKE EVERY other generation of Americans since 1865, we live in a time of tension and change regarding the meaning and memory of the Civil War and the age of emancipation. What John Hope Franklin once called "the verdict of Appomattox" is still not a completely settled subject, and perhaps it never will be.[1] The purpose of this essay is to suggest ways of understanding the place of Augustus Saint-Gaudens's monument to Robert Gould Shaw and the Fifty-fourth Massachusetts in the broad landscape of Civil War remembrance, to outline the context of the 1890s in which it was unveiled, and to reflect on the meaning and memory of the memorial a century later.

We live in a time when public struggles over the content and meaning of the past—between history and heritage—have important political stakes. It is as though we are living, once again, through one of those eras when old certainties have dissolved and many of the institutions, empires, or ideologies that had defined much of the geopolitics of the world have collapsed into a new order, the outlines of which we can only dimly see. The growing American pluralism (now more often called multiculturalism or the "browning" of America) inspires many of us and frightens others into retreat or attack. At the end of this century, and of the millennium, the question of what stories are welcome in the national narrative is a widely debated one. Many are unsure that a master, national narrative is worth imagining anymore at all. Melancholia and anxiety are, and perhaps always have been, the underside of great and exciting change. This is not a new problem; in this historical moment, our culture seems to be doing what others have done in similar circumstances—it is looking backward in search of identity, legitimacy, meaning, and hope, when looking forward is too confus-

ing or frightening. Scholars, teachers, and public historians should celebrate this enthusiasm for the past, harness it in the interest of learning
and understanding in every way possible. But this should be done with
no illusions; the marketplace for history is vast and turbulent, and often
members of the academy are playing only small parts in a cast of thousands.

For many reasons, this is a telling historical moment in which to
reflect on the Shaw Memorial. The unsuccessful call of Governor David
Beasley of South Carolina in late 1996 for removal of the Confederate
battle flag flying over the state capitol indicates that a politician's fate
in some Southern states may hinge on his or her position on the viabil-
ity of the Confederate heritage. Beasley was defeated in his November
1998 bid for reelection. In Virginia, Governor George Allen Jr. declared
April 1997 Confederate History Month for the third year running amid
considerable controversy, racial division, and an NAACP protest. In
April 1998 Virginia's new governor, James S. Gilmore III, issued a similar proclamation, honoring the sacrifice of Confederate soldiers but
adding this time a declaration that "slavery was a practice that deprived
African Americans of their God-given inalienable rights [and] which
degraded the human spirit." The inclusion of the statement about slavery prompted R. Wayne Byrd Sr., president of Virginia's Heritage Preservation Association, to call a news conference at the Richmond capitol
to denounce Gilmore's portrayal of slavery as an "insult." "Southern
life on a plantation," said Byrd, was more properly remembered as a
time when "master and slave loved and cared for each other and had
a genuine family concern."[2] Academic historians are well advised to
remember that although paradigms may change fundamentally in their
interpretive discipline, in the larger realm of public history and memory, great myths have durability beyond their control.

Saint-Gaudens's masterpiece, with its images of twenty-three black
U.S. soldiers, their individuality and collective purpose captured almost
miraculously in that relief, has special resonance again today. While a
growing movement in the popular culture, led by the Sons of Confederate Veterans organization, claims that thousands of "black Confederates" served the Southern cause, we need to keep clear in our minds
Saint-Gaudens's vision of the men of the Fifty-fourth regiment marching,
in the words of art historian Vincent Scully, as "all one will moving
forward."[3] We should always be open to new interpretations, but we also
have to be ready to declare whether historical claims are supported by
adequate evidence. Moreover, we need to understand the relationship
of such claims to the racial politics of our own time, to the ways the
present sometimes determines the past, to the ways that some Ameri-

cans are always seeking to give new legitimacy to the Confederacy, and thereby to current political motives.

In curricula, roundtables, book clubs, film, and tourism, and among collectors and reenactors, the Civil War may be as popular in historical interest as it has ever been. In the 1890s when the Shaw Memorial was unveiled, the South's "Lost Cause" mythology had achieved a remarkably wide appeal; it had captured a broad segment of the American historical imagination, and the "loss" of the war by the South had become for many (including Northerners) a "victory" over the experiment of racial equality during Reconstruction. As a public memory, a web of organizations, public rituals, and monument building, the Lost Cause became a civil religion, a heritage community formed in the Reconstruction South out of the chaos of defeat. As a version of history, the Lost Cause allowed white Southerners in the post-Reconstruction era to form a collective identity as victims and survivors. As the story went, the Confederacy had been defeated only by superior numbers and resources; its heroism on the battlefield represented the true continuity of state sovereignty from the founding fathers, and its principal legacy in the New South era was the white supremacy necessary to control the children of Reconstruction (black and white).

Lost Cause mythology had many opponents who kept alive a victorious, emancipationist, Unionist legacy of the war, especially Frederick Douglass, the former abolitionist, and the carpetbagger and novelist Albion Tourgée, as well as a variety of reformist newspapers, black churches, intellectuals, and some fringe elements of the Republican party. But those voices lost ground steadily in civic life, in public commemorations, and in history textbooks down through the 1890s. Douglass vehemently had warned of this trend as early as 1870, when he reacted to the first wave of Confederate monument-building and the growing secular sainthood of Robert E. Lee. "The spirit of secession is stronger today than ever," Douglass contended. "It is now a deeply rooted, devoutly cherished sentiment, inseparably identified with the 'lost cause,' which the half measures of the government towards the traitors has helped to cultivate and strengthen." And by 1884 Tourgée worried that the national history already had been perverted by the spirit of sectional reconciliation. The North, Tourgée complained, was "too busy in coining golden moments into golden dollars to remember a past that is full of the glory of noble purposes." "The South," he said, "surrendered at Appomattox, the North has been surrendering ever since."[4]

In the 1990s the Lost Cause may have transfigured once again (it has had many lives) into yet another revival of our culture's eternal fascination with the Confederacy, its "rebellion," its heroes and causes, and its cult of fallen soldiers. As legacy and symbol, the Confederacy has also played a major role in the ways Americans confront or evade the dilemma of race. In a wonderfully wry voice, the current Southern novelist Allan Gurganus writes: "Trust me. The South is no place for beginners. Its power of denial can turn a lost war into a vibrant, necessary form of national chic." Gurganus is among the many white Southerners resisting the current Confederate revival. Ruefully he chides his fellow Southerners to give up on the Confederate battle flag, as well as other symbols and lore, especially what he calls the South's "secret power: our habit of anticipating defeat while never accepting it." In our own time, we can see that the Shaw Memorial may have at least another century of useful work to do—by its very presence as a work of art and as a public declaration of specific and enduring meanings of the Civil War. As Booker T. Washington said in his dedication speech at the unveiling, "the full measure of the fruit of Fort Wagner, and all that this monument stands for," will never be realized until blacks and whites have achieved genuine forms of equality of economic opportunity and have learned to fully embrace each other's humanity. Similarly, writing in the 1920s, the critic Thomas Beer may have been prescient when he said that though the American Civil War "ceased physically in 1865, its political end may be reasonably expected about the year 3000."[5]

If the landscape of Civil War memory is so scarred, yet ever replenished; so cluttered with monuments rooted in artistic formula and social forgetting, yet also full of monuments that move us emotionally, why is this memorial unique? Where does it fit in the competing narratives of what some of us would still call America's national history? The Shaw Memorial and the events it commemorates compel us to acknowledge that wars have meanings that we are obliged to discern and that nations still have histories and once had (and may still have) a need for a sense of mission. Questions such as these force us to confront others that are central to African American history. Why did it take total war on such a scale to begin to make black people free in America? How did a struggle between white Northerners and Southerners over conflicting conceptions of the future of their societies become, for nineteenth-century blacks, a struggle over whether they had any future in America? Many younger students ask, Why did black men in the middle of the nineteenth century have to die by the thousands in battle or of disease in order to be recognized as men—not as citizens, just as men?

Answers to these questions lie deep in our political and cultural history and deep in the nature of racism itself. The answers will not be found in a kind of teeter-totter approach to history that considers the contribution of one group, and then another group, and then another in isolation. The search for answers to these questions might reveal a narrative of authentic *tragedy* at the heart of the Civil War, and therefore at the center of American history. Americans rarely have been fond of seeing their history as tragic; this forward-looking, expanding republic with great resources and a providential sense of its destiny has allowed little room for treating the darker, fated collisions and bitter contradictions in our past. Victory narratives—of conquest, of social and economic progress—have always sold best in the American marketplace; they have been good for commerce, good for foreign policy, and good tools of immigrant assimilation. It may be only human and the product of modern sensibilities to seek one's identity in a victory narrative out of the past. But we also have to be ready to explore how this use of the past for the formation of personal and national identity may be peculiarly American. "Americans love a tragedy," William Dean Howells wrote, "as long as it has a happy ending." And no one ever captured the tragic sense one can attain in gazing at Saint-Gaudens's monument as well as W.E.B. Du Bois did in *Black Reconstruction* (1935), where he wrote: "How extraordinary, and what a tribute to ignorance and religious hypocrisy, is the fact that in the minds of most people, even those of liberals, only murder makes men. The slave pleaded; he was humble; he protected the women of the South, and the world ignored him. The slave killed white men; and behold, he was a man!"[6]

The tyranny of slavery brought America to the bloodletting of 1861; the tyranny of racism, and the necessity to resist it, brought the men of the Fifty-fourth in 1863 to Camp Meigs, near Boston, and to that magnificent march down Beacon Street, captured for all time on this monument. The tyranny of war, and the inexorable demands that the men of the Fifty-fourth display their manhood, sent them charging against the parapet at Battery Wagner. If America is about new beginnings for fundamental ideas, if the Civil War was a second founding of the American republic and a "new birth" of freedom, then the story of the Fifty-fourth regiment and the Shaw Memorial is not about a *contribution* to the story. It is about our national promises and betrayals, about the civic ideology at the heart of our society, and about the *transcendence* that makes all tragedy meaningful. The men of the Fifty-fourth Massachusetts, and those of many other black regiments, embodied a whole cluster of meanings; they carried the highest aims of the Union cause and inevitably became the perfect target for what the Confederate cause sought to preserve. Probably only war could have wrought such a moment of truth in the nineteenth century, and hence the fate of the Fifty-fourth.

Their heroism was not merely the exhibition of physical courage in battle; it was their audacious faith to join up, salute, train, suffer, and give their lives for the chance to establish their own human dignity and their claims of belonging in their own land. Their deaths gave a new name to, and started a new narrative of, the idea of racial equality. If one looks very carefully at the faces on the monument, one can feel their determination, their lonely courage, the diversity of their ages and backgrounds—in short, their humanity—as they move forward toward death. There is no hesitation in their step; they seem to represent an idea we are not at all comfortable with in the 1990s: the notion that people can be asked, indeed, that it might be fated and necessary that they die for ideas.

Our own century since 1897, the most violent in modern history, has left us weak and sometimes wordless in the face of the violence we have committed as a species. Sometimes our own culture in the United States, as well as those in other nations, have simply refused to face that history, and sometimes we have stood up to it responsibly. In the case of the Civil War, understanding it requires a narrative told *through* the full story of emancipation, not around it, hovering above it, or packaged in feel-good notions of how America was simply living out its destiny of progressive freedom. That narrative cannot be served up with pure moral clarity; it has to accommodate evil and good, fierce hatred and deep compassion, great loss and great attainments. It has to be a narrative of tragedy, one that takes seriously the mystery of human suffering and accounts for the knowledge and change born from that suffering.

This tragic sensibility has to be something Saint-Gaudens understood in giving us this monument. After observing the unveiling in May 1897, and particularly after watching the survivors of the Fifty-fourth march to the monument, Saint-Gaudens recorded his thoughts with rapture:

> There stood before the relief 65 of these veterans . . . the Negro troops . . . came in their time-worn frock coats. . . . Many of them were bent and crippled, many with white heads, some with bouquets. The impression of those old soldiers, passing the spot where they left for the war so many years before, thrills me even as I write these words. They faced and saluted the relief, with the music playing "John Brown's Body." . . . They seemed as if returning from the war, the troops of bronze marching in the opposite direction . . . and the young men in bronze showing these veterans the vigor and hope of youth. It was a consecration.[7]

To those who look closely, and who know some history, the Shaw Memorial still has these elements of the sacred, of true consecration, of a kind of transubstantiation—not of bread and wine, but of the past into the present. The eternal fascination and nostalgia for Civil War history is often rooted, ironically, in a transgenerational yearning for a time when Americans were so alive with hatreds and passions, when they killed each other and overturned their society in epic proportions. The Shaw Memorial gives us at the very least an object through which to contemplate our own positions in that yearning.

Fifteen years after Battery Wagner, in 1878, Frederick Douglass delivered a Memorial Day speech in Madison Square in New York. Douglass appealed to military pathos and to the notion of heroic soldiers' sacrifice. But more than that, he demanded that his audience remember that the Civil War had been a struggle of ideologies on both sides. The conflict had been "a war of ideas," Douglass declared, "a battle of principles. . . a war between the old and the new, slavery and freedom, barbarism and civilization." It "was not a fight," he insisted, "between rapacious birds and ferocious beasts, a mere display of brute courage and endurance, but it was a war between men of thought, as well as of action, and in dead earnest for something beyond the battlefield." Although no single white Southern mind existed in the wake of the war, many ex-Confederates, ironically, agreed with Douglass (albeit from entirely different perspectives). In 1867 Edward A. Pollard, wartime editor of the *Richmond Examiner,* concluded his long book, *The Lost Cause,* with a warning to all who would ever try to shape the memory of the war. "All that is left the South," said Pollard, "is the war of ideas." The war may have decided the "restoration of the union and the excision of slavery, but the war did not decide Negro equality."[8] Thus, as the memory of the war became so deeply contested, the Shaw Memorial was so necessary in 1897 and remains necessary today and for generations to come.

This focus on ideology illustrates one of the oldest and most important questions in Civil War remembrance: do we remember the *meaning* of the war, or just the *fight?* Would we rather feel—or see—the spectacle of battle, or face the unending challenge of its moral and political consequences? Are we ennobled by Saint-Gaudens's relief or deflected by it? When we look at the memorial, does our eye follow Shaw on his eternal ride into military glory, as with "wren-like vigilance, a greyhound's gentle tautness," leading "his black soldiers to death, he cannot bend his back," as Robert Lowell put it in his great poem? Or, rather, do we see those black soldiers' faces arched forward and with William James in his 1897 dedication speech "almost hear the bronze Negroes breathe?" To which kind of meaning does our gaze lead? Which kind of details do we see or evade? Which kind of memory, to borrow

Veterans of the state's African American Civil War regiments passing in review at the dedication of the Saint-Gaudens monument to Robert Gould Shaw and the Fifty-fourth Massachusetts Regiment, May 31, 1897. Congressional Medal of Honor winner William H. Carney is carrying the United States flag. Photograph by James H. Smith and William J. Miller. Courtesy Massachusetts Historical Society.

again from Lowell, "sticks . . . in the city's throat": the meaning or
the fight?[9]

Douglass anticipated this kind of separation in popular memory in
his greatest wartime speech, "The Mission of the War," delivered many
times across the North in 1863–64: "A great battle lost or won is easily
described, understood, and appreciated, but the moral growth of a great
nation requires reflection, as well as observation, to appreciate it." It
was as if Douglass had somehow already anticipated the thousands of
regimental histories, battle memoirs, and veterans' reunion rituals of
the late nineteenth century, not to mention the industry of Civil War
nostalgia in our own time. His argument would echo again and again
in African American memory of the war. At the height of the 1868
presidential campaign, Benjamin Tanner, editor of the American Methodist Episcopal Church's *Christian Recorder*, issued a robust reminder
to the Civil War generation and those to follow. "The Abolition of Slavery, the Civil Rights Bill, and the Enfranchisement of colored men of
the South," he declared, "are measures which, in the future pages of
history, will outshine the lustre of Gettysburg, of Vicksburg, of Sherman's march, and of Appomattox Court House. Indeed without those
great acts of legislation, these victories would be almost unmeaning.
Feats of arms are glorious only as they make way for the advance of
great principles."[10] What we need today are more movies, books, and
journalism suggested by Douglass's and Tanner's nineteenth-century
historical priorities and fewer five-hour epics on the battle of Gettysburg, more public history interpretation that speaks to the political and
racial meanings of the Civil War and less that repeats the endless man-
tra of soldiers' sacrifice and reconciliation.

One hundred years ago, when this monument was unveiled, it took
its place almost alone, thematically, in the landscape of Civil War memory. By 1897 the sectional reunion was virtually complete, founded on
a racial apartheid that was becoming the law and practice of the land.
Hundreds of small regimental monuments dotted the landscape on
dozens of former battlefields, as well as in countless cemeteries, and
brought an abstract calm to busy town squares. Several giant equestrian
statues of Civil War generals already stood on the avenues and in front
of the court houses of major cities. Most Southern governors and many
congressmen and senators were Confederate veterans. Here and there
in the South, a lone black politician was still elected to office, one even
to the U.S. Congress (in North Carolina in 1896). But the slow wave of
explicit disfranchisement laws, followed by an ever more specific series
of segregation laws, had begun to roll over southern political life. By
1897 the farmers' revolt and the populist movement, which had threat-

ened to realign American politics on class and racial lines, had run its
course in almost every Southern state as the country faced yet another
cycle of economic depression. The *Plesssy vs. Ferguson* Supreme Court
decision, authorizing the "separate but equal" doctrine, was but a year
old when Boston turned out to honor the survivors of the Fifty-fourth.

In spite of the cunning practices of Jim Crow's visible and invisible
structures in the 1890s, blacks made long strides in education and property ownership; their churches grew in several denominations, and intellectual life flowered among a new generation of blacks educated in
both Southern and Northern schools. But in the great sectional reunion
that swept over American cultural and political life, there were no
"truth and reconciliation" commissions, no national forums or teach-
ins about racial healing to balance the endless rituals of sectional healing—apart from those that either offered accommodation to the new
regime of racial separation or could simply build small worlds behind
it. The Blue and the Gray long since had been "clasping hands across
the bloody chasm" of mutual soldiers' valor. But as Du Bois said in *The
Souls of Black Folk* (1903), "no man clasped the hands" of another, and
equally important, set of veterans—former slaves and former masters,
and the children of both who, according to Du Bois, lived in a condition
of "hatred" at the beginning of the twentieth century.[11]

By the mid-1890s it was only the rare Northern Memorial Day speech
that did not pay equal honor to the Confederate and the Union veterans,
as a means of continuing both the spirit of sectional reconciliation
and commercial growth. On the night before the unveiling of Saint-
Gaudens's monument in Boston, Henry Lee Higginson, Civil War veteran, entrepreneur, friend of Colonel Robert Gould Shaw, and frequent
ceremonial speaker, delivered the official oration in Sanders Theater at
Harvard University. He paid a moving tribute to Shaw and the black
soldiers who had "atoned," he said, "for the sin of slavery." Higginson
could lay such a burden of atonement on the men of the Fifty-fourth
only because in the beginning of the speech he had absolved white
Southerners of any specific responsibility. Higginson intended nothing
"harsh to our brothers of the South," for "the sin of slavery was national,
and caused the sin of disunion."[12] This viewpoint, the idea that somehow the Civil War had come by acts of natural law and inanimate forces,
had helped to pave the road to reunion. The doctrine of original sin has
a way of implicating everybody and absolving everybody all at once. No
one had been truly wrong; heroism and devotion alone had rendered
everyone right, North and South. In view of a war where no one was
deemed wrong, and where the defeated side had gained one political

victory after another for twenty years, we can begin to see the unique position the Shaw Memorial occupied in 1897. In a popular culture infused with white supremacy and the spirit of sectional comity, and in a legal system now governed only by a "thin disguise" that would promote racial hatred and discrimination, as Justice John Marshall Harlan put it in his famous dissent in *Plessy,* Saint-Gaudens's monument took its place as an inspiring exception.

At the beginning of the 1890s, many black writers, editors, and orators, as well as their white allies, resisted this American reunion forged out of the betrayal of the Civil War constitutional amendments and the deepening racial inequality. All who would resist the new regimes of race relations knew they faced a hardened version of recent history. The young journalist and civil rights activist Ida B. Wells showed that she knew it in her writings about the "thread bare lie" at the heart of white Southerners' excuse for lynching. The young African American educator Joseph Price (who founded Livingstone College in Salisbury, North Carolina, and died too young) may have captured the legacy of Reconstruction best in 1890 when he declared: "The South was more conquered than convinced; it was overpowered rather than fully persuaded. The Confederacy surrendered its sword at Appomattox, but did not there surrender its *convictions.*" At the end of the decade, Charles Chesnutt, in his novel *The Marrow of Tradition* (based directly on the Wilmington, North Carolina, riot and massacre against that city's black community in 1898), offered a trenchant summation of America's twisted and violent racial condition. The "weed" of slavery had been cut down, Chesnutt wrote, but "its roots remained, deeply imbedded in the soil, to spring up and trouble a new generation." As lynchings grew in frightful numbers, those "weeds" seemed to sprout all over the American landscape, not only in the South. Only four days after the unveiling of the Shaw Memorial, a large mob in Urbana, Ohio, a town some forty miles from Columbus, broke into a jail housing a black man named Charles Mitchell, who had been accused and convicted in a trial lasting a "few minutes" of assaulting a white woman. Although two in the mob were killed, a detachment of the Ohio National Guard could not stop the fury. Mitchell was hanged from a tree in the town square on June 4, 1897.[13]

As we think of the Shaw Memorial's appearance on the landscape of Civil War memory in 1897, we need to account for the distance between the inhumanity and death inflicted on Charles Mitchell in Ohio and the honor paid to Sergeant William H. Carney—the first black winner of the Congressional Medal of Honor—and his comrades. Hard as it is

to tell, they are parts of the same narrative, and they have to be connected. As we imagine the scenes in Urbana, Ohio, we can wonder with
Lowell, in "For the Union Dead," whether that town had its requisite
Civil War monument—one of "the stone statues of the abstract Union
soldier" adorning the town square, where "they doze over their muskets
and muse through their sideburns."[14]

The context of the unveiling in 1897 might be brought into even
sharper focus by looking at other, equally important, distances in the
interplay of Civil War memories. In late 1895 in Fort Mill, South Carolina, a hundred miles or so inland from Battery Wagner (where originally there had been a plan to build a memorial to Shaw), a monument
to the "faith and loyalty" of the Southern slave in the war was erected.
According to the *Charleston News and Courier*, the granite shaft stood
in the town square, next to monuments to the Confederate soldier and
one to Confederate women, as "the most significant and unique" of
Southern war memorials. Honor paid to "faithful slaves" became a standard element at Confederate reunions, in popular lore, and at community festivals; several "loyal slave" monuments soon dotted the Southern landscape by the early twentieth century. Indeed, the image of the
"loyal slave" and the "old time plantation Negro"—fashioned end-
lessly in the popular fiction of Thomas Nelson Page, in regular newspaper articles, and in stories in the *Confederate Veteran* magazine—had
become a mythic icon of American culture by the time the Shaw Memorial appeared. The United Daughters of the Confederacy lobbied
Congress for many years to build a "National Mammy Monument" in
the District of Columbia. An appropriation for such a monument passed
the U.S. Senate in 1923, but failed in the House of Representatives.
The model for the mammy memorial, designed by artist George Julian
Zolnay, consisted of an elaborate fountain, a sitting figure of a mammy,
and three children assembled about her. Originally planned for a site on
Massachusetts Avenue at Sheridan Circle, the mammy memorial never
became part of America's permanent remembrance of slavery.[15]

Moreover, in February 1896 the White House of the Confederacy was
reopened and dedicated as a museum in Richmond, Virginia. Created
by the Ladies Memorial Society and the United Daughters of the Confederacy, the mansion occupied by Jefferson Davis during the war became the repository of sacred relics and the ideology of the Lost Cause.
At the dedication, Virginia governor Charles T. O'Ferrall paid tribute to
the steadfastness of Southern womanhood and delivered a kind of "New
South" appeal for preserving a heritage and facing the future. A longer
oration followed by the former Confederate general Bradley T. Johnson.

Johnson served up a combination of unreconstructed white supremacy and Confederate triumphalism that would have baffled or offended much of the audience at the unveiling in Boston a year later. To him, nothing was "lost" about the South's cause. "The world is surely coming to the conclusion," announced Johnson, "that the cause of the Confederacy was right." White Southerners had merely "resisted invasion" and had never fought for slavery, he contended. With a historical logic that came to dominate both scholarly and popular understandings of the meaning of the war and its aftermath, Johnson declared slavery "only the incident" of the conflict, never its cause. And as that logic goes, he could therefore conclude that it was the North that had forced a contest of "race domination" on the South. Johnson summed up the legacy of the Civil War in a declaration in which many Americans had come to at least benignly acquiesce: "The great crime of the century was the emancipation of the Negroes."[16]

Within three weeks of the unveiling of the Shaw Memorial in Boston, the United Confederate Veterans organization held its seventh annual convention in Nashville, Tennessee, June 22–24, 1897. Several thousand veterans and their families gathered for a festival, not dedicated to the Lost Cause so much as intended to honor a noble legacy of heroism and to celebrate a flourishing memory of a righteous cause. In 1897 the *Confederate Veteran*, published in Nashville, claimed a circulation to 161,332 homes across the South and elsewhere in the nation. The keynote speaker at the reunion of 1897 was Governor John H. Reagan of Texas, a former member of Jefferson Davis's cabinet in the Confederacy. He took as his primary theme the causes of the Civil War. Reagan delivered a long survey of how "African slavery" did cause the war, but only as an "inheritance" entailed upon the South by Europe. The agony and agitation the nation suffered over slavery had been caused by antislavery Northerners. Then Reagan caught his second wind: "You must understand that I do not make this recital for the purpose of renewing the prejudices and passions of the past, but only for the purpose of showing to our children and to the world that the ex-Confederates were *not responsible* for the existence of African slavery in this country and were *not responsible* for the existence of the great war which resulted from the agitation of that question, and that they were neither traitors nor rebels."[17] Within the same month Saint-Gaudens could weep with joy and transcendence as he watched the black veterans march in front of his monument, and an ex-Confederate official could announce ceremoniously and sincerely that the South was absolved of any responsibility for the war or for the slavery the men of the Fifty-fourth had died to

destroy. The meaning of Battery Wagner had been captured in bronze
forever in Boston, but its meaning will likely remain a battleground in
our own time and beyond.

The conflicts and distances between historical memories are ultimately why such memories matter. The Shaw Memorial, therefore, is
not merely a monument we can pass by as yet another emblem of our
ancestors' vague or forgotten deeds. As we think about why the memorial is different, we need to remember that whatever the motives of the
committee that sponsored it (over the course of fourteen years), whatever Saint-Gaudens's deepest intentions, however we react to Shaw's
preeminence on horseback, the memorial entered a debate, a landscape
of remembrance where armies of memory and forgetting still contended for high stakes. The monument is different; the regiment fought
for ideals that seem higher than the mere abstractions we see through
our own eyes in all the thousands of other Civil War monuments we
pass by in our towns and cities. The Fifty-fourth's memorial is different
because it helps tell the narrative of emancipation. It takes Oliver Wendell Holmes's idea of a "soldiers' faith" and converts it into a moral
purpose larger than the late nineteenth century's craving for the manly,
strenuous life. It allows us to risk seeing soldiering as a testing of ideas,
instead of merely notions of masculinity. It enables us to see the human
aims in that war as well as its beastliness. As we reflect on this memorial's uniqueness, we might also exercise some caution. At the time of
the war, of course, black soldiers carried the burden of the expectations
of their alleged "difference." They were the "experiment" in whether
black men could fight, learn discipline, lead, face danger, and so forth.
Their "traits" were under constant scrutiny. In a piece in *Century Magazine* written in conjunction with the unveiling of the Shaw Memorial,
Thomas Wentworth Higginson, who had commanded the First South
Carolina Volunteers during the war, related the story of General Rufus
Saxton's receiving a long list of questions about the behavior of his black
Union troops in South Carolina. Saxton ordered his secretary to cross
out all the questions and at the bottom of the page simply write, "They
are intensely human."[18]

At this century mark in the life of a great memorial, and well into the
second century of the story it commemorates, hope rests on historians'
ability to reach broad publics with education and acts of remembrance.
Greater appreciation and hope might also be drawn out of all the poetry
and writing inspired by the Fifty-fourth's story and this sculpture. We
might draw our own challenge from the tattered hope that no poet will
ever again be moved to write, as Paul Lawrence Dunbar did in 1900 in
his poem, "Robert Gould Shaw":

Why was it that the thunder voice of Fate
   Should call thee, studious, from the classic groves . . . ,
Far better the slow blaze of Learning's light,
   The cool and quiet of her dearer fane,
Than this hot terror of a hopeless fight,
   This cold endurance of the final pain,—
Since thou and those who with thee died for right
   Have died, the Present teaches, but in vain![19]

MARILYN RICHARDSON

TAKEN FROM LIFE

Edward M. Bannister, Edmonia Lewis,
and the Memorialization of the
Fifty-fourth Massachusetts Regiment

When I turned to address the survivors of the coloured regiment who were present, and referred to Sergeant Carney, he rose, as if by instinct and raised the flag [he had saved at Battery Wagner.] It has been my privilege to witness a good many . . . sensational demonstrations . . . but in dramatic effect, I have never seen or experienced anything which equaled this. For a number of minutes the audience seemed to entirely lose control of itself.

> Booker T. Washington, *Up from Slavery: An Autobiography,*
> describing a scene at the 1897 unveiling of Saint-Gaudens's monument
> to the Fifty-fourth Regiment

THE IMPULSE to publicly commemorate the heroism of the Massachusetts Fifty-fourth at Battery Wagner quickly took hold in the minds of African American soldiers and civilians, North and South. The first effort to raise a monument to Robert Gould Shaw began within days of the battle. The men of the Fifty-fourth, although still unpaid and in many cases with families back home dependent upon charitable contributions of food, clothing, and financial assistance for day-to-day survival, pooled their meager resources to raise $2,832. Their comrades in the Fifty-fifth Massachusetts added another $1,000. A notice further encouraging this enterprise went out from the Beaufort, South Carolina, headquarters of Union commander Brigadier General Rufus Saxton in late July. Addressing the "Coloured Soldiers and Freedmen in this Department," he shared with them his conviction that the "truths and principles for which [Shaw] fought and died, still live and will be vindicated" and urged the recently freed slaves to "pay a last tribute of respect to [his] memory . . . by appropriating the first proceeds of your labour as free men, towards erecting an enduring monument to the hero, soldier, martyr. . . ."[1]

Over the next two months, blacks in the town of Beaufort and former slaves from throughout the rural areas of the Sea Islands, as well as those who fled there from inland plantations, even as they endured the precarious fate of refugees, contributed another $300.[2] Ohioan Frances D. Gage, a pioneering writer and lecturer on behalf of abolition, temperance, and women's rights, traveled to the South as a journalist when four of her five sons enlisted in the Union army. While serving as the Sea Islands correspondent for Henry Ward Beecher's newspaper the *Independent,* she was persuaded by General Saxton to take charge of the welfare of five hundred freedmen on Parris Island. In early September she wrote to Francis George Shaw, describing a gathering in an "unplastered and unpainted church," at which some of that amount was raised. In response to a sermon on the subject by Reverend James Lynch of Baltimore, the son of a slave mother and a white father, members of the congregation "[each] came forward with the mite to be added to the other mites, for the good work. Our people are poor," she continued; "many are ill at this time, and could not come out; and yet, I am proud to say, twenty-seven dollars were given." One of the 120 congregants present that day was "old Flora, eighty-five years a slave," who expressed her amazed delight at "de wite man dying to git us free, and we a buildin' him a big, great stone!"[3] When the plans for a stone monument to be erected on Morris Island were canceled, for reasons ranging from the difficulty of building on the shifting coastal sands to the hostility of the local white population to support among many black donors for an educational enterprise, the money went instead to found the first free school for black children in Charleston; the donors named it in honor of Shaw.[4]

Back in Boston, Joshua B. Smith, a black man who had worked for the Shaw family for some years before establishing a successful catering business, began a movement immediately following the assault on Battery Wagner to erect a monument in the city where the regiment had been recruited and trained. Smith was a radical abolitionist who had taken a leading role in the organized resistance to the Fugitive Slave Act of 1850, including the armed rescue of the apprehended runaway Shadrach Minkins. He discussed his idea with Senator Charles Sumner, who urged him to hold off on his plan until the end of the war. In October 1865 Smith, committing five hundred dollars of his own funds, joined with Sumner and others to organize a planning committee and raise the thousands of dollars necessary to commission a prominent sculptor to design and execute the monument. Although he did not live to see the completion of Saint-Gaudens's masterpiece, Smith, who was elected Cambridge representative to the state legislature in 1873, was recognized by African Americans throughout the country as the initiator of the evolving commemorative project.[5]

Two black artists living and working in Boston were among those who shared with Smith and his Southern counterparts the immediate impulse to memorialize the men who undertook the all-but-hopeless attack on Battery Wagner. That both the painter Edward Mitchell Bannister and the sculptor Edmonia Lewis were moved to create enduring public images in response to the exemplary valor of the regiment reflected the deep significance for blacks of the taking up of arms at last on their own behalf. Like those soldiers and civilians who pooled their dwindling financial resources, the artists who took to their studios with similar urgency understood that Shaw and his troops were men whose stories must never be lost to America's historical memory.

The landmark historical compendium *The Colored Patriots of the American Revolution,* published in 1855 by Bannister's and Lewis's friend William Cooper Nell, would have served as a vivid reminder of just how easily the story of the participation of blacks in all of this country's wars, often with outstanding courage and distinction, was erased from history and popular memory. Recognizing the significance of preserving African American history in statues and monuments as well as in books and documents, Nell and Smith had long worked in the interest of lasting public representation of black contributors to the making of America. In the early 1850s the two had composed and circulated petitions to the Massachusetts state legislature calling for a monument to Crispus Attucks, the black man killed in the 1770 Boston Massacre. Among blacks, Attucks was known as "the first to defy; the first to die."[6] Of Attucks and all of the black men who served in the armies of the Revolution, Nell wrote, "no attempt has . . . been made to preserve a record. They have had no historian. With here and there an exception, they have all passed away, and only some faint traditions linger among their descendants."[7] Nell's diligent research resulted in a volume of over three hundred pages of primary and secondary documentation of black achievement from the colonial era to the 1850s. A patron of the arts, an amateur playwright, and a founder of Boston's black Histrionic Society, Nell, whose 1855 appreciation of Bannister in *Colored Patriots of the American Revolution,* was the first published notice of the young painter, fully understood the importance of the arts in establishing a record of black participation in virtually all aspects of American life. Having himself watched the Fifty-fourth board the ship *DeMolay* for the voyage to South Carolina, and having proclaimed that occasion to be "glory enough for one day; aye, indeed for a lifetime,"[8] Nell would have heartily encouraged both Lewis and Bannister in their work of depiction and remembrance.[9]

Of the two black artists, Bannister had arrived in Boston first. Born about 1826 in New Brunswick, Canada, Edward and his younger brother, William, were raised by their mother following their father's death in 1832. Along with interests in music and literature, young Bannister developed an early passion for drawing, which, he later recalled, he often indulged at the expense of his other studies. By the time he was

Edward Mitchell Bannister, after 1869. The Rhode Island Historical Society.

ten years old, according to art historian Juanita Marie Holland, young Bannister's drawings of friends and family had won him some local acclaim.[10] By 1850 the Bannister brothers were living and working in Boston, a city with a long history of African American political activism as well as a recognized center of American artistic and intellectual life. Described by William Wells Brown as a man who was "spare-made and slim, with an interesting cast of countenance, quick in his walk and easy in his manners,"[11] Bannister supported himself with work as a hairdresser and later, as a photographer. Initially refused formal training by area art teachers, he managed to study and develop his artistic gifts on his own.

In 1857 Bannister married the highly successful businesswoman Christiana Carteaux, who owned hair salons in Providence, Rhode Island, and in Boston. His contemplative formal oil portrait of his wife is one of the highlights of Bannister's early career. Together they grew increasingly active and influential in both abolitionist and artistic circles.[12] Madame Carteaux, as she was known professionally, regularly organized participatory musical and theatrical evenings with such prominent African American friends as abolitionists Lewis and Harriet Hayden, portraitist William H. Simpson, Bannister's early patron Dr. John V. DeGrasse, attorney George L. Ruffin, and Nell. Bannister, Nell, Ruffin, and Simpson joined in the display of their musical talents. Billed as the Crispus Attucks Quartet, they were popular performers at political rallies and various civic celebrations.

In November 1864 Christiana Carteaux Bannister led the organization of a fair held by the Boston Colored Ladies' Sanitary Commission to benefit the members of the state's African American regiments, the Fifty-fourth and the Fifty-fifth Massachusetts and the Fifth Massachusetts Cavalry. There was a great need for such a fund-raiser to support the black soldiers, who had only weeks earlier resolved the dispute that had led them to serve without pay for a year and a half rather than accept less than white soldiers were paid. The event was an unqualified success. The leading black newspaper in the country, The *New York Weekly Anglo-African,* called it the "greatest fair ever held in Massachusetts by colored people." A correspondent described the hall as filled with tables sponsored by both black and white women's groups from throughout the state, all brimming with eye-catching items for sale. "As we enter Summer Street," the correspondent continued, "a large flag bearing the inscription 'Colored Soldier's Fair' meets the eye. On entering Mercantile Hall we behold a beautiful view. . . . On the North side a table extends the whole length, the center of which is the 'President's Table' being under the charge of Mrs. Bannister . . . assisted by

Christiana Carteaux Bannister, oil portrait by Edward M. Bannister, ca. 1870.
Courtesy Bannister Nursing Care Facility, Providence, Rhode Island.

Miss E. Ruffin [and] Mrs. Wm. Wells Brown." Following accounts of the
abundance and variety of goods to be found throughout the hall and the
listing of the names of distinguished participants, the final paragraph
of the report focused on an important artistic contribution to the exposition. "Directly in the rear of the speaker's stand," it began, "is a large

three-fourth length portrait of Col. Shaw the hero of Fort Wagner." The reporter offered an enthusiastic critical opinion, declaring the painting to be "a fine specimen of art," and went on to say that it had come from the studio of a black artist. Although the painting is not further described, it is emphatically identified as "the work of Mr. E. M. Bannister, our talented artist." To date, this portrait has not been located, and so it is particularly tantalizing to learn that it was both a popular and a critical success. "It attracts much attention," the reader is told, "and is highly spoken of by the profession."[13]

What we do have, however, thanks to its publication, between November 1864 and January 1865, in the *Boston Daily Advertiser*, the *Liberator*, and the *Anglo-African*, is a poem inspired by Bannister's painting, written by antislavery activist Martha Perry Lowe.[14] The young Martha Perry, later the wife of Unitarian leader Charles Lowe, was a graduate of Mrs. Sedgwick's School in Lenox, Massachusetts. Elizabeth Sedgwick, a progressive educator, prided herself on turning out independent, creative, and socially conscious young women. The Lowes were close friends of Dr. Henry I. Bowditch and his family, staying with them for a time before Charles accepted the pulpit of a church in Somerville, Massachusetts. Through Bowditch they would have known the Shaws. With the coming of the war, Reverend Lowe went south to serve as a chaplain to the Union troops and to work with the Freedman's Aid Society.

Martha Lowe, who worked in support of women's rights, temperance, and Unitarian organizations, as well as on behalf of blacks and Indians, was known in the Boston area as a dedicated and prolific, if not particularly gifted, poet. Her first collection of verse, *The Olive and the Pine*, on subjects inspired by an extended visit to Spain (the olive) and by her love for the hills and shores of New England (the pine), along with a selection of "Miscellaneous Poems," appeared in 1859.[15] Such poems as "The Virgin of Murillo," "The Two Pictures," "Ribera's Picture of an Old Monk," and "Scheffer's Picture of Dante and Beatrice" show that the contemplation of paintings often served as encouragement to her own muse.

THE PICTURE OF COL. SHAW IN BOSTON

> Buried with his negroes in the trench!
>   There he lies, a score of them around him;
> All the fires of bondage this shall quench;
>   Could a monument so well have crowned him?
> Sight to make a father's bosom throb—
>   There he stands upon the canvas glowing!

Sight to make a noble mother sob—
    Tender eyes, their glances on her throwing!
There he stands, so eloquent and mute,
    Modest, and yet looking in our faces
Undisturbed and calmly as doth suit
    One who did not ask the world's high places!
There he gazes, soldier-like and bold,
    Not a whit ashamed to die with him—
Him, the man of color, bought and sold;
    Not a bit ashamed to lie with him!
Look upon him Nation of the free!
    Surely, this shall cure thee of thy meanness;
Look upon him, Nation yet to be,
    Crying out, remorseful, "Oh, my leanness!"
Sleep serenely, with thy country's sigh,
    Noble martyr to the nation given!
With thy little company on high
    Thou shalt traverse all the plains of heaven!

Certainly a deeply felt response to the portrait, though no proliferation of exclamation marks can transform it into a work of literary merit, the poem is a crude but valuable contemporary document that combines a lament for Shaw with approbation for the work of a black artist. Lowe's introductory reverie upon Shaw's death both condemns and appropriates Confederate general Johnson Hagood's alleged remark that Shaw had been "buried with his niggers." The colonel, joined with his troops in death and ignoble burial, is raised, by transcendent paradox, to a nobility beyond the stain of any indignity. Lowe is nonetheless quick to establish, with her initial exclamation of dismay, her understanding of the clear demarcation between white and black, officer and troops, superior and inferior. Even though, in a burst of Bostonian chauvinism, she all but declares the circumstances of Shaw's death and burial alone sufficient to bring an end to "All the fires of bondage," Lowe obviously shares the compass of emotions ranging from horror to ambivalence felt by even the most sympathetic whites at the thought of the Brahmin colonel's eternally integrated resting place. There is no question here that he alone would be "crowned" by any monument that might be erected at the battle site.

Lowe's perception of the historical event precludes any mention of the fallen black soldiers' military prowess or their status as free men; they are Shaw's "little company"; they are "[men] of color, bought and sold," with whom any other white person would be rightly embarrassed at the thought of sharing a common grave. It is Shaw's extraordinary nobility of soul that renders him "Not a whit ashamed" and elevates him to the status of a "Noble martyr to the nation given!" Somewhat more subtly, though, Lowe laments the inadequacy of any style or type of monument theretofore imagined to interpret in bronze or stone the constellation of complex emotional responses to the assault on Battery Wagner and its aftermath. Eventually, of course, it was precisely such recognition of the unique experience of Shaw and the Fifty-fourth Massachusetts that led Saint-Gaudens to imagine and execute a new and original form of commemorative sculpture.

Lowe's choice to write about the work of art as well as its subject, along with her fulsome praise within the poem for the painting itself, suggest that to her mind this portrait, in its immediate intensity, is indeed a more apt locus of remembrance than would be a formal monument. Curiously, she makes no reference to the painter's race. Did she know when she first saw the picture that the artist was black? Probably so, given her history of helping to organize such Sanitary Fairs. She might simply have expected him to understand and accept the outrage to white sensibilities that is one key to the dramatic momentum of her elegy. Certainly she does not explicitly distinguish between the artist she finds capable of such affecting work and the shame-provoking soldiers she describes; all together, this is a compliment Bannister must have found peculiarly disconcerting.

Edmonia Lewis was a young woman whose mother was of black and Ojibway descent and whose father was a black man from the West Indies. Educated at Oberlin College and before that in a progressive preparatory course at New York Central College in McGrawville in upstate New York, Lewis was a radical thinker and activist committed to both abolition and women's rights. As a student at McGrawville (as the college was generally known), she studied under Charles Reason, George Vashon, and William Allen, three leading black intellectuals of their day and the first hired as faculty members at an integrated college. She and her classmates were further influenced by Frederick Douglass, who championed the school in his newspaper, the *North Star,* and who was a familiar presence on campus, as was his friend Gerrit Smith, a substantial contributor to the funding of this interracial coeducational academic enterprise. Amelia Bloomer, whose innovative clothing was adopted by many of the female students, and Lucretia Mott were among those who, as visiting lecturers and supporters of the school, spoke of the ability and the responsibility of these young men and women to challenge the oppression of blacks and women in this country. Still in her early teens, Lewis joined with other students and faculty in assisting the escape of fugitives on the Underground Railroad on their journey through northern New York to Canada. She enrolled next at

Oberlin, where both town and college were centers of ceaseless, controversial, and at times physically dangerous antislavery agitation. At both schools she was a serious student of art and music.

Lewis arrived in Boston in early 1863 with letters of introduction to William Lloyd Garrison and others of his circle, black and white. Under

Edmonia Lewis, ca. 1870. Courtesy Massachusetts Historical Society.

the tutelage of a friend of Garrison, sculptor Edward Brackett, whose heroic bust of John Brown was widely admired, she spent months refining her anatomical drawing and clay modeling skills. Brackett encouraged her to copy Houdon's famous bust of Voltaire. She soon advanced to her own designs for terra-cotta medallion portraits of champions of black liberation, including Brown, Charles Sumner, and Wendell Phillips.

By the summer of 1864, Lewis was ensconced in her own work space in the Studio Building at Tremont and Bromfield Streets in downtown Boston, the same building in which Bannister had his studio. In response to growing interest in her work, she had placed a notice in the *Liberator*, inviting "the attention of her friends and the public to a number of medallions of John Brown, just completed by her."[16] At the time she undertook her portrait bust of Shaw, her earliest known work in marble, Lewis was no longer studying with Brackett. Working from photographs of Shaw, she was casting about for a new teacher and asked fellow Studio Building occupant Anne Whitney to critique aspects of her work.

Because none of Lewis's papers or journals have come to light and only a few of her letters have been located, much of what we know about this artist's life and experience is gleaned from references to her in the correspondence of white friends and acquaintances. Along with comments revealing the more casually accepted prejudices of the day against blacks and Indians, many of those letters consciously and unconsciously express the great cultural ambivalence elicited by such a profoundly anomalous figure. "She wants," wrote Whitney to her sister Sarah, "to salaam me as her teacher." This supporter of the abolitionist movement, defender of women's rights, and herself the creator of a large allegorical statue, *Africa*, then delivered a brisk little character sketch. Lewis, Whitney continued, "is very much of an aboriginal, grateful, vengeful, a little cunning . . . I like her in spite of her faults, and will help her all I can. . . . I wish she were a little less of an aborigine about the ordering of her wigwam."[17]

Lydia Maria Child, the zealous essayist, novelist, journalist, and social reformer, was also an indefatigable writer of letters to scores of friends throughout the nation and abroad. She took up Lewis as somewhat of a protégé and a cause, making it her business to keep this most unusual artist and her work in the public eye through frequent articles and notices in such newspapers as the *Liberator* and the *National Anti-Slavery Standard*, as well as through correspondence with prominent abolitionist patrons of the arts. She wrote admiringly of the qualities of "life" and "expression" in Lewis's early work, including her bust of Voltaire, and of the exotic young sculptor's "eye for the form of things."[18]

Lewis spent the spring and summer working on her bust of Shaw. Calling upon her recollections of the departing regiment marching proudly to the strains, both rousing and poignant, of "John Brown's Body" and studying *carte de visite* photographs, she eventually achieved a fine likeness of the fallen Brahmin hero. So absorbed was she in the task that she commented to her frequent visitor, Child, on the psychic as well as intellectual energy she found herself investing in the project. "If I were a spiritualist," she told her, "I should think Colonel Shaw came to aid me about that bust, for I thought and thought and thought about how handsome he looked when he passed through the streets of Boston with his regiment; and I thought and thought and thought how he must have looked when he led them to Fort Wagner; and at last it seemed to me as if he was actually in the room."[19] Child, as Lewis knew, was deeply involved in the spiritualist movement, complete with seances and table rappings, so Lewis's well-chosen comments soon found their way into print under her mentor's byline. Elsewhere Child pronounced Lewis's portrait of Shaw "very good, without making allowances for circumstances [of Lewis's gender, race, and lack of experience]."[20]

Encouraging though she might be, Child could be an energetic critic indeed. Visiting her at home one day, Lewis discovered that her patron had sawed off a number of inches from her copy of the Shaw bust, a brusque but apparently effective bit of retouching on which Lewis tactfully remarked, "Why didn't you tell me of that before I had finished? How much you have improved it."[21] Since she had, only moments before, discovered an entire album of Shaw family pictures that Child had withheld from her, hoping to discourage the Shaw project at its inception, the "aborigine" might well be commended for her considerable show of restraint. "Edmonia," Child wrote to the late colonel's mother, "was a little piqued that I had not lent [the photographs] to her while she was making the bust."[22]

The portrait bust, inscribed by Lewis with the words "Martyr for Freedom," was a great popular success. Even John Greenleaf Whittier, who because of his ardent Quaker pacifism refused to so much as look at an armed man during the course of the Civil War—with the sole exception of Shaw on parade with his soldiers as they departed for the front—wrote to Child that he had seen "the bust of Col. Shaw that thee spoke to me of at the colored fair. It struck me as excellent."[23] His comment is all the more remarkable since he had refused to make any public comment, however indirect, on anything pertaining to the war, for fear he might inspire "some further impulse to slaughter."[24]

The fair to which Whittier refers is, of course, the same one at which Bannister's painting was on display. By fortuitous coincidence, Lewis's

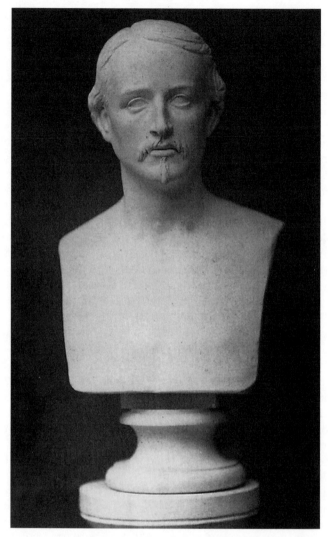

Marble bust of Robert Gould Shaw by Edmonia Lewis, 1864.
Courtesy Massachusetts Historical Society.

work also elicited a poetic response. Anna Quincy Waterston, the daughter of former Harvard president Josiah Quincy and the wife of the Reverend Robert C. Waterston, greatly admired the young sculptor; her own portrait bust in marble was one of the first works Lewis would later complete at her studio in Rome.[25] Waterston's paean to Lewis and her art was widely reprinted, including appearances in the *National Anti-Slavery Standard*, the *Liberator*, and the *Anglo-African*.

EDMONIA LEWIS

(The young colored woman who has successfully
modeled the bust of Col. Shaw)

> She hath wrought well with her unpracticed hand,
>   The mirror of her thought reflected clear,
> This youthful hero Martyr of our land.
>   With touch harmonious she has moulded here
> A memory and a prophecy—both dear:
>   The memory of one who was so pure
> That God gave him (what only can belong
>   To an unsullied soul) the right to be
> A leader for all time in Freedom's Chivalry;
>   The prophecy of that wide, wholesome cure
> For foul distrust and, cruel wrong,
>   Which he did give his life up to secure.
> 'Tis fitting that a daughter of the race
>   Whose chains are breaking should receive a gift
> So rare as genius. Neither power nor place,
>   Fashion or wealth, pride, custom, caste nor hue
> Can arrogantly claim what God doth lift
>   Above these chances, and bestows on few.[26]

Waterston emphasized the artist and the artist's subject equally, championing the cause of that most improbable phenomenon—a young black woman aspiring to a career as a sculptor. She placed Shaw and Lewis together as chosen recipients of special gifts from God—heroic martyrdom for him, artistic genius for her, not only making them, in this particular context, equals in their separate spheres, but also making each gift dependent upon the fulfillment of the other: his death breaks her chains; her art justifies his sacrifice. To Waterston's mind, Lewis both vindicates and preserves the memory of the historic event.

Their images of the white colonel brought considerable attention to the two black artists and served to further both of their careers. At the same time, the response to their depictions of Shaw would have given them insight into the ways in which the twin themes of martyrdom and commemoration entered the public consciousness. Both the painter and the sculptor understood that the possibilities of memorialization and historical immortality for the black men of the Fifty-fourth were intrinsically bound up with the martyrdom of Shaw. Within days of his death, General Saxton had eulogized Shaw as "hero, soldier, martyr."

Lowe and Waterston proclaimed him a martyr; it was a designation that had not only made the rounds by the time they wrote, but had also become a kind of Homeric epithet prefacing Shaw's name. Lewis, in turn, carved on her finished portrait the attestation "Martyr for Freedom," suggesting that she accepted the fact that in this particular Protestant hagiography the name of Shaw would lead all the rest. The surviving men of the Fifty-fourth and their loved ones, plus the families of the slain men, no doubt realized that although in sheer numbers the loss of black lives wreaked the most widespread personal devastation, the personification of the regiment that would secure its survival in memory was that of their fallen leader, not—yet—of his black warriors.

From the start, the mission of the Fifty-fourth had taken on strong overtones of a holy crusade and a religious duty. Among the flags the soldiers carried was a white banner showing on one side the Massachusetts coat of arms and on the other a golden star and a golden cross with the explicitly religious device *In hoc signo vinces* beneath.[27] A vocabulary of intense spirituality, evoking a widely felt sense of foreboding, is an integral part of the vivid descriptions, recorded early on, of Shaw and his men marching to the Boston waterfront. Sarah Sturgis Shaw, seeing her only son ride past at the head of his regiment, exclaimed, "What have I done that God has been so good to me?" Shaw's sister Ellen watched with a sense of exalted resignation as the men passed the Shaw family home at 44 Beacon Street. "His face was the face of an angel," she later wrote, "and I felt perfectly sure he would never come back." Henry I. Bowditch wrote in his diary that as the regiment moved along Boylston Street, "I got from [Shaw] that lovely, almost heavenly smile."[28] Declared the ardent pacifist Whittier, "He seemed to me beautiful and awful, as an angel of God come down to lead the host of freedom to victory."[29]

The black troops were praised and admired for their splendid military bearing, for the high level of their training, and for their eagerness to prove themselves in battle. But the volumes of description of that historic day lack specific accounts of response to individual black soldiers. However much members of the African American families and communities for which they fought and died kept their images burnished bright in such private remembrances as photographs, family stories, and generations of namesakes, these men were, in life and death, anonymous to the majority of whites, who perceived them as without significant differentiation or individuation.

It would appear that Augustus Saint-Gaudens shared and codified that insidious sense of the black masses as a generally undifferentiated presence in the larger society. Working from models hired in New York, he made dozens of plaster and bronze portrait heads of black men, many of which were incorporated into the memorial. Although the anonymous faces are individual and finely delineated, they are not the faces of men who had enlisted in the Fifty-fourth. He worked directly from numerous photographs of Shaw, but Saint-Gaudens apparently chose to forgo the hundreds of photographs of black recruits in uniform that were readily available to him. Captain Luis F. Emilio's comprehensive 1891 regimental history, for example, includes at least twenty-five such pictures, each captioned with the soldier's name, rank, and company.[30] The frontispiece illustration is a dramatic portrait of Sergeant William H. Carney standing with the flag he rescued at Battery Wagner. There are even photographs of a drummer boy and a young fife player, singular images indeed, but apparently not sources for the figure of the monument's drummer. With photography still an evolving medium and source of interest for so many artists in other media as it continued to yield up its secrets and possibilities, one can only wonder whether Saint-Gaudens, perhaps leafing through the work of Matthew Brady, ever considered or attempted a more literal representation of some of Shaw's men.[31] Each had a story to tell; many of those stories are with us still.

Two among the hundreds of such photographs are those of Charles and Lewis Douglass, their family origin certainly as notable in its way as Shaw's. Surely their father, Frederick Douglass, whose thunderous call to arms urged black men into a war that had become a massive slaughter of both blue and gray troops, trembled as his own boys signed their names to the roster of new recruits. As the Fifty-fourth prepared for battle, it was manifestly clear that the unprecedented and unrelenting toll of mounting casualties on both sides meant that the chances of any new units returning unscathed were remote indeed. One widely read eyewitness report by a black combatant, describing the attack on Fort Wagner as well as discussing life in the regiment immediately prior to that battle, is Lewis Douglass's July 20 letter to his parents, which his father printed in the August 1863 issue of *Douglass' Monthly*. Saint-Gaudens could not have wished for a stronger expression of character, sensibility, and heroic determination as inspiration to attempt to capture the spirit of the man in a bronze portrait. Toward the end of his account, Lewis Douglass wrote:

> Saturday night we made the most desperate charge of the war on Fort Wagner, losing in killed, wounded and missing in the assault three hundred of our men. The splendid 54th is cut to pieces. All our officers with the exception of eight were either killed or wounded. . . . I had my sword sheath blown away. . . . The grape and cannister, shell and minnies swept us down like chaff, still our men went on and on, and if we had been

properly supported we would have held the Fort. . . . If I have another opportunity I will write more fully. Good bye to all. If I die tonight I will not die a coward.
Good bye.

Lewis[32]

Fortunately, both brothers survived the war. The thoughtful analysis and insight Saint-Gaudens brought to bear upon the depiction of Shaw, the attempt to discern and make manifest aspects of the intrinsic character of the man, were all denied Lewis Douglass and the other black members of his regiment. As glorious as the conception of the design unarguably is, there is a peculiar psychological dissonance in the care Saint-Gaudens lavished upon the portraits of black men randomly selected to stand in for apparently interchangeable "types" whom he simultaneously immortalized in bronze and obliterated as individuals. Shaw is a unique and exalted equestrian figure; his troops are a marching chorus of honored symbols.

From a mid-twentieth-century vantage point, African American historian Benjamin Quarles was moved to redefine the partially emerged figures as expressions of potential. "[These] black comrades in arms," he writes, "were fighting for freedom in the round—not a low relief freedom for themselves alone, or for their group alone, or for the Union alone, but for freedom wherever there was oppression."[33] As Quarles's brilliant trope demonstrates, every monument speaks of both the past and the present. The facets of design and significance are forever understood in unanticipated ways by succeeding generations of viewers and critics. Certainly, with the twentieth-century addition of the names of the fallen blacks to those of the whites on the reverse of the monument, the men now named participate in a muffled roll call that echoes down the years and back to the sands of Morris Island. Further, contemporary racial politics make us more likely to recognize that even as anonymous symbols, there is a way in which Saint-Gaudens's soldiers comprise a politically radical as well as aesthetically inventive element of his composition. In depicting the literal fact of the grand progression of black soldiers through the streets of the "Cradle of Liberty," the artist incorporated into his design levels of meaning he could not have consciously foretold, juxtapositions whose national import coalesced only in the tribulations of Reconstruction. For the first time in American public statuary, row upon row of marching black men, each of them armed, ready, and capable of using their weapons, are forever passing in disciplined ranks before the citizenry of the nation; it is a scene then and now as edifying to black viewers and as subliminally disconcerting to many white Americans as was once the thought of Shaw and members of his regiment thrown into a common grave.

The *Anglo-African's* report on the Boston Colored Ladies' Sanitary Commission Fair followed its account of Bannister's painting of Shaw by noting a related piece. "A small statue representing Sergt. Carney of the 54th regiment, in a kneeling attitude holding up the colors lest they touch the ground, is to be seen on one of the tables; this is the work of Miss Edmonia Lewis of this city." Like Bannister's painting, this work has never been located. When Lewis made her sculpture, however, Carney, from New Bedford, the first black American to be awarded the Congressional Medal of Honor, was undergoing the mysterious process

Sergeant Major Lewis Henry Douglass and Private Charles Remond Douglass in uniform. Courtesy Moorland-Spingarn Library.

Storming Fort Wagner, chromolithograph by Louis Kurz and Alexander Allison, 1890.
Courtesy Boston Athenæum.

of becoming a living iconic figure. Widely reproduced illustrations of
the highly stylized (and inaccurate) "Assault on Fort Wagner" showed
two heroic figures at the apex of the struggle—one white, doomed; one
black, destined to survive and to recount with horrific immediacy the
circumstances of Shaw's martyrdom. Depicted by the popular lithogra-
phers Alexander Allison and Louis Kurtz with an idealized simultaneity, a symbolic reportorial freeze-frame shows Shaw's moment of martyrdom in a helpless backward free fall, stylistically ceding the apex of
the composition to Sergeant William H. Carney, who was lunging forward, sure-footed, to meet the future bearing aloft the flag he had moments before rescued from the fallen standard bearer.[34]

"The Regiment had gotten but a short distance," wrote Sergeant Carney in a description of the events he was invited to recount at Fourth of
July observances throughout his life, "when we were opened upon with
musketry, shell, grape, and canister, which mowed down our men right
and left . . . as a scythe would mow the thick grass. . . . As the color-
bearer became disabled, I threw away my gun and seized the colors,
making my way to the head of the column. . . . The musket balls and
grapeshot were flying all around me as they struck the sand would fly

in my face. In less than twenty minutes I found myself alone struggling upon the rampart while all around me were the dead and wounded."[35] As the news of Shaw's death was confirmed—early reports of the battle had erroneously claimed that he was wounded but alive—so too did word spread of Carney's bravery and of his determined affirmation as he

Sergeant William H. Carney, winner of the Congressional Medal of Honor, ca. 1906. Courtesy Carl J. Cruz, a descendant of Carney.

was helped, badly wounded, into the field hospital, that "the old flag never touched the ground, boys."[36]

Although it was the idealized bust of Shaw that advanced Lewis's reputation and, through the sale of copies and photographs, brought her the funds to travel and study abroad, the Carney statue is her first recorded narrative work, her first full-length, though not life-size, figure. Above all, it is the first known depiction by any sculptor—and therefore all the more significant because it is from the hand of a black woman—of the singular experience of a specific, named, and in turn nationally recognized individual African American soldier depicted in a free-standing three-dimensional work, a black man fighting for Quarles's ideal of "freedom in the round."

Lewis commemorated the man and the moment. She could not have calculated the phenomenal import this one man among thousands of black veterans would acquire with the passage of time. Booker T. Washington, in his startled response to the exuberant outpouring of honor and acclaim accorded Carney and the rescued flag, bears witness to the persistence of the public's memory of the scene of death and valor conjoined atop the ramparts of Battery Wagner. Sergeant Carney, rising to his feet there at the 1897 dedication of the memorial, holding aloft the very flag he had snatched from dishonor, was a figure come to life from Saint-Gaudens's heroic frieze, able still to tell his singular tale. No wonder that "for a number of minutes the audience seemed to entirely lose control of itself." Should Lewis's statue be found, the identity of its subject would be as clear today as when the work was modeled; aspects of its significance, however, can only now be recognized in light of our evolving understanding of the myriad social and psychological facets of the commemorative impulse. The presence at the 1864 Boston Colored Ladies' Sanitary Commission Fair of Bannister's painting of Shaw, Lewis's bust of Shaw, and her figure of Sergeant Carney constitutes an exceptional moment in African American artistic and social history. That their endeavors were recognized and acknowledged by the public and the press, black and white, as substantial work by professional black American artists marks a unique nineteenth-century conjunction of art, race, and politics.

By the end of the 1860s, Edward Bannister's career had gained considerable momentum. In 1869 he and his wife moved to Providence, Rhode Island. There he continued to produce work in a wide range of genres from portraits to landscapes to seascapes to animal scenes and still lifes. He became a prominent member of the Providence Art Club, the forerunner to the Rhode Island School of Design. In 1876 his painting *Under the Oaks* won the first-prize medal for painting at the Philadelphia Centennial Exposition, where Lewis enjoyed a great success with her life-size depiction *The Death of Cleopatra.* The rude reception of Bannister by the judges and arts patrons until he was identified as the prize-winner showed that there were, a decade after the close of the war, many victories still to be won by African Americans. He died in Providence in 1901; in tribute, his friends organized a memorial exhibition of more than one hundred of his works.

As for Edmonia Lewis, from the sale of plaster copies and photographs of her bust of Shaw, and with the help of abolitionist patrons, she soon raised enough money to sail to Europe in the summer of 1865, there to further develop her skills as a sculptor. She settled in Rome, where she lived for the rest of her career, making frequent trips back to the United States to exhibit and sell her work. She became the first black American to gain an international reputation as a sculptor. During the 1870s Lewis worked in a studio near Rome's Piazza Barberini at number 9 via San Nicola Tolentino. Saint-Gaudens's studio was in an adjacent building at number 4.[37] Lacking at this point any documentation of neighborly visits, we can only nod in agreement with critic and connoisseur Lincoln Kirstein, who remarked in 1973 that in his opinion Saint-Gaudens would have been familiar with her bust of Shaw.[38] What we can document is that although an entire generation would pass away between the end of the Civil War and the dedication of Saint-Gaudens's great monument, the heroism of the Fifty-fourth Massachusetts Regiment was recorded, even as battles raged, in the work of two black artists painting and sculpting images from a decisive moment in the nation's history to which they had borne witness and which they were determined to rescue from oblivion.

AUGUSTUS SAINT-GAUDENS
AND THE SHAW MEMORIAL

T HE SHAW MEMORIAL, a bronze Civil War monument in high
relief, is arguably Augustus Saint-Gaudens's finest work and the
greatest public sculpture in America. It honors Robert Gould
Shaw and the black soldiers of the Fifty-fourth Massachusetts Regiment who fell on July 18, 1863, in the disastrous assault on Battery
Wagner in South Carolina. Other contributions to this volume view the
piece in the context of politics, literature, music, and film; this essay
provides new facts regarding the creation of the monument.

Less than a fortnight after the Wagner debacle, Massachusetts senator Charles Sumner considered commemorating young Shaw's demise
with a work of art. In a letter of condolence to Francis George Shaw and
Sarah Blake Sturgis Shaw, Robert's father and mother, Sumner wrote,
"In his case the heroism is enhanced by the cause in which he fell &
the companions by whom he was surrounded. I mistake much, if this
incident does not take a place in history & also in art. . . . Nobody can
give so generously to country & to human freedom without compensa-
tion, which must last as long as consciousness or memory."[1] Sumner
also penned a letter that same day, July 29, to Edward Lillie Pierce, a
Boston abolitionist and lawyer, in response to the news of the attack on
Battery Wagner: "I cannot be consoled for the loss of Shaw. But where
better could a young commander die than on the parapet of an enemy's
fort which he had stormed? That death will be sacred in history and
in art."[2]

The movement to immortalize the colonel and his troops was generated by Joshua B. Smith, who had been employed by the Shaw family
and who became a successful caterer and an important figure in Boston's
black community. Smith, who promised to donate funds of his own for
the monument, sought further financial support from fellow African
Americans. With the help of Sumner and other local notables, a committee was assembled. In the autumn of 1865, a meeting to discuss a
memorial to Shaw was held in the council chamber in the State House
in Boston, chaired by Governor John Andrew, who had been instrumen-
tal in forming the Fifty-fourth Regiment. The minutes of that session
stated: "The monument is intended not only to mark the public grati-

tude to the fallen hero, who at a critical moment assumed a perilous responsibility, but also to commemorate that great event, wherein he was a leader, by which the title of colored men as citizen-soldiers was fixed beyond recall."[3] Edward Atkinson, an economist nominated by Sumner, served as the treasurer of funds raised for the memorial and subsequently compiled a narrative of the monument. Although Atkinson had not been in attendance at the gathering, according to his account, he was informed that there had been "some difference of opinion as to the kind of statue or memorial which should be procured."[4]

During a subsequent meeting in October at the Union Club in Boston, William Wetmore Story, the Cambridge-bred and Harvard-educated neoclassical sculptor, was selected as the artist for the monument[5] upon the recommendation of Sumner, his friend and mentor. Story's career was on the rise, spurred on by the splendid reviews that his *Cleopatra* (1858) and his *Libyan Sibyl* (1860) had received at the 1862 International Exhibition in London.[6] Story initially envisioned a traditional freestanding equestrian statue cast in bronze, as documented in correspondence between Sumner and Story. In late October 1865 Story, then living in Rome, communicated to Sumner that if the rider were to be about eight feet high with the horse being larger in scale, the cost of the caster's expenses might be between ten and twelve thousand dollars, with the entire estimate from twenty-five to thirty thousand dollars.[7] Story's diary showed several entries from January 1866 related to the Shaw: "Working at sketch of Shaw"; "Photographed statuette of Shaw"; "Cast sketch of Shaw on horseback"; and "Sent letters with photos of statues of Everett & Shaw to Sumner".[8] However, Story learned that the funds to furnish the monument would not be forthcoming: "I am afraid from what I hear indirectly that the subscription will not be made up, & I shall be sorry for many reasons if this be the case for it is a noble subject—I should have great pleasure in making it."[9] Had the design and execution of the Shaw monument proceeded in rapid fashion, it would have been one of the relatively few bronze works by Story, who was known principally for his sculpture in marble.[10]

Following the death of Governor Andrew in 1867 and that of Senator Sumner in 1874, attempts to advance the planning of the sculpture stalled, and Story had moved on to other commissions. Nevertheless, by 1876, through wise investments, the Shaw fund surpassed seven thousand dollars, allowing Atkinson to propose a rekindling of the initiative for a monument. He designated John Murray Forbes, Colonel Henry Lee, and Martin P. Kennard (all men sympathetic to the creation of a memorial) as an executive committee. Forbes became chairman of the newly organized group, and Atkinson, though not formally part of the committee, became both its treasurer and secretary. With what must have been a spreading of the word that a revival of the Shaw enterprise was in the air, by early April 1878 Martin Milmore had prepared a three- or four-foot-high equestrian statue of Shaw in plaster which was on display in his Boston studio.[11] Milmore, who had distinguished himself with a bust of Charles Sumner (1865)[12] and with three Civil War pieces, the *Roxbury Soldiers' Monument*, dedicated in 1868 at Forest Hills Cemetery in Roxbury, Massachusetts; *Sphinx* (1872), at Mount Auburn Cemetery in Cambridge, Massachusetts; and the *Soldiers' and Sailors' Monument*, erected on Boston Common in 1877, was one of the foremost sculptors in the city at that moment. For the monument on the Common, one of the bas-reliefs shows "The Departure for the War" with figures of Governor Andrew and Robert Gould Shaw, and in the panel representing "The Return from the War" are portraits of Sumner and Joshua B. Smith. It may not be too far-fetched to surmise that it was Smith who proposed that Milmore execute the equestrian statue of Shaw.[13] Although the *Boston Evening Transcript* reported a year later that Milmore would model the equestrian statue of Shaw,[14] apparently the sculptor's scheme was not taken beyond this stage, and with the death of Smith three months thereafter on July 5, 1879, Milmore lost the individual who may have been his staunchest advocate. Since the executive committee feared that the cost of an equestrian statue would exceed the funds that had accrued (less than twelve thousand dollars by the end of 1878), the committee considered limiting the project to either a standing statue or a bas-relief.[15]

At this point, the Shaw family, which had expressed slight interest in the undertaking, offered a suggestion as to who might be put forward as the sculptor. Atkinson imparted to Forbes: "It has come to my knowledge that Mrs. Shaw would be well pleased to have Launt Thompson chosen as the artist to make the statue of Col. Shaw. The fund is now sufficient and some action should be taken—May I ask the committee to come to a decision not only in regard to the artist but also as to the place for the statue."[16] Thompson was no doubt familiar to Sarah Shaw for having made in 1866 a marble bust of Robert B. Minturn, who had died on January 9 of that year and who had been the father-in-law of Sarah's daughter Susanna.[17] Thompson had established a solid reputation in New York as a sculptor of naturalistic bronze portrait busts and statues and was also responsible for several significant monuments in honor of military figures killed in the Civil War, such as the life-size bronze of Major John Sedgwick, unveiled in 1868 at the U.S. Military Academy at West Point, and the full-length statue of General Winfield Scott (1870–1873), for the Old Soldiers' Home in Washington,

D.C. Thompson was living in Florence when Sarah Shaw recommended him to Atkinson, but nothing came of her proposal. Of note, he returned to America in 1881, succumbed to alcoholic binges and to mental illness, and died in a state hospital for the insane in Middleton, New York, in 1894.[18]

Anne Whitney's involvement with the Shaw monument was a product of her own antislavery convictions as well as her relationship with the writer and abolitionist Lydia Maria Child, who was a close friend of Colonel Shaw's parents. A champion of the oppressed and a firm believer in social change, Whitney's oeuvre prior to her model of Shaw included *Africa* (1864) (destroyed) and *Toussaint L'Ouverture* (about 1870), now lost. At the urging of Child, and with no commission in hand, Whitney started by August 1880 to model a horse in a studio at her family's home in Belmont, Massachusetts. Whitney wrote in early December 1880 to Maria Weston Chapman, organizer of the Boston Female Anti-Slavery Society: "But the horse is—Yes he is worth your seeing now—& all the more I feel the imperfection of the rider & must when I have finished the other attend to him—I have him in my mind's eye—& know by that token that he will take shape. What a pleasure to work in the Ideal! Portraits to the rear!"[19]

The executive committee lacked a precise vision of the monument and could not decide whether it should be an equestrian statue, a bas-relief, or a standing figure.[20] In a fascinating letter to Whitney, the abolitionist Wendell Phillips, who knew Lee, Forbes, and Kennard, discussed Lee's ideas for the piece: "I had long talk [*sic*] with Lee. He objects to monument 1st because a statue wd not be discriminating in what it tells—Wants a bust & under it bas relief showing Shaw at the Fort leading blacks—etc. etc. . . . He promised to come & see the Horse—for he said he was not obstinately wedded to his notion—."[21]

Whether or not Lee ever inspected the animal, Whitney continued with her model, put Shaw on the horse, and went so far as to have the composition cast in bronze. Though Whitney readied her figure, presumably at her own expense, with the expectation that there would be an open competition for the commission, none came to pass.[22]

In the meantime, Henry Hobson Richardson, the renowned architect and neighbor of Atkinson, was engaged as the designer of the architectural framework for the monument. It was Richardson who had collaborated with Saint-Gaudens for a variety of patrons and who strongly endorsed him as the sculptor for the memorial. Beginning on February 24, 1881, a series of letters between Richardson and Saint-Gaudens documents the negotiations and progress regarding the commission for the Shaw.

Anne Whitney, *Robert Gould Shaw*, bronze model, [1882?]. Present location unknown. Courtesy Wellesley College Archives.

On March 9, in a letter to Saint-Gaudens, Richardson said that he had "written to Mr. Atkinson asking him if the 14th will be convenient to him and if not to appoint a day on which you can meet the Shaw monument committee"; on March 11: "I have just received a note from Mr. Edward Atkinson. He does not seem to think it necessary for you to meet all the members of the Shaw monument committee at the first conference. He therefore asks you to lunch with him, Col. Lee and

myself at the Union Club, Boston, on Monday the 14th inst." The committee apparently wished to see evidence of Saint-Gaudens's work, because Richardson reported to Saint-Gaudens in July that the "five photographs of the Farragut Monument [which had been unveiled to popular
acclaim in New York on Memorial Day, 1881] were duly received. . . ."
By November of 1881, Saint-Gaudens had met with Atkinson, had begun to think about the "tablet," and wanted to get together with Richardson to discuss it.[23] The widely published drawing from Richardson's
office in the Houghton Library featuring an equestrian Shaw was completed by mid-April 1882.[24] On his own, Saint-Gaudens made a number
of equestrian drawings and sketch models, which were modified considerably after being criticized by Shaw's family; they felt the young colonel should not be presented in a manner customarily reserved to honor
men of the highest rank.[25] During June and July of 1882, correspondence
between Atkinson and Saint-Gaudens disclosed the sculptor's hesitation to provide the Shaw committee with a model unless he was officially entrusted with the monument. It was a delicate dance; before
the committee hired Saint-Gaudens, they simply desired a satisfactory
model. They did agree, however, that they would not solicit other sculptors unless Saint-Gaudens's efforts proved unacceptable, a possibility
Atkinson thought would be extremely "remote."[26]

Saint-Gaudens was uncomfortable with making a model without being certain that he had secured an order because of a disappointing
experience with an earlier commission. In 1875, he had entered a model
in a competition in Boston for a statue of Charles Sumner. After requesting models of a seated Sumner, the project's committee members
decided that they wanted a standing figure instead. Saint-Gaudens was
infuriated and vowed that he would neither enter future competitions
nor submit sketches until a commission had been awarded to him.[27]

Although Anne Whitney was of the impression that there would be
an open competition, the Shaw committee became convinced that Saint-
Gaudens would not prepare a model unless he was designated the sculptor for the memorial. Accordingly, no competition took place. Atkinson
remarked that "the surest way to carry out our plans would be to select
an artist without confusing ourselves with any competition."[28] Further,
he told Forbes, "Realizing most fully that competitions were generally
unsatisfactory and that Committees were apt not to concur even when
reduced to so low a number as three, I promoted the contract with St.
Gaudens in the terms with which you are familiar."[29]

By the spring of 1883, the general configuration of the relief had been
finalized, and Saint-Gaudens appeared to be deeply engrossed in the
Shaw commission. The sculptor had learned that while in action in

South Carolina, the colonel had been on foot alongside his regiment. In an attempt to dignify the catastrophic truth of the saga and to create an equestrian, which he keenly wanted to do, Saint-Gaudens reached back two months earlier in the story to record the actual departure from Massachusetts. He struck upon the image we know today, with Shaw on horseback leading his men out of Boston. The rendition is close to the original mental picture Sumner had of the monument. He had conveyed to Atkinson that the "work should consist of a statue of Colonel Shaw mounted, in very high relief upon a large bronze tablet."[30] Typical of his working method, when portraiture was involved, Saint-Gaudens obtained photographs of the sitter and his clothing. For example, he wrote to Shaw's sister Josephine Shaw Lowell in the fall of 1883: "I will want the coat again when I begin work—."[31]

Saint-Gaudens's model was accepted in 1883. With the fund for the monument at seventeen thousand dollars, a contract was drawn and dated February 23, 1884. It stipulated that for a fee of fifteen thousand dollars Saint-Gaudens would execute a life-size memorial of Shaw, made of stone and bronze in a high bas-relief, in accordance with sketches the sculptor had delivered to the committee in April 1883. It also outlined that the memorial would be erected in front of the State House and be not less than ten feet high (excluding the base) and eleven feet wide. It called for the monument to be finished and set in place within two years from the date of the contract.[32]

The committee assumed that Saint-Gaudens's full attention would be directed toward the monument's termination, but the sculptor was ambitious and very much in demand. During this same period, Saint-Gaudens was working on other key pieces, such as the *Puritan* for Springfield, Massachusetts (for which he signed a contract in November 1884) and a statue of Abraham Lincoln for Chicago; each was dedicated in the autumn of 1887.

The deadline for completion of the monument in February 1886 came and went. Several months later, on April 27, Richardson died. In early June, to appease the committee, Saint-Gaudens sent a photograph of what he intended for the Shaw monument and noted he would mail two others, as well as some photographs of the *Puritan*, which he trusted would induce the members to "feel kindly and bear patiently with me."[33] Saint-Gaudens made little headway on the Shaw relief, although he exerted himself feverishly in the 1880s and 1890s and brought forth a sculpture of consequence each year between 1886 and 1893. Among these, in addition to the *Abraham Lincoln* and the *Puritan*, are various portraits, of which the many versions of *Robert Louis Stevenson* is one, as well as the *Adams Memorial* in Washington, D.C., and the gilded sheet copper weathervane, *Diana,* now in the Philadelphia Museum of Art.

In the fall of 1886, Shaw's sister Josephine, in concert with her mother, suggested to Lee that the location of the monument be changed from the front of the State House to the Boston Common, either on the Parade Ground or at the corner of Charles and Beacon Streets: "Might it not go across the Charles St. & Beacon St. corner, with a gate each side of it, one on each street, or, if that would be too inconvenient, would not the Charles St. side, somewhere between the middle gate & Beacon St., be a good place?" She opined that the bas-relief could face the Common with a seat beneath it, and, on the other side, on Charles Street, there could be a second seat "and the names of all the officers and men of the Fifty fourth, who were killed, on the back of the Monument."[34] Describing himself as the "hyphen" between Saint-Gaudens and the committee, Atkinson relayed to Saint-Gaudens the eagerness of Josephine's mother to have the placement of the monument moved from in front of the State House and reiterated how dissatisfied the committee was with the slow progress on the memorial.[35]

It was not until late 1891 that the site for the monument was finally settled upon. For a while, there was a movement to put it inside the "new part of the Statehouse," to avoid, as Atkinson dreaded, "the sparrows, dirty little beasts. They will nest behind the main statue."[36] Saint-Gaudens made clear his preference that the monument be situated where it ultimately went.

The shift from one side of Beacon Street to the other had enormous significance. By switching the location of the monument from the State House side of Beacon Street to the side of the street adjacent to the Boston Common, the city of Boston, rather than the state of Massachusetts, became its proprietor. This, however, caused trouble regarding Saint-Gaudens's choice of his friend Charles McKim to be the replacement for Richardson as the advisory architect. Atkinson explained the circumstances:

> There are some difficulties which I have kept mainly to myself in the present condition of things. Mr. McKim being St. Gaudens' friend and consulting architect, opened the way through his brother-in-law Mr. Meyer, for obtaining the grant from the city in which success was attained to my very great surprise; but now the present Mayor and the City Government as a whole are somewhat in antagonism to McKim for the reason that the Public Library has so outrageously exceeded his original estimate of its cost. It is therefore necessary to proceed with great caution and not to put McKim forward as St. Gaudens' consulting architect. His personality must be suppressed so far as it is possible. Therefore as soon

as the model is absolutely ready . . . Mr. St. Gaudens himself and not Mr. McKim, will *through me* submit the plans to the Mayor for his approval, and I have little or no doubt of securing it.[37]

What had begun with Story, a Brahmin sculptor, ended up with two New York artists, Saint-Gaudens and McKim. However much the committee attempted to arrange for the commission go to one of their own, outsiders took over, took too long, and overspent. It was a painful reminder that Boston's status as a force in the American art scene was undeniably diminishing.

By 1892, the Shaw committee's indignation with Saint-Gaudens was mounting. In a letter to Saint-Gaudens's wife, the long-suffering Atkinson spoke of the committee's uneasiness. "One of the Committee, Mr. Kennard, has lately visited the studio, and he was a good deal disheartened to witness some signs of a large new work which may have been undertaken by your husband; . . . an equestrian statue of General Sherman. This I hope he will be charged with, but certainly *not until the Shaw Monument is completed*."[38]

Later in 1892, the United States government asked Saint-Gaudens to design a medal for prize winners at the World's Columbian Exposition in Chicago in 1893. Convinced that no one in America, including himself, could produce a medal of quality, Saint-Gaudens initially declined the invitation.[39] Shortly thereafter, he came round and resolved to compose the medal, calculating that it would take a mere three months, which proved to be an underestimation.[40] Saint-Gaudens explained his decision to Atkinson in November 1892, but the Shaw committee was incensed by a flurry of correspondence from the architects Richard Morris Hunt and McKim and other prominent men connected with the Exposition. They requested Saint-Gaudens's freedom for a brief interlude to render the nation a service by executing this three-inch medal. For years, Saint-Gaudens had labored on other commissions; seemingly, the committee became aware of them only after they had been effectuated.

Evidently, Saint-Gaudens's other commissions often went unnoticed by guests to his studio. The reasons for this were clarified in his *Reminiscences*. "I began work on it [the Shaw] at once, and soon it took up the entire width of the studio, . . . with behind it a platform about eight feet high, on which I placed whatever statue I had to do that would ultimately be on a pedestal. . . ."[41] Thus, in the intervening time, whenever the Shaw committee went to Saint-Gaudens's New York studio to examine their piece, all they saw was the huge expansive breadth of the relief; until the aforementioned visit of Kennard during which he set eyes on the *Sherman* (which was eventually dedicated in 1903 in Grand Army Plaza, New York), no other works were discernible.

Despite objections by the committee, Saint-Gaudens proceeded with the modeling of the Columbian Exposition medal in early 1893. Atkinson defended the sculptor's actions, declaring that Saint-Gaudens was engaged with the medal exclusively in the evening and at night. Most importantly, Atkinson reassured the committee members that the creation of the medal would not interfere with the carrying out of the Shaw monument, which was slated to be delivered on schedule for the thirtieth anniversary of the regiment's departure from Boston.

As Saint-Gaudens toiled in the summer heat, Atkinson continued to play the unpleasant role of intermediary between Saint-Gaudens, the committee, and the city of Boston. So disturbed was he by the delays that he yearned to "never be called upon to deal with an artist again."[42] By October, Forbes was exasperated enough to propose to Atkinson that a radical solution to their woes might be warranted. "I would gladly join in a subscription to build a second monument to Shaw at some other suitable place, if Miss Whitney still has her very good sketch of Shaw on horseback and would undertake the work, or if Daniel [Chester] French, sculptor of the Concord Minute Man, would give us an impromptu statue to be ready about as soon as the St. Gaudens bas-relief, or at least during the probable life-time of some member of the Committee."[43] Days, months, and years slipped away, and the committee members were unavoidably busy with other matters in their lives.

Yet, until the Shaw's unveiling in 1897, the approach of every May raised the expectation that the monument might be dedicated on the anniversary of the Fifty-fourth's leave-taking of Boston. As time elapsed, and the bronze was finally brought to fulfillment, there was no question that it was a masterpiece; Atkinson perceptively assessed its position. "As a work of art we think this great *alto rilievo* will take a very high rank, perhaps the first place in the art of this country. . . ."[44]

The Shaw was the epitome of everything an artist dreams of achieving: it combined inventiveness of design, brilliant technique, and universal emotive power. Saint-Gaudens's sensibility was very different from that of the well-born Story, Whitney, or French; in that may lie the heart of the Shaw Memorial. Saint-Gaudens was an Irish-Catholic immigrant whose exquisite being could understand the plight of the black, whose deftness as a modeler could individualize the soldiers' portraits, and whose imagination and soul could relate their story with an unmatched empathic and spiritual bond.[45]

Saint-Gaudens arrived in America with nothing and then rose to the pinnacle of America's artistic community. He was charming and was endowed with memberships in private clubs, such as the Century Club in New York; however, the unusual emotional range and charge of his work sprang from his humble origins and his outsider's view. What could be more striking than the juxtaposition of the troops, Shaw and his men, whose backgrounds were worlds apart, joined together for a noble cause? Even more so today than one hundred years ago, the enlisted men's heads are telling proof of Saint-Gaudens's enormous talent.

In the 1960s and 1970s, the Shaw was in a deplorable condition, as were the spirits of Boston, torn apart by the school busing issue. Then in 1980, spearheaded by the Friends of the Public Garden and Common and the Boston Art Commission, an effort to restore and preserve the sculpture commenced. Following the Latin root for "monument," which means "a reminder," the Shaw resonated with the aim to heal not just the bronze, but the wounds of a divided city. As the momentum grew, a

Augustus Saint-Gaudens, The Shaw Memorial, bronze, 1884–97, Boston Common (pre-restoration). Photograph by Kathryn Greenthal, 1978.

newly formed committee to rehabilitate the memorial determined that the names of all the men of color from the Fifty-fourth Regiment who died in battle at Battery Wagner should at last be carved on the reverse of the monument.

From the beginning, it was the mission of the Shaw family to pay homage to the soldiers, along with their son. As early as the autumn of 1863, when plans had already been submitted for a monument to the regiment on Morris Island in South Carolina, Francis Shaw voiced his opinion about whose names should be recorded on the memorial. He was of the belief that "the monument, though originated for my son, ought to bear, with his, the names of his brave officers and men, who fell and were buried with him. This would be but simple justice.[46] The idea to immortalize the infantry was never lost sight of by the Shaws during the lengthy years of waiting for the work on the monument to be accomplished. Josephine Shaw Lowell had shared her thoughts about the issue in a letter to Henry Lee in 1886 and again on October 30, 1892: "I am 'concerned' about the inscriptions on the 54th Monument, and getting no comfort from Cousin John Forbes about it, I turn to you. I want very much to have the names of all the men of the 54th killed at Fort Wagner & afterwards, put on the base at the back—it seems to me due the privates. . . . [Her instincts told her that there would then be] no excuse for the feeling that it is only men with rich relations and friends who can have monuments."[47]

In so many ways, Atkinson was the unsung hero in the history of the Shaw Memorial. He was farsighted enough to comprehend that the piece would need maintenance and had tried without success, seemingly due to problems associated with the nearly insurmountable task of getting the bronze finished, to build an endowment for the perpetual care of the monument.[48] Moreover, having feared that the release of McKim's name as consulting architect would raise questions because of his cost overruns related to the building of the Public Library in Copley Square, Atkinson appreciated that McKim's handsome design must be properly acknowledged and concurred with Colonel Lee about this. Atkinson recommended that Lee write to McKim to express their thanks for his service and that a copy of the letter be included in a pamphlet report that was to be published.[49] Above all, it was Atkinson who took the most active part in the wearisome and torturous tale of bringing the monument to completion. He kept after Saint-Gaudens when it appeared that the work would never come to fruition, and it was Atkinson who recognized that Saint-Gaudens had gone beyond expectations. He observed how much the piece had profoundly exacted from the sculptor: "It grew in size and in scope. He [Saint-Gaudens] has

Augustus Saint-Gaudens, Head of the Flying Figure for the Shaw Memorial, plaster,
probably 1897. Private collection. Photograph by Kathryn Greenthal, 1999.

kept himself poor and put half his life into it."[50] Atkinson arranged for
supplemental moneys to further compensate the sculptor, who received
a total sum of twenty-two thousand dollars.

In the end, the long passage of time yielded a mutual admiration and
gratitude between Atkinson and Saint-Gaudens. After the unveiling
and a much earned rest, the sculptor, as was his usual generous practice,
made a gift of his work to Atkinson.

> I send to you today a cast of the full size head of the flying figure [the
> alterations of which had considerably postponed advancement on the
> relief] on the Shaw Monument. A fragment like that loses a great deal in
> its separateness from the rest of the body and the surroundings with
> which it has been composed, but such as it is I beg you to accept it. It
> will show in a small measure my deep appreciation of your kindness and

patience with me through the years that have spread themselves out since the day we first talked about the Shaw Monument in Boston."[51]

On May 31, 1897, Saint-Gaudens arrived in Boston two days after the unveiling of his *Peter Cooper Monument* in New York. Busy as ever, a few weeks thereafter, he went to Chicago for the dedication of yet another major commission, the *General Logan*. Although Saint-Gaudens lived until 1907, none of his other works ever matched the Shaw.

THOMAS J. BROWN

RECONSTRUCTING BOSTON

Civic Monuments of the Civil War

"THIS TOWN of Boston has a history," observed native son Ralph Waldo Emerson. "It is not an accident, not a windmill, or a railroad station, or cross-roads tavern, or an army barracks grown up by time and luck to a place of wealth; but a seat of humanity, of men of principle, obeying a sentiment and marching loyally whither that should lead them; so that its annals are great historical lines, inextricably national."[1] Emerson's juxtaposition of the "historical" and the "national" underscores the basis of community in his radically subjective thought. To have a history, to constitute a nation, was to be "a seat of humanity," to realize a trait of the universal soul. "Our admiration of the antique is not admiration of the old, but of the natural," Emerson argued; "every man passes personally through a Grecian period" in communion with the same "national mind" that informs Greek history, art, and literature.[2] Notwithstanding the conflicts and upheavals in its annals, Boston was similarly no mere product of circumstance but a geographic correlative for an ideal city upon a hill, transcending "time and luck" to connect all individuals who obeyed a sentiment and marched loyally whither that should lead them.

The Civil War presented a crisis for this understanding of Boston. Lewis Simpson has perceptively suggested the ways in which Emerson's immersion in the war, and his effort to claim it as a victory for New England, compromised the quest for transcendence he had inherited from the Puritans. As Emerson fused the meaning of his homeland to a specific event, the historicism of the nineteenth century overwhelmed the promise of a timeless fulfillment of human potential, much as the Union cause absorbed New England into the modern nation-state. Narratives of triumphant nationhood celebrating ethnic purity, abolitionist virtue, and martial prowess displaced zeal for the sovereignty of the mind. Simpson portrays the war-fevered Emerson as a tragic casualty of the retrospective age he had once denounced, unable to recognize that "the destruction of the ideal" is "the great modern subject."[3]

The score of major Boston monuments commemorating the Civil War provide a useful parallel to the pattern that Simpson describes in Emerson. Dedicated in three distinct waves during the half-century after 1865, the monuments present an extended effort to place the city in historical and national context. In the first phase of remembrance, the unsuccessful attempt of antebellum elites to reassert leadership demonstrated the prestige of historicism and the decay of the local traditions that had informed Emerson's idealism. The canonization of abolitionists in the second round of monuments even more squarely located the significance of the city at a particular point in time and associated it with particular relative values. The third set, an ethnically charged celebration of military heroes, subordinated the community to a nation-state defined merely by force. Ironically, however, the sole monument to share in all three corruptions of Emerson's civic vision was also the only one that embodied the meaning he had attributed to Boston.

1

The monuments erected in Boston immediately after the Civil War, sponsored by the Unitarian and Whig elite from which Emerson had emerged, reflected tendencies of local culture that he repudiated as well as elements on which he built. The statue of a sphinx dedicated in 1872 at Mount Auburn Cemetery in remembrance of the "Great War of American Conservation" best illustrated the Whiggish deference to the past that Emerson disdained. Since opening in 1831, Mount Auburn had incorporated into its ideological landscape an ambitious affirmation of American nationhood, defined largely as an extension of Boston. The cemetery commissioned much of the monumental sculpture to be seen in the Boston area during the 1850s, including portrait statues of John Winthrop, John Adams, James Otis Jr., and Joseph Story, exemplars of local culture and icons of American national identity. The Civil War memorial at Mount Auburn similarly commemorated "the uprising of a great people," in the words of the inscription supplied by Jacob Bigelow, the guiding spirit of the cemetery. To depict this coalescence, Bigelow instructed sculptor Martin Milmore to "restore for modern application the image of the ancient Sphinx." The message was clear: in the Civil War, the Brahmins honored at Mount Auburn had lifted the United States into the ranks of the great civilizations of history. The sphinx stood "on the dividing ridge of time," Bigelow wrote; the allegorical form that "has looked backward on unmeasured antiquity, now looks forward to illimitable progress." This imitative grandiosity was the antithesis of the self-reliance that Emerson urged. "The Sphinx must solve her own riddle," he warned.[4]

More ambiguous in its implications for Emerson's idea of Boston was

Martin Milmore, *The Sphinx*, 1872. Courtesy Mount Auburn Cemetery, Cambridge, Massachusetts.

the heroic statue of his one-time idol Edward Everett dedicated in the Public Garden in 1867. The orator, scholar, statesman, and Harvard president had long been regarded as a singularly representative figure, as indicated by Oliver Wendell Holmes's quip that Bostonians "all carry the Common in our heads as the unit of space, the State House as the standard of architecture, and measure off men in Edward Everetts as with a yardstick." By the outbreak of the Civil War, however, Everett's readiness to accommodate Southern demands on slavery issues had badly tarnished his reputation, and he symbolized the moral failure of all Whigs who followed the line of Daniel Webster. He might easily have become a lackluster supporter of the Union effort and drifted by

1864 into opposition to the Lincoln administration, as did many of his close friends and political associates. Instead, he became one of the most energetic and powerful spokesmen for the Union cause, earning what proved to be the unenviable assignment to deliver the principal address at the dedication of the cemetery on the Gettysburg battlefield. The world little noted and did not long remember what he said there, but at his death in January 1865, contemporaries thought his war record a stirring story of redemption. "If I have ever uttered anything in deroga- tion of Mr. Everett's public character . . . ," declared William Cullen Bryant, "I now, looking back upon his noble record of the last four years, retract it at his grave." John Greenleaf Whittier agreed that "only within the last four years I have truly known him."[5] Former Whigs pounced on the opportunity to raise a monument to Everett and, after a remarkably successful public subscription campaign, commissioned a statue by William Wetmore Story.

The selection of Story, finalized at the Harvard commencement in July 1865, ensured a monument that would embody the self-perception of the Boston elite. Eager to produce his greatest work for his native city, Story carried forward the tribute to the Athens of America that he had begun several years earlier when he sculpted his bust of Theodore Parker in the character of Socrates. The monument committee vetoed his plan to portray Everett in a toga, but Story inscribed his neoclassi- cism into the composition by depicting Everett with his arm uplifted in an epic gesture prescribed by the conventions of formal rhetoric. Many observers easily made the invited comparison with the Vatican statue of Demosthenes.[6]

If the Everett statue resembled the Mount Auburn Sphinx in its strain to connect the triumphant Boston of the Civil War with the great civilizations of antiquity, the focus on the orator as an ideal type identi- fied a vital source of local culture. As the embodiment of oral remem- brance, Everett stood not merely for a defining moment in history but for the force of living memory; following standard practice, he delivered his two-hour addresses without notes. The heroic orator—absorbing the past into his character to ennoble his audience—personified Emer- son's view that history could be a subjective dimension of personal ex- perience. The most successful performances in this role had been Web- ster's famous addresses at the Bunker Hill monument, the archetype of civic commemoration in Boston. "There was the Monument, and here was Webster," noted Emerson, ". . . and the whole occasion was an- swered by his presence."[7]

Harvard Memorial Hall, which honored the students, alumni, and faculty who had died for the Union, developed on a grander scale the historicized nationalism and cultivation of oratory expressed by the Everett statue. The similarity was hardly coincidental, for the Committee of Fifty that sponsored the Everett statue and the Committee of Fifty that built Memorial Hall shared the same chairman and twelve other members, including Jacob Bigelow of Mount Auburn cemetery.[8] As the sphinx and the Everett statue had invoked Egypt and Greece,

William Wetmore Story, *Edward Everett*, 1867, Boston Public Garden.
Courtesy Library of Congress.

Memorial Hall embraced Gothic models to announce the golden age of America.[9] Oratory figured prominently in this construction project, which also marked an important step in the expansion of Harvard into a national university. The three-part building included a large dining hall, a commemorative vestibule, and an academic theater, presumably a training field for future Edward Everetts. Decorating the polygonal exterior of the theater were rondels with portrait busts of orators representing seven great civilizations, including Demosthenes, Cicero, and Webster.

The cultural nationalism of Memorial Hall minimized two competing approaches to remembrance of the Civil War. It avoided allusions to the antislavery movement, which had bitterly divided the antebellum leadership of the city. Abolitionist John G. Palfrey urged Harvard president Charles William Eliot to use the rondel busts to honor Samuel Adams, James Otis Jr., and other graduates who had devoted their talents "to the service of that cause of freedom to which Harvard College had consecrated them," but Eliot replied that his purpose was to highlight intellect and civic leadership through the art of oratory, not to dramatize an ideology of emancipation. The second motif skirted by Memorial Hall was the valor of soldiers. Budding military historian John Codman Ropes resigned from the Memorial Hall committee in disgust after the rejection of his counterproposal for "a monument in the shape of a military trophy made of Brass." Charles Eliot Norton, an important contributor to the final design, summarized the prevailing view that "the memorial should be one which did not suggest victory or triumph in war, but the sacrifice of life for a cause wholly disconnected with ordinary warfare, and above it." E. Rockwood Hoar's address at the laying of the cornerstone in October 1870 and Charles Francis Adams's speech at the dedication of the building in July 1874 expressed similar viewpoints. Appearing only four months after he had been dismissed from Grant's cabinet as a result of the presidential feud with Charles Sumner, Hoar updated the longstanding Whig distrust of military influence in public life by emphasizing that Harvard soldiers had followed no improper ambitions and wishfully predicting that "the war, with its actors and its victims, is passing into history."[10]

The political stance and commemorative style of the old-line elite withstood the same challenges at the *Soldiers' and Sailors' Monument* on Boston Common, the principal monument financed by the city during the decade after the war. Hammatt Billings's initial 1866 design for the monument proved to be too vigorously abolitionist and militaristic to be built. It featured a shaft surmounted by a statue of Liberty carrying a sword and raising a laurel wreath signifying victory. Reliefs at eye level entitled "The Charge" and "Emancipation" echoed the themes of combat and the destruction of slavery by force. The plan aroused considerable protest that it would disrupt sectional reconciliation. Henry Rogers, chairman of the Harvard Memorial Hall building committee, and Abbott Lawrence, a cousin of the chairman of the Harvard Memorial Hall finance committee, both headed petitions opposing Billings's monument. Rogers testified against the design before the city council, and Lawrence hired an attorney who helped to stop the project after an early budgetary overrun.[11]

In the ensuing struggle over the form of the monument, veterans pressed the city to commemorate them with a memorial hall in which they could place war relics, display portraits of comrades, and conduct meetings. But the city council responded that Faneuil Hall, the long-time civic forum, was the only genuine locus of community memory of the war. "To no other structure could such associations be imparted by any official action," the council maintained.[12] Similarly, Martin Milmore's winning design managed to invoke the power of oratory while downplaying antislavery ideology and military valor. Milmore eliminated Billings's armed figure of Liberty and the panels of "The Charge" and "Emancipation," substituting a somber figure of America and reliefs that featured civilian topics such as "The Sanitary Commission" no less than the contest of arms. These reliefs included more than three dozen portraits of prominent Bostonians grouped at imaginary moments. The panel on the front side of the monument presented a fictitious departure of volunteers led by General Benjamin F. Butler and joined by future martyrs Thomas Cass, Charles Russell Lowell, and Robert Gould Shaw.[13] The montages of local celebrities called to mind the most conspicuous work of Whig art in the city, G. P. A. Healy's monumental painting in Faneuil Hall of *Webster Replying to Hayne,* which similarly portrayed prominent city residents—including some of the same personalities who appeared on Milmore's reliefs—as spectators. Through this convergence, the mobilization of the community became an extension of the heroic oratory that formed the strongest connection between the traditional local culture and Emerson's transcendent Boston.

Although initially persuasive within the narrow circles that controlled the commemorative campaigns, the appeal to Whiggish forms of remembrance failed dismally when presented to the public for approval. Far from demonstrating the maturity of a great civilization, the principal monuments suffered repudiation even by their sponsors. The Mount Auburn Sphinx, the last major didactic project at the cemetery, marked the end rather than the beginning of an era in the expan-

Martin Milmore, *The Departure for War*, relief panel on Soldiers' and Sailors' Monument, 1877, Boston Common. Courtesy Massachusetts Historical Society.

sion of Boston culture. Charles Eliot Norton later criticized acidly the Harvard Memorial Hall he had done so much to help create, and architect Henry Van Brunt came to consider the building notable primarily for its documentary value as an example of the brief heyday of the Gothic revival. At first the public applauded the *Soldiers' and Sailors' Monument* on Boston Common, but the unsparing attacks of art critics eventually reversed the tide of opinion.[14]

Most telling was the overwhelming denunciation of the Everett statue. The *Atlantic Monthly* called the invited comparison with the Vatican Demosthenes "humiliating," and the *Boston Evening Transcript* published a long series of articles, letters, and squibs ridiculing the statue.[15] Everett's admirers hastened to emphasize that the flamboyant pose did not accurately represent his dignified and graceful gestures. The attack on the statue, however, expressed a more fundamental belief that the heroic orator as a civic type did not warrant praise. One contributor to the newspaper debate over the statue noted that Everett "is known to the present generation chiefly as an orator, yet this is not his greatest claim to remembrance. . . . He will be judged in the future by the more enduring memorials he has left." Another letter-writer, reporting that Story had imagined Everett delivering the peroration to his famous address on Washington, suggested the addition of an inscription that would situate the composition in time and shift its focus from the art of oratory to Everett's patriotism.[16] The statue continued to serve as a reminder of the disappointed dreams of the Athens of America until city authorities removed it from the Public Garden and exiled it to Dorchester in the twentieth century.

2

The second round of Civil War monuments in Boston responded to the perceived flaws of the first set. Most conspicuously, the initiatives launched between 1874 and 1888 dramatized a different meaning of the war by shifting the thematic emphasis from the vindication of Whig leadership to the triumph of the antislavery movement. Changes in the style of remembrance accompanied the new substantive focus. Ambitious historical allusions ceased to dominate commemorative designs, and the marriage of built memorials and oral memory dissolved. At the same time, the increasingly consolidated community of professional artists—which had played an important role in the failure of the first round of monuments—began to exercise a growing influence over the sponsors of new projects.

The economic and social structure of Civil War commemoration changed little during this period. Private contributions remained the chief source of financing for almost all projects. Throughout the first two phases, the city council directly appropriated funds only for the *Soldiers' and Sailors' Monument* and for an obelisk in a cemetery plot dedicated to former soldiers without other means of burial. The city commissioned statues of Samuel Adams (1873) and Josiah Quincy (1879), but no Civil War memorials, with the income from the modest endowment left by Jonathan Phillips for beautification of the streets.[17] The commonwealth did not initiate any Civil War monuments. A small circle of sponsors continued to dominate the remembrance of the conflict in the civic landscape. The passage of time and the increased attention to abolitionism naturally affected membership in this group, although the continuities were often striking. The nine-member committee to raise funds for a monument to William Lloyd Garrison included three men who had earlier served on the Edward Everett committee.[18]

The antislavery wave of Civil War monuments began to take shape upon the death of Charles Sumner in March 1874. After a successful subscription drive, the promoters of the proposed memorial tried to avoid the debacle of the Everett statue by holding a juried design competition. The proceeding resulted in the commissioning of a portrait statue by Thomas Ball, which was placed in the Public Garden in December 1878.[19] The death of William Lloyd Garrison in May 1879 inspired another commemorative campaign, which culminated in the dedication of Olin Warner's statue on Commonwealth Avenue in May 1886. Garrison's death also prompted one Republican to donate to the city a copy of Thomas Ball's *Emancipation Group*, dedicated three years earlier in Washington, D.C., as the Freedmen's Memorial to Abraham Lincoln.[20] Two other efforts to honor abolitionists proved partly successful. Plans for a monument to Theodore Parker followed soon after the Garrison initiative, but a statue designed for Boston Common during the 1880s went instead to the First Unitarian Church of West Roxbury in 1902. A campaign to commemorate the controversial Wendell Phillips after his death in 1884 stalled for lack of contributions, although it laid the groundwork for the statue placed in the Public Garden in 1915.[21]

The shift from the veneration of antiquity to the celebration of abolitionism more closely matched the sympathies of Emerson, who joined in the call for a Garrison memorial, but the new monuments remained different from his description of Boston as "a seat of humanity" unbounded by time. A Boston that stood for the overthrow of slavery did not transcend history but found definition in history; it typified the modern nation that "tends to transform itself into an idealized version of its historical reality," exalting the particular relative values that the culture deems salvational.[22] Indeed, the antislavery monuments moved further away from Emersonian idealism by rejecting the role of the heroic orator, the strongest link between Emerson and the Whig monuments. The Sumner and Garrison statues were dedicated, as one report gratefully put it, "without any cheap effusion of ceremony and speechifying."[23] Neither monument represented its subject in the act of delivering an address, nor did the Parker statue, despite the importance of oratory in the careers of the antislavery leaders.

Daniel Chester French's statue of Wendell Phillips illustrates the indifference to public speaking as an art of civic representation and the transition to a Boston identity grounded specifically in abolitionism. Like Everett, Phillips was a remarkably versatile and mesmerizing speaker, although the delivery styles of the two men differed as much as their politics. One admirer of Phillips's calm, conversational demeanor reported that he looked "like a marble statue, cool and white." French, however, took no interest in the commanding power of the heroic orator and instead depicted a man possessed by a cause. His Phillips holds a slave's broken chain as a theatrical prop; he leans forward with animation, ready to pound the table. When a visitor to French's studio complained that the statue looked nothing like Phillips's speaking manner, French replied that "whether it is a faithful portrait of the man himself or not, I should like to represent what he stood for in the zenith of his power and usefulness. . . . I am going to make my anti-slavery hero as inspiring as I know how."[24]

If different in aims from the monuments commissioned in the years immediately after the war, the commemorative projects of 1874–88 met with a comparably hostile reception. The competition for the Sumner statue turned into a disaster. Sumner's close friend William Wetmore Story refused to participate because he considered the premiums for submissions inadequate, and the judges ignited a storm of protest by reversing an initial decision in favor of Anne Whitney's seated composition of the senator. Critics scorned Thomas Ball's winning portrait as a poor imitation of outdated Italianate models; one writer called the Sumner statue in the Public Garden "the acme of plastic inanity." Reviews of Ball's *Emancipation Group* were equally critical.[25] Although Olin Warner's statue of William Lloyd Garrison received plaudits for following the increasingly influential precepts of the École des Beaux-Arts, the seated image of the benevolent, aging liberator captured little of the intensity of the antislavery crusade and aroused correspondingly little enthusiasm.[26]

The continued dissatisfaction with public sculpture in the city led to the formation of the Boston Memorial Association (BMA) in 1880 as a means to bring together traditional sponsors of monuments and the community of artists and critics. The elite membership included such active supporters of the antislavery monuments as Republican wheel-horse Alexander Rice, who had headed the committee that presented the Sumner statue to the city, and such prominent commentators on art as W. P. P. Longfellow, editor of *American Architect and Building News.* The first project undertaken by the BMA, the monument to Theodore Parker, aimed to realize the grand civic theme so dismally repre-

Daniel Chester French, *Wendell Phillips*, 1915, Boston Public Garden.
Courtesy Harvard College Library.

sented in Thomas Ball's recent works and also to offer cities throughout the country instruction "in selecting public works of art with intelligent discrimination."[27]

Rather than consolidating political and artistic leadership, however, the BMA succeeded only in creating a target for the Irish resentment of Brahmin condescension. Conflict erupted over a project closely related to the antislavery memorials, the Boston Massacre Monument authorized by the state legislature in May 1887 and dedicated on Boston Common in November 1888, which was generally recognized as a tribute to Crispus Attucks, a central figure in the political culture of black abolitionists in Boston. The Boston Massacre Monument received only lukewarm support from the BMA leadership.[28] But Irish members of the city council who derided Robert Kraus's composition as "an insult to the race it was intended to commemorate" naturally turned their fire from the little-known sculptor to the BMA, for Kraus had also received the commission for the Theodore Parker statue. "I do not believe in memorial societies or other societies being given charge of these monuments," declared one Irish member of the city council. "We should act on our own judgment, rather than take that of the so-called aesthetic people in this city."[29]

As such remarks indicated, by 1888 the bitter ethnic and class conflicts of Boston pervaded the environment for the creation of public monuments. Democrats of Irish ancestry had controlled the city council since the beginning of the decade; in 1884 they had elected the first Irish-born mayor, Hugh O'Brien, who would remain in office for five consecutive terms. Rejecting the leadership of educated elites and recoiling from the celebration of the abolitionist crusade, the Irish put forward a new vision of Boston expressed through a different approach to remembering the Civil War.

3

Legendary ward boss Martin Lomasney touched off the third wave of Civil War monuments in Boston shortly after the death of Philip Sheridan, the leading Union hero of Irish ancestry, by proposing in September 1888 that the city erect equestrian statues of Sheridan and Grant. The initiative struck at an antimilitary strain in Boston commemoration that had deepened in the aftermath of the Sumner-Grant feud, which in itself had culminated in a struggle over the remembrance of the Civil War in the regimental flags of the army. When the city council accepted Thomas Ball's statue of Sumner, one member noted that "in looking at the lives of great men, we are too apt to judge of them by great and daring victories upon the battlefield, and by the positions they must have attained by the slaughter of their fellow creatures."[30] The circle that dominated public art in Boston showed little interest in tributes to Union soldiers. The deaths of national heroes like David Farragut (1870), and figures with Massachusetts associations like Joseph Hooker (1879), John A. Winslow (1873), and William Francis Bartlett (1876), did not prompt monument campaigns. Most strikingly, although most predictably, Boston abstained from the scramble that broke out in New York, Philadelphia, Chicago, Saint Louis, and other Northern cities to honor Grant at his death in 1885.

When the city council warmly invited veterans' organizations to testify on Lomasney's proposal, the Brahmin-Irish conflict dominated the three public hearings held in December 1888. Assailing the idea that Boston possessed a civic identity distinct from the nation-state headquartered in Washington, Lomasney emphasized American loyalties and sought to measure the city against the rest of the country. "The city of Boston is behind the times," Lomasney argued. "It is behind New York, it is behind Philadelphia, it is behind St. Louis in erecting statues to the generals of our army."[31] The clash figured especially prominently in discussions of possible locations for the proposed monuments. Council members and witnesses repeatedly proposed Copley Square—the Back Bay cultural showcase surrounded by the new Museum of Fine Arts, Henry Hobson Richardson's Trinity Church, and the Boston Public Library then under construction—as an appropriate site. One observer sighed sarcastically that "if Copley Square must have the earth, I think we might as well put one of the statues there." Another witness suggested that statues of Grant, Sheridan, and Farragut might be placed in the corners of one of the Copley Square triangles. Similarly, council member Thomas Keenan suggested placement of the Sheridan statue on the new Charles River embankment, "over by the classic city of Cambridge."[32] These discussions represented a contest over social space marking, an attempt by the monument supporters to reclaim or at least neutralize the sites of privileged institutions.

Soon after the city council approved partial funding for statues of Grant, Sheridan, and Farragut in February 1889, the Irish majority took another step in its challenge to the antimilitary traditions and exclusive places of the Brahmin caste. Learning that the veterans of the all-Irish Ninth Massachusetts Infantry Regiment had commissioned a cemetery memorial for its commander Thomas Cass, who had fallen at Malvern Hill, a city alderman insisted that the statue be erected in the Public Garden alongside Everett and Sumner. The Society of the Ninth Regiment expressed some hesitation about this prominent placement of the work, which had been executed by a stonecutter of modest ambitions. After a fierce controversy over the artistic quality of the sculpture, the council ordered Cass to the front lines of the Public Garden to prove, as one legislator said, that there was "no spot or place within the limits of the city that is too sacred for his features to be put there in granite."[33]

In addition to protesting the suitability of the Cass statue for the Public Garden and trying unsuccessful legal maneuvers to block the use of city funds to honor Grant, Sheridan, and Farragut, traditional elites lashed out more broadly against the tendency of commemorative politics in 1888–89. Local author Arlo Bates satirized the corruption of public art in his novel *The Philistines*, which revolved around a bargain tying together the commission for an allegorical statue of America and the diversion of a railroad line to benefit a manufacturer. William R. Richards led a lobbying campaign to insulate art from politics through the establishment of the Boston Art Commission, a state agency that entrusted the chief officers of the Museum of Fine Arts, the Boston Public Library, the Boston Society of Architects, and the Massachusetts Institute of Technology with veto power over the placement of artworks on city property. The trend-setting legislation contributed to a sharp decline in the number of monuments placed on city land after 1890. In one of its first important decisions, for example, the Art Commission provided Copley Square with permanent protection from ethnic invasion by ruling that no statues would be allowed in the contested public space.[34]

Moreover, the Brahmins met the Irish challenge directly by shifting their own commemoration of the Civil War era to military themes. Aware that founders of the Museum of Fine Arts had bruised some feelings shortly after the war by rejecting a request to set aside one gallery for portraits of Union heroes, the trustees of the Boston Public Library invited veterans to donate mementos of their fallen comrades for display in the new building and devoted its grand staircase to a tribute to the Second and Twentieth Massachusetts Infantry Regiments, units recruited largely from Beacon Hill.[35] Much of the commemorative counteroffensive, including not only the establishment of the Boston Art Commission but also the appropriation of public funds for additional monuments, built on the Republican advantage in the state legislature. The skirmish following the death of Benjamin Butler in 1893 typified the pattern of Irish initiative and Yankee response. The Democratic proposal for a statue, forcefully opposed by Henry Lee Higginson, Moorfield Storey, and Francis A. Walker, was also undercut by an appropriation for an equestrian statue of Joseph Hooker, a Massachusetts native although he had spent little time in the state after his youth.[36] During the renovation and expansion of the State House in the last decade of the century, the capitol increasingly became a fortress of military monuments, manned by Hooker and two Union generals who had played leading roles in Republican politics, Charles Devens and Nathaniel Banks. The transformation of Oliver Wendell Holmes's "hub of the universe" reached a climax in the addition of a memorial hall displaying the regimental colors of the state and statues of Massachusetts military heroes William Francis Bartlett, Thomas G. Stevenson, and John A. Winslow.[37]

Although keeping pace with the local Irish challenge, the new military emphasis represented a startling departure from previous attempts to define an autonomous Boston through commemoration of the war. Charles Francis Adams Jr. lamented the abandonment of local for federal standards, reflecting that "never since it was placed there have I passed by the front of the State House without feeling a sense of wrong and insult at the presence, opposite the head of Park Street, of the equestrian statue of Hooker." He sighed that a statue of Charles Russell Lowell "would have represented something typical of Massachusetts."[38] At the same time, the oratorical tradition once associated with public monuments in Boston had given way to such anti-intellectual performances as the stump speech delivered by John F. Fitzgerald in Faneuil Hall at the dedication ceremonies for the Thomas Cass statue and the excruciatingly detailed battle reminiscence delivered by General Charles P. Mattocks after the lavish parade celebrating the Joseph Hooker statue. On Memorial Day 1895, Oliver Wendell Holmes Jr. delivered his address "The Soldier's Faith" in Harvard Memorial Hall. Standing in the structure that Charles Eliot Norton had once hoped to consecrate to a cause far removed from ordinary warfare, Holmes argued that "the ideals of the past for men have been drawn from war, as those for women have been drawn from motherhood. For all our prophecies, I doubt if we are ready to give up our inheritance."[39] Insofar as it located civic identity in the Civil War, Boston now represented itself as what Emerson had said it was not, "an army barracks grown up by time and luck to be a place of wealth."

4

The thirty-two-year-long effort to create a Boston monument to Robert Gould Shaw continued through all three rounds of Civil War commemoration, and each wave left an imprint on the memorial dedicated on

May 31, 1897. The cumulative result of these stages, however, contrasted sharply with its Whiggish, abolitionist, and military cohorts in representing the historical and national significance of the city.

Like the Mount Auburn Sphinx and Harvard Memorial Hall, the original plan to erect an equestrian statue of Shaw fused the sentimental culture of bereavement to a local assertion of national identity. Joshua B. Smith, who was not only one of the most prominent black abolitionists in Boston but also a personal friend of the Shaw family, started the call for an equestrian monument because of his fervent desire "to see [Shaw's] statue on horseback erected on Boston Common, as he last saw him at the head of his regiment on Beacon street." Charles Sumner combined this nostalgia with a claim of Bostonian leadership in the nation when he took charge of the effort to realize Smith's idea in October 1865. The projected monument overlooking Charleston harbor might directly evoke the sacrifices at Battery Wagner, Sumner noted, but a monument recalling the departure of the Fifty-fourth Massachusetts from Boston would highlight "where the martyr was born, and where the regiment was born also." Defending Smith's plan against other proposals for a tribute to Shaw, the senator advocated the equestrian design as a republican adaptation of a commemorative form restricted in Europe to members of a royal family. "As an American citizen he belonged to our sovereignty, and we fitly celebrate him with the highest honors," Sumner emphasized. The award of the commission to William Wetmore Story, who had accepted the Edward Everett assignment only three months earlier, illustrated the Whiggish nationalism underlying the project as well as the dominant influence of Sumner.[40]

This initiative collapsed within a few months, a victim of Sumner's mismanagement and his political rivalry with John A. Andrew, and only after the death of the senator did the campaign revive in the surge of antislavery commemoration. Appropriately, former abolitionist Maria Weston Chapman made the first substantial gift to the monument fund after treasurer Edward Atkinson began to accept new donations in January 1876. Most important, Atkinson reconstituted the monument committee to include two key members of Andrew's wartime administration, John Murray Forbes and Henry Lee Jr., with local art connoisseur Martin P. Kennard assuming a subordinate role. Although related to the Shaws and glad to please them by completing the monument, Forbes and Lee sought not merely to honor their kinsman but also to dramatize the pivotal importance of the acceptance of African Americans into the Union army, a policy strenuously urged by Andrew. For the most part, Lee and Forbes pursued this objective through a protracted discussion of the inscriptions for the monument. Applying the same priorities to the problem of form, the new committee attached less significance to the equestrian motif than had Smith and Sumner, for according to Lee, a statue of Shaw on horseback "would not be discriminating in what it tells." Lee initially favored instead "a bust & under it bas-relief showing Shaw at the Fort leading blacks."[41] But the new committee typified the patterns of art patronage as well as the ideological goals that characterized the second phase of Civil War monuments—Lee and Atkinson were members of the BMA, and Kennard was the president for almost the entire life of the organization—and by early 1881 the group had begun to cede responsibility for the design of the memorial to professional artists. Their deference to Henry Hobson Richardson's recommendation of Augustus Saint-Gaudens for the commission, and their acquiescence in the sculptor's insistence that he would not provide a model until he had signed a contract, reflected the increasing authority of the artistic community influenced by the École des Beaux-Arts.[42]

The final stages of the Shaw project took place amid the class and ethnic conflicts that spurred the proliferation of military monuments. The lengthy debate over the inscription for the Shaw Memorial often revolved around the differences between the elites who walked along Beacon Street and the broad range of people whom Forbes and Lee expected to see the monument only from Boston Common. The monument also joined more directly in the Yankee response to the Irish commemorative initiative, for a Beacon Hill legislator persuaded the city council to divert almost half of the Grant-Sheridan-Farragut fund to finance Charles McKim's architectural setting for Saint-Gaudens's relief.[43] The remaining money paid only for a statue of Farragut, dedicated in 1893 in a waterfront park in South Boston. In the end it was the Shaw Memorial that thwarted Martin Lomasney's plan to celebrate Grant and Sheridan on the Boston landscape.

The multilayered development of the Shaw Memorial makes it tempting to regard the monument as a composite emblem of the ideological, ethnic, and statist forms of nationhood opposed to the transcendent Boston of Emerson, whose poetry is inscribed on the edge of the monument terrace.[44] To the contrary, however, Saint-Gaudens's work offers a meditation on the persistence of the ideal amid the historical consciousness of the nineteenth century. Indifferent to the tribal pride of the Brahmins and often insensitive to principles of racial equality, the sculptor approached his subject primarily as a problem in art.[45] He sought to advance the naturalism animating his widely praised statue of Farragut (1881) while incorporating the allegorical and classical vocabulary of nationhood. He devoted much of the long gestation period of the Shaw Memorial to the challenge of dissolving time in the repre-

William Rimmer, *Warriors against Slavery (Dedicated to the Fifty-fourth Regiment)*,
1863. Courtesy Museum of Fine Arts, Boston, Gift of William R. Ward.

sentation of a specific historical event. His solution effectively imagined the moment of nationhood as the enactment of the universal
promise that Emerson identified with Boston.

After the Shaw family rejected Saint-Gaudens's initial plan for an
equestrian memorial, the sculptor creatively reconsidered the original
purposes of the monument advocated by Smith and Sumner. He expanded the proposed allusion to Shaw's departure from Boston into an
astonishingly lifelike tableau of the regimental procession down Beacon Street, fortuitously placed at almost the very spot where Governor
John A. Andrew had reviewed the troops that he had done so much to
organize. Saint-Gaudens's verisimilitude withstood exacting scrutiny
on such questions as whether the relief showed the soldiers' canteens
on the wrong hip and Shaw riding on the wrong side of his men. In
focusing on the hour of departure, Saint-Gaudens did not merely adapt
a European motif of nationhood, as Sumner had proposed; instead he
renewed a powerful image of the making of a people, the mobilization
of citizen volunteers. This motif appeared in many works of art related
to the Civil War. William Rimmer, for example, had made a widely

noticed allegorical drawing of the advance of the Fifty-fourth Massachu-
setts during the recruitment of the regiment, and Shaw had appeared in
Martin Milmore's sentimental front panel of the *Soldiers' and Sailors'
Monument* on Boston Common.[46]

Saint-Gaudens's composition, however, more directly acknowledged
and revitalized the great ideal treatment of the subject, François Rude's
Departure of the Volunteers in 1792, unveiled on the Arc de Triomphe
in 1836. Rude's masterpiece, under scaffolding for restoration at the
time of the Shaw Memorial dedication, needed the rehabilitation that
Saint-Gaudens offered. The dynamic relief popularly known as *The
Marseillaise* was perhaps the most famous artistic representation of
nationhood in the nineteenth century. As Truman H. Bartlett noted in
1878, it had long been "regarded as the grandest work of sculpture of
the kind in the world." But Rude's ensemble was losing its grip on the
sensibility of Saint-Gaudens's generation; a critic in *American Architect and Building News* commented in 1889 that the supercharged alle-
gory "decidedly approaches clap-trap." Saint-Gaudens, who had temporarily lived in a studio near the Arc de Triomphe while attending the
École des Beaux-Arts, nonetheless urged his students to absorb the influence of Rude and singled out *The Departure of the Volunteers* as one
of the works of sculpture he most admired.[47]

Saint-Gaudens linked his Shaw Memorial to Rude's work not only
by representing the same theme but also by paralleling its unusual form
as a high relief fused with sculpture in the round. The deepening of
the relief was Saint-Gaudens's most significant change from the sketch
approved by the committee and the source of much of the delay in execution. As the soldiers increased in importance, their steady march inten-
sified the powerful forward energy that characterizes Saint-Gaudens's
panel no less than Rude's group.[48]

Although the thematic and formal similarities of the two monuments provided a basis for emphasizing contrasts as well as continuities,
the figure flying above the regiment clearly expressed Saint-Gaudens's
desire to assert the persistence of the ideal. His commitment to this
element of the composition was extraordinary. He reworked it several
times despite the impatience of the monument committee and the
sharp criticism of his friend Paul Bion, who argued that it did not belong
in the modern realistic composition, and he continued to modify it in
versions of the sculpture that followed the dedication of the Boston
monument. The revisions sought to avoid misinterpretation of the figure as a simple foreshadowing of the fate awaiting the regiment. Placing
an olive branch rather than a palm in the arms of the figure, Saint-
Gaudens expressed satisfaction in February 1897 that "it looks less

'Christian martyr-like.'"[49] The figure embodied a much broader conception of the transcendence attainable through the volunteers' collective
exercise of will.

As Edward Griffin has shown, the allegorical image also played an
important role in Saint-Gaudens's invocation of classical counterparts
to his volunteers. "I still think that a figure, if well done in that relation

François Rude, *Departure of the Volunteers,* Arc de Triomphe, 1836, Paris.
Giraudon/Art Resource, New York.

to the rest of the scheme, is a fine thing to do," the artist insisted at one point. "The Greeks and Romans did it finely in their sculpture."[50] Beyond this general reference to the classical union of the real and the ideal, the winged figure flying above the men made the Shaw Memorial an amplification of the reverse side of the medal of the Society of the Cincinnati. Saint-Gaudens reinforced the allusion by inscribing on the panel "omnia relinqvit servare rempvblicam," the motto of the organization of Revolutionary War officers and their descendants, in which Shaw's ancestry entitled him to membership. Although frequently traced to Shaw's father, who had suggested it in 1863 for the proposed monument in South Carolina, the inscription reflects the unity of conception in Saint-Gaudens's relief. The sculptor did not adopt Francis G. Shaw's primary suggestion for an inscription, the motto of Massachusetts, and during the long debate within the committee over the inscriptions, he sought to keep the panel clear of text. At the unveiling, the inclusion of the Latin motto came as a surprise to the monument committee.[51]

The integration of the Cincinnatus story into the Shaw Memorial, deftly highlighting the classicism that Story had strained to dramatize in the Edward Everett statue, complemented the adaptation of Rude's *Departure of the Volunteers* in incorporating the ideal vocabulary of nationhood. Saint-Gaudens did not merely equate the triumphant Union with its political counterparts emerging from the American Revolution, the French Revolution, and the wars of the Roman republic; he envisioned the procession down Beacon Street on May 28, 1863, as an exemplar of the timeless formation of a community of conscience. Transcending the ethnic, ideological, and statist definitions of nationhood on which it drew, the monument luminously represented Emerson's ideal Boston, a movement of "men of principle, obeying a sentiment and marching loyally whither that should lead them."

5

The brilliant oratorical finish sealed upon the Shaw Memorial at its dedication was even more contrary to the trend of Civil War remembrance in Boston than the fulfillment of the long-frustrated ambition to represent the city in a great work of public art. Planning for the dedication ceremonies generally followed the military pattern of commemoration in the 1890s. Although Edward Atkinson firmly rejected Oliver Wendell Holmes Jr. as the principal orator in light of his "brutal" address at Harvard Memorial Hall, the monument committee sought to plan the program around a speech by a veteran, to be followed by Booker T. Washington for "what might be considered a response on behalf of

Pierre L'Enfant, drawing of proposed medal for the Society of the Cincinnati (reverse), 1783. From the archives of the Society of the Cincinnati.

his race." The committee soon settled on Colonel Thomas Livermore. When he declined, the committee deferred to the wishes of the Shaw family and invited William James, a decision perhaps based less on his intellectual stature than on his eligibility as the brother of the regimental adjutant severely wounded at Battery Wagner. James's own absence from the war, a source of deepest anxiety for him, evidently remained a matter of considerable concern to Atkinson and to Shaw's former comrades in the officer corps, who petitioned the committee for a representative on the program. The veterans eventually settled for an address by Henry Lee Higginson at Harvard Memorial Hall on the evening before the unveiling.[52]

Eager to revisit a formative crisis of his life in the maturity of his powers, James embraced the role of the heroic orator defining the legacy of the Civil War. He sent Booker T. Washington and committee member Henry Lee a flurry of notes emphasizing the importance of "the *ensemble* of the ceremony" and seeking to influence the arrangements. He unsuccessfully urged the committee to hold the dedication ceremony in the open air near the monument as a more dramatic setting than the Music Hall. His preparations for his own performance included a careful review of Shaw's letters and Sarah Sturgis Shaw's compilation of newspaper and poetic tributes to her son. More strikingly, he made his oration the only major address that he delivered by heart in a long career of public speaking. His concern about the content of his speech matched his attention to the theater of the event. Although fully alive to the pathos of "the last wave of the war breaking over Boston, everything softened and made poetic and unreal by distance," he aimed for "something a little higher than the usual flourishing of proper names and the flag, which are sure to bring down conventional applause." He fended off requests that he mention key individuals who had helped to form the regiment, and he revised his text repeatedly to strike a balance between pleasing his audience and avoiding trite formulas. When rumors about the drafting process prompted criticism of his plans, James sighed that "it would take an Emerson to do anything original on such an occasion."[53]

James turned to Emerson not only for a model of the public intellectual but for the keynote of the dedication address. At his centenary tribute to Emerson six years later, James identified a passage from "Voluntaries" as the best expression of "the insight and creed from which Emerson's life followed": "So nigh is grandeur to our dust, / So near is God to man." If he saw this poetic reflection on the Fifty-fourth Massachusetts as the essence of Emerson, James conversely found the dominant theme for his Shaw Memorial oration in what he would call the "bugle-blast" of the Concord sage, "the sovereignty of the living individual."[54] Gently warning against excessive admiration for "the common and gregarious courage" that Shaw shared with many other soldiers in the war, James devoted his highest praise to "that lonely kind of courage" shown by Shaw in leaving his secure place in an institution he revered, the Second Massachusetts Infantry Regiment, to instill his character in the Fifty-fourth Massachusetts. While making his remarks "as 'abolitionist' in tone as anyone can desire," James considered the problem of freedom in broad philosophical terms. His Shaw dispelled racial injustice, but he achieved his greatest victory over the pressures toward social conformity that threatened to constrict his personal development. That self-reliance made Shaw, no less than his African American troops, an exemplar of "our American religion," which James defined as "the faith that a man requires no master to take care of him, and that common people can work out their salvation well enough together if left free to try."[55]

For James, as for Emerson, the ascendancy of the individual culminated in a history shaped by principle and will rather than circumstance. The climax of the address assailed one of the most powerful forms of nineteenth-century historicism, social Darwinism, in an incisive critique of war "as a school of manly virtue." War had for millennia exacted the subordination of the individual to the group; it was "the gory cradle of mankind, the grim-featured nurse that alone could train our savage progenitors into some semblance of social virtue, teach them to be faithful one to another, and force them to sink their selfishness in wider tribal ends." The cumulative experience of humanity reinforced this "battle-instinct." "How could it be otherwise," James asked, echoing Holmes's address two years earlier, "when the survivors of one successful massacre after another are the beings from whose loins we and all our contemporary races spring?" The example of Shaw, however, suggested an alternative vision of society ordered not by this erratic, destructive "instinct" but by an exercise of will cohering in "habit." James's emphasis on the habits of fairness and vigilance, drawing on his account of habit as "the enormous fly-wheel of society" in *The Principles of Psychology* and anticipating his essay "The Moral Equivalent of War," sought to shift the safeguard of community from an inherited impulse to self-perpetuating acts of judgment. "The nation blest above all nations" was one in which "the civic genius of the people does the saving day by day."[56]

James's slap at American militarism, delivered from a stage crowded with fifty former or present officers, including his old debating opponent Wendell Holmes, in itself required no small measure of the civic courage he praised in Shaw. Conquering anxieties about his own war record and possible adverse reaction to his mugwumpery, he boldly staked a claim to moral leadership on a central political issue of the day, the rising tide of imperialism. The epitome of the sovereign individual, the orator mobilized history into an extension of personal experience, dissolved the years between 1863 and 1897, and cast himself as the representation of his subject.

In the brief prayer with which he closed his address, James devoted his final lines to the connection between the legacy of the Civil War and the hopes of the founders of Boston. Should Americans preserve the habits commemorated by the Shaw Memorial, he declared, "so may our ransomed country, like the city of the promise, lie forever four-square under Heaven, and the ways of all the nations be lit up by its light."[57] The civic landscape shaped by commemoration of the Civil War had offered little to sustain faith in the transcendence envisioned by the Puritans or by Emerson, but the monument on Beacon Hill at last held out a hope that "great historical lines, inextricably national" might still radiate from Boston.

UNCOMMON SOLDIERS

Race, Art, and the Shaw Memorial

O N MEMORIAL DAY in 1897, when ceremonies to honor Civil War veterans were taking place at war memorials across the country, a new monument was unveiled on Boston Common, a monument to Colonel Robert Gould Shaw and the regiment he commanded, the Fifty-fourth Massachusetts Infantry. The orator of the day, Harvard philosopher William James, compared the new monument with the more typical Civil War memorials already ubiquitous in the Northeast and elsewhere in the United States—the equestrian monuments to great generals, on the one hand, and the common-soldier monuments, with their generic figures of the ordinary foot soldier, on the other hand. The monument to Shaw and his regiment, James declared, was different. Shaw was not a general, and the men he commanded were not ordinary soldiers but African Americans mustered into the most important regiment of black soldiers raised in the North; Shaw and many of his troops had died together in the assault on Battery Wagner, one of the earliest large-scale engagements of African American troops in the Civil War. And so this was no ordinary monument to military valor. The soldiers in this monument, James argued, represented "the profounder meaning of the Union cause." These soldiers had fought not just for a flag but for a moral cause that transcended mere territorial loyalties; they had fought to free the nation of what James called the "social plague" of slavery.[1]

The monument James praised was indeed unique. It was the first monument in the nation to show African American soldiers in full uniform, and it was a uniquely artful solution to the whole problem of the war memorial—in effect synthesizing the great-officer monument and the common-soldier monument into one startlingly new depiction of a cohesive military unit. This is why the name "Shaw Memorial" is so inadequate: the monument is much more than a tribute to one individual.

Two aspects distinguish the monument most dramatically from the run-of-the-mill Civil War memorial: its interracial subject and its unique artistry. I address these two issues—race and art—from the perspective of the late twentieth century, since that is a perspective we cannot avoid. At least one scholar has argued from this perspective that the monument is a racist work.[2] How do we put such a conclusion to the test? How do we go about interpreting an extraordinary and carefully designed monument that takes on racial issues avoided or hidden in standard war memorials? Our challenge, one hundred years after the monument's erection, is to use both historical knowledge and the evidence of our eyes—as we actually look at the monument's design—to help shape or control our interpretation of its content. I navigate one possible route through this methodological and political thicket, in the hopes that readers will test the argument themselves, debate it, and form their own conclusions.

There are as many possible interpretations of a work of art as there

Augustus Saint-Gaudens and Charles F. McKim, The Shaw Memorial, 1897, Boston Common. Courtesy Library of Congress.

are individuals to interpret it. This is a truism of "reception theory," which argues that the meaning of a text (or a design) is actually completed not by the author or artist but by the reader (or the viewer). Even if we accept this truism, however, there is no need to surrender entirely to the relativist conclusion that anything goes. Not every interpretation is equally valid: some are more informed or more perceptive than others, and some take better account of the visual evidence in plain view and the documentary evidence buried in archives.

Let us start, then, by looking at the visual evidence—specifically, the huge bronze relief designed by the sculptor Augustus Saint-Gaudens for the monument to Shaw and the Fifty-fourth Massachusetts Regiment. The panel is set in a sophisticated architectural frame, originally conceived by the architect Henry Hobson Richardson and then redesigned by Charles McKim; on the back side of the frame is a series of lengthy inscriptions. But it is above all Saint-Gaudens's sculpture that defines the monument's content, not simply because it is so compelling but also because in the nineteenth century that was how monuments were generally understood: as sculptural images of heroes. The design, as already emphasized, is unique. It represents an infantry march with Shaw, the commanding officer, on horseback and his soldiers on foot, the whole scene displayed in profile and contained within one panel. Shaw is of course the leading figure in the composition, because he is front and center and in the highest relief; but he does not literally lead the march. Shaw rides beside his troops as they all move together toward their destiny in one narrative image.

The foot soldiers obviously represent a well-drilled and disciplined unit, clad in uniform, marching in step, their faces all directed straight ahead. But as one looks more closely at the panel, the amazing diversity of the individual soldiers becomes apparent. They defy military standardization, on the one hand, and racial caricature, on the other. Their blackness is not a leveling trait, in other words, but a field in which the sculptor chose to create a rich interplay of internal differences. Thus, if we examine the work from right to left, we see the drummer boy juxtaposed with the sergeant behind him, the youngest member of the group with the oldest, smooth skin with beard, short stature with height; but if we read into depth, other more subtle contrasts emerge too: of facial hair and of cheekbone, nose, and eye shape. The procedure the sculptor used for faces is essentially the same one he applied to every detail of the body and its uniform and equipment. Hat brims are flipped and twisted to create variations of pitch and curvature; guns are tilted at slightly different angles so that they cross or spread; blankets are rolled in various shapes and set on the pack in different ways. In this fashion the overall impression of uniformity—of identically clad soldiers marching perfectly in step, rhyming each other's body movements—is changed and enriched by a kind of contrapuntal assertion of diversity.

The soldiers fill the width of the panel, but they do not entirely control it. There are really two rhythms in this march, masterfully interwoven: the steady tread of the foot soldiers carrying their gear, and the light but powerful step of the horse bearing Shaw. The soldiers lean their whole bodies slightly into the march, counterbalanced by the pack straps, which pull against their shoulders. We are made to feel the weight they carry, and how they manage their burden in a series of controlled, disciplined movements; as they step forward, their trousers rise and fall in rumpled folds on heavily creased shoes. The horse, by contrast, fairly glides, its tail and raised leg moving in a perfectly timed pattern of opposing arcs. The animal naturally towers over the troops and moves with ease. The only strain betrayed by its sleek surface of vein and muscle is the pressure on its neck created by Shaw's taut reins, which check the horse's strength and keep it from outpacing the men beneath. Shaw thereby rides absolutely motionless, propelled not by his own body but by the superior energy of the steed. While everyone else angles forward, he remains fixed upright, ramrod straight, in the saddle. This creates perhaps the most startling effect of the whole panel: Shaw becomes a still center in the midst of an otherwise moving tableau. He is swept along, we know, by its collective movement, and yet abstracted from it.

Now at this point I should stop and admit that what began as a "description" of the work has already become highly interpretive and thus is open to debate. The scholar Albert Boime, for example, also has noted the difference between the erect bearing of Shaw and the forward angle of the foot soldiers, but he argues instead that the soldiers are "listless and somewhat rumpled looking." I disagree: the reason the soldiers do not spring forward with backs perfectly erect is that they are marching, conserving their strength as they carry themselves and their equipment in a measured tread. When viewed within the context of the narrative, they come across to me as disciplined, not listless. Boime's notion that the troops are "listless" is a crucial step in a larger argument that he makes, the conclusion being that the relationship between Shaw and the troops is a racist hierarchy. In this view the African American soldiers in the relief function merely as a foil by which to measure the superiority of the white hero above. Boime needs to persuade us, however, that the representation of Shaw and the representation of the troops are diametrically opposed to each other: he is up above, they are down below; he is erect, they are listless. Ultimately, Boime argues that in this comparison the troops lose their very humanity; he claims that the black men and the horse merge into one mass of subhumanity. He points our attention particularly to the visual rhyme between the horse's hind leg and the soldiers' retreating legs in back.[3]

Here again my analysis of the visual evidence differs considerably. Boime overlooks the many ways in which the horse and the troops remain visually distinct, in their movements, in their surface quality. And even more importantly, he does not see that this particular visual rhyme is one of a whole pattern of such rhymes meant to knit together all the various planes of the relief, including Shaw's. The diagonal of the sword, for example, so prominent at the front of the relief, rhymes the horse's leg below and the rifle barrels above, thereby helping to unite foreground and background—commander, horse, and troops—in one harmony.

Despite these unifying devices, it is still obvious that Shaw does indeed have a superior status in this relief, the status of a commanding officer. So although the sword helps to link Shaw with the rest of the march, it is also a mark of his distinction. The sword was a deliberately antiquated weapon chosen to embellish the officer's regalia precisely because it signaled the officer's removal from the actual business of killing, which the troops instead were trained to undertake. The detail of the sword reinforces what the interwoven rhythms of the whole have already established: Shaw at once belongs to the march and transcends it. He rides with his troops but is elevated above them, his head reaching up into the realm of the angel who floats over the men and guides their march. For Saint-Gaudens, the figure of the angel was crucial; he stood by it despite the opposition of committee members and even friends.[4] It enabled Shaw to become a mediating figure between the register of the real below—the concrete realm of the male body under physical strain—and the register of the ideal above—signified by the weightless female body divinely propelled. Shaw thus passes between the realms of mortality and immortality, between oblivion and eternity. Whereas he moves ahead with his troops toward an inevitable death, he alone is singled out for everlasting fame.

This distinction between the commander and his troops in the relief panel has a racial and racist dimension because black soldiers in this war, with few exceptions, were not allowed to be commanders; the whole idea of command or leadership was impregnated with assumptions of white privilege. Yet, what is so extraordinary about Saint-Gaudens's panel is that it maintains this distinction in status without reducing the soldiers to a mere foil. If we compare the panel to Thomas Ball's so-called *Emancipation Group* (1879), also located in Boston, the point becomes clearer. Ball took a familiar image of enslavement, that of the kneeling, seminude black man, and contrasted it point by point with the heroic figure of Lincoln up above. The black man is defined not as a person in his own right, but as a *lack* of those attributes of personhood that Lincoln has in abundance: verticality, clothing, paper, and book, hence independence, power, and civilization.[5] In Saint-Gaudens's panel, by contrast, the soldiers have their own signs of social legitimacy and power—uniforms, guns, disciplined action, determination. And they have a compelling presence and individuality that African Americans had never before had in public sculpture, that common soldiers, black or white, had never had in the generic monuments erected to honor them. If one took the panel and simply changed the faces from African American to Anglo-American, it would still be a groundbreaking tribute to the common soldier. Indeed, if the soldiers' bodies were identified as "white," it would probably not occur to anyone to read them negatively, in opposition to the figure of the commanding officer.

The "blackness" of the soldiers' bodies serves as a kind of container into which viewers can pour their own anger or prejudices, sometimes in a way that actually flouts the visual evidence in front of them. For example, in 1913, the critic Charles Caffin contrasted what he called the "doglike trustfulness" of the troops with "the serene elevation of their white leader."[6] This interpretation moves from visual evidence into the realm of pure fantasy. I have a hard time imagining how doglike trustfulness could ever be depicted in a sculpture of anything other than a dog; much less do I see it in these faces. Boime actually uses this quotation from Caffin as more ammunition against the monument, but it is misguided to give such an absurd description any critical weight. Caffin's observation is simply a racist misreading that tells us more about the critic than about the monument.

Having spent some time considering the visual evidence, we need to ask whether it is possible to find any documentary evidence that can supplement or amplify what the object itself tells us. The most obvious step is to consider the artist himself, to try to discover what he thought about the work he made. Although this seems eminently reasonable, in practice it is full of pitfalls. If there was ever a good example of Picasso's dictum "Don't talk to the driver," Saint-Gaudens is it. He did not talk much about his work, publicly at least, but he did leave behind a memoir containing several anecdotes about his work on the Shaw Memorial, especially about the black men who modeled for him. These anecdotes are essentially a series of racist slurs and jokes made at the expense of the men who became the models for the soldiers we see on the relief. In his recounting, the sculptor lumps together the horse and the African American men and writes that "all furnished me with the greatest amusement." The horse was amusing to ride, and the "darkeys" were amusing for their ignorance, superstition, and deceit, though Saint-Gaudens was careful to remark that "they are very likable, with their soft voices and imaginative, though simple, minds."[7] Now if one already sees the relief as a racist hierarchy, it is easy to understand how Saint-Gaudens's racist stories offer more support for the case. But we need not accept this equation of the artist's mental attitude with his work. There is a clear difference between Saint-Gaudens's representations of the models in print and his representations of them in bronze. In the memoir he stereotypes the men, and the humor is supposed to work precisely because the (white) readers are expected to recognize and accept the stereotypes. In the relief panel, by contrast, the artist was not interested in creating any generic types, negative or positive. In fact, Saint-Gaudens was interested in the African American soldiers precisely because they broke the generic mold of the white soldier repeated countlessly in other soldier monuments. Saint-Gaudens resisted that kind of standardization in his art; his own artistic philosophy compelled him to individualize the soldiers rather than stereotype or caricature them as he did in the memoir.

I do not mean to overlook Saint-Gaudens's racism, but rather to argue that an unpredictable process of artistic problem-solving and labor came between the artist's preconceptions and his final product. His artistic discipline took him in a new and unexpected direction. As a social being, he was thoughtless, mimicking the racist beliefs of his milieu; as an artist, he was extraordinarily thoughtful, compelled to search out the humanity even of people he would ridicule in his gentlemen's club.[8]

This is not to say that the notion of artistic intention is worthless, or that we should not talk about it at all. But the notion of artistic intention should not be reduced to what the artist happened to say or be thinking about at a particular time. Intention must be broadened to encompass—at the very least—the artist's training, how the artist conceptualized the artistic task, and the process by which the artist revised the work under internal pressures as well as pressures from outside.[9] If we look at all these intentional factors in Saint-Gaudens's case, they help explain the paradox of how a racist white man could produce the first and most compelling images of African American soldiers in American sculpture.

To help us, we have a large, though by no means complete, archival record that documents the long and tortuous process by which the final design for the monument emerged. I have described this process in detail elsewhere, so here I concentrate on a few points salient to the issue of intention. The first point to stress is that when the campaign for a monument began in Boston in 1865, the sponsors conceived of the work not as a monument to the black regiment but to the white hero Shaw, who had become (after John Brown) the most famous martyr of the abolitionist cause. Interestingly, the prime mover behind the project at its inception was an African American businessman in Boston, Joshua B. Smith; after pledging a good deal of his own money and raising funds in the local African American community, he enlisted the aid of the famed abolitionist senator from Massachusetts Charles Sumner. Both Smith and Sumner were adamant that the monument should be an equestrian statue of Shaw, and they managed to beat back the objections of those who felt that such a traditional image of military glory was inappropriate for an abolitionist hero.[10]

It was not until the early 1880s, after a long period in which the project lay dormant, that this conception of the monument began to shift. By this time Smith and Sumner had both died, but the monument fund had grown to the point where a project was now feasible. The architect Henry Hobson Richardson began work on a design, and he brought in Saint-Gaudens to collaborate on the sculpture; Saint-Gaudens, by his own admission, also wanted to do a traditional equestrian statue. In April 1882, the monument committee—now in the hands of a group of Boston Brahmins—announced a design. Not surprisingly, it featured an equestrian statue of Shaw (set in an arch), but also three relief tablets below the statue illustrating the history of the black regiment—its departure, the battle at Battery Wagner, and the return of the survivors. A sketch from Richardson's office shows a very similar plan, with two instead of three relief tablets. Shaw remained the leading figure in this design, of course, but the commemorative intention had expanded to encompass the narrative history of the regiment extending even after Shaw's death and raising the issue of the black soldier and his civic status.[11]

This design was soon abandoned. According to Saint-Gaudens, the Shaw family objected to the plans for an equestrian statue, believing that Shaw had not attained sufficient military rank to merit such a representation; it would appear "pretentious."[12] Saint-Gaudens then rethought the problem and devised a solution that would integrate into one image the two separate elements of the 1882 design. The sculptor hit upon the idea of representing an infantry march with Shaw on horseback and his soldiers on foot, the whole scene in one large relief panel.

Office of H. H. Richardson, design for the Shaw Memorial (ca. 1882), pen and ink.
Courtesy Department of Printing & Graphic Arts, The Houghton Library,
Harvard University.

In this way the commemorative content shifted further, as Shaw and
the troops now melded into one sculptural statement.

It is ironic that the traditional white-hero monument contemplated
by Joshua B. Smith had evolved, in the hands of a group of Brahmins
and an elite white sculptor, into a monument also commemorating
the black soldiery. The Brahmins clearly understood the change and
welcomed it; for them the shift from a lone equestrian statue to a narrative relief was not a compromise but an opportunity to enrich the monument's meaning. Committee member John M. Forbes wrote five years
before the monument's completion:

> The original intention was to have a statue. By tacit consent we have
> changed to a bas-relief, which includes soldiers differing to that extent
> from the original plan. Col. Lee asks what I think it is intended to record?

I think the change from a statue to a bas-relief permits us to make it a memento for those who fell at Fort Wagner, and also to make it serve as a record of the Era which the outgoing of the regiment from Boston, and its only memorable battle some sixty days later, marks; but always with Col. Shaw the leading figure in the Memorial.[13]

Neither Saint-Gaudens nor the committee went into the project expecting to commemorate African American soldiers, but they ended up doing just that because of a series of unexpected events and the artistic responses they provoked. Nonetheless, even with the format of a single relief panel showing the regiment and its commander together in a march, Saint-Gaudens could have decided to minimize the role of the

Augustus Saint-Gaudens, plaster cast of sketch model for the Shaw Memorial, date unknown. Courtesy U.S. Department of the Interior, National Park Service, Saint-Gaudens National Historic Site, Cornish, New Hampshire.

foot soldiers in the composition. Indeed, his plaster sketch, probably done in 1883–84, shows the regiment in very low relief, a kind of background screen for the heroic figure of Shaw. Why then did the sculptor over the next decade bring the soldiers into high relief and devote years of work to individualizing their portraits? In his memoir, Saint-Gaudens explained: "In justice to myself I must say here that from the low-relief I proposed making when I undertook the Shaw commission, a relief that reasonably could be finished for the limited sum at the command of the committee, I, through my extreme interest in it and its opportunity, increased the conception until the rider grew almost to a statue in the round and the negroes assumed far more importance than I had originally intended."[14] It is reasonable to infer that, for Saint-Gaudens, the shift from a single equestrian statue to a relief format was not a disappointment but rather an opportunity, just as it was for the Brahmin committee. For the committee, it offered an opportunity to expand the commemorative intention to represent more explicitly the real power and accomplishment of abolitionism and to remind the world of Boston's role in it. For Saint-Gaudens, who as far as we know had nothing invested in abolitionism or Boston's civic image, the opportunity was an artistic one: an opportunity to create a uniquely artful war memorial. Since the 1880s, standardized soldier monuments had come increasingly under attack from both critics and artists, and Saint-Gaudens was certainly sympathetic to those who deplored the cheap industrial reproduction of soldier monuments by monument companies and mail-order firms. The Shaw Memorial can be understood as a systematic assault on the conventional character of the particular type of war memorial that had become so predominant after the Civil War. The more Saint-Gaudens focused on representing the foot soldiers and individualizing them, the more unusual and ambitious the monument became. Their "blackness" once again was not a problem but an opportunity, for it distinguished them even more from the generic white soldier in the standardized war memorials.[15]

Saint-Gaudens's interest in bringing the troops into higher relief and treating them as individuals may well have been the reason he made one other crucial decision: to arrange the whole march in profile. Although he never abandoned his plan to have the equestrian figure of Shaw in the front and center of the panel, he did experiment with various possibilities within this general scheme, one of which was a three-quarter perspective with Shaw at the head of the march leading his troops.[16] In addition to being technically complicated, this solution would have of necessity pushed the troops much farther into the background. By shifting to a profile view, the sculptor had to situate Shaw's figure *alongside* his troops if Shaw was to remain in the center. This decision, in turn, not only permitted the soldier figures to emerge from the background but also created a composition in which officer and troops move together, side by side, toward their joint destiny. If Shaw had led the march, he would have controlled the rhythm of the whole; but with the rhythm of the march set by the drummer boy at the head, the soldiers following behind have a life and will of their own; the equestrian figure of Shaw then becomes a subtle counterpoint rather than the conductor of the band. And from this contrapuntal arrangement comes the creative tension of the panel: although Shaw is singled out—elevated and differentiated—he is bound together with the troops on the ground in a common mission that is represented most profoundly by their compelling material presence.

Ultimately we can trace convincing artistic reasons for every step Saint-Gaudens took as he devised a solution to the problems posed by the monument. This is not to elevate art above ideology or to insist that art is somehow pure and free of ideology. Rather, it is to explain how a particular artistic compulsion could actually overcome the artist's own deep-seated racial beliefs, inculcated in him by his culture. If art has a liberating force, it is this: it can compel people to reexamine what they think they already know. Saint-Gaudens's monument may not have changed his consciousness, but it has, in some small way, changed ours. By accident and by design, a great work that still speaks to us today came into being.

JAMES SMETHURST

"THOSE NOBLE SONS OF HAM"

Poetry, Soldiers, and Citizens at the End of Reconstruction

Abraham Lincoln called upon the colored men of this country to reach out their iron arms and clutch with their steel fingers the faltering banner of the Republic . . . Ah! then, my friends, the claims of the Negro found the heart of the nation a little more tender and responsive than now. But I ask Americans to remember the arms that were needed then may be needed again.

Frederick Douglass, "The United States Cannot Remain
Half-Slave and Half-Free" (1883)

I would sing a song heroic
Of those noble sons of Ham,
Of the gallant colored soldiers
Who fought for Uncle Sam!

Paul Laurence Dunbar, "The Colored Soldiers"

HISTORIAN Sidney Kaplan observed that after the 1897 dedication of Augustus Saint-Gaudens's monument on Boston Common, a new generation of poets, white and black, responded to it and "the saga of the Fifty-fourth with a new sense of consecration." African American writing on the Fifty-fourth Massachusetts Regiment and the black Civil War soldier, however, long preceded Saint-Gaudens's work. Moreover, the meaning and purpose of black writing on the Fifty-fourth Massachusetts and Saint-Gaudens's monument differed markedly from the work of white poets.[1] In theme, tone, and purpose, this black poetry served unique political, cultural, moral, and artistic ends. In the highly contested cultural landscape of the post–Civil War era, the work of African American poets became verbal statues, indispensable "monuments in the mind." Like Frederick Douglass's speeches and writings in the 1880s and 1890s, African American poetry commemorated black sacrifice and bravery and promoted African American citizenship.[2]

African American poetry from the 1870s to 1900 emerged out of the political and cultural wars that raged over Southern white repudiation of Reconstruction and over the rise of the Jim Crow system of legal segregation that disfranchised blacks throughout the region. A wave of poetry by black authors used images of the Fifty-fourth Massachusetts Regiment and the black Civil War soldier to affirm African American citizenship and manhood. While African American poets, especially during the last two decades of the nineteenth century, explored the meaning of black military service, their white counterparts largely focused on the Fifty-fourth's white commander, Robert Gould Shaw. By the close of the century, however, African American poets had largely abandoned the rhetoric of citizenship for bitter elegies that reflected the unfulfilled promises of Reconstruction.

Many of the first poems about Shaw and the Fifty-fourth Massachusetts Regiment appeared shortly after the Union attack on Battery Wagner in South Carolina on July 18, 1863. They represent Shaw as an abolitionist martyr redeeming America from the stain of satanic slavery, often with Shaw literally ascending into heaven, as in Epes Sargent's "Colonel Shaw: On Hearing That the Rebels Had Buried His Body under a Pile of Twenty-Five Negroes" (1863):

> There, where the smoke from Sumter's bellowing guns
> Curls o'er the grave, which no commingled dust
> Can make less sacred. Soon his monument
> Shall be the old flag waving, and proclaiming
> To the whole world that the great cause he died for
> Has nobly triumphed,—that the hideous Power,
> Hell-born, that would disgrace him, has been hurled
> Into the pit it hollowed for the Nation,—
> That the Republic stands redeemed and pure,
> Justice enthroned, and not one child of God
> Robbed of his birthright, freedom![3]

Like many of the poems composed by white authors during the war, such as Elizabeth Sedgwick's "Buried with His Niggers!" and L. H.'s "To Robert Gould Shaw, Buried by South Carolinians under a Pile of 24 Negroes," Sargent's poem presents a Christlike Shaw whose physical contact with black bodies in death provides white readers a shocking intensity.

Those white authors who focused on the black soldiers tended to represent them as agents of freedom, as did Ralph Waldo Emerson in "Voluntaries" (1863).

> She will not refuse to dwell
> With the offspring of the Sun;
> Foundling of the desert far,

> Where palms plume, and siroccos blaze,
> He roves unhurt the burning ways
> In climates of the summer star.
> He has avenues to God
> Hid from men of Northern brain,
> Far beholding, without cloud,
> What these with slowest steps attain.
> If once the generous chief arrive
> To lead him willing to be led,
> For freedom he will strike and strive,
> And drain his heart til he be dead.[4]

These poems share the Protestant primitivism displayed in antebellum and postbellum American literature from Harriet Beecher Stowe's *Uncle Tom's Cabin* (1853) and *The Minister's Wooing* (1859) to W.E.B. Du Bois's *Souls of Black Folk* (1903), wherein African Americans are seen as possessing special spiritual gifts that they can provide to America in exchange for freedom.[5]

During the 1860s, few African Americans appear to have written formal poems about the Fifty-fourth Massachusetts. In fact, the only extant poem by a black author published during the war is "The Massachusetts Fifty-Fourth" by Frances Harper, arguably the most important African American poet before Paul Laurence Dunbar and one of the best-selling black poets of all time. The poem, originally published in the New York *Weekly Anglo-African*, "establishes a moral symmetry, following in the Christian tradition of death and rebirth."[6] This use of a Protestant rhetoric of martyrdom and redemption was similar to that seen in white authors who wrote of Shaw and the Fifty-fourth. However, in Harper's poem the redemptive figure of Shaw (or even the more generic "chief" of Emerson) is absent, replaced by a collective figure of the black troops, whose blood would heal the republic.

> Oh! not in vain those heroes fell,
>   Amid those hours of fearful strife;
> Each dying heart poured out a balm
>   To heal the wounded nation's life.
>
> And from the soil drenched with their blood,
>   The fairest flowers of peace shall bloom;
> And history cull rich laurels there,
>   To deck each martyr hero's tomb.
>
> And ages yet uncrossed with life,
>   As sacred urns, do hold each mound
> Where sleep the loyal, true, and brave
>   In freedom's consecrated ground.[7]

The replacement of Shaw with black troops and the lack of a white presence sharply distinguishes Harper's work from the majority of poems about the Fifty-fourth published during the Civil War. It imputes to the black soldiers a subjectivity, a self-consciousness, and an agency lacking in nearly all the poems by white writers. Harper's poetry also differs from that of her white contemporaries by her refusal to use Shaw's burial with his black troops in a mass grave either for shock effect or to emphasize Shaw's presumed Christlike qualities. Nonetheless, Harper's piece shares with those other works a personification or figuration of the idea of freedom by the black troops.

In the years immediately after the Civil War, the Fifty-fourth Massachusetts and the black Civil War soldier almost disappear as subjects of American poetry. Those writers who do invoke the unit are nearly all, so far as I can tell, African American—few white poets wrote about the Fifty-fourth (and none at length) until after the dedication of the Shaw Memorial in 1897.[8] The epics of James Madison Bell, an influential antebellum black leader, *The Progress of Liberty* (1866) and *The Triumph of Liberty* (1870) are among the few poems that address the Fifty-fourth's history before 1877.[9] In both poems, not only is slavery the civic curse that caused the Civil War, but also the black soldier is the essential component in the redemption and renewal of the republic. In both poems, the Fifty-fourth assumes special importance as the only black unit mentioned by name. As in Harper's poem, there is a focus on the African American troops and no mention of Robert Gould Shaw, emphasizing the agency of the black soldiers without a white intermediary. Also like Harper's "Massachusetts Fifty-Fourth," Bell's poems objectify or personify freedom and liberty, but being free is not defined simply as not being a slave. Instead, it is explicitly extended to the idea of citizenship, particularly in *The Triumph of Liberty.*

> There is no right a freeman has
> So purely sacred as his choice.
> How e'er bereft he'll cling to this,
> And in its potency rejoice;
>
> For in its exercise he stands
> The peer of titled wealth and state,
> How e'er possessed of spreading lands,
> Or gifted they in high debate—
>
> He is their peer, however grand,
> Or much upon themselves they dote,
> For there's no station in our land
> Which ranks a man above his vote.[10]

Both poems end fulsomely praising the republic—*The Triumph of Liberty* includes an almost ludicrous catalog of its great natural resources ("And hail to thy Streamlets"), its technological and economic advances ("And hail to thy Telegraph"), and its governmental institutions ("And hail to thy Magistrates, Judges, and Courts").

Joshua McCarter Simpson's "Let the Banner Proudly Wave," an "air" included in *The Emancipation Car* (1874), similarly figures the black soldiers as redemptive agents of freedom, emphasizing a "rights of man" republicanism rather than the Northern Protestantism that characterized Harper and most of the white poets writing about Shaw and the Fifty-fourth.

> We've stood and fought like demons,
>   Upon the battle field;
> Both slaves and Northern freemen
>   Have faced the glowing steel.
> Our blood beneath this banner
>   Has mingled with the whites,
> And 'neath its folds we now demand
>   Our just and equal rights.[11]

Although the themes of freedom and slavery appear in the poem, Simpson also expands upon the idea of citizenship. He reminds the reader that freedom and citizenship are not interchangeable concepts (legally or culturally) in the United States and observes that not all black soldiers had been legally slaves—and hardly any remained so once in the army. The Fifty-fourth Massachusetts was a regiment of free men, many of whom had been born in the North; relatively few ever had been slaves.[12] This observation is missing in the earlier poems, where an opposition between slavery and freedom exists and the "Afric" slave struggles for his freedom. Both Harper's poem ("Bearers of a high commission / To break each brother's chain") and those by white authors include that struggle. Simpson, however, reminds us that to be free—in the sense of being a "freeman"—is not the same as being a citizen with "just and equal rights." Freedom might be a constitutive element of American citizenship, Simpson observes, but many categories of people in the United States did not enjoy anything approaching full citizenship, including unnaturalized "white" immigrants, "nonwhite" immigrants, African Americans, Native Americans, and women. They might be free in the sense of not being slaves, but they were not citizens. Thus, for Simpson, as for later black writers, African Americans are entitled to citizenship, not merely freedom, because they have earned their status as citizens through the sacrifice of the black Civil War soldiers.

They earned the right in the same way that native-born whites gained citizenship rights through the sacrifice of the patriots of the American Revolution. Of course, these writers were not opposing "freedom" to "citizenship," but identifying the first as a necessary precondition for the second. The recognition that the two conditions are not the same gained new poignancy with the rise of Jim Crow and mass African American disfranchisement.

Bell's poems may be "uniformly soporific," as literary scholar Joan Sherman claims, and in many respects Simpson's poetry is weak and disappointing.[13] Nonetheless, their poems are important forerunners of the poetry of later African Americans who use the Fifty-fourth Massachusetts and the black Civil War veteran to assert their claims to citizenship and "Americanness." They are unlike black and white writers such as Emerson, Booker T. Washington, and the early Du Bois, who understood freedom as a precondition for the former slaves to develop the self-consciousness necessary for citizenship. Bell and especially Simpson demand "citizenship now," founded on the sacrifice of the black Civil War soldiers and on a republicanism that invokes the democratic and republican rhetoric embodied in the Declaration of Independence. This emphasis on citizenship and Americanness over an idealized and unspecified freedom is the distinguishing mark of much African American literature during Reconstruction.

Simpson's poem and Bell's epics notwithstanding, the post–Civil War wave of poems about the Fifty-fourth and the black Civil War soldier did not really begin until congressional Reconstruction had ended. Traditionally, historians have set the formal end of Reconstruction with the Compromise of 1877. To end partisan rancor and avoid renewed warfare, Republicans and Democrats sent Rutherford B. Hayes to the White House in exchange for a promise not to use Federal power and the army to guarantee the political rights of African Americans in the South.[14] But we might also fix the end of Reconstruction as a viable ideal with the final consolidation of Jim Crow and the disfranchisement of the mass of African Americans in the South at the close of the nineteenth century and the beginning of the twentieth.[15] If Reconstruction is taken to mean that era in which the federal government actively intervened in state and local government in the South, largely for the purpose of establishing African American citizenship, then Reconstruction ended in 1877. However, it is also clear that African Americans and their allies did not see Reconstruction as a lost cause until well after the Compromise of 1877. Black poets like Simpson employed a rhetoric of citizenship that contested attempts to end Reconstruction and to effectively limit the political and social rights of African Americans. The

Fifty-fourth Massachusetts came to embody African American claims
to citizenship earned with blood. Thus, when I write here of late Reconstruction or a late-Reconstruction rhetoric, I refer to this period from
the late 1870s to the early 1890s when formal Reconstruction had died
but the ideal and some black political gains of Reconstruction endured.

This late-Reconstruction rhetoric can be seen clearly in Albery
Whitman's *Not a Man and Yet a Man* (1877). Whitman's epic is particularly interesting for its mixture of Protestant jeremiad, parable, quasi-
scientific or medical rhetoric, echoes of Longfellow's *Hiawatha* and
Cooper's *Last of the Mohicans*, neomedieval romanticism, and republican rhetoric of citizenship. Whitman focuses his story on Rodney, a
slave of African and European descent (with his European "blood" pre-
dominating) who is a mixture of Leatherstocking, Uncas, Hiawatha,
and Ivanhoe.[16] The final section of the poem, "The End of the Whole
Matter," begins with Rodney, a victorious black Union officer, encountering his former master, Aylor, wounded and dying on the battlefield.
As Aylor dies, he is tormented by the memory of his torture of Rodney
and his rape of Rodney's lover and (later) wife, Leoona. Seeing Rodney,
Aylor begs for water and forgiveness, which Rodney gives as Aylor dies
in his arms. This parable of forgiveness is immediately followed by a
call for a reconciliation that acknowledges the valor of both sides.

> And now my country let us bury all
> Our blunders sad beneath grim battle's pall.
> Gathered beneath the storm's heroic folds,
> While our dear land an aching bosom holds,
> Let us forget the wrongs of blue and grey,
> In gazing on the grandeur of the fray.
> Now the vanquished his repentant face
> Lean in the victor's merciful embrace,
> And let the victor, with his strong arm heal
> The bleeding wounds that gape beneath his steel.
> And may no partial hand attempt a lay
> Of praise, as due alone to blue or grey.
> The warrior's wreath may well by both be worn,
> For braver man than either ne'er was born.[17]

In Whitman's call to forget "the wrongs of blue and grey" on the battlefield, he does not call upon Americans to forget what he sees as the root
cause or sin of the war, slavery. Rather, as in the opening parable, it is
necessary for the sinners to confess and repent their sins before they
can be forgiven. For Whitman's speaker the war was necessary, even
divinely inspired.

> The war was God-sent, for the battle blade,
> Around the seething gangrene, Slavery, laid,
> By Heaven's arm, this side and that was prest,
> Until the galling shame dropt from the Nation's breast.

The jeremiadic Protestantism of this passage would not have been out of place in many of the earlier poems that mentioned the Fifty-fourth, the black soldier, and Robert Gould Shaw—though the use of the metaphor of disease rather than a Christlike figure of redemption was unusual, but not unique.[18] What is unique is the manner in which that Protestant rhetoric merged with a rhetoric of citizenship and government that cast God as the divine surgeon who uses the instrument of the Union Army to heal the body politic.

> War was inevitable, for the crimes
> That stained our hands (and in the olden times
> Engendered) now were Constitutional,
> And spreading thro' the Nation's body all.
> Deep rooted where the vital currents meet
> Around the heart of government, their seat
> Evaded Legislation's keenest skill,
> Or bent the stoutest edge of human will.
> 'Twas then that God the raving Nation threw
> Upon her own war lance and from her drew,
> By accidental providence, a flood
> Of old diseases that lurked in her blood.

This medicalized jeremiad is immediately preceded by a passage mixing medicine and medieval romance in which African American soldiers are represented as an integral part of the instruments through which God drew out the infection of slavery:

> And where our sons their battle lances drew,
> Fought not their sable comrades bravely too?
> Let Wagner answer 'mid the reeking storm
> That mingles with black dead proud Shaw's fair form.
> Ask it of Fisher, and a thousand more
> Brave fields that answer with their lips of gore.
> And while America's escutcheon bright,
> Is bathed in war-won Freedom's glorious light,
> Forget it not, the colored man will fight.
> More patriotism Sparta never knew,
> A lance more knightly Norman never threw,
> More courage never armed the Roman coasts,
> With blinder zeal ne'er rode the Moslem hosts,

> And ne'er more stubborn stood the Muscovite,
> Than stood the hated negro in the fight.

The "lances" of the (presumably) white soldiers mirror those of the black troops. The medievalism of "lances" resonates with the mixture of medicine and Protestantism in the following section, again suggesting that both the black and the white troops are instruments of God. The new connection and equality between black and white is emphasized in the image of Shaw. Here, Shaw is not so much a Christ figure but, rather, symbolic of the disintegration of racial division, suggestively linked to the dead black troops by the word "mingles."

Strangely enough, the voice of Whitman's speaker identifies with white readers, the "we" whose "sons" were joined by their "sable" comrades. Yet this sort of identification fits the general recognition of the bravery of soldiers on both sides of the Civil War and the call for forgiveness and reconciliation. The poem is addressed, then, in large part, not simply to the former abolitionists of the North and partisans of the Union, but also to the former soldiers and supporters of the Confederacy. For Whitman's speaker, however, the only way that reconciliation can work is for the sin of slavery—and any other restriction of citizenship on account of race, religion, or ethnicity (if not gender)—to be erased after repentance on the part of the sinners. This can be seen most clearly as the poem ends in a combination of medievalism and radical republicanism:

> Free schools, free press, free speech and equal laws,
> A common country and a common cause,
> Are only worthy of a freeman's boasts—
> Are Freedom's real and intrinsic costs.
> Without these, Freedom is an empty name,
> And war-worn glory is a glaring shame.
> Soon where yon happy future now appears,
> Where learning now her glorious temple rears,
> Our country's hosts shall round one interest meet,
> And her free heart with one proud impulse beat,
> One common blood thro' her life's channels flow,
> While one great speech her loyal tongue shall know.
> And soon, whoever to our bourne shall come,
> Jew, Greek or Goth, he here shall be at home.
> Then Ign'rance shall forsake her crooked ways,
> And poor old Caste there end her feeble days.

Again, as in many of the early poems invoking the Fifty-fourth and the black soldier, freedom is objectified in an abstract manner. Yet this objectification and abstraction is undermined with the claim to citizenship that flows both from natural rights and from the efforts of black (and white) soldiers. Any restriction of the rights of people residing within the United States, whatever their race, religion, or nationality, makes a mockery of America and threatens to bring another divine intervention, presumably as in the Civil War. Thus, Whitman is not merely commemorating the valor of black soldiers, or even reminding the reader of the evil of slavery. He is arguing for the preservation of Reconstruction and against any future system that would threaten the citizenship of African Americans or any other Americans.

During the 1880s, the use of the Fifty-fourth Massachusetts Regiment and the black Civil War soldier in poetry diminished greatly, though they continued to appear in African American prose works. The only poem by an African American author during those years that I have discovered is James Monroe Trotter's "Fifty-Fourth at Wagner." Trotter, a former officer in the Fifty-fourth's sister regiment, the Fifty-fifth Massachusetts, invokes the Fifty-fourth to express an Afrocentric quasi-nationalism, rather than a rhetoric of citizenship.

> Momentous hour! A race on trial, which oft in this and other lands
> Had filled the deadly breach, had helped to burst foul slavery's bands!
> O shades of Attucks, Salem, Hannibal, O grand Toussaint,
> Thy valor's lost, thy fame is nought, if these now prove faint![19]

Trotter shares with other black poets a focus on the rank and file of the Fifty-fourth rather than on Shaw. However, the near-nationalist exclamations and apostrophes of Trotter, with their emphasis on manhood, resemble more the verse found in Marcus Garvey's early-twentieth-century *Negro World* than other poetic treatments of the Fifty-fourth by postbellum African American writers.[20]

By the 1890s, black citizenship was doomed in the South. The erection of segregation's legal infrastructure, especially disfranchisement, elicited a renewed defense of Reconstruction and its legacies by African American writers. Probably the best-known response came from Frances Harper. Her popular 1893 novel *Iola Leroy* strongly featured the heroism and sacrifice of black soldiers in the Civil War. Harper's feminism, which posited black women as crucial participants in the cause of African American empowerment, added a dimension to the discussion of Reconstruction and citizenship that was missing in the work of male African American writers who used the figure of the black soldier.

Representations of the Fifty-fourth Massachusetts and the black soldier returned to African American poetry in the 1890s. A minor effort, "The Old Flag" (1890), by George Clinton Rowe, is significant as one of the very few poems about the Fifty-fourth by either a black or a white author that names a black soldier—or any member of the Fifty-fourth other than Robert Gould Shaw.[21] "The Old Flag" is a brief praise poem for William H. Carney, the black sergeant wounded in the assault on Battery Wagner who bore the regimental colors back to the Union lines, where he exclaimed, "The dear old flag has never touched the ground, boys!" (Carney was the first African American to be awarded a Congressional Medal of Honor.)[22] Rowe celebrates not only the bravery of "the noble hero of our race" but also the patriotism and the Americanness of Carney—and by extension, of all African Americans.

There is a strange doubleness to Rowe's poem. At times he uses the word "our" to mean the people of the United States ("our country—South and North"), presumably encompassing something like the reconstructed and reconciled republic of Albery Whitman. At other times, "our" seems to refer specifically to African Americans ("our race"). Thus, the "we" of the poem, and by extension of the imagined audience of the poem, seems indeterminate. Perhaps this doubleness or indeterminacy is intended to trouble both categories, making it an early statement of black "double-consciousness," which would shortly be articulated so powerfully in Paul Laurence Dunbar's "We Wear the Mask" (1895) and W.E.B. Du Bois's *Souls of Black Folk* (1903). "The Old Flag" is unlike most poems about the Fifty-fourth and black soldiers in that freedom does not figure directly at all. Rather, the poem is dominated by a rhetoric of bravery and patriotism, with a notion of citizenship implied by the patriotism.

Undoubtedly, the poet laureate of the black Civil War soldier is Paul Laurence Dunbar. He wrote at least a half-dozen poems about African American veterans of the Civil War or the Fifty-fourth Massachusetts, or both, as well as poems commemorating black soldiers in the Revolution and the Spanish-American War. In fact, one might mark the beginning of Dunbar's literary career with the publication of "Our Martyred Soldiers" at age sixteen on June 8, 1888. It was ostensibly a poem to all Union soldiers, though, as in the work of Rowe, "our" here carries with it a sense of racial dualism or doubleness. Dunbar's interest in the subject likely originated in his father's fascinating career. Joshua Dunbar returned to the United States from Canada after escaping from slavery on the underground railroad. He enlisted in the Fifty-fifth Massachusetts Regiment and later transferred to the Fifth Massachusetts Cavalry (both African American units).[23] Beyond any personal identification with the black Civil War veteran, Paul Laurence Dunbar employed the image of the black soldier to defend the goals of Reconstruction. After the abandonment of Reconstruction, Dunbar reappropriated the Fifty-fourth Massachusetts, the black soldier, and, for the first time in his career, Robert Gould Shaw, to bitterly elegize Reconstruction's demise.[24]

Dunbar became intensely engaged with his material, giving it a concreteness and specificity missing in the works of other poets, black or white. In Dunbar's early poems dealing with black soldiers, those soldiers fight for citizenship, not merely freedom.

> Yes, the Blacks enjoy their freedom,
>   And they won it dearly, too;
> For the life blood of their thousands
>   Did the southern fields bedew.
> In the darkness of their bondage,
>   In the depths of slavery's night,
> Their muskets flashed the dawning,
>   And they fought their way to light.
>
> They were comrades then and brothers,
>   Are they more or less to-day?
> They were good to stop a bullet
>   And to front the fearful fray.
> They were citizens and soldiers,
>   When rebellion raised its head;
> And the traits that made them worthy,—
>   Ah! those virtues are not dead.[25]

Here, in "The Colored Soldiers," first collected in *Majors and Minors* (1895), the sacrifices of black soldiers became an argument for their right to citizenship. Though Dunbar would later write a tribute to Lincoln, he insisted that citizenship was not a gift to African Americans—and as such, something that could be taken away—but a status earned. Again, as in the work of such black poets as James Madison Bell and Joshua McCarter Simpson, there is an implied connection to the patriots of the American Revolution, whose sacrifice made citizenship an inalienable right, not something granted by a king or a queen—or even a benevolent president.

Beyond the issue of citizenship, there is, as in Simpson's "Let the Banner Proudly Wave," an essential claim to a common Americanness of black and (loyal) white through the metaphor of blood mixing on the battlefield ("And their blood with yours commingling / has enriched the Southern soil"). This metaphor argues against a notion of citizenship and national identity based on skin color or other racialized notions, reminding Northern whites that their common sacrifice was with their fellow black Unionists (not with white Confederate soldiers), creating a new bond of blood.[26]

"The Colored Soldiers" is one of the prime examples of Dunbar's politically and poetically optimistic early phase, "We Wear the Mask" notwithstanding. Like other Dunbar poems from this period, such as "Ode to Ethiopia" and the elegy "Frederick Douglass," "The Colored Soldiers" is assertive, uplifting, proud, and commemorative while looking forward into a promising future (if Americans, particularly African Americans, stay the course). These poems honor black achievement and black potential and call upon other Americans to do the same.

The tone of Dunbar's poems dealing explicitly with the politics of race in the United States radically changed as the decade wore on. Two events in particular signaled the final setting of segregation and black disfranchisement. The first was the 1896 Supreme Court decision in *Plessy vs. Ferguson* upholding the constitutionality of Jim Crow segregation. Though it was only one in a series of retreats from Reconstruction by various branches of the federal government (e.g., the Compromise of 1877 and the 1883 Supreme Court decision striking down the Civil Rights Act of 1875, which outlawed segregated public accommodations), the 1896 Supreme Court decision marked a final hardening of segregation's legal infrastructure. It was more than a decade before the establishment of the Jim Crow system was complete throughout the South, but the ruling in *Plessy* marked the end of any hope that Reconstruction could be reinvigorated or its remaining fragments preserved.

Ironically, the second event was the dedication of the long-awaited Shaw Memorial on Boston Common in 1897. It produced, as Sidney Kaplan observed, a flurry of poetry commemorating Shaw and the Fifty-fourth, including the first significant group of such poems by white authors since the Civil War. Not surprisingly, given Shaw's centrality to the monument, these poems by black and white authors heralded a return both to elegy and to a focus on the regiment's first commander. There remained, however, a broad distinction between African American authors, who, like their black predecessors, emphasized the black rank and file and elegized Reconstruction as well as Shaw, and white authors, who emphasized Shaw and elegized an earlier (and often ideal) America, without any specific reference to Reconstruction themes.

As Dunbar implied in "The Unsung Heroes," the black rank and file soldier is absent from the poetry written by white authors after the dedication of Saint-Gaudens's monument. In these poems, such as Richard Watson Gilder's "Robert Gould Shaw," Thomas Bailey Aldrich's "An Ode on the Unveiling of the Shaw Memorial on Boston Common," and Robert Underwood Johnson's "Saint-Gaudens," Shaw becomes a heroic object abstracted from historical context. In Aldrich's poem particularly, one is hard pressed to find any reference to the historical moment in which Shaw's heroism took place or any allusion to the cause for which he fought (other than a single oblique mention of "his dusky braves"). These poems even fail to note the black troops on the monument, an aspect so striking that Robert Lowell's "For the Union Dead" would assert that in William James's speech at the dedication, James "could almost hear the bronze Negroes breathe." In an ironic sense, most of the works produced in response to the dedication of the Shaw Memorial might be seen as emblematic of the compromises with Jim Crow and the "New South" made—even in the heartland of abolitionism—at the turn of the century. These poems honor a hero without a cause, in dramatic contrast to virtually all earlier poems on the subject. They also avoid the issues of Reconstruction and black citizenship, which played so large a part in black literary treatments of Shaw, the Fifty-fourth, and the black soldier generally.[27]

The one poem by a white contemporary that expressed any concern for the black soldier and the end of Reconstruction was William Vaughn Moody's "Ode in Time of Hesitation." Unlike the poems of Aldrich, Gilder, and Robert Underwood Johnson, "An Ode in Time of Hesitation" connects the memorial to a specific historical past in a headnote beneath the title: "(After seeing at Boston the statue of Robert Gould Shaw, killed while storming Fort Wagner, July 18, 1863, at the head of the first enlisted negro regiment, the Fifty-fourth Massachusetts.)"[28] Also unlike Aldrich, Gilder, and Johnson, Moody described the bronze relief of Shaw and the black rank and file of the Fifty-fourth in brief but arresting detail:

> This bright March morn I stand,
> And hear the distant spring come up the land;
> Knowing that what I hear is not unheard
> Of this boy soldier and his negro band,
> For all their gaze is fixed so stern ahead,
> For all the fatal rhythm of their tread.
> The land they died to save from death and shame
> Trembles and waits, hearing the spring's great name,
> And by her pangs these resolute ghosts are stirred.

Moody's work was as much an elegy to a past era as to Shaw and the Fifty-fourth Massachusetts. For Moody, however, it was not the end of Reconstruction, the emergence of Jim Crow, or what Dunbar termed "the new slavery" of the South that marked the debasing of America, but the seizure of American overseas colonies, especially the Philippines, in the wake of the Spanish-American War. He linked Shaw and the Fifty-fourth to an idealized American past in which force served the righteous but more generalized cause of freedom and democracy, rather than to the specific fight to end slavery. "An Ode in Time of Hesitation" concludes on a jeremiadic note, promising that the heroic dead will return to bring disaster on the nation unless it turns from its imperialist course. Though threatening, in the manner of traditional jeremiads, the poem still holds out a possibility of choice. Thus, without specifically engaging the contemporary state of African American citizenship or freedom, Moody uses the image of Shaw and the Fifty-fourth to emphasize the debasement of an ideal America by imperialist avarice and alienation from a spiritualized essence—much as Robert Lowell would do decades later in "For the Union Dead."[29] There remains in Moody, however, a chance for repentance and spiritual rebirth.

Dunbar's later poems carry on a gloomy and often critical dialogue with the work by white poets about Shaw and the Fifty-fourth. It is quite possible that Moody's poem directly influenced Dunbar's "Robert Gould Shaw"—or that at least Dunbar had Moody's work in mind, since "An Ode in Time of Hesitation" appeared in the *Atlantic Monthly* only a few months prior to the publication of Dunbar's work in 1900. Certainly, the honored war dead who are invoked most clearly in Moody's poem are those whose dream of citizenship was subverted in the South, not in Puerto Rico or the Philippines. Dunbar may well have seen Moody's appropriation of the figures of Shaw and the black soldier as thoroughly draining those figures of their original meaning.[30]

Dunbar is also far more pessimistic than most of his contemporary poets on the possibility of American renewal or redemption. In the only substantial poem directly about the black soldiers that Dunbar wrote in "dialect," "When Dey 'Listed Colored Soldiers" (1899), the poem's voice is that of the black "folk" wife or lover of an African American soldier named Elias. The speaker recalls in an elegiac narrative the enlistment and departure of Elias, some of the human costs of the war, and Elias's death in action. As in the poetry of James Madison Bell and Albery Whitman, there is a metonymic reconciliation wherein the sorrow of the speaker is linked to that of the family of her former master, who also suffered loss in the war:

> Mastah Jack come home all sickly; he was broke for life, dey said;
> An' dey lef' my po' young mastah som'r's on de roadside,—dead.
> W'en de women cried an' mou'ned 'em, I could feel it thoo an' thoo,
> For I had a loved un fightin' in de way o' dangah, too.

Den dey tol' me dey had laid him some'r's way down souf to res',
Wid de flag dat he had fit for shinin' daih acrost his breas'.
Well, I cried, but den I reckon dat's whut Gawd had called him for,
W'en dey 'listed colo'ed sojers an' my 'Lias went to wah.[31]

There is a moral—one might say human—equality implied by the metonymy of suffering in which the black speaker asserts that she feels the same emotions as her former masters. Despite the empathy of the speaker for the suffering of her former owners, she clearly retains an image of the Civil War as a holy war against the evil of slavery. This claim to a common humanity, the admission of a feeling of civic responsibility toward the republic on the part of Elias and the speaker, and the sorrow mitigated by a sense of a higher duty clash with the still-common assessment of Dunbar's dialect poems as accommodationist—even racist—misappropriations of black culture, or at best only indirect criticisms of slavery and racism. Dunbar's critics fail to see in this poem his radical imputation of consciousness to the black folk, both male and female. He presents this folk consciousness without the supervisory presence of the elevated, literate (often "mulatto") African American figure common in so many representations of the black soldier, as in Albery Whitman's epics and Harper's *Iola Leroy*. The introduction of the contested civic position of women, both black and white, in the Reconstruction and immediate post-Reconstruction periods gives the poem an important dimension lacking in most of the contemporary literature, including Dunbar's later poems, which are primarily concerned with notions of manhood.

Despite the imputation of an equality between former slave and master and the sense of civic duty, a claim to citizenship—as opposed to only freedom—is not much in evidence. Of course, if asked by someone whom she could trust, the speaker (and Dunbar) would have declared that African Americans deserved citizenship. The poem could be taken as an implicit argument for full African American citizenship. But unlike the case of "The Colored Soldiers," that argument remains at best only implicit, reminding the reader of the distance between what African Americans in the South deserved and what they could expect.

This essentially pessimistic, though proud, vision can be seen in Dunbar's response to the Shaw Memorial and to the new burst of poems about Shaw and the Fifty-fourth Massachusetts Regiment by white writers. One of Dunbar's most frequently reprinted poems was the elegiac Petrarchan sonnet "Robert Gould Shaw" (1900).[32] In many respects, the opening octave of the sonnet appears to have more in common with the Civil War–era elegies to Shaw by white writers than with the work of earlier black poets, including Dunbar's own. The Fifty-fourth's black rank and file are present only as the "unlettered and despised droves," while Shaw is seen in the familiar position as sacrificial redeemer.

> Why was it that the thunder voice of Fate
>   Should call thee, studious, from the classic groves,
> Where calm-eyed Pallas with still footstep roves,
>   And charge thee seek the turmoil of the state?
> What bade thee hear the voice and rise elate,
>   Leave home and kindred and thy spicy loaves,
> To lead th' unlettered and despised droves
>   To manhood's home and thunder at the gate.[33]

The poem differs from most elegies to Shaw in replacing "freedom" with "manhood" as the key word. In this respect, the poem recalls Emerson's notion of Shaw's leadership and the Fifty-fourth as a rite of initiation into full humanity, although the emphasis on "manhood" also has much in common with the rhetoric of African American nationalism as it developed in the late nineteenth and early twentieth centuries.[34] This emphasis anticipates the turn in the concluding sestet: manhood achieved is something not easily taken away, unlike freedom or citizenship in the new post-Reconstruction South (and much of the North). This turning marks the poem's shift from an elegy for Shaw to one for Reconstruction and African American citizenship in the South.

> Far better the slow blaze of Learning's light,
>   The cool and quiet of her dearer fane,
> Than this hot terror of a hopeless fight,
>   This cold endurance of the final pain,—
> Since thou and those who with thee died for right
>   Have died, the Present teaches, but in vain![35]

Dunbar sees Shaw buried with his nameless and forgotten black troops once again. Of course, these soldiers had names, as Dunbar knows well from his family history. He implicitly suggests here, as he would state in "Unsung Heroes," that these black "droves" are rendered nameless through a national forgetfulness. The ending, then, is one of defeat—or, at best, a deferred dream of citizenship.

Though that bitterness and despair distinguish Dunbar's poem from other elegies to Shaw, "Robert Gould Shaw" strikes a tone much like that of other Dunbar poems of the same era, such as "The Haunted Oak" (about lynching); another angry, yet pessimistic elegiac sonnet,

"Douglass" (in contrast to the combative optimism of the 1895 "Frederick Douglass"); and "To the South: On Its New Slavery." It is also close in spirit to the one nondialect poem Dunbar wrote at this time directly on the subject of the black Civil War soldier, "The Unsung Heroes."[36] As in "Robert Gould Shaw," the black soldiers who fought and died at Battery Wagner, Fort Pillow, and Port Hudson achieve a divinely sanctioned manhood through their sacrifice—but without a white intermediary ("They fought their way on the hillside, they fought their way in the glen / And God looked down on their sinews brown, and said, 'I have made thee men'"). The poem closes with a plea to God to inspire the memory of the soldiers' sacrifice (and manhood) in those poets who have "not the fire to smite the lyre and sing them one brief strain." The final note of the poem is one of pessimism in which the speaker sees no likelihood of such poems being written, Dunbar's efforts notwithstanding, short of divine intervention. Given the number and kind of poems written about Robert Gould Shaw by white authors, Dunbar's criticism seems even more pointedly bitter.[37]

With the works of Moody and Dunbar, the black Civil War soldier declines as an important trope in American poetry. The black Civil War soldier, unlike the black abolitionist, the slave revolt leader, and the fugitive slave, virtually disappeared from American poetry. Two exceptions were elegies to Shaw by African American writers, Benjamin Brawley's "My Hero" (1915) and Henrietta Cordelia Ray's "Robert G. Shaw" (1910), slight poems that marked the exhaustion of a subgenre. They made little effort to engage the complexities of the political situation of African Americans at a time when segregation and disfranchisement coexisted with the Fourteenth and Fifteenth amendments to the Constitution guaranteeing full citizenship and the right to vote to all native-born (male) Americans. The poems view the struggle waged by Shaw and the Fifty-fourth as distant and mythical. Brawley represents the attack on Battery Wagner as a scene from Arthurian legend with Shaw as Galahad, shorn of the historical detail that marked Albery Whitman's use of a similar neomedieval rhetoric. Ray's poem is more in tune with the works commemorating Shaw written immediately after the dedication of the Saint-Gaudens monument; it repeats themes found in Dunbar's "Robert Gould Shaw" but with an upbeat ending.[38]

After 1915 the Civil War veteran nearly disappears from African American poetry. The 1930s and 1940s saw a renewal of historiographic interest in African American participation in the Civil War, particularly in the work of scholars influenced by the Communist Left, such as W.E.B. Du Bois's *Black Reconstruction* (1935) and the early studies of Herbert Aptheker.[39] But there was no corresponding renewal in poetry

by black or white writers, even in the Popular-Front-influenced, historically oriented poetry of the late 1930s and early 1940s. During this
period black poets, including Sterling Brown, Melvin Tolson, Langston
Hughes, Margaret Walker, and Robert Hayden, invoked Frederick Douglass, Nat Turner, Gabriel, Harriet Tubman, Sojourner Truth, Cinqué,
and Crispus Attucks, but not the soldiers who helped achieve black
freedom in the Civil War and who once held such a significant place in
the work of black poets.

Ironically, the poetry inspired by the Shaw Memorial best known
today, John Berryman's "Boston Common" (1942) and Robert Lowell's
"For the Union Dead" (1960), appeared several decades after "Robert
Gould Shaw" and "An Ode in Time of Hesitation." Lowell's and Berryman's poems meditated on the possibilities of heroism in the modern
era. Both poets used Shaw and the Fifty-fourth much as Moody did, as
an image of an ideal America and the difficulty, if not impossibility, of
a noble act in the contemporary United States. And in both cases, the
black soldiers following Shaw appear relatively unimportant and indis-
tinguishable, "Negroes without name," as Berryman said without the
bitter irony of Dunbar. However, these poems were themselves sepa-
rated from each other by decades and were not part of a broader usage
of the Fifty-fourth Massachusetts or the black soldier such as existed
from 1863 to about 1903.[40]

In many respects, the tropes of the Fifty-fourth Massachusetts Regiment and the black soldier employed during the second half of the
nineteenth century marked a unique period in African American poetry. As literary critic Robert Stepto emphasized, much African American literature is characterized by what he called the pregeneric myths
of freedom and literacy.[41] In text after text one sees enacted an African
American journey toward freedom and literacy. It is often a literal journey from the South to the North, from the country to the city, from the
legal status of slavery to a more ambiguous (in antebellum America)
status of freedom, from being a thing or a brute to being accepted as
fully human. This geographical, spiritual, and legal journey also moves
from the African American folk of the South toward an uncertain indi-
vidualism associated with the North, best seen in the autobiographies
of Frederick Douglass. There is also another narrative of a physical and
spiritual journey common in African American literature: the return
journey South to the folk.[42] This symbolic journey away from individu-
alism, deracination, and the separation of instinct and intellect moves
toward community, group identity, and the natural world. The second
is in many respects a reaction to the first and has dominated much

African American literature from James Weldon Johnson's *Autobiography of an Ex-Colored Man* (1912) until the present.

The poetry invoking the Fifty-fourth Massachusetts and the black Civil War soldier is a departure from the narratives of literacy and freedom and from the literary journeys North and South. Tropes of freedom and literacy often appear in these poems, but, as in Dunbar's work, there is a transcending of both categories. The soldiers have earned citizenship with their blood, not merely freedom (which they could be said to have possessed, since they were already legally free in many if not most cases), and it is manhood, not literacy, that they have attained through sacrifice in a divinely sanctioned duty. Again, these poems do not oppose freedom to citizenship but are arguments against a notion of freedom that would not include full citizenship or would defer it until some future date when white citizens deemed African Americans "ready." Similarly, these works are not opposed to literacy (they are poems, after all) but are implicitly opposed to a concept of literacy that might serve as a bar to African American citizenship—as it did in fact.

But there is no return to the South and the "folk." The soldiers of the Fifty-fourth returned only metaphorically to the South (many actually saw it for the first time), and they neither embraced nor rejected a folk identity. Their identity as citizens and Americans (and African Americans) was not represented as dependent on the adoption or rejection of a particular cultural identity but on their actions in the defense of the republic and in attacking the institution of slavery. In this, their claim to citizenship was much like that of Irish American and German American soldiers, whose varying relationships to mainstream American culture did not influence their de jure (if not de facto) citizenship.

The final value of the Fifty-fourth Massachusetts Regiment and the black Civil War soldier to American poetry resides not solely in reclaiming the history of two important and interrelated tropes in African American literature. They are also barometers for changes in the ideology and poetics of black writers in the second half of the nineteenth century. Representations of the Fifty-Fourth and the African American soldier clearly demonstrate how black and white authors interacted and influenced one other while maintaining distinct sensibilities and traditions. In short, the poetic usage of the black Civil War soldier complicates our assumptions about American writing that, in the past, too often absolutely segregated literary "traditions" or too easily erased cultural distinctions—assumptions that all too often dog our vision of literature and literary traditions in the United States.

III

Renewing Immortality

DENISE VON GLAHN

THE MUSICAL MONUMENT OF CHARLES IVES

That men may listen to the striving in the souls of black folk.

W.E.B. Du Bois, *Souls of Black Folk*

E ARLY IN the second decade of the twentieth century, American composer Charles Ives wrote a poem and a piece celebrating the memorial to Robert Gould Shaw and the Fifty-fourth Massachusetts Regiment.[1] He entitled his composition "The 'St. Gaudens' in Boston Common (Colonel Robert Gould Shaw and His Colored Regiment)." It, along with "Putnam's Camp, Redding, Connecticut," and "The Housatonic at Stockbridge," formed his *First Orchestral Set*, better known as *Three Places in New England*. Each of the three pieces commemorated a place in the Northeast that had a specific meaning for Ives. "Putnam's Camp" memorialized a Revolutionary War encampment nestled in a small town close by Ives's family home. Ives's uncle, Lyman Brewster, was a commissioner of Putnam Park and an indefatigable proponent of its preservation.[2] By the beginning of the new century the camp had been turned into a popular park frequented by local school and church groups. "The Housatonic at Stockbridge" was a personal paean to the scene of a honeymoon walk that Charles and Harmony Ives took the summer after their marriage. Ives used those memories, and verses from a poem by Robert Underwood Johnson, as sources for one of his most intense orchestral miniatures. In his autobiography, *Memos*, Ives explained the import of that sylvan setting.[3]

The third site captured in *Three Places in New England* was "The 'St. Gaudens' in Boston Common," Ives's thoughtful response to a place, an event, and an artwork rich with personal, regional, and national significance. In it Ives probed issues that were close to his heart. Unusual among artistic tributes of the time, Ives's poem and piece celebrating Saint-Gaudens's historic bas-relief focused attention on the men of the regiment rather than on the martyred colonel. They may be the first works inspired by the monument to confront the issue of race, which lies so close to the surface of the bas-relief and the Civil War.[4] "The 'St. Gaudens' in Boston Common (Colonel Robert Gould Shaw and His Colored Regiment)" is Ives's prescient, private perspective on a public memory.

CHARLES IVES AND THE MONUMENT

Charles Ives was born in Danbury, Connecticut, in 1874 to a family that could trace its lineage to the earliest English settlers. He identified closely with New England and found its history and haunts sources of personal comfort and artistic inspiration. Ives's interest in the Civil War in the early years of the second decade of the twentieth century was no doubt fueled by media stories that covered various fiftieth anniversaries associated with the war, but it was also deeply personal. According to family legend, Ives's father had been the youngest bandmaster in the Union army and had been singled out by General Grant for special comment. Regardless of the story's veracity, Charles Ives embraced fully the romanticized notion of his father's having had a small but distinguished role in the conflict. Beyond this specific filial connection to the war, however, Ives could boast of his extended family's long commitment to abolitionism and could relate stories of relatives who had assisted runaway slaves.[5] Born nine years after the verdict of Appomattox, Ives sought his own role in the history-defining struggle.

When the Saint-Gaudens bas-relief was unveiled in 1897, Ives was twenty-three, and he could probably identify with the twenty-six-year-old Shaw, a regional and national hero whose biography was common knowledge. Both men enjoyed comfortable upbringings and benefited from Ivy League educations—Shaw at Harvard, Ives at Yale—both were reared in highly regarded families with traditions of social consciousness and action, both identified strongly with the Union cause, and both, for whatever combination of reasons, felt a responsibility to become personally involved in the Civil War. Born too late to play a more conventional role, Ives's involvement took the form of artistic expression. This essay seeks to illuminate how Ives's compositions comment on the war and the monument. It is about art that is inspired by art and history.

TWO ARTISTIC EXPRESSIONS

Ives's most specific response to Saint-Gaudens's sculpture can be gleaned from an original poem he wrote to accompany the music. "Moving,—Marching—Faces of Souls!" is unique in Ives's oeuvre as the only free-standing, full-length poem he composed.

Moving,—Marching—Faces of Souls!
Marked with generations of pain,
Part-freers of a Destiny,
Slowly, restlessly—swaying us on with you
Towards other Freedom!

The man on horseback, carved from
A native quarry of the world Liberty
And from what your country was made.

You images of a Divine Law
Carved in the shadow of a saddened heart—
Never light abandoned—
Of an age and of a nation.

Above and beyond that compelling mass
Rises the drum-beat of the common-heart
In the silence of a strange and
Sounding afterglow
Moving—Marching—Faces of Souls![6]

Although Ives never clarified whether he actually saw the monument in Boston before composing the verses or the piece, his poem is remarkably sensitive to the visual image; it emphasizes the quiet power the bronze regiment wields over the observer. Of course, evocative descriptions of the monument were readily available in a number of magazines and newspapers.

It is also not known whether the composer was familiar with any of W.E.B. Du Bois's early writings that appeared in *Atlantic Monthly* or *Dial* or with their collective appearance in *Souls of Black Folk* in 1903. Ives's prominent use of the word "souls" and his reference to the "shadow," a returning image in Du Bois's prose, give one reason for pause. The composition of a full-length poem by Ives is exceptional enough to allow for unusual circumstances behind its conception. These unknown factors aside, it is obvious that the men of the regiment are most important to Ives; it is they who capture his imagination and speak most clearly to him. This comes across in both words and sound.

In the poem direct reference to Colonel Shaw is limited to the line "The man on horseback." By contrast, three of Ives's four stanzas focus on the men of the Fifty-fourth. He sees the "generations of pain" that mark their faces; he responds physically to the men "swaying . . . on with [them] / Towards other Freedom!"; he talks to them, "You images of a Divine Law." He hears the pulsing rhythm of their "common-heart." It is not the high-born hero who captivates Ives; it is, instead, the less celebrated soldiers, the individuals who bear the common heart. So vivid in bronze, so undeniable in prose—how to capture these individual "Faces of Souls" in sound? An extramusical program might help.

A POSSIBLE PROGRAM FOR THE PIECE

Ives provided generous commentary in *Memos* for the other pieces in *Three Places in New England,* but such remarks are conspicuously absent for "The 'St. Gaudens.'" Does this mean that Ives intended no explication of this piece or that he thought none was necessary? Did he assume that his poem was explanation enough? *Memos* editor John Kirkpatrick suggested otherwise when he observed that remarks regarding "The 'St. Gaudens'" would probably have appeared on a page that is missing from the typed transcriptions of Ives's dictated comments.[7] It is likely, therefore, that Ives envisioned some kind of extramusical chronicle. Thus, although suggesting a program is potentially controversial, it is entirely consistent with Ives's own approach to other works, in which he guides listeners through pieces with detailed narratives.

The music Ives composed is unusual in its own way. "The 'St. Gaudens'" is among Ives's most introspective works: subdued, restrained, sober—characteristics not regularly associated with the irascible composer. Ives creates an aural environment that encourages deliberate, unhurried, thoughtful contemplation of the monument. He wants us to stop and think. Given the undeniable temporal nature of music— music acquires its meaning by unfolding in and through time—such quietude requires a bit of sonic legerdemain. Ives accomplishes his artistic objective by using a technique that minimizes the irresistible, dynamic, linear motion of music normally associated with traditional Western harmonic and rhythmic behavior and maximizes a sense of stasis, balance, and equipoise. Robert Morgan has identified this compositional technique as "spatial."[8] In such a sound world, listeners are not consumed with where the music is heading as much as they are content to be where the music is. Not as extreme as some Eastern-inspired minimalist music (once known as trance music), which simultaneously sharpens and dulls a listener's awareness of the passage of time, this is music clearly within the Western tradition. It allows for a degree of disengagement with surrounding events though not attempting a complete break with earthly reality.

The music of "The 'St. Gaudens'" emerges extremely slowly and softly. Listeners cannot be certain whether they have caught the beginning of the work or whether they have come upon something already under way. The ambiguity is profound. For whereas the events commemorated in the monument occurred decades earlier—they are part of the historical record—it is only when an observer engages with the sculpture or a listener thoughtfully considers the music that the resonance of those events is apprehended or heard. (The listener's moment of perception is similar to the observer's moment of realization.) Though nearly inaudible, the opening music is of utmost importance because it contains information essential to understanding Ives's thinking about the piece. Significantly, Ives devotes the first moments to introducing the individual soldiers. Struggling to be heard, a cryptic, soft-spoken musical idea materializes as if from history itself; it takes shape and grows in meaning with successive appearances.

And how do these individual souls make themselves known? Ives corporealizes the men by borrowing the falling-rising three-note gesture that begins the chorus of Stephen Foster's 1860 song "Old Black Joe." Some might think this song inappropriate in a piece purportedly praising black soldiers. Its romanticized version of a slave's memories "when my heart was young and gay" grates with the reality of slave life. But without ignoring that dissonance, Ives makes us hear the familiar song anew. None other than W.E.B. Du Bois cited "Old Black Joe" as an exemplar of "the range of white America [that had] been distinctly influenced by the slave songs [and had] incorporated whole phrases of Negro melody." Du Bois understood "Old Black Joe" and "Swanee River" as songs in which "the slave spoke to the world."[9] The Connecticut Yankee composer understood as well the power of that voice and quoted the music that accompanies the words "I'm coming" from Foster's plantation song. Over and over, listeners hear a wordless "I'm coming," "I'm coming." With a simple gesture, Ives has called attention to the essential "I."

"Old Black Joe"

Though there is no defense for the idealized picture of slavery painted by Foster's lyrics, there is perhaps a way of looking at Ives's music that makes the use of the song's chorus consistent with Ives's abolitionist inheritance and acceptable to our modern sensibilities.[10] Just as Ives's response to the Civil War was deeply personal, so was his interpretation of the monument. As stated before, to Ives the bronze relief was not a generic collection of black soldiers; these were individual human beings, individual souls made so real by Augustus Saint-Gaudens that you wish you knew each soldier's name.[11] And Ives created a group of individual men with the numerous soloistic entries of the three-note gesture associated with the words "I'm coming."

In the first sixteen measures of the piece, the three-note motive enters at seven different pitch levels; each "I'm coming" is distinctive. Though through rigorous training in the first months of 1863 the men of the Fifty-fourth eventually developed into a unit, Ives reminds us with his music that each man came to the endeavor by himself. As we hear the three notes enter on different instruments, from different places in the orchestra, we are reminded that the recruits came from all over the nation and beyond to join the Fifty-fourth Massachusetts Regiment. Ives's expansive musical statement reminds us that this was no provincial movement; this was a national effort.

After using the opening measures of the piece to clear time and space for a contemplation of individuals as captured by Saint-Gaudens, Ives changes compositional gears approximately a third of the way through and creates a musical narrative reenacting the ill-fated assault at Battery Wagner. The soft, slow, ambiguous rhythms and harmonies that characterize the first section of the piece are gradually overtaken by louder, more assertive, and metrically secure music. As if matching the metamorphosis of individuals into a military regiment, Ives's music solidifies. The "I'm coming" motive that permeated the opening of the piece is joined by another Civil War song, George Frederick Root's 1861 "Battle Cry of Freedom." It is no mere happenstance that the tunes Ives draws upon were written during the Civil War period or that they referred to that conflict. Ives's borrowings are regularly selected for their chronological authenticity, their topical appropriateness, and their motivic linkages.[12] His musical-dramatic webs are carefully considered and tightly woven. It comes as no surprise, then, to find that the chorus of "The Battle Cry of Freedom" (the line beginning "The Union forever"), incorporates the same falling-rising three-note motive found in "Old Black Joe."

"Rally Round the Flag Boys" ("The Battle Cry of Freedom")

The Un - ion for-ev - er, Hur - rah boys, hur-rah! Down with the Trai - tor,

As the music moves seamlessly from one source tune to the next, transitioning on the shared melodic gesture, the drama advances through a listener's association of multiple texts with the same music. Whereas "I'm coming" focused on individuals, "The Union forever" focuses on the developing community of men. The "I" of "Old Black Joe" has become "we" in "The Battle Cry of Freedom":

> Yes *we'll* rally round the flag, boys,
> *we'll* rally once again,
> Shouting the battle cry of Freedom,
> *We* will rally from the hillside
> *we'll* gather from the plain,
> Shouting the battle cry of Freedom.
>
> The Union forever, Hurrah boys, hurrah!
> Down with the Traitor,
> Up with the Star;
> While *we* rally round the flag, boys,
> Rally once again,
> Shouting the battle cry of Freedom.[13]

Published accounts of the regiment's actions provided Ives with all the information he needed to create a sonic equivalent of the attack on Battery Wagner. A consistent feature of these accounts was the reference to Shaw and his men as they struggled along the beachfront until they finally gained the parapet. A letter from Lieutenant James W. Grace, Company C of the Fifty-fourth, provides details for the musical program:

> When we arrived within one thousand yards of Fort Wagner, we laid down waiting for our support to come up. We laid there about thirty minutes when we were ordered to rise up and charge the works, which we did at double quick time with a tremendous scream. When we arrived within a short distance of the works, the Rebels opened on us with grape and canister accompanied with a thousand muskets, mowing our men down by the hundreds. This caused us to fall back a little, but we soon made another rush to the works, when we received another tremendous discharge of musketry, and also grape and canister. Such a tremendous fire right in our faces caused us to fall back . . . a good many of our men went on to the works and fought hand to hand with the Enemy.[14]

The letter refers to three attempts by soldiers of the Fifty-fourth to rush the Confederate earthworks. Likewise, starting about two-thirds of the way through his piece, Ives makes three attempts to drive the music further and further upward, as if to gain the parapet. In the first attempt, the music rises in pitch and volume; the rhythms become more agitated and push the music forward. We hear the suggestion of a distant bugle call—a logical musical gesture to announce a military action. But the music, like the men, falls back. A second attempt starts a semitone higher and gains ground, as it were, rising from the pitch G in flutes and violins to the C a fourth above. Though sounding more urgent, the music once again fails to reach its goal. The third and final surge lifts the music up an octave while increasing the volume from very soft to very loud—the one point in the music where the volume does venture outside a soft and controlled dynamic palette. In the background listeners hear the bass drum deliver its thudding cannon blasts. Here too, Ives stayed close to written accounts of the conflict, which described the men coming under unforgiving attack by cannon fire.

Besides descriptions of the regiment's efforts to take the Confederate stronghold, turn-of-the-century published accounts were uniform in their presentation of the swift and deadly events that followed immediately upon Colonel Shaw's reaching the high point. A single line in an 1897 story in *Century* magazine captured the scene most tersely: "He waved his sword, cried out, 'Forward, Fifty-fourth!' and fell dead."[15]

Ives's music dramatically parallels this scene—the virtual simultaneity of the regiment's tactical achievement and Shaw's sudden death. Once again, his music focuses on the power of the individual. Ives's recreation of the third and final attempt to gain the parapet captures the conflicting emotions that must have been felt by men who were committed to their mission, and confronted with the likelihood of death. Quivering tremolos, intensifying volume, broadening rhythms, and tonal ambiguity define the music; and still the piece moves unequivocally toward resolution on a C chord. At the climactic moment, a single dissonant note B from a horn pierces through the mass of sound. It negates harmonic closure; it denies us our goal. Like the men of the Fifty-fourth, we are refused a satisfying resolution. But at the same time, with one note Ives reminds us of the real focus of the piece. It captures the power and pain of individual actions. The one note could be Shaw, but for Ives it could just as easily be any man of the black regiment, any one of the faces of souls. The one note reinforces the notion of the first person singular, the "I."

Ives's sonic portrayal goes beyond the most overt pictorializations. Three other musical events in the piece appear to record the scene at Battery Wagner quite faithfully: a series of descending lines, the reappearance of "The Battle Cry of Freedom," and the dissolution of sound into silence. In Ives's third attempt to gain the parapet, he introduces numerous descending passages—melodic lines that gradually become lower in pitch. In fact, almost as many lines descend as ascend to the climactic moment. Records show that nearly three hundred of the six hundred troops who charged the fort were killed, wounded, or captured. Perhaps Ives was trying to depict casualties suffered by the Fifty-fourth in the many musical lines that fall away.

The trombone line may also contain clues to Ives's programmatic intentions. Just three measures before the dramatic-musical climax, it presents a fractured but tenacious rendition of the music that accompanies the words "the Union forever" from the chorus of "The Battle Cry of Freedom," where the men are enjoined to "Rally 'round the flag." The music stubbornly presses onward and upward. Accounts of the soldiers' charge often mentioned the valiant efforts of Sergeant William H. Carney to keep the flag aloft. Although severely wounded in the assault, Sergeant Carney returned the national colors to the troops behind the battle line with the memorable words "The old flag never touched the ground, boys."[16]

Ives captures the deadly defeat of the Fifty-fourth with the sudden dissolution of all musical activity. As the lives of so many men were snuffed out, so too is all sound. But this is not a silence of quietude and repose; it is a silence full of reverberation and energy. Two measures after the thunderous climax, listeners are left to reflect upon events both musical and historical in the "strange and sounding afterglow" that Ives evokes in his poem.

The death of Colonel Shaw and so many of his comrades weighed heavily on the surviving soldiers. Corporal James Henry Gooding of the Fifty-fourth wrote of the soldiers' feelings in a letter from Morris Island to the *New Bedford (Mass.) Mercury*, dated July 24, 1863, just six days after the encounter at Battery Wagner.

> We have since learned . . . that Colonel Shaw is dead—he was buried in a trench with 45 of his men! Not even the commonest respects paid to his rank. Such conduct is in striking contrast to the respect paid a rebel Major who was killed on James Island. The Commander of the 54th regiment had the deceased rebel officer buried with all the honors of war granted by the regulations; and they have returned the compliment by tossing him into a ditch. . . . The men of the regiment are raising a sum to send the body of the Colonel home, as soon as Fort Wagner is reduced. They all declare that they will dig for his body till they find it. They are determined this disgrace shall be counteracted by something noble.[17]

The soldiers' plans never came to pass, because Shaw's parents insisted that their son's body remain buried where he fell—with his men. But Ives follows his version of the battle with "something noble" that recognizes the achievement as well as the sacrifices of the soldiers.

Emerging from the shocked silence, Ives's musical regiment begins
"moving—marching" once again like the soldiers in the last line of his
poem. Listeners are tugged along by a heavy-treaded march to the
much-slowed-down choruses of "Rally Round the Flag" and Henry Clay
Work's "Marching Through Georgia" (1865): "Hurrah! Hurrah! We
bring the Jubilee! Hurrah! Hurrah! the flag that makes you free!" The
chorus of Work's piece shares the familiar falling-rising third gesture
that characterizes the other two source tunes, although it actually begins with a repeated rising third before it descends once and rises again
and again. The irrepressible rising third of Work's victory anthem is a
powerful musical portent of the soldiers' and the union's refusal to be
defeated by the struggle.

"Marching Through Georgia"

"Hur-rah!   Hur-rah!   we bring the Ju-bi-lee!   Hur-rah!   Hur-rah!   the flag that makes you free!"

Soft dynamics, a slow tempo, and a repeating short, drooping figure
in the cellos and the string bass combine to cast a funereal pall over the
music. Even this effort seems too much, and the solemn march dis-
solves five measures after it begins. At the moment the halting march
dissipates, Ives has the first violin sing out the melody of another Civil
War period song, a Stephen Foster tune that he also used in a most
loving musical homage to his adored father. Ives turns to Stephen Foster's "Massa's in de Cold Ground" and quotes the melody of the second
half of the chorus. "All the darkeys am a weeping, Massa's in de cold
ground." Our present-day sensibilities are offended at the thought that
Ives was equating Shaw with a plantation "Massa." But that reading
would be misinformed and incorrect. In quoting this tune, Ives was
attempting to suggest that the soldiers felt a reverential attitude toward
Shaw similar to what Ives felt toward his own father. Whether or not
this was true of the men of the Fifty-fourth, such an interpretation is
completely consistent with Ives's well-documented, idealized version
of his father-son relationships.[18] But the use of this tune at this particular moment in the musical narrative may suggest an additional meaning: at the same time when Shaw and his men are buried at Battery
Wagner, so too is slavery buried. And that burial would be something
that Ives celebrated. As with other borrowed tunes, this quoted phrase
manifests the descending minor third gesture. Unlike the other falling-
rising motions, this one, like slavery, never rises.

With his musical-historical reenactment complete, Ives gradually returns to a contemplation of the men and the monument. The regiment leads the way advancing from the past into the present, from Battery Wagner to Boston Common. Once again Ives reminds us of his focus on the men. He recalls the opening sounds of the piece with the "I'm coming" motive, just as the final line of his poem recalls the first. But in this second experience, the music has changed. Contemplating events has deepened our understanding of the moment in history, and by extension it has deepened our understanding of the monument and the ideals it epitomizes. Ives imagines that listeners have been uplifted by their new awareness, so he literally raises the last "I'm coming" motive to a new pitch level in the final measure. The music wafts in a realm of unearthly enharmonics much like the allegorical figure that floats above the bronze men in the bas-relief.

The monument was a rich and complex source of inspiration for Ives, so affecting that he created two responses. His poem tells us unambiguously what touched his heart, but his music speaks more movingly. With the simplest of musical gestures, he identifies the men. He acknowledges their autonomy. He recognizes their separation from him, their distance in time and life experience. He applauds their collective effort. And he concedes their sustained power over him and the nation. He understands that they have something to teach. "Slowly, restlessly—swaying us on with you / Towards other Freedom!" Ives's men of the Fifty-fourth Regiment are our conscience; the grief they awaken belongs to the entire nation.[19] Though captives of a society, of a war, and of a bronze monument, the "Moving,—Marching—Faces of Souls!" bear a message that is dynamic and immediate and lasting. The men are not a faceless collection, but rather a gathering of individuals, individuals vested with power. For the idealistic composer from Connecticut, this means Americans. Ives charges us to move with the men of the Fifty-fourth to "The drum-beat of the common-heart." With "I'm coming" echoing transcendentally, the piece looks forward to a time when that will occur.

ART, HEROISM, AND POETRY

The Shaw Memorial, Lowell's "For the Union Dead,"
and Berryman's "Boston Common:
A Meditation upon the Hero"

THE DEATH of Robert Gould Shaw became the subject of many poems, but here I discuss the single great poem it has occasioned, Robert Lowell's 1960 elegy "For the Union Dead." Lowell's poem, which explores the relation between heroism and the art commemorating it, concerns not only Shaw and his regiment, the Fifty-fourth Massachusetts, but also the 1897 Shaw Memorial bas-relief by Augustus Saint-Gaudens. Appended to my consideration of Lowell's poem are a few remarks on a 1942 poem written by Lowell's contemporary John Berryman. Berryman set his World War II poem at the Shaw Memorial; this youthful (and unsuccessful) poem, by a poet who eventually wrote in a different style altogether, will help to suggest how and why Lowell's poem has taken on permanent aesthetic value.

Lowell writes "For the Union Dead" in the light of two earlier, and daunting, artworks. I say "two artworks," because "For the Union Dead," though it has in view Saint-Gaudens's distinguished monument as a model for its own being, silently competes also, as its title suggests, with Allen Tate's 1928 "Ode to the Confederate Dead." Tate was Lowell's teacher and mentor in poetry at Kenyon College; his ode is ceremonious, "high," and "noble" in the best commemorative tradition. Like Tate's poem, the other precedent poems on the Fifty-fourth Massachusetts, by black and white poets alike, also took a high tone. In the commemoration by Lowell, however, Shaw, though no less exalted, is allowed human responses to his predicament as the commander of the regiment; and the poet centers the poem around his own life, as well as around Shaw's.

FOR THE UNION DEAD

"Relinquunt Omnia Servare Rem Publicam."

The old South Boston Aquarium stands
in a Sahara of snow now. Its broken windows are boarded.
The bronze weathervane cod has lost half its scales.
The airy tanks are dry.

Once my nose crawled like a snail on the glass;
my hand tingled
to burst the bubbles
drifting from the noses of the cowed, compliant fish.

My hand draws back. I often sigh still
for the dark downward and vegetating kingdom
of the fish and reptile. One morning last March,
I pressed against the new barbed and galvanized

fence on the Boston Common. Behind their cage,
yellow dinosaur steamshovels were grunting
as they cropped up tons of mush and grass
to gouge their underworld garage.

Parking spaces luxuriate like civic
sandpiles in the heart of Boston.
A girdle of orange, Puritan-pumpkin colored girders
braces the tingling Statehouse,

shaking over the excavations, as it faces Colonel Shaw
and his bell-cheeked Negro infantry
on St. Gaudens' shaking Civil War relief,
propped by a plank splint against the garage's earthquake.

Two months after marching through Boston,
half the regiment was dead;
at the dedication,
William James could almost hear the bronze Negroes breathe.

Their monument sticks like a fishbone
in the city's throat.
Its Colonel is as lean
as a compass-needle.

He has an angry wrenlike vigilance,
a greyhound's gentle tautness;
he seems to wince at pleasure,
and suffocate for privacy.

He is out of bounds now. He rejoices in man's lovely,
peculiar power to choose life and die—
when he leads his black soldiers to death,
he cannot bend his back.

On a thousand small town New England greens,
the old white churches hold their air
of sparse, sincere rebellion; frayed flags
quilt the graveyards of the Grand Army of the Republic.

The stone statues of the abstract Union Soldier
grow slimmer and younger each year—
wasp-waisted, they doze over muskets
and muse through their sideburns . . .

Shaw's father wanted no monument
except the ditch,
where his son's body was thrown
and lost with his "niggers."

The ditch is nearer.
There are no statues for the last war here;
on Boylston Street, a commercial photograph
shows Hiroshima boiling

over a Mosler Safe, the "Rock of Ages"
that survived the blast. Space is nearer.
When I crouch to my television set,
the drained faces of Negro school-children rise like balloons.

Colonel Shaw
is riding on his bubble,
he waits
for the blessèd break.

The Aquarium is gone. Everywhere,
giant finned cars nose forward like fish;
a savage servility
slides by on grease.[1]

In leading the regiment, Shaw suffers a violation of his privacy; his motive is duty, not love; his virtue is less an abolitionist fervor than a Roman *pietas.* Lowell's poem is itself conspicuously Roman, adopting as its epigraph the motto of the Society of the Cincinnati, which, though it is incised on Saint-Gaudens's monument in the singular, is rephrased by Lowell in the plural—"They left all things to serve the common weal"—so that it applies not only to Shaw, who was by inheritance a member of the society,[2] but to all the members of the Fifty-fourth Massachusetts. During the city of Boston's recent restoration of the bas-relief, the names of the black soldiers of Shaw's regiment who died at Battery Wagner were incised on the reverse of the monument; this act follows an impulse comparable to Lowell's in his poem, asserting that individual heroism must be seen as part of a collective heroism. Civic degradation, too, even if perceived in individual instances, is also collective. A decayed aquarium here, an excavated Boston Common there, ugly parking lots everywhere are, for Lowell, signs of an underlying collective corruption that has attacked Boston, and not only Boston but the United States as well. It is a corruption visible in the dropping of the atomic bomb and in white resistance to school desegregation in the South.

Shaw's monument "sticks like a fishbone in the city's throat." It is an affront to the present, embodying as it does an ethic of the commonweal that is always in danger of being undermined. The State House, inadequately propped, shakes against "the garage's earthquake." The contrasting of a noble past and a fallen present is not a new thing in elegy, but most elegists of the past, including the many nineteenth-century elegists of Shaw, invariably represent themselves as on the side of the angels; they become the spokespersons for the values embodied in Shaw. In earlier laments for Shaw, the evil role is played sometimes by the Confederate authorities who intended, by burying Shaw in a common ditch with his "niggers" (their word), to dishonor him; sometimes by corrupt public officials who (in William Vaughan Moody's 1900 "Ode in Time of Hesitation") pursue the Spanish-American War; and sometimes (as in Paul Lawrence Dunbar's 1900 sonnet) by Americans who remain racist in sentiment and action.

Robert Lowell is the first elegist of Shaw to place himself individually among the corrupt, though he delays this move until very late in the poem, until the moment when he is watching television. The source of greatest social fracture in the United States as Lowell writes the poem in 1960 is the desegregation of the schools following the 1954 Supreme Court decision in *Brown vs. Board of Education,* and Lowell sees on television "the drained faces of Negro school-children." He cannot show himself in a heroic role: instead, he is a savage worshiping the new American idol, television. "When I crouch"—and he lets the damning verb drop almost casually—"When I crouch to my television set, / the drained faces of Negro school-children rise like balloons." For all his admiration of Shaw, Lowell cannot, given his own marginal and disordered life as a person subject to chronic returns of manic-depressive illness, write autobiographically as a first-person representative perpetuator of Shaw's heroic civic virtue. Instead, Lowell depicts himself as helpless before the vandalizing of a venerable part of his city (the Common where Emerson had his vision)— as helpless as he was when the South Boston Aquarium of his childhood visits was allowed to die, as helpless as he was when his country dropped the atomic bomb on Hiroshima—an act now revoltingly co-opted into an advertisement for the indestructibility of a Mosler safe. Once, the ruling citizens of the Boston oligarchy (drawn from families such as the Shaws, the Winslows, and the Lowells) governed almost as by dynastic right. But now the poet's civic presence—even though he is descended from Winslows and Starks as well as from Lowells—is as anonymous as anyone else's, and the government of Boston has irrevocably passed from those of English descent to those of Irish descent. The pangs Lowell feels as he sees his city fall to a new government, as he watches his childhood scenes (the aquarium, the Common) destroyed, as he finds himself a person of no civic consequence and no heroic action, motivate the poem along with his nostalgia for the early days of the republic.

Lowell carefully does not name the Irish in his poem, though it would have been obvious to his audience that it was the Irish political machine that—with graft and corruption, subsequently exposed—allowed the construction of the parking garage under the Common, and it was the Irish who (although South Boston was their own territory) had let the South Boston Aquarium go to rack and ruin; it was the Irish who—in their vulgarly large and sharklike cars—were sliding through Boston with savage servility. Yet Lowell knew, especially from his own earlier residence in Louisiana, that it was his own ethnic group—English-descended Protestants—who were the very persons resisting desegregation in the South. Suggesting his complicity in that crime by passively prostrating himself before the television reporting it, Lowell suggests that no heroic posture is available to the modern American. "There are," he bitterly reports, "no statues for the last war here." The Korean War was a profoundly unheroic one in public estimation. And when Lowell looks to the future, he has no comfort to offer: the end is nearer; the ditch is nearer.

Lowell's historic glance, which concludes in an envisaged apocalyptic end, sweeps back to the American Revolution through the Latin motto of the Cincinnati, the village churches with their air of sparse, sincere rebellion, and the graveyards of the Grand Army of the Republic. The Revolutionary Era is his Golden Age, before the country fell into the division of the Civil War. And yet in the Civil War the Union side at least preserved an idealism commensurate with that of the Revolution, and that past civic belief in heroism is commemorated in the generic statues of a Union soldier on almost every town green in New England. However, those conventional statues symbolizing collective ideals grow, in Lowell's fantasy, slimmer and younger every year, and soon will (by extrapolation of this regression) vanish altogether. Saint-Gaudens's bas-relief, both in shape and in content, is sturdier; it stands foursquare, and its equestrian central figure—comparable to the single Union soldier cast in bronze and standing in town centers—is backed by its massed supporting infantrymen. Shaw's family declined an equestrian statue of Shaw alone in favor of a monument honoring both the regiment and its leader.[3] The envisaged cooperation of the races adds something strong to individual heroism; but it is in Saint-Gaudens's vision as an artist, rather than in an actual collective civil idealism in contemporary Boston, that the idea of heroism is now being perpetuated.

In writing his poem, Lowell suppresses the visible allegorical sign of heroism that Saint-Gaudens placed on the bas-relief—the female figure of Victory bearing a single crown. As she floats above the human figures, she is the representation of a permanent ethical value, the visible embodiment of the eternal possibility of heroism. Her crown waits always, in the ethereal world, ready to be bestowed on the next candidate for civic veneration. By suppressing her, Lowell obviates her function; as the poet looks around his city, he sees no possible new hero awaiting her coronal.

These are not appetizing views; and that Lowell recited them in Boston in 1960, during a civic occasion, the Boston Arts Festival, makes them doubly biting. They are a rebuke to all civic boosterism. They are also a rebuke to the easy patriotism of the more mediocre elegies on Shaw, those that engaged in no personal reflection about the present state of the country. (The two notable poetic exceptions to thoughtless patriotism were the elegy written by Paul Laurence Dunbar—who saw that the values for which Shaw had died were still unenacted in America—and the ode by William Vaughan Moody, who saw that the United States's oppression of the Filipinos was a disgrace to the American government.)

What can be said, then, about Lowell's view of heroism if he cannot act heroically in his own person, must (unlike the other elegists) exclude himself from collective virtue, must even show himself degraded before the television screen? And what can be said for a poem that dares not affirm the allegorical, eternally available presence of civic virtue, a poem that shows past New England statues of "abstract" Civil War soldiers, generalized to the point of pious unreality, asymptotically approaching, as the years pass, a vanishing point?

I propose that Lowell's poem is a resurrection rite intending to resuscitate both Shaw and his monument. In 1960 the Shaw Memorial was not a conspicuous part of tourist Boston; even educated native Bostonians could not have told you where it was located or who Shaw was. The Lowell of "Life Studies," composing portraits of his family, had personal reasons for writing the poem: Colonel Shaw's sister Josephine had married Charles Russell Lowell, Shaw's comrade-in-arms. (Charles Russell Lowell's uncle Robert [brother of the poet James] was Robert Lowell's great-grandfather.) But the poem aims also to rescue a significant Boston artwork. Lowell knew that unless artworks are from time to time refurbished and brought anew to public attention, they tend to vanish into the scenery. This is true of poems as well as of monuments, and poets are constantly reburnishing the poems of the past as they draw them up into renewed visibility from the forgetful abyss—as, in this instance, Lowell reminds us of Allen Tate's "Ode to the Confederate Dead" by writing a poem of the North to counter his teacher's poem of the South.

How does Lowell accomplish his resurrection of the Fifty-fourth Massachusetts and their monument? He does it very simply—by bestowing on them the present tense:

> Their monument sticks like a fishbone
> in the city's throat.
> Its Colonel is as lean
> as a compass-needle.

Until this moment in the poem, not only has the present tense belonged to corrupt Boston—"The old South Boston Aquarium stands / in a Sahara of snow now"—but till now, Shaw and his men inhabited a historical past tense: "Two months after marching through Boston, / half the regiment was dead." Later in the poem, Shaw and his men will inhabit the past tense once again:

> Shaw's father wanted no monument
> except the ditch,
> where his son's body was thrown
> and lost with his "niggers."

This is the Fifty-fourth Massachusetts as an item in the historical record, fixed in the chronicles of a past war.

But in the present tense, the regiment is a living part of modern Boston: "Its Colonel is as lean / as a compass-needle." And his men are on alert:

> When he leads his black soldiers to death,
> he cannot bend his back.

Why does the dead colonel now merit the present tense? Because this is not the dead colonel of history, but rather the colonel on the monument, and the monument has found a way—through the power of its sculptor's genius—to make the colonel and his men living presences imposing themselves on us. Monumental artworks (such as the statues of the abstract Union soldier) are often conventional and empty, gradually losing their power to move us as memory of their era fades. The Shaw Memorial could be as dead as many of its fellow statues in New

England if it were not a work of genius. Lowell does not mention the twelve years' work that Saint-Gaudens put into the monument, but anyone who has visited the sculptor's studio in Cornish, New Hampshire, will see that Saint-Gaudens went far beyond the usual preparation for a bas-relief. For example, he modeled in the round, as a complete sculpture, the head of each black soldier—and those sculptures are very distinctive, individual, fully imagined, and beautiful. Each of the infantrymen was a whole three-dimensional person to Saint-Gaudens, even though in the monument the soldiers would be represented only in shallow relief. It need hardly be said that it was uncommon in nineteenth-century America to expend such aesthetic effort on a portrait of anonymous blacks. The ethereal figure of Victory bearing her crown was not nearly so real to Saint-Gaudens as were Shaw and his men: there is no full modeling of her.

The structure of Lowell's poem is that of a struggle between corruption and virtue, each aesthetically imagined. This structure is most fully seen at the close, as the last two stanzas show a face-off in the present tense between Colonel Shaw and the shark-like cars gliding through Boston (now one enormous aquarium): he is rising on his bubble, they nose forward like fish. The colonel waits for the last judgment, that end which is getting nearer, when his tensely maintained bubble of virtue will be allowed to break and his long, severe maintenance of the iconic force of virtue will be ended. But till then he will remain forever in the present progressive tense—not existing as the mere fact represented by the phrase "Colonel Shaw rides" but portrayed in the active self-balancing of "Colonel Shaw is riding." This is not the past-tense Shaw of the historical record but the present-tense Shaw of ongoing sculptural energy. Without the spiritual force that Saint-Gaudens first, with an effort of empathetic imagination, absorbed from the story of Shaw and his regiment and then, with a second effort of aesthetic imagination, poured out of himself into his sculptured re-presentation of heroism, there would be no Colonel Shaw riding still in Boston; instead, Shaw's last ride would have been that past-tense one through Boston, two months before his death.

What does Lowell's hailing of Saint-Gaudens's accomplishment tell us about the poem "For the Union Dead"? Lowell hopes, of course, that his resuscitation of both the historical Shaw and the sculptural Shaw will once again give the hero a new lease on life within the legend of Boston, will reinsert him into 1960. The poet's thought-through arrangement of tenses is a verbal technique comparable to Saint-Gaudens's intense modeling in the round. Each artist asks, How can I pour the spirit into the fact? Without imagination aided by technique, the historical fact remains inert and gradually perishes, as it does in the well-meant but ill-realized conventional statues of the abstract Union soldier.

When we inquire into the difference between Lowell's poem and that of his teacher, we recall that Tate's elegy in a country churchyard is an ode, that is, a poem that addresses a "you"—in Tate's case, the collective "you" of the Confederate dead. Lowell's poem is not an ode to but an offering for the Union Dead. The dead are not addressed by Lowell as the dead; they are seen, through the grace of art, as living. Tate's dead are permanently buried; they "shift [their] sea-space blindly / Heaving, turning like the blind crab." Tate's is the losing side, of course; yet that alone is not enough to make his soldiers permanently dead; there was virtue in Confederate bravery, too. As Tate says, "Invisible lyric seeds the mind / With the furious murmur of their chivalry."[4] Yet the poet cannot desire to resurrect that chivalry: it was spent in too equivocal a cause, and the stain of slavery is upon it. Tate's poem—which is really an elegy for a fatally mistaken culture—becomes as it closes an elegy for himself as well:

> Leave now
> The shut gate and the decomposing wall:
> The gentle serpent, green in the mulberry bush,
> Riots with his tongue through the hush—
> Sentinel of the grave who counts us all!

Could a great sculptor have created a bas-relief of a Confederate hero and his men that could compete in aesthetic power with the Shaw monument? Lowell's poem suggests that the Confederate cause could not encapsulate sufficient universal appeal over time, and sufficient virtue, to inspire a committed artist. Saint-Gaudens, himself the son of an Irish immigrant to Boston, had to imagine and identify with the resurgent virtue of the Fifty-fourth Massachusetts before he could conceive their monument, had to invest it with his own passion. As for Lowell, before he as poet can imagine and inscribe with conviction his own present tenses, he has to identify not only with the civic virtue of Colonel Shaw and his men but also with the power of Saint-Gaudens to endow Shaw, through the aesthetic merit of great sculpture, with present relevance. In his homage in honor of the Union dead, Lowell implicitly questions the aesthetic potential of his teacher's ode to the Confederate dead. He also suggests that it is only in great art and sculpture that the values of the past can live on: neither historical chronicle nor mediocre generalized civic art can keep the heroism of a vanished past alive. Lowell hopes that in his poem, as in Saint-Gaudens's bronze,

Colonel Shaw and the Fifty-fourth Massachusetts can live on to remind us of "man's lovely, / peculiar power to choose life and die."

IN A CONTRASTING poem, the young John Berryman had earlier contemplated the Saint-Gaudens monument. It is likely that Lowell knew Berryman's 1942 war poem "Boston Common: A Meditation upon the Hero," and it is possible that his own reaffirmation of the value of the aristocratic virtue of Shaw and the aesthetic virtue of the Shaw Memorial is in part a refutation of Berryman's wish that the common man, rather than the leader, be the hero of our time and of Berryman's declaration that heroism is self-sufficient and needs no aesthetic commemoration.

Berryman's stately poem is written in eighteen eight-line irregularly rhymed stanzas, each bearing, in Yeatsian fashion, its own Roman numeral, making each a stable "station" of meditation on the new sort of hero needed for democratic contemporaneity. It opens on a February night, with a view from below of the Saint-Gaudens bas-relief, before which a vagrant lies asleep on the pavement:

> Slumped under the impressive genitals
> Of the bronze charger, protected by bronze,
> By darkness from patrols, by sleep from what
> Assailed him earlier and left him here,
> The man lies.[5]

In this "Dramatic bivouac" for "the casual man" (as Berryman puts it), the phrase "the casual man" moves this poem in the ambience of W. H. Auden; and Berryman's subsequent use of the generic name "Jack" for the vagrant puts the poem within the frame of one of Gerard Manley Hopkins's poems ("Man Jack the man is, just, his mate a hussy"). That poem, "The shepherd's brow," is one of those treating the common man—Harry Ploughman, Felix Randal, the navvy, the soldier. Unlike Lowell, Berryman has abandoned any nostalgia for the vanished New England aristocracy that generated Colonel Shaw: what the Second World War needs is the image of "the possible hero" that can be produced from the democratic "casual man." The nineteenth-century bas-relief shows Shaw and his "Negroes without name" reduced by the crucible of their common fate, Berryman affirms, to "a common character": Shaw's men

> Imperishable march below
> The mounted man below the Angel, and
> Under, the casual man, the possible hero. (42)

But how is the casual man to become the possible hero? Berryman is vague on that process. Though the man may seem to lie passive, "in shapeless failure," something or other may transform him—or perhaps has already transformed him and has given him heroic acts in his past:

> May be this man
> Before he came here, or he comes to die,
> Blazing with force or fortitude
> Superb of civil soul may stand or may
> After young Shaw within that crucible have stood. (42)

As the poem progresses, an unnamed voice breaks in to rebuke Berryman for his wish for another heroic monument like the one erected in memory of Shaw. Memorials, the voice reminds Berryman, are "accidents of history," consoling only to the living; the hero needs no monument, because the light of his heroism suffices to itself; he needs no record, since his perishing is his immortality. As the voice says,

> "The light is where it is,
> Indifferent to honour. Let honour be
> Consolation to those who give,
> None to the Hero, and no sign of him:
> All unrecorded, flame-like, perish and live." (43)

With this dismissal of the need for artworks to glorify the hero, Berryman's eyes return to the shape "defeated and marvellous, of the man I know, / Jack under the stallion":

> We have passed him by,
> Wandering, prone, and he is our whole hope. (44)

As he calls the vagrant "The heart of the Future beating" (44), the poet rises to a socialist rhetoric of faith in the common laborer, seeking, in Audenesque tones,

> The face towards which we hope all history,
> Institutions, tears move, there the Individual. (45)

However, the apotheosis of the laborer—"Rise / Homeless, alone, and be the kicking working one" (45)—can scarcely compete in aesthetic force with the silent purposeful presence of Colonel Shaw and his men. In spite of his prediction of a socialist apocalypse, Berryman, while still contemplating the vagrant sleeping under the Shaw Memorial, looks to the common fighting man on the sands of European beaches being taken by American assault to reconcile the heroisms of the nineteenth century (commemorated in William James's account of the dedication

of the Shaw Memorial) and the twentieth century (now being acted out
in the liberation of Europe):

> Helpless under the great crotch lay this man
> Huddled against woe, I had heard defeat
> All day, I saw upon the sands assault,
> I heard the voice of William James, the wind,
> And poured in darkness or in my heartbeat
> Across my hearing and my sight
> Worship and love irreconcilable
> Here to be reconciled. On a February night. (46)

Berryman's poem founders in a fundamental incoherence: it offers no
reason for its own existence. If heroes need no monuments, if battle-
death is its own redeeming conflagration, then there is no need for this
poem, except as consolation to survivors (a reduced aim). Berryman
forgoes the wish to worship the hero as an exceptional man (the aim of
the Shaw Memorial); instead, he wants to love the anonymous common
man he has found in an ignominious position, "helpless under the great
crotch" of Shaw's horse, "Slumped under the impressive genitals / Of
the bronze charger." Recognizing in himself the persistent nostalgic
wish to worship, Berryman declares that his own motive in writing the
poem is to bring into harmony his aesthetic veneration of a heroic past
and his socialist love of the present-day worker: "Worship and love
irreconcilable / Here to be reconciled." The infinitive of reconciliation
remains a future possibility, along with the manifestation of the "possible hero" from the sleeping vagrant. The artwork itself melts into a
negligible phenomenon, saved from the helplessness of its own mixed
motives only by the appearance of the nameless voice declaring the
hero's independence from commemoration.

Lowell and Berryman were of an age, but Berryman's socialist rhetoric is of its 1942 moment and comes from a writer in his twenties, still
under the sway of his mentors Auden, Hopkins, and Yeats. Lowell's far
more accomplished poem is that of a man in his forties, who has already
created a marked and mature style. That both writers felt a need to
come to terms with the Shaw Memorial and with the form of heroism
it represented suggests the importance of Saint-Gaudens's work in both
artistic and ethical terms to serious American writers with ties to Boston. If we are disposed by these two poems to ask when public poetry
succeeds, we can answer that unless such poetry engages a fundamental
problem of the lyric poet's own sensibility, it will remain merely the
sort of pious rhetorical piece that we encounter in Berryman's well-
meaning, but inert, youthful poem. Because Lowell's poem comes to

grips with his nostalgia for his family heritage and his anger at the vandalism of the Irish toward Boston civic spaces and his guilt at the segregationist policies of the South, it catches fire interiorly. Because it feels its way inside Colonel Shaw's own mixed feelings about his duty, it makes its hero human. Berryman does not engage his own inner demons in his poem, nor does he render his socialist vagrant a believable person. The "abstract Civil War soldier" of Lowell's poem, fading into insignificance because he is carved without artistic energy, has his counterpart in the "abstract homeless citizen" of Berryman's poem, a creature of the program of socialist realism about whom Berryman cannot write with lyric conviction.

MARTIN H. BLATT

GLORY

Hollywood History, Popular Culture, and the Fifty-fourth Massachusetts Regiment

A S AN ACCURATE historical portrayal of the Fifty-fourth Massachusetts Regiment, *Glory* is way off the mark. However, the filmmakers did not intend to produce a documentary of the regiment. Their aim was to provide a dramatic interpretation of the significant role African Americans played in the Civil War; they were successful in realizing that objective. *Glory* is a powerful, engaging war movie that employs the combat film framework to tell a story of courage and valor. In making the white regimental leader, Colonel Robert Gould Shaw, the focal point of the film, the filmmakers demonstrated that they are complicit with the rest of Hollywood in the way black subjects are represented in film. Ultimately, the greatest contribution of *Glory* was to stimulate tremendous interest in this important chapter in U.S. history. With broad video and forthcoming digital video disc distribution, the film continues to provoke new ways of thinking about the role of African Americans in our nation's past.

Glory, released in 1989 by Tri-Star Pictures, was produced by Freddie Fields and directed by Ed Zwick from a screenplay by Kevin Jarre. Zwick's credits include the television series *thirtysomething* and the films *About Last Night . . . , Courage under Fire*, and *The Siege*. Matthew Broderick portrayed Colonel Shaw, the narrator and chief protagonist of the film. An excellent group of actors portrayed a fictionalized ensemble of black soldiers of the Fifty-fourth, including Denzel Washington as the embittered ex-slave Trip; Morgan Freeman as the Southerner Rawlins, a gravedigger who eventually becomes the regiment's sergeant major; Andre Braugher as Shaw's educated Beacon Hill friend Searles; and Jihmi Kennedy as the uneducated Sharts from South Carolina. Washington's gripping portrayal earned him an Academy Award for Best Supporting Actor and turned out to be a breakthrough performance for him. He subsequently worked with Zwick in *Courage under Fire* and *The Siege. Glory* also received Academy Awards for Best Cinematography and Best Sound. Director of Photography Freddie Francis achieved great success in shooting the film's remarkably authentic battle scenes. The soundtrack by James Horner featured a haunting theme and the voices of the Harlem Boys' Choir.

The opening scene of the film is at Antietam Creek, Maryland, in 1862. Wounded during the battle, Shaw hears in a field hospital that Lincoln is about to free the slaves. Later, at home in Boston at a Beacon Hill reception, Massachusetts governor John Andrew, an abolitionist and a friend of Shaw's parents, introduces Shaw to the abolitionist Frederick Douglass. Andrew asks Shaw to head a black regiment, and after a brief period of reflection he accepts. The scene then shifts to training camp in Readville, Massachusetts, where Shaw recruits a tough Irish drill sergeant, Mulcahy, to train and discipline the men. Shaw orders that Trip be publicly flogged for an unauthorized departure from camp even though he was on a search for shoes for himself. Subsequently, upon the advice of Rawlins, the colonel forces the local quartermaster to release shoes for all the men. On payday Shaw joins his men in refusing to accept any pay because the government has paid the black troops less than the white troops.

After long-awaited uniforms arrive, the regiment marches out of Boston in spring 1863 to its first assignment south in Beaufort, South Carolina. There is little action, and it becomes clear that the regiment is to be confined to service as a labor force. The regiment's first engagement is the sacking and burning of Darien, Georgia, under the command of James Montgomery. Horrified by this action, Shaw confronts his commanding officer with irregularities and succeeds in securing a transfer. At James Island, the regiment repels a Confederate force. Union commanders decide to attack Battery Wagner outside of Charleston, South Carolina. Shaw volunteers to lead the charge despite his men's exhaustion and the suicidal nature of the assault. On July 18, 1863, the Fifty-fourth manages to breach the parapets of the Confederate stronghold briefly but then is repulsed in fierce fighting with heavy casualties. The Confederates bury the fallen Shaw with his men in a mass grave. A closing graphic states: "The Massachusetts 54th lost over half of its number in the assault on Fort Wagner. The supporting white brigades also suffered heavily before withdrawing. The fort was never taken. As word of their bravery spread, Congress finally authorized the raising of black troops throughout the Union. Over 180,000 volunteered. President Lincoln credited these men of color with helping turn the tide of the war." The movie credits roll with varied still shots of the Shaw/ Fifty-fourth Massachusetts Monument on the screen.

ORIGINS AND DEVELOPMENT OF THE MOVIE

How did Hollywood come to make the movie *Glory?* There are differing accounts. According to an article in *Civil War Times Illustrated,* in 1985 prolific movie producer Freddie Fields, who had previously produced *Looking for Mr. Goodbar, The Year of Living Dangerously,* and *American Gigolo,* and screenwriter Kevin Jarre, whose credits include *Rambo II,* were in Boston on business. As they walked through Boston Common and up the granite steps leading to Beacon Street, the article reports, their attention was caught by the breathtaking sight of the Saint-Gaudens monument. "We both felt the same thing," said Fields. "Perhaps there was a movie here. The monument was impressive." "We researched Shaw and the 54th Massachusetts and found this wonderful, unknown story of the Civil War." From that point on, Fields related, getting the movie made became a "four-year passion." He characterized the story of *Glory* as a "major moment of African-American heritage, unknown, overlooked or suppressed in history . . . a story of American heroism, of black and white men brought together in a common objective." One of the books he says the film was based on, Peter Burchard's *One Gallant Rush,* was published in 1965, so the history had hardly been suppressed. He is perhaps considering the story's absence from American popular culture to be suppression. The film credits acknowledge that the movie was based on Burchard's book, Lincoln Kirstein's volume on the monument, and the letters of Robert Gould Shaw. The movie opens with these lines: "Robert Gould Shaw, the son of wealthy Boston abolitionists, was 23 years old when he enlisted to fight in the War between the States. He wrote home regularly telling his parents of life in the gathering Army of the Potomac. These letters are collected in the Houghton Library of Harvard University." Kirstein received assistance by way of corroboration and help with a number of details from Burchard. According to Peter Burchard, after the release of *Glory* Leslie Katz, Kirstein's editor, told Burchard that Kirstein had hired Kevin Jarre to write the script in an effort to see to it that a major motion picture about Shaw would be written and produced. According to the movie's press guide, several years prior to the movie's release in 1989, Jarre met Kirstein, who inspired him to write the script. Moved by Kirstein, the founder and general director of the New York City Ballet, who had known some of Shaw's family as a youth, Jarre wrote the initial screenplay in a few weeks. In 1985 Fields acquired rights to the film and, after a few unsuccessful efforts, managed to convince Tri-Star Pictures to take on *Glory.*[1]

Once the draft screenplay was in Fields's hands, *Glory* underwent an extensive development process driven by Fields and Zwick. Leslie Katz reported to Peter Burchard, who was uncertain as to the accuracy of these comments, that Kirstein was not "paid a cent for his contribution to the making of the movie" and did not like the final product. It is difficult to determine Kirstein's precise role and final assessment of the film. It is clear, however, from an examination of two draft scripts and the final film, that extensive reorganization and rewriting took place, as occurs with most Hollywood products.[2] It is interesting that Burchard found out about the movie only after filming was under way and made his discovery via an article in the *New York Times*. At any rate, Burchard did connect with Fields and provided extensive comments on the first script, authored solely by Jarre. His input greatly improved the final product. Burchard also composed a piece for the Tri-Star press kit. In return for his contributions, the filmmakers generously allowed the imagery of the movie to adorn the paperback reissue of Burchard's book.[3]

It is informative to compare the Jarre script, the later rewrite, and the final product. Early in the Jarre script there is an absurd scene with what Burchard calls "preposterous dialogue" where in Harvard Yard Shaw confronts two Southerners, fellow Harvard men, who have their black slaves in tow. It was Burchard's influence, it seems, that was responsible for the omission of this entire scene.[4] Jarre places John Brown in a confrontation with Shaw over the depth of his abolitionist convictions at an early 1860s Beacon Hill party. The martyr Brown, of course, had been executed in December 1859. Once again, Burchard was able to sway the filmmakers, and all references to Brown were deleted. In dramatizing the creation of the unit, the movie creates a distortion that truly minimizes the magnitude of the regiment's achievement. Rather than forming in the fall and winter of 1862, as the movie portrays, it was not until February 1863 that the effort really got going, and the majority of the men did not arrive in camp until late April 1863. Since they left for South Carolina on May 28, at best the men had less than two months to train. In shorter time than any other Union regiment, the unit was created and trained to the army's highest standards. In distorting the time frame to advance the story line, the film grossly underplays what the men of the unit achieved in a remarkably brief period of time. Jarre wrote the script scorning the most elementary study of chronology, and later rewrites retained the narrative error about the period of training. Cut out of Jarre's script was a ridiculous scene of Shaw with a camp prostitute in Massachusetts and also a relationship between Shaw and the black Charlotte Forten, an actual historical figure who came from the North to teach freed slaves. (To be fair, there is some basis for speculating about a relationship between Shaw and Forten, since she was quite taken with him. However, his recent marriage and the propriety of the times in all likelihood would have precluded such a liaison.) Jarre's script included an unnecessarily heavy-handed scene of Shaw in the Union Army participating in the return of fugitive slaves. Presumably Jarre felt that this scene would provide viewers with a motive for Shaw's later commitment to the Fifty-fourth. Fortunately, this bit of inaccuracy also did not make it to the final product. Shaw's family had impeccable abolitionist credentials; his depth of commitment did not match that of his parents but was strong nonetheless. Shaw's mother, who exerted great influence on him, at first had been given a significant role in the script; rewriting led to her virtual disappearance. Whatever the significance of losing the talents of Jane Alexander, who played Sarah Shaw, the overall decision to focus the film on Shaw and the Fifty-fourth was a good one. The rewrite of the Jarre script gets to the war much more quickly and the final film even more rapidly.

Overall, the revision process made *Glory* essentially a war movie that also to a certain extent highlighted the problem of racism in nineteenth-century America. This shift accelerated the narrative pace of the movie and emphasized the elaborate battle scenes, which the *Glory* team excelled in producing. It also made *Glory* less a film about Robert Gould Shaw and more a film about all of the men of the Fifty-fourth Massachusetts.

IS *GLORY* GOOD HISTORY?

In many respects, the film is a poor reflection of the history of the regiment and its context. Where the filmmakers are most open to criticism is their choice to make Shaw, the white commanding officer, the hero of the film. In their depiction, Shaw takes only a few moments to decide to accept Governor Andrew's offer to command the regiment; in reality, reaching his decision was a lengthier and more complex process. It is a typical Hollywood approach to choose a white hero when making films whose ostensible subject matter is people of color. The film *Missing* was a taut, compelling drama that exposed the brutality of the Pinochet regime in Chile and the U.S. complicity with the official state violence. However, the two stars, who give outstanding performances, are both white (Jack Lemmon and Sissy Spacek). No Chilean is given a substantial part to play. A dramatic film about Steve Biko, the South African martyr, portrays white South Africans as its central protagonists. *Ghosts of Mississippi,* a film that focuses on the murdered civil rights leader

Medgar Evers, highlights the white prosecutor who eventually brought Evers's murderer to justice; James Woods's portrayal of the Klan murderer is by far the most compelling part of the film. *Mississippi Burning*, whose subject is the murder of black and white civil rights workers James Chaney, Andrew Goodman, and Michael Schwerner, stars white FBI investigators. And the litany could go on and on. What are we to make of this pattern? For one thing, the people who produce Hollywood movies are part of the entertainment industry, which wishes to create a product that sells. Films that feature stories about whites and star whites typically sell better than films such as *Malcolm X*, by Spike Lee, an exception that proves the rule. Thus, in some respects the Hollywood industry is racist, which should not seem surprising, given the pervasive racism in the overall American culture. As historian Patricia Turner declared, "It's hard to think of a single, successful commercial film in which a black hero is allowed to be the successful agent of change in any aspect of the oppression of his or her people."[5]

Closely related to the decision to make Shaw the hero and focal point of the film as narrator and central protagonist is how the filmmakers chose to represent the black enlisted men of the Fifty-fourth. Turner noted, "To use the much-quoted but very appropriate adage coined by Ralph Ellison, the real men of the 54th are *invisible* in this film." Director Zwick oddly characterized the film as faithful to the regiment's history: "So often history has to be in some ways manhandled or perverted so as to serve dramatic truths. And here was a story which unto itself, literally, with its beginning, middle and end, told a complete story and one that was utterly compelling."[6] Ample evidence was available to the filmmakers to remain faithful to the historical record, but instead they chose to create a composite group of fictional characters. The four black soldiers featured in *Glory* experience the male bonding of training and bloody combat often played out in Hollywood war films. However, the historical truth might well have proved to be much more interesting. Frederick Douglass's two sons both served in the Union Army; Lewis Douglass, who actually served as sergeant major in the Fifty-fourth and whose letters are extant, fought in and survived the battle of Battery Wagner. William H. Carney, another member of the regiment, received the Congressional Medal of Honor, the first black to receive it, for his valor in rescuing the national flag despite the multiple wounds he sustained.

There is no question that the actors in *Glory* were sensitive to these criticisms. Denzel Washington recalled that during production, "I did express my concern to Ed [Zwick] and Freddie [Fields] that the movie not be about whites, and I think the script reflects this."[7] Morgan Free-

Colonel Robert Gould Shaw (played by Matthew Broderick) leading the Fifty-fourth
Massachusetts in the charge against Battery Wagner in *Glory.*
Courtesy Museum of Modern Art, Film Stills Archive.

man replied to critic Roger Ebert's charge that the movie focused too much on the white point of view:

> I don't have a problem with that. He [screenwriter Kevin Jarre] wrote it from a place he could write a story from, the only place he could get a grip on it from. You cannot reasonably ask a white writer to do it differently. Now, if we're going to start citing some unfortunates, it might be unfortunate that a black writer didn't write it, but if a black writer had written it, there's a good chance he wouldn't have found a producer. So there you are. This is a movie that did get made, and a story that did get told, and that's what is important.[8]

Historian Barbara Fields deplored the conversion of the regiment from one consisting of free men into one of fugitive slaves. Had Lewis Douglass been included as a character, his very presence would have "blasted the fiction of the fugitive slave regiment as an illiterate, inarticulate, and politically naïve group of enlisted men." If there was one thing that the movie could not encompass, it was a substantial African American male figure, "who from the very outset could stand up and speak for himself."[9]

Asa Gordon of the Douglass Institute of Government noted: "I have attended several screenings of *Glory* in the presence of black youths and adults who clearly absorbed the film's negative messages devaluing education as a means to improve the status of African Americans in our society." He reported that he had heard some black youths use the term "snowflake," with which Trip taunted Searles, as a way to deride fellow blacks interested in intellectual pursuits.[10]

Glory not only ignores the actual individual enlisted men of the regiment but also creates a misleading impression of its makeup. Three of the four fictional soldiers highlighted in the film are former slaves from the South; in fact, four-fifths of the Fifty-fourth Massachusetts were Northerners who had been free throughout their lives. The film turns its back on the vitally important communities of African Americans in the nonslaveholding states. It depicts the only black Bostonian in the ensemble, Searles, as pathetically effete and incompetent.

Glory can easily mislead viewers into thinking that the Fifty-fourth Massachusetts was the first group of blacks to fight in the Union Army, when in fact that distinction belongs to two other groups, the First South Carolina Volunteers, organized in 1862 and commanded by Boston abolitionist Thomas Wentworth Higginson, and the Louisiana Native Guard. Barbara Fields asserted that one fact stands out in the history of the Civil War and is clearly demonstrated in Higginson's history of his regiment: "It was the clear-mindedness with which slaves understood the political dynamics of the war, far ahead, I may say, of Abraham Lincoln and most of the politicians."[11]

Another deplorable aspect of the history depicted in *Glory* is the virtual absence of Frederick Douglass, the extraordinary abolitionist leader who served as a major recruiter for the regiment and whose son was an important combatant in the Fifty-fourth. In the little that we do see of Douglass, he is depicted as an older man who has virtually nothing to say. In fact, at the time that the recruitment was being organized, Douglass, a riveting orator, was a vigorous organizer in the prime of his life. For him, according to David Blight, the black soldier was "the principal symbol of an apocalyptic war, liberating warriors who alone made suffering meaningful, a physical force that gave reality to millennial hopes." Blight wondered how the makers of the film could have missed the possibilities offered by a scene of Douglass addressing black recruits. Imagine, Blight wryly commented, "the use of less apocalyptic music and more of Douglass's apocalyptic voice."[12] There was indeed a recruitment scene depicting Douglass addressing a group of young black men in Syracuse, New York, that was shot for the film but omitted in the editing process. The scene is included in the video *The True*

Story of Glory Continues, a documentary companion to *Glory* that is addressed later in the essay.

One of the most dramatic scenes in the entire film is the whipping of Trip after he has run away from camp in search of shoes. However, historian Joseph T. Glatthaar, whose overall view of *Glory* is positive, called the flogging of Trip "wholly inaccurate." It was the most disturbing scene in the movie, Glatthaar maintained. "Congress outlawed whipping [in the military] in 1861. The soldier did not desert—he was absent without leave, which was the most common offense. He would have been entitled to a hearing, and the chances are that the most punishment he would have received would have been a month without pay or confinement." Glatthaar documented several instances in other black regiments of black soldiers rebelling against mistreatment, rebellions that led to charges of mutiny and to execution. But this scene with Trip constituted a gross distortion.[13]

A glaring omission from *Glory* that serves to decontextualize the history in the film is the absence of any discussion of the draft riots in New York City, which occurred just before the attack on Battery Wagner. Shaw's mother and sisters were forced to flee their Staten Island home, and the nephew of one of the black men in the regiment was killed by rioters.[14] If the filmmakers had been interested, they could have introduced this sobering historical note. The fact that the film glibly depicts white Union troops who had scuffled with the black Fifty-fourth earlier in the drama cheering them on as they march to their destiny on the beach at South Carolina only makes the problem of racism and the history of the unit more problematic.

Glory leaves the viewer with the distinct, visceral impression that the entire black regiment was wiped out at Battery Wagner. As this volume and many other studies demonstrate, that is completely inaccurate: the Fifty-fourth fought on until the end of the Civil War. Further, the movie's closing graphic misleadingly states that the fort remained in Confederate hands, whereas the Union siege eventually led to its evacuation in September 1863. Ironically, however, the evacuation of Charleston, in which "elements of the Fifty-fourth and Fifty-fifth, another black regiment, were among those who marched triumphant into the city," did not result from the fall of Wagner but rather from Sherman's triumphant march from the west.[15]

THE STRENGTHS OF *GLORY*

With all of its historical limitations, *Glory*'s great strengths make it a significant contribution to American culture and its ongoing conversation over race. *New York Times* film critic Elvis Mitchell concluded that "what we have to look at is that *Glory* started a conversation and provokes discussion, which is part of the duty of art." He characterized the film as a "good movie about a great subject," which transported and moved viewers in fundamental ways. The ensemble of black actors, Mitchell asserted, was outstanding. "I saw it with a group of kids from Los Angeles. You could feel—you could taste the excitement in the room, and that's when we have got to realize the power of movies."[16]

Glory is a powerful, dramatic film that makes a very important point: blacks fought in the Union Army and played a pivotal role in the central event in U.S. history. They proved their manhood and demonstrated by their willingness to fight and die with valor that they were an integral part of America. This film reveals in a manner no viewer can mistake or overlook that blacks fought for their freedom in the Civil War. African Americans did not have freedom bestowed upon them but rather won it on the battlefield and on the stage of history. *Glory* makes these basic historical insights palpable. In response to historical criticisms, producer Fields declared that the filmmakers had a challenging objective: "to make an entertaining film first. Social messages and history can be very boring, but if you put them in an entertaining film, people will learn some history and take away a message." He argued that "you can get bogged down when dealing in history. Our objective was to make a highly entertaining and exciting war movie filled with action and character."[17] Judged by the criteria that Fields identifies, the film must be termed a success.

Glory makes a significant contribution to popular understanding of the African American role in the Civil War. Edward Linenthal eloquently stated this case, reprising some of Morgan Freeman's comments cited earlier.

> We cannot bemoan the historical literacy of Americans and then complain too bitterly when Hollywood takes a daring step for Hollywood and produces a film that has without any question sparked in the American mind interest in this story. How many people went to *Glory* without ever knowing that blacks fought for the Union in the Civil War? And even though Frederick Douglass was flattened, and even though they were not [depicted as] free people of color, this story provided a spark in the minds of young and old to make them go and read, to learn about this, to begin—and whose responsibility is it to teach them about this? It's our job as historians to deepen and add complexity to the story. This is what public history is about and it is our responsibility to do so. Hollywood has its limitations, and films, like every other kind of memorial work,

which *Glory* was, remember and forget, the same way that historians or monuments remember and forget.[18]

James M. McPherson asked, "Can movies teach history?" For *Glory*, he replied, the answer is yes. "Not only is it the first feature film to treat the role of black soldiers in the American Civil War, but it is also one of the most powerful and historically accurate movies ever made about that war." McPherson acknowledged that the film is not accurate in its portrayal of the history of the Fifty-fourth, but the filmmakers, he contended, chose to tell a story "not simply about the Fifty-fourth Massachusetts but about blacks in the Civil War." The movie in some ways is really not about the Fifty-fourth but rather is a metaphor for the black experience in the war. Indeed, the film quite openly and directly confronts the problem of racism in American culture by characterizing many Union Army commanders as deeply prejudiced. If the actual historical players were much more racist than the movie communicated, the fact that the topic was engaged seriously at all is worth applauding. Associate Producer Ray Herbeck asserted that the point of *Glory* was to characterize the phenomenon of the U.S. Colored Troops, a majority of whom were former slaves. From McPherson's viewpoint, with this goal as their objective, they succeeded admirably.[19]

Other historians have praised the film while simultaneously offering critical comments. David Blight called *Glory* a "war movie, a Civil War platoon drama that follows certain predictable formulas. But it is also a war movie that says that sometimes wars have meanings that we are obligated to discern." However haltingly or sketchily, it was at least an "initial Hollywood attempt to confront some central questions of African-American history: why did it take total war on such a scale to begin to make black people free in America? Or, why did black men in the middle of the nineteenth century have to die in battle, by the thousands, in order to be recognized as men?" If *Glory* did not do much to answer these questions, most voices in American cultural life do not even begin to discuss these difficult issues. Despite valid scholarly criticisms, wrote William S. McFeely, the film is certainly a celebration of involvement and valor and, as such, should be viewed positively.[20]

In the closing credits of the film, the producers extend special thanks to historian Shelby Foote, who served as a consultant during production. He considered the battle details especially praiseworthy. Peter Burchard raised the interesting point that Foote may have been featured as a historical consultant in order to highlight a Southerner as the filmmakers sought support nationwide for the film—even though Foote's expertise in African American history is not distinguished.[21]

Foote's comment pinpoints a great strength of the film: the authenticity with which *Glory* depicts battle scenes, whether it is the Fifty-fourth's first baptism of fire at James Island, South Carolina, or their ill-fated assault on Battery Wagner. These battle scenes seem graphically and brutally true to life. In *Glory*, Richard Bernstein wrote in the *New York Times*, war is clearly hell. Producer Fields hired Ray Herbeck, himself a reenactor, as associate producer and historical/technical coordinator and gave him a substantial budget to ensure authenticity. Herbeck commented in the *New York Times* that this was "the first film to show the life of the common Civil War soldier—white or black—in such detail." Hollywood, he commented, does not often let "historically minded people get involved to this extent." With the help of many, Herbeck coordinated the development of a group of black Civil War reenactors who appeared in the film.[22] The film credits declared: "The producers gratefully acknowledge the invaluable contribution of the thousands of living history reenactors from 20 states whose donation of time, equipment, and Civil War combat experience made this film possible."

Tumult and emotions of combat depicted in *Glory*. Courtesy Museum of Modern Art, Film Stills Archive.

THE IMPACT OF *GLORY*

According to Ray Herbeck, the film cost approximately $20 million to produce and took in roughly $35 million. To break even, he argued, a film has to double its budget. However, the film has proved quite successful in television broadcasts and videocassette sales and rentals since its release in 1989.[23] It seems safe to speculate that the movie was ultimately a profitable venture, although not what Hollywood would consider a blockbuster.

Based on the continuing marketability of *Glory,* Columbia Tri-Star has decided to release it in digital video disc (DVD) format. DVD has emerged as the fastest-growing format ever and is regarded as the eventual replacement for the videocassette. It should become the preeminent home viewing product because of two unique features: high-quality resolution and great capacity to store information. The major film studios are producing selected backlist titles and major new films in the DVD format. The DVD version of *Glory,* to be released sometime in 2001, will include the film itself; interviews with Ed Zwick, Morgan Freeman, and Matthew Broderick; a new documentary entitled *Voices of Glory;* and a previously produced documentary, *The True Story of Glory Continues. Voices of Glory,* featuring historian James Horton, focuses on the refusal of the men of the Fifty-fourth to accept wages lower than those of white soldiers and their eventual triumph on this issue.[24]

The popular press considered the film a success. *Glory* received some negative reviews, but the positive assessments predominated. Vincent Canby in the *New York Times* called *Glory* a "beautifully acted, pageantlike" film. He made special note of the climactic battle scene: "The attack on Fort Wagner, which is the climax of the movie, comes as close to anything I've ever seen on screen to capturing the chaos and brutality that were particular to Civil War battles." *Glory,* Canby concluded, is "celebratory, but it celebrates in a manner that insists on acknowledging the sorrow. This is a good, moving, complicated film." Although disturbed by some of the film's shortcomings, David Nicholson, writing in the *Washington Post,* called *Glory* "a long overdue treatment of black participation in the Civil War," which corrects the "omission of a significant chapter in American history from popular culture." David Ansen, writing in *Newsweek,* described *Glory* as a handsome, intelligent movie that "demands attention: it opens our eyes to a war within a war most of us never knew about." Richard Schickel in *Time* was struck by the depictions of battle: "*Glory* is at is best when it shows their [referring to the men of the Fifty-fourth] proud embrace of 19th century warfare at its most brutal. Director Edward Zwick graphically demonstrates the absurdity of lines of soldiers slowly advancing across open ground, shoulder to shoulder, in the face of withering rifle volleys and horrendous cannonade. The fact that the Fifty-fourth finally achieves respect (and opens the way for other black soldiers) only by losing half its number in a foredoomed assault on an impregnable fortress underscores this terrible irony." Stanley Kauffmann in the *New Republic* saluted *Glory* by noting that it was "not a mere exploitation of a historical circumstance with modern relevance, not a made-for-TV thesis tract" but rather an "authentic, patient, bloody, and moving work." Writing in *Commonweal,* Tom O'Brien characterized *Glory* as a "no-fuss example of how to teach inclusive history and document a minority group role in preserving America."[25]

The film *Glory* has had a long-term, positive impact, stimulating both the visibility of and interest in the story of blacks in the Union Army. The influence has been demonstrated in a variety of areas: historical reenactment, public sculpture, genealogy, archives, books and publications, curricula, films and videos, and public programs.

Civil War historical reenactment dates back to the nineteenth century and was an almost totally white phenomenon until the making of *Glory.* William Gwaltney of the National Park Service was one of the organizers of Company B, Fifty-fourth Massachusetts Regiment, for the movie. He recalled that when "we left the film, it was not so much the movie that we were fixated on but the history. And we had great feelings of pride in having participated" in the making of *Glory* and "redoubled our efforts to tell the story." The experience of being part of the filmmaking, Gwaltney recounted, "gave the men of Company B and other [black reenactors], the opportunity to become involved in special events in museums, education, in parades, special programs, in various reenactments, changing the stakes in the hobby."[26] Though the "hobby" remains overwhelmingly white, a small but active group of black reenactors clearly bring unique commitments and a special energy to Civil War historical reenactment.

In the summer of 1998 in the Shaw neighborhood, a black community in Washington, D.C., the African-American Civil War Memorial Freedom Foundation, dedicated "Spirit of Freedom," a new monument to the blacks who fought in the Union Army. It features a "bronze statue of black soldiers in front of three low semicircular granite walls covered with stainless steel plaques listing . . . all of the black soldiers who served . . . plus the 7,000 white officers they served under." The project will eventually include a heritage center adjacent to the memorial, which is intended to complement the memorial with historical displays and presentations. The central organizer of the project, Washington, D.C., city councillor Frank Smith Jr., developed an interest in the black soldiers who fought in the Union Army while a young civil rights worker with the Student Non-Violent Coordinating Committee in Mississippi during the 1960s. Inspired by the movie *Glory*, Smith engineered passage of a local bill calling for the memorial in 1991 and then succeeded in gaining congressional authorization for the $2.5 million project in 1992. Clearly, the 1989 release of *Glory* proved immensely helpful in developing the necessary political momentum for these actions.[27]

As a direct result of the activities of the African-American Civil War Memorial Freedom Foundation, Jean Douglass Greene and Jeanette Braxton Secret established the organization Descendants of African-American Union Soldiers/Sailors and Their White Officers in the Civil War, 1861–1865. Greene is the great-granddaughter of Frederick Douglass, and Secret is the great-granddaughter of Iverson Granderson, who served in the Union Navy. The purpose of the organization is to promote research and publications and to honor and commemorate African Americans who served in the Union military. Secret is the author of a guide on how to conduct such research.[28]

In September 1997 the National Gallery of Art in Washington, D.C., placed on display in a beautifully presented exhibit the restored plaster cast of the Shaw Monument, on long-term loan from Saint-Gaudens National Historic Site in Cornish, New Hampshire. The plaster cast had remained outdoors for decades until the park decided in 1993 that they could no longer run the risk of continued exposure to the elements and the ongoing deterioration of this invaluable piece. The Saint-Gaudens Memorial Trustees, in collaboration with the National Park Service, began a fund-raising effort, which resulted in the restoration of the plaster and the casting of a bronze replica for display in Cornish. There can be little doubt that the 1989 release of *Glory* provided significant impetus to these efforts, which were primarily driven by the deterioration of the plaster and the then upcoming centennial of the monument's installation in Boston. Matthew Broderick, who portrayed Shaw in the film, was featured at the National Gallery opening.[29]

Teachers across the country successfully utilize *Glory* in their classrooms, and the film is also a formal part of school curricula. Award-winning secondary school teacher James Percoco of Fairfax County, Virginia, shows *Glory* at the end of the Civil War unit in his U.S. history class. For him the film is a powerful depiction of a story that has long been overlooked in the classroom. Before screening the film for students, Percoco summarizes the historical inaccuracies and advises his students "that this film is not a documentary, but rather a producer's or director's *interpretation* of the past." The film leads to "all kinds of wonderful discussions with students" concerning why the filmmakers chose to omit Lewis Douglass, why they depicted the men of the Fifty-fourth as largely former slaves, and why filmmakers created a story that leads to the false impression that Battery Wagner was the regiment's only major engagement. In short, experience has shown that *Glory* serves as an extremely effective classroom tool. It is interesting to note that Percoco utilizes the edited version created for the classroom because his "school district has a policy against showing films that are rated R."[30]

"Utterly enveloped, inspired, and swept away" by *Glory*, businessman-educator George Gonis in 1998 produced a dress-up cap that enables young people to imagine themselves as the black and white brothers of the Fifty-fourth. His firm Round Robin, which designs toys and learning products and produces children's literature, includes the "CAPtive Readers" series, "a collection of history-inspired headwear paired with over-sized, laminated bookmarks—each bookmark packed with factual information, vintage photographs, colorful graphics, and a reading list for three age groups." Gonis claims that the cap is "one of the few non-book products available for kids that addresses the evils of bigotry and the heroic struggle for abolition, civil rights, and brotherhood." Winner of a Parents' Choice award, the Fifty-fourth cap and bookmark have been extremely well received.[31]

The film also gave new life to another account of the regiment and led to a modern edition of Shaw's letters. Saint Martin's Press published Peter Burchard's excellent book *One Gallant Rush* in 1965 and over the course of a quarter-century sold between four and five thousand copies of the book. Since the book was reissued in 1989 upon the release of *Glory*, with the film depicted on the front cover, more than fifty thousand copies have been sold. This is perhaps one of the most dramatic demonstrations of how a popular film can stimulate enormous interest in a serious piece of historical work that had previously received little exposure. In the preface to his edited collection of Robert Gould Shaw's letters, Russell Duncan noted that in "the book's earliest stage—two weeks after the premiere of the movie *Glory*," the University of Georgia Press "encouraged me to move quickly on the project."[32] The film also renewed interest in Luis F. Emilio's nineteenth-century history of the regiment, sparking several reprint editions.

A survey of some of the institutions holding significant archival materials relevant to Shaw and the Fifty-fourth reveals that in all cases usage of the materials skyrocketed after the release of *Glory*. In large part because of *Glory* and, to some extent, the Ken Burns public television series *The Civil War,* there was a significant increase in the number of researchers examining materials pertaining to African American troops at the National Archives and Records Administration (NARA). Indeed, Budge Weidman, project manager of the Civil War Conservation Corps, reported that Shaw's military service record was so frequently examined as a direct result of *Glory* that it had to undergo conservation before it could be microfilmed. Weidman's corps, composed of members of the National Archives Volunteer Association, has undertaken the massive project of preparing for microfilming approximately two thousand boxes of records relating to the U.S. Colored Troops. Weidman recounted that as a result of the film she personally has fielded an increased number of calls about the men of the U.S. Colored Troops, most of them from descendants of African Americans who served in the Civil War.[33]

Glory also sparked the creation of two National Park Service database projects connected with the African-American Civil War Memorial Freedom Foundation. On September 10, 1997, the Park Service announced the completion of the first phase of the "Civil War Soldiers and Sailors Names Index" project and placed more than 235,000 African American Civil War servicemen's names on its Web site. The Web site includes regimental histories of 180 African American Union regiments, with hyperlinks between soldiers' names, the regiments they served in, and the battles the regiments fought in. In addition, the National Park Service, Howard University, and the Department of the Navy have formed a partnership to compile the names of African Americans who served in the Union Navy.[34]

Susan Halpert of Houghton Library, Harvard University, related that *Glory,* which included "strangely large credits for Houghton at the beginning of the film," had a major impact on her research facility. According to her there were a huge number of requests to examine Shaw's letters at the time of the movie's release in 1989. Another peak occurred when the movie was released on the video market. Every year since the film's release, Houghton staff have noticed a strong interest in the Shaw letters. Requests are made in person and often via phone or letter related to History Day projects. History Day is a national competition, sponsored by education groups, the National Park Service, The History Channel, and many other groups, which has stimulated the interest of young people in history. Often screenings of *Glory* in schools will trigger a burst of interest. The letters are now on microfilm, and inquirers are frequently referred to Russell Duncan's book. Donald Yacovone of the Massachusetts Historical Society reported that since 1989 the society has witnessed a marked increase in requests to examine its collection of Shaw letters and the papers of Luis F. Emilio, whose book on the Fifty-fourth remains the fullest treatment of the regiment.[35]

To capitalize on *Glory*'s success and, perhaps, to compensate for the film's shortcomings as history, Tri-Star Pictures issued a video, *The True Story of Glory Continues*, narrated by Morgan Freeman. Ray Herbeck, who wrote and produced the documentary, believed that it should "enhance the experience of the feature film" and noted that the two are marketed together, perhaps one of the first times a studio has employed this marketing approach. Several of Lewis Douglass's letters are quoted. The documentary treats the history of the Fifty-fourth after the assault on Battery Wagner; includes a scene dropped from *Glory* where, at a recruitment rally, Frederick Douglass exhorts young black men to enlist; and features many images and the names of several enlisted men of the regiment. The documentary addresses the financial hardships on the home front that arose because of the men's refusal to accept unequal pay. The work also focuses on the black reenactors and their efforts to educate Americans about this important chapter of American history. Overall, the documentary effectively employs illustrations, photos, and dramatic footage.[36]

Sparked by the film *Glory*, Judy Crichton, executive producer of public television's *American Experience*, developed a documentary on the Fifty-fourth. *The Massachusetts 54th Colored Infantry*, produced by Jackie Shearer, who worked on the civil rights documentary series *Eyes on the Prize*, and Laurie Kahn-Leavitt, once again was narrated by Morgan Freeman.[37] This documentary, a conscious and successful attempt to correct the history that *Glory* portrayed, serves to set the regiment in its proper historical context. In his scripted introduction, series host David McCullough carefully stated:

> Our film tonight deals with two large misconceptions about the Civil War. The first is that black people before the war all lived in slavery in the South, when in fact there were 500,000 free blacks about evenly divided between North and South.
>
> The second misconception is about the term "abolitionist." Abolitionists, we learned in school, were high-minded white northerners—ministers, editors, society women, Bostonians mainly—and to be sure, a great many were. But many, too, were free northern blacks and with the onset of the war came the greatest, most influential abolitionist force by far—thousands of black men in blue uniforms, carrying Springfield rifles, volunteers, that is, soldiers of their own free will, serving in the Grand Army of the Republic. No one advocated the abolition of slavery more than they and in time, they came by the tens of thousands.

Trip (played by Denzel Washington) and fellow soldiers shred their pay
vouchers rather than accept unequal pay in *Glory.* Courtesy Museum of
Modern Art, Film Stills Archive.

Our film . . . is about the famous 54th Massachusetts Volunteers, the
first black northern regiment to go into action. They were the men in
the movie *Glory.* This is their true story, pieced together as it's never
been before—from newly found photographs, old letters and diaries uncovered by producer Jacqueline Shearer and from the proud history
passed down to the living descendants of the 54th.[38]

McCullough was referencing *popular* misconceptions, assumptions
among many Americans who do not read scholarly books or, possibly,
any history at all. The documentary makers did not claim to have presented new historical evidence. Rather, their work frames the story of
the regiment in a way that Hollywood chose not to do. The story of free
blacks in the North and their centrality in the abolitionist struggle is
central to an accurate historical picture of the Fifty-fourth. This is the
narrative that the Shearer work provides.[39]

The documentary effectively and movingly communicates the history of the Fifty-fourth. It outlines the rich community life of Boston's
free black community on Beacon Hill, demonstrates the strength of
abolitionist activity among free African Americans, portrays the recruitment efforts of free black leaders, and highlights the history of

several men of the Fifty-fourth, as well as activities of the regiment. Several descendants of men of the Fifty-fourth, including Carl Cruz, whose ancestor was William H. Carney, are prominently featured, as are such scholars as James Horton, Barbara Fields, and Massachusetts state representative Byron Rushing. Other consulting scholars included Edwin Redkey, Leon Litwack, and Sidney Kaplan.

In a moving scene of the sort missing from *Glory*, narrator Morgan Freeman relates in a voice-over that during the summer of 1865 Major Martin R. Delany, a prominent African American abolitionist who recruited for the Fifty-fourth and the army's highest-ranking African American, went to Charleston to visit his son in the Fifty-fourth. Delany addressed Port Royal ex-slaves in the church that Charlotte Forten had used as a schoolroom. Laurence Fishburne, powerfully portraying the voice of Delany, exclaims, "I want to tell you one thing. Do you know that if it was not for the black man, this war never would have been brought to a close with success to the Union and the liberty of your race if it had not been for the Negro? I want you to understand that. Do you know it? Do you know it? Do you know it?"[40]

Other televised programs on the Fifty-fourth followed. The History Channel produced a 1993 documentary entitled "The 54th Massachusetts" as part of its *Civil War Journal*. Narrated by Danny Glover, this solid program also sought to fill in the history missing from *Glory*. Prominent voices in the program belong to scholar James Horton and William Gwaltney of the National Park Service, who provide excellent historical commentary. Though not overall as sophisticated as the public television program, "The 54th Massachusetts" successfully relates the basic historical context of the regiment, the composition of the men who served in the Fifty-fourth, the assault on Wagner, and the significance of the Fifty-fourth in U.S. history.

More recently, the production of *Glory* made possible the great success of Boston's 1997 centennial celebration of the Saint-Gaudens monument to Robert Gould Shaw and the Fifty-fourth Massachusetts Regiment. Certainly the film heightened interest in the monument. Appeals to major funders and supporters were made easier because all shared the experience of the film. Without this common awareness, backing for the project might have been difficult to obtain, perhaps impossible. All major aspects of the centennial program—the public ceremony featuring General Colin Powell, the largest gathering ever of black Civil War reenactors, and the public symposium—represented one of the city's most important public commemorations. To African Americans, it validated, though belatedly, the black contribution to American history. It also led to the production of two television programs focused on the event and the meaning of the Fifty-fourth—"Return to Glory," a joint production of WCVB-TV in Boston and the Museum of Afro American History, and a documentary program produced by the black public affairs program of the local public television station, WGBH-TV. Even this volume of essays from the centennial celebration is a result of the impact of *Glory.* Interestingly, in each of the eight panels in the public symposium, which were on a wide variety of subjects, the one topic that consistently arose, often with strong feelings, was the movie *Glory.* At the final symposium session, which focused on *Glory,* William Gwaltney acknowledged that there are numerous deficiencies in the film but concluded that because of the movie, "people talk, and people are still talking, and we're talking about it again today. *Glory* means a lot of things to a lot of people."[41]

Gwaltney was correct in his observations. I do not think we can ask more from a Hollywood movie than what *Glory* has delivered and continues to deliver.

THOMAS CRIPPS

GLORY AS A MEDITATION ON THE SAINT-GAUDENS MONUMENT

A BOVE ALL, one is struck by the persistent, even enduring, political clarity of Augustus Saint-Gaudens's monumental homage to the abolitionist spirit of Boston. Even the social order remains precisely *there:* the erect, mounted, patrician white officer leading stolid, purposeful African American soldiers who are leaning into their task at hand. Yet this bronze bas-relief marvel of composition describes more than a stereotyped detail of stratification along racial lines. Robert Gould Shaw's pose is no mere indicator of class and race—his is also the military seat prescribed by the army's manual; as for the blacks, they march not as an anonymous chorus to Shaw's Gawain on a private quest but as individuated black *men* marching on their own behalf—as though we can hear the strains of "The Battle Cry of Freedom" over the scene before us. We know they march in the cause of freedom for men and women like themselves—indeed, we are taught this by the monument.[1]

I make this seemingly obvious point that a fine piece of public sculpture in fact makes *its* point to generation after generation of viewers because so many artistic and social forces seem to act against such an outcome. At every turn we see evidence that the civic spirit that once formed the collective will to memorialize has diminished. Indeed, there has been a slow erosion of civic space—the suburban "gated community" having intruded into the *bürgerische Öffentlichkeit,* the public space that the German theorist Jürgen Habermas sees as the sine qua non of any truly open society. Clashes of political will contribute to postponements in placing and even bringing to fruition all manner of public sculpture. Maya Ying Lin's Vietnam Veterans Memorial in Washington, D.C., and, nearby, Howard Peaslee's Marine Corps War Memorial come to mind. Public gatherings and rituals that once honored specific persons and events have coagulated into generalities such as "Presidents' Day" and "Veterans Day" that serve mainly as occasions for "one-day only" retail sales. This drift away from public commonality and its rituals was accompanied, according to the Harvard economist John Kenneth Galbraith in *The Affluent Society* (1958), by a predictable condition of private affluence and public squalor fueled by a persistent plea for ever lower taxes. In tandem with and perhaps induced by these trends, a generation of particularistic, one-issue political parties has diminished the capacity of major parties to speak for a national polity. The result has been a generation of weed-grown concrete slabs set in disused crannies of valueless realty, each shabbily honoring the dead of some war upon which a small sector of well-wishers might agree.

In place of the formerly lively civic life acted out in public spaces, the chosen media of collective expression have become lone—perhaps even lonely—exercises in watching moving images of public celebration. On television we watch in endless reruns the celebrants in the spring and summer of 1945 cheering the end of World War II; we gather for sporting events in dens and taverns to watch crowds of fans celebrate triumphant games played always somewhere else.[2]

Finally, in this sketch of a mood antithetical to the liberal idealism caught in Saint-Gaudens's monument, one must include a sense that if the North won the Civil War, the South won the peace that followed. Whether we take note of the ease with which the defeated South after Reconstruction found alternative means of social control of freed African Americans or the facile portrayal of a white Southern version of black character in the form of generations of minstrel shows, movies filled with black buffoons and servants and song-and-dance men, or even the gradual assimilation of white Southern "country music" into the national taste culture, we have no choice but to see a persistence of dissent from the broadly catholic sentiments expressed in Saint-Gaudens's monument.

We may see this regional particularism in the public sculptures not only of the states of the old Confederacy but even in a "border state" such as Maryland. A single monument to the black abolitionist Frederick Douglass stands in the quadrangle of Morgan State University, cut off from "white" eyes; the black Supreme Court justice Thurgood Marshall is remembered by means of a berobed statue at, as some black critics say, the *back* door of a federal office building; and a similarly lone figure of the black jazz singer Billie Holliday looks into a gritty lot in the older ghetto of Baltimore. No Saint-Gaudens celebrated the abolitionists of the state, such as the black Harriet Tubman and Henry Highland Garnet or the white Quakers Samuel Hopkins and Elisha Tyson, or for that matter the twenty-five thousand free African Americans (of a total black community of more than twenty-seven thousand) who lived and worked in Baltimore at the time of the 1860 census.

Rather, we find a vast "Confederate Hill" in one of the city's oldest cemeteries, where the veterans of the First and Second Maryland Cavalry, CSA, lie buried under testaments to "duty." The most celebrated,

Lieutenant Colonel Harry Gilmore, later police commissioner of the city, is venerated as "Our Gallant Harry"—"Dauntless in battle, / Splendid in success / Constant in defeat." Elsewhere in the broad avenues of the city stand the Confederate Soldiers and Sailors Monument with a Nike-figure embracing a dying warrior ("Glory Stands beside Our Grief," says the pedestal); and in a glade across the Baltimore Museum of Art, a dual equestrian statue, fully twenty feet in height, of Robert E. Lee and Thomas "Stonewall" Jackson–"great generals and Christian soldiers [who] waged war like gentlemen," as its pedestal says.[3]

I draw this contrast between Baltimore and Boston not only in order to argue the obvious point that both victorious causes and lost causes raise their heroes' memories, but also to point out that the achievement of Saint-Gaudens's sculpture was its singular authority in asserting a provincial Boston spirit that had become not only a national war aim but also a symbol of an eventual American social goal.

How do we reassert this moral (and political) authority in an age of the electronically driven moving image, whether in darkened auditoriums or in ever smaller primary groups seated before flickering video screens in anomic, privatized "rec rooms"? These dim havens pass for the public space—Habermas's Öffentlichkeit—in which a communal sense of the past can be shared.[4] Moreover, in order to reach a broad enough polity, this moving image must be a popular "movie." It cannot be a visual dissertation. The historicity of such an offering would be lost to all but a few students, and the program's brief fifty-seven-minute duration could do little to capture the nuance and ambiguity that a knowledgeable scholar might expect.

The late Jacqueline Shearer's video production, The Massachusetts 54th Colored Infantry (1991), for all its considerable merit, must accommodate the casual attention of the generalists who watch The American Experience on television (or later rent it from Blockbuster). Thus, television programmers must, even more than moviemakers, strive for a "high concept," a hook on which to hang the focus of the audience. This angle, as expressed in its "billboards" and "teasers," claims to fill a gap "in the history books" or even to provide a corrective to "what you learned in school." Thus the narrator of Shearer's documentary, David McCullough, half-seated in his book-lined study with its aged upright typewriter, tells us that the program will use "newly found" sources to correct two "misconceptions": first that all African Americans were slaves and, second, that they stood on the sidelines during the war. Of course, a dutiful reader might not only be familiar with such works as John Hope Franklin's Free Negro in North Carolina

(1943) and Dudley Cornish's *Sable Arm: Negro Troops in the Union Army, 1861–1865* (1956), but would likely also know that Franklin's *From Slavery to Freedom* (1947) and Benjamin Quarles's *Negro in the Making of America* (1964) took up these topics and that all four works have been in print for decades.

Shearer's video opens on Douglass, John S. Rock, and others in meetings on Beacon Hill. A "talking head" asks, as though quoting them, "How can we turn this to become a violent struggle to end slavery," while ignoring Douglass's distancing himself from John Brown. "It is gallant to go forth singlehandedly," Quarles quotes from Douglass's letter to Brown, "but is it wise?" I do not mention such neglect of nuanced black debate as a cavil against a good film, but merely as a reminder that the medium by its nature invites declarative statements rather than the shadings that a scholarly monograph allows by virtue of *its* nature.

Glory as *movie* is closer to Saint-Gaudens's sculpture with respect to both method and intended audience response. Together the two media, the one static and offered to its public in a civic space, the other narrative and extended, reach for their audiences' sentiments. Their shared artistic goal is an evocative credibility rather than an authenticated dissertation. A tolerable credibility requires only that the details *ring* true rather than claim truth: the trigger housings and the flash pans of the muskets, the badges on the kepis, the mundane details of Boston teatime as well as Carolina campfires allow us to believe that the accompanying story seems true enough to carry the freight of its meaning. "Fakery in allegiance to truth," Henry Luce said of his popular cinematic magazine of the mid–twentieth century, *The March of Time*. Luce, although he expressed it a bit crassly, shared this notion with Saint-Gaudens (and other sculptors of public imagery) and with Edward Zwick, director of *Glory*.[5]

Sculpture and movies, indeed all art forms, are alike in another way: they are subject to editing. The moviemaking truism "When the shooting stops, the cutting begins" might readily apply to plastic arts. Cramming in everything in a quest to be "real" or authentic can only slow the action. Compare, for example, Saint-Gaudens's warriors with Gutzon Borglum's homage to the heroes of *all* of America's wars; it sits in and monopolizes Military Park in midtown Newark, New Jersey. Apart from its vivid display of technical skill in rendering in the round a daunting number of figures drawn from every American combat experience, it somehow loses itself in the details of costume, weaponry, and signs of the passage of time. Every moviegoer must recall such an instance of the "busy" sort of film that inspired the anonymous wisecrack about

Cecil B. DeMille's struggle "to weave Moses into the War of the Roses." Only through this painful paring away, this distillation, can the artist actively seek the difference between detail and essence, fact and meaning. Only then may image become metaphor, thereby allowing the artist to think *with* history rather than merely about it.

Curiously, both of these media took years to reach this essence of their racial politics, each passing through an era of Thermidorean reaction in which racial liberalism contended with a sentimentality toward the "lost cause." The Shaw monument had been preceded by scores of military memoirs, biographies, novels, and apologia ranging through a "life and letters" of Stonewall Jackson and memoirs like John Esten Cooke's *Wearing of the Grey* to Thomas Nelson Page's *Two Little Confederates* for children. Lost in the clatter of saber and the blare of trumpet was the essence of the final abolitionist meaning of the war, which Saint-Gaudens's work was meant to revive.[6]

Gutzon Borglum, *Wars of America*, bronze, 1926, Military Park, Newark, New Jersey. Saint-Gaudens's rigorous focus on what William James called "the profounder meaning" of the Civil War contrasts with Borglum's monument to all of America's war dead, an imposing achievement that resisted paring down to a single theme. Courtesy The Newark Museum and Art Resource.

By the time of its unveiling, Boston itself had grown less hospitable to African Americans. True, Senator Henry Cabot Lodge annually introduced his "Force Bill" aimed at reducing representation in states that disfranchised blacks. And William Monroe Trotter's newspaper, the *Boston Guardian*, gave angry voice to black aspiration. But for every Negro like Clement Morgan who sat in local councils, thousands of others never attended Boston's elite schools or rose out of its servant classes. The men of the family of the black scholar Benjamin Quarles, for example, were porters in the Boston subway and waiters on the Fall River Line; these occupations were paths to black manhood for Quarles himself (although he did attend Boston English). Harvard, as though of two minds, awarded W.E.B. Du Bois its first black Ph.D. but honored the famous Booker T. Washington (who spoke at the unveiling) with only an M.A.

The point here, of course, is not to uncover Boston's feet of clay beneath the monument but rather to point out the pervasive antipathy that tinged almost every racial encounter. For their part, movies in their first half-century purveyed the visual rhetoric of this chauvinism, which crested in a love feast of intersectional harmony during the semicentennial of the Civil War, 1910–15. In that age, no black soldier leaned into his stride, musket shouldered, with the same élan that Saint-Gaudens gave his little troop. If anything they were "structured out," in James Snead's term.[7] Early on in this cycle of Civil War movies, the role of African Americans was circumscribed into a narrow range of servile behavior. Most pointedly so was *His Trust* and *His Trust Fulfilled* (both 1911), released in two parts as a sop to exhibitors still chary of any length longer than two reels. Together, the two films were a primer on what whites thought they knew about black men, both in slavery and in a seemingly unwanted freedom. No African bluecoats here. "George"— the one whose trust is fulfilled—is a bent, woolly-headed slave who takes over a plantation in his master's absence. He defends the place against Yankee marauders, saves the white women from their burning house, shields them against the arrogance of newly freed black rowdies, and, unbelievably, draws upon his "savings" to educate the daughter of his absent master, then marries her off to a highly eligible English gentleman. Why a film grounded in such invincible ignorance of black life? The filmmaker was the infamous D. W. Griffith; the times were, in Rayford Logan's view, the "nadir" of black fortunes in this country; lynchings had become commonplace; black protest seemed to founder until the enfolding of several activist groups in 1909 into the National Association for the Advancement of Colored People.[8]

Far from being a lone instance of white chauvinism or a dernier cri of the Southern "lost cause," Griffith's movies were a sampling of five years of scores of such treacly homages to the semicentennial. Typically, in *The Confederate Spy* (1910), the slaves are "happy, contented, and well cared for," and one of them, old Uncle Daniel, saves the plantation from Yankee foragers "for massa sake and little missa." Their titles throb to the drumbeat of their message: *Uncle Pete's Ruse* (1911), *Old Mammy's Secret Code* (1912), *A Slave's Devotion* (1913). Whenever emancipation intrudes, it is glossed or made mawkish as in Vitagraph's literal rendering of *The Battle Hymn of the Republic* (1911), which drops the line "to make men free," or in *Lincoln the Lover* (1914), in which a "darkey" gazes "lovingly" at Lincoln dozing before his hearth.

As though a coda to this crescendo of sentimental Southern chauvinism, D. W. Griffith's epic of the Civil War and Reconstruction, *The Birth of a Nation* (1915), appeared at the end of the cycle. Far more bluntly, on an unprecedented scale and at an uncommon length of three hours, it offered its regional message to the entire nation. As asserted by Thomas Dixon, the Southern preacher and author of the novels that had inspired and informed the script, the film sought "to teach the North . . . the awful suffering of the white man during the Reconstruction period."[9]

Its release also aroused and thrust together in common cause the remnants of Boston's abolitionist heritage and the rising political consciousness of African Americans. With its arrival on Tremont Street, protesters filled the street between the Shaw monument and the State House, disrupting showings, pressing its maker to cut racially offensive scenes, and finally inducing the state legislature to pass a law prohibiting the slander of any ethnic group.

At first centered in Boston, this militant activism soon grew into a national movement, with Trotter's *Boston Guardian* serving as its voice. The Boston NAACP acted as a clearinghouse and fund-raiser for movements in other cities. Joining with Booker T. Washington's secretary, Emmett J. Scott, several Bostonians took up the project of making a filmed rebuttal to *The Birth of a Nation*, a proposed epic of the role of Africans in the story of humankind, to be entitled *The Birth of a Race* (1918). Prof. Albert Bushnell Hart of Harvard volunteered the use of his research library. W.E.B. Du Bois agreed to help with the script. And Oswald Garrison Villard, a descendant of the abolitionist William Lloyd Garrison, offered his services, at least until the onset of World War I called him to Washington. For a time they engaged the attention of both Universal Pictures and the philanthropist Julius Rosenwald, the first Jewish senior officer of Sears Roebuck.

Sadly, for the moment, *The Birth of a Race* proved terribly disappointing, and the Confederate sentiments of the era persisted in movies almost unopposed during the twenty years between the World Wars in a moss-grown Hollywood of misty epics. They grew as Hollywood itself grew. They included local color sketches like *Hearts in Dixie* (1929) and Stark Young's novel *So Red the Rose* (1935), which Paramount Studios bought to rival David O. Selznick's plans for *Gone with the Wind*; theatrical chestnuts such as Charles Dazey's *In Old Kentucky* (1927, 1935); Broadway musicals such as *Showboat* (1927, 1936, 1951) and *The Green Pastures* (1936); social dramas such as *Cabin in the Cotton* (1932) and Lillian Hellman's play *The Little Foxes* (1941); comedic star vehicles for Will Rogers and his black malapropist sidekick Stepin Fetchit, such as *Judge Priest* (1934) and *Steamboat round the Bend* (1935), and similar pictures for Shirley Temple and *her* black foil, Bill Robinson, such as *The Littlest Rebel* (1935) and *The Little Colonel* (1935).

This homage to Dixie survived until World War II, when black advocates, ranging from the pages of the *Pittsburgh Courier* to the halls of the Office of War Information, called for a "Double V"—simultaneous victory over both foreign fascism and domestic racism. The NAACP served as a go-between, lobbying both in Hollywood and in Washington for an altered black cinema image more in keeping with wartime propaganda slogans that called for "tolerance, brotherhood, and unity." Moreover, early on, they had come to see this emerging racial liberalism as capable of survival in the postwar world as well. Not to put too fine a point on it, within their odd complex of art, industry, and commerce, some of them sought a version of William James's "moral equivalent of war."

Examples of the evolving mood appeared even before the war. The Hollywood producer Walter Wanger and Walter White of the NAACP—each was "Dear Walter" to the other—played roles in the era. White exacted pledges from the studio "moguls" for more egalitarian casting while Wanger cut movies to fit the times. The result of their work showed throughout the war. Wanger's *Sundown* (1941), for example, was drawn from an African colonialist yarn in the prewar *Saturday Evening Post*. But by the time of its release in late 1941, Wanger had managed to include the German Afrika Korps threat to the Suez, as well as liberalizing its racial angle. As though requested by the NAACP, a British officer at his post in East Africa violates the custom of segregating Arabs, telling his Arab guest that "the England that's going to win this war is going to do away with a lot of this nonsense."

By midwar four of the major Hollywood movies that consciously put forth war aims—*Bataan, Sahara, Crash Dive,* and *Lifeboat*—carefully integrated the armed forces almost a decade before their actual integration. And by the war's end, when a revival of cinematic expressions of Southern sentimentality seemed imminent, liberal critics were poised. When Walt Disney's *Song of the South* (1946), a Technicolor fable based upon Joel Chandler Harris's "Bre'r Rabbit" tales, appeared, Bosley Crowther, veteran critic of the *New York Times*, bristled. "You've committed a peculiarly gauche offense," he wrote. "Put down your mint julep, Mr. Disney."[10]

Following the war, various surveys of Hollywood audiences revealed an emerging taste for what historian James T. Shotwell called "the thinking picture." Thus, even before the emergence of television as a threat to box office receipts, the studios began to stray from the older escapist genres, such as musicals, and to take up what critics called "message movies"—films like *The Naked City* (1948) that were shot on gritty locations rather than in sterile studios; films like *The Lost Weekend* (1945) that were derived from harshly realistic novels; or those like *The Snake Pit* (1948) that took up some social issues. In 1949 alone, a rash of race-angled movies of this genre went into release: *Pinky, Lost Boundaries, Home of the Brave*, and *Intruder in the Dust*. By early 1950 Sidney Poitier, the actor who almost defined the era, made his debut as an intern charged with murder when a racist patient in his care mysteriously dies. The genre lasted until the 1960s, when, with the exhaustion of the Civil Rights Movement, it spent itself on an almost apolitical cycle of "blaxploitation movies." In a way, *Glory* signaled a return to the values of the generations of both Saint-Gaudens and the World War II "Double V."

Certainly its makers thought so. *Glory* began, according to its producer, Freddie Fields, on the steps of the State House in Boston. While there on another mission, he and his writer Kevin Jarre saw the monument, and "we both felt the same thing," a sense that the monument made manifest "this wonderful, unknown story of the Civil War." Never mind that a student of the period would have known of Peter Burchard's durable *One Gallant Rush: Robert Gould Shaw and His Brave Black Regiment* (1965); their *feelings* drove them, not the stuff of history. Indeed, only belatedly did they call upon Burchard, and then only to save their picture from odd gaffes such as a John Brown who lived longer in the script than in life.[11]

Their goal was not authenticity but credibility. Even then, their concern extended only so far as to capture on film what they, and for that matter Saint-Gaudens, William James, Booker T. Washington, Robert Lowell, and any sensitive latter-day tourist, felt as they contemplated the stone and bronze pile on Boston Common: "the profounder meaning of the Union cause," in James's words on that day.

Steven Spielberg, in a recent interview, spoke to the nagging issue of what to leave in or take out. His well-crafted account of the slave revolt aboard the *Amistad* (the title of his movie) was a disappointment at the box office despite its evocation of an antique (and misappropriated) federal-period ambience, subtleties of characterization, complexities of both the politics and the law of slavery and abolition, and the rousing coda of images of the eventual destruction of slavery that put filmmaker, film, and audience on the side of the angels. Why did it flop? "I kind of dried it out," he told an interviewer, "and it became too much of a history lesson."[12]

But what to cut? What to keep? What to heighten or sharpen or accent? And what to play diminuendo? In the writing of either history or fiction, the aims of the medium may dictate what to "punch up" (as the actor John Garfield said of scripts he read). But when one writes history-as-fiction, the quandary deepens, the choices clash, the certainties stammer. Ask Jane Alexander, the distinguished actress who saw her supporting role as Shaw's mother evaporate into a bit part.

Or consider how to play the abolitionist Frederick Douglass, the hero of every student of African American history. I missed him, and have said so in another place.[13] But in Jarre's and Fields's view, *Glory* is not his movie; it is Shaw's and the Fifty-fourth's. Perhaps with this in mind, they chose to play Douglass as the leonine sage of the era rather than the still-young stalwart that he would have been in the mid-1860s. His look is that of the veteran icon of the postwar Republican Party rather than, say, the black-haired, hot-eyed radical of the frontispiece of his *My Bondage and My Freedom* (1855). As much as we might have wished to hear him give a farewell speech as he sent his own son off with the Fifty-fourth, perhaps to die, this fiery Douglass might have carried the viewer away from the centrality of the Fifty-fourth. Besides, he had spent much of late 1862 and early 1863 recruiting in New York, and although he visited the Fifty-fourth's Readville encampment a couple of times and saw their ship off to Beaufort, he seems not to have addressed either the troops or the Boston community. The filmmakers had even shot a sequence of him as a recruiter in Syracuse but cut it—"structured him out," Snead might have said—for the sake of tightening the focus on the regiment. That is, they were making a movie, not a monograph.[14]

Glory was not Douglass's first contact with the cutting room floor. World War II had brought with it a mood of, as propaganda catchwords put it, "brotherhood, tolerance, and equality." In fact, David O. Selznick, the producer of *Gone with the Wind* (1939), had told his first-draft scriptwriter, Sidney Howard, that he wished for Negroes "to come out on the right side of the ledger" in these "Fascist-ridden times." Prodded by the NAACP, the Office of War Information pressed Hollywood to play to the mood of the times.[15] In such a fleeting moment of black influence in both Washington and Hollywood, a young black radio writer, Carlton Moss, was touted to the Pentagon as a prospective writer of their own propaganda film, with which they hoped to dampen racial antipathies between their black and white troops. Bravely (or naively), Moss borrowed the title of his first draft from Douglass's stirring appeal for volunteers for the Fifty-fourth Massachusetts infantry regiment, *Men of Color to Arms!*

But the army knew what it wanted, and soon so too did Moss, so the title became more prosaic: *The Negro Soldier.* Nonetheless, it was a startling movie in its time and one that the NAACP not only fought to have recut into a usable civilian version but also lobbied to have freely given to postwar social activists and public schools. But of course, Douglass would have been too hot an image for an orientation film meant to cool racial antagonisms. So his slogan and his image faded from the final cut, and the Civil War itself, with its capacity still to raise interracial and intersectional passions, became almost a throwaway line merely accompanying a shot of the cold stone of the Lincoln Memorial. Critics on the left, nevertheless, touted it as "the best ever done," although James Agee found it "pitifully, painfully mild."[16]

Just as Moss felt compelled to make a persuasive film that redefined a black meaning of World War II, so Freddie Fields committed himself to making "an entertaining film"—a meditation on Saint-Gaudens's monument and its "profounder meaning of the Union cause," but nonetheless, a *movie.* In this sense the movie echoed the music of the era. From the patriotism of "Rally 'Round the Flag, Boys" the music grew ethereal, even sacral, in voice.

That is, by the time of Lincoln's address at Gettysburg in November 1863, when he consecrated the cemetery in the name of "a new birth of freedom," Julia Ward Howe's "Battle Hymn of the Republic" had become the North's anthem of choice. For her the war had become "a glory in His bosom that transfigures you and me." She all but asked soldiers to join the hallowed dead of Gettysburg as a testament to evolving war aims. "As He died to make men holy," she wrote, "let us die to make men free." As she heard the "profounder meaning" that James saw on Boston Common in 1897, so Fields and Jarre and the director Edward Zwick sought to vivify it on film.

And yet *Glory* appeared almost a century later. It followed wars whose propaganda expressions included making "the world safe for democracy" and a "Double V," as well as an African American civil rights movement that more than any previous American social movement

In keeping with Saint-Gaudens's casting in monumental form of the abolitionist ideals of Boston, the filmmakers of *Glory* took care to locate the origins of the Fifty-fourth in the ambience of the city, as in this scene of the regiment departing for war. Courtesy Museum of Modern Art, Film Stills Archive.

expressed itself in the moving image. Indeed, one television producer spoke of his medium as "the chosen instrument of the civil rights movement." *Glory*, then, had little choice but to replicate the interracial nature of the social history of the century following the unveiling of the Fifty-fourth's monument.

This, apart from issues of historical details, artistic license, and the obligatory truncations and warpings required by the medium, was the central purpose of the movie: to render the profounder meanings of 1897 into the clear, interracial terms of the late twentieth century. Thus, each set-piece, neatly constructed vignette, or dramatic incident seemed placed to teach Colonel Shaw and his men about each other.[17] This is the burden of the entire "backstory" prior to the main titles. At Antietam Creek, Shaw behaves well and receives a minor wound—his "red badge of courage." He is prodded awake by a black man dressed in slaves' motley (played by Morgan Freeman, so we know he will be among Shaw's tutors in the Fifty-fourth). Later his scratch is treated while through a scrim a screaming soldier is having a limb sawn off.

Abolition only just seeps into his head in a casual conversation in which we learn that the Emancipation Proclamation will free the slaves— "some of 'em, anyway."

Back home in Boston, Shaw floats through a party of swells as though in a mannered Restoration comedy. Governor John A. Andrew is there, along with a rather blandly regal Douglass.[18] Every gesture seems mumbled or compromised. Shaw is asked to command a colored regiment; he hears that such a move might be "unpopular"; he palters, finally seeming merely to go along. In his first pep talk to the assembled, as yet ununiformed or trained troops, he invokes God, not to free the slaves but "to restore the Union."

Shaw, we see, knows only free black Bostonians, including his closest friend, an apocryphal Thomas Searles (Andre Braugher). Thereafter, the viewer is allowed to infer that only African Americans on the bottom rung of life are the most authentically "black." Thus, license is given to break with history and create a regiment mainly from slave runaways, for only they can teach Shaw the ropes. He confirms this in voice-overs of his letters home. "I don't know these men—their music, their camaraderie—I miss Boston," he says, by which he means Boston and its certainties of race, class, and group.

At every turn he meets white men for whom the sight of black troops is an affront or an absurdity, each incident allowing us to see his own incremental learning. Idling soldiers haze his "niggers." Major Forbes, Shaw's second in command, says of his fictional white sergeant major, "The Irish are not noted for their fondness for the coloreds." The Union quartermaster himself seems hellbent on denying the troops not only weapons but even shoes. In fact, the absent shoes provide one of Shaw's most deeply felt lessons. He has decided to make an example of a soldier who has returned from an absence without leave (in search of shoes), a soldier who happens to be the most embittered of the ex-slaves. Officiously presiding over the whipping of the rebellious soldier, Shaw sees—too late to back off—that the soldier's back is laced with lash marks from beatings administered by the last white man who had held dominance over him: his owner.

Shaw's education continues after the Fifty-fourth steams southward to Beaufort. In yet another vignette, he sees his fellow officers fighting in the "profounder cause" harbor a casual racism. One of them—in reality, Colonel James Montgomery—orders the regiment to sack and burn the town of Darien, Georgia. He is a vengeful Kentuckian, thus a Unionist but one who by experience is "naturally" suited to command these "little monkey children." Yet Montgomery has a flash of misunderstanding: when he frees his men to loot and burn, they feel entitled to bully and manhandle the rebel women who resist (perhaps even to rape them; the viewer is not allowed to know). In order to redraw a line between black men and white women, the officer wordlessly shoots one of his own soldiers, reducing Shaw to mute astonishment.

Soon Shaw—by now he is surely meant to be "us," the viewers—is learning rapidly. As far back as Readville, he took the troops' side in a dispute over discriminatory pay scales by tearing up his pay voucher. Moreover, Shaw has risked court-martial by threatening a quartermaster and forcibly confiscating supplies and uniforms. So by the time they reach Battery Wagner, the site of their eventual apotheosis into the secular saints that Saint-Gaudens memorialized, they are indeed a regiment, one eager to assault the ramparts of this sentinel at the mouth of Charleston Harbor. And Shaw now openly admires "their character, their strength of heart," which once had been bafflingly inaccessible to him.

By now the filmmakers have ransacked history in search of fitting anecdotal vignettes that might carry some dramatic point or be bent to the task of revealing some facet of character. The great Port Royal experiment of General Rufus Saxton, a Yale man who encouraged slaves to farm abandoned lands while making a place for Laura Towne and Charlotte Forten and their New England sisters to teach them the ways of free men and women, is given a snapshot presence.[19] The Yankee soldiers who once hazed the black troops now cheer them onward with a "Give 'em hell, 54th!"

Most artistically manipulative in its intention was a decision to have Shaw announce to the regiment that the Confederacy intended to pursue a policy of treating black soldiers as runaways and rebels and their white officers as inciters of servile insurrection, thereby denying them the protection of the laws of war. This dramatization—based on fact—allows the viewer to fear the worst, perhaps summary executions in the field, thus heightening the drama. The Lincoln administration had attempted to blunt the threat by announcing that each execution so ordered would result in the shooting of a Confederate prisoner. The policy in the North was never implemented, however, even when black soldiers suffered death at the hands of their Southern captors.

Out of this movie patchwork of legend, history, and fiction came the transfiguration that Howe wrote of in her hymn and that the speakers at the unveiling saw in Saint-Gaudens's work. And in order to preserve the moral victory embedded in the heroic but vain assault on Battery Wagner, the moviegoer is told in a coda that the fort never succumbed to assault by any subsequent force.

Perhaps the filmmakers' most creative rendering of an aspect of the monument to Shaw and the Fifty-fourth occurred in a sequence that was almost postmodern in its insistence on a complex, multilayered black identity. It is the eve of their charge across the open beach before the earthen fort. The soldiers know their manhood is at stake in the impending assault and that they must hold fast against a surely withering fire. This defining moment indelibly marks them as both black and soldiers. The scene is a prayer meeting around their campfires where in classic, revival-style, black call-and-response mode, each of the principals testifies and prays for courage. The churched and the unchurched, the Boston sophisticates and the folkish runaways, the calming older men and the rebellious firebrands all testify, pray with simple eloquence, and brace one another's courage. It is this mood we find embedded in the differentiated faces, the purposeful stride, and the ordered ranks on Boston Common, with Shaw clearly in their midst but not entirely *of* them. This, rather than the eventually repulsed assault on Battery Wagner, is the true climax of *Glory*. It is something that Saint-Gaudens would have wished if statues could move and speak.

At the onset of their charge across the open ground, the density of the layers of their identities is clear. They are marching under both the American flag and the guidon of the all-black Fifty-fourth. They are both a force in themselves and larger than themselves: they are Africans, Americans, ex-slaves, avengers, soldiers—and men. We see this complexity in the character of the soldier who has been whipped for his absence in search of shoes. He has been whipped both by slavemasters and by soldiers in the blue uniform he is wearing. Together these men belong to a white tribe that by its seeming nature has done harm to his black tribe. Yet he must choose one over the other and not only die in the charge across the beach but also with his last breath take up the flag from a fallen comrade. Thus, their cadenced march across the sands at the quick, beautifully shot and edited as it was, is but the denouement of the prayerful sequence that came before. It is a demonstration of what we already know the troops to have become.

We can see all of this affirmed in Tri-Star's companion film, *The True Story of Glory Continues* (1996). At the very top of the short film, Morgan Freeman's raspy-timbred voice asserts that after the Emancipation Proclamation the United States was "on the side of angels." The camera is panning over a Victorian library that we are to take as Lincoln's study, as Freeman points up the drift from "Union forever" as a slogan to "The Battle Cry of Freedom." The filmmakers want us to know that theirs has been a meditation on actual history, even though in fictional terms. They show us their out-takes, perhaps to see why they cut often powerful images from the release print, among them Douglass's recruiting speech in Syracuse.

Have I ended by arguing a century after Saint-Gaudens that a movie shown in a darkened theater is the medium of choice for memorializing our most cherished sentiments? I suppose so. The most American of art forms, "the movies," with their mingling of art, industry, and commerce, do seem to be our preferred public art. This is to diminish neither Saint-Gaudens nor his age, but only to recognize that our public art emerges from a reproducible industrial culture and a resulting taste culture. Its icons are as unique as, say, Picasso's *Guernica,* yet as numberless as Andy Warhol's Campbell's soup cans. The movies that derive from this milieu of popular culture, in which history seems a barely tolerated art form, need offer us not authenticity but only a veneer of credibility grounded in plausible details that testify to its "reality." One of my most persistent memories dates from forty-five years ago during the ordeal of basic training with the 101st Airborne Division. We were shown an abridged print of MGM's *Battleground* (1949), which celebrated the 101st's role in the Battle of the Bulge, Hitler's last futile campaign in World War II. Its potted history was meant to stir many of us to volunteer for jump-school, and it was successful. I imagine that Cecil B. DeMille's *Ten Commandments* (1923 and 1956), an annually rerun epic, fulfills a similar purpose of seeking a cohesive community in the hyperindividuated late-twentieth-century America.

In much the same way, Joe Rosenthal's Pulitzer Prize–winning photograph of the Marines raising a flag atop Mount Suribachi at the height of the Iwo Jima campaign and Howard Peaslee's Marine Corps War Memorial at the Quantico Marine base, which was inspired by Rosenthal's photograph, are indeed touching homages to heroism. But *The Sands of Iwo Jima* (1949) by B-movie director Alan Dwan, starring John Wayne, during its last half-century of reruns has surely touched millions more Americans than the distinguished works of Rosenthal and Peaslee have.

These last images suggest that American culture at the onset of a new millennium is woven of strands of high culture and popular culture that had once seemed incompatible. Consider that Rosenthal's photograph was created in the heat of combat; Peaslee's sculpture followed from it; but Dwan's movie, because of its endless life cycle of reruns and inexpensive videocassettes, provided the prism through which millions of viewers annually turned over in their minds' eyes the meanings of World War II. Perhaps also this need for some image drawn from life inspired veterans of Vietnam to protest the cold abstraction of Maya Lin's memorial and to demand some graspable image. The result was

Frederick Hart's companion sculpture, which now stands with Lin's geometric black slab. Her angular planes inscribed with the names of the American dead memorialize our loss of them, but Hart's three soldiers march in rumpled, mud-caked uniforms, gaunt faces incapable of celebrating their war; nevertheless, all three, like Saint-Gaudens's Fifty-fourth, lean forward into their stride. It is as though the rhythmic figures express the truth of the war in Vietnam while at the same time mourning the saddest of American wars. In this sense, the two monuments seem linked to each other as Saint-Gaudens's Fifty-fourth and Fields and Zwick's *Glory* are linked: the former speaking to a public that embraced the high culture of Boston, the latter spreading its sentiments to a new audience of millions for whom movies are their iconic agency. The German philosopher Walter Benjamin viewed this merger of unique art and mass-produced art with some dismay. The singular work of art "has a presence in time and space, a unique existence at the place where it happens to be," thereby becoming, he wrote, "inseparable from its being embedded in the fabric of tradition." But he worried that mass art diminished the aura of art. *Glory,* by its example, however, invites us to think about the one through the eye of the other.[20]

CATHY STANTON AND STEPHEN BELYEA

"THEIR TIME WILL YET COME"

The African American Presence
in Civil War Reenactment

As the sun rose on May 31, the camp began to stir. The cooks built up crackling hardwood fires, and fresh coffee became the first thing in every soldier's mind. The men happily visited the cookhouse for a warm cup, instead of using the precious ration each one jealously carried in his haversack.

The major was up with cup in hand to greet the men. "Good morning, lads," he said. "Well, this is the day we've been planning for two years. I want to thank you for being here, for traveling so far to be in Boston."

The sergeant major, saluting the major, handed him the morning reports. "Sir!" he barked. "All of the companies have reported, sir."

Just over a mile away at the State House, work crews finished the last details of the platform where the dignitaries would review the troops and address the crowds. The platform, so tall that men had to climb into the trees and tie back the branches, commanded the corner of Park and Beacon Streets. Anxious cleaning and polishing left the parade route and Boston Common sparkling.

At nine o'clock the regimental adjutant carried the national colors to the center of the parade ground in the middle of the encampment. The first sergeants gave the call to fall in. As each company formed and marched into place, the colors moved to the center. After a flawless inspection and drill, the major gave the last instructions for the day. "Men, you see around you the largest body of black soldiers yet assembled. We are all here for one reason: to remember those brave men that history has all but forgotten. It is your commitment and pride that everyone will see."

The march to the State House began at Park Square, where the regiment formed, turned right, and stepped off. It proceeded through the downtown business district, and when it turned onto Washington Street, the thunder of drums froze shoppers in place as rank after rank of soldiers passed. Filled with pride and a sense of mission, the blue-clad columns of men advanced past City Hall and turned onto Trem-

ont Street. Once on Tremont, the major sent back the order to look sharp. Now the time had come. The color sergeants unfurled the flags in the brisk, warm breeze. Spotless brass glittered in the sun. The men pulled and straightened their equipment as the officers dressed the ranks.

From the start, the major had been at the head of the column. It seemed strange to him that a white man should lead this martial parade of black soldiers. Yet he knew that he had the trust of the men and that he would not let them down. "Lord," he said, "so much planning, so much work. Please let me do what I need to do." Turning back, he looked at the long blue lines. "What a sight!" he thought. "I am so fortunate to be here."

As the regiment resumed its march up Park Street toward Beacon, the major could see that both sides of the street and the expanse of lawn before the State House had filled with people. "Head of the column to the left!" he called, and the men of the Fifty-fourth Massachusetts Volunteer Infantry turned the corner in front of the State House. The crowd drew one long breath and then broke into cheers.

The officers of the regiment, swords drawn, saluted the dignitaries as they passed the platform. The soldiers, ramrod straight, marched on. Following close behind, a column of cavalry tightened their formation, their horses straining at the bit. The black cavalrymen sat proudly in their saddles, sabers at the ready.

The soldiers moved into the small space in front of the platform. This would be the test of whether the men had mastered the drill. Each company commander gave the order "Countermarch by files left," and the battalion turned and doubled back. The swelling crowd had pushed into the street, leaving less room than the major had anticipated. He knew the formation needed every foot of space. "Just a few more feet," he thought. As he gave the order "Battalion, halt!" 150 pairs of leather brogans took a last step in unison. "Front, order arms, parade rest!" The men pivoted their muskets to the left; officers dropped the points of their swords, and all was quiet.

Time had come full circle. Before the platform stood two hundred men and women in nineteenth-century military and civilian dress, juxtaposed with the twentieth-century dignitaries. Behind the platform loomed the timeless Saint-Gaudens bronze image of the Fifty-fourth's black soldiers and their young colonel, who had marched through these very streets more than 130 years earlier.[1]

I N RECENT years, historical reenactors have become a familiar feature on the commemorative landscape. Yet their motives baffle many who encounter them. Why, spectators often wonder, would anyone want to relive anything as agonizing as the American Civil War—or any war? What prompts reenactors' sometimes fanatical devotion to "authenticity?" What happens when reenactment touches on still unresolved tensions over regionalism, gender roles, and, of course, race? Why do black reenactors choose to revisit an era when blacks' claims to citizenship and even humanity were rejected by most white Americans? This essay addresses the questions of motivation, identity, and interpretation raised by the African American presence in the Civil War reenactor community.

In adopting Civil War personas, black reenactors, like their historical models in the Fifty-fourth Massachusetts Regiment and elsewhere, enter a field originally claimed by and for whites. They play their Civil War roles only temporarily: the war always ends when the weekend is over. But their reenactment experiences can tell us a great deal about the present state of race relations in America. We explore here how the

Troops passing in review before General Powell at the monument to Shaw and the Fifty-fourth, 1997. Courtesy National Park Service.

black minority's experience of reenactment compares with the white majority's and consider the phenomenon of reenactment as a complex response to the many social changes of the past half-century. Although our central focus is on questions of race, this study of African Americans in reenactment also reveals more general contemporary patterns in Americans' changing relationship to their past.

ROOTS OF REENACTMENT

Although modern Civil War reenactment has developed only since the Civil War centennial of the 1960s, amateur performers have represented the war in different ways ever since the guns stopped firing. Scholars of this type of cultural performance have shown that, far from being mere reflections of "real-life" circumstances, these performances constitute dynamic moments when social relationships are negotiated and renegotiated, often with significant consequences for the cultures that produce them.[2] The various forms of Civil War reenactment, then, can reveal a great deal about changing views of the war and changing American social conditions.

The first "reenactments" of the Civil War were by the veterans themselves, and the first such large-scale public performance was the Grand Review in Washington, D.C., in May 1865, marking the Union victory. At this two-day parade of Union regiments, federal officials continued their wartime discrimination against black regiments, excluding them from participation. The few blacks who were included were either presented as little more than laborers or as individuals exploited for comic relief. As Stuart McConnell reports, "Two large black soldiers . . . for example, were displayed 'riding on very small mules, their feet nearly touching the ground.'" "Contraband" (escaped slaves) included in the Grand Review were dressed in outlandish clothes, many also riding mules. Some observers commented on the absence of the black units, and one journalist with the *Philadelphia Inquirer* concluded that "by some process it was arranged that none of them should be here. . . . They can afford to wait. Their time will yet come."[3]

That time did not come in the remaining years of the nineteenth century, the period of the veterans' greatest activity in commemorating the war. Some radical members of the Grand Army of the Republic (GAR), the leading association of Union veterans, did advocate for the rights of black veterans within the organization, and activists like Frederick Douglass spoke occasionally at GAR encampments and meetings. But nearly all GAR posts were segregated by race, and black veterans who applied to white posts for membership were routinely rejected.

As one study of the GAR observed, "the same wave of reconciliation sentiment that was inspiring Blue-Gray reunions and Confederate veterans' homes in 1890 was also heightening GAR ambivalence about race relations." Veterans who regarded a thorough reconstruction of the South and black suffrage as their wartime legacy did not feel obliged to support "social equality" in the North. Although many supported some version of political equality, most still adhered to the color line outside of politics.[4]

Many white veterans in the North and South believed that the social upheavals of the late nineteenth century threatened the values they had fought for in the war. The strongly conservative, nativist flavor of all veterans' activities—Union and Confederate—overwhelmed any lingering sectional tensions. In this atmosphere, black challenges from within their own organizations were particularly unwelcome to white veterans.

Nonetheless, discussion of race did find its way into veterans' activities. A heated debate over whether segregated posts should be official policy dominated the 1891 GAR national encampment. The color line continued to be upheld in practice although disclaimed officially. But the issue attracted national attention and caused an unusual airing of differing views on race within the GAR. One of those views, which would reappear among modern black and white reenactors, centered on the belief that shared military service could supersede racial divisions. Insisting that veterans should not adopt the segregation prevalent in churches, schools, and other fraternal organizations, former GAR commander William Warner maintained that these "are matters of sociability. Comrades, when these black or white men, or whatever color or nationality they may have been, shouldered the musket in defense of the Union, it was not a question of etiquette, a question of sociability. It was a question of patriotism and loyalty." But such social change was more symbolic than actual. Blacks remained on the fringes of official white veterans' activities. Moreover, their presence in the historical record of the Civil War continued to be provocative and troubling for many whites who sought to portray the war through commemoration and performance.[5]

PAGEANTS

Unease over race was also evident in American pageantry, a hugely popular form of public performance in the first two decades of the twentieth century. Historical pageants often featured episodes that linked local and national histories and tended to reflect many Americans' buoyant belief in progress. Although the Civil War was a frequent subject in pageant scenes, battle recreations were less common than vignettes of camp or home-front life. Rarer still were episodes dealing with the causes of the war or with black Americans' role in it. There were exceptions. A 1913 pageant in Newburyport, Massachusetts, featured four floats devoted to African American and abolitionist history. A Springfield, Massachusetts, pageant of 1908 included black Civil War veterans reenacting the assault on Battery Wagner. One observer speculated that the pageant revealed a "glimpse of America of the future which is to come out of this mingling of races and race-ideals."[6]

But this optimistic assessment of the American melting pot would not be successfully sustained. Many white pageant organizers, whether liberal or conservative, remained ambivalent about racial equality or disheartened by the failed promises of emancipation and Reconstruction. Like the organizers of the Grand Review in 1865, most pageant organizers found it easier to rely on stock comic black figures in pageants or to ignore African Americans completely. The result, clearly, was to widen the gap between black and white life in America. The gigantic 1914 pageant celebrating Saint Louis's 150th anniversary, for example, "sharpened the differences between black and white residents" and contributed to the adoption of legal segregation in the city two years later.[7]

Some black performers and organizers responded to blacks' virtual exclusion from social or popular pageantry by orchestrating their own pageants. W.E.B. Du Bois, contending that "the American Pageant Association has been silent, if not actually contemptuous, of efforts to use pageantry as black folk drama," wrote and directed "The Star of Ethiopia," a black history pageant that premiered in 1913 as part of the NAACP's celebration of the fiftieth anniversary of the Emancipation Proclamation. But this event was also an exception. In general, pageantry remained a white form of cultural expression that ignored African Americans and helped erase the black contribution to American history from popular white consciousness.[8]

CONTEMPORARY REENACTMENT

The same racial cultural patterns held true for the modern phenomenon of Civil War reenactment, which originated in the "heritage phenomenon" following World War II.[9] Civil War roundtables, battlefield tourism, and black powder weapons clubs all gained popularity during this period when many middle-class Americans became historical pilgrims in search of some authentic sense of connection with the nation's past.

The Civil War centennial in 1961–65 was the catalyst for a new kind of cultural performance. Wearing makeshift Civil War uniforms, enthusiastic amateur performers (including National Guardsmen and members of black powder clubs such as the North-South Skirmish Association) joined to recreate Civil War battles. Despite the official disapproval of the National Park Service, which expressed concern over safety and historical accuracy, and a tapering off of interest after the Civil War centennial, the nucleus of a Civil War reenactment community formed in those years.

Activity within this community remained sporadic during the next decade. Few Americans could find pleasure in mock battles while the nation fought a costly and troubling real war in Vietnam. Not until after the Vietnam era did interest in recreational reenactment revive, and then the Revolutionary War bicentennial, not the Civil War, provided the focus. During the bicentennial years of 1976–81, experienced reenactors were joined by younger men, who had come of age after World War II. That important generational shift has, to a large extent, shaped contemporary reenactment.

As in the Civil War centennial, the younger generation of reenactors was almost entirely male and white. One author of this essay, who joined the reenactment community in the 1970s, recalls encountering only one bicentennial-era black reenactor, a man who portrayed a freedman in a British infantry regiment. Ethnic and feminist challenges to traditional versions of American history had not fully penetrated popular American historical consciousness, and reenactors still presented the past as a tale of white men's deeds.

With the end of the bicentennial in 1981, many reenactors turned their attention to the Civil War. Most of the structures and practices of the Civil War reenacting community developed during the cycle of large battle reenactments staged to commemorate the 125th anniversary of the war in 1986–91. Civil War encampments are now staged across the country (and also outside it) throughout the year, with reenactor attendance ranging from two or three people to more than ten thousand. Some events are organized by reenactors; for others, they are recruited and sometimes paid a fee by event organizers, which often include historical societies or other civic groups. Film producers, schools, and museums also increasingly make use of reenactors' unique form of "edutainment" in their own presentations of history.[10]

The Influence of *Glory*

Although Civil War reenactment remains primarily a white male activity, the 1990s saw significant changes in the reenactor population.

Women, in both combat and noncombatant roles, have added female perspectives to the depictions of Civil War reenactments. Since the popularizing of the story of the Fifty-fourth Massachusetts in the 1989 film *Glory,* black reenactors have joined the reenactment community in increasing numbers. Just as the mobilization of black soldiers late in the Civil War sparked a critical national discussion of race, the recent presence of blacks in the reenactor community has drawn attention to a dimension of the Civil War story that many white reenactors have minimized: the role of race and racism in the conflict.

The African American presence in Civil War reenacting emerged almost entirely from the making of *Glory.* Like the makers of previous Civil War movies, the film's producers recruited a number of white reenactors to serve as skilled extras. But since nearly no experienced black reenactors existed at that time, film producers raised four companies to portray the enlisted men of the Fifty-fourth Massachusetts.[11] Just as the Civil War centennial gave birth to modern reenactment, *Glory* became the driving force for a distinctly African American element in reenacting.

Currently, five companies of the Fifty-fourth Massachusetts Regiment have been organized, joined by about ten companies of other black Civil War–era units. The meeting of past and present creates an unusual internal dynamic in these units. Until very late in the Civil War, no black commissioned officers existed in the Union army. But in today's black reenactment regiments, African Americans have assumed leadership both in founding and running the organizations. This result is a dual level of leadership in which white "officers" take charge on stage but have either equal or subordinate roles when the units are offstage. This dual leadership—performative and administrative—often operates in white units as well. The factor of race, however, makes it a necessity in African American units, requiring all members of these groups to accept the paradox of "followers" who lead and "leaders" who must follow.

It is important to emphasize that the "integration" of the reenactor community takes place in varying degrees and at different levels. Both black and white reenactors find their most intense experiences of camaraderie within their own units. This fact, along with the historical separation of black and white regiments, means that blacks and whites may camp near one another at reenactments and take to the field at the same time, but they experience little interchange on the field. At small, low-key events, there may be more intermingling, even to the extent of black and white reenactors "fighting" side by side, in defiance of historical precedent.[12] At larger or more tightly scripted events, historical

Reenactors fire muskets in battalion formation, 1997. Courtesy National Park Service.

Civilian reenactors at the Centennial Celebration of the monument to Shaw and the Fifty-fourth, 1997. Courtesy National Park Service.

conventions are usually more closely observed, for reasons of both accuracy and preference. For instance, at the annual February reenactment of Florida's Battle of Olustee, where the Fifty-fourth Massachusetts and the Eighth U.S. Colored Troops played critical roles, large numbers of black reenactors participate. They camp together to follow the historical model and have become more closely acquainted over the years as a result. In all cases, "integration" is complicated by the need to simulate nineteenth-century race relations and by the tendency of the closest reenactor relationships (as in the military) to form within units rather than between members of different units.

Striving for historical accuracy creates additional challenges and new opportunities for contemporary reenactors. A small number of reenactors portray both slaves and free blacks who fought for the Confederacy; another handful are beginning to choose roles as "contraband" or other civilians. As with white reenactor groups, women in black units are finding new roles. In Boston's Company A of the Fifty-fourth Massachusetts, a group of women organized originally during the Shaw/Fifty-fourth Centennial Celebration now reenact as the Colored Ladies' Baptist Relief Society. During the 1997 event, the two hundred black Civil War reenactors from around the country who encamped at Charlesbank Park on Boston's Charles River Esplanade represented about 85 percent of all black reenactors in the United States. The gathering led to new discussions about the broader organization of black units within the Civil War reenactment community. It is precisely this point—black reenactors' search for a place within the larger Civil War community and the country's historical consciousness—that reveals some of the most important findings of this study and helps illuminate the ways in which Americans continue to struggle with the legacy of the Civil War.

Perceptions of the Past and Present

Before the 1960s American history was generally taught and understood as a chronicle of the actions of white men. Despite the work of pioneering historians like W.E.B. DuBois, George W. Williams, Herbert Aptheker, Bell Irwin Wiley, Benjamin Quarles, and others, there was little public awareness of the active role that African Americans had played in the Civil War. During the 1960s ethnic minorities, feminists, and liberal historians challenged American structures of power in both social and scholarly domains. The ferment of social change produced radical new interpretations of the past, along with new critiques of the "traditional" values upheld in older versions of American history.

The most striking difference between black and white reenactors can be seen in their responses to this "new" history. For blacks, recent trends in the writing of history have meant the recovery or discovery of a past that had been largely lost to them. As one Fifty-fourth Massachusetts reenactor recalled, "When I went to school I was never taught any black history, any whatsoever. That was quite a few years ago; I am 51 now. I think a lot of it was recorded but it was swept away someplace after it was recorded. That is the way this country has always been." Other black reenactors' statements echo this sense of rediscovery and a feeling of mission—even obligation—about reclaiming their lost history. "There is a whole segment of our ancestors, coming out of slavery, that is totally missing," one man said. Another added, "I don't think that the real men got their due. Thanks to the reenactors they have risen the awareness of black participation in the Civil War. Within the last ten years there has been a proliferation of books on this subject. Before this you could hardly find anything. We are bringing to the forefront the accomplishments, the achievements of these men that have gone largely unrecognized." Many black reenactors clearly sense the psychic costs of their unrecognized legacy. One woman stated, "We [African Americans] have a very low self-esteem already. Knowing who you are and having a foundation, knowing that you have a wonderful history, makes you a stronger person. It helps you identify and be proud of what your race can do." Another woman wondered, "How can you feel good about anything if you don't know your history? If you don't have a true history, you cannot have anything. We don't have a true history." Many black reenactors also recognize that these gaps in history have affected white Americans as well as blacks. As one man in a Fifty-fourth Massachusetts company remarked, "It is important . . . to know that blacks were not passive observers, all slaves waiting to be emancipated. This is an impression that most of the public have, both blacks and whites. . . . It is equally important when dealing with the public, when working with people of European descent or African descent to get that same message out. Although they may have a different perspective the message is the same and it is important."

White reenactors' response to the "new" history is more complex. If black reenactors see themselves as leading a charge to capture a lost heritage, many white reenactors believe they are fighting a rearguard action on the contested field of American history. This is not to imply that all white reenactors are overtly hostile to more inclusive versions of history, although some undoubtedly are. It is far more common to encounter white reenactors who accept or even applaud the inclusion of new voices in the historical record but who nonetheless cannot let go of older images of the past because those images played such an important role in the shaping of the reenactors' own ideals and identities. White reenactors possess a highly ambivalent attitude toward contemporary historical scholarship. They welcome the new insofar as it supports what they loved about the old: the heroism of the citizen-soldier; the unquestioned goodness of the nation; the virtues of self-reliance, capitalism, and democracy that they see illustrated in the traditional story of the American past. Tension arises, however, when newer versions of history contest those values, leaving their very truthfulness in doubt.

Some white reenactors respond to these vexed issues directly, usually by vehement denials that race was a central factor leading to the Civil War. Another strategy—one that may explain reenactors' fascination for the minutiae of historical presentation—is to move the whole subject of the war to a materially oriented, value-free framework, where the debate over hand- versus machine-sewn buttonholes becomes more important than that of right versus wrong. No matter how they feel about recent challenges to traditional visions of American history and values, many reenactors search for unassailable ways to express those visions, even if it means reducing historical discussion to microscopic levels of detail. As one white male reenactor expressed his desire for a value-free history, "I think that our systems try to apologize for what we've done and who we are and what made us what we are, instead of just saying, 'This is what happened, this is what they were thinking, may have been right or wrong, let's not make a judgment today on what they did.' If we want to teach ethics, that's another course. But to teach history, it's facts. . . . They try to take a slant on it now."

African American reenactors present no threat to the reenactment community's view of itself or of American history so long as they are depicting qualities such as gallantry, loyalty, martial decorum, and other "bedrock" values. But when black reenactors' presence or discourse brings questions of race and morality to the fore, they inevitably disturb a community that prefers to avoid such issues and interpretations. The general acceptance of black reenactors in the community suggests that those "bedrock" values are shared across race lines. But blacks also meet with occasional hostility, and certainly with widespread wariness, from their white counterparts. No matter how compatible they may be in many ways, they still represent moral and social dilemmas that most white reenactors have tried to expunge from their depictions of the Civil War.

Black reenactors sometimes exhibit their own ambivalence about the social shifts of the past half-century. Some blacks (particularly the few who have recently begun to portray Confederate soldiers) may themselves be looking for a history free of the troubling need to make judgments about the moral meaning of slavery and the Civil War. In general, though, African American reenactors embrace these meanings, whereas white reenactors tend to avoid them. The "new history" offers blacks an ever-increasing sense of support and validation; for white reenactors, that sense of being fully supported by the historical record is more a fond memory than a reality. As Jim Cullen has suggested in his discussion of how white reenactors use the Civil War story to express traditional visions of American society, many seem to fear

> that in this increasingly diverse society, events such as the Civil War (which so many European Americans hold near and dear to their hearts, and in which they have such personal, familial, or assimilationist interests) may become less relevant. In this light, reenacting becomes a ritual . . . by which a majoritarian United States reassures itself that it, too, has a past, and that that past is as dramatic, interesting, and important as the alternative, multicultural pasts that are increasingly competing with it. . . . [The] Civil War has become a banner around which millions can rally, a point of reference that can shore up a center that fears it may not hold.[13]

White reenactors, then, no matter how supportive they are of the ideal of inclusion, often feel that it is accomplished at the expense of the history they love. Blacks, meanwhile, sense that the *Philadelphia Inquirer's* prophecy after the exclusion of African American troops from the 1865 Grand Review is on the verge of fulfillment—"Their time will yet come."

Gender Identity and Reenacting

Despite the considerable number of women who participate in Civil War reenactment, the spirit of the community is essentially masculine. One female reenactor, content in her support role as a civilian, admitted, "It's a guys' thing . . . it's male-driven, it's male-dominated, it's male-oriented." It is over questions of gender identity that black and white reenactors, no matter what their other differences, most readily find common ground.

Of all the challenges to "traditional" American structures and values in recent decades, the challenge to definitions of masculinity is perhaps the one that Civil War reenactors feel most keenly. One reenactor explained part of the reenactment appeal by confessing that

> the white Anglo-Saxon male of today really doesn't know what he's supposed to be. Society says one thing, families say another, the media says another, his significant other says another. I think a lot of the younger

guys, young to middle-aged guys, are just looking for a simpler day, to where they can go out and not feel guilty about, you know, being quote-unquote "a man." . . . One of the things that's missing in today's society is there are no codes of conduct. Do you hold the door open for a lady? Well, you take a risk when you do.

An ex-Marine, when asked how it felt when a contemporary woman refused a male's offer of protection or support, replied: "Doesn't matter: protect and defend you we will. And if you resent it we're profoundly confused and put off. . . . Refusing the proffered protection from a man is to partially emasculate him."

The reenactors quoted above are white. But it is clear that black male reenactors share with their white comrades an intense appreciation of the masculine camaraderie found in reenacting. "I think that reenacting is a male thing, not a black thing or a white thing," said one black member of a Fifty-fourth Massachusetts company. The idea of "being a man" runs through the comments of reenactors of both races. "Comradeship between the men is most important. That is the way it was back then, especially with the black soldiers," remarked another Fifty-fourth Massachusetts reenactor. Speaking of Civil War soldiers in general, a white reenactor felt that "[to enlist] was what was right, and to be a man that's what you did, and you did it and that was that." The same individual explained his own military service by saying, "There's pride and there's duty, and I served my time, and my father did, and his father did, and my mother's father did, and it just goes right down the line." A black combat veteran explicitly connected his own military service with his identification with Civil War soldiers: "By the time you get to boot camp and once you're in the Marines for a while, you have this built-in pride and this built-in idea of respect for other Marines, and you love being with other Marines. . . . And I can kind of relate that back to the 54th because they had a common bond, a common respect."

For many adult male reenactors, mentoring younger men is an adjunct to the idea of "being a man." Those who see military or paramilitary experiences as valuable rites of passage take their roles as mentors and advisers to younger reenactors with utmost seriousness. "Kids today need somebody to look up to, somebody who is a hero in your life," one black Fifty-fourth Massachusetts reenactor commented, adding that Civil War soldiers could provide those heroes. And many adult male reenactors also see themselves, if not as heroes, then at least as models who may help to point a young man in the right direction.

Just as men and women of post–World War II generations are caught

Encampment of black troops at the Boston Esplanade during the Centennial
Celebration of the monument to Shaw and the Fifty-fourth, 1997.
Courtesy National Park Service.

between older and newer definitions of American identity, men of these
same generations are uneasy about changing definitions of manhood.
Many white males feel strongly that they are being made to shoulder
blame for everything now perceived as wrong in American history. But
black men, too, especially those who identify strongly with military
roles and models, may have similar difficulties in absorbing the effects
of feminism in public and private life. Both black and white male reenactors find relief in being able—if only on occasional weekends—to
present themselves as soldiers, patriots, rebels, protectors, or gentlemen without having to worry who may be offended. An unapologetic
masculinity is central to Civil War reenactment.

A comparison of the reception of African Americans within the reenactment community and reenactors' response to women who choose
roles as disguised Civil War soldiers best illustrates the centrality of
masculinity to historical reenactment. White reenactors may resist
attempts to make race central to the story of the Civil War, but there
has been no overt challenge to blacks' right to take the field. Despite
hearing occasional hostile remarks masked as "authentic" nineteenth-

century speech, "most of what I have experienced has been positive," one member of a black unit affirmed. "We have been respected."

By contrast, women who choose combat roles have provoked a heated, decade-long debate—punctuated by occasional lawsuits—that is far from resolved. Many female reenactors do take the field in uniform, with varying degrees of credibility, but their presence can be a very sore point with men who resent the invasion of one of the last male refuges. "When women are present, the differences are subtle but there nonetheless," wrote a columnist for *Camp Chase Gazette*, Civil War reenacting's monthly magazine. "It puts a finger smear onto our window into the past."[14] White reenactors who may be uncomfortable or hostile about sharing a camp with blacks are clearly reluctant to say so publicly, but there has been no such reluctance in airing opinions about women in the ranks.

A black woman who put forward the idea of wearing a uniform within a company of the Fifty-fourth Massachusetts quickly discovered how jealously male reenactors guard the soldier role for themselves. "I wanted to be a soldier," she said. "I wanted to tote a gun. And they were really freaking out! . . . I wanted to play that role, because I'm a tomboy at heart, and I'm very comfortable in that role. And they're like, 'Oh, no, no, no, no, no!'" This woman eventually found a less controversial place for herself as a civilian reenactor. In this role, she and her female comrades now find that "We're not a threat. And that's what [the men in the unit] say to us, that we've added to them, we've brought attention to them, recognition to them, by doing our own separate thing and not competing, not wanting to be them. . . . We complement them. We're not trying to take over their roles."

If some social changes of the past fifty years divide black and white reenactors, others—particularly those involving gender—seem to unify the races. (Indeed, some female reenactors also seek relief from the confusion of shifting modern gender roles. Women, like men, often describe reenacting as a way to step temporarily into more clearly defined patterns of social behavior.) Those who initiated Civil War reenactment in the early 1960s were, perhaps, able to be more straightforward in their presentation of "traditional" roles and values. Or perhaps even then the stirrings of change prompted many men to find refuge in performed versions of American history and masculinity. By the time "baby boomers" began to reenact in the 1970s and 1980s, tension over cultural definitions of gender had become a fact of everyday life. Some Civil War reenactors successfully negotiate this tension in their "real" lives. For others, it is more problematic. But it seems fair to say that virtually all, black and white, feel a sense of connection to traditional definitions of masculinity and share a need to incorporate those definitions—at least symbolically—into their images of themselves.

Military Service

Perceptions of history most vividly divide black and white reenactors, and expressions of gender identity most strikingly unite them, but the subject of military service generates both unity and division and is, perhaps, more typical of the unresolved state of American race relations.

Both black and white reenactors enter into Civil War reenactment's military atmosphere and the idealization of the American citizen-soldier. Many reenactors of both races are children of World War II veterans; they are saddened by the dissonance between their early positive images of the American soldier and their own coming of age during the Vietnam era. Most male reenactors entered young adulthood willing to go to war if their country called them, only to find their sense of duty deeply shaken during the 1960s and 1970s. Many found ways to avoid military service, and even those who did serve could not maintain unambivalent patriotism in the face of the troubling realities of the Vietnam War. One black Marine Corps veteran, who now reenacts as a member of the Fifty-fourth Massachusetts, revealed that, at least initially, "I felt strongly that if we were [in Vietnam], there was a reason for us to be there." In hindsight, though, he believes, "we should either have went in there and fought the war the way we know how to fight a war or we should not have been in it at all. And I lean more toward maybe we should not have been in it at all."

For these baby boomers, reenacting the Civil War provides a positive vicarious experience of war and military service. It is one that gives reenactors connections to comrades and country of the kind that their fathers' generation had during World War II, without the soul-searching that accompanied the nation's foray into Southeast Asia. The idea that reenactment rehabilitates or substitutes for real-life military experience can be heard in both general and specific comments from reenactors. One black member of a Fifty-fourth Massachusetts company addressed the relationship between Vietnam and Civil War reenactment.

> You know, a lot of the guys in the [reenacted] 54th were in the service, but the Civil War thing really, like, woke them up. See, a lot of them didn't believe in the Vietnam era type thing—now they don't, anyway. But the Civil War thing, once they touch bases with it, it glues them to it and they just can't stop. . . . And I don't understand what that means, but I just think the Civil War has much more, something going for the

people, in my opinion, than Vietnam. Because Vietnam I think was somebody else's war.

Reenactors frequently draw the parallel between their hobby and the experience of real military service. "The camaraderie that you find in the real military, the closest I've come to finding it in the outside world is in reenacting, without a doubt," said an ex-military man who commands a Confederate unit. One young woman who had served with the Air Force agreed: "After six years in the military I find the atmosphere very, very similar. It has nothing to do with the fact that they're doing military roles. It has a lot to do with the fact that you all go out there and you suffer together." In this light, the heavy wool clothing, physical labor, and occasional foul weather that make up a large part of a reenacting weekend can be seen—as the actual military is seen by many—as a test of character and resourcefulness leading to strong bonds among those who share in it.[15] Instead of taking place in the context of an ambiguous foreign intervention, Civil War reenactment offers an idealized, home-grown struggle. In it reenactors can find American courage and gallantry on both sides, set in a danger-free context and framed by a narrative made comfortingly clear by nearly a century and a half of hindsight.

For many blacks and whites, reenactment is a substitute for the "good war" they grew up believing it would someday be their duty to take part in. Reenactment offers a chance for a reaffirmation of the citizen-soldier role and a way to combine that role with other elements of identity based on race, gender, regionalism, or ideology. For some, reenactment functions as a kind of symbolic veterans association, providing an outlet for stories and emotions that are difficult to share elsewhere. One black combat veteran, seriously wounded in Vietnam nearly thirty years ago, confessed:

> I never talked about the war when I got home. I wouldn't even talk to my kids when they asked me questions. . . . Only recently did I start talking about what went on in Vietnam. One night around the fire at a Civil War event with the 54th, we were talking about what went on during the day. . . . Before I knew it, I was drawing a connection to when I was in the service and I was telling the men, young and old, what had happened. They wanted to hear my story and I knew these guys, so the stuff that I held onto for so long came out.

In many ways, both idealism and disillusionment about military service can act as powerful bonds between black and white reenactors. But there are additional layers to black experiences in the American military that make the subject more complex. As the saga of the Fifty-fourth Massachusetts illustrates so clearly, blacks, like other ethnic minorities in the United States, have historically used military service as a means to gain full citizenship. That their efforts have not always been successful, and that racism persists despite their sacrifices, makes these soldiers more viscerally aware of the shortcomings in the system they are being asked to defend with their lives.

During the Vietnam era, those shortcomings were highlighted by antiwar activists and others who focused on American racism at home and abroad. Not only were blacks underrepresented in American public life, these critics pointed out, but they were also overrepresented among the soldiers sent into combat. And once overseas, those soldiers had to grapple with questions of ethnic alliances no less troubling than those they had left at home. One black Civil War reenactor and combat veteran remembered, "When I was in Vietnam and we would come into a village, the dark-skinned Vietnamese would come up to me and other black soldiers and point to his skin and then to mine and say, 'Lookee, lookee, same, same.'" Black American soldiers traditionally have had to fight the additional enemy of American racism, and it is this that lends a unique quality to black reenactors' portrayal of Civil War soldiers. Black baby boomers, like black Civil War soldiers, know how it feels to be caught between the desire to participate fully in traditions of manhood and the awareness that American structures of power have been arrayed against them. When they become "glued" to the subject of the Civil War, they pay homage to pioneers in an unfinished struggle, an element missing from white reenactors' depictions of the war.[16]

FROM THE 1865 Grand Review in Washington to the 1989 filming of Glory—and the subsequent decade of black participation in Civil War reenactment—enormous changes have occurred in the nation's perception of the black role in the Civil War. In Civil War–related public commemorations and historical reenactments, exclusion and ridicule are no longer the rule. As one woman in a Fifty-fourth Massachusetts reenactor group concluded, "We have now come to a point where we are comfortable with saying, 'Your ancestor was a slave holder and mine was a slave.' That's okay. We can accept that today. We now can talk openly about these things, where before we couldn't. We have gained a kind of comfort level." More complex, however, is the question of how this comfort level has been achieved. Black participation and acceptance into the world of Civil War reenactment has not been a simple linear move. Many lines of identity continue to be crossed and recrossed to create the place that African American reenactors occupy in this once all-white and still conservative community.

Members of Companies A and B, Fifty-fourth Massachusetts Regiment, at the monument to Shaw and the Fifty-fourth, 1997. Courtesy National Park Service.

Like all cultural performances, Civil War reenactment both reflects and negotiates the society's social struggles. When we consider the life experiences of contemporary reenactors, black and white, clearly their depiction of the Civil War is a response to World War II, Vietnam, and other contemporary social transformations that have shaped their lives. This response leads in two divergent directions. Disillusioned by Vietnam and recalling the patriotic certainties of their childhoods, reenactors remain in search of the "good war," with its intense camaraderie and unambiguous righteousness. At the same time, only the most determined escapists among them can block out the awareness that America never has been as moral as they all once believed. Through performance—a medium ideally suited to the acting out of paradox and multiple realities—reenactors search for heroes and certainties in a culture that has come to admit the limitations of both.

African American reenactors share these nostalgic needs with whites and find common ground in a personal quest for moral certainty in the past. Like their white counterparts, they use reenactment as a respite from the many complexities of modern life. Both white and black reenactors celebrate the citizen-soldier tradition, search for personal and family "roots" in the story of the Civil War, and share the camaraderie achieved through camping and performance. The "male bonding" within this hypermasculine, paramilitary environment often creates alliances that cross race lines. Ironically, it is a common ambivalence about social change—the effects of feminism or rapidly changing technology in everyday life—that helped make the racial integration of this largely white, conservative community possible.

But the African American presence in that community also raises unwelcome questions about the meaning of the Civil War and American definitions of freedom. What can we conclude from the fact that despite the tension caused by those questions, black reenactors generally have been accepted and respected by their white counterparts? First, for the majority of black and white reenactors, the need to discover and embody a heroic, "true" history may be stronger than the need to resolve vexed questions about race. In other words, within the community race is reduced to just one of many related factors that motivate reenactors. Second, the acceptance of black Civil War reenactors reflects a level of awareness among white reenactors—an awareness shaped during their youths in the 1960s and 70s—that no matter how one may wish it otherwise, no depiction of America can be complete without including those voices that challenge received accounts of the past. African American reenactors, then, serve as a conscience for the community, sometimes welcomed, sometimes resisted, but always in ways that resonate on some level with the white majority.

Civil War reenactment helps to facilitate a popular recasting and reintegration of the past in several important ways. The story of the Civil War itself is rich in the history of the struggle for racial equality. But for those who do not see race as central to the conflict, the story also offers ways to celebrate the valor of the American citizen-soldier, a figure honored by blacks and whites. Even reenactors who disagree about the meaning of the war can find themselves portraying it together. Through this medium, African Americans become contributors to a well-loved story and in the process gain a hearing for their demands for social justice. The inclusion of blacks in the Civil War reenactment community over the past decade not only has created a more accurate popular view of the Civil War but also has stimulated a reassessment of personal and national identity that will play an important part in the reenvisioning of America in the century to come.

NOTES

Foreword, by General Colin L. Powell

This foreword is based on an address General Powell delivered in Boston on May 31, 1997, at the Centennial Celebration of the Augustus Saint-Gaudens monument to Robert Gould Shaw and the Fifty-fourth Massachusetts Regiment.

1. Hal Goldman, "Black Citizenship and Military Self-Presentation in Antebellum Massachusetts," *Historical Journal of Massachusetts* 25 (summer 1997): 169 n. 29.

2. Ervin L. Jordan Jr., *Black Confederates and Afro-Yankees in Civil War Virginia* (Charlottesville: University Press of Virginia, 1995), 235.

3. Benjamin Quarles, *Frederick Douglass* (New York: Atheneum, 1968), 209.

4. Sergeant Major Lewis H. Douglass (1840–1908) joined the Fifty-fourth on March 25, 1863, and reached Battery Wagner's parapet in the fateful attack on July 18. Frederick Douglass's other son, Charles R. Douglass (1844–1920), trained in the Fifty-fourth but did not accompany the unit to South Carolina. He transferred to the Fifth Massachusetts Cavalry and served briefly in southern Maryland before his discharge for illness in 1864. John W. Blassingame et al., eds., *The Frederick Douglass Papers*, ser. 1, *Speeches, Debates and Interviews*, 5 vols. to date (New Haven, Conn.: Yale University Press, 1979–92), 3:586–87, 4:279 n. 1; Luis F. Emilio, *A Brave Black Regiment: History of the 54th Regiment of Massachusetts Volunteer Infantry, 1863–1865* (Boston: Boston Book Company, 1891), 339, 364; William S. McFeely, *Frederick Douglass* (New York: Norton, 1991), 103, 224–25, 230.

5. Quoting Confederate general Johnson Hagood. Emilio, *Brave Black Regiment*, 99.

6. Total Union casualties in the battle were 1,515; the Fifty-fourth lost 281 men including those killed, wounded, and captured. The Confederate defenders sustained only 181 casualties in the battle. Francis G. Shaw's letter to General Quincy A. Gillmore, commander of Union forces in South Carolina, is in Emilio, *Brave Black Regiment*, 102–3; for casualty figures, see 90–91, 392. Edwin Redkey places the Fifty-fourth's losses at 284.

7. The lyrics of this song appeared in the *Boston Transcript*, June 2, 1863.

Introduction

1. Frederick Douglass, "Men of Color, to Arms!" March 2, 1863, in *The Oxford Frederick Douglass Reader*, ed. William L. Andrews (New York: Oxford University Press, 1996), 225.

2. T. S. Eliot, "The Hollow Men," in *Collected Poems, 1909–1962* (New York: Harcourt, Brace, and World, 1970), 81–82.

3. William James to Henry James, June 5, 1897, in *The Correspondence of William James*, ed. Ignas K. Skrupskelis and Elizabeth M. Berkeley, 6 vols. to date (Charlottesville: University Press of Virginia, 1992–), 3:9.

4. Ralph Ellison, introduction to *Invisible Man*, 30th anniv. ed. (New York: Random House, 1982), xvii.

5. George William Curtis, "The Flag," *Harper's Weekly*, June 13, 1863, 371; Ralph Waldo Emerson, "Voluntaries," *Atlantic Monthly*, October 1863, 504–6; James Russell Lowell, "Memoriæ Positum: R.G.S, 1863," *Atlantic Monthly*, January 1864, 88–90; Lydia Maria Child, "A Tribute to Colonel Robert Gould Shaw," *New York Evening Post*, reprinted in *Memorial R.G.S.* (Cambridge, Mass.: University Press, 1864), 119–22; Francis Parkman dedicated *Pioneers of France in the New World* (Boston, 1865) to Shaw and two other kinsmen slain in the war.

6. Lewis Carroll, *Through the Looking-Glass and What Alice Found There* (London, 1872; reprint, New York: Random House, 1946), 73.

Citizenship in Black Boston at Midcentury, by James Oliver Horton

I would like to thank Lois E. Horton, Sabette Pitcaithley, Anthony Rotundo, Kate Stevenson, and Stephanie Batiste-Bentham for their timely, direct, and most helpful criticism of this article during its formative stages. Gayle Wald, Phyllis Palmer, and Denise Meringolo helped in my interpretation of the race and gender dimensions of nineteenth-century literature.

1. Quoted in James Oliver Horton and Lois E. Horton, *Black Bostonians: Family Life and Community Struggle in the Antebellum North*, 2d ed. (New York: Holmes and Meier Publishers, 1999), 127.

2. Don E. Fehrenbacher, *The Dred Scott Case: Its Significance in American Law and Politics* (New York: Oxford University Press, 1978).

3. Moncure Daniel Conway, *Testimonies concerning Slavery* (London: Chapman and Hall, 1864), 28–30.

4. Philip S. Foner and George E. Walker, eds., *Proceedings of the Black State Conventions, 1840–1865*, 2 vols. (Philadelphia: Temple University Press, 1979), 1:327.

5. Linda K. Kerber, "The Paradox of Women's Citizenship in the Early Republic: The Case of Martin vs. Massachusetts, 1805," *American Historical Review* 97 (April 1992): 349–78, quotation on 351.

6. Kerber, "The Paradox of Women's Citizenship," 349–78, 351.

7. For a discussion of African American rights in the Northern states, see James Oliver Horton and Lois E. Horton, *In Hope of Liberty: Culture, Community, and Protest among Northern Free Blacks, 1700–1860* (New York: Oxford University Press, 1997). Taney's opinion in the Dred Scott decision raised legal questions about the Massachusetts practice of providing blacks with documents indicating their citizenship, but the practice was not challenged in the

court before the Fourteenth Amendment to the Constitution made the question moot.

8. Phyllis F. Field, *The Politics of Race in New York* (Ithaca, N.Y.: Cornell University Press, 1982); Leonard P. Curry, *The Free Black in Urban America, 1800–1850: The Shadow of the Dream* (Chicago: University of Chicago Press, 1981); Paul Finkelman, "Prelude to the Fourteenth Amendment: Black Legal Rights in the Antebellum North," *Rutgers Law Journal* 17, nos. 3, 4 (spring–summer 1986): 415–82.

9. Field, *Politics of Race,* 37. Under New York's first constitution, the property requirements for voting were a $50 freehold to vote for a congressman and a $250 freehold to vote for a senator or a governor.

10. Horton and Horton, *In Hope of Liberty,* 101–24.

11. Horton and Horton, *Black Bostonians,* 125–38.

12. See George M. Fredrickson, *The Black Image in the White Mind: The Debate on Afro-American Character and Destiny, 1817–1914* (New York: Harper and Row, 1971).

13. Thomas Jefferson was not as likely to describe blacks in feminized terms as later apologists for slavery were. He was willing to concede that blacks were "at least as brave as whites" and "more Adventuresome," although he believed that might have resulted from their "want of forethought, which prevents their seeing a danger till it is present." Winthrop D. Jordan, *White over Black: American Attitudes towards the Negro, 1550–1812* (Chapel Hill: University of North Carolina Press, 1968), 436.

14. Larry E. Tise, *Proslavery: A History of the Defense of Slavery in America, 1701–1840* (Athens: University of Georgia Press, 1987). For an important discussion of the evolution of nineteenth-century American racial theory, see Joanne Pope Melish, *Disowning Slavery: Gradual Emancipation and "Race" in New England, 1780–1860* (Ithaca, N.Y.: Cornell University Press, 1998).

15. Eric L. McKitrick, ed., *Slavery Defended: The Views of the Old South* (Englewood Cliffs, N.J.: Prentice-Hall, 1963), 45.

16. McKitrick, *Slavery Defended,* 44.

17. McKitrick, *Slavery Defended,* 37.

18. Fredrickson, *Black Image in the White Mind,* 111. For a literary analysis of Stow's use of race and gender, see Myra Jehlen, "The Family Militant: Domesticity v. Slavery in Uncle Tom's Cabin," *Criticism* 31 (fall 1989): 383–400; Eric Sundquist, *New Essays on Uncle Tom's Cabin* (New York: Cambridge University Press, 1986).

19. As quoted in Fredrickson, *Black Image in the White Mind,* 117–18.

20. Harriet Beecher Stowe, "Sojourner Truth, the Libyan Sibyl," *Atlantic Monthly* 2 (April 1863): 473–81.

21. Carleton Mabee, *Sojourner Truth: Slave, Prophet, Legend* (New York: New York University Press, 1993), 76; Nell Irvin Painter, *Sojourner Truth: A Life, a Symbol* (New York: W. W. Norton, 1996), 125.

22. Theodore Parker, "A Sermon on Slavery," in Francis P. Cobbe, ed., *The Works of Theodore Parker,* 15 vols. (London, 1863–70), 5:4. Abolitionist Mon-

cure Daniel Conway openly advocated intermarriage as a means of taming the Anglo-Saxon spirit. See George M. Fredrickson, *The Inner Civil War: Northern Intellectuals and the Crisis of the Union* (New York: Harper and Row, 1965).

23. Thomas Wentworth Higginson, "The Ordeal by Battle," *Atlantic Monthly* 8 (July 1861): 94. For Higginson's later views on black soldiers, see Thomas Wentworth Higginson, *Army Life in a Black Regiment* (Boston, 1870; reprint, Boston: Beacon Press, 1962).

24. Theodore Tilton, *The Negro: A Speech at Cooper Institute, New York, May 12, 1863* (New York: American Anti-Slavery Society, 1863), 11–12.

25. Marilyn Richardson, ed., *Maria W. Stewart, American's First Black Woman Political Writer* (Bloomington: Indiana University Press, 1987), 57, 64.

26. Deborah Gray White, *Arn't I a Woman? Female Slaves in the Plantation South* (New York: W. W. Norton, 1985).

27. Horton and Horton, *Black Bostonians,* 8–13; W. Jeffrey Bolster, *Black Jacks: African American Seamen in the Age of Sail* (Cambridge, Mass.: Harvard University Press, 1997).

28. Horton and Horton, *In Hope of Liberty,* 116.

29. James Oliver Horton, *Free People of Color: Inside the African American Community* (Washington, D.C.: Smithsonian Institution Press, 1993), 108.

30. Horton and Horton, *In Hope of Liberty;* Horton and Horton, *Black Bostonians;* Shirley J. Yee, *Black Women Abolitionists: A Study in Activism, 1828–1860* (Knoxville: University of Tennessee Press, 1992).

31. Horton and Horton, *Black Bostonians,* 107.

32. Horton and Horton, *Black Bostonians,* 74.

33. Wilbur H. Siebert, *The Underground Railroad* (New York: Macmillian, 1898), 246.

34. *Liberator,* November 1, 1850.

35. Horton and Horton, *Black Bostonians,* 135.

36. Quoted in James Oliver Horton and Lois E. Horton, "The Affirmation of Manhood: Black Garrisonians in Antebellum Boston," in Donald M. Jacobs, ed., *Courage and Conscience: Black and White Abolitionists in Boston* (Bloomington: Indiana University Press, 1993), 127–53, quotation on 146.

37. See Gary Collison, *Shadrach Minkins: From Fugitive Slave to Citizen* (Cambridge, Mass.: Harvard University Press, 1997); Horton and Horton, *Black Bostonians,* 111–23, quotation on 112.

38. Horton and Horton, *Black Bostonians,* 130–31.

39. John A. Andrew to Edwin M. Stanton, May 15, 1863, in Henry Greenleaf Pearson, *The Life of John A. Andrew: Governor of Massachusetts, 1861–1865,* 2 vols. (Boston: Houghton, Mifflin, 1904), 2:74–75.

40. *Liberator,* March 12, 1858.

Profile of the Fifty-fourth Massachusetts Regiment, by Edwin S. Redkey

The author gratefully acknowledges research grants from the American Philosophical Society and the National Endowment for the Humanities. Much of the research on which this essay is based was conducted during my year as a Scholar in Residence at the Schomburg Center for Research in Black Culture.

1. Luis F. Emilio, *A Brave Black Regiment: History of the Fifty-Fourth Massachusetts Volunteer Infantry, 1863–1865*, 2d ed. (Boston: Boston Book Company, 1894).

2. The most relevant records in the National Archives are the compiled service records, RG 94; descriptive rolls and regimental books, Fifty-fourth Massachusetts Regiment, RG 94; and pension records, RG 15. This essay is founded on my research in these materials for a larger study of the Fifty-fourth.

3. *War of the Rebellion . . . Official Records of the Union and Confederate Armies*, 128 vols. (Washington, D.C.: Adjutant General's Office, 1880–1901), ser. 3, 3:45 (hereafter *OR*).

4. The nationwide recruiting network created by Stearns continued to enlist blacks after the Fifty-fourth was filled. The Fifty-fifth Massachusetts Infantry and the Fifth Cavalry, along with the Fourteenth Rhode Island Heavy Artillery and the Twenty-ninth Connecticut Infantry, shared the same broad base as the Fifty-fourth. After the summer of 1863, other Northern states created their own black regiments that more closely reflected statewide populations, plus what freed slaves they could recruit. By the end of the war, Southern ex-slaves composed most African American regiments.

5. Technically, "Fort Wagner" was constructed as a battery, not a fort. Confederates referred to "Battery Wagner," but in Union reports it was usually "Fort Wagner." The officers and men of the Fifty-fourth consistently called it a fort, and most writers ever since have followed their example. I will do the same.

6. Russell Duncan, ed., *Blue-Eyed Child of Fortune: The Civil War Letters of Colonel Robert Gould Shaw* (Athens: University of Georgia Press, 1992), 319; Emilio, *Brave Black Regiment*, 19–20.

7. Bell Irvin Wiley, *The Life of Billy Yank, the Common Soldier of the Union* (Baton Rouge: Louisiana State University Press, 1952), 303.

8. See James Oliver Horton and Lois E. Horton, *In Hope of Liberty: Culture, Community, and Protest among Northern Free Blacks, 1700–1860* (New York: Oxford University Press, 1997), chap. 5.

9. *OR*, ser. 3, 2:513–20.

10. U.S. War Department, *U.S. Infantry Tactics for the Instruction, Exercise & Manoeuvres of the Soldier . . . For the Use of Colored Troops of the United States Infantry* (New York: D. Van Nostrand, 1863), 15.

11. *OR*, ser. 1, vol. 28, pt. 1:362.

12. Accurate casualty figures for the Civil War are notoriously difficult to produce; battle reports and official histories differ widely in their counts of the killed, wounded, and missing men of the Fifty-fourth. The numbers reported here result from a careful study of the regimental and individual records, both service and pension files. The counts, especially for the attack on Fort Wagner, may seem low compared to the common belief. For example, James M. McPherson, in *Battle Cry of Freedom* (New York: Oxford University Press, 1988), 686, reported that the Fifty-fourth "lost nearly half its men" at Fort Wagner.

But that casualty estimate includes those wounded and missing as well as those killed or mortally wounded. Furthermore, according to Colonel Hallowell, only 600 men of the Fifty-fourth made the charge, not the full regiment. The missing 400 included camp guards and sick men left at Saint Helena Island, the wounded from James Island, and a work detail unloading supplies on Morris Island. Hallowell reported that the enlisted men suffered 256 casualties at Fort Wagner. The statistics given in Captain Emilio's book counted the regiment's total casualties at Fort Wagner as 281 killed, wounded, and missing. My count shows 284 casualties that night. The differences in these numbers result from using different sources, applying different categories of injury, and calculating errors. However they are counted, indeed nearly half the men who attacked the fort became casualties. *Brave Black Regiment,* 75, 91, 392.

13. Affidavit of F. R. Livingston and E. Groomer, pension file of Thomas Jackson. See also Eric T. Dean, *Shook over Hell: Post-Traumatic Stress, Vietnam and the Civil War* (Cambridge, Mass.: Harvard University Press, 1997), esp. chap. 6.

The Pay Crisis and the "Lincoln Despotism," by Donald Yacovone

1. This essay is based on my *Voice of Thunder: The Civil War Letters of George E. Stephens* (Urbana: University of Illinois Press, 1997). I want to thank the press for its generous permission to reproduce material from the book in this essay. I also wish to thank my coeditors and my wife, Cory Burke Yacovone, for their helpful criticism.

2. The best biography of Andrew remains Henry Greenleaf Pearson, *The Life of John A. Andrew, Governor of Massachusetts, 1861–65,* 2 vols. (Boston: Houghton, Mifflin, 1904), and the fullest treatment of the regiment is still Luis F. Emilio, *A Brave Black Regiment: History of the Fifty-Fourth Regiment of Massachusetts Volunteer Infantry, 1863–1865,* 2d ed. (Boston: Boston Book Company, 1894).

3. W. W. H. Davis, *History of the 104th Pennsylvania Regiment* (Philadelphia: W. W. H. Davis, 1866), 182; *Anglo African* quoted in C. Peter Ripley et al., eds., *The Black Abolitionist Papers,* 5 vols. (Chapel Hill: University of North Carolina Press, 1985–1992), 3:59.

4. Ira Berlin et al., eds, *Freedom: A Documentary History of Emancipation, 1861–1867,* ser. 2, *The Black Military Experience* (Cambridge, Eng.: Cambridge University Press, 1982), 362–64; Herman Belz, "Law, Politics, and Race in the Struggle for Equal Pay during the Civil War," *Civil War History* 22 (September 1976): 197–213.

5. George E. Stephens to Robert Hamilton, August 1, 1864, in Yacovone, *A Voice of Thunder,* 321.

6. George E. Stephens to Robert Hamilton, August 7, 1863; August 1, 1864, in *A Voice of Thunder,* 252–54, 320; *New York Tribune,* September 8, 1865, quoted in Emilio, *A Brave Black Regiment,* xii. Few white regiments, the *Tribune* stated, "would have born it for a month."

7. Robert Gould Shaw to John A. Andrew, March 31, 1863; July 2, 1863; Edward L. Pierce to John A. Andrew, August 3, 1863, Executive Department letters, Massachusetts State Archives.

8. Richard H. L. Jewett to Eliza Nutting Jewett, August 9, 1863, Richard H. L. Jewett papers, Boston Athenæum; Sergeant Frederick Johnson to John A. Andrew, August 10, September 4, 1863; John Mercer Langston to John A. Andrew, June 28, 1863, Executive Department letters, Massachusetts State Archives; Emilio, *A Brave Black Regiment*, 351. Andrew's response to Langston's letter appears in William Schouler, *Adjutant General's Report* . . . (Boston: State of Massachusetts, 1864), 66–72.

9. Mrs. L. A. Grimes to John A. Andrew, n.d., Mary E. Clark to John A. Andrew, November 15, 1863; John Murray Forbes et al., to John A. Andrew, November 11, 1863, Executive Department letters, Massachusetts State Archives.

10. John Ritchie's journal, September 27, 1863, *New York Tribune*, September 29, 1863, in 54th Massachusetts Regiment papers, 1:262, Massachusetts Historical Society; Luis F. Emilio diary, September 29, 30, 1863, Philip and Betty Emilio family collection (privately held).

11. George E. Stephens to Thomas Hamilton, October 3, 1863, in Yacovone, *A Voice of Thunder*, 278–80.

12. George E. Stephens to Thomas Hamilton, October 3, 1863, in Yacovone, *A Voice of Thunder*, 278–80, 282.

13. Luis F. Emilio diary notes, October 31, 1863, in 54th Massachusetts Regiment papers, 2:n.p., Massachusetts Historical Society; Edward N. Hallowell to Albert G. Browne Jr., August 2, 1863, Executive Department letters, Massachusetts State Archives; Lieutenant Colonel Henry Lee Jr. to John A. Andrew, September 18, 1863, John A. Andrew papers, Massachusetts Historical Society.

14. Recollections of Alfred S. Hartwell, n.d., Alfred S. Hartwell papers, Hawaii State Archives; John A. Andrew to Quincy A. Gillmore, December 3, 1863, Edward W. Kinsley papers, Duke University; John Whittier Messer Appleton letter book, December 13, 1863, John Whittier Messer Appleton papers, West Virginia University Library; J. H. Stephenson to John A. Andrew, November 20, 1863; Edward N. Hallowell to John A. Andrew, November 23, 1863, Executive Department letters, Massachusetts State Archives; Luis F. Emilio diary, December 12, 1863, Philip and Betty Emilio family collection.

15. *War of the Rebellion . . . Official Records of the Union and Confederate Armies*, 128 vols. (Washington, D.C.: Adjutant General's Office, 1880–1901), ser. 1, 28:127–28; *Liberator*, May 20, 1864; George L. Stearns to John A. Andrew, July 30, 1863, Executive Department letters, Massachusetts State Archives; George Washington Williams, *A History of the Negro Troops in the War of the Rebellion, 1861–65* (New York, 1888; reprint, New York: Bergman Publishers, 1968), 120–24, 154–55.

16. Charles B. Fox, letter extracts, August 14, 1863, Charles B. Fox papers, Massachusetts Historical Society; William H. Dupree and Charles L. Mitchell to Burt G. Wilder, April 12, 1909, Burt G. Wilder papers, Cornell University.

17. John A. Andrew memo, December 5, 1863; Norwood P. Hallowell to John A. Andrew, December 7, 1863; H. Ware to Robert R. Corson, December 5, 1863; N. P. Cowell to John A. Andrew, May 4, 1864, Executive Department letters, Massachusetts State Archives.

18. J. H. Stephenson to Dr. Le Baron Russell, January 26, 1864, Edward W. Kinsley papers, Duke University; "Fort Green" to Editor, August 21, 1864, in *Christian Recorder*, September 24, 1864; George E. Stephens to Robert Hamilton, May 26, 1864, in Yacovone, *A Voice of Thunder*, 304–12.

19. Charles Sumner to Francis W. Bird, February 22, 1864, Charles Sumner papers, Houghton Library, Harvard University; George E. Stephens to Robert Hamilton, March 6, 1864, in Yacovone, *A Voice of Thunder*, 298–300.

20. "Picket" to Henry Highland Garnet, June 30, 1864, in *New York Weekly Anglo-African*, July 30, 1864; *New York Weekly Anglo-African*, April 30; July 16, 30, 1864; 55th Massachusetts Regiment, orderly books, RG 94, National Archives; Edward N. Hallowell to Aurora, December 25, 1864, Hallowell papers, Haverford College.

21. *Liberator*, April 8, 1864; Charles B. Fox letter extracts, April 28, 1864, Charles B. Fox papers, Massachusetts Historical Society; Edward N. Hallowell to Luis F. Emilio, [?] 1864, 54th Massachusetts Regiment papers, vol. 4, Massachusetts Historical Society; Howard C. Westwood, *Black Troops, White Commanders, and Freedmen during the Civil War* (Carbondale: Southern Illinois University Press, 1992), 142–66.

22. Howard C. Westwood, "The Cause and Consequence of a Union Black Soldier's Mutiny and Execution," *Civil War History* 31 (September 1985): 222–27, 233, quoting Andrew; George E. Stephens to Robert Hamilton, March 6, 1864, in Yacovone, *A Voice of Thunder*, 299.

23. John Whittier Messer Appleton letter books, April 12, 1864, 210, John Whittier Messer Appleton papers, West Virginia University Library; Luis F. Emilio diary notes, April 26, 1864, 54th Massachusetts Regiment papers, vol. 2:n.p., Massachusetts Historical Society.

24. John Whittier Messer Appleton letter book, April 18, 1864, in 54th Massachusetts Regiment papers, vol. 2:n.p., Massachusetts Historical Society.

25. Luis F. Emilio to his father, April 29, 1864, Philip and Betty Emilio family collection; Samuel Harrison to Robert Hamilton, April 14, 1864, in *New York Weekly Anglo-African*, April 23, 1864; *New York Weekly Anglo-African*, May 7, 1864; Anonymous to John A. Andrew, March 25, 1864, Executive Department letters, Massachusetts State Archives; Thomas D. Freeman to William Freeman, March 26, 1864, Thomas D. Freeman to Martha, April 25, 1864, typescript copies, American Antiquarian Society.

26. An anonymous sergeant to Elijah Weaver, May 29, 1864, in *Christian Recorder*, June 25, 1864; Alfred S. Hartwell, "Recollections," ms., Alfred S. Hartwell papers, Hawaii State Archives; typescript notes, June 12, 1864, Charles B. Fox letter book, Burt G. Wilder papers, Cornell University.

27. Frederick Douglass, *The Life and Times of Frederick Douglass* (1881, 1892; reprint, New York: Collier Books, 1962), 346–48, quoting Lincoln; George Hale to John A. Andrew, May 29, 1864, John A. Andrew to George W.

Smally, February 22, 1864, Executive Department letters, Massachusetts State Archives, quoting Andrew.

28. *New York Weekly Anglo-African,* August 13, 27, 1864; Ripley et al., *Black Abolitionist Papers,* 3:65.

29. Berlin et al., *The Black Military Experience,* 398–402, quotation on 402; "Bay State" [55th Mass.] to Robert Hamilton, April 10, 1864, *New York Weekly Anglo-African,* April 30, 1864.

30. 55th Massachusetts Regiment descriptive book, Company I, RG 94, National Archives. Details of this account are from the documentation in Baker's and Henry Way's court-martial trials, RG 153, National Archives.

31. Wallace Baker Court Martial, RG 153, National Archives; 55th Massachusetts Regiment orderly books, Company I, RG 94, National Archives.

32. General Order No. 43, Alfred S. Hartwell, in 55th Massachusetts Regiment orderly books, RG 94, National Archives; George Thompson Garrison diary extracts, June 19, 1864, *New York Daily News,* June 27, 1864, in notes of Luis F. Emilio, in 55th Massachusetts Volunteer Infantry Association of Officers records, box 1, Massachusetts Historical Society; "Picket" to Henry Highland Garnet, June 30, 1864, in *New York Weekly Anglo-African,* July 30, 1864; George E. Stephens to Robert Hamilton, June 18, 1864, in Yacovone, *A Voice of Thunder,* 316–18.

33. Hartwell is quoted in his letter of May 10, 1864, in 54th Massachusetts Regiment papers, 1:549, Massachusetts Historical Society; Charles B. Fox diary, June 18, 1864, vol. 2, Charles B. Fox papers, Massachusetts Historical Society; Thomas Appleton journal notes, June 18, 1864, George Thompson Garrison diary extracts, June 1864, 55th Massachusetts Volunteer Infantry Association of Officers records, box 1, Massachusetts Historical Society; 55th Massachusetts Regiment orderly books, RG 94, National Archives; Schouler, *Adjutant General's Report* (1866), 566.

34. George E. Stephens to Robert Hamilton, August 1, 1864, in Yacovone, *A Voice of Thunder,* 320.

35. Norwood P. Hallowell to John A. Andrew, May 17, 1864, Executive Department letters, Massachusetts State Archives.

36. John Whittier Messer Appleton letter book, May 12, 1864, 223, John Whittier Messer Appleton papers, West Virginia University Library; John Ritchie journal, May 12, 1864, in 54th Massachusetts Regiment papers, vol. 2:n.p., Massachusetts Historical Society; Richard H. L. Jewett, May 14, 1864, Richard H. L. Jewett papers, Boston Athenæum.

37. John Whittier Messer Appleton letter book, May 19, 1864, 226–27, John Whittier Messer Appleton papers, West Virginia University Library; John Whittier Messer Appleton papers, May 19, 1864, John Ritchie journal, May 21, 1864, in 54th Massachusetts Regiment papers, vol. 2:n.p., Massachusetts Historical Society.

38. Edward N. Hallowell to John A. Andrew, June 4, 1864, 54th Regiment letter book, RG 94, National Archives; Edward N. Hallowell to H. Ware, May 28, 1864, Executive Department letters, Massachusetts State Archives.

39. J. H. Hall to Elijah Weaver, August 3, 1864, in *Christian Recorder,* Au-

gust 27, 1864; J. H. B. D. to Elijah Weaver, May 24, 1864, in *Christian Recorder*, June 11, 1864; Isaac White to John A. Andrew, July 31, 1864, Executive Department letters, Massachusetts State Archives.

40. John Whittier Messer Appleton letter book, n.d., 281, John Whittier Messer Appleton papers, West Virginia University Library; J. Gregory Smith to John A. Andrew, April 25, 1864, James Freeman Clarke to John A. Andrew, June 27, 1864, Union League of New York petition, n.d., Executive Department letters, Massachusetts State Archives.

41. John A. Andrew to Edward W. Kinsley, April 25, 1864, newspaper clipping, Edward W. Kinsley papers, Duke University; John A. Andrew to Charles Sumner, February 16, 1864, John A. Andrew to Abraham Lincoln, May 27, 1864, Executive Department letters, Massachusetts State Archives.

42. Charles Sumner to John A. Andrew, Sunday 1864; Charles Sumner to John A. Andrew, June 18, 1864, Executive Department letters, Massachusetts State Archives; Charles Sumner to Thomas Wentworth Higginson, June 22, 1864, in Beverly Wilson Palmer, ed., *The Selected Letters of Charles Sumner*, 2 vols. (Boston: Northeastern University Press, 1990), 2:245–46.

43. The first quotation is in Lewis Hayden to Alfred S. Hartwell, May 17, 1864, Alfred S. Hartwell papers, Massachusetts State Library; Albert G. Browne Jr. to Luis F. Emilio, April 26, 1864, Philip and Betty Emilio family collection; Alexander Price to Ambrose E. Burnside, November 2, 1864, Edward W. Kinsley papers, Duke University; Kinsley quotation in Edward W. Kinsley to William Logan, July 19, August 10, 1864, Edward W. Kinsley collection, letter book, box 1, Moorland-Spingarn Research Center, Howard University; *Liberator*, May 20, 1864.

44. Berlin et al., *The Black Military Experience*, 367; Charles Sumner to John A. Andrew, Sunday 1864, Executive Department letters, Massachusetts State Archives.

45. John Ritchie journal, August 31, 1864, in 54th Massachusetts Regiment papers, vol. 3:n.p., Massachusetts Historical Society; typescript notes, Charles B. Fox letter book, August 23, 1864, Burt G. Wilder papers, Cornell University; Berlin et al., *The Black Military Experience*, 368.

46. *New York Tribune*, November 17, 1864; *New York Weekly Anglo-African*, December 3, 1864; *Christian Recorder*, November 12, 1864; Luis F. Emilio diary notes, September 29, 1864; John Ritchie journal, October 5, 1864, 54th Massachusetts Regiment papers, vol. 3:n.p., Massachusetts Historical Society; James Monroe Trotter to Edward W. Kinsley, November 21, 1864, Edward W. Kinsley papers, Duke University; untitled typescript song, October 16, 1864, Burt G. Wilder papers, Cornell University.

The Shaw Family and the Fifty-fourth Massachusetts Regiment, by Joan Waugh

This essay is based on Joan Waugh, *Unsentimental Reformer: The Life of Josephine Shaw Lowell* (Boston: Harvard University Press, 1997). I would like to

thank Donald Yacovone, Thomas J. Brown, and Martin H. Blatt for their helpful criticism.

1. Quotation from Edward Waldo Emerson, *The Life and Letters of Charles
Russell Lowell* (Boston: Houghton, Mifflin, 1907), 288–89, emphasis mine.

2. Quotation from Henry James, ed., *The Letters of William James,* 2 vols.
(Boston: Atlantic Monthly Press, 1920), 2:60; Robert Hughes, "American Re-
naissance Man," *Time,* January 13, 1986, 68; Burke Wilkinson, *Uncommon
Clay: The Life and Works of Augustus Saint Gaudens* (San Diego: Harcourt
Brace Jovanovich, 1985), 59.

3. Richard Watson Gilder, "To Mrs. Francis George Shaw," January 23, 1903,
in Shaw Family Letters, Boston Athenæum. A selected example of literature
reflecting the idealistic view of the family includes Thomas W. Higginson,
Edward T. Atkinson, and William A. Coffin, "The Shaw Memorial and the
Sculptor St. Gaudens," *Century Magazine,* May 1897, 176–200; William James,
"Robert Gould Shaw," in *Memories and Studies* (London: Longmans, Green,
1911), 37–61; Richard Benson and Lincoln Kirstein, *Lay This Laurel: An Al-
bum on the Saint-Gaudens Memorial on Boston Common, Honoring Black
and White Men Together Who Served the Union Cause with Robert Gould
Shaw and Died with Him July 18, 1863* (New York: Eakins Press, 1973); Luis
F. Emilio, *A Brave Black Regiment: History of the Fifty-fourth Regiment of
Massachusetts Volunteer Infantry, 1863–1865* (Boston, 1894; reprint, New
York: Arno Press, 1969); James Russell Lowell, "Memoriæ Positum: R.G.S,
1863," *Atlantic Monthly,* January 1864, 88–90; Robert Lowell, "For the Union
Dead, 'Relinquunt Omnia Servare Rem Publicam,'" in *Life Studies and For
the Union Dead* (New York: Farrar, Straus, and Giroux, 1964), 70–72; *The Mon-
ument to Robert Gould Shaw: Its Inception, Completion, and Unveiling,
1865–1897* (Boston: Houghton, Mifflin, 1897); Robert T. Teamoh, *Sketch of the
Life and Death of Col. Robert Gould Shaw* (Boston: Grandison and Son, 1904);
Robert Penn Warren, *Legacy of the Civil War: Meditations on the Centennial*
(New York: Random House, 1961), 81–82. Two recent works include Ludwig
Lauerhauss Jr., "Beyond Glory: How the Homeric Vision of Augustus Saint-
Gaudens Expressed in His Boston Common Memorial to Civil War Colonel
Robert Gould Shaw and His African American Soldiers of the Fifty-Fourth
Massachusetts Regiment Inspired the Century-Long March of an American
Epic" (1996), in Waugh's possession; an abridged version of this essay was pub-
lished as "The Shaw Memorial in American Culture," in *The Shaw Memorial:
A Celebration of an American Masterpiece* (Ft. Washington, Pa.: Eastern Na-
tional, 1997), 47–68; Edward Zwick and Marshall Herskovitz, *Glory* (Los
Angeles: Tri-Star Productions, 1989).

4. Robert Gould Shaw to Sarah Blake Shaw, November 18, 1856, Robert
Gould Shaw Papers, Houghton Library, Harvard University. The revisionist in-
terpretation of Robert Gould Shaw and the Shaw family is found in the follow-
ing works: Albert Boime, *The Art of Exclusion: Representing Blacks in the
Nineteenth Century* (Washington, D.C.: Smithsonian Institution Press, 1990);
Peter Burchard, *One Gallant Rush: Robert Gould Shaw and His Brave Black*

Regiment (New York: St. Martin's Press, 1965); Russell Duncan, ed., *Blue-Eyed Child of Fortune: The Civil War Letters of Colonel Robert Gould Shaw* (Athens: University of Georgia Press, 1992); Russell Duncan, *Where Death and Glory Meet: Colonel Robert Gould Shaw and the 54th Massachusetts Infantry* (Athens: University of George Press, 1999); George M. Fredrickson, *The Inner Civil War: Northern Intellectuals and the Crisis of the Union* (New York: Harper and Row, 1965); Lewis P. Simpson, *Mind and the American Civil War: A Meditation on Lost Causes* (Baton Rouge: Louisiana State University Press, 1989); Stephen J. Whitfield, "'Sacred in History and Art': The Shaw Memorial," *New England Quarterly* 60 (March 1987): 3–37; Donald Yacovone, ed., *A Voice of Thunder: The Civil War Letters of George E. Stephens* (Urbana: University of Illinois Press, 1997).

5. Sarah Shaw quoted in Adelaide Weinberg, *John Elliot Cairnes and the American Civil War: A Study in Anglo-American Relations* (London: Kingswood Press, 1969), 167; Duncan, *Blue-Eyed Child of Fortune*, xxi–xxiii.

6. Henry Lee Higginson, quoted in Bliss Perry, *Life and Letters of Henry Lee Higginson* (Boston: Atlantic Monthly Press, 1921), 531.

7. Simpson, *Mind and the American Civil War*, 68; Sarah Shaw quoted in Otto Friedrich, *Clover* (New York: Simon and Schuster, 1979), 68; Duncan, *Blue-Eyed Child of Fortune*, xv. Every scholar of the Shaw family owes a debt of gratitude to Russell Duncan for his superb editing of Robert Gould Shaw's letters and for his informative introduction. I differ, however, with his interpretation of the relationship between Frank and Sarah and between Rob and his parents.

8. My analysis of gender and family in nineteenth-century America has been shaped by the following works: Ruth H. Bloch, "American Feminine Ideals in Transition: The Rise of the Moral Mother, 1785–1815," *Feminist Studies* 4 (1978): 101–26; Mark C. Carnes and Clyde Griffen, eds., *Meanings for Manhood: Constructions of Masculinity in Victorian America* (Chicago: University of Chicago Press, 1990); Nancy F. Cott, "Passionlessness: An Interpretation of Victorian Sexual Ideology, 1790–1850," *Signs* 4 (1978): 219–36; Carl Degler, *At Odds: Women and Family in America from the Revolution to the Present* (New York: Oxford University Press, 1980); Stephen M. Frank, "'Rendering Aid and Comfort': Images of Fatherhood in the Letters of Civil War Soldiers from Massachusetts and Michigan," *Journal of Social History* 26 (fall 1992): 5–31; Joseph M. Hawes and N. Ray Hiner, *American Childhood: A Research Guide and Historical Handbook* (Westport, Conn.: Greenwood Press, 1985); Mary Lynn et al., eds., *A Century of Childhood 1820–1920* (Rochester, N.Y.: Margaret Woodbury Strong Museum, 1984); Thomas E. Jordan, *Victorian Childhood: Themes and Variations* (Albany: State University of New York Press, 1987); Joseph F. Kett, *Rites of Passage: Adolescence in America 1790 to the Present* (New York: Basic Books, 1977); Karen Lystra, *Searching the Heart: Women, Men, and Romantic Love in Nineteenth-Century America* (New York: Oxford University Press, 1989); Colleen McDannell, *The Christian Home in Victorian America, 1840–1900* (Bloomington: Indiana University Press, 1986); Steven Mintz, *A Prison of Expectations: The Family in Victorian Culture* (New York:

New York University Press, 1983); Jacqueline S. Reinier, *From Virtue to Character: American Childhood, 1775–1850* (New York: Twayne Publishers, 1996); Anne C. Rose, *Victorian America and the Civil War* (New York: Cambridge University Press, 1992); Carroll Smith-Rosenberg, *Disorderly Conduct: Visions of Gender in Victorian America* (New York: Knopf, 1985).

9. Sarah Blake Shaw to Robert Gould Shaw, February 6, 1863, Sarah Blake Shaw Papers, Houghton Library, Harvard University.

10. Francis G. Shaw to Harry Bowditch, undated, Bowditch Memorial Collection, Massachusetts Historical Society; Francis G. Shaw to William Lloyd Garrison, November 4, 1863, William Lloyd Garrison papers, Boston Public Library. I am grateful to Donald Yacovone for bringing these two letters to my attention.

11. The depiction of the Shaw family is taken from chaps. 1–3 of Waugh, *Unsentimental Reformer*. See also Richard Mather Bayles, ed., *History of Richmond County, Staten Island New York, from Its Discovery to the Present Time* (New York: L. E. Preston, 1887); Mary Caroline Crawford, *Famous First Families of Massachusetts*, vol. 1 (Boston: Little, Brown, 1930); Charles Gilbert Hine and William T. Davis, *Legends, Stories, and Folklore of Old Staten Island* (Staten Island, N.Y.: Staten Island Historical Society, 1925); *Memorial Biographies of the New England Historic Genealogical Society*, vol. 2 (Boston: New England Historic Genealogical Society, 1881); Bradford Adams Whittemore, *Memorials of the Massachusetts Society of the Cincinnati* (Boston: Massachusetts Society of the Cincinnati, 1964).

12. A first-person account of Fuller's "mixed" conversations can be found in Caroline Healey Dall, *Margaret and Her Friends or Ten Conversations with Margaret Fuller upon the Mythology of the Greek and Its Expression in Art* (Boston: Roberts Brothers, 1895). For background on Fuller and her circle, see Charles Capper, *Margaret Fuller: An American Romantic Life: The Romantic Years* (New York: Oxford University Press, 1992); Ralph Waldo Emerson, William Henry Channing, and James Freeman Clark, eds., *Memoirs of Margaret Fuller Ossoli*, 2 vols. (Boston: Phillips, Sampson, 1852); Robert Hudspeth, ed., *The Letters of Margaret Fuller*, vol. 4. (Ithaca, N.Y.: Cornell University Press, 1988).

13. As quoted in Mary Caroline Crawford, *Romantic Days in Old Boston* (Boston: Little, Brown, 1910), 13. The Shaws' Brook Farm days have been described in Henry Steel Commager, *Theodore Parker* (Boston: Little, Brown, 1936); Sterling F. Delano, *"The Harbinger" and New England Transcendentalism: A Portrait of Associationism in America* (London: Associated University Presses, 1983); Zoltan Haraszti, *The Idyll of Brook Farm as Revealed by Unpublished Letters in the Boston Public Library* (Boston: Trustees of the Public Library, 1937); Lindsay Swift, *Brook Farm: Its Members, Scholars, and Visitors* (New York: Macmillan, 1900).

14. Josephine Shaw Lowell to Thomas Barwick Lloyd Baker, September 17, 1879, Thomas Barwick Lloyd Baker Records, Gloucestershire County Record Office, Gloucester, Eng.; Louis Ruchames, ed., *The Letters of William Lloyd*

Garrison, vol. 4, *From Disunionism to the Brink of War, 1850–1860* (Cambridge, Mass.: Harvard University Press, 1975), 334–35.

15. Lydia Maria Child to Louisa Gilman Loring, June 24, 1849, and Child to Ellis Gray Loring, December 3, 1849, in Patricia G. Holland and Milton Meltzer, eds., *The Collected Correspondence of Lydia Maria Child 1817–1880* (Millwood, N.Y.: Kraus Microform, 1980), 27/753, 27/766.

16. There is a growing literature on the important link between middle-class female religiosity, social reform movements, and politics in nineteenth-century America. See Norma Basch, "Marriage, Morals, and Politics in the Election of 1828," *Journal of American History* 80 (1993): 890–918; Ann Braude, "Women's History *Is* American Religious History," in Thomas A. Tweed, ed., *Retelling U.S. Religious History* (Berkeley: University of California Press, 1997), 87–107; Lori D. Ginzberg, "'Moral Suasion Is Moral Balderdash': Women, Politics, and Social Activism in the 1850s," *Journal of American History* 73 (1986): 601–22; Daniel W. Howe, "The Evangelical Movement and Political Culture in the North during the Second Party System," *Journal of American History* 77 (1991): 1216–39; Glenna Matthews, "'Little Women' Who Helped Make This Great War," in Gabor S. Boritt, ed., *Why the Civil War Came* (New York: Oxford University Press, 1996), 31–50.

17. Sarah B. Shaw to Charles E. Norton, September 27, 1899, Charles Eliot Norton Papers, Houghton Library, Harvard University. This aspect of feminist marriages is explored in Blanche Glassman Hersh, *The Slavery of Sex: Feminist-Abolitionists in America* (Urbana: University of Illinois Press, 1978). See also Deborah Gold Hansen, *Strained Sisterhood: Gender and Class in the Boston Female Anti-Slavery Society* (Amherst: University of Massachusetts Press, 1993); Laura McCall and Donald Yacovone, eds., *A Shared Experience: Men, Women, and the History of Gender* (New York: New York University Press, 1998); and Jane H. Pease and William H. Pease, *Ladies, Women, and Wenches: Choice and Constraint in Antebellum Charleston and Boston* (Chapel Hill: University of North Carolina Press, 1990).

18. The quotation is in Louisa Lee Schuyler, "Mrs. Lowell's Early Life and Her Connection with the State Charities Aid Association," *Woman's Municipal League Bulletin* 4 (1906): 5. Francis George Shaw, "To the Women of the Boston Anti-Slavery Fair," *Harbinger* 1 (October 4, 1845): 268–76, quotation on 269. Frank Shaw's contributions can be found in volumes 1, 2, 3, 4, and 6 of the *Harbinger*.

19. Elizabeth Gaskell, "Robert Gould Shaw," in *Macmillan's Magazine* 9 (1863): 113–17, quotation from 114. My thanks to Dr. Marianne McLeod Gilchrist for alerting me to Gaskell's article and for sharing her own insights about the Shaw family. Marianne McLeod Gilchrist, "The Shaw Family of Staten Island: Elizabeth Gaskell's American Friends," *Gaskell Society Journal* 9 (1995): 1–12.

20. Gaskell, "Robert Gould Shaw," 113. This type of worry about girls was common. Anne M. Boylan, "Growing Up Female in Young America, 1800–1860," in Hawes and Hiner, *American Childhood*, 153–84. Nineteenth-century parents were particularly concerned about the transmission of their religious

values and beliefs to their children. See Mary Lynn, "Children, Childhood, and Change in America, 1820–1920," in Lynn et al., *A Century of Childhood*, 1–32; Kett, *Rites of Passage*; and Reinier, *From Virtue to Character*.

21. Studies of the differences between the socialization of young men and women in the Victorian age include Jordan, *Victorian Childhood*; Barbara Finklestein and Kathy Vandell, "The Schooling of American Childhood: The Emergence of Learning Communities, 1820–1920," in Lynn et al., *A Century of Childhood*, 65–95; Anne Scott MacLeod, "The Caddie Woodlawn Syndrome: American Girlhood in the Nineteenth Century," in Lynn et al., *A Century of Childhood*, 98–119.

22. Steven Mintz wrote: "We discovered that relations within the Victorian families we studied took on a distinctive pattern of filial rebellion and accommodation. What we found was the filial rebellion directed against a father at the onset of adulthood, far from signaling a lack of identification between family generations, was a vehicle for the transmission and internalization of cultural patterns between generations." Mintz contended that this rebellion was mainly against fathers because they represented the public. But in Shaw's case both of his parents represented the "public" world of reform and religion. Mintz, *A Prison of Expectations*, 196.

23. Robert Gould Shaw to Sarah Blake Shaw, November 5, 1854, Robert Gould Shaw Papers, Houghton Library, Harvard University; *Letters: Robert Gould Shaw* (Cambridge, Mass.: Houghton Library, Harvard University, 1864), 40.

24. *Letters*, 29. Robert Gould Shaw to Josephine Shaw, July 31. 1861, Robert Gould Shaw Papers, Houghton Library, Harvard University.

25. *Letters*, 113.

26. As quoted in Burchard, *One Gallant Rush*, 21.

27. Hine and Davis, *Legends, Stories, and Folklore*, 69–79; "The Riot in Staten Island," *New York Tribune*, July 17, 1863.

28. Charles Eliot Norton, ed., *Orations and Addresses of George William Curtis*, 2 vols. (New York: Harper and Brothers, 1894), 1:15–16. Burchard, *One Gallant Rush*, 24.

29. Robert Gould Shaw to Sarah Blake Shaw, April 18, 1861, Robert Gould Shaw Papers, Houghton Library, Harvard University.

30. As quoted in Henry Greenleaf Pearson, *The Life of John A. Andrew: Governor of Massachusetts, 1861–1865*, 2 vols. (Boston: Houghton Mifflin, 1904), 2:74.

31. Quotations in Pearson, *Life of Andrew*, 2:75. See James M. McPherson, *The Struggle for Equality: Abolitionists and the Negro in the Civil War and Reconstruction* (Princeton, N.J.: Princeton University Press, 1964), for the best account of the abolitionists' role during the war and their efforts to raise black units. The story of the Union's efforts to raise African American regiments can be found in Joseph T. Glatthaar, *Forged in Battle: The Civil War Alliance of Black Soldiers and White Officers* (New York: Penguin Books, 1991).

32. Duncan, *Blue-Eyed Child of Fortune*, 283.

33. As quoted in Burchard, *One Gallant Rush*, 73.

34. Quotation in Burchard, *One Gallant Rush,* 73. This process of maturation has been described in Earl J. Hess, *The Union Solider in Battle: Enduring the Ordeal of Combat* (Lawrence: University Press of Kansas, 1997); James M. McPherson, *For Cause and Comrade: Why Men Fought in the Civil War* (New York: Oxford University Press, 1997).

35. Duncan, *Blue-Eyed Child of Fortune,* 123.

36. Duncan, *Blue-Eyed Child of Fortune,* 286.

37. Quoted in Duncan, *Blue-Eyed Child of Fortune,* 298.

38. Examples of Rob's letters to his father are in Duncan, *Blue-Eyed Child of Fortune,* 300, 303, 365–66, 376. For insight into father/son relationships during the Civil War, see Frank, "Rendering Aid and Comfort," esp. 5–8.

39. Robert Gould Shaw to Josephine Shaw, September 11, 1861, Robert Gould Shaw Papers, Houghton Library, Harvard University. Reid Mitchell, *The Vacant Chair: The Northern Soldier Leaves Home* (New York: Oxford University Press, 1993), 37.

40. Quoted in Weinberg, *John Elliot Cairnes,* 142–43.

41. Sarah Blake Shaw to Robert Gould Shaw, February 6, 1863, Sarah Blake Shaw Papers, Houghton Library, Harvard University.

42. As quoted in Weinberg, *John Elliot Cairnes,* 167.

43. Quoted in Paul C. Nagel, *This Sacred Trust: American Nationality, 1798–1898* (New York: Oxford University Press, 1971), 221.

44. Frank Shaw's involvement with Henry George is documented in letters between the two men in the Henry George Papers, Manuscripts and Archives Division, New York Public Library. See also Anna George de Mille, *Henry George: Citizen of the World,* ed. Don C. Shoemaker (Chapel Hill: University of North Carolina Press, 1950). Shaw's death was reported in the *New York Times,* November 9, 1882.

45. For an account of Curtis's activities during these years, see John M. Dobson, "George William Curtis and the Election of 1884: The Dilemma of the New York Mugwumps," *New York Historical Society Quarterly* 52 (1968): 215–34; see also Robert Charles Kennedy, "Crisis and Progress: The Rhetoric and Ideals of a Nineteenth-Century Reformer, George William Curtis (1824–1892)" (Ph.D. diss., University of Illinois at Urbana, 1993). For Barlow, see Allen Johnson, ed., *Dictionary of American Biography,* 11 vols. (New York: Charles Scribner's Sons, 1964), 1:608.

46. "Mrs. Anna Shaw Curtis," obituary, *New York Times,* August 24, 1923; "Mrs. Susanna S. Minturn," obituary, *New York Times,* October 17, 1926; "Mrs. E. S. Barlow, 90, Reformer Is Dead," obituary, *New York Times,* January 13, 1936. A small sampling of letters to Ellen Shaw Barlow from Henry James and Grover Cleveland can be found in the Shaw Family Letters, Boston Athenæum.

47. "Lenox Summer Resident Dies Suddenly in Boston," March 19, 1907, *Berkshire Eagle;* George H. Tucker, *A History of Lenox* (Lenox, Mass.: Lenox, Massachusetts Library Association, 1992), 49. I am grateful to Cornelia Brooke Gilder for bringing this information to my attention.

48. Josephine Shaw Lowell to Edward W. Ordway, September 27, 1905, Edward W. Ordway Papers, New York Public Library.

49. Josephine Shaw Lowell to Edward M. Shepard, January 24, 1903, no. 13, Edward M. Shepard Papers, Rare Book and Manuscript Library, Columbia University.

50. Josephine Shaw Lowell to Norton, December 31, 1902, Norton Papers, Houghton Library, Harvard University.

51. As quoted in *Monument to Robert Gould Shaw*, 30–31.

The Shaw Memorial in the Landscape of Civil War Memory, by David W. Blight

1. John Hope Franklin, "A Century of Civil War Observances," *Journal of Negro History* 47 (April 1962): 98.

2. On Governor David Beasley's efforts to remove the Confederate battle flag from official use, see Allan Gurganus, "At Last the South Loses Well," *New York Times*, December 8, 1996; Jack Hitt, "Confederate Semiotics," *Nation*, April 28, 1997. For information on Governor George Allen's proclamation in the state of Virginia, I have relied on conversations with John Coski, librarian and director, the Museum of the Confederacy, Richmond, Va. For the Byrd quotation and for James Gilmore's proclamation, see "Slavery 'Abhorred,' Gilmore Says," *Washington Post*, April 10, 1998. I thank James O. Horton for providing information on Gilmore and the Virginia controversy, and I thank Thomas J. Brown for clarifying my understanding of Beasley's efforts in South Carolina. On the current enthusiasm for the Civil War, see Tony Horwitz, *Confederates in the Attic: Dispatches from the Unfinished Civil War* (New York: Pantheon, 1998). And on Civil War memory generally during the first fifty years after the conflict, see David W. Blight, *Race and Reunion: The Civil War in American Memory* (Cambridge, Mass.: Harvard University Press, 2001).

3. Vincent Scully, art historian emeritus, Yale University, quoted from an address delivered at the unveiling of a restored casting of the Shaw Memorial, St. Gaudens National Historic site, Cornish, N. H., July 13, 1998 (author's notes). On "black Confederates," see Charles Kelley Barrow, J. H. Segars, and R. B. Rosenberg, eds., "Forgotten Confederates: An Anthology about Black Southerners," *Journal of Confederate History Series* 14 (1995); Richard Rollins, ed., "Black Southerners in Gray: Essays on Afro-Americans in Confederate Armies," *Journal of Confederate History Series* 11 (1994); and Ervin L. Jordan Jr., *Black Confederates and Afro-Yankees in Civil War Virginia* (Charlottesville: University Press of Virginia, 1995). Also see the Web site of the Sons of Confederate Veterans, "Black History Month: Black Confederate Heritage," http://www.scv.org/scvblkhm.htm (February 1997); and Dan Hoover, "Civil War Controversy: Blacks in Rebel Gray," *Greenville (S.C.) News*, March 2, 1997 (clipping provided by John Coski).

4. Frederick Douglass, "Wasted Magnanimity," *New National Era*, August

10, 1871; Albion Tourgée, *Continent* 5 (April 2, 1884): 444; and *Continent* 6 (July 30, 1884): 156.

5. Gurganus, "South Loses Well"; Booker T. Washington, "A Speech at the Unveiling of the Robert Gould Shaw Monument," Boston, May 31, 1897, in Louis R. Harlan, ed., *The Booker T. Washington Papers* (Urbana: University of Illinois Press, 1975), 4:287; Thomas Beer, quoted in Daniel Aaron, *The Unwritten War: American Writers and the Civil War* (New York: Knopf, 1973), xiii. An excellent essay on the contexts in which the Shaw Memorial emerged is Stephen J. Whitfield, "'Sacred in History and in Art': The Shaw Memorial," *New England Quarterly* 60 (March 1987): 3–27.

6. Howells is quoted in Allan Gurganus, *Oldest Confederate Widow Tells All* (New York: Ivy Books, 1984), epigraph; W.E.B. Du Bois, *Black Reconstruction in America, 1860–1880* (1935; reprint, New York: Atheneum, 1969), 110.

7. Saint-Gaudens quoted in Sidney Kaplan, "The Sculptural World of Augustus Saint-Gaudens," *Massachusetts Review* 30 (spring 1989): 36. On Saint-Gaudens, see Whitfield, "Sacred in History," 8–10; Robert Hughes, "American Renaissance Man," *Time*, January 13, 1986; Burke Wilkinson, *Uncommon Clay: The Life and Works of Augustus Saint-Gaudens* (San Diego: Harcourt, Brace, Jovanovich, 1985); Kathryn Greenthal, *Augustus Saint-Gaudens: Master Sculptor* (New York: Metropolitan Museum of Art, 1985); and Theodore J. Karamanski, "Memory's Landscape," *Chicago History* 26 (summer 1997): 54–72.

8. Frederick Douglass, "Speech in Madison Square," Decoration Day, May 30, 1878, Frederick Douglass Papers, Library of Congress, reel 15; Edward A. Pollard, *The Lost Cause: A New Southern History of the War of the Confederates* (New York, 1867; reprint, New York: Bonanza, n.d.), 750, 752.

9. Robert Lowell, "For the Union Dead," in *Norton Anthology of American Literature* (New York: Norton, 1980), 1:842; William James, "Robert Gould Shaw," delivered in Boston, May 31, 1897, in *Memories and Studies by William James* (New York: Longmans, Green, 1911), 40.

10. Frederick Douglass, "The Mission of the War," delivered in New York City, February 13, 1864, in Philip S. Foner, ed., *The Life and Writings of Frederick Douglass* (New York: International Publishers, 1952), 3:401; Benjamin T. Tanner, "The Issues before the People," *Christian Recorder*, September 19, 1868.

11. W.E.B. Du Bois, *The Souls of Black Folk* (Chicago, 1903; reprint, Boston: Bedford Books, 1997), 54–55.

12. Henry Lee Higginson, "Robert Gould Shaw," an address delivered in Sanders Theater, May 30, 1897, in *Four Addresses by Henry Lee Higginson*, (Boston: Merrymount Press, 1902), 72–73, 102.

13. Ida B. Wells, *Southern Horrors: Lynch Law in All Its Phases*, in Trudier Harris, comp., *Selected Works of Ida B. Wells-Barnett* (New York: Oxford University Press, 1991), 17; Joseph C. Price, "The Race Problem Stated" (1890), in Carter G. Woodson, ed., *Negro Orators and Their Orations* (New York: Russell and Russell, 1940), 490, emphasis mine; Charles Chesnutt, *The Marrow of Tradition* (Ann Arbor: University of Michigan Press, 1969), 269–70; *Boston Evening Transcript*, June 4, 1897.

14. Lowell, "For the Union Dead," 842.

15. "A Monument to the Southern Slave," from *Charleston News and Courier*, in *Baltimore Afro-American*, August 3, 1895. Six or seven "loyal slave" memorials of various kinds have been identified across the South. I am indebted to James Loewen for sharing his information on such monuments. On the Fort Mill monument, see Kirk Savage, *Standing Soldiers, Kneeling Slaves: Race, War, and Monument in Nineteenth-Century America* (Princeton, N.J.: Princeton University Press, 1997), 155–61. "Faithful slave" stories and reminiscences became a regular feature in the *Confederate Veteran*, which began publication in 1893. For some examples, see *Confederate Veteran* issues of May, December 1899; March 1903; March, September, July 1905; March 1906; August, October 1909; October, December 1914. On the national "Mammy Monument," see *Goldsboro (N.C.) Argus*, July 8, 1923; *New York Amsterdam News*, August 22, 1923; *New Orleans Southwestern Christian Advocate*, October 4, 1923.

16. Speeches by O'Ferrall and Johnson, in a pamphlet from the dedication ceremonies, *In Memoriam Sempiternam* (Richmond, Va.: Confederate Museum, 1896), 44, 47, 50, copy in the library of the Museum of the Confederacy, Richmond, Va.

17. *Confederate Veteran*, July 1897, my emphasis in the Reagan speech.

18. Thomas Wentworth Higginson, "Colored Troops under Fire," *Century Magazine* 54 (June 1897): 199.

19. Paul Lawrence Dunbar, "Robert Gould Shaw," in Jay Martin and Gossie H. Hudson, eds., *The Paul Lawrence Dunbar Reader* (New York: Dodd, Mead, 1975), 320.

Bannister, Lewis, and the Memorialization of the Regiment, by Marilyn Richardson

1. "Tribute To The Late Col. Shaw," letter dated July 27, 1863, printed in *Douglass' Monthly* 5 (August 1865): 853.

2. Benjamin Quarles, *The Negro in the Civil War* (Boston, 1953; reprint, New York: Da Capo, 1989), 19.

3. Frances D. Gage, in *Memorial R.G.S.* (Cambridge, Mass.: University Press, 1864), 153–55. See also the entry on Frances Dana Barker Gage (1808–84) in Edward T. James et al, eds., *Notable American Women: A Biographical Dictionary*, 3 vols. (Cambridge, Mass.: Belknap Press, 1971), 2:2–4.

4. Richard Benson and Lincoln Kirstein, *Lay This Laurel: An Album on the Saint-Gaudens Memorial on Boston Common Honoring Black and White Men Together Who Served the Union Cause with Robert Gould Shaw and Died with Him July 18, 1863* (New York: Eakins Press, 1973), unpaginated.

5. See Kirk Savage, *Standing Soldiers, Kneeling Slaves: Race, War, and Monument in Nineteenth-Century America* (Princeton, N.J.: Princeton University Press, 1997), 196–97, for a discussion of Smith's work on behalf of the monument to Shaw and the regiment.

6. A monument dedicated to all of those slain in the Boston Massacre was

eventually erected on Boston Common in 1888. African American attorney Butler Wilson was central to seeing the project through. See Boston (Mass.) City Council, *A Memorial of Crispus Attucks, Samuel Maverick, James Caldwell, Samuel Gray, and Patrick Carr from the City of Boston* (Boston: Printed by Order of the City Council, 1889).

7. William C. Nell, *The Colored Patriots of the American Revolution, with Sketches of Several Distinguished Colored Persons: To Which Is Added a Brief Survey of the Condition and Prospects of Colored Americans* (Boston: Robert F. Wallcut, 1855), 9.

8. Quarles, *The Negro in the Civil War*, 12.

9. Juanita Marie Holland, "Breaking through the Veil: African-American Artist Edward Mitchell Bannister," catalog essay in Juanita Marie Holland and Corrine Jennings, eds., *Edward Mitchell Bannister: 1828–1901* (New York: Harry N. Abrams, 1992), 11. Holland is the foremost scholar on Bannister's life and work, and "Breaking through the Veil" is the only thoroughly researched and documented study of the artist to date.

10. Holland, "Breaking through the Veil," 17.

11. Quoted in Holland, "Breaking through the Veil," 22.

12. Bannister's portrait of Christiana Carteaux Bannister is in the Newport Art Museum in Rhode Island and is illustrated in Holland, "Breaking through the Veil," 16.

13. *New York Weekly Anglo-African*, November 5, 1864, 1. The article is signed "G. W. P." and dated October 20, 1864.

14. *Martha Perry Lowe, In Memoriam 1829–1902* (Cambridge, Mass.: Riverside Press, 1903), includes a biographical sketch along with a collection of eulogies and brief reminiscences of Lowe.

15. Martha Perry Lowe, *The Olive and the Pine* (Boston: Lothrop, 1859).

16. *Liberator*, January 29, 1864, 19.

17. Anne Whitney to Sarah Whitney, August 9, 1864, Wellesley College Archives.

18. Lydia Maria Child, "A Chat with the Editor of the Standard," reprinted from the *Anti-Slavery Standard* in the *New York Weekly Anglo-African*, January 21, 1865, 4.

19. Lewis quoted by L. M. Child in the *Liberator*, January 20, 1865.

20. Lydia M. Child to Sarah Sturgis Shaw [Robert Gould Shaw's mother], November 3, 1864, in Milton Meltzer et al., eds., *Lydia Maria Child: Selected Letters, 1817–1880* (Amherst: University of Massachusetts Press, 1982), 446.

21. Lydia M. Child to Sarah Shaw, April 8, 1866, in Patricia G. Holland and Milton Meltzer, eds., *The Collected Correspondence of Lydia Maria Child, 1817–1880* (Millwood, N.Y.: Kraus Microform, 1980), 64/1717. Subsequent copies of the bust conformed to the altered dimensions. See, for example, the 1867 version in the collection of the Museum of Afro American History in Boston.

22. Lydia M. Child to Sarah Shaw, April 8, 1866, in Holland and Meltzer, *Correspondence of Lydia Maria Child*, 64/1717.

23. John Greenleaf Whittier to Lydia M. Child, November 15, 1864, in John B. Pickard, ed., *The Letters of John Greenleaf Whittier* (Cambridge, Mass.: Belknap Press, 1975), 2:486.

24. Lincoln Kirstein, "The Memorial to Robert Gould Shaw and His Soldiers by Augustus Saint-Gaudens," in Benson and Kirstein, *Lay This Laurel*.

25. Lewis's circa 1866 portrait bust of Anna Quincy Waterston is in the collection of the National Museum of American Art, Smithsonian Institution, Washington, D.C.

26. Waterston's poem was possibly first published in the *National Anti-Slavery Standard*, December 24, 1864. I am indebted to Professor Allen Flint of the University of Maine at Farmington for this citation.

27. Quarles, *The Negro in the Civil War*, 11.

28. Quoted in Peter Burchard, *One Gallant Rush: Robert Gould Shaw and His Brave Black Regiment* (New York: St. Martin's, 1965), 93.

29. Burchard, *One Gallant Rush*, 94.

30. Luis F. Emilio, *A Brave Black Regiment: History of the Fifty-Fourth Regiment of Massachusetts Volunteer Infantry, 1863–1865*, 2d ed. (Boston: Boston Book Company, 1894).

31. The Hollywood film *Glory* neatly paralleled Saint-Gaudens's formula, even as it attempted to "bring the monument to life." Ignoring whole archives of information on specific individuals, Shaw's story is told with relative fidelity, including quotations from his actual correspondence, whereas to a man, the black characters are prototypes from central casting. There is no mention in the film of Sergeant William H. Carney.

32. *Douglass' Monthly* 5 (August 1863): 2, 4.

32. Quarles, *The Negro in the Civil War*, 20.

34. In December of 1865, the sculptor T. H. Bartlett wrote from New York City to the adjutant-general of Massachusetts requesting the name of an officer of the Fifty-fourth Massachusetts who might give him information concerning Carney's heroism. "It would," he wrote, "make a splendid subject for a statuette." In William Wells Brown, *The Negro in the American Rebellion* (Boston: Lee and Shepard, 1867), 209. Truman H. Bartlett was a Boston sculptor and the biographer of William Rimmer, sculptor and famous teacher of artists. He was the father of the better-known sculptor Paul Bartlett. See Wayne Craven, *Sculpture in America* (Newark: University of Delaware Press, 1984), 428. Both Lewis and Bartlett conceived of a work of considerable detail but modest scale.

35. From a three-page manuscript by Carney in the collection of the Museum of Afro American History in Boston, uncataloged, n.d., probably from the 1880s.

36. Emilio, *Brave Black Regiment*, caption to frontispiece photograph of Sergeant Carney with the flag from Battery Wagner.

37. *Roman Times*, October 28, 1871, 3. Newspaper listing of addresses of artists' studios for the convenience of tourists.

38. Lincoln Kirstein, March 9, 1973, response to a query addressed to the Boston Athenæum. Collection of the Boston Athenæum.

Augustus Saint-Gaudens and the Shaw Memorial,
by Kathryn Greenthal

1. Charles Sumner to Francis George Shaw and Sarah Shaw, July 29, 1863, Shaw Family Papers, Boston Athenæum.

2. Edward L. Pierce, ed. *Memoir and Letters of Charles Sumner*, 4 vols. (Boston: Roberts Brothers, 1877–93), 4:142.

3. *The Monument to Robert Gould Shaw: Its Inception, Completion, and Unveiling, 1865–1897* (Boston: Houghton Mifflin, 1897), 7.

4. *Monument to Robert Gould Shaw*, 8.

5. *Boston Evening Transcript*, October 23, 1865.

6. This marble version of *Cleopatra* is in the Los Angeles County Museum of Art, and this marble version of the *Libyan Sibyl* is in the Metropolitan Museum of Art.

7. William Wetmore Story to Charles Sumner, October 26, 1865, Charles Sumner Papers, Houghton Library, Harvard University.

8. William Wetmore Story Diaries, no. 5, January 1, 22, 23, 29, 1866, Harry Ransom Humanities Research Center, University of Texas at Austin.

9. William Wetmore Story to Charles Sumner, January 25, 1866, Charles Sumner Papers, Houghton Library, Harvard University. Along with the letter, Story sent some photographs and a sketch for the equestrian statue, which he described as "only a design for composition." The photographs and the sketch are not included in the Houghton Library's collections.

10. See Jan M. Seidler, "A Critical Reappraisal of the Career of William Wetmore Story (1819–1895), American Sculptor and Man of Letters" (Ph.D diss., Boston University, 1985), 612–13, for a discussion of the Shaw commission vis-a-vis Story.

11. See *Boston Daily Advertiser*, April 11, 1878. I am grateful to Thomas J. Brown for having brought the information about Milmore's plaster model to my attention.

12. The bust of Sumner is in the Senate Wing of the U.S. Capitol.

13. Ernest Rodenburgh III made this suggestion to me.

14. *Boston Evening Transcript*, April 17, 1879.

15. Newspaper clippings in the Anne Whitney "Scrapbooks," 2:99, referred to in Elizabeth Rogers Payne, "Anne Whitney: Nineteenth Century Sculptor and Liberal," typescript, Anne Whitney Papers, Wellesley College Archives, 1241.

16. Edward Atkinson to John Murray Forbes, July 7, 1880, Edward Atkinson Letterbooks, Massachusetts Historical Society.

17. The bust of Minturn was presented to the Union League Club in New York City by twenty-five members; Minturn, a merchant and ship owner, had been the club's first president in 1863. S. Parkman Shaw, Robert B. Minturn of Boston, and Arthur Lawrence, librarian and archivist of the club, were most helpful in providing information about Minturn and the commemorative bust.

18. For the most recent review of Thompson's life and career, see David B.

Dearinger, "Launt Thompson," *American National Biography*, 24 vols. (New York: Oxford University Press, 1999), 21:562–64.

19. Anne Whitney to Maria Weston Chapman, undated, Payne annotated "[Dec. 5, 1880]," Anne Whitney Papers, Wellesley College Archives.

20. Payne, "Anne Whitney," 1240.

21. Wendell Phillips to Anne Whitney, February 27, [1881?], Anne Whitney Papers, Wellesley College Archives.

22. Payne, "Anne Whitney," 1241.

23. Henry Hobson Richardson to Augustus Saint-Gaudens, February 24, March 9, 11; July 18, 1881; Augustus Saint-Gaudens to Henry Hobson Richardson, November 29, [1881], Saint-Gaudens Papers, Dartmouth College Library.

24. "The drawing for the Shaw Memorial is completed and has been placed in the hands of Messrs Doll & Richards to be framed." Henry Hobson Richardson to Edward Atkinson, April 19, 1882, Edward Atkinson Papers, Massachusetts Historical Society.

25. Homer Saint-Gaudens, ed., *The Reminiscences of Augustus Saint-Gaudens*, 2 vols. (New York: Century, 1913), 1:332.

26. See letters from Edward Atkinson to Augustus Saint-Gaudens, June 2, 12; July 18, 28, 1882, Edward Atkinson Letterbooks, Massachusetts Historical Society, and two letters from Augustus Saint-Gaudens to Edward Atkinson, June 10, 1882, Edward Atkinson Papers, Massachusetts Historical Society.

27. *Reminiscences of Augustus Saint-Gaudens*, 1:174. Ironically, it was Anne Whitney's seated model that won the anonymous competition for the Sumner statue. However, after the committee learned that the winning model was the work of a woman, the committee claimed that they had really desired a standing statue. The commission went to Thomas Ball, whose standing figure of Sumner now resides in Boston's Public Garden. Some twenty-five years after the Sumner competition, Anne Whitney's model was enlarged, slightly modified, and installed in Harvard Square in Cambridge.

28. *Monument to Robert Gould Shaw*, 10.

29. Edward Atkinson to John Murray Forbes, June 16, 1892, Edward Atkinson Letterbooks, Massachusetts Historical Society.

30. *Monument to Robert Gould Shaw*, 9.

31. Augustus Saint-Gaudens to Josephine Shaw Lowell, October 26, 1883, Shaw Family Papers, Boston Athenæum. See also Kathryn Greenthal, *Augustus Saint-Gaudens: Master Sculptor* (New York: Metropolitan Museum of Art, 1985), 44–56, for a discussion of Saint-Gaudens's working methods.

32. Contract between the trustees of the Shaw Memorial Fund and Augustus Saint-Gaudens, February 23, 1884, Saint-Gaudens Papers, Dartmouth College Library.

33. Augustus Saint-Gaudens to Edward Atkinson, June 3, 1886, Edward Atkinson Papers, Massachusetts Historical Society.

34. Josephine Shaw Lowell to Henry Lee, October 1, 1886, Miscellaneous Papers, Massachusetts Historical Society.

35. Edward Atkinson to Augustus Saint-Gaudens, November 5, 1886, Edward Atkinson Letterbooks, Massachusetts Historical Society.

36. Edward Atkinson to Augustus Saint-Gaudens, December 9, 1891, Edward Atkinson Letterbooks, Massachusetts Historical Society.

37. Edward Atkinson to John Murray Forbes, June 16, 1892, Edward Atkinson Letterbooks, Massachusetts Historical Society.

38. Edward Atkinson to Augusta Homer Saint-Gaudens, January 18, 1892, Edward Atkinson Letterbooks, Massachusetts Historical Society.

39. *Reminiscences of Augustus Saint-Gaudens*, 2:66.

40. For the history of the creation of the medal, see Kathryn Greenthal et al., *American Figurative Sculpture in the Museum of Fine Arts, Boston* (Boston: Museum of Fine Arts, 1986), 229–31.

41. *Reminiscences of Augustus Saint-Gaudens*, 1:332–33.

42. Edward Atkinson to John Murray Forbes, August 29, 1893, Edward Atkinson Letterbooks, Massachusetts Historical Society.

43. John Murray Forbes to Edward Atkinson, October 9, 1893, Lee Family Papers, Massachusetts Historical Society.

44. Edward Atkinson to Thomas Livermore, December 29, 1896, Edward Atkinson Letterbooks, Massachusetts Historical Society.

45. Greenthal et al., *American Figurative Sculpture*, 216–17.

46. See Francis George Shaw to Rufus Saxton, November 25, 1863, in *Memorial R.G.S.* (Cambridge, Mass.: University Press, 1864), 178. Thomas J. Brown kindly reminded me of this letter.

47. Josephine Shaw Lowell to Henry Lee, October 30, 1892, Lee Family Papers, Massachusetts Historical Society.

48. Edward Atkinson to Henry Lee, June 30, 1894; Edward Atkinson to Augustus Saint-Gaudens, January 2, 1895; June 6, December 14, 1896; Edward Atkinson to Josephine Shaw Lowell, January 26, 1897; Edward Atkinson to William James, February 5, 1897, all in Edward Atkinson Letterbooks, Massachusetts Historical Society.

49. Edward Atkinson to Henry Lee, June 5, 1897, Lee Family Papers, Massachusetts Historical Society.

50. Edward Atkinson to Daniel Appleton, February 5, 1897, Lee Family Papers, Massachusetts Historical Society.

51. Augustus Saint-Gaudens to Edward Atkinson, September 22, 1897, Edward Atkinson Papers, Massachusetts Historical Society. The plaster head, long thought to be lost, and listed as "non localisée" as recently as 1999 (see *Augustus Saint-Gaudens 1848–2907: Un maître de la sculpture américaine* [Musée des Augustins, Toulouse, and Musée national de la coopération franco-américaine, Château de Blérancourt], 135), is in a private collection. Following the receipt of the cast, Atkinson queried Saint-Gaudens: "If I should desire to have this head cast in bronze, would you agree, and what would it cost?" Edward Atkinson to Augustus Saint-Gaudens, October 12, 1897, Edward Atkinson Letterbooks, Massachusetts Historical Society. Six days later, Atkinson wrote again to the sculptor: "Colonel Lee was at my house yesterday afternoon and greatly admired the cast of the angel's head, advising on the conclusion which I had already reached, *not* to have it put in bronze. I shall get a skilled mechanic to make a wooden box pegged inside at the different points so as to

sustain the thin plaster at every part and hang it up. I wish you would send me a little bit of plaster that could be put down at one corner with your name inscribed and date. I want it signed." Edward Atkinson to Augustus Saint-Gaudens, October 18, 1897, Edward Atkinson Letterbooks, Massachusetts Historical Society. Saint-Gaudens did indeed send to Atkinson a plaster section, which is inscribed "TO · EDWARD · ATKINSON / AGVSTVS · ST · GAVDENS," and it was fitted into the lower right-hand corner of the piece.

Civic Monuments of the Civil War,
by Thomas J. Brown

The author would like to thank Marty Blatt, David Blight, Gaines Foster, Richard Fox, Kathryn Greenthal, Louis Masur, Stuart McConnell, Kirk Savage, Nina Silber, James Smethurst, Michael Vorenberg, and Donald Yacovone for comments on previous versions of this essay.

1. Ralph Waldo Emerson, "Boston," in *The Complete Works of Ralph Waldo Emerson*, ed. Edward Waldo Emerson, 12 vols. (Boston: Houghton, Mifflin, 1903–4), 12:188.

2. Emerson, "History," in *Complete Works*, 2:25 ("admiration"), 2:24 ("every man"), 2:14 ("national mind").

3. Lewis Simpson, *Mind and the American Civil War: A Meditation on Lost Causes* (Baton Rouge: Louisiana State University Press, 1989), 87.

4. Jacob Bigelow, *An Account of the Sphinx at Mount Auburn* (Boston: Little, Brown, 1872), 7 ("restore"), 13 ("dividing ridge" and "looked backward"); Emerson, "History," in *Complete Works*, 2:4. Daniel Walker Howe, *The Political Culture of the American Whigs* (Chicago: University of Chicago Press, 1979), chap. 4, describes the Whig view of history. Blanche Linden-Ward, *Silent City on a Hill: Landscapes of Memory and Boston's Mount Auburn Cemetery* (Columbus: Ohio State University Press, 1989), emphasizes the centrality of Whig culture in the shaping of the cemetery.

5. Holmes quoted in David Herbert Donald, *Charles Sumner and the Coming of the Civil War* (New York: Knopf, 1960), 206. Bryant and Whittier quoted in *Boston Evening Transcript*, January 19, 24, 1865.

6. Jan M. Seidler, "A Critical Reappraisal of the Career of William Wetmore Story (1819–1895), American Sculptor and Man of Letters" (Ph.D diss., Boston University, 1985), 650–60. Seidler notes that Story may also have intended for the composition to invoke the recently excavated *Augustus of Primaporta*.

7. William H. Gilman et al., eds., *The Journals and Miscellaneous Notebooks of Ralph Waldo Emerson*, 16 vols. (Cambridge, Mass.: Belknap Press, 1960–82), 10:397.

8. Charles G. Loring chaired both committees. In addition to Bigelow, the overlap group included Robert C. Winthrop, James Lawrence, Francis E. Parker, Sidney Bartlett, Richard Henry Dana Jr., William Amory, John G. Palfrey, Samuel H. Walley, J. Ingersoll Bowditch, Oliver Wendell Holmes, and Thomas G. Appleton. Sidney Everett, who was not a member of the committee honoring his father, served as secretary of the Memorial Hall committee. *Boston Eve-*

ning Transcript, January 18, 1865; Waldo Higginson, "Memorial Hall—Part I," in *The Harvard Book*, comp. F. O. Vaille and H. A. Clark, 2 vols. (Cambridge, Mass.: Welch, Bigelow, 1875), 2:51–52.

9. Robert B. Shaffer, "Ruskin, Norton, and Memorial Hall," *Harvard Library Bulletin* 3 (spring 1949): 213–31. See also Bainbridge Bunting, *Harvard: An Architectural History* (Cambridge, Mass.: Belknap Press, 1985), 86–92.

10. John G. Palfrey to Charles W. Eliot, February 19, 1876; Charles W. Eliot to Henry B. Rogers, June 4, 1876; John Codman Ropes to Charles Eliot Norton, June 12, 1865, all in Miscellaneous Records of the Committee of Fifty, Harvard University Archives; Shaffer, "Ruskin, Norton, and Memorial Hall," 215. Hoar quoted in *Boston Journal*, October 6, 1870. On Whig concerns about military leaders, see Howe, *Political Culture*, 87–95.

11. City of Boston, *Report upon a Design for a Soldiers' and Sailors' Monument*, City Doc. no. 103 (1866), 5–7; City of Boston, *Report upon the Remonstrances against the Erection of a Monument*, City Doc. no. 123 (1866); *Boston Daily Advertiser*, December 22, 1866. All cited city documents are available in Littauer Library, Harvard University.

12. City of Boston, *Report of the Joint Special Committee on the Erection of an Army and Navy Monument*, City Doc. no. 98 (1870), 5.

13. *Dedication of the Monument on Boston Common Erected to the Memory of the Men of Boston Who Died in the Civil War* (Boston: Printed by Order of the City Council, 1877), 43–54.

14. Linden-Ward, *Silent City on a Hill*, 287–93; Shaffer, "Ruskin, Norton, and Memorial Hall," 228–31; Thomas J. Brown, "The Real War Will Never Get into the Statues," *Reviews in American History* 26 (December 1998): 703–4.

15. "Sculpture in the United States," *Atlantic Monthly* 22 (November 1868): 560; *Boston Evening Transcript*, November 22, 30; December 2–5, 11, 16, 1867.

16. *Boston Evening Transcript*, December 5, 13, 1867.

17. *Erection and Dedication of the Soldiers' and Sailors' Monument in the Army and Navy Lot, in Mount Hope Cemetery, Belonging to the City of Boston*, City Doc. no. 80 (Boston: Printed by Order of the City Council, 1867). The city did spend forty-five hundred dollars from the Phillips Fund for fencing and grading around the copy of Thomas Ball's *Emancipation Group* donated by Moses Kimball. *Reports of Proceedings of the City Council of Boston for the Municipal Year 1879* (Boston: Rockwell and Churchill, City Printers, 1879), 502.

18. The overlapping members were Martin Brimmer, William Endicott Jr., and Henry P. Kidder. *Message of the Mayor, Transmitting a Communication from a Committee of Citizens, Presenting a Bronze Statue of William Lloyd Garrison to the City*, Boston City Doc. no. 119 (1886), 1.

19. *Boston Evening Transcript*, December 23, 30, 1878.

20. *Boston Evening Transcript*, May 30, July 9, 1879; *Proceedings of the City Council of Boston for 1879*, 392, 418, 441–43; *Bronze Group Commemorating Emancipation. A Gift to the City of Boston from Hon. Moses Kimball. Dedicated December 6, 1879*, City Doc. No. 126 (Boston: Printed by Order of the City Council, 1879).

21. *Boston Evening Transcript,* June 27, 1879; *Exercises at the Dedication of the Statue of Wendell Phillips, July 5, 1915* (Boston: City Printing Department, 1916).

22. Simpson, *Mind and the American Civil War,* 86–87. On Emerson's support for the Garrison memorial, see *Message of the Mayor . . . Presenting a Bronze Statue of Garrison,* 1. Emerson had previously served on the Committee of Fifty to build Harvard Memorial Hall.

23. *Boston Evening Transcript,* May 14, 1886.

24. James Brewer Stewart, *Wendell Phillips: Liberty's Hero* (Baton Rouge: Louisiana State University Press, 1986), 186; Daniel Chester French to Charles William Eliot, January 28, 1914, French MSS., Library of Congress.

25. Seidler, "Career of William Wetmore Story," 615; William Howe Downes, "Monuments and Statues in Boston," *New England Magazine* 11 (November 1894): 361–62, 369; Truman H. Bartlett, "Civic Monuments in New England: Part 2," *American Architect and Building News* 9 (June 18, 1881): 292; Truman H. Bartlett, "Civic Monuments in New England: Part 3," *American Architect and Building News* 9 (June 25, 1881): 304; Eleanor Tufts, "An American Victorian Dilemma, 1875: Should a Woman Be Allowed to Sculpt a Man?" *Art Journal* 51 (spring 1992): 51–56. The scathing comments of Wendell Phillips are quoted in *Bacon's Dictionary of Boston* (Boston: Houghton, Mifflin, 1886), 381–82.

26. *Boston Evening Transcript,* May 10, 1886; December 29, 1888.

27. *The Constitution of the Boston Memorial Association, as Amended and Adopted December 2, 1885, with the List of Officers and Members* (Boston: Printed for the Association, 1885); *American Architect and Building News* 9 (February 12, 1881): 73–74. I am grateful to David L. Franks, Mark C. Lamphier, and Susan Rovzar for assistance in researching the Boston Memorial Association.

28. *Boston Evening Transcript,* November 8, 1888; October 24, 1889; November 6, 1890; Oliver Ames to Henry Lee, August 29, 1888, Lee Family Papers, Massachusetts Historical Society.

29. *Reports of Proceedings of the City Council of Boston for the Municipal Year 1888* (Boston: Rockwell and Churchill, City Printers, 1888), 1035 (December 27, 1888); *Reports of Proceedings of the City Council of Boston for the Municipal Year 1889* (Boston: Rockwell and Churchill, City Printers, 1890), 551 (May 13, 1889).

30. *Boston Evening Transcript,* January 3, 1878.

31. *Report on the Subject of Erecting Statues to the Memory of Generals Grant and Sheridan,* Boston City Doc. no. 138, December 27, 1888, 34.

32. *Report on Statues to Grant and Sheridan,* 21, 30, 34, 39.

33. Daniel George Macnamara, *The History of the Ninth Regiment, Massachusetts Volunteer Infantry* (Boston: E. B. Stillings, Printers, 1899), 423–24; *Proceedings of the City Council of Boston for 1889,* 951.

34. Arlo Bates, *The Philistines* (Boston: Ticknor, 1889). The mayor also sat on the Boston Art Commission as originally organized. It was reconstituted in 1898 to provide for the mayor to choose from persons nominated by these four organizations and the Boston Art Club. *American Architect and Building*

News 60 (May 21, 1898): 58, 62; *Notice from the Art Commission of Disapproval of the Placing of the Statue of Columbus in Copley Square,* Boston City Doc. no. 168 (1892). Mayor Josiah Quincy resolved the controversy over the Cass statue by obtaining city funding in 1896 for a new monument. Beaux-Arts sculptor Richard E. Brooks's portrait statue of Cass was placed in the Public Garden in 1899.

35. *Report on the Erection of an Army and Navy Monument,* 4–5; Herbert Small, comp., *Handbook of the New Public Library in Boston* (Boston: Curtis, 1895), 22.

36. *Boston Evening Transcript,* March 25, 1896.

37. See generally Ellen Mudge Burrill, *The State House, Boston, Massachusetts,* 9th ed. (Boston: Wright and Potter Printing, 1927).

38. Charles Francis Adams, *Charles Francis Adams, 1835–1915: An Autobiography* (Boston: Houghton, Mifflin, 1916), 161–62.

39. *Boston Evening Transcript,* November 12, 1889; *The Equestrian Statue of Major General Joseph Hooker Erected and Dedicated by the Commonwealth of Massachusetts* (Boston: Wright and Potter Printing, 1903), 129–65; Oliver Wendell Holmes, "The Soldier's Faith," in *Speeches by Oliver Wendell Holmes* (Boston: Little, Brown, 1896), 58.

40. *Boston Daily Advertiser,* October 3 (Sumner quotations), 9 (Smith quotation), 18, 1865; *Boston Evening Transcript,* October 7, 17; November 4, 1865.

41. See *Boston Daily Advertiser,* October 18, 1865, for criticisms of Sumner by Henry Lee Jr., Henry Ingersoll Bowditch, and Samuel Gridley Howe, all of whom quickly left the monument committee to which Andrew had appointed them. Chapman's contribution of one hundred dollars was preceded only by an anonymous gift of five dollars. "Contributions to the Shaw Monument Fund," [May 1897], MS. Memorandum, Lee Family Papers. Wendell Phillips to Anne Whitney, February 27, [?], Anne Whitney Papers, Wellesley College. I am grateful to Kathryn Greenthal for this reference. Norton to Lee, March 18, 1876, Lee Family Papers, expresses concern about the possible abandonment of the equestrian plan and calls for a statue that would portray Shaw as he was last seen in Boston.

42. On these negotiations, see Lois Goldreich Marcus, "The *Shaw Memorial* by Augustus Saint-Gaudens: A History Painting in Bronze," *Winterthur Portfolio* 14 (spring 1979): 8.

43. John M. Forbes to Lee, June 5; August 10, 15, 1892; Forbes to Edward Atkinson, December 11, 1893, all in Lee Family Papers; *Reports of Proceedings of the City Council of Boston for the Municipal Year 1891* (Boston: Rockwell and Churchill, City Printers, 1891), 1238–39, 1259. Atkinson later chortled that "an Irish common Councilman heartily approved 'the commemoration of the brave young colored man who led members of his race to the war.'" Atkinson to Daniel Appleton, February 5, 1897, Lee Family Papers.

44. Simpson, *Mind and the American Civil War,* 69, 95.

45. Stephen T. Riley, "A Monument to Colonel Robert Gould Shaw," *Proceedings of the Massachusetts Historical Society* 75 (1963): 27–38, describes the frustration of the monument committee with the sculptor's priorities and

pace of work; Albert Boime, *The Art of Exclusion: Representing Blacks in the Nineteenth Century* (Washington, D.C.: Smithsonian Institution Press, 1990), 205–9, scrutinizes Saint-Gaudens's racial views.

46. "The Monument to Colonel R. G. Shaw," *American Architect and Building News* 57 (September 11, 1897): 89. On Rimmer's drawing, see Jeffrey Weidman, "William Rimmer: Critical Catalogue Raisonné," 3 vols. (Ph.D. diss., Indiana University, 1981), 3:809–15. Another well-known example of the mobilization theme is Thomas Nast's monumental painting *The Departure of the Seventh Regiment to the War, April 19ᵗʰ, 1861* (1869), also an event in which Shaw participated.

47. Truman H. Bartlett, *About Monuments* (Boston, 1878), 11; S. Beale, review of *François Rude*, by Alexis Bertrand, *American Architect and Building News* 25 (February 9, 1889): 70; Homer Saint-Gaudens, ed., *The Reminiscences of Augustus Saint-Gaudens*, 2 vols. (London, 1913; reprint, New York: Garland Publishing, 1976), 1:64; 2:18, 49, 51, 263. Robert Gildea, *The Past in French History* (New Haven, Conn.: Yale University Press, 1994), 134–41, discusses the ways in which commemoration of the 1792 mobilization helped to construct a French nationalism that had profound influence elsewhere.

48. Marcus, "The *Shaw Memorial*," 19, notes the formal similarity between the two monuments but fails to recognize the thematic relationship because the essay mistakenly assumes (1, 4 n. 7) that Saint-Gaudens intended to represent the regiment at the time of the assault on Fort Wagner rather than at the departure from Boston.

49. Marcus, "The *Shaw Memorial*," 10–16.

50. Edward M. Griffin, "Cincinnatus and the 'Shaw Memorial': Monument as Emblem in Saint Gaudens, Dunbar, and Lowell," in *The Telling Image: Explorations in the Emblem*, ed. Ayers L. Bagley, Edward M. Griffin, and Austin J. McLean (New York: AMS Press, 1996), 181–82.

51. Francis George Shaw to Rufus Saxton, November 25, 1863, in *Memorial R.G.S.* (Cambridge, Mass.: University Press, 1864), 178; Atkinson to Lee, June 11, 1897, Lee Family Papers.

52. Atkinson to Lee, October 8; December 3, 1896 ("brutal"); January 5; March 3, 23, 1897; Atkinson to Committee, December 29, 1896 ("what might"); January 21, 1897; Josephine Shaw Lowell to Lee, January 4, 1897; Henry Lee Higginson to Atkinson, March 22, 1897, all in Lee Family Papers.

53. William James to Lee, March [?] (*"ensemble"*), 7 ("an Emerson"), 30, 1897; William E. Barton to William James, May 14, 1897, all in Lee Family Papers; William James to Booker T. Washington, March 8, April 16, 1897 ("flourishing"), in Louis R. Harlan, ed., *The Booker T. Washington Papers*, 14 vols. (Urbana: University of Illinois Press, 1972–89), 4:264, 271–72; William James to Henry James, June 5, 1897 ("last wave"), in Henry James, ed., *The Letters of William James*, 2 vols. (Boston: Atlantic Monthly Press, 1920), 2:60–61; Linda Simon, *Genuine Reality: A Life of William James* (New York: Harcourt Brace, 1998), xi–xvi, 276–79.

54. William James, "Address at the Emerson Centenary in Concord," in *Memories and Studies* (New York, 1911; reprint, New York: Greenwood Press,

1968), 23–26, 33, quotations on 23–24, 26, 25. R. W. B. Lewis, *The Jameses: A Family Narrative* (New York: Farrar, Straus, and Giroux, 1991), 140–41, 560, discusses the significance of Emerson's "Voluntaries" to the James family.

55. William James to Washington, April 16, 1897, in Harlan, *Booker T. Washington Papers*, 4:272; William James, "Robert Gould Shaw," in *Memories and Studies*, 57 ("lonely"), 43 ("faith").

56. James, "Robert Gould Shaw," 56 ("school," "cradle," "survivors"), 57 ("battle-instinct"), 58 ("nation blest"), 61 ("habit"). George M. Fredrickson, *The Inner Civil War: Northern Intellectuals and the Crisis of the Union* (New York: Harper and Row, 1965), 229–38, places James's oration on Shaw in the context of the development that led to "The Moral Equivalent of War."

57. James, "Robert Gould Shaw," 61.

Race, Art, and the Shaw Memorial,
by Kirk Savage

1. *Exercises at the Dedication of the Monument to Colonel Robert Gould Shaw* (Boston: Municipal Printing Office, 1897), 40, 42. James actually claimed that the Fifty-fourth was the "first Northern negro regiment," but it was preceded by a regiment mustered in Kansas.

2. Albert Boime, *The Art of Exclusion: Representing Blacks in the Nineteenth Century* (Washington, D.C.: Smithsonian Institution Press, 1990).

3. Boime, *Art of Exclusion*, 209.

4. John M. Forbes, in particular, disliked the angel figure and the way in which Shaw's hat intersected with it: "I should like to make it a condition that that dev[ilish]. . . . angel should be got out of the way of Robert Shaw's hat." Forbes to Henry Lee, June 15, 1892, Lee Family Papers, Massachusetts Historical Society. Saint-Gaudens's artist friend Paul Bion told him to remove the figure and wrote that "your priestess merely bores me." Homer Saint-Gaudens, ed., *Reminiscences of Augustus Saint-Gaudens*, 2 vols. (London: Andrew Melrose, 1913), 1:344.

5. This monument is a replica of the Freedmen's Memorial to Lincoln erected three years earlier in Washington, D.C. For more on the genesis of the design, see Kirk Savage, *Standing Soldiers, Kneeling Slaves: Race, War, and Monument in Nineteenth-Century America* (Princeton, N.J.: Princeton University Press, 1997), 77–81, 114–119.

6. Charles Caffin, *American Masters of Sculpture* (Garden City, N.Y.: Doubleday, 1913), 11.

7. Picasso quoted in Michael Baxandall, *Patterns of Intention: On the Historical Explanation of Pictures* (New Haven, Conn.: Yale University Press, 1985), 41. *Reminiscences of Augustus Saint-Gaudens*, 1:333, 335.

8. When an earlier version of this paper was delivered at the Centennial Celebration symposium, a member of the audience made an interesting objection to this point. My remarks reminded him of a standard defense made of racist supervisors in workplaces: if they make racist remarks at work, that does not mean that their *professional* conduct is motivated by racism; to him this

distinction between personal and professional conduct on the job was insignificant. I concur, but I see the case of the Shaw Memorial in a different light. Ultimately, we are not judging Saint-Gaudens's behavior but his work, the material product of his labor. Thus, although Saint-Gaudens's professional behavior toward his models does indeed seem racist, the monument he made with those models need not be.

9. See Baxandall, *Patterns of Intention*, esp. 41–42.

10. For more discussion of the development of the design, see Savage, *Standing Soldiers, Kneeling Slaves*, 196–201. An earlier effort by the regiment, freed slaves living in the vicinity of Battery Wagner, and Northern blacks to erect a monument to Shaw was abandoned, and the accumulated funds went toward establishing a school for former bondspeople in Charleston. See Savage, *Standing Soldiers, Kneeling Slaves*, 195, 196–97.

11. *Reminiscences of Augustus Saint-Gaudens*, 1:332. *Boston Evening Transcript*, April 25, 1882 (my thanks to Thomas J. Brown for passing on this reference to me).

12. "I, like most sculptors at the beginning of their careers, felt that by hook or crook I must do an equestrian statue, and that here I had found my opportunity. Therefore I proceeded with this theory until the Shaw family objected on the ground that, although Shaw was of a noble type, as noble as any, still he had not been a great commander." *Reminiscences of Augustus Saint-Gaudens*, 1:332.

Interestingly, scholars (including myself) have not yet fully corroborated this story in archival documents. We do know from the surviving archival record that the monument committee in the 1880s did consult with the Shaw family. A letter from the monument treasurer, Edward Atkinson, to Saint-Gaudens dated November 5, 1886 (Atkinson Family Papers, Massachusetts Historical Society), makes this clear. An earlier letter from Saint-Gaudens to Shaw's sister, Josephine Shaw Lowell, dated October 26, 1883 (Boston Athenæum), confirms that she had already seen his plaster model for the monument and this was even before Saint-Gaudens had signed a contract with the monument committee (my thanks to Joan Waugh for showing this document to me). Nothing in the archival record suggests that Saint-Gaudens's account is false.

13. Forbes to Lee and M. P. Kennard, September 30, 1892, Lee Family Papers. Forbes's comments were part of the committee's long debate over the monument's inscriptions. The committee members fought hard with each other and in the process reflected openly on the meaning of the monument. But for all their differences over details, they agreed on the essentials—that the monument commemorated far more than Shaw himself and that the black troops were critical to its significance.

14. *Reminiscences of Augustus Saint-Gaudens*, 1:333.

15. For more on this argument, see Savage, *Standing Soldiers, Kneeling Slaves*, 192–93.

16. Lois Goldreich Marcus, "The *Shaw Memorial* by Augustus Saint-Gaudens: A History Painting in Bronze," *Winterthur Portfolio* 14 (spring 1979): 16.

Poetry, Soldiers, and Citizens at the End of Reconstruction, by James Smethurst

1. Sidney Kaplan, *American Studies in Black and White: Selected Essays* (Amherst: University of Massachusetts Press, 1991), 118. Also see Steven Axelrod, "Colonel Shaw in American Poetry: 'For the Union Dead' and Its Precursors," *American Quarterly* 24 (October 1972): 523–37; Chadwick Hansen, "The 54th Massachusetts Volunteer Infantry as a Subject for American Artists," *Massachusetts Review* 16 (autumn 1975): 745–59; Allen Flint, "Black Response to Colonel Shaw," *Phylon* 45 (fall 1984): 210–19; Stephen J. Whitfield, "'Sacred in History and in Art': The Shaw Memorial," *New England Quarterly* 60 (March 1987): 3–27; Gary Scharnhorst, "From Soldier to Saint: Robert Gould Shaw and the Rhetoric of Racial Justice," *Civil War History* 34 (December 1988): 308–22.

2. David W. Blight, "'For Something beyond the Battlefield': Frederick Douglass and the Struggle for the Memory of the Civil War," *Journal of American History* 75 (March 1989): 1156–78. Blight writes, "But memories and understandings of great events, especially apocalyptic wars, live in our consciousness like monuments in the mind. The aging Douglass's rhetoric was an eloquent attempt to forge a place on that monument for those he deemed the principal characters in the drama of emancipation: the abolitionist, the black soldier, and the freed people" (1176).

3. Epes Sargent, "Colonel Shaw: On Hearing That the Rebels Had Buried His Body under a Pile of Twenty-Five Negroes," *Boston Evening Transcript*, August 4, 1863, 2.

4. Ralph Waldo Emerson, *Poems* (Boston: Houghton, Mifflin, 1904), 206–7.

5. Du Bois, for example, writes in *The Souls of Black Folk* (Chicago, 1903; reprint, New York: Penguin, 1982), "The history of the American Negro is the history of this strife,—this longing to attain self-conscious manhood" (47). Later in the same chapter, he names the special gifts of African Americans to the United States as faith, humility, good humor, and spiritual strivings.

6. Donald Yacovone, "Sacred Land Regained: Frances Ellen Watkins Harper and 'The Massachusetts Fifty-Fourth,' A Lost Poem," *Pennsylvania History* 62 (winter 1995): 102. Although Harper's poem is the only one I have discovered that mentions the Fifty-fourth and was published during the war, Joshua McCarter Simpson's "Let the Banner Wave," in *Anti-Slavery Ballads* (1874; reprint, Miami: Mnemosyne, 1969), features a subtitle indicating that it was written shortly after Lee's surrender at Appomattox.

7. For a full accessible text of Harper's poem (which originally appeared in the October 10, 1863, issue of the *New York Weekly Anglo-African*), see Yacovone, "Sacred Land Regained," 105–6.

8. I have been able to discover few poems mentioning Shaw and the Fifty-fourth written by white authors between the end of the war and the dedication of the memorial. One is by S. R. Bartlett, *The Charge of the Fifty-Fourth* (Chicago: n.p., 1869), which originally was published in only fifty copies. Others are John Hay's "Advance Guard," which first appeared in *Harpers* in 1871, and

Thomas Wentworth Higginson's "Memorial Ode," which was read at a Boston Memorial Day ceremony in 1881. Both Hay's and Higginson's poems, which contain only brief mentions of Shaw and the Fifty-fourth, are primarily about other (white) martyrs of the Civil War. For the text of Hay's poem, see *The Complete Poetical Works of John Hay* (Boston: Houghton, Mifflin, 1917). For a copy of Higginson's poem, see John Davis Long, *Memorial Day: Oration by Gov. John D. Long. Ode by Thomas W. Higginson* (Boston: Lockwood, Brooks, 1881).

9. For a short sketch of Bell, who achieved a certain fame for his dramatic public readings of his epics, and a brief analysis of his poetry, see Joan R. Sherman, *Invisible Poets: Afro-Americans of the Nineteenth Century* (Urbana: University of Illinois Press, 1974), 80–87.

10. James Madison Bell, *Poetical Works of James Madison Bell* (Lansing, Mich., 1901; reprint, Freeport, N.Y.: Books for Libraries Press, 1970), 146.

11. Joshua McCarter Simpson, *The Emancipation Car* (Zanesville, Ohio, 1874; reprint, Miami: Mnemosyne, 1969), 144. As noted elsewhere, the subtitle "Let the Banner Proudly Wave" makes the claim that the poem was written shortly after Lee's surrender. I have chosen to deal with this poem as part of the cultural conversation of the mid-1870s, when the poem was first published (so far as I can tell). Whatever the precise date of composition, the author certainly felt that the poem was germane enough to the moment of the mid-1870s to warrant its inclusion in the collection. Certainly the readers of the poem interpreted it within the framework of Reconstruction and its debates rather than that of the rather uncertain period at the end of the Civil War.

12. For a history of the Fifty-fourth (by a former officer of the regiment) that was itself a monument of the sort that David Blight describes in his essay, see Luis F. Emilio, *A Brave Black Regiment: History of the Fifty-Fourth Regiment of Massachusetts Volunteer Infantry, 1863–1865* (Boston, 1891; reprint, New York: Arno Press, 1969).

13. Sherman, *Invisible Poets*, 83.

14. Eric Foner, *Reconstruction: America's Unfinished Revolution, 1863–1877* (New York: Harper, 1988), 564–601.

15. One possible ending for Reconstruction could be 1901, when the last black Southern congressman before the post–Civil Rights era, George White of North Carolina, left office.

16. For a brief discussion of Whitman's poem, see Sherman, *Invisible Poets*, 117–21.

17. Albery Whitman, *Not a Man and Yet a Man* (Springfield, Ohio, 1877; reprint, Upper Saddle River, N.J.: Gregg Press, 1970), 206–7, 213–14. Subsequent quotations of Whitman's poetry are also from this work.

18. For example, Martha Perry Lowe in an 1864 poem, "The Picture of Colonel Shaw in Boston," which appeared in both the *Boston Daily Advertiser* and the *Liberator*, wrote, after seeing a picture of Shaw, "Look upon him, Nation of the free! / Surely this will cure thee of thy meanness." *Liberator*, November 25, 1864, 192.

19. *Boston Commonwealth*, December 8, 1883.

20. Why there were few poems about the black soldier in the 1880s when the Jim Crow system began to take shape is unclear. Certainly, as the epigraph to this essay indicates, African American intellectuals and political leaders used the black soldier in their attacks on the new segregation and the curtailment of black civil rights. However, it may be that the sheer accumulation of Jim Crow laws, practices, and resurgent racism as the 1880s wore on eventually provoked a return to the powerful figure of the African American veteran. It is worth noting that both black and white prose writers increasingly employed imagery of Civil War veterans in their works of the late 1880s and early 1890s. Frances Harper's novel *Iola Leroy* (Philadelphia, 1892; reprint, New York: Oxford University Press, 1988) is the most prominent example. One could also cite the appearance of historian George Washington Williams's *History of the Negro Troops in the Rebellion* (New York: Harper and Bros., 1888) and Emilio's *Brave Black Regiment.* Both Williams and Emilio were Civil War veterans of African American units. James Monroe Trotter, "The Fifty-Fourth at Wagner," *Boston Commonwealth,* December 8, 1883. See also Yacovone, "Sacred Land Regained," 110 n. 52.

21. George Clinton Rowe, *Our Heroes: Patriotic Poems on Men, Women, and Sayings of the Negro Race* (Charleston, S.C.: Walker, Evans, and Cogswell, 1890), 47–48. Rowe also wrote—in the same collection—"The Reason Why," about a standard-bearer of the First Louisiana Regiment, U.S. Colored Troops, who died defending the regimental colors in the 1863 assault on Port Hudson, Louisiana. Since Rowe's text is virtually unavailable in print form (the same is true of the works of other African American writers discussed here, with the exception of Harper and Dunbar) it is most readily accessible through the Chadwyck-Healey Literature Online (Lion) service's *African American Poetry (1750–1900).*

22. Hondon B. Hargrove, *Black Union Soldiers in the Civil War* (Jefferson, N.C.: McFarland, 1988), 155–56.

23. Addison Gayle Jr., *Oak and Ivy: A Biography of Paul Laurence Dunbar* (Garden City, N.Y.: Doubleday, 1971), 6–8.

24. For example, Dunbar, along with Simpson, was one of the few writers to allude to the broader, distinguished career of the Fifty-fourth beyond the suicidal, if heroic, attack on Battery Wagner. He mentioned, for example, the 1864 battle of Olustee, Florida, where the bravery and discipline of the Fifty-fourth saved a Union army from a complete rout.

25. Paul Laurence Dunbar, *The Complete Poems of Paul Laurence Dunbar* (New York: Dodd, Mead, 1913), 51.

26. It is worth noting that this era featured not only the institution of Jim Crow and the disfranchisement of African Americans in most of the South, but also an increasingly ardent debate about the relationship between race and citizenship. The new intensity of this discussion was fueled largely by the immigration of millions of people from southern and eastern Europe and featured a rhetoric that spoke of the "Hibernian race," the "Teutonic race," the "Jewish" or "Semitic race," the "Syrian race," and so on. Ultimately, this debate led to the establishment of immigration laws in the 1920s that severely limited the

ability of southern and eastern Europeans (and others) to enter the United States. Thus, the issue of race, blood, and citizenship dominated the thinking of Americans in the North as well as in the South. For a study of the debate, see Matthew Frye Jacobson, *Whiteness of a Different Color: European Immigrants and the Alchemy of Race* (Cambridge, Mass.: Harvard University Press, 1998).

27. Aldrich's and Gilder's poems are collected in *The Poems of Thomas Bailey Aldrich* (Boston: Houghton, Mifflin, 1907), 410–13, and *The Poems of Richard Watson Gilder* (Boston: Houghton, Mifflin, 1908), 268–69, and Robert Underwood Johnson's may be found in *Saint-Gaudens: An Ode and Other Verses* (New York: Century, 1910).

28. *The Poems and Plays of William Vaughn Moody* (Boston: Houghton, Mifflin, 1912), 1:15.

29. However, Lowell's lines "When I crouch to my television set, / the drained faces of Negro school-children rise like balloons," referring to the civil rights struggles in the South during the 1950s and early 1960s, indirectly allude to the failure of Reconstruction, which is missing in Moody's poem. Robert Lowell, *Selected Poems* (New York: Farrar, Straus, and Giroux, 1977), 137.

30. Dunbar, like many other African Americans, was ambivalent about American participation in the Spanish-American War. On one hand, he wrote poems praising Theodore Roosevelt and, especially, the black soldiers who fought in the war. However, he also criticized what he called a "new attitude" engendered by the war that made white Americans perfectly willing to let black soldiers fight and die but not vote or exercise the other prerogatives of full citizenship. It is worth noting that in both cases Dunbar used the figure of the black soldier in much the same way that he always had, suggesting that he would have resisted any move to shift the meaning of that figure. For a brief discussion of Dunbar's attitude toward the war, see Willard B. Gatewood Jr., *Black Americans and the White Man's Burdens, 1898–1903* (Urbana: University of Illinois Press, 1975), 110.

31. *Complete Poems of Dunbar*, 183–84.

32. These poems appeared most frequently, though not exclusively, in Boston-based magazines and journals, such as the *Atlantic Monthly* and the *Boston Journal*.

33. *Complete Poems of Dunbar*, 221.

34. Probably the most famous literary example of this nationalist or nationalist-influenced rhetoric of manhood in the early twentieth century is Claude McKay's 1919 poem "If We Die," which concludes with the couplet "Like men we'll face the murderous, cowardly pack, / Pressed to the wall, dying, but fighting back!" *Liberator*, July 1919, 21. However, even a casual glance at the poetry published in *Negro World*, the mass weekly newspaper founded by nationalist leader Marcus Garvey in 1918, will confirm that McKay's conflation of manhood and racial self-assertion was part of a much larger literary (and political) phenomenon.

35. *Complete Poems of Dunbar*, 221.

36. "The Unsung Heroes" was first collected along with "Robert Gould

Shaw," "Douglass," "The Haunted Oak," and "To the South" in *Lyrics of Love and Laughter* (New York: Dodd, Mead, 1903).

37. This trope of forgotten and unsung heroes or martyrs reappeared in later African American poetry, perhaps most directly in Countee Cullen's 1933 "Scottsboro, Too, Is Worth Its Song," in *The Medea and Other Poems* (New York: Harper, 1935), 96–97.

38. It is also unclear when Ray actually wrote her sonnet-elegy to Shaw. She was of an earlier generation than Brawley, with a poetic career dating back to the 1870s. She published her first book in 1893. The volume, *Poems* (New York: Grafton, 1910), in which "Robert G. Shaw" appeared was her second and last collection. In short, it is quite possible that Ray wrote the piece during the flurry of poems about Shaw in the last years of the nineteenth century.

39. Aptheker was a Communist Party member in the 1930s and 1940s when he wrote his pioneering works on African American slave revolts and black participation in the American Revolution and the Civil War. Du Bois had a more troubled relationship with the Communist Party when *Black Reconstruction* (New York: Harcourt, Brace and Company, 1935) appeared in the mid-1930s—though he became associated with the Communist Left in the 1940s. Indeed, the Communist Party and its newspapers and journal were severely critical of Du Bois's work. However, Du Bois's study clearly displays a Marxist influence derived in no small part from the new cultural prominence of Communism in the early years of the Great Depression.

40. It could be argued that Lowell, through his relationship to Shaw (whose family intermarried with the Lowells) and his investment in family history in the Civil Rights era, engaged the earlier literary tradition. But even in this case, it was a retrospective engagement rather than a contemporary one.

41. Robert B. Stepto, *From behind the Veil: A Study of Afro-American Narrative* (Urbana: University of Illinois Press, 1979).

42. Later this journey also came to include the return to the ghetto from some (generally) "white" space.

The Musical Monument of Charles Ives, by Denise Von Glahn

1. Assigning precise dates to Ives's compositions presents many difficulties. The composer's habit of redating a piece as revisions were made often suggests conflicting evidence to musicologists determined to find the original date of composition. For the purposes of this essay, it is sufficient to know that Ives worked on "The 'St. Gaudens' in Boston Common (Colonel Robert Gould Shaw and his Colored Regiment)" over a period of years commencing as early as 1911.

2. Lyman Brewster married Charles Ives's Aunt Amelia, sister of Charles's father George. Brewster brought his own unassailable family pedigree and social status to the Ives family. In addition to his highly regarded professional work as an attorney, Brewster served in the state Senate and supported numer-

ous social and cultural causes in and around the Danbury, Connecticut, area. He provided an important role model for Charles Ives of a successful business-man who was committed to the arts.

3. Charles E. Ives, *Memos*, ed. John Kirkpatrick (New York: Norton, 1972), 87.

4. Gary Scharnhorst states emphatically: "Only once during these years did the memorial inspire an artist to front the race issue directly. In a dirge entitled "The 'St. Gaudens' in Boston Common," Charles Ives emphasized the slow tramp of the footsore soldiers as they march toward the front. He thus struck a note long silent in the hoopla over Shaw." "From Soldier to Saint: Robert Gould Shaw and the Rhetoric of Racial Justice," *Civil War History* 34 (December 1988): 321.

5. Among the family stories is one about Ives's Aunt Sarah. As the tale goes, she organized a group of women who successfully rescued a captured slave from almost certain return to the South. Another refers to Charles's father, George, who befriended Henry Anderson Brooks, a young black boy whose mother had done laundry for George's Union Army troop. In *Memos* Ives details how his father taught Brooks to read and write and eventually took him home with him to Danbury, where he sent him to school. See *Memos*, 53.

6. Charles E. Ives, *Three Places in New England*, ed. James B. Sinclair (Bryn Mawr, Pa.: Mercury Music Corporation, 1976), 1. Over the course of the last few decades, *Three Places in New England* has been recorded by numerous orchestras and conductors. Among the most thoughtful performances is that by Orchestra New England under the direction of James Sinclair, who, in addition to being a conductor, is chief editor of Ives's *Critical Editions* and overseer of the monumental *Descriptive Catalogue of the Music of Charles Ives* (New Haven, Conn.: Yale University Press, 1999). As a conductor and scholar thoroughly familiar with Ives's spirit and thought, Sinclair brings a unique sensibility to the music. See James Sinclair, dir., *The Orchestral Music of Charles Ives*, Orchestra New England, Koch International Classics, 3–7025-2 (1990).

7. John Kirkpatrick hypothesized that remarks would have appeared on page 31 of source "T." "T" is the symbol provided by Kirkpatrick in the preface to *Memos* for Florence Martin's first set of typed pages transcribed from notes taken from Ives's dictation. See Ives, *Memo*, 16–17, 83–85.

8. Robert P. Morgan, "Spatial Form in Ives," in *An Ives Celebration*, ed. H. Wiley Hitchcock and Vivian Perlis (Chicago: University of Illinois Press, 1977), 145–58.

9. W.E.B. Du Bois, *The Souls of Black Folk* (Chicago, 1903; reprint, New York: Signet Classic, 1995), 270.

10. One should not assume that Ives felt any responsibility to soften Foster's images or remake Foster's reputation. It is likely that Ives would have considered such a salvage effort unnecessary, misguided, and patronizing. Ives's interests were purely musical ones. He saw the potential for identifying black soldiers in a familiar, concise, textually appropriate musical gesture and made the gesture his own.

11. William McFeely expressed similar sentiments (perhaps more poetically) in his remarks about the soldiers of Saint-Gaudens's monument at the Hope & Glory Conference, May 29, 1997.

12. According to *The Charles Ives Tunebook*, a volume cataloging the popular, military, classical, and sacred source tunes that Ives used in his compositions, George Frederick Root's song "The Battle Cry of Freedom" was written in 1861 and first published in a Root and Cady publication of 1862. C. M. Cady was a partner first in a publishing firm with George Frederick Root's older brother E. T. Root and later with George Frederick Root himself. See Clayton Henderson, *The Charles Ives Tunebook* (Warren, Mich.: Harmonie Park Press, 1990), 67. For commentary on Ives's use of quoted materials, see H. Wiley Hitchcock, *Music in the United States: A Historical Introduction* (Englewood Cliffs, N.J.: Prentice-Hall, 1969), 171; and H. Wiley Hitchcock, *Ives: A Survey of the Music* (New York: Institute for Studies in American Music, 1977), 86–87.

13. George Frederick Root, "The Battle Cry of Freedom," in Henderson, *Charles Ives Tunebook*, 67, emphasis mine.

14. Quoted in James Henry Gooding, *On the Altar of Freedom: A Black Soldier's Civil War Letters from the Front*, ed. Virginia M. Adams (Amherst: University of Massachusetts Press, 1991), 39–40.

15. "The Hero," *Century* 54 (1897): 314.

16. Frontispiece to Luis F. Emilio, *A Brave Black Regiment: History of the Fifty-Fourth Regiment of Massachusetts Volunteer Infantry, 1863–1865* (Boston: Boston Book Company, 1891).

17. Gooding, *On the Altar of Freedom*, 41.

18. For a discussion of Charles Ives's association of George Ives with Stephen Foster, see two essays by Stuart Feder, "Thoreau Was Somewhere Near: The Ives-Thoreau Connection," in Edmund A. Schofield and Robert C. Baron, eds., *Thoreau's World and Ours: A Natural Legacy* (Golden, Colo.: North American Press, 1993); and "Charles Ives and Henry David Thoreau: 'A Transcendental Tune of Concord,'" in Philip Lambert, ed., *Ives Studies* (Cambridge, Eng.: Cambridge University Press, 1997). For a thorough discussion of the father-son relationship enjoyed by Charles and George Ives, see Stuart Feder, "Charles and George Ives: The Veneration of Boyhood," in Stuart Feder, Richard L. Karmel, and George H. Pollock, eds., *Psychoanalytic Explorations in Music* (Madison, Conn.: International Universities Press, 1990).

19. The individuated faces of Saint-Gaudens's monument serve much the same purpose as the 57,661 names carved on Maya Lin's Vietnam Veteran's Memorial in Washington, D.C., if more subtly. In both cases the artists remind visitors that the cost of war is individual life.

Art, Heroism, and Poetry,
by Helen Vendler

1. "For the Union Dead," in Robert Lowell, *Selected Poems* (New York: Farrar, Straus, and Giroux, 1977), 135–37. I have written at more length about

"For the Union Dead" in "Reading a Poem," in *Fieldwork: Sites in Literary and Cultural Studies,* ed. Marjorie Garber, Rebecca L. Walkowitz, and Paul Franklin (New York: Routledge, 1996), 129–36.

2. Steven Axelrod, "Colonel Shaw in American Poetry: 'For the Union Dead' and its Precursors," *American Quarterly* 24 (October 1972): 523–37. See 530.

3. Axelrod, "Colonel Shaw in American Poetry." Referring to and quoting from an 1897 article by William A. Coffin ("The Shaw Memorial and the Sculptor St. Gaudens," *Century Magazine,* n. s., 32 [June 1897]: 179, 181), Axelrod concludes that "the family felt that the memorial should not glorify a single man, but should rather 'typify patriotic devotion, and embody a modern spirit with heroic attributes'" (530–31).

4. Allen Tate, "Ode to the Confederate Dead," *Collected Poems: 1919–1976* (New York: Farrar, Straus, and Giroux, 1977), 20–23.

5. "Boston Common: A Meditation upon The Hero," in John Berryman, *Collected Poems, 1937–1971,* ed. and with an introduction by Charles Thornbury (New York: Farrar, Straus, and Giroux, 1989), 41. Subsequent quotations from this work, cited parenthetically in the text, also refer to this edition.

Glory: Hollywood History and Popular Culture, by Martin H. Blatt

1. C. Peter Jorgensen, "The Making of *Glory,*" *Civil War Times Illustrated* 28 (November–December 1989): 53–54; Peter Burchard, *One Gallant Rush: Robert Gould Shaw and His Brave Black Regiment* (New York: Saint Martin's Press, 1965). Richard Benson and Lincoln Kirstein, *Lay This Laurel: An Album on the Saint-Gaudens Memorial on Boston Common, Honoring Black and White Men Together Who Served the Union Cause with Robert Gould Shaw and Died with Him July 18, 1863* (New York: Eakins Press, 1973). Peter Burchard to Martin Blatt, July 19, 1998. Tri-Star Pictures, *Glory* Press Guide, 1989, 16; Jim Cullen, *The Civil War in Popular Culture: A Reusable Past* (Washington, D.C.: Smithsonian Institution Press, 1995), 153; Douglas Brode, *Denzel Washington: His Films and Career* (Secaucus, N.J.: Birch Lane Press, 1997), 80–82.

2. Jorgensen, "Making of *Glory,*" 54; Burchard to Blatt, July 19, 1998. I was unable to acquire a text of the final shooting script. I did obtain from a Los Angeles book dealer two scripts, *Glory* by Kevin Jarre, and *Glory* by Kevin Jarre—rewrite by Edward Zwick and Marshall Hershkovitz. Warnings on both scripts indicate that no portion of the script may be quoted or published without prior written consent. So, I refrain from doing so; instead, I paraphrase or provide summaries.

3. Burchard to Blatt, July 19, 1998.

4. Burchard to Blatt, July 19, 1998.

5. See Patricia Turner, *Ceramic Uncles and Celluloid Mammies: Black Images and Their Influence on Culture* (New York: Doubleday, 1994). For her discussion of *Mississippi Burning,* see 168–71; for her discussion of *Glory,* see

172–76. Patricia Turner, panel presentation, "History on Film: *Glory* and the Fifty-fourth Massachusetts Regiment," part of public symposium, "The Monument to Robert Gould Shaw and the Fifty-fourth Massachusetts Regiment: History and Meaning," Boston (hereafter, public symposium), May 30, 1997.

6. Turner, *Ceramic Uncles and Celluloid Mammies*, 174. Although the "real men" of the Fifty-fourth such as Lewis Douglass and William H. Carney were indeed invisible in the film, the black soldiers as played by Freeman, Washington, and others came across much more vividly than the white officers. Zwick quoted in Robert Seidenberry, "Glory," *American Film* 15 (January 1990): 58.

7. Brode, *Denzel Washington*, 88.

8. "Morgan Freeman," in *The 1991 Movie Home Companion*, ed. Roger Ebert (Kansas City, Mo.: Andrews, McMeel, and Parker, 1990), 641.

9. Barbara Fields, presentation in panel, "The Impact of African-American Soldiers on the Civil War," public symposium, May 29, 1997.

10. Asa Gordon to Blatt, May 27, 1997.

11. Fields, public symposium.

12. David Blight, "The Meaning of the Fight: Frederick Douglass and the Memory of the Fifty-fourth Massachusetts," *Massachusetts Review* 36 (spring 1995): 147–48.

13. Joseph Glatthaar is the author of *Forged in Battle: The Civil War Alliance of Black Soldiers and White Officers* (New York: Free Press, 1990). He is cited in David Nicholson, "What Price *Glory*?" *Washington Post*, January 21, 1990.

14. Cullen, *Civil War in Popular Culture*, 163.

15. Burchard, *One Gallant Rush*, 150.

16. Elvis Mitchell, presentation in panel, "History on Film: *Glory* and the Fifty-fourth Massachusetts Regiment," public symposium, May 30, 1997.

17. Jorgensen, "Making of *Glory*," 59.

18. Edward Linenthal, presentation in panel, "Changing Memories of the War, 1863–1897," public symposium, May 29, 1997.

19. James McPherson, "*Glory*," in Mark Carnes, ed., *Past Imperfect: History according to the Movies* (New York: Henry Holt, 1995), 128, 130; Ray Herbeck, telephone interview by Blatt, June 5, 1998.

20. Blight, "Meaning of the Fight," 143. William McFeely, "In the Presence of Art," *Massachusetts Review* 36 (spring 1995): 165.

21. Richard Bernstein, "Heroes of *Glory* Fought Bigotry before All Else," *New York Times*, December 17, 1989; Peter Burchard, telephone interview by Blatt, July 3, 1998. Foote served as a principal narrator of the Ken Burns public television series *The Civil War*.

22. Bernstein, "Heroes of *Glory*." Jorgensen, "Making of *Glory*," 55; Herbeck quoted in Glenn Collins, "*Glory* Resurrects Its Black Heroes," *New York Times*, March 26, 1989; Herbeck, interview by Blatt, June 5, 1998.

23. Herbeck, interview by Blatt, June 5, 1998.

24. Peter Nichols, "Getting to Know the Sights and Sounds of DVD," *New*

York Times, November 21, 1999; telephone interview by Blatt with Margaret Roberts, producer, *Voices of Glory*, October 22, 1999; telephone interview by Blatt with Dan Kavanough, Mirage Productions, October 29, 1999.

25. Vincent Canby, "Black Combat Bravery in the Civil War," *New York Times*, December 14, 1989. Nicholson, "What Price *Glory*?" David Ansen, "*Glory*," *Newsweek*, December 18, 1989, 73. Richard Schickel, "*Glory*," *Time*, December 18, 1989, 91. Stanley Kauffmann, "Comrades in Arms," *New Republic*, January 8, 15, 1990, 28. Tom O'Brien, "At War with Ourselves: *Glory* & *Fourth of July*," *Commonweal*, February 9, 1990, 85.

26. William Gwaltney, presentation in panel, "History on Film: *Glory* and the Fifty-fourth Massachusetts Regiment," public symposium, May 30, 1997. In a bizarre twist, a Washington, D.C., paper reported in 1998 that there had been a growing number of blacks reenacting with Confederate units, in part as a response to *Glory*. The article fails to demonstrate a large groundswell, and Civil War historian James McPherson noted that black participation in the Confederate Army may have "happened on an unofficial and limited basis, but it was not a regular, sizable component of the Confederate Army." Eddie Dean, "The Black and the Gray," *Washington City Paper*, vol. 18, no. 28, July 17–23, 1998.

27. Richard Stevenson, "Civil War Regiment Receives Capital Tribute," *New York Times*, July 12, 1998; "For Black Soldiers, A Fight for Recognition," *Boston Globe*, July 12, 1998; Estella Duran, "Glory, in Granite and Bronze," *Boston Globe*, July 19, 1998.

28. Jeanette Braxton Secret, *Guide to Tracing Your African American Civil War Ancestor* (Bowie, Md.: Heritage Books, 1997).

29. *The Shaw Memorial: A Celebration of an American Masterpiece* (Ft. Washington, Pa.: Eastern National, 1997). See 37 for the condition of the plaster. For a discussion of *Glory*, see Ludwig Lauerhauss Jr., "Commemoration," in *Shaw Memorial*, 47–66, esp. 62–66.

30. *Glory* is featured in Wendy Wilson and Gerald Herman, *American History on the Screen: A Teacher's Resource Book on Film and Video* (Portland, Maine: J. Weston Walch, 1994), 21–28; James Percoco, telephone interview by Blatt, December 23, 1998; James Percoco, *A Passion for the Past: Creative Teaching of U.S. History* (Portsmouth, N.H.: Heinemann, 1998), 84.

31. George Gonis to Martin Blatt, October 1, 1999; Round Robin press release, Milwaukee, Wis., spring 1999.

32. Burchard, interview by Blatt, July 3, 1998; Burchard to Blatt, July 19, 1998. Russell Duncan, ed., *Blue-Eyed Child of Fortune: The Civil War Letters of Colonel Robert Gould Shaw* (Athens: University of Georgia Press, 1992), xvii.

33. Budge Weidman to Blatt, undated; Richard Peuser to Blatt, June 17, 1998; Susan Cooper, "Records of Civil War African American Troops Inspire Major Archival Project," *Record* 3, no. 2 (November 1996); Budge Weidman, "Preserving the Legacy of the United States Colored Troops," unpublished manuscript, n.d. See Donald Yacovone, "I Am a Soldier Now," [Civil War Con-

servation Corps], *American Legacy* 3 (fall 1997): 46–49. On Ken Burns, see Robert Brent Toplin, ed., *Ken Burns's The Civil War: Historians Respond* (New York: Oxford University Press, 1996).

34. John Peterson, "African-American History in the Civil War Soldiers and Sailors Partnership," *Cultural Resource Management* 20, no. 2 (1997); Joseph P. Reidy, "The African-American Sailors' Project: The Hidden History," *Cultural Resource Management* 20, no. 2 (1997).

35. Susan Halpert, telephone interview by Blatt, June 23, 1998; Donald Yacovone, telephone interview by Blatt, June 23, 1998.

36. Herbeck, interview by Blatt, June 5, 1998.

37. Laurie Kahn-Leavitt, telephone interview by Blatt, June 5, 1998.

38. Script, "The Massachusetts 54th Colored Infantry," *The American Experience,* show no. 403, air date October 14, 1991, 1.

39. Kahn-Leavitt, interview by Blatt, June 5, 1998.

40. Script, "Massachusetts 54th Colored Infantry," 6.

41. Gwaltney, public symposium.

Glory as a Meditation on the Saint-Gaudens Monument, by Thomas Cripps

1. See Deborah Chotner and Shelley Sturman, *Augustus Saint-Gaudens' Memorial to Robert Gould Shaw and the Massachusetts Fifty-fourth Regiment* (Washington, D.C.: National Gallery of Art, 1997), for a well-crafted provenance of a "patinated" and restored plaster version of the monument that accompanied its unveiling in September 1997 at the National Gallery in Washington.

2. A good history of the changing nature of the exhibition of movies may be found in Douglas Gomery, *Shared Pleasures: A History of Movie Presentation in the United States* (Madison: University of Wisconsin Press, 1992); see also his "Coming of Television and the 'Lost' Motion Picture Audience," *Journal of Film and Video* 38 (summer 1985): 5–11.

3. For an homage to this Confederate presence in Baltimore, see Mabel Jones Tracy, *The Monumental City's Confederate Monuments to the War between the States* (Baltimore, privately printed, 1987), particularly 3–10, 21.

4. The notion of a diminished public or civic space and its link to movies has coalesced into a generalized "reception theory" that may be found in a growing literature. See, for example, Bruce Austin, *Immediate Seating: A Look at Movie Audiences* (Belmont, Calif.: Wadsworth, 1989); and as influenced by Jürgen Habermas, Miriam Hansen, *Babel and Babylon: Spectatorship in American Silent Film* (Cambridge, Mass.: Harvard University Press, 1991); Lizabeth Cohen, "Encountering Mass Culture at the Grassroots: The Experience of Chicago Workers in the 1920s," *American Quarterly* 41 (March 1989): 6–33; and, as applied to African Americans, Dan Streible, "The Harlem Theatre: Black Film Exhibition in Austin, Texas, 1920–1973," in Manthia Diawara, ed., *Black American Cinema* (New York: Routledge, 1993), 221–37.

5. Luce quoted in Erik Barnouw, *Documentary: A History of the Non-Fiction Film* (New York: Oxford University Press, 1983), 121.

6. The definitive work on this theme remains Edmund Wilson, *Patriotic Gore: Studies in the Literature of the American Civil War* (New York: Oxford University Press, 1962), whose title, curiously, comes from the anthem of the state of Maryland–"Maryland My Maryland" (set to the melody of "Oh Tannenbaum"). The "gore" of the title is the blood shed on April 19, 1861, defending Baltimore against an "invading" army, the Sixth Massachusetts, which was marching from one railway station to another on its way to Washington. The song, still sung by Maryland schoolchildren, warns of Lincoln's aggression: "The despot's heel is on thy shore, Maryland." See Wilson, *Patriotic Gore*, 400–401, for excerpts; also see Beta Kaessmann, *My Maryland: Her Story for Boys and Girls* (Baltimore: Maryland Historical Society, 1953), 432–33.

7. First discussed in James A. Snead, "Recoding Blackness: The Visual Rhetoric of the Black Independent Film," in *Whitney Museum of American Art: The New American Filmmakers Series*, program no. 23, the printed program for a Whitney Museum series; and posthumously in James A. Snead, *White Screens, Black Images: Hollywood from the Dark Side*, ed. Colin McCabe and Cornel West (New York: Routledge, 1994).

8. Rayford W. Logan, *The Betrayal of the Negro from Rutherford B. Hayes to Woodrow Wilson* (original title, *The Negro in American Life and Thought: The Nadir, 1877–1901*) (New York: Collier Books, 1954, 1965), 350–51, 361–62.

9. Dixon quoted as voice-over in the documentary film *Black Shadows on a Silver Screen* (Washington, D.C.: Post-Newsweek Television, 1976); on Griffith's film and its response, see Thomas Cripps, *Slow Fade to Black: The Negro in American Film, 1900–1942* (New York: Oxford University Press, 1977), chaps. 1–2.

10. Drawn from Cripps, *Slow Fade to Black*, and Thomas Cripps, *Making Movies Black: The Hollywood Message Movie from World War II to the Civil Rights Era* (New York: Oxford University Press, 1993). Crowther quoted in *New York Times*, December 8, 1945, clipping in National Association for the Advancement of Colored People Records, Library of Congress.

11. C. Peter Jorgensen, "The Making of *Glory*," *Civil War Times Illustrated* 28 (November–December 1989): 53–54. For an extended account of the origins of the movie, see Jim Cullen, *The Civil War in Popular Culture: A Reusable Past* (Washington, D.C.: Smithsonian Institution Press, 1995), 155.

12. Quoted in Stephen J. Dubner, "Spielberg: Stephen the Good," *New York Times Magazine*, February 14, 1999, 42.

13. Thomas Cripps, "Frederick Douglass: The Absent Presence in *Glory*," *Massachusetts Review* 36 (spring 1995): 154–63.

14. For a sample of images of Douglass and for an account of his travels during the course of the assembling of the Fifty-fourth, see William S. McFeely, *Frederick Douglass* (New York: Norton, 1991), the signatures between 146–47 and 274–75, and 224–27. See also Benjamin Quarles, *Frederick Douglass: Challenge and Response* (Baltimore: Morgan State University Press, 1977), 7. On

Quarles himself, see Thomas Cripps, "A Certain Style: Benjamin Quarles and the Scholarship of the Center," *Maryland Historical Magazine* 93 (fall 1998): 289–300.

15. Selznick to Howard, January 6, 1937, in Rudy Behlmer, ed., *Memo from David O. Selznick* (New York: Viking Press, 1972), 151; discussed in Cripps, *Making Movies Black*, chap. 1.

16. Interview between Moss and Cripps, cited in Cripps, *Making Movies Black*, chap. 4; Agee quoted in Cripps, *Making Movies Black*, 112.

17. See Robert Burgoyne, *Film Nation: Hollywood Looks at U.S. History* (Minneapolis: University of Minnesota Press, 1997), 16–37, for a thorough analysis of the representation of racial identity in *Glory*.

18. Here is Douglass's scene, if he is to have one, but he is played as a thoughtful sage rather than at the height of his powers.

19. The still definitive account of this eventually vacated social experiment is Willie Lee Rose, *Rehearsal for Reconstruction: The Port Royal Experiment* (New York: Oxford University Press, 1964).

20. Walter Benjamin, "The Work of Art in the Age of Mechanical Reproduction," in Hannah Arendt, ed., *Illuminations*, trans. Harry Zohn (New York: Harcourt, Brace, and World, 1968), 222, 225. On Frederick Hart, see Tom Wolfe, "The Artist the Art World Couldn't See," *New York Times Magazine*, January 2, 2000, 16–19.

The African American Presence in Civil War Reenactment, by Cathy Stanton and Stephen Belyea

1. It is perhaps worthwhile here to clarify our approach to the use of reenactors as sources of information for this paper. The description of the 1997 encampment and parade was written from the perspective of Stephen Belyea, who participated in the centennial event in the role of military commander. He also interviewed fellow reenactors in two companies of the Fifty-fourth Massachusetts in 1998. Cathy Stanton conducted interviews with both black and white reenactors during 1996–98 as part of a two-year ethnographic fieldwork project. All interview sessions were taped and transcribed; tapes and transcriptions are in the possession of the authors. Because this study was informed by the discipline of anthropology, we have chosen to follow anthropological conventions and quote interview sources anonymously. We were less concerned with confidentiality and analyzing individual experiences within the reenactment community than with our purpose of examining a generalized experience of African Americans in Civil War reenactor culture. We recognize that there is a wide range of beliefs and practices among reenactors; our use of anonymous sources is not intended to suggest that one reenactor can possibly speak for all. But insofar as there are clearly identifiable patterns of belief and practice within the reenactor community, we have chosen interview material that speaks for those patterns. For a similar rationale of anonymously quoted interview material, see Richard Handler and Eric Gable, *The New History in*

an Old Museum: Creating the Past at Colonial Williamsburg (Durham, N.C.: Duke University Press, 1997), 26–27.

2. See Roger Abrahams, "Toward an Enactment-Centered Theory of Folklore," in William Bascom, ed., *Frontiers in Folklore* (Boulder, Colo.: Westview Press, 1977); John J. MacAloon, "Cultural Performances, Culture Theory," in John J. MacAloon, ed., *Rite, Drama, Festival, Spectacle: Rehearsals toward a Theory of Cultural Performance* (Philadelphia: Institute for the Study of Human Issues, 1984); Victor Turner, *Dramas, Fields, and Metaphors: Symbolic Action in Human Society* (Ithaca, N.Y.: Cornell University Press, 1974); and Victor Turner, *From Ritual to Theatre: The Human Seriousness of Play* (New York: Performing Arts Journal Publications, 1982).

3. Stuart McConnell, *Glorious Contentment: The Grand Army of the Republic* (Chapel Hill: University of North Carolina Press, 1992), 8–9.

4. McConnell, *Glorious Contentment*, 213.

5. National encampments were large-scale annual reunions at which veterans camped together in brief, idealized versions of Civil War camps, remarkably similar to contemporary Civil War reenactments. Confederate veterans held comparable reunions each year. McConnell, *Glorious Contentment*, 217.

6. David Glassberg, *American Historical Pageantry: The Uses of Tradition in the Early Twentieth Century* (Chapel Hill: University of North Carolina Press, 1990), 63.

7. Glassberg, *American Historical Pageantry*, 197.

8. Glassberg, *American Historical Pageantry*, 132.

9. Michael Kammen, *Mystic Chords of Memory: The Transformation of Tradition in American Culture* (New York: Knopf, 1991), 535.

10. The Civil War reenactor community in the United States is essentially a loose affiliation of independent small groups. In many cases the individual groups join to form brigade or battalion structures in order to facilitate large-scale military maneuvers, but reenactors' primary loyalties tend to be with their own units. Standards of authenticity are constantly debated within the reenactor community, although "authenticity" is frequently an issue through which more contemporary or personal concerns are negotiated. The general consensus of the community is that "nonperiod" items must be hidden from view whenever camps are open to spectators and should be used sparingly during nonpublic hours, in order to help create a more convincing illusion of the past for everyone in camp.

Estimates of the total number of Civil War reenactors have ranged from Jim Cullen's estimate of 20,000 to reenactor estimates of 40,000. A 1998 "mega-event" in Gettysburg attracted more than 20,000 participants. Jim Cullen, *The Civil War in Popular Culture: A Reusable Past* (Washington, D.C.: Smithsonian Institution Press, 1995), 186. For discussions of the development of contemporary reenactment, see Jay Anderson, *Time Machines: The World of Living History* (Nashville: American Association for State and Local History, 1984); R. Lee Hadden, *Reliving the Civil War* (Mechanicsburg, Pa.: Stackpole Books, 1996); and Cullen, *Civil War in Popular Culture*. Other information in this section is drawn from personal observation and conversations with long-time reenactors.

11. Company A was the "camera" company, comprised of professional actors rather than amateur reenactors. Company B consisted of experienced reenactors and new recruits who intended to use their experience on the film as a starting point for future involvement with reenactment. In lieu of pay, many negotiated to keep the uniforms and equipment supplied by the film company. Company B remains an active reenactment unit of the Fifty-fourth Massachusetts in the Washington, D.C., area. Company D was formed largely of unemployed men from Savannah, Georgia, and Jacksonville, Florida (including some from Jacksonville drug rehabilitation programs). This group was used for "deep background" and was issued inauthentic equipment. Company I consisted of active-duty soldiers from a nearby military base. According to a participant, these men "required very little training or supervision to turn them into convincing members of the 54th Massachusetts." David Jurgella, "One Week of 'Glory.'" *Military History Illustrated, Past and Present* 26 (July 1990): 18.

12. Only by accident, as during the retreat at the Battle of Olustee, Florida, were soldiers in black and white regiments thrown together during combat.

13. Cullen, *Civil War in Popular Culture*, 199.

14. Jonah Begone, "The Vandals at the Gates," *Camp Chase Gazette*, May 1998, 56–57.

15. The officer in charge of Company D during the filming of *Glory* related how the shared experiences of the ill-equipped "deep background" extras, who were excluded from other units' camaraderie, eventually coalesced into a feeling of group unity and pride among themselves. The men asked to be taught the drill and tactics that were already familiar to the reenactors. "At the end of the week, before heading out to the beach for the final night's filming, I thanked 'Co. D' for their efforts and told them I was proud to have been associated with the film, and with them. They responded with 'three cheers for the Captain' and marched over the boardwalk with feet stamping in time to a chant of 'Company D, Company D.'" Jurgella, "One Week of 'Glory,'" 20.

16. There are other instances of reenactors' viewing their performances in similar ways. For example, some female reenactors who choose soldier roles see themselves as recovering the memory of pioneers in the field of gender equality. Hispanics, Jews, and other ethnic minorities sometimes celebrate their forebears' efforts to gain greater acceptance in American society, much as blacks do. Southern nationalists may use reenactment to promote the idea of regional independence. We are talking here about paying homage to cultural pioneers, which may be quite different from historical revisionism. In general, however, this spirit of paying homage to pioneers in an unfinished struggle is much more typical of black reenactors than of whites.

CONTRIBUTORS

STEPHEN BELYEA is currently head of the Art Department at Boston's Cathedral High School, where he also teaches classes focusing on issues of racism in America. He has been involved in "living history" projects for more than twenty years.

MARTIN H. BLATT is the Chief of Cultural Resources/Historian at Boston National Historical Park. Among his books are *Free Love and Anarchism: The Biography of Ezra Heywood* (1989) and (co-editor) *The Meaning of Slavery in the North* (1998). A leader in the field of public history for two decades, he has developed museum exhibits, popular publications, audiovisual productions, and a variety of special programs.

DAVID W. BLIGHT, Professor of History and Black Studies at Amherst College, has written widely on abolitionism, American historical memory, and African American intellectual and cultural history. Among his many works is *Frederick Douglass's Civil War: Keeping Faith in Jubilee* (1989). His most recent book is *Race and Reunion: The Civil War in American Memory* (2001).

THOMAS J. BROWN, Assistant Professor of History at the University of South Carolina, is the author of *Dorothea Dix, New England Reformer* (1998).

THOMAS CRIPPS, University Distinguished Professor retired at Morgan State University, has written five books, among them *Slow Fade to Black: The Negro in American Film, 1900–1942* (1997). He also has authored many articles and television scripts, including *Black Shadows on a Silver Screen* (1976), which won gold medals at several international film festivals. He has been a fellow of the Rockfeller, Guggenheim, and Daedalus Foundations, the Woodrow Wilson International Center, and the National Humanities Center.

KATHRYN GREENTHAL, former Assistant Curator in the Department of American Paintings and Sculpture at the Metropolitan Museum of Art, is a Trustee of the Augustus Saint-Gaudens Memorial in Cornish, New Hampshire. She also was a member of the committee formed in 1980 to restore the Shaw Memorial. Among her publications are *Augustus Saint-Gaudens: Master Sculptor* (1985); *American Figurative Sculpture in the Museum of Fine Arts, Boston* (1986) (coauthor); and "Augustus Saint-Gaudens et la sculpture américaine," in *Augustus Saint-Gaudens 1848–1907: Un maître de la sculpture américaine* (1999).

JAMES OLIVER HORTON, Benjamin Banneker Professor of American Studies and History at George Washington University, is also Director of the African American Communities Project of the National Museum of American History at the Smithsonian Institution. He is the author of *Free People of Color: Inside the African American Community* (1993) and coauthor with Lois E. Horton of *In Hope of Liberty: Culture, Protest, and Community among Northern Free Blacks, 1700–1860* (1997).

GENERAL COLIN L. POWELL, twelfth Chairman of the Joint Chiefs of Staff from 1989 to 1993, was the youngest person and the first African American to hold the most senior position in the armed forces of the United States. While on active duty he served Presidents Reagan, Bush, and Clinton in top advisory positions. He has become one of the nation's most popular public speakers, and his 1995 autobiography, *My American Journey,* is a best-seller. In 1997 he became chairman of America's Promise—The Alliance for Youth, a not-for-profit organization dedicated to helping young people gain access to the resources they need to become successful adults.

EDWIN S. REDKEY, emeritus Professor of History, Purchase College, State University of New York, has written widely on African American history. Among his books is *A Grand Army of Black Men: Letters from African-American Soldiers in the Union Army, 1861–1865* (1992). His essay in this volume is part of a larger work in progress on the Fifty-fourth Massachusetts Infantry Regiment.

MARILYN RICHARDSON is a former curator of Boston's Museum of Afro American History and the African Meeting House on Beacon Hill. The African Meeting House was a recruitment center for the Fifty-fourth Massachusetts Regiment. She has taught and lectured nationally and internationally on African American cultural and intellectual history. Her publications include *Black Women and Religion* (1980) and *Maria W. Stewart, America's First Black Woman Political Writer* (1987).

KIRK SAVAGE is Associate Professor of the History of Art at the University of Pittsburgh. He is the author of *Standing Soldiers, Kneeling Slaves: Race, War, and Monument in Nineteenth-Century America* (1997).

JAMES SMETHURST, Assistant Professor of English at the University of North Florida, is the author of *The New Red Negro: The Literary Left and African-American Poetry, 1930–1946* (1999). He is presently at work on a study of the rise of the Black Arts Movement and other nationalist literary movements in the 1960s and 1970s.

CATHY STANTON is a freelance writer who has produced many works in genre fiction, playwriting, and other areas. She recently completed a master's degree in cultural anthropology at Vermont College, focusing on Civil War reenactment as a form of cultural performance, and is a doctoral candidate in history and anthropology at Tufts University.

HELEN VENDLER, A. Kingsley Porter University Professor at Harvard University, is the author of books on Yeats, Stevens, Herbert, Keats, Heaney, and Shakespeare and is the editor of *The Harvard Book of Contemporary Poetry.* She is a frequent contributor to the *New York Review of Books,* the *New Republic,* and other journals. Her North Carolinian great-grandfather Joshua Brothers fought in the 24th Massachusetts Regiment during the Civil War; his brother Jesse fought for the Confederates; both survived the war.

DENISE VON GLAHN, Assistant Professor of Music History at Florida State University, specializes in twentieth-century and American music. Her articles on Charles Ives and his music have appeared in *Musical Quarterly* and *American Music.* She is completing a book entitled *The Sounds of Place: New Perspectives on the American Cultural Landscape,* which addresses the issue of place as a source of inspiration for American composers.

JOAN WAUGH, Associate Professor of History at the University of California at Los Angeles, is the author of *Unsentimental Reformer: The Life of Josephine Shaw Lowell* (1997). She is conducting research for a book on Ulysses S. Grant as a symbol of American nationalism.

DONALD YACOVONE, Associate Editor for the Massachusetts Historical Society, has written on the history of abolitionism, reform, gender, and nineteenth-century African American history. Among his recent books is the life and letters of an African American soldier in the Fifty-fourth Massachusetts Regiment, *A Voice of Thunder: The Civil War Letters of George E. Stephens* (1997).

INDEX

A SEASON OF DELIGHT

A SEASON OF DELIGHT

JOANNE GREENBERG

HOLT, RINEHART AND WINSTON
NEW YORK

C. 2

Library of Congress Cataloging in Publication Data
Greenberg, Joanne.
A season of delight.
I. Title.
PS3557.R3784S4   813'.54   80-20421
ISBN: 0-03-057627-X

Chapters 1 and 2 were first published in slightly
different form in *Ploughshares.*

A limited first edition of this book
has been privately printed.

First Trade Edition

Designer: Amy Hill
Printed in the United States of America
1 3 5 7 9 10 8 6 4 2

BL

JL 15 '81

To David and Alan
with Love and Pride and Wonder

A SEASON OF DELIGHT

When Grace Dowben, the middle-aged
mother of two estranged children,
meets Ben Sloan, the new Jewish fellow
member of a local volunteer fire and
rescue squad, their camaraderie grows
into love.

1

I used to dislike shopping, the rushing here and there, and all the details to remember. Now it's almost pleasant. I shop in the morning when the stores are uncrowded and the early light gleams off the beige brick and glass of the storefronts. Since Joshua and Miriam are grown and gone, there's less to do and I can see the young mothers, some of them harried and embattled, with a sympathy that will soon, very soon, become nostalgia. I like the silence and order of the house now that I'm used to it. Saul and I sit close together at his end of the table. We thought we would have less to talk about when the children were gone, but it turned out not to be so. The daily happenings still interest us and we are able to pay more attention to the greater events.

Rosh Hashanah, the Jewish New Year, has just passed; these are the Days of Awe, the days between the New Year and Yom Kippur, the Day of Atonement. In the old times, people faced this week in terror. They cried aloud in the synagogues, they ran weeping to their neighbors, pressing unpaid debts upon them before it should be too late and their measuring by the

1

Lord be over and the mark against them made and blotted. We don't weep now. Debt is fashionable and we are decorous, rational, and fearless, but it's still possible to dream old-fashioned nightmares during the week of Awe. I am forty-eight and the freedom and wealth of my life here are shadowed during this week with smoke whispering from the chimneys of Camps I have never seen. I was thinking when I got out of the car, suddenly, of a fragment of a memorial poem in our prayer books, and this day about me, so paradoxically blue and golden, makes me pause. My grandparents' villages are gone. This Gilboa is in Pennsylvania and it's autumn with the mellow warmth of late summer still in it. I go in to my shopping.

The stores are in a covered mall but the mall is lit by skylights and it is pleasant. Down the long center gallery are places to sit and there are trees and shrubbery planted under the skylights. The people on the squad know that Thursday I'm out of service until noon, so my pace is leisurely but not idle. Store to store, steadily. I'm a good housewife. With a list.

But when I come out of the supermarket, the sadness from that poem, which has been standing off like the rain over the hills to the west of us here, has moved back in on me. Our New Year is a poignant time. So I change my mind. Instead of going directly to the car and home, I go to one of the mall's benches and sit down. I want to think about the holiday a little more, to give it its time.

There's a young man approaching the bench. I smile a little, in acknowledgment, and move over. To my surprise, he comes up to me and I see that the basket he is carrying is not for shopping but has flowers and leaflets in it. He takes one of these leaflets and hands it to me. There's a picture of a boy and a girl on it.

"Excuse me, ma'am," he says politely, "but did you know that millions of our children are hooked on drugs?"

My hand almost starts for my purse and the donation I think he wants, but then I remember and my heart sinks.

2

"You're not the Salvation Army or the teen center or any drug program," I say, and the words come out as tired and sad as I feel them. "You're the Unification Church."

"We do a lot of good," he says. "We have programs in all the major cities for drug addicts and runaways."

"You steal Jews," I say.

He has been taught to answer such things, but he misguesses me.

"We're not anti-Semitic," he says. "I myself had a Jewish background. My parents are Jewish."

We are both surprised and he is mortified when I begin to cry. The tears are so sudden and so overwhelming that they have come up into my eyes and flowed over before I know it, as though they had been waiting in ambush for this boy's arrival. My glasses are steaming over but my voice is still steady, and while I have it, I have him.

"Hitler killed one-third of us. A language, a culture, a way of life. Only our dispersion saved us from complete extinction. Now, through that awful tear in our people, more are flowing away. Don't you see that?"

"We don't seek—"

"*You* don't, you poor sap," I cry, "but *they* do. Somewhere in Illinois my son is dressed in yellow and is chanting someone else's ancestral language. His head is shaved for ritual reasons. He and you eat and don't eat for ritual reasons. You are burlesque artists, parodists!"

"Judaism is a bankrupt faith!"

"When did you invest a moment of yourself in it?"

It's no good and I see it. He can't see my visions or understand my pain. Free and equal, I know, I know. "I am I and you are you."

My voice is compromised now. I'm crying outright. Blushing wildly, he leaves me. Like any good American, he is unnerved by the public demonstration of emotions, except in groups. A Jewish mother weeping is his metaphor for hell, a banality he cannot endure. And I, too, am American. I can't sit blubbering and blind in a shopping-center mall at eleven in the morning for no visible reason. So I blow my nose, dry my eyes and my glasses, and drive home.

No more about the Illinois renunciate! But my mind drifts as I drive. He has given over his name, an ordinary Jewish name by which other Jews can know him and Christians too, as one of a people, a line, a tradition, a curse, a sorrow, a glory, a law. His new names are Sanskrit. He doesn't realize it but he comes two generations too late. How popular he might have been in Munich in 1934. He is that once most enviable of forebears, an Aryan. It is an irony I cannot share with him or with Eichmann or with Hitler, ghosts with whose ghosts I am saddled. It occurs to me that it has been three days since I last thought of Joshua-Sanjit. Three days without anguish and now the anguish returns.

Miriam also has gone into a world where Jews disappear. She is liberated from her husband and works at a women's center in California. I admire her commitments to battered wives and rape victims and the exploited of the Third World. Sadly for me, none of her commitments involves the continued existence of her own people. The blacks and Chicanos with whom she castigates me multiply in all their variety and rich profusion. The poor of the world are not an endangered species. Her former husband was not Jewish and she laughed at me when I begged her to consider raising Kimberley, who is legally so, as a Jew. It wasn't for me, I said, but for the people, so that Hitler would lose again, would lose forever.

"Everything has to change," she said, "some things have to die out, I guess."

Did I tell her that about Biafra, about the American Indians, that she should say it about *my* minority? *My* people? Is there anyone more lonely than the champion of an unfashionable cause?

4

Unaccountably, as I ride, the day opens outward. The autumn smells its briny apple-smell, but the sun is still in summer. I have the windows open and though I was angry and sobbing twenty minutes ago, there was a relief in the tears and I feel better for them, close to the day and the center of my life. Saul and I didn't die when Miriam met a man and moved in and then married without our presence. I made apologies to the family, to my mother who blames me for the loss, to all the aunts and uncles, and went on living. Joshua quit college and found the tide that carried him so far away, and we didn't die then, either. We only spoke a little more quietly when we sat together at dinner. We live like modern nobility, in the ancestral castle. There are certain rooms shut off for warmth and because of the upkeep. We remember those rooms, every inch of them, and everything with which they were furnished, but we don't often unlock them and we try to live all the more warmly in the rest of the house. Try.

When I get home, I back into the driveway, so the car faces out. I go into the house and before I unload my groceries, I check the call box. No red light. I call Rita Neri, our dispatcher. I am home.

"O.K.," she says, and we hang up. I'm in the fire and rescue service of this district. There's a dispatch box in the stairwell, and a red gumball light on the roof of my car. If there is an auto wreck or a fire or a heart attack or a serious fall or a sudden illness in Gilboa or the farms or suburbs around it any time of the day or night, I'll hear about it on the call box and I'll go and help deal with it. I've been on the squad for five years, and the whole district including "The Loop" of the Interstate is heavy with anecdote for me.

I unpack my groceries then and put them away. There's no class today, nothing special for me to do, and although I know I should study or do the windows or write letters, I do none of these things. I sit down at the kitchen table and let the day wash over me.

Last year, our student rabbi spoke about the High Holidays and gave examples of *galut*—exile. The harvest festival of Succos, soon to come, would find our evenings too cold to sit, as the celebration decrees, under the stars in magical booths hung with bunches of grapes. It is balmy in this season in Jerusalem, but one does not stay dreaming starward, somnolent and peaceful in these latitudes. Half an hour in a *succah* in this Gilboa and hypothermia would set in. To be unable to celebrate the feast correctly, seasonably, is exile, he said, be we ever so wealthy and at peace, be our neighbors ever so warmly disposed to us; our exile is the more poignant for being subtle and peripheral to our lives.

It was a good sermon and must have been partly true or I wouldn't have remembered it. But God is everywhere and He has arranged recompenses for His exiles. The wine-crisp tang of autumn does not blow through Jerusalem. Hallelujah the hills. Haifa has hills too, but they never blaze with a thousand fires in a hundred tones of rose-gold, flame and orange, yellow, purple, and umber. My exile lies in fragrant piles on my doorstep and breaks beneath my feet in the snap-twig wood-smoke mornings of my father's chosen land.

I think now would be a suitable time to cry. The house is clean and in order. Saul isn't due home for hours. I could get the old pictures of Joshua and Miriam out of the boxes in the attic and set them around me and remember the hope and the work and the planning and the good intentions, the new starts, the books we read, the pangs of conscience we suffered. It's too late. I have cried my cry already in front of another woman's fool and it's all over. The phone rings. I smile. Had I been crying, whoever it was would have caught me at it.

It's Riva, my mother-in-law. Poor woman; she was never very religious but because she's Saul's mother, she feels she owes it to her position to uphold the values of her generation.

"Grace, Yom Kippur is this Thursday and I haven't settled the plans in my mind. What are we planning to do?"

"I think things will go pretty much as they did last year, evening and Yom Kippur Day. Some people will want to go home after the service and break the fast with their families. For those who want to stay, there will be a light meal, dairy. If you want to stay, we will too. In any case, I'm down for a potato pudding and a salad."

"When Elia was alive it was so much nicer. We all stayed then. Now— And I wish we didn't have services at the town hall. It's so—"

"I know," I say, "but right now there is no other place. We've gotten too big for Bert and Joan's basement."

"It was nice there."

I know what she means. Five years ago, the Jews of Gilboa, Russian Grove, and Tarrant together numbered no more than twenty families, and of these, only half were observant. For years we met warmly and intimately in the Finegolds' rumpus room. The "Sisterhood" was four women, the "Hebrew School" eight kids and a teacher, but a new housing development came in between Tarrant and Gilboa and Jews from the suburbs west of Midlothian found it pleasant to come east on the Interstate to us instead of going to the city. Two years ago, we found we had to look for another place. Since then, we have been meeting in a corner of the town hall basement. There are cooking facilities there and lots of chairs; there are no religious reminders to distract us, but we are dwarfed in the large hall. The sound we make, even praying all together, doesn't fill half the space. We are conscious as never before of ourselves as a minority, a decimated minority. Could this be the reason for the memorial poem to rise in my mind before its time, this feeling that we are flowing away through the terrible wounds of Hitler's tyranny and Stalin's murders and our own sloth and social dislocation and the blandishments of other faiths?

"I know, Riva, but what can we do? I'm grateful the town

fathers let us meet down there. They could have gotten stuffy and talked about separation of church and state. I wish there were a bigger house or a smaller hall that would have us." She sighs into the phone. My signals go up. "What's the matter—is something wrong?"

"No—no. I suppose it's the end of summer. Whenever I have to put on a heavy sweater in the morning, I remember I'm an old lady. Elia used to say, 'One foot in the grave and the other on a banana peel.'" We talk for a while longer—something she isn't saying, isn't ready to say—and when we hang up I find I'm tense and tired. I put up a cup of tea and have a piece of the cake Saul brought home last night. Food, the Jewish tranquilizer. I should be grateful; it could have been booze. Leaving the kitchen door open, I go out to the little porch in back and sit down.

Saul is home. I hear the mailbox slam shut because he knows I sometimes forget the mail. I haven't this time. I smile. There's a silence as he comes up the walk and then there is the sound of his step on the front porch and then the door opening. He's early. This past year he's been taking off for a couple of hours on the days when the store is open 'til nine. I want him to come out here where I'm sitting. I want to tell him about the young man with the flowers and the Jewish parents. We've been through twenty-five years together, a war, death and birth, hopes blossoming, hopes in blight. I want to tell him this, too, but I'm worried that he'll take it the wrong way. Men have strange ideas about the fragility of women. I don't want him to see my weeping as more than it was. But what it was, I don't yet know myself. Now I hear him moving through the house. It makes me smile again. He'll glance at the mail on the hall table, then come into the kitchen and take the cracked mug, the big one with his name on it that the children gave him one birthday long ago, and he'll pour himself a cup of coffee and soon he'll be out here to sit in his sprung old chair and look out over the field and down the long hill to where Gilboa's main streets, hidden by trees, lift their few spires and building tops. Beyond Gilboa, the bypassing freeway arches. To the east of the fields it comes around to us close on the other side. We hear the traffic as a low, constant hum. It's getting a little cooler. I call to him, and as I do, I decide I'll wait until I know what my tears were for before I burden him with them.

We've been so close for so long that it is only in flashes that I see him aging, and I have one of these as he comes toward me. How gray he is now! There are wrinkles around his eyes. It must be the same with me, although I don't really see it. In another twenty years, if we are lucky, we will both be old. I ask him about his day.

2

Saul grew up in Gilboa. It was a small Pennsylvania farm town before Midlothian got big with the heavy industry of World War II. Elia Dowben came here in 1912 and set up a dry goods and clothing store. Over the years, the dry goods business was taken over by chains, but the old man, a Russian Jewish peasant from Shedletz, turned out to have a designer's eye for style and an intuitive sense of the wants of his customers. The clothing store flourished. Three years later, he contacted a marriage broker in New York who supplied him with a wife, Riva, from a place called Shedletz "so she would be compatible." They and their children were the only Jews in Gilboa until the mid-forties. I was raised in Chicago. I met Saul in college and came to Gilboa, to what my family still considers an exile worse than the Babylonian. I like the town and the sense of community that, although changed and diluted by the new populations, is still subtly present here and there and still speaks in an older voice in the fire department and the church and the private relationships between neighbors. It roots Saul, centers him. As I thought it might, his voice has restored some peace to the afternoon.

We sit quietly together and watch the day go down in mellow light. The Caetanos' teenage daughter is entertaining her friends and the music drifts across to us mellowed, sweetened by distance. Saul tells me about his day, an ordinary day. I have a book but I put it by. It's more important just now to study exactly how the golden field gets its shadows and how the shadows pull long and then how the sun goes behind the hills on the way to Midlothian. When the sun goes, the shadows are destroyed. Then everything stands in equal light, a glow in which each visible thing is made real, complete, itself. And because the year has turned, there is a little haunting coolness when the light goes. We are a little higher than the town; we get the light later, so we wait, Saul and I, for the first lights to be lit down there. The district. My Chicago relatives are aghast at my being a "fireman." It seems bizarre to them, although there are middle-aged women doing fire-rescue all over the country. I like the work for many reasons, one of them being that I am able, by virtue of what we do, to look out over Gilboa and onto the great loop of the Interstate exit by exit and know that it is, at this moment, within the widest limits possible, at rest.

On Tuesday, I sign myself out for the twenty-four hours of the holiday. I call Rita for rescue and C. A. Bordereau for fire, and tell them that I will be out of service from sundown tomorrow night to sundown Thursday. "Sundown? When exactly is that?" C. A. cries. Very Talmudic.

"A Jewish sage says it's when you can't tell a light thread from a dark one in natural light," I answer.

C.A.'s voice becomes formally serious. "Oh, Jewish holidays—" he says, "religious reasons." He pauses and then remembers. "What is this holiday? I thought it came last week."

"Last week was the new year and this week is the Day of Atonement."

Religious matters are very serious to C.A. Four generations

of the Bordereaux supplied a full complement of nuns and priests from this parish. Because religious observance is as important as election or damnation to him, his voice always falls when he talks about such matters. As an old-fashioned Catholic, he doesn't need or wish explanations of what we "do" on various holidays. He assumes it is Divine Mystery. Saul remembers him from school as desperately shy, too big for any of the desks after the fourth grade. I know him as competent and dedicated. "Well," he says, "happy Yom Kippur."

"Thank you," I answer.

I think as I clean the house the next day that I should get myself ready for the holiday, stop thinking about classes or cleaning or rescue, take what advantages there are in the serenity of an empty house, and slow down so that I can overtake the holiday at its pace, walking. Saul will be home at five-thirty. We'll eat and then go to the evening service. We might even go down over the field while it's still light, the shortcut that our kids and the ones who still live on these streets take to school.

The alarm, two ululant wails, and the sheriff's man: "Attention Gilboa Fire and Rescue. You have a first aid at the Methodist Church, Federal and Larch." The call is repeated. I am in my red rescue coat and out the door before the end of the second call. It's six blocks to the church, but there are as many turns, and even with red light and siren, dangerous at this time of day. When I get to the church, Geri Pines, the squad captain, and some of the others are there. Geri radios to the rest of the squad to stand down; we will not need any more people.

We go inside and a woman motions us down to the basement. Then I remember the day, yes, Wednesday, Altar Guild day, and there they are, around the table at their newest project, the raffle quilt for the repair of the leak on the south wall. We stop for a moment. Who is it? Who among all these old women is it? I try to deny—they will not let me. They stand aside, away from her, as they never would do for one of their living friends in trouble. It is Violet, my friend Violet Cleve, my first friend in Gilboa. She's sitting at her place at rest in her chair. Her hands are on the quilt the women are making. She looks no different from her usual self. I go over and feel for a pulse. None. She's cold. Her legs have stiffened. I know we could not resuscitate her. I know what it would take to try. I shake my head. Geri comes over and listens, then feels at the legs. "How old a woman was she?" Geri asks. I open my mouth to say "seventy," but Addie Arvis says, "Ninety-five. She was ninety-five." Of course. The years, the years have gone by.

"She's been sitting here quietly dead for half an hour at least," Geri says. It's a statement that tells the squad we will not start work on her. It's something on which we all must agree and we all do. The ladies haven't wanted to move her. They are standing back, murmuring at the suddenness. Geri goes out to call the coroner from Midlothian. Someone must stay until he comes and I ask to let it be me. We ease Violet over onto a bench, and cover her. Since the death was unexpected, state law takes over. There's nothing more to do.

I sit and wait, thinking how satisfying rescue is except when there is nothing to be done—except when the pain and death are those of a friend.

Saul is in the kitchen when I come home. "I heard about Violet and knew you must have been with her. I thought if you were late, I'd start dinner. You won't want to be cooking, now."

"Where but in a small town could you get communication like this without a phone?"

"Speed of sound." We smile at one another.

Down over the field and the hill is the back way to the town hall, to services. We talk about Violet, how she and I met, and my coming as a bride to Gilboa. How hard I worked to belong to it all, to make Saul's friends mine, his parents mine, to remember all the names and traditions. We laugh at my false starts, my joining the Garden Club—I, who didn't know a rose from a peony. He wonders again how Violet and I took to one another in a shy, surprised way. She was old, even then. She was First Family, we were new—only a generation in Gilboa. We had nothing obvious in common and even Saul was surprised at our friendship. I learned Gilboa through Violet's eyes. I learned to relax and let it come—people, the town, the farms around, the hills, glades, forests, flowers, rocks, streams, ponds that were for her familiar, part of a vaster scheme in the goodness of God. I got pregnant and caught up in motherhood, but when the seasons changed, the two of us would always go out together as official witnesses to the change and the continuity of things. "I wonder what Joshua is doing tonight."

"Chanting."

"I wonder if he knows it's Kol Nidre."

"Grace—"

"Animals lick their wounds and in my ambulance the victims keep touching the broken arm, working the sprained wrist surreptitiously to see if the pain's still there, still just as bad."

"It wasn't our fault and it isn't now."

"Whose, then?"

"Grace, don't do this, please," Saul says. "You're moving my broken arm, too." I have brought back the Days of Awe. A sweet ramble over a wild-wheat-scented hillside is not part of our tradition. Is guilt? People say so. It's the oldest Jewish joke we know. My Orthodox grandparents mourned the two children who fled away to America's secularism and married "strangers." They declared them dead. It was bizarre and I wouldn't do it, but my generation is so rational that it allows no grief at all. "Everyone makes his choice," we tell one another. We are all free as hell and instead of weeping we shrug.

When we get to the hall, I look for Riva. She says it's silly for us to come and pick her up and I've let her convince me, but when I don't see her here I worry. All around me neighbors are greeting one another, but there are many I don't know, people from Midlothian or its closer suburbs who come here because the congregation is small. I look around. We are doing well in "exile." People look happy and peaceful. There are no haunted faces among us. Oh, here comes Riva, dressed for the occasion. Years as Elia's wife never touched her taste in clothes, which has been a lifelong cry against the poverty and drabness of her youth. She loves to have birds and flowers flying across her dresses, yellow turbans, colored shoes. For years, Saul tried, by buying clothes for her, which she never wore, to modify her unmodifiable style. When Elia died, we gave up and she did, too. When Dowben's clothes are not bright enough, she goes to the shopping center. Bold as brass.

But as I look at her objectively, I sense a change. The loud colors have gone louder still. I know she has been having trouble seeing lately; I wonder if her vision has gotten worse. Perhaps she needs these colors because they are all she can see.

It's a beautiful service, Kol Nidre. Our man, not a rabbi but a young student, is earnest and well-meaning, but he has little feeling yet for resonances. He leads the prayers, but doesn't tell us in what way they are linked, why they have, some of them, to be repeated. Riva stands between Saul and me and I stand next to Mr. Levine and look into his prayer book. When the Al Chet comes, the recitation of sins, I cry. I always do, quietly, while Saul looks on, partly jealous, I think. In the older tradition, in Chicago, in the small side-street shuls—some of them brought over entire and alive from this or that specific village in the Pale—everyone cried, men and women unabashedly. But the younger generations, my mother's and mine, were scornful of such carryings-on. We were afraid of how it looked and what the Gentiles would think, and so decorum came to the second generation and the third, a revelation so vast it covered the whole land and now only the very old weep aloud, and Grace Dowben weeps quietly and Saul Dowben watches her partly embarrassed and partly amused and partly jealous and partly moved. Why do I cry? Because I have always cried. Why have I always cried? I don't know.

Saul comes with me to the morning service but after the noon break he decides to stay home. I am fasting; he is not. He praises my strength of character, but I don't fast out of zeal so much as habit. I thought I'd stop when I no longer had children for whom to provide an example. The Sisterhood's meal after the evening service includes my pudding and salad, which means I have to bring them to the hall sometime during the afternoon. Some clever rabbi a thousand years ago must have urged this union between food and faith.

Riva, too, is gone, drawn away in a net of excuses. It makes me laugh. My children's style was confrontation. When Miriam didn't wish to go to services or to school or to visit my parents, she gave me an hour's speech about hypocrisy, the middle class, and institutionalization. Riva's style—the style of her generation—is more comfortable: "I should go, really, but—" and I am shown how impossible it is to do what she does not wish to do. The outcome is the same, but I like Riva's "reasons" better. They are less tiresome and self-righteous.

In any case, it means that I'm there alone for the memorial service and we say the broken Kaddish that intersperses the Hebrew words of the prayer with the names of death camps and places of persecution, so many places on our journey that Jews must remember because our tormentors will not. Light as smoke wafts the little memorial poem, and the poem for the children we lost. If the highways and the heart attacks and the booze and the bridge abutments gave me a thousand a day to rescue, I couldn't make up one of the cities of my lost people in a lifetime.

I look around. There are young people here, although I read that in America the median age of our people is now forty. Will we all get old, old as the age-old caricatures of us, and glimmer away quietly into history, more quietly than even our tormentors wish? I look around again. There are children here—not enough, never enough. There are young people here, but not mine, not mine.

The break comes. I go home to rest, but don't. Many people will be coming for the final service, drawn by that clever custom, dinner at the end. Average Jews, we are very good cooks. I bake my potato pudding and make the salad. The afternoon is warm, sweet and golden with sunlight, but the memorial words hang over it and the names of the camps and the curl of that smoke just out of hearing, just out of sight. None of the graves are here, not even Elia's, who has been dealt with in the practical modern way. In the old country during this time we would all be out visiting the graves of our dead to conjure them as witnesses to our year. Look, Grandma, how tall my youngest is; look, Grandpa, I've gotten old myself. My generation and the two before it have millions more ghosts to conjure, all the little children of the poem, all the others. What would I tell such ghosts, I wonder? What would they tell me?

They would stand against the wall of the Caetanos' house, the house next door, which is brick. They would be dressed in those familiar black-and-white-striped outfits, but they wouldn't be the people themselves, they would be the grainy black-and-white photographs from those times. Nothing would move on them when the wind blew, no little wisp of hair from the child's face, no garment. They would be a small group, my conjured ghosts, not an attempt to understand a continent full of people. Four or five, no more: a child, young woman, maybe two men— one a grandfather, old and bearded. I would say, "Shalom aleichem." Nonsense. An American's homemade ghosts speak English. I can expect no flavoring dialects dead with their villages, with Mezeritch and Zoromin. Zoromin is smoke. I would say, "Don't chide me for my children. Some of yours also fell away. And please don't demand strict observance from me, in your pain that the price for being Jews was so high for *you*, observant or not." The woman I have conjured beckons. There's a sound from her as she clears her throat of smoke and earth. "There were," she says in a voice no more than a whisper, "children to have been born to me. I never nursed a child . . ." Then, surprisingly, the boy speaks in a high child's voice: "Taddeus and I had a sled, but the Germans came before the snow and there was never—"

"—at the height of my profession," the older man cries, "with my mind opening so wide I could almost feel it—experimental work that was altogether new, a whole new understanding of—"

"—He sold me the land," the younger man interrupts, "and threw in the barn, it was such a wreck. I would have made—" and as in a fugue, their whispers blend and are lost, and then they fade again to nothing.

What a strange conjuring! The ghosts of this holiday haven't cursed me—I thought they might. I'm not the kind of Jew an Orthodox Jew would recognize, but . . . my woman would have an opinion of someone who spent Yom Kippur afternoon talking to ghosts and letting her potato pudding burn in the oven.

I pack up my bowls and baking dishes and put them in the car. As I do, I try hard to remember us when we were a family, not just fragments, when we would walk these Yom Kippur afternoons, Elia and Riva and Miriam and Joshua and Saul and I, over to the Finegolds' for services. What were we like together? Were we happy to be with one another or was it all the way Joshua characterized it when I saw him last: "I had no life as a Jew; my life was empty."

I think back, I try to remember clearly what was said, who laughed, who scolded, if there was any pleasure in the day, any feeling of the presence of God; any sense of union with a people and a law that— Then I think of the boy at the shopping center and I'm crying again before I know it. Wonderful, perfect. I can go back to services looking puffed and blotchy in the wrong country and a century too late. Grace is the perfect name for me; Grace, queen of timing. No wonder Miriam spent her last year here with her eyes rolled toward heaven in that strained patience look that used to drive me mad. But it makes me stop crying because I have remembered in that look of Miriam's a parody of my own. Enough. It's time to go back. I drive the five blocks to the town hall and get out and begin to unload. No one is here yet. I will be able to make two trips to the car and then sit outside on the steps and think about the service to come.

But when I have unloaded and put the food where it belongs and sat down with my prayer book, I feel the presence of the ghosts glimmering around me. "Listen!" the woman cries to me, "I never bore children!"

So there it is again. Children. Why else would such images rise, but to tell me my wound is more than a private pain; a blow, another blow to a bleeding people. "No, you listen!" I cry to them without sound. "This memorial is yours more than my own father's, more than my own grandparents'! What do you want from me, three hundred sixty-five Yom Kippurs a year? You're here, horrified, standing in judgment of what I am—what I've done. I loved my children as much as you did yours—what can I do for you now? What can pay back your suffering? Leave my wounds alone, don't touch them. My pain is sufficient for me, more than sufficient. What can I say to you that isn't choked with tears?"

The child turns to one of the men. "I tried to tell her about the sled, about my sled, but all she wants to talk about is how we died."

"It's natural, with such deaths, such millions of deaths," the younger man says.

"It isn't fair!" the older man cries to him. "*They* imposed that horror on us and we are victims forever. I was more than that, a whole rich life, a life of textures, of discoveries! My own people are making of me the numbers on my arm!"

They are all turned inward arguing with one another, their

fingers and hands flashing up and down in the sun-latticed corner where they stand half-visible in the blue and golden light. I feel ludicrous—my own ghosts in an argument with one another; they are paying no attention to me at all. And then the woman turns into the light until she is plain. "Men!" she sniffs. "Listen to them. Theoretical. They are spinning theories now. The sun will go down and spin them off into the air, theories and all."

"What do you want?" I ask her.

"That you remember us not only as horror stories. In our unlived lives there are millennia of joy. Couldn't you live a little of it, a little each day, each of you? You who remain?"

"How can I live your joy?"

"How else? As your own. Take delight . . ."

The sun is going down. Unconscious of it, the men are still arguing. The woman smiles. "Happy Yom Kippur," she says.

3

Violet Cleve's funeral is a town event. After all these years, I have forgotten this town's need for communal events. It's a hunger that still separates us from the suburbanites who shop here and live near us. The ladies of our Garden Club bring out every flowering and leafing plant they have; gardens are stripped. All morning the men of the town labor with cachepots and vases. The Methodist Church looks like a green bower.

It's packed. Jammed into a pew made for half the present number, I see here and there most of Gilboa Fire and Rescue. The mayor is here, and Sheriff Ups. The school has been let out early. Serena at the post office must simply have closed her window and come. But, it's not a day to grieve. No one is grieving. Neighbors are chatting, the Garden Club preening, Pastor Dodge has hearers who have never been his before nor will be again. Sheriff Ups is mending fences, the mayor gently, deftly campaigning. Beside me, my ghosts are standing. I know why they are here and what they are witness to, but they are a metaphor no one in this church shares with me.

Pastor Dodge begins. The readings and prayers are familiar and expected. It's the sermon that saddens and disappoints me. I wanted the pastor's remarks to be special for Violet. If I had my way, the people here would rise one by one and remember her. How did the pastor really see her? Was she more to him than a stylized old-fashioned lady? Why are you here, C.A.? What do you remember of her, forty years ago when you were ten and she was fifty-five? Was she a terror about that garden of hers? Or did she let you steal grapes from the blue gloom of the arbor she used to have? Ghosts have demanded of me that there be no general deaths, no more mass graves. The pastor is a nice man, but he is putting Violet in a mass grave. "A kind and gentle spirit," he is saying. When? Where? To whom? I begin to get angry. Descriptions like that are made of any woman needing burial, any old woman. Where can I go with my testimony about who Violet was and what she said?

Eventually, it's over. I go out with Geri and Claude and Rita, and we stand outside the church. "Are you going to the graveyard?"

"I'd like to go," Rita says.

I'm surprised.

"I want to go, too," Geri says, "but who'll stay and cover the district?" It's a familiar question, a constant discipline we have all gotten used to.

Claude nods. "The Sharps are here and I'll stay." We smile. Done, then.

We drive to the cemetery two miles out of town in Rita's new car. I ask her how she came to know Violet. Even in a town like this, there are still mysteries.

"I never knew her except to say hello to at the store or on the street. I'm here for my grandfather. My grandfather used to say, 'The Italian has a big appetite and a long memory.' Back in the twenties, they came here from Tarrant. The town didn't freeze up against them, but it was cool. 'Except for the lady,' Nonno used to say, 'the lady make us to be citizens.' Miss Cleve went to see Nonna. She hired the kids to do odd jobs. To me it sounds like exploitation, but for them it meant recognition, a place in the community. Soon, people got used to seeing the Neris. Only later did the other mill people come, the Ruggieros, DiBellos, all the rest. The old folks are gone, and Mom isn't well, so I'm here as a stand-in." I smile. I am getting older. I remember "the old folks" well.

Geri says, "That old broad was a symbol of everything I'm fighting, everything I hate."

"How come?" I am dumbstruck.

"All those 'ways'—what my ex-husband grew up expecting— the batted eye, the demure smile, the delicate lady role."

I try to answer, knowing I can't. "She didn't play the role. She was the real thing. I think we only *make* the roles when we can't be the real thing. And anyway, is wanting those virtues so bad?"

"Not if you don't mind drowning in honey."

"When I think of Violet I feel calmed, quieted. I wish I was more like her—gentler than I am."

"Why shouldn't she have been gentle? She was Queen of the Garden Club and Grande Dame of Gilboa."

"She was a spinster in a small town, a woman with a reputation to live up to. I think she made a virtue of necessity and accepted what she was. I think that twenty-five years later, she looked at herself and saw that the virtues she had made of necessity had magically turned into real virtues. I think that made her laugh."

"Brrrrr! Virtue!"

"You can't get away with that, Geri. I've seen *you* at work. You're as gentle in your way as Violet was in hers. The difference is in the style, not the content." Rita laughs.

"Shut up, Rita," Geri says. Rita laughs again.

At the cemetery we stop in wonder. The Garden Club has made the burial place like a wedding bower. The way to the grave site is posted with bouquets and fall arrangements. "I bet the ladies are angry as hell she didn't die in early summer," Geri whispers, "when the roses were out."

"This is better for them. Taxes the creativity. Spurs the ingenuity." I like the idea of flowers at a grave, although traditional Jewish funerals don't have them. Years ago in Chicago, our rabbi had said, "The deaths of men should not occasion the deaths of other living things." If I were to be true to the metaphor of my people the way Rita has been to hers, I would tear a piece of my clothing or a ritual scrap attached to it. Jewish mourners flutter in the wind. Their hair is left to blow; they are ragged with loss.

On the way home from the funeral, we stop at the firehouse to restock one of the trucks. C.A. passes, and seeing the door open, stops and comes in. Orley Flett is with him. When Orley comes, I feel Geri go a little stiff beside me. Orley greets C.A., nods at me, and stares for a moment at Geri with an expressionless face.

Around us like ancestors, the pictures of the men of Gilboa Fire line the walls. Fathers and sons since 1857, they stand in front of the new horse-drawn pumper, the new steam model, the new horseless, the new diesel. Good, stout machines. Good, stout men. Fire-eaters. During the First and Second world wars, women had been allowed to drive the trucks and do firehouse maintenance, but they were not members. When fire fighting began to change to fire-rescue, the issue of women members split many of the volunteer services. In Gilboa, a woman named Margaret Orange applied to be a fireman in 1970. Her application was posted as political humor on the bulletin board. Early in 1972, Serena Hansen and Anna Hamer applied. They were women with husbands in the department. They argued that with the new, lighter hose-couplings and lightweight hoses, they were as capable of operating equipment as the men. Furthermore, they were available during working hours when the department was weakest. Their applications were held "pending further discussion." In the spring of 1972, I applied. The firemen knew that discussion couldn't be tabled indefinitely, so they let us take the training for a year instead of the usual six months. I think they were surprised by our courage and ability. We were conditionally accepted in 1973 by a one-vote margin. There have been, significantly, no group pictures after that time. No woman's face is on the firehouse wall. Some of the firemen still do only fire fighting; some of the rescue people do no fires; and in some, the old anguish remains. C. A. Bordereau is still uneasy with us; Orley still sees his two categories of women: mothers and whores. Which are we?

He seems to know which kind Geri is. At accidents she's assertive like a man. Afterward, she smokes cigarettes and, Orley suspects, pot. She swears. She drinks. She is divorced and unashamed of it. They stay out of each other's way, but the air between them vibrates. So they stand among the engines, surrounded by pictures of Orley's heroes and Geri's antagonists, and stare down the caricatures they present to one another. I go to the office to talk to C.A. about a lost blanket.

"That was a nice funeral," he says. "I guess this town won't see the like of a great lady like that again."

"I guess not."

C.A. nods. His weight makes him overwhelm the office a little. With the two of us in the small room, it's crowded. "I liked what Mr. Dodge said about her."

"I wish he'd been more *personal*. What was she like when you were a kid?"

C.A. shrugs. "Well, *you* know, she always dressed just so. Passin' her on the street, she'd say hello, but then there'd always be somethin' more, somethin' nice—"

I have edged him out of the office. Geri moves toward us. I can feel her defensiveness as she stands there. "If I hear the word 'lady' one more time today—" For a minute, I wish the women's liberation movement had hours like a business, nine to five, and on weekends and holidays time out from the confrontation, the freezing of thoughts into slogans.

But C.A. doesn't seem to mind. "Miss Cleve had a way of showing the nice side of things—"

"Yes, she did," I say.

C.A. smiles. "But you know, she was always *old* to me. I used to think when I was a kid, that she was so old and fragile she would break apart one day—her bones. It scared me. A couple of times I had dreams about it, her suddenly falling down and not having no shape because her bones was all gone inside her. Nightmares, you know."

"Really?"

"It got so bad I told my dad about it. The next time he had work in Midlothian, he took me with him, and on the way back he just marched me into the hospital and told 'em I needed to see a bone specialist. Well, I guess they figured I was sick. We gone up and seen this doctor and my dad told him. Well, the doctor's eyes come open, but he took me in the room where they study the X-rays, and for maybe half an hour we just looked at X-rays of old people's legs and spines. I don't know what it proved, but I didn't have no more of them dreams. I kept seein' Miss Cleve, an' she didn't die an' her bones didn't crumble away, and I guess it taught me how strong gentle people can be. When Jeannie come along, I guess I seen that in her, that I maybe never would have if not for Miss Cleve."

We don't say anything. We are moved, all the more because Jeannie Bordereau is a broad, a cute dumb broad, and C.A. sees Violet in her.

"She done a lot for the Garden Club, too," Orley says. "The flowers she done for the schools—Shakespeare plants and that."

C.A. laughs. "I grew up thinkin' every Catholic church had a fig tree in the chancel."

"I never knew that it was Miss Cleve. I thought it was the

Garden Club's original purpose all these years."

"It was all her, the schools and the churches. She never let on. I know because my ma talked about it."

I'm touched by C.A.'s story. Violet was so fragile-looking it was no wonder a boy raised in C.A.'s teeming, loud house should have seen her flesh as insufficient and her bones as bird bones, too light to support a person through the world. I tell him my story. Geri comes over to listen.

"Once, it was an April morning, maybe fifteen years ago, I had a box of remnants to take over to Violet for the quilt ladies at the Altar Guild. It was one of those glowing spring mornings—a light, fresh wind and the smell of earth. I went up Cleve Road the back way, and I heard her in the yard talking softly to herself, noting the new things that had come up, and suddenly, she stopped, and I heard her say, 'Oh, my, isn't it wonderful!' And then there was a sound I couldn't identify, and I went close. I saw her, the wizened, wrinkled, fragile old lady, standing by her lilac bush. The buds had shaken open in the warm wind, the very first ones, and she was *applauding* them, the way a delighted child would."

"That's *too* childlike for me," Geri says.

Why can't I show her these differences? She's so intuitive, so perceptive about other things! "It's the very opposite of child-like. It's not innocence, it's simplicity refined." I stop. C.A. is beginning to look uncomfortable. Perhaps he thinks it isn't right to talk about people's motives this way.

Geri is smoking. She is doing it because Orley is here.

"All right," I say. "You want the dark sides, too, do you? I don't know many; I'm sure they were there. Musically, she was illiterate. Her taste in art was sappy-Victorian. She was responsible for that ghastly picture of Jesus in the vestibule of the Methodist Church. Why the congregation didn't sue her and the artist for slander, I'll never know. Her taste, except for flowers and quilts, was awful. I wouldn't let her choose an article of clothing for me, a set of dishes, or a knickknack for the mantel, but spiritually, she was what one of my ancestors described as 'a well of sweet water.' "

I'm scandalizing C.A. "It ain't right, you goin' on this way! What does it matter what she thought about *dishes*? Miss Cleve was a wonderful woman!"

"We're saying good-bye, C.A., that's all. It's only our way of saying good-bye."

"Well, it's a mighty mean way of doin' it, if you ask me. It ain't right to speak ill of the dead." And C.A. gets up. "I got to get busy around here." He calls out to Orley, but Orley has done what he had come to do and has gone. C.A. can't help a quick look of irritation at Geri. Orley Flett used to spend all his free time at the firehouse, hours cleaning and polishing the trucks and waiting for cronies to stop by. The Old Boys' Club days are over. The beer cooler is now stocked with soft drinks and the pool table is gone. No one sits in the open doorway in nice weather, smoking and reading the paper, tip-tilted on a kitchen chair. In his heart, C.A. approves of the changes, and I know it, but now he sighs and moves away among the trucks.

Our team—how different we are from one another! Away from the wreck, the fire, the alarm box, we can scarcely guess at the force that unites us, fuses us into the strange family we have become.

Geri is staring after C.A. "I've never heard that man say so much at one time since I've known him."

"I shocked him, telling you about Violet's bad taste in home furnishings." We look at one another and begin to laugh.

Then Geri says, "In all the doings today, I forgot to tell you. Two more people want to come on the squad. One of my nurses over at the nursing home says she's interested and yesterday a young man came by and said he would like to join."

"Who is he?"

"He's new in the area, he says. Got long hair and a beard. I told them both to come to Wednesday's meeting."

"Good. By the way, Dowben's is having a sale this weekend and I'll be helping, so I'll be across the street from the ambulance."

"Do you like working with Saul in the store?"

"People in accidents are nervous and fearful, and some of them react with defensiveness and hostility. People buying clothes are nervous and fearful, and some of them react with defensiveness and hostility. The only difference is that in the ambulance, we command the scene, and at the dress shop, the victim does." I get up.

"Thanks, Grace."

"For what?"

"For getting C.A. to talk. He never would have said all that to me alone."

"Isn't that what death is supposed to do for the living?"

"I never knew death was supposed to *do* anything."

"It's there, you might as well use it."

"Housewife!"

I plan to go home and do a little cleaning, but I'm so close to the store I decide to go over and be with Saul for a while. My taste in clothes is poor and the whole town knows it, but as a general assistant I'm better than most. If there's a long lull, I'll hang the new stock and write the new prices on the sale stuff and tell Saul, as we work, about the Moonie in the Pinecrest Mall.

4

Miriam is calling from California. She asks how we are and I tell her. It all sounds trivial. I decide to broach the subject of Riva. Riva is well, but losing her vision, and she's defensive, ashamed about it in some way. Frightened of being a burden, she denies and denies. I tell Miriam some of the ploys I have tried, to get Riva to a doctor. So far they have all failed. Miriam sighs, and I can almost hear the little habitual click of her impatience, a gesture with the thumbnail and the fingernail snapped from under it—she has used it for years.

"Mother, I think you're fostering dependence in Grandma, and Grandma's tradition encourages it. She's not going to overcome her problems if she has you and Dad to fall back on all the time!" She goes on to tell me that Riva needs to have her consciousness raised, to understand the politics of her situation. I say that, to Riva, the situation is personal and has no politics. Miriam tells me that it's this kind of thinking that has kept women imprisoned in their cultures for generations. She is working toward the day when they will all be free and none of them dependent. And what if one of them should get old or be sick? I ask. "The society would have a way—"

"All right, but here in Gilboa, I'm society and this is my way."

"Well, you see the success you're having. Did I tell you? We didn't get the state grant we put in for."

"Oh, too bad."

"All those damn forms to fill out—a demonstrated need, and then nothing."

"I suppose there are many competing needs—"

"They'd do it for men!" she cries.

Her self-centeredness irritates me. I sigh into the phone. Three thousand miles away she hears the sigh. I'm sorry then that I have allowed it. "Oh, there is more news—town news. Violet Cleve died last week."

"Good Lord, I thought she went years ago. Wasn't she that wispy old thing who used to give away flowers all the time? She came to school and talked about the flowers in Shakespeare's plays, and she gave us a big vine in a pot that was supposed to bloom but didn't. She called us 'dear children.' Tommy Bordereau was sitting in the back with his hand up Mary Ellen DiBello's dress, and she's calling us 'dear children.' The class broke up laughing."

"Do you know the quilt we have on your bed? She and the ladies of the Altar Guild made it out of your outgrown dresses so that when you grew up she said you could remember—could still have, in a way, the clothes you had worn as a child. The dogwood bush we have is from her stock."

"She was certainly a town character all right. Didn't she use to take us on those awful nature walks when we were small? Wasn't she the one?"

"The whole town came, almost everyone. She was my first friend here, besides your father. The first friend I made on my own."

"I hardly know what you would have in common with her, she was so old-fashioned."

"Oh, worse than that. She was unfashionable."

31

"Mother, I didn't mean to be unsympathetic. It's that town, all of it frozen like a bunch of living statues, unchanging."

"But it has changed; I just told you."

She doesn't answer.

We talk about her work at the women's center—it is vital work, providing the abused and alcoholic and divorced and drug-wrecked and raped women with a place to go for comfort and safety and support. Anyone who does such work is worthy of praise. Why, then, do I hang up the phone so full of anguish and go upstairs to the room that had been Miriam's room, where the old quilt still lies at the foot of the bed, and finally cry for the loss of Violet Cleve?

The ambulance meetings are held at the firehouse the first Wednesday of the month. Sometimes they are routine, sometimes full of confrontation and argument. We study our runs for the month; we talk about breakdowns in communication, support problems, patient assessment, and treatment, "learning," Rita says, "at the tops of our voices."

In the back of the room, I see the two new people sitting apart, their eyes wide. "The patient was flat on his back, even though he was not technically immobilized. His neuros were good, and he didn't complain of pain," Jack Sharp is saying. "Nothing in the mechanics of the injury—"

"Dumb luck!" Rita cries. I jump in.

"I was there, and as Jack says, it looked like simple fainting. He was helping to guide a beam into place on a construction site when he suddenly fell over, according to the witnesses. I thought about a heart problem, because there was chest pain. We took him in for that and kept him still for that, even though, atypically, he did not want to sit up."

"We have to be aware," Geri says, "that what we are seeing without X-rays or monitoring machines may not be what the injury is."

We pass on. "Antonelli," Jack reads, "the saloon fight—"

"I wanted to talk about that one," Claude says. He describes the problem. Geri asks who made the run, and what we thought about it. I was involved and am interested in the discussion, but as it goes on, I see that people are trying for something that can never make sense for a group like ours. Outside of several unrealistic suggestions, I see no way we can operate differently. I sit still and wait with nothing "constructive" to offer.

"Grace, what do you think?"

"I haven't *thought* much about this; I *felt* a lot, and that's been getting in my way. I *felt* betrayed. These guys were tough strangers. They were in a fight, and in the ambulance one of them attacked the other. The local boys who get drunk and fight have a whole code of unwritten laws about when and when not to play macho. I was guiding an oxygen line and holding an I.V. bag, getting ready to hang it. I had no hand free to defend myself. I had cleared the line and was changing hands with the I.V. when one patient went for the other patient and knocked me over. I suppose that because I have been told so often not to fall on a victim, I fell sideways into the cabinets." I hear an intake of breath from the back of the room. "I've talked about this to people informally, and I did have to sit in the emergency-room lounge for a while calming down afterward but the squad can't start doing karate or putting every drunk in restraints because of something like this." I turn slightly and look toward the back where the two new people are sitting. Their faces are carefully neutral. No gesture or posture declares them. I turn back and we go on. Most of the rest are ordinary runs. Old Man Rabush, a diabetic farmer out on the pike, has spited his wife again by not taking his insulin; the usual number of drunks and sleepers on the long straight of the freeway have gone off the road downhill of where it bellies out to bypass the town. Kids have fallen from swings, slides, roofs, refrigerators. Older people eat too much and young ones drink too much. Two attempted suicides in the new development. We saved both; I wonder what the outcomes will be. If there's any deep frustration in our work it's that we see people in a crucial two hours of their lives, but unless they are neighbors, never after. Did the husband of the runaway with the broken back find her and were they reconciled? We will never know. Did they ever find the driver of the car that ran the cyclist down? The story ends for us there. We know that the cyclist lived, no more. Claude is talking about squad finances. I drift off and begin to doodle on the pad I am carrying: Hebrew letters and words. Hebrew has no present indicative of the verb *to be*. As we speak, we are speaking of what has, in that instant, become the past. I thought of that bit of grammar when I learned about the heartbeat. The sound of the heartbeat is the sound of the valves of the heart slamming shut. When we hear the heart "beat," its blood has already been pumped. Time was. Time was when I was young. Time was when my daughter was tactless and my son a yellow-robed renunciate. I return to the discussion.

Geri is introducing the guests. She asks them to tell us their names and something about themselves. The nurse gives her name. She's interested, she says, because she wants more varied experience. She has an advanced first aid card, but little emergency training. Would we answer some questions she has: Is there a chain of command? We give the names of officers and their duties, but Claude tries to get to the reality of the experience. The officers coordinate things and have final decision, but there is, on an accident scene, a kind of natural consensus. Is there a day crew and a night crew? Jack answers that some people work days and some nights at regular jobs. There are many fewer day people, of course, but if Linda means are there rigid divisions, the answer is no. When people are home, they ride. When the accident needs few people, the rest go home.

There is a look, half-puzzled, half-fearful, beneath the careful guest-blandness of Linda's face. I see what it is, and remember how loose it all seemed, at first, how random—no orders, nothing sure or set. I put my hand up. "I know it sounds like a game of jackstraws, all up in the air and all down on the ground in no order, but the looseness is really part of a form that's imposed by the accident itself. Come and watch us a few times. I can have someone call you when we are running."

It doesn't help. If anything, Linda looks more frightened than ever. Behind her, I see the young man and realize we have forgotten him. "Do *you* have any questions?"

"Yes," he says slowly. "How many runs do you do a month?"

"About ten—less than Midlothian, more than Tarrant."

"Not enough to support a paid service?"

"No." With all the hair on his face, it is hard to tell his expression.

"Tell us something about yourself," Geri says.

"Well," he starts, "my name is Sloan—Benjamin. I'm from California. I worked in a national park there, search and rescue. I have a California EMT card. I'd like to come and observe, but I have no phone."

"Where are you staying?" Geri asks.

"I just got a job at Longhill and I'm staying there, at one of the houses."

Geri doesn't bat an eye. Longhill—the place has bad associations for all of us, but to our credit, the silence is all we allow. Because of that silence and something I can't name, I say, "Perhaps we can give him a spare alarm box so that he can hear calls and come and observe for a while."

It is not unprecedented for prospective members, but none of the prospective members is so complete a stranger; none has been at Longhill. There is silence. A long silence. "Look," he says. "If it's a problem, I could put a deposit on the box. The kids at the school are disturbed, but we have a good relationship, and I'm sure they won't mess with it. I can see from your point of view, though, why you'd be worried about it."

Breath out. We relax. It isn't the kids, and maybe he knows it, but he has brought some of our worries out in the open and gone halfway toward an answer about his own permanence. Claude shrugs. "Anybody want to make a motion?"

When we are leaving, I go to the young man. "I'm Grace Dowben. I live off Garibaldi. When an accident is north of Marshaltown Pike or Mundy, you can go to the corner of Cleve and Federal from where you are, and I'll pick you up."

"I have no car," he says, "at least not for the moment. I can wait on Van Riper, though, when you are going that way."

"O.K.," and I smile at him. He doesn't smile back but it doesn't bother me. There is something about his seriousness that I like.

"How did your meeting go?" Saul is sitting up in bed reading, waiting for me.

"The dustup I expected about one of the runs. Two possible new members. One of them, I think, is Jewish."

"Did he say?"   .

"No, and his name isn't, but there's that feeling." Saul smiles.

In the old days, we would have known; the differences now are much subtler, but still there: eyes, faces, voices, an inflection, a movement of the hands; not sure, but there. Usually. "He works at Longhill—a young man in his twenties, I would say. I stupidly neglected to offer him a ride home, even though I knew he had no car."

"Longhill—I hope he's not one of the druggy ones."

"I don't think so. The other prospect is a nurse who works with Geri. I think our ways frighten her—not enough structure."

"Speaking of structure, why don't you come to bed? I'll show you something you've seen thousands of times before."

"Braggart—if it's what I think it is."

"Too bad you know my story, all my moves."

"Your story is a classic, your moves, too. It all gets better with repetition." We laugh. Old jokes, married jokes.

Before we go to sleep, he says, "I hope none of *your* drunks hit any of *our* bridges tonight."

36

5

There is a man in the house, someone in the house disturbing—then I am awake and it's the call box. I have missed the alarm tone and the dispatcher is talking about location. Exit 18, the road to Russian Grove. I have my night kit under the bed. I can slide it out and be half-dressed before I am out of bed—keys and wallet on the nightstand—but the dressing isn't done smoothly this time. I bump my head, hit edges that hadn't been there before, stumble in the dark.

Outside, the night wakes me. How cool it's gotten these nights into morning in late autumn. As I run to the car, I'm struck with time, its passing, the seasons here and gone; a month, a year, ten, twenty. It runs as I do, intent on something else. The car's lights put out the stars and darken the world. Work, not dreams. I drive down Federal, silent and motionless, closed for the night, past the firehouse, its door gaping, its left front tooth, the rescue truck, gone into action. My car radio is suddenly busy with message; crack and stab of static and the voices of friends. Then, Claude at the scene: "One victim, no serious injuries. All other units stand down."

I kill the emergency lights and slow down and then stop. I am coming to the ramp. The dispatcher is saying, "All Gilboa units, stand down," but at least one Gilboa unit is now wide awake, having been armed for combat and fired into a flashing-red-lit night. The target is gone, and I am left to disarm. I make the swing around west on the freeway. I will go up quiet old Vere and then Van Riper, past the sleeping farms and Longhill. Maybe that Sloan is out waiting. If he hasn't taken his call box with him, he won't know that the squad has been stood down. It must be early in the morning; there are very few cars. I look over to the right down to the old highway and Mundy Road, a dead end—Gilboa's Lovers' Lane. It is empty. When I come to the next exit, I pull off and turn down under the ramp. The road goes to dirt, the world suddenly into a countryside peace and calm. Vere is a dark, wooded lane, seldom traveled now. The Ochsners live in a battered farmhouse off this road, but there's no light showing. I begin to feel my tiredness, a slow releasing of muscles I hadn't known were bound up in the thrust to get me to my work. The radio goes again. The fire units are closing down one by one, the squad, car by car, like the muscles of my arms and face, relaxing. I turn off Vere and onto Van Riper. Down the road, I can see the light at the turnoff to the school. The road is empty. If he had come out at all, he must have gone in again. As I pass, I look to see if there are lights on in any of the houses, but my own headlights and the single light far down the road at the school make the dark beyond them too dark to see anything. I had never thought about that paradox before.

Longhill is a place of paradoxes. In the 1930s and forties, there was a primitive summer camp there. In the fifties, a church took it over and built a large main building and cabins, and it was used for retreats. The people who ran the place dealt little in town and the visitors, of course, did not leave the retreat. In the early sixties, Longhill was deserted, visited by chipmunks and the initiates of the high school fraternities. Farmers ran stock on its fields. The town began to think of it almost as public land. People fished the creek and there was even talk about damming it up for swimming.

And then came the communes. First, there was a group that called itself Tomorrow: a group of idealistic young people who planned to farm it. They threw up a tent town around the cabins and kept the main building as a communal barn. The land was cleared in a month with a dedication that amazed me. Elia, who had known farmers in Europe and America, shook his head: "All energy, no pacing." The "farmers," it turned out, were disenchanted college professors who had never farmed before; they should have called themselves Yesterday. They hated all technology. They plowed and sowed by hand, broadcast, in the ancient, poetic, wasteful way, and the birds ate the seeds. They didn't spray or fertilize with chemicals. Internal dissensions wore them out through the winter, and by February, there were only three couples there. I got the story from one of the women who came by in April selling beadwork to raise the money to leave town with her child. I tried to convince her to stay. "But there's nobody here," she said at last, "they've all gone on."

"But you could move into town—"

"But there's nobody here.—"

What they had built with more haste than knowledge and more love than wit, caved in that summer. The second commune started fresh. They were mystics of some kind who also lived in the old cabins for a while, but they did not build, they dug. They dug caves and food pits and religious pits. Martin Diers from the county health department sent complaints to the state; but the land was zoned agricultural then, and broad allowances had always been made for the farmers. The mystics (by now, the place had another name: Centering) began to be joined by others, runaways and commune-samplers, who built new things and moved into the old camp and church structures and into huts built over the mystics' pits. The field in front became a parking lot for junked cars, abandoned at journey's end. A few of the residents made their way into town to panhandle money to support themselves. There were fights. Rumor lay over Longhill like a fog. They weren't friendly to the few of us who tried to come, and even less so to the official inquirers, the school people, and the health department. And the town mouths milled away. Did we know there were orgies there, drugs, incest, immorality of every kind? In November, soon after I joined the squad, there was the Longhill Night. It was actually early morning, about the same hour as it is now. I remember riding in night-sweat silence, but we could see the fire all the way from town. It had spread from one of the cabins to the trees near it, crowning them. It had dropped flaming limbs onto the old cars and into the dried, overgrown autumn fields. By the time the fire had been reported, it had destroyed most of the area. Three departments were ten hours fighting it.

There were four victims in the cabin where the fire started; about twenty others, homeless, ended up in the town hall. It was their condition that focused our feelings. The four dead had been so deeply drugged that they had been burned alive. Experts from Midlothian told us that. But the survivors were ragged, filthy, and stinking, not with fire but with sloth and disease. All of them had lice; most of them had worms. For a week, they stayed in the town hall while various state health authorities came and went. People were angry and frightened. There were moves to pass ordinances to protect the land. We had saved two or three of the sturdier cabins on the south side. It was possible that a new commune . . .

But nothing happened. The mid-seventies burnt themselves away in other places. Three years ago, John Ferguson at the county clerk's office told Macy Ups that the land had been sold. To a corporation. We wondered if that meant a housing development. I hoped not. I liked being surrounded by the countryside to the west of Gilboa. The area was filling up with suburbs and shopping malls, but to the south and west, there were still meadows and woods.

The corporation was Longhill School, an experimental school for disturbed children run by what gossip told us were idealistic and radical methods. By that time, the word *idealistic* conjured for us the smell of burned bodies and unwashed feet; *radical*, the sight of roaches skating in the rancid grease of cooking pans, and for me, the memory of a line of lice walking down a small child's neck.

The school built a building and moved in. As was almost traditional now, neither its staff nor its students sought to become part of the town. They did all their shopping at Pinecrest. They had no account at our bank, said "Amen" at none of our churches, stood in no lines at our strawberry festivals, corn roasts, or Garden Club rummage sales. That was why we were surprised when Benjamin Sloan said he wanted to join us. Since he isn't in the road waiting, perhaps he hadn't come out at all. Geri had given him a call box because of me—maybe he had thought better of the whole thing and turned the voices off and let the sleep flow in upon him again, the night now darker and more silent because of the momentary contrast of light and noise.

I feel myself collapsing inward, too. The ancestral drugs are washing away in the tides of my blood. The clever hormones that have been keeping me wide awake and warm, continent and competent, are gone. I am cold now, and aching for a toilet. The road jogs south at the back of town; there are houses, all dark now. I turn down Garibaldi and into our road. The street has no name; our house is at the end. The kids used to call it Bullwinkle Boulevard, and if ever the street is paved and officially titled, I will press for that name.

The house is orderly and quiet. I unlace my boots and walk

out of them, and then the clothes fall away. I'm suddenly very, very tired. I put everything back in the night kit, turn out the alarm light, and go up to sleep.

On Saturday, when pious Jews are in prayer, separating the Sabbath from the week, I'm helping Saul in the store. We have a busy morning, town women mostly, and an even busier afternoon, mostly the women from the developments. In the beginning, there was a great difference in the clothes they wore. It had been Elia's gift when the new developments came in the fifties to see the difference between town and suburb, and to buy well for both. It enabled us to weather the competition of dress stores in the shopping centers that came in later, and the fear all over town of what would happen to Gilboa's merchants, but tastes began to merge. Now it's possible for a Gilboa woman to travel to New York or Los Angeles and not have her wardrobe give her away instantly as a resident of a town of less than ten thousand population. When I made that observation to Elia before he died, and meant it, I think it was one of the crowning moments of his life. Saul doesn't have Elia's dramatic flair, but he has solid knowledge of his customers and a good eye. He likes women and it shows; he is not a parodist.

I enjoy helping. The town laughs at my lack of a sense of style, but I know my neighbors and the store is a friendly place. I ring up sales and wrap up purchases, but Saul is the judge. They stand before him for his nod or the shake of his head. "Turn again. Oh, yes. This one, not the other." Sometimes I have a pang because I haven't the ability to help him more, but Saul seems to worry less than I. "At least I've gotten you to stop wearing those baggy shirts."

"I joined Gilboa Fire and Rescue so I could dress this way."

"Don't think I haven't suspected that."

Saturday afternoons are usually quiet and I don't expect a call, but at about three o'clock the alarm goes off. Accident with injuries on Van Riper, one-half mile east of Longhill. We have the town's two streetlights rigged to our alarm, so when it rings at the firehouse, they both turn red. I am out the door and across Federal into the firehouse. Orley is coming up the street for the light fire truck, Claude and Rita from opposite directions to jump into the ambulance. It is always a moving and comic sight to me, like one of those timed sequences in old movies: short people running west, tall people running east, all in desperate seriousness, their expressions rapt and earnest, almost colliding; and from other places, other people, avoiding by inches a giant sprawl. They scramble in and I pull away, turning on the siren as I go up Federal until the road ends at the back of town. I turn right onto Van Riper. The road goes to dirt, and we jiggle and bump in the ruts.

"I can take it slower—" I cry to Claude in the back.

"No." His voice sounds like the voices of people on trampolines. "I'm O.K."

Two miles out we see the wreck. A car has gone over in the ditch. I pull up behind it. An officer is there and so is the "observer," Benjamin Sloan. He has done a quick examination of the three victims, seen there is nothing life-threatening, and has a good, concise evaluation. I am surprised and pleased. Claude and Rita have come up and heard him, and now they are able to go where the need is. They start vitals on their victims. The girl is crying, shaking with tears. "One minute we were just going along, and the next we were all—I was falling and Dino was in the air—"

"It was one of our kids," Benjamin murmurs beside me. "He'd had a bad morning and wandered out here. He was in the road and these people swerved to avoid him. They were going too fast, that's all—"

We load. Others have come to help. "Saturday is usually well attended," I say to Benjamin. With three in the ambulance, there isn't room for an observer. He knows it and begins to turn away. "Listen," I call to him, "you did a fine job. You saved us a lot of time. Thanks." He turns again, and this time smiles. It is almost an unwilling smile. He ducks his head and his hand goes up. "We'll see you," I say.

"Yeah."

The ambulance pulls away. I see him standing looking after us.

By the time I get back to the store, it's time for me to leave. I usually quit at six or so on Saturdays to go home, light candles for Havdalah, the final service separating the Sabbath from the rest of the week, and make supper for Saul and Riva. During the early years, it was something of a festival meal, all six of us. Although Saul and Elia worked Saturdays, we wanted to mark the time somehow. Now there are three, and the two women on perpetual diets.

I fix the table. It is after sundown, but one of my compromises, of which there are so many, is to say that sundown is celebrated when *I* am ready and not before. Sundown at our house is when Saul and Riva come in, usually at seven. On Saturday nights, we celebrate the traditional, exquisite, short farewell to the Sabbath, and then we eat. As I put out the wine and spice box, there is a knock at the door, and then the person outside discovers the bell and rings also. When I open the door, there is the young man—Benjamin. He looks uncomfortable. "I, uh—somebody left a kit out there—it wasn't anything vital—bandages and stuff, but I didn't know if you would need it and I thought someone would miss it—"

I ask him in. I'm embarrassed for the squad—all those people, and no one checking the scene. He is still a stranger, and I don't like us to look bad in front of him.

I take the kit from him and put it on the bottom stair. "My husband and mother-in-law will soon be home, but I was just going to have a cup of coffee. Let me make you some, too."

"That would be nice." We start through the dining room.

His shyness makes his feet big, and he clumps. He is far from the table, but I feel his anxiety that he might knock something over. "Oh!" he says. "Braided candles."

"They're called Havdalah candles. See? Three wicks. It's a ceremony Jews have to end the Sabbath." I have said the word; will he echo it?

"Uh, I know; I've heard of it. I've just never seen it. My family is . . . I'm Jewish." I am able to smile because I am in front of him, and he can't see my face.

"I didn't know—Sloan isn't a particularly Jewish name." Then he laughs, a laugh nothing like the competent, intelligent worker at the accident, and nothing like the uncomfortable visitor at the door. It is a deep, satisfying laugh. He laughs like a fat man with his whole body.

"No one has reminded me of it for years," he says. "When my grandfather came to Ellis Island they asked him his name and he said 'Shlomo.' The Immigration Officer—"

"Oh, yes," I say, and laugh, too. "I heard of a man named Hitchcock whose name had been Yitzchak before. It's good that your grandfather told you his real name, too. Look, it's almost time for them to come. Stay over and have Havdalah with us and eat some supper."

"I'd like to, but I can't. I'm on duty tonight and someone's covering me while I'm here. I shouldn't even be drinking this coffee. Havdalah. Sabbath. My grandfather's real name is one of the few things I know about us. As a Jew, I'm a liar. People expect me to know—to believe certain things."

"To know, yes, but not necessarily to believe. Belief is a gift with us."

"It helps, though, if you believe."

"It helps if you are rich and handsome, too, but—" I smile and shrug. I think he's surprised. He finishes his coffee and goes to the sink and puts the cup in it. I wink a greeting to his mother across the space he cannot see.

"I have to go now," he says. "The kids are waiting."

"Sometime I'd like to hear about the school."

"I feel like apologizing to somebody for today—the kid, I mean. He had no business out there."

"It could happen anywhere."

"Yes, but well—the school wants to be based on love, trust, and freedom, and sometimes—he could have been killed, and then the kids driving the car—"

"Mothers and fathers the world over have been through that," I say. He nods. "Thanks for returning the kit. I liked what I saw out there, the way you work."

"I like the way you all work, too."

"Then we'll see you the next time under the bridge or off the road."

"Yes," he says, and we go out again through the dining room set for Havdalah. I can see him this time trying to take it all in, the little side table with the ceremonial things, the wine and spice box, braided candles. When I open the door, the cold and darkness flow in at us.

"It's so cold—I forgot you have no car. I can run you back—"

"No, I'm running. I like to. Thanks for the coffee." And he is gone, jogging up the street. I can hear his footsteps for a few seconds after he has been claimed by the darkness.

When Saul and Riva come, I can see they are upset. Besides the accumulated pressures of the busy day, and my defection, I can guess it is their new assistant. It's a problem we didn't have until recently. There have always been so few jobs for young people in Gilboa that those there were, were seen as choice, and vied for. A high school boy needing money for college had an ideal chance at Dowben's. For years we had the town's best. Now, for whatever reason, there has been a succession of indolent and bored children, who work with an air of martyred patience. It angers Riva and disgusts Saul, and now I feel guilty because of the run.

I take their coats and let them talk for a while. Riva is furious. "If we let him go, what will we get? Another one just like him—like the one we had last, and the one before that?"

"What do you want me to do then?" They fret with it back and forth until I have to break in.

"Excuse me, but Havdalah is ready." So we stand for a few moments, calming ourselves, and while I stand I wonder if there was ever a time and place in which it was possible to keep, without compromise, the gift of the Sabbath, to suspend, for that space of time, all daily cares, all worries and heartaches, to lay down the burdens, literally and figuratively, to relearn delight, to rest, to converse on topics that did not include blame or hard feelings? We invented Sabbath and gave it to the world, and now—Saul lets go; I can see him easing his face, relaxing, but Riva's face is still tight in the candlelight, and I remember Miriam and Joshua, also unready, unwilling to let the great world go for an hour, no less a day, the lust-filled, death-filled world of television, or the ordinary world of phone calls and busy-ness. I remember so many times when we tried to make a Sabbath—and failed. The children hated it, Riva and Elia hated it, and in the end we admitted we were doing it for them and gave it up, keeping only the Friday night meal and this Havdalah—two gates that were supposed to open and close on a magic garden, but now guard nothing. Had there ever been a time in Jerusalem or Bet Shearim, in Sura or Pumbedita, in Prague or Zoromin when one banished by Law and in fact the sorrowful and the sorry for a single day each week?

We eat. During dinner, I tell them about Benjamin Sloan whose father's father had been named Shlomo and who worked at Longhill and had seen in our house his first Havdalah candle.

6

Now Benjamin is often waiting at the Longhill road on Van Riper as I go by. Sometimes he catches rides with Larry. Sometimes he is in a light coat, thrown on in a hurry. He stands at the fringes of accidents helping to lift, holding equipment, or simply watching, a little apart. He looks so forlorn, not a spectator, not a worker, that I feel sorry for him at these scenes where there is nothing for him to do. The others on the squad have begun to recognize and greet him. He is still shy, rarely smiling. "When you don't work with the patient," he says once in the wolf-cold of a predawn run, "when you're not driving or loading or holding an I.V. or something, you have time to think about the victim philosophically—his family, his trouble, your own tiredness, the work you've left."

"Have you been doing emergency work long?"

"Never like this. I worked in a park, I think I told you, a national park, a very small one. Picnickers would get lost or fall—broken bones, sometimes kids O.D.ing, no auto wrecks."

"Having seen us—"

"I like the way you work. I'd like to join."

"Have you talked to that nurse, Linda?"

"Yes, we met after one of the first ones. I think she was put off by the looseness of it all. She was looking for someone to give orders, one consistent leader."

"There are leaders—"

"But not the same ones on each accident. The freedom is the very thing I like; there's not one law set down for the way things should work."

"We've tried, but each accident is different in ways impossible to predict or plan for."

"I know." And he smiles the rare smile.

At the November meeting, his application is voted on, and when I go home from the meeting, I tell Saul he has joined. "You're full of plans, aren't you? You want to get him into the Jewish congregation. After that, there will be a girl, won't there, and you've seen a house, haven't you, and how many kids do you plan for them?"

"Very funny."

"Oh, nothing crass, nothing overstated. Who are you going to get to drop a glove, leave an empty space on the cotillion dance card? Don't you know he's probably shacking up with some chick up there at the school? The old days of understatement are over. They all make out like mink."

"I admit, I'd like to see him in the congregation, but there are no girls here."

"Wait till the other yentas see him: A beard? Is he a hippie? Does he take drugs? Which ones?"

"Are you calling me a yenta?"

"Every Jewish woman over thirty is a yenta. It's something genetic, I believe. I used to think it was the water or the food we ate. I've fed you carefully for twenty-five years, given you good water, clean air, a wholesome, simple environment with simple, wholesome companions, and what do I get— instant yenta."

"You see me sitting with the greats, do you?"

"Every bit as big as Lou Epstein."

I make a face at him; Lou Epstein is the congregation's resident pest. When Miriam married in California, and Lou found out, she called and gave me an hour of good advice. God forbid that she finds out about Joshua. She thinks he's still in college. I know she devils Saul at the store, asking questions about both of them. He looks at me and grins. I look at him and wink. Old jokes, family phrases. Our pleasure with one another has gone so far inward over the years that very little of it shows on the surface. We seem dull but we are not; we are inward; the deepest source of our joy is the twenty-five-year knowledge we have of one another, and that the sources of our pain are the same. I remember that it was Miriam who called us dull. "I wouldn't want a relationship as boring as yours and Dad's." I was astounded. I had tried to tell her, "Like good bread, not in the spread, in the bread itself, all in the texture, the flavor of the bread itself." She had only given that heavenward stare that I, God help me, had taught her.

Saul takes me by the hand. He leads me to the alarm box and turns it off. He is making what Miriam's generation would call a nonverbal statement.

How do I love thee, let me count the ways—laughing and teasing, in anger, sometimes not well, out of boredom, sometimes out of boredom beautifully. In the early nights of Joshua's leaving, we ground out sorrow on each other's bodies. Rarely, but sometimes, in a terrible loneliness, bearing that loneliness like another organ of sight or hearing. We have loved in sudden, shaking passions and in long, slow, meditative times, very tenderly. We are well matched, but not like the heroes and heroines of the modern novel; we seldom reach orgasm together. We aren't experts, but we know what we like, and the alarm box with its little pop of static as it's turned off has become an erotic message for us. Sometimes we go to it together; sometimes, walking behind me up the stairs, Saul will turn it off and the click will begin my thought. Then afterward, before sleep, I'll go down and turn it on again, and be passingly sorry I do work that binds me so tightly to the world.

When I get up this time, I go to the window first. The night is icy. Hoarfrost covers everything in a light, deceptively rough dusting. This, too, marks a change. In my pre-rescue days, I would have stayed at the window reveling in the subtle beauty of monochromatic gray-on-gray, feeling the textures of the familiar world change before me. It is beautiful, I can still see that, but now I dread what I see. How could so rough-seeming a surface go so mysteriously, murderously slick underfoot and under the wheels of a car? Knife-cold, knife-smooth, I know, and now my enemy. If someone drinks too much tonight, or falls, or shoots a lover, or if just on toward morning the tiny electrical charge being fired sixty-five times a minute in a single heart in these eight square miles should suddenly stop firing or change its rhythm, I will have to fight all this damned beauty. To risk—I don't want to think about it. Let Saul worry. That's his part to do. I smile a wolf-smile and remember Winston and Julia in *1984*. Winston at the ultimate moment of pain and terror screams: "Give it to Julia—give the pain to Julia!" He has betrayed her. And I betray Saul, sleeping the spent sleep after love. I go down and click on the world.

The subject is water, pouring over stones, clean and cool sheeting like pane-glass over a sill of stone, congealing with bubbles like molten glass at pool-places under. . . . What? I am standing up wreathed in my pool-stream-river dream and it has all broken into noise and cold. It's a call, oh, God, not out there in the adversary night! The voice comes again; they always say it twice, the dispatchers; they know how many of us are riding swift and sweet on the muscling arms of water.

I am dressed and out. The night is locked in cold, giving

nothing. I am not cold in it. Not yet. Ancestral drugs. Ancestors even older than Jews. The car half-starts painfully, protesting. Slow oil, slow steel, both cold, come on, damn you. Finally. The accident is near Exit 17 and I am traveling as fast as I dare down Van Riper, somewhere between a stall and a skid, when I see Benjamin standing at his place outside the school turnoff. I slow down, wondering if I will slew over to the side and bury myself in the ditch, whether, when I stop, I will be able to start again. He gets in quickly, and we do start slowly, the physics deciding, after a long moment of hesitation, to give us friction on the ground and not a spin. I drive more cautiously with him here, wondering why as I do so. "We'll soon get heat. I have the heater on."

"I think the rule is that the heater kicks in when you get to the accident," he says. We are halfway down Vere.

"Look out to the left and see if you see a light. Larry might still be here."

"No, it's dark."

"O.K., here we go." We pick up speed and get on the freeway. There have been one or two check-ins as we ride; now a voice, Claude's, surer than the others have been.

"Gilboa units. This accident is off 17 at the entrance to Pinecrest. I'm setting flares. Victims are still in the street." Victims. Plural. I hear Ben beside me, breathing in and out, trying not to breathe too fast. We come off the freeway and top the hill. Down at the bottom we can see the flares past the service road when the car hits a soft dip of some kind. Suddenly there is no wheel and no brake. We're out of control. Then the car is pulled sideways down the grade. Frictionless, we spin silently, like ghosts, waiting for the crash, the impact, the overturn. We seem to be hung in centrifugal force, waiting. At last we stop and we're at the bottom of the hill, facing up.

"Are you all right?"

"Yes, are you?"

"I'm O.K."

"So that's the tango," Ben says. "I like the moves, but it's hard to get the rhythm right without the music."

"We've got to get out of here. In another minute three cars and an ambulance will be on top of us and they probably won't be able to stop any better than we did." I turn the key. The car grinds over once, dies again, then starts. We see lights at the top of the hill. The ambulance; we are grinding and rocking, but not moving. "Get on the radio!" I cry.

As he speaks into it, the ambulance begins to come down. From here we can see the slick spot and we watch the ambulance hit it and lose control, but instead of side-skidding, it skids straight and goes on past us at a terrifying rate. Behind it are two cars and behind them the fire truck. Ben uses the radio again, and C.A. answers us in the truck and cuts his siren. The cars have already started down. The first one, Rita's, goes over half on the shoulder trying to avoid the slick spot, but in the middle of the hill gets stuck in the sandy bank there and slews over sideways; the second car is halfway down when the driver—I don't know who—realizes his problem. Avoiding Rita's car, he will almost surely hit mine. Before he can decide, he hits the slick. At his speed, the car spins instantly. Still spinning, it turns past Rita's. If I could only move—the car is headed straight for us when it seems to hit another patch of ice and begins spinning faster. Then it stops. It is nose to nose with us but I haven't felt a bump. It's Jack Sharp. Over the radio, I hear C.A. in the fire truck laconically.

"If you kids is through down there, I'll come by for you." The big truck goes into four-wheel drive and lumbers up the left shoulder. It comes down slowly, in complete control. C.A. knows he's on the radio, monitored by the sheriff and the State Police. "Leave your lights on. When we see what's goin' on up the road, I'll come back and pull you all out."

Like any other survivors, we come out slowly, cautiously. I almost want to put my hands in the air. C.A. is calling the police to tell them the road is impassable. We all get in the truck, Rita, Jack, Ben, and I in the squad section. C.A. turns back to us, no longer needing to be careful for the sheriff. "You kids shouldn't be funnin' at an accident scene. Get on in the house—tomorrow you'll all have colds!" How I love to work with men. How I love their gallantry under pressure. Ben with his joke, C.A. now and a dozen times before. Where did they learn such a joyful way of setting themselves against their fear?

The two victims are young and very drunk. They've been thrown out of the car and are lying yards away from it and each other and shouting across the empty space. The ambulance crew is already attending to them, so I begin to make arrangements for loading. Ben goes, but is back in a moment. "They're ready to splint. She has a fractured humerus and a possible dislocation of the knee. He has a possible pelvis, but if there's bleeding, it's very slow."

"O.K. He'll go on a board on the gurney. She'll get the stretcher."

"Listen," Ben says, "they think those kids are drunk, but they're not. I mean I think it's something else."

"What, then?"

"There's a combination of uppers and downers, mostly Valium, that the kids mix up themselves—I saw a lot of it out at the park."

I work while he speaks. "Are you sure?"

"I think so, yes."

"O.K., let's go." We roll the cot out of the ambulance for the boy, and get the splints. I go to Geri. "Ben says this isn't alcohol but dope—a combination."

"It looks like alcohol because of the slurred speech," Ben says, "and the unreactive eyes, but I really think not, or not only."

"What can we expect?" Geri asks.

"Wild changes in vitals, almost from minute to minute. Sometimes, they say, sudden arrests."

"Get in the ambulance," Geri says, "and look those two over. You, too, Ben—see what you think."

They are loading. The boy and girl are both talking away, occasionally comforting one another loudly like two jolly drunks at a beer bash. Ben is as jolly as they are, but when I go past him, he says into my ear, "She's taken more than he has. They'll both need oxygen soon."

I get things ready and go out to tell Geri. "I'm at sea on this. Ben seems to know what's happening. I'd like him with me. He needs the runs anyway to work off his probation. I know he's new, but—"

"Both of you go in back. Claude and I will go up front in case they do arrest." Geri calls the hospital on the radio.

We are almost ready to go. The jolly-good-fellow mood has gone from the back of the ambulance. It's confession time. "I love you," the girl is weeping to Ben. "I don't love Ned, that sonofabitch, because I just fuck with him. I don't love him. I love you."

"I love you, too," Ben says, and caresses her hair. The boy is singing a rock song about suicide, I think, and weeping copiously.

"Are you sure this isn't vodka?" I whisper. "Or grain alcohol?"

He shakes his head. "Smell them."

There is a booze smell, but something else I can't identify. Her respirations have dropped from thirty a minute to eight. His have gone from twelve to twenty-five. Ben talks to her while I put an I.V. in. I explain how it works. She doesn't want to hear anything from me. I remind her of her mother. Ben explains again. We start.

We begin to stink. The heat in the ambulance has melted the frozen moisture on our clothes to an almost palpable vapor. Wet wool, sweat, fresh blood, the smell of shock, and their breaths—
"Ozone!" I cry. "That's what it is!" Ben grins at me.

"Ozone!" the boy intones. "I want to go there, to the planet

Ozone, close to the sun!" We talk about it for a while, and I finish my assessment. If he's bleeding, it's very slow; he seems fairly stable within the rise and fall of blood pressure and respirations that Ben has predicted. She varies more rapidly. Sometimes her heartbeat is too rapid to count. Any minute she might go into fibrillation. All she has is her youth. She asks Ben his name and then continues with him the kind of love talk adolescents use at thirteen or fourteen, franker than in my generation, but with the same superheated coyness. He is playing back and I find myself smiling.

She says, "I love you, darling," and he answers, "I love you, too, Terry."

The hospital at Midlothian is twenty-five miles away, and because the roads are bad, the trip is long tonight. They are not in pain yet, and they should be. The hardest job we do is probably keeping someone awake who wants to drift off into sleep or unconsciousness. We poke and prod, joke, and make them talk. Now that the manic effect of the drugs has worn off, the bottom sides of their vitals are well into the shock zone. We increase the oxygen and raise the drip rate on the I.V.'s. It's all we can do.

It's been a bad night for everybody. The examination stations at the emergency room are full, and patients are spilling over into the corridors. We plead for ours that their vital signs are unstable, and we are given a place. We get them undressed and do a final set of vitals. Geri lies in wait for a doctor and zips him in to us between other examinations. It's Macomb. I don't like Macomb. "What did they take?"

"I don't know," Ben says, "but it looks like L.A. Popcorn."

"What the hell is that?"

"A relaxant-tranquilizer like Valium, a phenobarbital, and a heavy stimulant, and then an amphetamine, and then Tylenol. When you take three of each and ten Tylenol, it's a handful—like popcorn."

"Do you know when they took these?"

"We've been trying to find out through the ride. They've lost any sense of time, but the rush phase usually goes for about three-quarters of an hour, and that was before the accident . . ." Macomb glares.

With anyone but Macomb, it would have been easier. The younger doctors are used to working with us, seeing us as less well-trained but not less experienced in our very narrow way. They have the avuncular stance of teachers, proud of their brighter students. Macomb resents us bitterly. Years of medical school, internship, residency, he now has to listen to the un-anointed talk about absorption rates. He has cut Ben off for no reason. It angers me. "If you're through with us, sir, the district is unattended." We get our run sheet signed, and go back to the ambulance. I am furious.

But the excitement of the run is wearing off, and I am also wet and tired. "You guys want coffee? Let's go into the nurses' lounge and get some." We move clumsily. I see how tired we all are. The tension of our own near-accident is beginning to release itself in an almost tremulous exhaustion. Geri and Claude ask Ben about L.A. Popcorn.

"I didn't mean to come on like an expert," he says quietly. "The park where I worked had a lot of kids, and they did a lot of drugs. The park police were spread too thin to do anything but confiscate what they saw and to help with overdoses. I was there for the county as a kind of troubleshooter."

We feel like people in a monastery whose doors have suddenly been opened. Our overdoses are the common drugs, tranquilizers and sleeping pills, but the new things, the chemistry-set things that talented amateurs make and sell themselves, worry us only in the literature, not in our experience. We listen, as Dr. Macomb would not listen, to Ben's description of signs and symptoms, absorption rates, treatments succeeding, treatments failing. He speaks succinctly, without self-praise. Geri asks him if he will present something to the group at the next training. On our way out, a nurse stops us. "Gilboa Rescue, there's a call for you at the desk."

Geri goes over and comes back grinning. "C.A. has gotten all the cars back to the firehouse. He wants me to tell you it is illegal to start a used car lot on a county road. Violates the zoning." We laugh.

On the way home, I show Ben how to fill out the forms, the state's and ours. We have turned out all but the small work light, and when we are finished, we turn that out and ride on in the dark. I tell him I'm sorry about Macomb. He laughs that mellow laugh in the darkness. "I thought it was the beard."

"It was really the tutu and the open-toed shoes," I say.

"Admit it, it wasn't really the shoes; it was the nail polish—you don't have to save my feelings—the little smile faces painted on the big toes."

"You did something I could never do."

"What was that?"

"You lied because she needed it."

"Lied—how?"

"All that about how much you loved her. She wanted to hear it and you told it to her."

"She didn't really mean me. She was talking to someone in her fantasy."

"But I couldn't say 'I love you' to someone I didn't love. That sounds self-righteous, I know. I should be free to say what a patient needs to hear. You were very good with her, by the way."

"I doubt you've had my experience with drug overdoses—not only as a job, but all through school. In high school, I had to talk down lots of friends of mine who were loaded. I was sometimes loaded too." He sees my eyes widen in spite of myself. "Maybe Gilboa didn't have the drugs other places did, but in any case, your kids probably wouldn't have let you in on their drug experiences."

"We had drugs in Gilboa and programs at the school and folders from the P.T.A. I don't know if our son used drugs or not. The town preferred to believe no drugs were here. Only when something happened—a death in one case, psychosis in another—did we know, did the town know, I mean. My own kids said nothing. When I asked them about those others—their classmates—they shrugged."

I hadn't meant to go so far. In the dark, there aren't faces or bodies, only voices. I didn't want mine to carry pain, only simple, objective facts. We're both sitting on the squad bench with a pile of blankets between us. I hear him shift beside me and I hope it isn't because he catches the pain and is embarrassed by it.

"Will you be able to sleep in a little tomorrow?" I ask.

"I doubt it. The kids'll wake me up. They'll come over and pound on my door. Part of the reason I came on this squad is that I wanted to show them there are other parts to the world. The kids are angry and bitter but they're not psychotic. The work I do is so—so—amorphous. Along with showing them that they aren't the center of the universe, that they don't have to be, I wanted to do something physical and direct."

"Do you tell *those* kids you love them?" I am kidding him a little, enjoying it.

"All the time. It's something the director is very big on, that the kids know they're loved. The director says that love is a human right."

"Like peace and freedom?"

"Absolutely."

"Automatic and equal, to each kid, no matter what?"

"Yup."

"And you believe that's desirable, or even possible?"

Why am I arguing, defending a point that needs an arguer far more skilled than I—or a better mother.

"I don't know, but I try."

"Perhaps it's a generational difference. I don't think of those things as a right, only a lucky accident. Tell me, do all the kids have to love *you*?"

"Well, no, but . . ."

"So it's all one way? You have to give all this with no responsibility on their side?" I stop myself. It's his business, not mine. I am defending only the gate to my own pain. "Good God, I'm sorry! It's 4:00 A.M. I'm tired and wet and scared of getting back in my car and wondering if maybe you're scared of driving with me after what happened and what almost happened before. Forgive me. It's just bad manners."

He laughs his good laugh. "Lady, now you do sound like my grandmother. People don't talk about manners anymore."

"Well, maybe they should!" I cry, and we both laugh.

"About the love thing—I've never heard anyone say what you said."

"The old-time hypocrisy was faith. Now, it's love." I groan. "Where did I get so wet?"

"Want an old park trick? Use some of that spray-can waterproofing on your working turnout. It really helps."

"*I'm* supposed to tell *you* all that housewife stuff!"

"Sure!"

The ambulance pulls up at the firehouse and we get out. My car is parked in the area the firemen use. It's perfectly straight, wheels turned in, in C.A.'s deft, self-sufficient way. Ben gets in as though we had never skidded sideways down a hill, turning, and then waited for horrors to happen. Men. There's a note on the windshield: YOUR FRONT LEFT TIRE WAS FLAT. THE SPARE'S ON IT NOW. TELL MURPH TO CHECK ALIGNMENT, TOO. SHE'S WORE TO THE OUTSIDE—C.A.

"You ready to go?" I ask.

"Might as well. It's too late to do nothin' else. Saloons all closed. Pool hall ain't open yet." He is mimicking Orley. We pull out slowly and head home. "Leave me at the school road," he says. "There's that hill down to my house and the ground there is chewed up."

"You don't like the way I drive down hills!" For a moment he looks at me, thinking I might be serious, and then I can feel him smiling in the dark behind the beard.

"I want to run a little—to wind down."

"I'll run, too, when I get home. The bathtub."

I creep in quietly. It will soon be getting light, and I lie down beside Saul knowing it's only for an hour or so. He turns and puts out his hand to touch me. "Tough run?"

"A little. Drug overdose. I had a flat, too, but C.A. changed the tire."

"You didn't have any trouble, did you?"

"No, just the flat." He pats me and rolls over, already asleep. Before I fall asleep myself, I have a few minutes to ponder the nature of deception.

Once a month, I take Riva into Midlothian to look around. Disguising myself in hat and hose, I take her to the museum and then out for a nice lunch and some shopping in the afternoon. Riva likes traditional Jewish food, although she hates to cook. We always stop at the big deli on Converse Avenue and pick up a good-sized order. "Under gourmet foods. My mother would have died laughing." It *is* pretty funny. The makeshift of the wretched poor of Europe—giblet soup, beet soup, stuffed cabbage, potato knishes—"and they charge like sin!"

"*You* don't want to stand folding cabbage leaves, do you?"

"God forbid."

"Make a day."

"Thursday looks good. What about you?"

"I never have anything to do, so I'm always free."

I fight a desire to defend our treatment of her. "O.K., Thursday it is."

"What do you think of this?" I ask Saul. "We go to the museum, then to the big library in Midlothian. I know they have a cassette collection and also the books with the extra large print. If I can get the librarian over there to go with her—to show without suggesting, we might be able to get her interested."

"Watching you try to be devious is worth the price of admission. Go ahead and good luck. If only we could get her to the doctor—"

"Until her sight gets worse and she's forced to do something, I can only try things like this."

"If only she wasn't so frightened—"

"If only . . ."

7

It's a bright, mild day a week before Thanksgiving. I've gotten up early and straightened the house, made breakfast, and seen Saul off to work. Riva and I will do the town and this time maybe I can convince her to stop denying that her eyesight is going, that she is narrowing her life to the size of her apartment. We plan to leave at nine-thirty. I'm wearing my good-looking new pants suit and am about to leave. The alarm goes off. It's rare to get a call this early. I run through the roster quickly in my mind. Geri is working, so is Claude. Rita can get off, but she is sick, and the Sharps are out of town. I have to go. Accident with injuries, the sheriff's dispatcher says, a mile out Cleve Road. I put my squad jacket over the new outfit and leave. I know Saul will hear and see the ambulance and will call Riva. If I'm lucky, it will be something light and we'll get started a little later. As I go down Federal, I hear the ambulance coming up toward me. I pull over, jump out, and flag it down. It's Ben. "God, am I glad to see you!"

"Same here."

"I was downtown in the drugstore. I had my alarm box with me. It went off like the Fourth of July."

By this time we've turned east and have started into open country. There's Violet Cleve's house. I take a quick look as we pass. The Garden Club has dressed the ground and pruned the fruit trees. I nod a greeting. We come to the crest of the hill and look down. At the very bottom is a tangle of cars and the red lights of police. "What's going on down there—it looks like something odd."

As we come closer, I see past the police car. A farm tractor with a harrow attachment must have come out of the little side road on the left. A sports car going at a tremendous speed has rear-ended it and gone underneath it. "You won't be able to get by," I say. "You'd better pull up behind this car."

Bischoff from the State Police comes over. "Hello, Grace." He is a little pale, I think. "You got two, we got one. Your two aren't hurt too bad. Ours is caught up in the broken-off ends of that harrow. It's why we threw the blanket up over the back of it there. We got the coroner coming. Yours are here."

The farmer is more frightened than hurt. I don't know his name, but I've seen him in town now and then. Hearing nothing else in the noise of his tractor, he'd made the turn onto Cleve and a moment later found himself popped out of the seat. He had grabbed the steering wheel and hung on and managed to stop the engine. Both arms are broken. The other victim, the driver of the sports car, has a broken wrist and has mashed his foot under one of the pedals. He is also very drunk.

Because we're working at the rear wheel of the tractor, the presence of the impaled man looms over us. We can't see him; the officers have covered him, and it's dark under the blanket in the tangle of machinery. I see Ben look up into that tent several times while we work on the farmer. The sports car driver is numb and muttering. He knows his companion is dead, but he hasn't accepted it. As we work, Claude comes. He helps us with the driver and the loading, but he has to get back to school. The school principal is taking his class.

"Can we wait one minute?" Ben looks at me. "I've never

seen a corpse, I mean—" He's pale, as pale as Bischoff is. "If I'm going to be in this work, to do this—"

"You want to get it over with," Claude says. "Let me explain it to the cops, then. If it's O.K. with them, we'll take the time." He goes over to the police and we see him pointing our way and then to the blanket, speaking. They look at us and nod.

"Who'll get the body out of there?" Ben whispers.

"The coroner's men. Bischoff and Jesperson will probably have to help, and that's why they look so bad."

We're standing by the ambulance looking in at the patients. Claude comes. "Be quick," he says. "Go ahead." We climb up on the back of the tractor and I pull the blanket away a little. Ben takes a good, long look.

"O.K.?"

"O.K.," he says. We get down carefully, very carefully. "Are they always—do they always look yellow like that?"

"Yellow or gray. The blood pools quickly in cases like this, in whatever parts are lower. Hanging the way he is—"

"Listen, the patients—are they all right? I mean, can we—can we just walk for a minute?"

"Do you want to be alone?"

"No, no; I—just for a minute."

So we flank him, touching him on either side but not holding him, and we walk. "The smell there—"

"It's a quintessential auto wreck," I say. "Gasoline, anti-freeze, blood, booze, and the smell of bodies in shock, a subtle but penetrating blend." We laugh for no reason, to prove that we can. "Are you ready? Can you drive?"

"Yes." He looks at us, one side and then the other. "Thanks."

"Go thank the cops," I say, "they understand it all." To my surprise, he does.

"Is he going to be O.K.?" Claude asks. "I really need to get back."

"We'll be fine. I want Bischoff and Jesperson to get to know the bearded freak, and I want the bearded freak to get to know the local fuzz."

"Lady, you're thinking all the time."

"That college money wasn't no waste, y'know. I may live in town but I got a city brain. You go back and learn them kids, now. I got this sitchaytion in my hand." We laugh again, a way of telling each other we don't like yellow corpses, young corpses there was no way to save.

Ben drives; I work in the back. The driver of the sports car sobers up long enough to realize what he has done and he cries—not a drunkard's cry, but a series of long, racking sobs— and the farmer cries, too, because he has not too many years ago been young and drunk himself. The death and pain of it are still completely personal. Official retribution, the law, insurance, license revocations, settlements, and accountings are waiting miles away. On the road, we're like rafters, skiers, hang-gliders, in pain rather than joy. But the pain is unalloyed, uncompromised, in a sense, free.

And Ben has seen his first corpse. He has arranged to see it when there were only two of us there so that should he shame himself, it wouldn't be before the whole squad. How foreign that is from the way I think! C. A. Bordereau, who disapproves of Ben's clothes and beard, would have done the same. I've seen my corpses, too, but never as a test to be passed for other people. Perhaps I knew all along that had I cried or vomited or fainted or gone shock-white, it would have been forgiven me because I was a woman. There are worse things in this work than a victim already dead, but we've made Ben a good beginning. We've walked with him a little and on the way back I'll let him talk it out.

I don't get home until noon; I call Riva right away. "I'm sorry— we can go tomorrow, but if you're really set on it, there's still time—"

"Never mind; I heard the siren and knew you were off on that rescue work. I'm sure that's very important. Your family's needs must seem very ordinary beside that."

She's half right and that half hurts. "I'm not canceling our trip, I'm postponing it one day."

"Tomorrow's Friday. You won't want to go out and then come back late because you'll have to clean for Shabbos and prepare dinner. You didn't think of that."

"The victim didn't think of it. Riva, in a funny way, I'm trying to guarantee that no one I know and love will ever lie unattended in a wreck somewhere or fall on the street with a heart attack and be passed by. We're preventing it in Gilboa and other people are preventing it all across the country. I want to take you to Midlothian. You're right about tomorrow. Let's make it Monday. The art store and the library particularly."

"Saul told me you want me to try those cassette books. You think you can solve my problems like that?"

"God forbid. I only want to make what you want to do easier for you."

"Yes, all right, I know. I'll be over tomorrow as usual."

Riva is grateful to me and I know it and her gratitude weighs on her heavily, so that she is uneasy with it and attacks for no reason. Knowing it doesn't stop the twinge of anger I feel. But then I begin to think about the accident, reliving it in a strangely peaceful way. I think about the two of us walking with Ben, and later about Ben in the ambulance talking out his horror to me. It is the deep, satisfying sharing that one does, in fantasy, with gentle daughters and loving sons.

8

Geri is sitting at my kitchen table drinking coffee. We're supposed to be discussing supply and inventory for the ambulance. It's pettifogging work we both hate. "I want to ask you something. A salesman Saul knows is coming to dinner Thursday. He's single and a charming man. Would you like to meet him?"

Geri laughs. "In your combat boots and coat, which are generally what I see you wearing, I forget how very old-fashioned you are." ·

"How do people meet these days?"

"How did you and Saul meet?" I tell her.

We met at the university. As Jews in a world of non-Jews, we had to be more subtle and formal than our friends. I had to find out what kind of name Dowben was. Saul asked his friends about me, I about him. It was all very elaborate, and now it sounds as antique as the minuet. I wonder how it's done now.

"I go out occasionally," Geri says, "but I'm not looking for anything serious. I'm having too much fun to get married. One of these days, Orley Flett, skinny, worn and wizened, is going to be struck dumb with a mad passion for me, and I want to be ready."

I ask her where she's going for dinner on Thanksgiving. She's working. Since Miriam and Joshua won't be home, I'd planned to ask some others. Riva will be there, and Ben had said he would come. For the last few years, Violet Cleve has been included, and I miss her.

"You planned to invite me and this possible young man, huh?"

"Well, possibly."

"I think that's sweet."

"Sweet is not one of your words."

"How would you like to grow up a *Garland*?"

"I thought Geri was short for Geraldine. Garland is a lovely name."

"It is, for a *sweet* girl who walks around wafting clouds of delicate perfume, a girl always in soft focus, a girl who never sweats."

"God, Geri, we parody the old-fashioned virtues and then we hate the parody. I'm not wild about the name Grace either. Fear not. There are few Garlands and Graces being started today. My granddaughter's name is Kimberley, a name so foreign to me as to constitute a kind of insult."

"Do you see her often?"

"Only when I go out to them in California—four times. Kimberley is six, and I don't think she knows me. It's sad, but not tragic. Miriam would be miserable living here or even in Midlothian. I know it, and consistent with my plan to be, as Saul's father used to say, up-to-date-one-hundred-percent-modern, I am not grieving, or if I am—"

"I didn't know old-fashioned people were so practical."

"I learned to be practical. The perspective changes when you raise children."

"Does it?"

"A woman's got to change when she sees a penis go from being an erotic object to a toilet training problem to a source of anxiety and back again. It's why there are so many dippy old broads walking around."

"With all that, you like to preserve things. The holiday, for instance, in the old-fashioned way. Turkey and all of that."

"Of course, my dear. 'On Thanksgiving Day, the crème de Gilboa society was present at the holiday table of Grace Dowben, one of Gilboa's social elite. The gracious hostess appeared in a dress for the first time in months. Among those present were her handsome husband, whose sense of style has been assaulted by her daily since marriage; Riva Dowben, who, it is rumored, missed the house three times because she is too proud and shy to get her eyes examined; and Benjamin Sloan, educator, whose hair and beard, whichever is which, had been carefully combed for the occasion and who appeared barefoot as a form of self-expression. Ever the spontaneous hostess, the charming Mrs. D. left the turkey burning in the oven to oversee the extrication of three winos overturned in a ditch. A quarter of the guests left with her and the party continued in the new location for several hours.' "

"By that time, the crème was a little sour?"

Thanksgiving is my favorite American holiday. It's serious but not solemn, and like the good Jewish holidays, it features food and family. The turkey and the corn, the nuts and the sweet potatoes are all acceptable to kosher Jews; the traditional activities are ours also—we are able to be as "traditionally American" as the Cabots and the Lodges. Riva says she'll come early to help me but I know she won't. She likes to be a guest, entertained by Saul with a drink and a story, and I like to hear her laughing with him. She has little gift and no liking for kitchen work and will usually dress so as to make doing it impossible. This time it's scarves, flowing here and there. She's a fire hazard, and she knows it.

Ben comes a little late. I've told Riva about him and she's prepared for the beard and the long hair and possibly for clothes stranger than her own. He is wearing very clean but faded jeans and an Indian shirt, also very clean, but of a gauzy, soft material, unironed, like a pajama top. For a moment they look at one another, hard. Then Riva smiles and Ben smiles and then she says that he looks like an Indian prince in reduced circumstances and he laughs that magical laugh and the afternoon flows warm from that beginning.

In wonder, I carry things in and out, listening to the three of them. Riva begins to tell stories not even I have heard about her girlhood in Shedletz, stories full of flavor and liveliness. We laugh often at the girl who could never get first things first in a town that demanded of its young girls piety instead of wit and dedication instead of adventure.

"I wanted to guess things—I loved mysteries, and in Shedletz, for a woman, there were none. I drove everyone crazy. To top it off, the reward for my wildness was that I was sent for by a rich merchant in Pennsylvania to be his bride." She draws the word out, luxuriating in the strange sound of it. "It was the biggest adventure of all. How could I not go? Does water run downhill? Who can stop it? Strangest of all to them, the groom was no ordinary man, living among others in a city. You must remember that to Shedletz came daily letters from New York, from Chicago, and Philadelphia. Some immigrants came back and our people knew the names even of streets and sections in the big American cities. Not for me. For me a Bible town. There was even wondering if the Indians had the Bible to give such a name. What was I? A pioneer!" Nothing bitter, I notice in that laugh, and we all laugh with her.

As we eat, Saul, to my astonishment, begins to talk about Korea. He has never spoken much about it. Over the years it has come bit by bit, the worst parts in tiny, measured, manageable horrors, images mostly, not interpreted or summed up. After Riva's stories, his come as naturally as the leisure we have, the whole day.

"Korea was my time as a stranger—" he says. The sky has begun to lower early on, and by one o'clock a light snow begins falling softly on its soft, gray background. We sit at the table and later with some brandy before the fire in a magical isolation, a dream-time, as though no phone could ring, no door be knocked on, no alarm box go off. I'm caught up in the wonder of it—who could have predicted this? The snow falls undriven. We have the fire, and as the day darkens, we don't add other light. We sit close in an eveninglike intimacy into which we speak quietly.

"The combat was such a small part of the whole thing." We are silent. "What was real and constant were the men in the platoon and the company. I'd always thought of myself as being an average guy from an average town. In Korea, I lived, ate, slept with men from places so remote they had never before seen people to whom they weren't related. Some were barely literate, some were savages almost, rural savages and urban. We had a sprinkling of college men and one concert pianist, believe it or not. He was always looking for someplace where there was a piano. Most of the rest went and drank themselves into a stupor. I tried to learn the country."

"Was that difficult?"

"Yes, but not the way you think. The Koreans, when they found someone really interested in their culture, were eager to show, to teach, to share anything they could. Even the people in the smallest villages had an appreciation of their own culture and traditions and a wonderful folk art. The problem was us—me. The ordinary days were so dull and enervating, the army's hurry up and wait so arbitrary and reasonless, that most of the time I didn't have the energy or spirit to leave the group and strike out on my own. Also, I was young enough to want to belong even to a group with which I had very little in common. Combat buddies have a special relationship because of the danger and it makes for a kind of loyalty that doesn't come in the ordinary way of things." He turns to me. "You know that. Would you have the same feeling about C.A., for example, if not for the Gilboa Fire and Rescue?"

"C.A. has saved my life a couple of times and my hash at least a dozen."

"That's the point; you have the danger in common."

"War buddies," Ben says, and smiles. "I was never in a war, but in a sense, it followed me. The comradeship of it was missing and maybe it's part of what I like about rescue."

"What do you mean, war followed you?" At any other time, it might have been too rude a question, too personal and aggressive, but we are sailing, snow-shawled and invisible, in a mystical ship as free as strangers, as trusting as old friends, and the time is right for the question.

There are only three of us now. Riva is lying on the couch curled up like a child and sleeping. There are the sounds of her breathing and a little sigh now and then. In the whiteout that surrounds us, we seem conscious of everything, the hums of the house, the colors of the room, the satisfactions of the meal, the warmth, the relaxation of our bodies.

"I ran away from the Vietnam War, my war," Ben says. "I didn't go to Canada, where most of my friends went, but to Europe. I think I saw myself romantically in those days—singled out, cheated by fate. My dad had been in World War Two, in the navy, and he had been badly hurt—we didn't have the usual father-and-son relationship because of it."

Saul and I looked at one another. What is the usual father-and-son relationship? How does either of the sharers know if what they share is what they will remember having shared?

Ben goes on quietly. "I was raised with high expectations and it made me self-righteous. I was as self-righteous as a TV hero. War was bad and I was good and so I had a moral justification for whatever I did. I think I was scared stiff; just that, really, and I ran away. Europe was full of highly moral Americans between eighteen and thirty-five, many of whom were dealing in dope or other contraband. I had sworn I would never do that. I had also promised myself I would survive. I worked on farms in Portugal, as a janitor in a Spanish mental hospital, at a rope-works on the French coast—all were jobs that one way or another were a threat to survival." He stops, looks at us, then goes on. "I was against war and wanted to make my statement about that, so—don't laugh—I aimed myself toward the capital of peace, Switzerland." *He's* almost laughing now. "I thought it was so deep, that idea, such a unique personal vision." I hear, in the inflection, the sorrow he is not expressing. His tone is light. "When I got there, the place was overrun. It was like a convention. Every state in the Union had sent a thousand representatives with the same unique vision and the same empty pockets. My first instinct was to split. But I was living allegorically in those days, and I had no money, so I had to stay. There was no work. The cost of living was astronomical. Worse yet, the free-and-easy attitude Portugal and Spain had toward the poor didn't exist. No sleeping under bridges or 'waiting' in back of restaurants. No three-day jobs. No charity boxes with warm clothes in the basements of churches, and God, it was cold!"

"But the hotels—you speak English—"

"—and I was young and American, long-haired and bearded and moral and so obviously a resister or deserter; no hotel would touch me. They didn't want a hassle from the American tourists I would be serving."

"What did you do?"

"I ended up working in a bar in Berne, an after-hours dive. Berne is a very moral place, very upright and, in its lower spots, savage. I was a bouncer. I grabbed people from behind when they were arguing. I kicked the legs out from under noisy drunks and threw them into the alley out back. A job like that, unless it's balanced against something else—a happy home life, love, something—begins to be like a sickness. I'd run away from war, but it seemed to be all around me. The managers despised their 'help'—in my bar, there were three of us. We despised each other and ourselves. The patrons hated us—even the ones we saved from fights or worse. Sometimes one of us got beaten up by a customer and the patrons would cheer and stamp. Everyone seemed to be against us and we soon felt we were against all of them. Because the place served the lowest level of crooks and perverts, the police were always raiding it, subject to prearrangements we were never in on. They would 'question' us with fists or batons. The three of us were foreigners and didn't speak the local argot well enough to understand compli- cated criminal plans and all the rest, but that didn't stop them from giving us a working over every time they could. Some- times the guys we bounced got their boys together and waylaid us. No guns, but chains and knives. They wouldn't kill us, of course, because then the manager would only hire another Al- gerian jailbird, another Sudanese weirdo, another American moralist. They knew that if they beat us enough to scare us, we would think twice about giving them the shove the next time the manager made his funny little nod and finger-flick. I saved every cent I could to get out of there, but the cost of living was so high that I was trapped for months. The lowest jobs in the world are like that, a kind of peonage—"

"But your parents—couldn't you have—"

"As long as I had any power of choice at all, no. If I'd been given a long jail term or been desperately ill in a hospital, I might have called for help, but it's got to stop sometime, doesn't it, running to Mommy and Daddy? I'd gotten myself in; it was my job to get myself out."

"You could have gotten some money by dealing—dope or

women—" Saul says. He has been sitting very still, his face showing no expression. I can't tell what he is thinking.

"No," Ben says very quietly. I have the feeling he has not said these things aloud before. "I couldn't do that. I don't want to sound better than I am, but that was a line I had drawn and I knew if I stepped over it, I was lost and anything was possible. When you're that low and your world is that dangerous and ambiguous, there have to be lines you draw for yourself—unbreakable laws—that you'll keep your clothes clean, that you'll bathe every day, that you'll never use a fist on a woman, that you'll do no drugs, that you won't sell sex—yours or theirs—things like that. Sometimes there's only that to keep you from—God knows what."

I want to cry—not only about Ben but about Joshua, fled away into Sanjit's laws. Why did he need to get a law so binding and so exclusive? "Did your parents know any of this?"

"No. I wrote to them from Europe, of course. I told them where I worked, but not what I did. They'd been sympathetic with my war resistance because they thought it was a moral stand, which it wasn't entirely. Having denied war, it was as though its spirit followed me. After the bar, at which I worked for seven months—a long stay in that job—I went to Lausanne, then to Ouchy. Wherever I went, I got pulled into racial situations, prowar versus antiwar battles, hip versus straight fights—in bars, in workers' barracks, on the job even. The fights seemed to find me out. I had none of the camaraderie or purpose you talked about—only the combat zone boredom and tension. When I left war-torn Switzerland, I went to Sweden and then to France, and it was the same. In the end, I surrendered. I came home tired and beaten in more ways than one and got ready for prison. I thought I would be killed there by fights, but a kind God intervened. They take blood there for the physical. Mine was taken with a bad needle and I got hepatitis. Because I was so run down, I was very sick. I remember almost nothing of my jail term, which was served in bed, but there were no fights there, not one. They let me out early because of the hep. I think my parents threatened a lawsuit. America's war was over and so was mine. I haven't fought since."

We say nothing. The quietness with which he has spoken and the lack of anger gentle the fact, make them more sad than ugly. I don't want this singular day to end with me crying. I had seen Joshua after he was Sanjit, enveloped in rote answers and pieties—nothing like Ben Sloan, but the echoes seem strangely the same. Joshua had gone away to college and then left abruptly after less than a month. We didn't know he had left until our letters began to come back. We called the police. Reports were filed. After a nightmare month, we got a letter from him in Nogales, Mexico. He had left, he said, because his studies were empty and useless. He wanted to try the world for a while. He was gone a year. God knows what fights, what jails and illnesses he had before he took, in preference, the numbing rote of his new religion. When I am under control, I ask, "Did you ever tell your parents about this?"

He looks at me in a way that neither of my children would have at such a provocative question. It is an open look without defensiveness. "No, I couldn't bring myself to do that. I told a girl once, but both of us were drunk and neither of us was listening."

"But you're telling us." ·

"Yes, and I'm not drunk now."

"It's a good day for it," Saul says. "The turkey, the fire, and the snow." I want to kiss him. He knows what I am feeling, all the places where the points of guilt and pain are still fixed.

"And the people," Ben adds, and I know he means it. It's all right then; I won't cry. Riva stirs and I get up to serve the dessert. While I am by myself in the kitchen, I think for a moment that I want to bring my ghosts to them. I've been visited now and then through the narrowing days of autumn.

Their presences are passive, offering nothing but their metaphor, special to me, their shapes at the sides of my eyes, their whisper in my ear about the joy I still have not defined. I think and then think again. It would sadden people, even while I insisted that the message was to "take delight." I'll tell them maybe, but not today.

As we are eating, I say, "Riva has told her war story, and Saul and Ben have told theirs. I have a war story, too, one nobody has ever heard." I look around the table. They are waiting, eager to hear. "It's the story of my first big run. To begin with, you should know that I went into rescue, *my* war, with all my life's unused idealism. I'd been on fires and done traffic control at accidents, but emergency medicine meant saving lives to me. I studied very hard, as you remember, did my clinical internship at the hospital in a kind of glow, the glow left over from a mothering no one needed anymore. Your war, Saul, was dry necessity; Ben's was fear and anger. I went into combat the way it must have been a century ago: my soul full of drums, flags, and music. I'd been qualified for a month but we had nothing really serious, and then one night the alarm went: 'accident with injuries off Mundy.' "

"I think I remember," Saul says. "That call wasn't your first, but I think I remember."

"Ben, do you know where Mundy is?"

"I've heard of it. It's over by Pinecrest, isn't it?"

"Yes, but the road dead-ends at the top of the hill. It's a lovers' lane and always has been, as far as I know. A special kind of accident happens there. The boys park up on the crest with their girl friends. They neck and pet and some of it gets fairly active. A hand or foot bumps against the gearshift and knocks it into neutral or out of park. If the emergency brakes are worn or not set, the car goes over the hill."

"I didn't know you knew about that!" Saul cries. "We used to call it chipmunk chasing."

"I think they have a new name for it now—a worse one. Since your day, the excavation for the highway and the culverts they put there have changed things. The fall used to be about fifty feet with a soft landing in Kempe's pasture. Now, it's more like a hundred to rocks and highway rubble."

"What happened?" Ben asks.

"The fire department gave us that hard light from its power plant—it was bright as day down into the gully. The scene was horrifying. Car parts marked the way down, great gouts pulled out of the hillside where the car had landed, turning over and going on to turn again and again. It had stopped against a boulder at the bottom, its doors sprung. It was hard enough getting down with equipment, but there was the terrible pressure for speed. The two of them had been thrown out near the bottom. I didn't know then how God loves the young, puts them on learners' permits, and abrogates the laws of physics on their behalf. I was sure they were both dead or dying. Others on the squad were going down—we had to be careful to avoid kicking dirt and rocks onto the victims below us. I got to the boy first, looking at him as I had been taught, but unable to keep from seeing beyond the medical evaluation, his youth, the horror for his parents if he should die. I spoke to him the way I had been taught, telling him that he had been in an accident and who I was and that I was there to help. He opened his eyes—how glad and grateful I was to see that! He drew a good breath and looked up at me out of his bloody face and said, 'Fuck off!' ".

Why aren't they laughing? I look around at them one after another, silent. Ben is smiling, I think, but maybe it's only his beard smiling. "Where did you learn such language!" Riva cries. "It's disgusting, such talk."

"It *is* disgusting," Saul says, "when I think of you getting up night after night, in rain and snow, going out and risking your life for a bunch of drunks and garbage-mouths, it makes me furious!"

"You didn't think that was funny—just a little? Well, I do, and I'm going to have another slice of this and then take the plates into the kitchen and have a little chuckle."

"I thought it was funny," Ben said, "but I thought it was a little sad, too. It obviously didn't hurt you too much because you're still on the squad. I guess I was looking at the scene, imagining it, and how your face must have fallen."

"It didn't, you know, or if it did, only for a second."

"What happened?"

"I burst out laughing." I look around the table. "Come on, team, perk up. I've got a dozen more war stories, all of 'em heartrendin'. No one is drunk in any of them, all the victims are grandmothers with Ph.D.'s—"

The phone rings. I hear everyone sigh. Thinking we had only been drifting silently through the day invisible and dream-protected, we had been taken by subtle tides back into port and here were the people and the complications. It's the school. They want Ben back; apparently there has been some trouble with one of the boys. When I come back to the table, I see that all of them are hoping it is nothing and no one, that we can go on to some other port in the dream-sea, still anonymous, disguised now by darkness and hidden in snow. I tell Ben and he sighs and goes for his coat. He's not easy with social thanks, and his is no more than peremptory, but I know, we all know, how good this day has been. The phone rings again.

9

After the early freeze and the Thanksgiving snow, the weather relents. I take Riva to Midlothian twice to shop, I clean out the storage room in the basement, go through my wardrobe and get rid of what I can't use. It has always depressed me to do it, but this time I feel lighter, agile and competent. It's the weather, I'm sure. Even an unhappy call from Miriam doesn't upset me. The women's center wants to make a film about consciousness raising, she says. The film will make a meaningful statement about the subtle and not-so-subtle abuses to which women are subjected by the male-dominated society. The trouble is that no one in the male-dominated government wants the nation to hear these painful truths. There is no funding available. Therefore . . .

"Darling, whatever gave you the idea that we have that kind of money?"

"But you have some savings, don't you?"

"Yes, but Riva doesn't. The savings we have need to be invested for profit because things are going up and we're getting older."

"But don't you see how important this is? Not only for the film and the people who will see it but for the women here, to raise their self-image? We have a perfect group for this project—women with such different problems and yet each keys in with the problem of being a woman."

"Do any of you know professional-level filmmaking?"

"No, that's the point. It will be amateur, rough, not slick like a Hollywood movie, and the sincerity will be there—"

It's all I can do not to gasp or laugh at that naiveté. "Darling, I could give you my emergency money, a hundred dollars. If that will help, you may have it."

"That won't pay for the film, even. We need a commitment, a base of support—you work with those ambulance women—there are older women in town who—"

Suddenly, in full light, I see her fantasy. The women of Gilboa, fettered by convention, crushed in stifling relationships and small-town boredom, could reach out to their sisters in the inner city. "Speak for us," they would say; "we are frozen in our hypocrisy, but you can be honest and free. Be our voices, cry our universal cry."

"Miriam, dear, I can't go from group to group in Gilboa raising money for you to make a film. The women on the squad work, but they would, if I asked, give me five or ten dollars out of their lunch money, their clothing or movie money. They would do it for me, because I asked. I won't ask. If you want to come back here and speak to the Garden Club and the church and the P.T.A. and raise the money, you're free to do it. I'll give you a hundred dollars privately. That's all I can do."

I try to sound tender and loving, but I know I sound the way I feel, like a kindergarten teacher talking to a first-day student about throwing clay. Why has she pushed me into this corner where I must refuse her once again? When I hang up the phone, I expect to be depressed and annoyed, but I'm not. The love and patience have gone one way long enough. It is possible that I am getting over my guilt-anguish at last. Perhaps I will soon be able to stop looking at other women's daughters without a pang. Oh God, perhaps I will someday be able to deal with the other lost Jew, renamed and recycled into a wheel of cockroaches and blue-faced gods. The signs go up and I turn my mind from it, but the good feeling stays with me. I'm a survivor and I will survive. There are things we might never have—grandchildren who know us, the knowledge that we are continuing our people, the special love of—forget it! forget it! and this time I do.

We make a day run in an icy fog to the mill on the northwest side of town. Two women in a knife fight. Ben, Rita, and I and, thank God, the cops. The air is blue with their language to us and each other. Jack drives. Even with restraints, Ben, Rita, and I have to sit on them to keep them from wiggling free. They spit at us, they scream. They are incontinent. I talk and talk, I reason and plead, but their hate is so terrible and their brains so poisoned that they are unable to save themselves, and we are forced to save them against their wills. I have seen drunken fights before, and even been part of the brawl in the ambulance last autumn, but these women are the hardest fighters I have ever seen. They would consent to their own maiming in order to destroy one another. It occurs to me that men fight through their boyhoods and learn that there is a tomorrow and they must count the cost. A feminist on television yesterday said that with women running the governments of the world, there would be no wars. I look at these two and think that with women running the governments of the world there would be no quarter.

Now and then I catch Ben's eye as we work. He smiles, encouraging me over the screaming women. I am not yet ready for compassion, and I am trying to keep myself from rage. The closed box of the ambulance is like a slaughterhouse: noise and the stench of blood and urine and of the chemicals of rage that seem to stimulate an answering anger in me. I think: Facial wounds, burns, torn flesh are not so ugly as this. There are always the eyes then, that see and follow and give the reason to save. Only death—I make myself stop. I try to discipline myself by working on them. They fight it all. I can't even get a pulse. Before I know it, I have left them again and am thinking about Violet Cleve.

It was years ago, a time in the fall. She was explaining to me the reasons why "willows whiten, aspen quiver." How sufficient everything was in the nature Violet loved. The leaf, she said, has to be spread to the sun, but the trees that grow in climates where the snow comes early and suddenly must have leaves that are able to turn at an angle to their branches to shed the snow, lest the weight of it break the branch and kill the tree. When the same world can hold Violet Cleve and these women, prayers of wonder should be said. I've begun to smile because of the memory of where I had been, on the hill above Violet's house, in a grove, rose-gold and fluttering; the day snapping-cold and the colors, colors of fire around me; and our joy, Violet's and mine, at the creation of such elegant sufficiency. Ben looks at me quizzically. "I'm sorry, I was daydreaming."

"Book says you should never do it, but under the circumstances, I won't tell."

At long last we come to the hospital and unload, almost gleeful that the responsibility of them and their ugliness will be slipping away from us. We go out in the cold and begin to clean up the ambulance.

"I want to fumigate this rig!" Jack cries. "Why are women so much worse than men?"

Rita turns to him. "Wanna hear my theory? It will solve the whole thing."

"Go on, you wacky broad, tell me."

I take off my wet hat and hit him with it. He grins at me. "You're beautiful when you're mad," he says.

84

"I'm beautiful all the time, and I'll beat up the lousy bum who says that I'm not! Go on, Rita."

"You boys have what the TV sociologists call role models for being drunk. In a sense, you're taught how to do it with some class. Women have no models for being drunk, only the model for being a bitch, so we have to use that one."

"Where did you get that theory, Rita?" Ben asks.

She smirks at him. "I made it up." Jack snorts.

"I made up a theory," I say, "about men in accidents. Because they have no instructions, they do imitations. The older men do Brando. Younger men do Newman, Redford, or Burt Reynolds; a much mellower image."

"I must dash off a note to Burt to thank him," Rita says.

"Say hello for me. Include my telephone number."

"I say, Benjamin," Jack says, "have you a theory?"

"No, Jack, none."

"None whatever?"

"None. I looked around this morning and realized that the theory I had been keeping by my bedside was gone. Someone must have made off with it."

"You've been walking around without one?"

"I'm afraid so, yes."

"Let's get out of here quickly before someone notices the deficit."

We've cleaned·up the ambulance, but it still stinks. "All those with theories," I cry, "should sit in front. In the back should ride those who do not have a theory."

"I'm sorry," Ben says, "but State Law 1.10 of the Ambulance Code says that them as rode in back going shall ride in front coming. It's called the equality of nausea statute."

In the end, we let Rita go up front with Jack, who is the driver of record. It's hateful to get back in the patient section. As soon as the heat goes on, the fumes wake from the corners. "Take my mind off my troubles," I say to Ben. "Tell me the story of your life." I'm enjoying our ease with one another, that he's Joshua's age, but not Joshua, not bitter or angry or defensive, all the things Joshua was, before he became passive and full of mystical rhetoric and even farther sealed away from us. There are some rare young who do not give pain. He sits on the jump seat, laughing.

"I was born," he says, "of poor but honest parents in a two-story colonial in New Canaan, Connecticut, in 1954."

In 1954, I was in college and Saul was in Korea. And New Canaan—"When I was a child in the late thirties," I say, "few Jews lived in New Canaan, Connecticut."

"What do you mean—was it unfashionable or something?"

"No, most of it was covenanted—forbidden to Jews."

"But that's impossible."

"No, it isn't. The lovely villages in the northeast, hundreds of them, were, by gentlemen's agreements or by covenants, closed to Jews."

"I thought only blacks—"

"No, not only blacks; Jews, Poles, Orientals, and in some places Catholics. All over the country, restaurants, hotels, resorts, some stores, many colleges were closed to us. The Ivy League universities had quotas to limit the numbers of Jews."

"But—"

"It's history no one wants to remember. We're learning to be neighbors now. Neither of us wants to spoil it."

"But I was—I grew up in New Canaan."

"I don't know the town or what it's like, but in 1940 my aunt and uncle married and tried to live there and were told very coldly by realtors to 'stay where it's healthy for Jews to be.' But they liked the smaller towns. They went to a dozen places and were told to go back to New Haven where there was a 'Jewish section.' Well, it wouldn't have worked out anyway. He was killed in the war. She went back to Chicago. All the suburbs ringing Chicago were restricted, too."

"But how did a person know which—"

"Many places said so, subtly or blatantly: SOGGY BOTTOM ES-
TATES: COVENANTS ENFORCED. THE RISING GORGE GOLF CLUB: RE-
STRICTED. There were scenes. People were 'discovered' and
asked to leave. We learned before we went out for an evening
where we could go and where we couldn't."

"But traveling—"

"When in doubt, people carried a picnic hamper and a ther-
mos, like the blacks did, and they stayed where they knew there
were Jews."

"But why did the Jews stand for it? Why did the
Christians?"

"It was the way things were. We got revenge by living well.
We made the most of the compensations. Our language and
Yiddish expressions and jokes were known to us alone. We
communicated with secret words in subtle ways over the heads
of the others. At the same time, we worked like hell to belong.
We straddled the fence."

"An uncomfortable position," he says. He has known none of
this before.

"Some people changed their names, killed their memories,
and passed, or tried to. What jokes we told about *them*! What
comfortlessness we saw awaiting them in the bland, careful
world in which no *mishpucha* was allowed—no families, no paradoxes, no secret pulse of life, and with betrayal around every
corner. All that seems as old-fashioned now as cambric tea and
cupping. The truths then were different. Few of us had any
social dealings with Christians."

"*Really?*"

"Really."

"It amazes me that that happened here, in America."

"It amazes me that you never knew."

"I thought the reason why we had everything new, our
neighborhoods and houses—that it was because—"

"Why?"

"Because the Jews were more materialistic than the older residents in the older neighborhoods."

"You never asked your family why the Jews were in the new houses and had the new money?"

"It's not something you have words for."

Suddenly, the alarm goes off again, piercingly from the radio up front. "Good God," Jack cries, "another one!" We're about three minutes from town. "First Aid, 101 Amsterdam Street," the dispatcher voice says dryly, with none of the consternation that we feel reflected in his tone. Jack turns on the lights and siren and we pick up speed.

It's the Tellers. I don't know them well. When we go inside, we see Sheriff Ups, and there are so many neighbors, I have trouble finding the victim. It's Mrs. Teller. She is sitting on a kitchen chair at the center of a considerable friendly uproar, very pale. Her hand is wrapped in a wet towel.

"I feel so silly," she says. I ask if I can send the neighbors home. "Oh, would you? I appreciate their concern, but—"

I see Doris Manning from the Garden Club. She does the job well. Ben has come in behind me.

"It's just my hand," Mrs. Teller says. "I was using the electric slicer and it got a piece of meat jammed into it and it stopped and I went to get the meat out—"

I unwrap the wet towel slightly and see that the cut has gone through the tendons and bones at the joint of the thumb. It is almost severed. I call Ben to get what we need to immobilize the thumb without severing its shred of tissue. It should lie in a natural curled position in opposition to the fingers. "Do you have anything in that dryer?"

"Yes, the laundry."

"Any socks?"

"Yes."

I ask Ben to get the laundry out and to put one of our blankets in to warm it. He has not understood at first, but does what I tell him and then sees the reasons.

"Oh, please, don't make me go out of here lying down!"

"O.K., but when we get into the ambulance, I think it will help. Ben, get me a pair of socks out of the dryer. Preferably white." He does. He is holding one in each hand. "Good, now ball them." He looks at me quizzically. Men. I suddenly become aware of our generational differences. "Make them into a ball, one inside the other. Never mind, bring them over and I'll show you." Mrs. Teller smiles at me, a quick, conspiratorial mother-smile. I see her good hand reach out instinctively to do the thing she has done thousands of times. I make the ball and put it inside the natural curve of the injured hand. The thumb lies almost in its normal position. I bind the hand well and sling and swath it to her chest.

"I feel so stupid," she says. We have wrapped her in the warmed blanket and draped her coat over her shoulders. "My daughters live in Russian Grove. They were coming to dinner tonight. I should call them."

"Better have someone do it, a friend. I want a hand specialist to look at this as soon as possible."

"Do you think they can save it—any of it—the use of it—it *is* my right hand." She looks at me pleading the case, as though I had any other choice than to do what I'm doing, as though we both know such an instinctive gesture could never result in so radical a loss.

"I hope so," I say.

A neighbor must have called Mrs. Teller's daughters because they are there when we get to the hospital. They help me undress her, laughing gently at themselves and each other in a soft, comforting, female way. "Look, Mom, what I came away in—this old top—"

"Is someone with the kids? You didn't come right away . . ."

"Now, you know better than that. They're with Jessie Prager."

"You did a bad thing, Mom, getting hurt. Vern was saying

this morning he was looking forward to the dinner you were going to set out. How am I going to break this news: last week's hash I put in the freezer!"

"You just fry some mushrooms and onions fresh and get some canned soup, mushroom, some of that and put that with it—"

Maybe it is watching these ordinary women or the tension of calls in such quick succession, but I have begun to ache with a loss that this mother does not know. If I had a thumb off or all the bones of my body broken, would my daughter come and make of the examining room something like a sewing corner on a Sunday afternoon? In the back bedroom where I taught her how to make doll clothes, the boxes of the scraps of her school dresses are waiting for my granddaughter, a stranger. Miriam is so brave and so energetic and so cold, liberated from everything that these women share. "Girls," Mrs. Teller is saying, "get to your father; he's sure to be worried when he comes home and finds blood all over the kitchen."

Ben looks in. They're ready to go. The specialist is outside. I realize I have been standing here to no purpose. Ben smiles at the women. "Don't worry; we cleaned up the kitchen a little and it wasn't as bad as you imagine it." I excuse myself.

"You've been wonderful to me," Mrs. Teller says. The daughters smile at me.

Then the doctor comes in. "Well, hello there, girls," he cries. I feel my jaw tighten.

I need to feel less alone, so back in the ambulance I ask Ben how the school people are taking his sudden exits in the middle of the day. "It's a hassle, but it's good for the kids, I think. It dumps all kinds of responsibility on the teachers and other aides, but the kids *are* seeing that there is a world out here, that other people have problems too. When I come back from something, I talk about it; I tell what the victims did and what we do—good and bad."

"It doesn't scare them? A world full of auto wrecks and jammed meat slicers, drunks with knives and other assorted horrors?"

"They've accepted it better than anyone thought they would. And they can laugh at me, running away in the middle of a ball game or this or that. Some good school spirit has come from Ben jokes: Ben is in the john and the call comes and he loses his pants. Ben's in the shower and he goes as is. My favorite: Ben's playing billiards and there's that beep-wail and he still has the pool cue in his hand and goes to the call and (1) pokes a cop in the eye; (2) splints a broken leg with the pool cue; (3) splints a broken arm with the pool cue and teaches the victim, a sweet little girl, to become a pool shark to the horror of her parents."

"Sounds like fun."

"Yes, but possibilities two and three were from boys who usually give nothing but violent and sadistic talk. There's good stuff going on at that school. There's a lot of fad and woolly theory but underneath it all, we're getting through to the kids."

"But you don't trust us townspeople to understand, do you? You don't come to our churches or stores, the library, the post office . . ."

"I guess not. We train them for outings in the big impersonal places: the shopping centers, Midlothian sometimes. The town is too much of a challenge right now, and there's a prejudice against Longhill, isn't there?"

"Yes, Longhill has quite a past: the isolation isn't new and there has been some genuine horror."

"Not just the school, then?"

"God, no, the name evokes a decade of bad dreams."

"Tell me."

I tell him. I tell him about Tomorrow and we laugh. It seems funny at this distance, all those earnest Ph.D.'s denying themselves even a tractor, cutting the electric lines between themselves and town, plowing with sticks, sowing seeds like

91

Mesolithic man. Finally, we are laughing so hard that Rita and Jack in the driver's compartment begin to tease us. "Gettin' rowdy back there!" Jack cries over the noise of the engine. "Next thing you know they'll be sendin' out for cold cuts and beer."

"Just cold cuts," Rita cries. "I think there are still fumes left from our first run. They're probably pie-eyed, riding back there."

We laugh again, and then I tell Ben about Centering, the automobile junkyard, the mystics' pits, the fire, the charred victims still sitting in their friendly circle, the stench of unburned garbage, the "natural" ecology of "natural" man: rats, lice, flies, and roaches, the living scalps of the children. "You saw all that?"

"I was the one who discovered the bodies. I was checking for hot spots. The fire was out by then. Later, I brought some of the families to the town hall and helped them get clean. We had to call the health department for chemicals to bathe them and then to fumigate the place."

"No wonder there's been that silence around me . . ."

"You felt it, then, when you first came to the meeting . . . I'm sorry . . ."

"Only slightly there. I thought it was me—my hair and beard, my clothes, but it's been all around me at times: the library, the coffee shop—nothing rude, just something."

"Have any of the other Longhill people felt it?"

"Frankly, few of them come to town as much as I do."

"Then we have a project: You want to heal the kids. It's phony to live near a town and never go there. I think the teachers need to be healed, too, and I want to heal Gilboa after all this time. We've suffered enough the fear of what other people's children can do. Let's fix things."

"It may take a long time."

"We can afford it." We pull up at the firehouse. "You've

started already by coming with us, by joining the town. People know you a little."

"I'd like to do it and I'd like to do something else, too."

"What?"

"When we're back here alone or when I have some free time, could I come over and ask you—talk to you about—about Judaism?"

"Sure," I say, as casually as though I had never lost a son. "Also, you can come to the services we have once a month in the town hall basement. And please come to the house for Shabbos any Friday night you want. Riva likes you and Saul does, too. And I'll be happy to tell you whatever I can."

"I can't come this week, but I'll clear next Friday night."

"Great," I say.

"Oh, yes, one more thing—" He is smiling down at me. "Never tell someone of my generation to ball a pair of socks!"

When I am safely home, I sit in the car for a while in awe. The town may need healing and the school may need healing, but who knows how deep our wounds are, Riva's and Saul's and mine? Are we being sent a son to ease the pain we have been bearing with no particular grace? I wasn't a Spock-mother, or a Ginott-mother, infinitely patient and reasonable and loving, but I gave the best I had. In a hospital room in Midlothian at this moment, two daughters are throwing pots and pans, knitting needles, and recipe cards at their mother's loneliness and fear, the way I once, in a dream, attacked an intruder.

What does Ben not know? What prayer does he need, what law, what ceremony? My mind is blazing with Sabbath lights.

10

We're sitting in my kitchen, telling war stories, Geri, Rita, and I. The air is thick with the smoke of combat. I know that in deference to me, it's tobacco. "As we were leaving, he said to me, 'Never tell someone of my generation to ball a pair of socks.' " We laugh. I feel happy and lucky today, partly because what I feared years ago hasn't happened.

Years ago, I used to watch my mother and her friends who met on Wednesday afternoons without fail to play bridge and, when it became fashionable, canasta. The talk was of clothing, housework, children, recipes, and health. Sometimes they went to matinees. One or two did fund raising for the synagogue; there were always teas or luncheons. What a dry rind of life it seemed to me, teas and card games! My mother still mourns for me, living in a small town where the better people are so few and the luncheons must be limp affairs indeed. "All the same faces all the time. *We* invite celebrated people and improve our minds."

They didn't then. They only had their small circle and a life without real work outside their homes. It's Sunday afternoon.

Rita and Geri are here, and we're telling war stories. I suppose what we say is no deeper or wiser or truer than what they said between the hands they dealt and played out with such savage concentration, loser to buy refreshments for the next week's play. But our scope is wider, our work immediate and urgent, and also away from the familial sources of our pain and pleasure. I can forget that I spoke to Joshua-Sanjit yesterday as one speaks to a stranger, receiving his impersonal, Oriental respect, placid and passionless as I told him my message. We're worried about Riva's health, and should something happen, would he be free to come? She would like to see him, I think, while she still has eyesight enough. He answers that the child of Krishna shows his responsibility to his worldly family by perfecting his inner gifts to their fullest. In a worldly environment, the spiritual life shrivels. He is not yet sufficiently perfected to be able to combat the worldly environment. I can see that age, blindness, and death are minor vicissitudes to him. Our lives and deaths are not in his philosophy, and he seems barely interested in them. In any case, he says, he would have to submit the question to higher authority. Many blessings are available from the deities who are all beauty and all truth.

I was blinded with paradox and had to sit in the upstairs bedroom for an hour until I could move out from under it. Stop a passing angel, open a fortune cookie, study the guts of birds, hope in the fall of straws, pull the wishbone of a twenty-pound turkey, what would I have conjured all these years for my children? That they have work in the world, a mission, a cause, a purpose. Because happiness is a by-product coming magically out of such work, such purpose. The angel smiles, the cookie crumbles, the guts arrange, the straws fan open, the bone breaks clean. Wish is answered. It is done: this. I sigh and turn to my friends.

"You know, if the genie of the lamp came to me and asked me what I wanted, I would say I wanted a lovely figure—minus twenty pounds. You know what would happen?"

"Yup," Geri says. "Gangrene in your right leg. It would have to be amputated and you'd lose the twenty."

Rita snorts. "Change your genie."

"It's a rotten genie but it's the only one who understands my hair."

"Grace, I thought you were past all that," Rita says. "Look at you. Two healthy kids, a husband—a nice husband, too—a house, work, enough money—"

They don't know what my children are doing, although I suspect they would admire Miriam, who is liberated and says "fuck" and "shit" a lot. I remember my mother's generation as no less protecting. Their keener pains and disappointments never lay among the discards of the thousand bridge games they played. They would sigh in their corsets, and once or twice, like prisoners under torture, half a word, half a name would pass their clenched teeth: "What a world for a mother!" The others, quickly, before the confession was out, would apply the biting stick: "Isn't it always—" "How true, yes, no day without its trouble." Geri and Rita have done the same thing—spared me and themselves. Yet I know that had I wished to speak, I would have been given a good and generous hearing. Sometimes the flayed prisoner confesses against his will. They want to be sure, I think, that I really want to speak. I do not. Krishna forbid.

I understand now that in their card games, my mother and her friends put wrangling children and bored husbands away for a while, even as they spoke of them. I want to do the same. Tell me a war story. The world is full of other women's fools.

We start to tell Geri about the two fighting women and I find myself drifting away, thinking about Ben and what I want to tell him. For these two days, I have been working it over in my mind now and again, in secrecy and delight, like a miser counting his treasure. Hebrew—he should learn some Hebrew and the old legends, of course. I told Joshua those legends when he was small and now he has forgotten them for someone else's. And Jewish history—American-Jewish history. Everyone thinks it started in 1908. Listen, Ben, the man who yelled "Land, ho" on Columbus's ship was a Jew. We had an admiral in the Revolutionary War who got the navy to outlaw flogging. The first free library—not Ben Franklin's, Judah Touro's. Have you ever heard—do you know about—?

Because I am up fiddling with the coffeepot, they don't notice I have left them. I pull myself back but the wash of joy has left a narrow, gleaming edge around the afternoon. I feel strange about it. I had come to associate young people with pain.

A night call. (They always happen at night, we tell each other, although our own statistics have shown us it isn't so.) I struggle into my clothes. The night is raspingly cold, ugly with fog. Why do I do this work? Why am I out here when the sane and the reasonable are sleeping? Why else are they sleeping but to lie safe and secret through the times when danger proclaims itself free in the world. What am I daring time after time? It's Woodridge, a development newer than Pinecrest, out Exit 18. I remember when all this was farmland. In the summer we came down—Van Bronchorst went all the way through to Russian Grove and we bought produce up this road. Where did all these people come from? In a childish defense against the newness and the change, I am unable to learn the names of the new streets in the developments—they all sound the same: Pine Way, Pine Court, Cherryvale, Cherrywood, Cherry Knoll. This is a place called Grant Road. If Ulysses S. Grant had been Ulysses S. Kransdorf, would there be Kransdorf Roads all over the North? Suggs? Terwilliger? I pull in. The ambulance is already there. I see Sheriff Ups outside. Claude comes out of the house.

"Are there enough people?" I ask.

"They need another woman in there; go in. Hurry."

Something is in the air, bad vibes, Ben would say, palpable in the fog we are almost lost in. I go cautiously into the house.

A small house, almost pathologically neat. I love neat houses, and I hate this one. It is sick, aseptic. In the back, I hear a man weeping loudly. I follow his sound. The bedroom. It's in shambles. The man is being held by Macy Ups's deputy, Ken Witz. "Forgive me, Connie, please! I love you, Connie!" He is trying to get to her. Around her is the furniture he has broken with her body—chairs, the dresser with its mirror shattered. She is unreasonably still conscious and Geri is having to be very careful, since so much of her is broken. I can't hear myself think. Can the man please be quiet—I want to get a blood pressure and lung sounds. For a few seconds, he is quiet and I bend in and start getting Connie's vitals. Then he breaks out again, sobbing and calling to her. There's another mood in the room. It's coming from Geri, a dangerous rage and something akin to panic. I feel it thrumming in the air and through the body of the woman on whom we are both working. I've seen Geri in situations of terrible injury, but never like this. I raise my head to look at her. Her face is expressionless, locked as code. Claude is at the door now. I look at him and he shrugs. She has sent him out, I think. "Get a scoop stretcher, Claude," I say. I lean in again. "Connie, we're going to put you on a special stretcher so you won't have to be moved when we lift you, O.K.?" Then, to Geri, "Do you want to go in on this? Claude and I—"

"No men with her!" Geri growls. "Women. Men have done enough!"

I would have thought not. I would have imagined that comfort at the hands of a sympathetic man at this moment might have a special meaning, but what do I know about the feelings of a beaten woman? Whoever goes, I don't think Geri should. She is too dangerous, too personally involved, but she is the squad leader. I also know just at that moment in the dead certainty of sudden insights as we slip the scoop beneath Connie and snap the sides together and raise her onto the gurney that Geri is seeing herself on the stretcher and her ex-husband at her side, weeping. She thinks this man is playing; I can see it in her look. His tight, white rage is over. He is playing to the jury, to Ken Witz and us. I'm not sure. As it is, I'm glad I can treat and leave, and not have to unravel this dance of rage and dependence, love and hate, passivity and aggression. Who will? Or will we see these people again? I'm falling in with Geri's mood.

Geri. She's overtreating. I've never seen her bustle like this, cleaning wounds that will only have to be cleaned again, arranging and rearranging the blankets, cooing, touching, reassuring with promises that might never be kept. The victim, Connie, barely conscious, lies beneath the fussing perhaps far enough so that it makes no difference, but I think not. I whisper once or twice to Geri, think helplessly about holding her back, about taking her into my arms as she would like to do to Connie, but I'm frozen into inaction. Such a move would be intrusive. She might resist me, might even fight.

"Geri—"

"Wait a minute—can't you see I'm busy here?"

"Geri, stop, please stop a minute—"

"Let me do this—you don't understand!"

"No, I don't understand, and that's the point."

How changed she is before me! The balanced, tolerant woman with whom I work easily and well is suddenly someone else and I'm paralyzed into inaction, unable even to think of a way to act. Is this what happens to the wives of these men, that their passivity is amazement and confusion? Behold, the sharer of secrets, the quiet, modest neighbor, the respectful son. the helpful, laughing brother. Can he undergo, for no reason, or no easy reason, this awful change? We are all familiar with this terror, so familiar that it's child's play: the wolf man at full moon, Dracula at sundown; Grimm's tales are haunted with relatives, mothers, and stepmothers who, when the word is uttered, the thought invoked, turn capes inside out in the black wind and fly to evil over all the hedges of normal law. They know no relationship, these people; nothing holds them.

Always we are told and tell each other that each of us has weaknesses, prejudices for or against. It's in the first lecture in training and a perennial coffee-room staple. He goes limp and panicky when faced with an injured child; she loses her professional calm when drunks are involved. Head injuries frighten you, chest injuries frighten me. But Geri— As we start to the hospital, she continues, vitals over and over again, sponging and fussing and murmuring and patting. Two I.V. lines where one would have done, almost in tears and yet not done with hating.

There are too many people in the coffee room. Claude, who had driven; some nurses, resting. Geri sits pale and tight-lipped in the corner; I am dizzy with tension. We are waiting for splints and equipment while the woman is X-rayed.

"He seemed upset at what he had done—the man," Claude says.

"I wonder how many times he's been *upset*," she answers bitterly.

I say, "I wonder about the first time—the first slap, trying it out, watching to see if she would take it."

Geri looks at me. "You're blaming *her*, aren't you—making it *her* fault, doing what they all do!"

"No, Geri, I'm not. I'm saying it's a relationship, that somehow he knows she'll take it and so he's free to do it."

"She loves him! Can't you see that!"

"And love forgives it all? Why do I see a moment when he's not quite out of control for her to say: I'm sorry, but I can't afford you. My heart will mend, my teeth won't. Good-bye."

"It doesn't happen that way—"

Claude has been looking at Geri and me, back and forth like the spectator in a tennis game, wondering, no doubt, if he should say something.

Geri has given away more than she wishes. The nurses are nervously shifting their positions, wondering if they should go or stay. The small room, furnished with hospital castoffs, is suddenly much too small. Claude murmurs something about checking on the equipment and leaves. The nurses finish their coffee break and leave also. "I'm sorry, Geri," I say.

She looks at me in simple wonder. "When am I through with it—when is it over? I put it away six years ago, came halfway across the country to get away from everyone I knew and all the associations I had, and here it is again."

"You weren't Connie—you couldn't have been, passively letting it all happen."

"Single women are supposed to have cats," Geri says slowly. "I don't. Do you know why? Because they catch little animals, squirrels and birds, and they make the little animals part of a game—the cat will only hurt them if they move, so their survival depends on their being perfectly still while all their instincts are keyed toward escape. The cat tries to make them move, but they won't. They won't until the tension between discipline and instinct becomes so great that anything is better than the tension. The little animal makes the break and the cat pounces and wins the game. It was Brian's game—something going wrong at work, someone he didn't like, bad service in a restaurant, an unsuccessful time in bed, and the tension would begin to wind and wind. Complete stillness, docility, passivity for days. Dinner to the minute, perfectly served, clothes cleaned, shirts folded, house immaculate—then the slip, the end run, all hell breaking loose. We both broke loose and I guess my knowledge of my part in it all kept me from fighting back. Grace—"

"What, Geri?"

"Don't tell the squad."

"If you don't take care of any more beat-up ladies. Let us do it—assign us."

"O.K."

"Is there a place in Midlothian, a safe-house for her to stay in?"

"I've told the mental health people about her; it's all we can do."

We don't speak much, riding home. I'm thinking about the secrets of women, the weeping in back bedrooms, generation after generation, and the causes so few and unchanging that one century blends into another and only the artifacts are there to tell the difference between Moses' day and mine. Has nothing changed then? I remember what Violet's generation bore. Under the hand-pieced quilts with their lovely names, how many dead children lay? That at least has changed; why not the cruelty with it? I sigh. None of it has happened to me or mine. I look in from the outside, uncomprehending and appalled.

Geri is ashamed. When Claude pulls the ambulance in and closes the door, she comes to me again. "I'm sorry, Grace—I'm so sorry."

At least I can deal with her apology. "You should be. *I* never go overboard, *I* have no weaknesses, *I've* never walked face first into my own past like a plate-glass window."   .

"Well, yes—I guess everyone, one way or another—"

We smile and thank Claude and go home.

I know my weaknesses as wife and mother, but what are they here? Where is the day into which I will run and meet something suddenly beyond the physical problems of broken bones or blocked airways, a horror that's mine, not theirs? There has always been that fear, each night, each day, that this one, the one I am riding to, will be the one that's beyond me. That fear, as much as the satisfaction I have in the work, has driven me into the medical books I read and the classes I take. Now there is the added knowledge that among the wreckage of smashed autos, household battles, and saloon fights, ghosts are waiting for me—ghosts less friendly than my ghosts of the Camps. The stakes have been upped but I am still in the game. Why?

I stare, grainy-eyed, at Saul across the breakfast table. The run has taken most of the night. It's Friday and I have Shabbos to get ready for. I can see that he's displeased. He knows I had to make the run. He is telling himself that it's not my fault, that no one who rides to save lives and help the injured should be faulted for it, but he is angry nevertheless; angry at my exhaustion and my lined face, at the inconveniences past and still to come, at the knowledge that should the alarm go off this moment, I would be gone in seconds with the breakfast crumbs still on my face. He wants to shout, but about what, to rage, but at whom? People who might have been dead are living by our efforts. I am not slothful or careless or unloving. He is balked. My heart goes out to him. No vengeful enemy could have constructed so elegant and devilish a torment. No enemy could build his pain so thriftily on the love that has weathered so much. I think about Joshua again and sigh. I want to ask Saul to forgive me but there is nothing to forgive and all he would have then would be the extra burden, my love as well as his own.

So what's the difference between a sinful life and a good one if they both exact such penalties? The drunken woman's husband sits silently at the table wishing to rage, knowing he shouldn't. The rescuer's husband cannot rage and wishes he could. And now I, too, am angry. This work is good and valuable. Its demands in time are constant but not overwhelming. I've figured my share of runs to be 2.6 times a week, not including training times, and some of them are over in less than an hour. What if I had a full-time job—how much less would I be able to provide the kind of home life Saul wants? It's only tiredness. I get up and start the day. Saul goes to work.

When I saw him last, I invited Ben to the Sabbath dinner. Now I wish I hadn't. I'm liable to fall asleep in the middle of the evening, to be dull and sluggish through the day. I start the cleaning upstairs as usual. There is plenty of opportunity, as I clean the bathroom, to look in both mirrors. I am shocked at what I see. The graceful, well-made figure I used to have has been gone for years, but it's as though I had never seen until now what came in its place—thickenings, rolls of flesh, no worse than other middle-aged women, but there, and there to stay. No wonder my clothes fit so differently now—I have not been dressing a womanly figure but a matronly one. And the face—it's not yet heavily lined under the graying hair, but there are creases, and I see for the first time that I'm not ending something, I am beginning something—my old-lady face, the face I will have in twenty years.

I'm not ready for that, not yet. I don't want to settle back the way my mother did, to the bridge games and the fearfulness. But why not? Behind the door in a year or two or ten may be the slow onset of the creeping diseases of age.

I knew I was getting older; I'd been having so much fun I didn't stop to look, or looking had not seen. On my fortieth birthday, when most women spend the day weeping, I saw no reason not to be glad; I baked a cake. At forty-five, it was the same. Why am I caught now at forty-eight in the net of my own wrinkles? Why today? Because I'm tired and disgusted, because Saul is angry over another broken sleep, because Ben is coming tonight and will see—my God!

Once, when I was fairly new on the ambulance, we were called to transport an epilepsy patient. He had convulsed again in the ambulance without regaining consciousness after the first seizure. We were worried about Status Epilepticus. When the second seizure was over, he was shivering. I covered him with a blanket. Still unconscious and never having seen me, he took hold of my hand and kissed it, bringing it to his lips in a delicate, courtly, and swift gesture, absolutely sure. The same blush comes now, a terrible heat all over my face from the roots of my hair and downward to my neck. Then, I had looked around quickly hoping no one had seen. Why? Now, I know I'm alone and a sure knowledge comes that no one blushes so over a son.

So I start to cry because I am tired and sad and alone, and lost. I shouldn't be lost. I have fallen in lust—it can't be anything more. I am the one this time, unconsciously kissing the hand that unfolds the warm blanket over me. I am a loving wife to a good man; how can I be in love with someone the age of my daughter? It's ridiculous, a reflex, as the kiss was a reflex, an act done out of pure animal relief at being warm and safe at last.

I turn back to the mirror. My ghosts tell me to be joyful, and goddamn it, I will be if it kills me. I look again. Joyful will not mean dyeing my hair or wearing a corset or getting a face-lift or having my fat shaved away. It won't mean my stopping being a fool, it won't mean submission—not yet—to the fear of illness. I look closer. The skin of my neck is not yet crepy, but it certainly is no longer the smooth, taut skin it used to be. What amazes me is that all those changes could have happened some time ago and I have so counted on seeing in the mirror what I have always seen that I did not mark the changes as they came. My eyes are very clear, the whites white and without broken vessels. They are not beautiful and have never been counted among my "good points," but now I turn away smiling because they are not old woman's eyes. As I turn, the light catches something. I turn back again and, in spite of myself, I start to laugh. It's on my left eye, on the far side of the sclera, very small but there, the little thickening, like the clear little ropiness in an egg white: it's *arcus senilis*, the aging eye. It's supposed to begin at forty-five or so. I'm forty-eight. It's three years late, unless I have been missing it for three years. Why am I laughing instead of crying?

I'm laughing because it's a joke, and when I see Ben again I will know it. Desdemona fell in love with Othello because he told her war stories. Ben told us his war stories and he and I have lived others. I have seen him outlined in the red and white beacon lights of the ambulance with these aging eyes, when their pupils were widened with the drugs of combat.

And then how the world glows! The warrior knows it guiltily; the policeman, before he burns out with the paperwork and the law's delays, the wing-walker, the speed cyclist, the fire fighter, the stunt pilot, the football player, and the professional stand-up comic, know that in the afterglow of these chemicals of combat every color is seen in its truest tones, every sound is heard; we are alert and alive as when we were children and saw the newly made morning world for the first time.

It isn't love, it's glands and ambulance lights. That will be clear at my next sight of him. What if that seizure case knew he had kissed me? He would have gone red with embarrassment. These are not proper thoughts; get on with it. The house needs to be dusted upstairs and cleaned downstairs and time is passing.

By two, I'm around the track and coming toward the straightaway. Order is made in my wake; there are rewards for long apprenticeship, a sometimes marvelous competence. In the work, passion will be lost and unreason left behind with the rooms' disorder. I cannot think what these thoughts about Ben may be except unreason and exhaustion. I am tired, Saul is irritated. It's only that. There's baking to be done, the cleaning to finish, the table to set, a bath and clean clothes—the Sabbath peace to summon and if it won't come, at least to simulate.

By five, it's ready; by six, I am, still feeling out of focus and self-conscious, and here comes Ben, passing the front window, dressed too lightly as usual and walking with his head down and his hands in his pockets. I like looking at him objectively when he is unaware of being seen. Even with the beard, he looks younger than he is and not at all like what he has been, a jailbird, a bouncer in an underworld dive, a man driven and despairing. It's what amazes me most about young people. On the television documentaries the dope addicts, prostitutes, killers, and thieves we see are young and ordinary-looking, and we are mesmerized by that difference between form and substance. Deep in my wishes I want the face to tell. I want to know the difference between good and evil as an absolute; I am titillated by the sweetness of those faces and the wideness of those eyes—look, not a sign, not a hint.

Then I know all this is nothing but a way of trying to blemish Ben in my mind, to defeat my feelings about him by using his life against him. A good try, objectivity. I want to run to the door and swing it wide and throw my arms around him. What is it like to be kissed by a bearded man? A proper opening of the door; a proper greeting. He smiles. He is happy to see me. How can I stand there and not revel in that smile? It would mean blushing as I did in the ambulance, going hot in the face, that color telling him things he shouldn't know, and he would laugh or be embarrassed. *Arcus senilis* in the left eye. I love you all the same. "Good Shabbos," I say.

I am no longer dragging. I could serve a roast ox to one hundred harvest men. We talk for a while about the Sabbath. He is serious about wanting to learn its traditions. What is there to tell—some stories I grew up with, some laws, some customs. "That bread knife looks like a saw."

"It is. The old people don't cut the Sabbath bread at all—they break it, but that's awfully messy and destroys the loaf."

"Why don't you use a knife?"

"Knives are weapons; a saw is a tool. Somewhere in the Talmud it says that weapons are to be forbidden at the Sabbath table. We've always liked neat little differences in words. You could kill someone with a saw, I guess, but it is not classed as a weapon. The whole point really is to separate—no, to differentiate—the Sabbath from the week."

He waits a long time, looking at me. He is trying not only to think it out, but to feel it, to see into the reason. Then he nods. "Berne," he says.

"How so?"

"In Berne the days were all the same. I think I talked about it Thanksgiving night, how you have to depend on your own discipline, the small ceremonies you make for yourself to keep from dying."

". . . and when you are wealthy and free and happy, it's a way of relaxing, to stop being too busy and too rational."

"My parents never—never once—"

"It's hard to see such a need in a place that—that isn't Berne."

Saul and Riva are late. Not since childhood have I had such joy-guilt. I ask Ben about his childhood and his parents. His years are the years of Miriam and Joshua, and I begin to see a glimmer of the country into which they grew. It's a landscape I barely recognize, a place of upheavals and assassinations, of plots and seeming conspiracies. Ben was in grade school when John Kennedy was shot. His teacher had to explain to the class why there would be sadness during this ordinarily happy season. His chief memory of it was the interruption of his football game after school because the parents of the neighborhood wanted their children close and quiet beside them for a time. Looting and shooting on television—the cities at war, later in high school and college, an anger in his teachers as they counted the national shames: poverty, injustice, racism. "It was after the big explosions—the Berkeley thing seemed antique to us. We knew they were angry and that we should be angry, too, but, besides the war, we weren't sure about what." He looks around the quiet house. "C.A. and I were talking and he mentioned that his kids went to school with yours."

I smile. "My daughter's name is Miriam. My son is Joshua. I suppose we're strange in that you won't see pictures of them anywhere. When they were small, I used to think it was silly to put out pictures when the living person was right there. Later, the kids said they didn't want any. Now that they're grown and gone, it's all I can do to keep from making idealized fantasies of the time they were here."

"My mother has me on the coffee table with my sister and brother."

"Bar Mitzvah pictures?"

"His is. Mine is a high school graduation picture."

"No beard?"

"No."

"What do you look like there?"

"A wimp. My mother says it's sensitive. Actually, it's a good picture of a scared, confused jerk, which is what I was at the time. They say the body never lies. Mine didn't, damn it."

Voices are at the door. I curse them inwardly and myself for wishing they hadn't come just now or all night. How does Ben see his mother and father and brother? Did he have a happy childhood there in New Canaan, Connecticut? What was it like in those new, new houses in that old town? He seems to have missed my neat side step. I didn't want to talk about Miriam and Joshua—to open closer pains just yet, and maybe never. But he has talked to C.A. They talked about me. I go to the door smiling.

Once again, it's a happy evening. Riva laughs often and Saul relaxes. I warm with love for all of them. It is the Sabbath peace—the peace the rabbis and sages wanted for their bruised people. Riva has forgotten the special songs, the z'mirot, and Saul and I never knew them, but there is still the essence of what they hungered after: good talk and joking and laughter. If Ben asks her enough times, I think Riva will search back and remember one or two and then we will sing. If he is with us a little longer, we will be able to forgive ourselves and each other for having lost the other children, for having given one another such grand promises and such great pain.

Saul and I clear the table and put away the perishables, leaving Ben and Riva in the living room. When we come back, we see that something has happened. Riva is flushed and on the verge of tears. "Look," she says, "look."

He has brought her a little cassette tape. I take it. Stories of Sholem Aleichem. "Where did you get this?" He is flustered now, because of the fuss—he truly didn't want it.

"As a school, we get lots of instructional aids catalogues and one is a literary series on cassettes. I just happened to spot this one."

"What a wonderful idea!" Riva cries. "Tapes for people who don't see to read so well!"

Saul and I catch eyes. All the times we tried, all the tactful trips to the library, the suggestions, the indirection, all resulting in defensiveness and anger. "You can't cure my problems!" she had cried to me bitterly. We smile, and I see Ben catch the look. Where did he get the charm for all this, the secret, quiet giving of gifts?

The joy of him sings in my blood. *Z'mirot*, Sabbath songs. This is an infidelity I have never imagined. My word is pictured so tritely—a man and a woman, undressing. It's afternoon. Into the little tray where the husband keeps his keys and change at night, the stranger's pockets are emptied. Out of habit she lies on the left side of the bed. The man lies where the husband should lie. The thought disgusts me. But now I know better. I have been half-unfaithful all evening, with all the pleasure we had. I wished Saul away, wished him and Riva gone so that I might be alone with Ben in this very house. All evening long I have wanted Ben's hands touching me, his warmth near me, his smile giving me gifts, all in a small secret space, dark until the lights grew and burst behind my eyes.

11

We don't see each other for five days. I measure out the time missing him, but not tormented. The time will swing him in his arc back again, a morning run, an ambulance cleanup. My duplicity is careful. I waited nine months for each child and twenty years for a son and a daughter. That patience, once a virtue I scraped out of necessity, is a real virtue at last. I yearn like any girl of nineteen, but I can wait.

Geri calls Tuesday night. There has been a run while I was shopping at Pinecrest. It was right after the rain started; an auto crash, three victims. The ambulance is a mess. "I'll be at work tomorrow but Rita is free and Ellie says she can get away after two in the afternoon. If you see any of the firemen down there, the vehicle can use a polishing, too." I smile. Geri seems to have made an interesting peace with her feelings about equality of the sexes. We are equal when it suits us to be. It's a truth not lost on either of us, so we are laughing when we hang up.

I can now call Ben legitimately, but I am suddenly struck shy. It's a bad idea anyway; calling him for favors is too wife-motherly, not clever. For years, my happiness in Gilboa was that I didn't have to be careful with anyone but Riva, not clever at all. Now, duplicity and cleverness will follow me all the days of my life. I have lost another kind of innocence.

Rita and Ellie and I clean up the inside of the ambulance. We laugh and talk and reminisce. Rita talks about one of the lawyers she works for. It is gossip, but funny and not hurtful. Ellie, who is a cook at the elementary school and has troubles at home, tells stories about food and the kids. The firehouse door is open but it's too cold to pull the rig outside.

We are just deciding whether we will wash the ambulance when Ben comes by. He has two of the boys from the school with him, kids of about thirteen or fourteen. He greets us first, a thing I know he wouldn't ordinarily do, and it makes me smile. He is suddenly half a parent himself and for the sake of the children is sacrificing his own comfortable reserve. He introduces the boys, who simply stand there. I see almost a parent's pain in his eyes. We wait for long moments, none of us knowing what more to do. Finally I say, "You're just in time. We've got one dirty ambulance and three tired women."

Ben looks relieved. "What do you say, guys; let's help. We're not due back at school for another hour or so."

"You can call from the dispatch room," I say, "and tell them where you are." He wants the boys to agree but they don't. They stand blankly, prisoners of a situation they have not foreseen and over which they have no control. They are terrified. I have begun to curse myself for having taken their basic normality for granted—that any boy of fourteen would want to work in a firehouse.

They had been standing at the door. Ben shepherds them inside. "They need us, guys, let's help them out." Silence. He will have to do it all. I come to him with three sponges and three rags and put them on the fender of the truck near where they are standing. Rita and Ellie have begun at the front of the ambulance. I hear snatches of their companionable talk. Ben and I start at the back.

"Should I fix the bucket for them?"

"No," he says, "they need to come some of the way by themselves."

The sun goes lower while we work, drawing off the east-facing buildings and leaving them to cold shadow. Rita turns on the lights and closes the great doors. "No use heating up the whole outside," she says.

As though at a code word, the boys move. "Where do—" "What should—" Ben doesn't show his surprise. "Grace, where's that other bucket?"

"Under the sink, over there. Make it easy on yourselves, fellas, fill it half full of hot water." They turn and go to the sink. "What was it?" I whisper.

"Too vulnerable on that open side, I guess."

We are soon working hard. With the door closed, the fire-house heats up quickly. The men have the thermostat set high, a great comfort to come in to after a run in the cold weather, but too hot for now. We take our jackets and coats off and apply ourselves. The boys don't talk much, but it's obvious they are enjoying us and the work. They are properly serious about the job they are doing. When one of them knocks over the bucket, there is a flash of fear and shame and a defensive anger. I have to tell him twice that water belongs on a firehouse floor before he will fill his bucket again. "It needed changing anyway," I say. "It was dirty." The boy looks at me to see if I am lying, but I am working again so he fills his bucket and starts in.

When the ambulance is soaped over, Rita goes for the hose. There is an ordinary faucet outlet on the wall as well as the two inch-and-a-half outlets from which we fill the trucks. When she turns on the faucet, we wait for water but nothing happens. "Follow your line out," Ellie says. "There's a kink in it." The kink is almost at the end and when Rita gets it, water sprays out all over Ellie. Ellie, soaking wet, narrows her eyes and then dashes for the old tanker. The new ones are made with pumps that won't work unless the motor is on. The old one has an independent pump and it is soon grinding away. The racket is terrible. Ellie has pulled ten feet of light reel-hose and stands holding it, her hand on the machine-gunlike trigger. "Git back, you scum!" she cries. "I'm takin' over this ship!" The boys, white-faced, disappear behind the side of the ambulance.

"Our people must arise against all persecutors," I say to Ben.

"Our people are always fighting with one another," he smiles, and overturns the bucket on my boot. The boys have come around the back side of the ambulance. I see that their sponges are sopping with the water from the floor.

"You're covered!" I cry at Ben.

"Old trick," he says. A sponge, perfectly pointed, hits him in the head. Then another. Ben returns one, I the other. I turn on Ben with my sponge, but he has gone after Ellie. It's a water fight at its most anarchic. The floor hose and reel-hose are at war with one another, spraying anyone in between. There are plenty of hiding places among the trucks, but the people at the hoses are soon moving among them, searching out victims. I am ambushed, caught in cross fire, but I get control of the hose and go after Rita. Russel, one of the boys, tries to get my hose by holding a bucket in front of him, but he is broadsided by his friend. Together they take the hose from me, but then Russel turns the hose on the other boy. Ben has the reel-hose. I creep up behind him and kink it. When he turns it up to look at the nozzle, I release the kink. To hell with love and loyalty, honor, constancy, kindness, and trust! Everyone is an island surrounded by water. We don't stop until we are drenched and worn out. We have all had time at the hoses, Russel has discovered "tactics" and is delighted, and more than once in the long melee the ambulance has been entirely rinsed off. When it's over, we stand shaking with exhaustion, steaming under the lights. My glasses are so fogged over that I am stone blind. There's no fight left in any of us. Rita sits down on the back running-board of the pumper. There is room for six or seven and we all sit there and let the heater, directly over us, blow warm air on us. I could swear there is a rainbow near the high ceiling. We steam in companionable silence. "Anyone know what time it is?" someone says after a while.

"There's a digital clock in the radio room."

"Anyone want to go in there and read it?"

"I will."

"When?"

"Later."

Silence. "Well," someone says, "the ambulance is clean."

"Yes, a most successful afternoon."

"Why are we all waiting here?"

"Do you know what's out there?"

"What?"

"A chilly evening."

"Good God! Why wasn't I told?"

I sit next to Ben and the boys. Once or twice during the combat, I have come in close and smelled the male smell of him, body and breath; the soap he used this morning and the sweat he is sweating now, and the under-smell that is an essence of him, like a pheromone. I am drawn, another of his species, to him, but in an embarrassment no gypsy moth ever felt. Surreptitiously, I breathe it in as we sit. It makes me long for him; it makes pictures in my mind. Do moths get such pictures? Do they see other moths naked and ready miles away under the moon? What pictures must those be to make them fly through tempests to such signals! Like mine! Like mine! Unlike the wind-ragged moth, I am forced to repudiate the sense that makes such longing. "Good God, man, you smell like a wet dog!" I say to him, smiling. He stares at me.

"Are you sure it is me—I?"

"No, it's all three of you."

He turns to the boys. "Gentlemen, we have been insulted. What does a gentleman do when he has been insulted?"

"Insults the woman back?"

"Wrong. He rises with dignity and splits. Madam," and he turns such a warm and loving pair of eyes on me that I am afraid I will go red, "we take umbrage at your remark—yes, umbrage. My companions and I are splitting." They get their jackets from the truck. "This all goes better," he tells them, "if your shoes don't squish when you walk." They tell us good night and leave.

A sadness comes over me. "Let's fill the truck; I've got to get home and get Saul's dinner." We work quietly, then say good night even more quietly, and venture out into a night that seems much colder than it really is. Only Rita will not have to tell anyone what happened—why she is wet through. Only she will not have to try to re-create the fun, to explain a ceiling rainbow to someone's patient condescension.

On the way home, I raise my ghosts. They have told me to rejoice, to take delight, and I do the best I can, but the means to do it are denied to me. I am wonderfully tired now but tomorrow I won't be able to re-create the feeling. If I taste a taste again or smell a smell, I will be able to identify it, but I won't be able to re-create it for myself at will. I want to hold more than the memory of this night; I want to feel the senses' joy of it again, the smells and touches, the abandon. Because there are many times of drought—seasons of despair. If I work at memory I can remember Saul standing beside me in the pouring rain by his car that had broken down saying, "Grace, I love you, wet as much as dry." I can remember the words but I can't re-create the rain or the rush of joy I had then or the sight of his face. This is a night I want to save, feelings, senses, all of it. When I see it again in my mind it will be like seeing a movie, third-person; *she* instead of *me* and no touch or smell or steaming clothes—the picture only. What a loss!

The four of them are standing by the bare lilac bush when I leave the car. Try as I will, I cannot evoke its summer leaves or springtime flowers, any of the twenty years of them. The night is cold and there's a mean little wind that cuts the face and whips the thin withes of the bush against the house. The ghosts are impaled by the branches and this time their clothes do move with the wind and they huddle to one another. "Oh, God, I'm sorry—I take back my complaint! Go away; I shouldn't have summoned you. I can't bear to see you cold—"

The older man speaks; his voice has shivering in it. "Would you really wish to be hung in the past? With your hoarded delight would come agonies better forgotten. Do you wish on yourself physical recall of all the falls and illnesses of your childhood? Would you have the courage to live one day more?" And too cold, they shred away quickly, blowing their fingers with a wreathing breath until they are wind itself.

I don't see Ben again until ambulance meeting a week later. Suddenly there are embarrassing problems. Should I change my seat and sit next to him? If I do, will it be noticed? I am usually early and he is usually late. I want to be free of these adolescent logistics, but need has made me fourteen again, watching the hall for Mark Boudeneau or Paul Janov. Will I pass him or stop? Will I look at him or turn away and pretend to be talking to my friends? Will I smile or not smile? Ridiculous. I sit down in my old place and curse the fever. Hamlet to Queen: "At your age the hey-day in the blood is tame, it's humble and waits upon the judgment." Hamlet's age is supposed to be upwards of thirty. The kid who delivered himself of that tidbit of wisdom wasn't a day over sixteen. Ben comes in. He looks smaller than he looms in my mind, which he fills like a hand held before the sun. Luckily, Rita and Ellie talk to him first, saving me the need.

"Did you have any trouble at the school, bringing the kids home wet like that?"

"Less than I thought from the administration, more from the

other kids. We have to deal with a lot of jealousy. Unfortunately, Russel and Clay didn't do anything to play down their parts in things." He smiles. "On points, though, I thought it was a big success—the other kids want to come down and see the firehouse."

"We can't always guarantee a water fight," I say.

He smiles. "I want the kids to learn that—that there are special days, but no special treatment. The experience taught me a lot, too. I had a fantasy of bringing some of the older ones in for a trip through the firehouse; that we would give them rides on the trucks and take them through the sheriff's office where the calls come. Since that afternoon, I'm not sure. I want them to see things and go places, but as ordinary kids, not special cases for whom people put themselves out in a special way."

"I agree. How can we help you?"

He's going to answer but Geri pounds the table and the meeting starts.

We have two extraordinary runs to discuss but aside from that the meeting is fairly routine. Rita, in an attempt to bring "order" to our meetings, has been demanding parliamentary procedure and for the past few months we have been drowning in a sea of details and rules. So I disappear. Hand in hand I run with Ben into the hills back of town, to the green glades that were Violet's favorite and where I have seen the sun-and-leaf pattern on her wrinkled face. Wood nymphs do age. They become as lined and brittle as old leaves, as transparent as the vein pattern left after the body of the leaf has been blown to powder by the autumn winds. In the springtime when the earth yearns, when the rain falls green and the fields move with bees—I am brought back too quickly. Ben is speaking, I'm not sure about what. I am struck again with the sadness that has been following me all day. When I first walked in that glade with Violet and thought that thought, Ben Sloan in New Canaan, Connecticut, was hanging dizzily to the edge of a coffee table, wondering if he might set himself free in the vast spaces of his parents' living room, actually to walk. I look at him. I am warming myself at a phantom fire. He's young and full of the joyousness of someone who has just found out he can have part of the world on his own terms. My pining is useless and ludicrous. If he knew of it, he would guffaw. I love Saul still and always have and will forever. This new passion is foolish, not a growing, a growth. The meeting moves to a discussion of the runs. I become interested in the talk.

Thanks to Rita, it's late when I get home. Saul has left the light on for me but a subtle flavor of his displeasure hangs in the air. No obvious clues, but I know. It should be a special glory to read so subtly marked a terrain. He likes me to go to bed when he does. If I'm not on a run, he likes that last word of the day with me. He knows I can't help it if the meetings run late. He thinks I stay even later, talking, rehashing runs. He had a last cup of coffee while he was waiting; look at the aggressive punctiliousness of that cup and plate in the sink. Perhaps he is so annoyed he can't sleep. I go up quickly. He has left the hall light on for me in his usual considerate way, but the dust motes that are falling through the light are heavy with injured feeling. I swear there is an odor, a subtle, acrid tang, of discontent.

But however injured he is, it is not so deep or so painful as to keep him awake. When I slide in beside him he only stirs for a moment and sinks again away. Instead of picking a fight with his sleeping spirit, I, too, sink away. In the knife-edged cold of this winter night, I am able to summon Violet's summer glade, the green gloom under the great trees, the soft mosses bearing infinitely tiny flowers. A Sunday afternoon that lasts all summer. Ben and I are reading, dreaming, making love, and the whole thing is catered.

Joshua calls from Illinois. His vow of poverty exalts him but the collect phone calls make Saul angry. It is all Sanjit-communication, impersonal and replete with special mystical language, the jargon of his new life. He is well, thanks to the Love of Krishna. Under the guidance of the Sunnyasi, whose perfect devotion is exemplary, he is calling to invite us to a feast, the unveiling and enthroning of new deities, an occasion of special devotion. Seen deities—a Jew's nightmare. "Jo—excuse me, Sanjit, I have something very personal to ask you. If it's *you* wanting *us* to come to see you, we will. If it means that before, or after, the ceremony, you'll stay with us, walk or sit and have general conversation, we'll come, but the last time I came, I got a pitch. There was nothing from you but mystical theology, a not-so-subtle way of keeping us at a distance, and from your friends, a not-so-subtle appeal for money. It's not a long trip, but it's a difficult trip for us psychologically, and if our reward at the end is not you, but a look at a devotee only, I'm afraid the thing is more of a pain than a pleasure."

He is silent, then he says, "But when you see how joyful it is to serve Krishna, how rapturous—"

"Not unless I get some of *you*, some private time with you in person—"

"But this loving servant is what I am."

"I know, and we thank you for wanting to include us in anything that's important to you, but it just hurts too much; can you understand that?" I get a sudden inspiration. "Sanjit, try to listen to this story: you meet a girl there, a devotee. After seeing her for a year, the authority approves of your marriage. In due time you have a child whom you raise with every kind of love you have. You think that your devotion to Krishna shines out to this child in everything you do. The child grows and you send him to the special school and then when he is raised he comes back to the temple. You want a relationship with this child, a new relationship now that he is growing up; you want him to be more like a friend and less like a dependent, yet because of the lifetime of love you have given him, you feel something very special for him, a special joy in seeing him. He tells you then that you have given nothing of value to him and that he wishes to remember nothing of you or the life you have forced him into, that he wants to go into the world and never hear the name of Krishna or think about the devotees and will obliterate from his behavior any hint of them. How would you feel, Sanjit?"

"That could never happen," he says simply.

"Why not?"

"Among other reasons, because a child raised in a Krishna-conscious way would be more advanced than that."

"Wonderful," I say. I can say no more. I tell him to think about what I have requested of him and let me know. Then I hang up and cry. Not in sorrow, or not only. I am angry as hell. What is it that has made him so smug? Autism of the imagination? Atrophy of the empathy? Somehow I still believe we get what we deserve—lives, governments, children. I have raised a hybrid—half angel, half idiot. And just my luck: The part that faces Illinois is the angel.

In the night as we slept, the Lord changed His mind and took away the world. When we wake up there is a whiteout. He has left the tree in front of our window, bare and rimed-white, but nothing else. Of the other houses on Bullwinkle Boulevard, nothing. Of the field behind us, nothing. It's more than a fog, less than a snow, and it seems total. No wind. It's ten degrees out. What the sages forgot to mention in Genesis I was the cold. "I don't know why I should open up today," Saul says. "In weather like this, who'll come?"

"Why not stay home then? If the day changes, you can always go in later. You haven't played hookey for a long time."

"Well, I have some inventory to do and there's always a little straightening—"

"If you stay home, I'll make waffles—"

I remember then that I'm supposed to take Riva into town

and after that to go to Tarrant to sign up for a course at the college there, but something nudges my elbow, a grandmother-spirit, wiser than I. Saul wants me to stay—to be wifely and close today. It's little enough to ask and he hasn't asked it. And he shouldn't need to. I am in need as well as he. "Here is a day—a free gift—how do you want to spend it—in healthful and creative work, i.e., cleaning out the attic, or would you just like to hang around?"

"A couple of hours of each and we could tell which we are doing because we could make love in the middle and anything before would be cleaning up and anything after would be hanging around."

We haven't made love in the daytime for years—not since the kids were small. It makes me feel daring and reckless. "Good thought," I say.

It's dark up in the attic and it would have been a little sad among the outgrown lives of the family, but for Saul's presence there. As we work, I tell him about Joshua's call. I don't mention the comparison I made or Joshua's answer about his nonexistent Krishna-conscious child, just the facts—they seem gentler that way, less maddening when I don't quote. "Would you like to go to see him again—would you like us both to go?"

"How do you feel?"

"I feel like an overweight, overage, overmatched fighter," he says. He is holding a pair of skates that could be the ones we got Miriam when she was nine or Josh when he was nine or could even have been Saul's own. "I get angry when I get hit, and I get sad when I get thrown down, but mostly I feel a kind of—amazement at it all. Punches come from out of nowhere. If I hit out I hit nothing and then a blow comes from some unexpected, uncovered side and I get knocked off my feet. Mirele going—"

He has called her by the old love name he used to use when she was a tiny, elfin girl, when she would come down to the store and try on the hats, eventually wearing one I swore he got for her and kept for whenever she came. "My hat, please." Rose-buds and lace over the braids and then the pony-tail, "my sha-poe," in a high, clear, imperious voice, her magical laughter hiding in the aftertones. Saul sighs. "I say to myself—she had to go. I didn't really expect her to stay in Gilboa—there's nothing here for her. But oh, God, the way she went, the distance and then that curt call, 'I'm getting married,' and you begging her to let us make the wedding. Dad dying, Ma closing up on life—Josh. And I say to myself, 'Josh had to make his choice. He lived here for all those years and the world had him for one year and this is what he chose. He was free to choose and this is his choice.' And you."

"Me?"

"The icier the day, the foggier the night, the more danger-ous the hillside—you can't see three feet ahead of you? That's when the call comes. No one is sure where the car went over? Search the dangerous hill, the rocks, in the dark. And I say to myself, 'How can you fault her?' Mrs. Tyndall still comes in and shows me how you saved her arm. Macy Ups never sees me without comparing you favorably to Florence Nightingale, and Doris Mercer tells me how hard you worked to save her little boy. You think I don't see bored wives in this town, angry at their husbands, driving everyone crazy with their frustrations? Shouldn't I be grateful for what you are, what you've done?"

"But—"

"—but the danger, the awful danger—and then on top of it, Riva." He tells me she has been coming down to the store every day, which I didn't know. Unable to read, restless and bored, she has been wandering in to see him, able to do little but find fault and get in everyone's way.

"I suppose I should go over there more often—"

"You like that work you do, your freedom—I wouldn't want you to change things to nursemaid my mother, who isn't sick but only bored and miserable. You'd be crazy in two weeks."

"Saul, why not hire some young people to read to Riva?"

"—not a high school kid, like our last assistant. She'd bean him."

"No, younger ones, pre-adolescent, and more than one."

"Kids?"

"Good kids. Let me go up to the grade school and try. If it doesn't work, I'll go to the junior high. Then I'll advertise in the library."

"Will she allow it—she's so defensive?"

"That will be your part. Put your foot down."

"You know, Grace, I think Ben could get her to do it."

Ben. I had worked myself free of him, hair, mouth, eyes, all morning, and now he is here again. When we get ready to go downstairs and make love, I may commit adultery because I will be thinking about Ben and not Saul, a thing I have been carefully avoiding for weeks—not because the thought is father to the act, but because the thought is child of the life. My life is decent and respectable, or was until recently; my thoughts were part of that life, cohered with it, belonged to it. I want to love Saul—I do love him. I want—

The crude sound is muffled up here, but it sounds all the same. The alarm. Saul looks at me and shrugs. What can he do? What can I do?

"The squad is running short this week—"

"I know," he says, "I know. It's icy as hell out there. Please—"

"I will—" but I am barely listening. I am halfway down the stairs.

Glare ice. Cracks in the pavement yawn and grin with it. Wires sing in the cold: "You have no control; is your luck that good?" The car gags with cold. Its fittings groan and screech. The wheels spin. They say: "You have no control. You have only luck. Is your luck that good?" I rock the car a little, gently.

The wheels take. I go. My heart is pounding. The accident is off Exit 18 on the way to Russian Grove. I call in and hear no other voices. Riding through town I lean on the horn in fear. Everyone is afraid to move to the side for fear of getting stuck. I can barely see ten feet into the icy fog, but then I hear the siren and a voice on the radio: Larry Ochsner, I think, wreathed in static. They are ahead of me in the crowded nothingness. A way opens to my horn. I go. I can barely read the road. Is this crossing Tulip or Marshaltown? No—there's Tulip; then I must be coming to Marshaltown. I almost lose the road twice looking for the small service exit under the ramp. This is madness; why am I doing it? I should be home and safe, not sticking my finger in fortune's eye! There are tiny waves of nausea beginning in my chest. I hear a few blurts of static, undecipherable. I radio in and give my location. I am unanswered. Who is there? Where am I now? Two minutes without vision and hearing and I have lost it all—time, place, direction. I am helpless and frightened. I nearly collide with the ambulance, lights and all. I have drifted far over on the shoulder; two feet farther and I would have been over, down the gully. We have arrived.

She has been thrown out of the car and is lying near the side of the road. I go to the cop—it's Bischoff. "Close this road or post someone—it's hell out here."

"We have Fire coming," he says, "I just toned it off." I go to the victim. She is lying in a fairly natural position. Larry and Ben are there. "You've got to move her fast," Bischoff says, "she's too far out in the road."

Something warns me—a look, a feeling. "How are you doing?" I ask her.

"Where's Lisa?"

"There's a kid," Larry says, "in the car. Looks O.K. I'll stay with her."

I tell the woman—her name is Barbara—that Lisa is being taken care of. I do a blood pressure and pulse while Ben gets a board and sandbags. I can't tell why, other than the force of the fall, but I feel funny about this one. The lady has been badly hurt but doesn't know it yet. "Where's Lisa?" I tell her again. The blood pressure is 140/86, the pulse is 90. The secondary check shows no reason for my anxiety. Bischoff is getting nervous.

"Why don't you move her?" I don't know why. I only feel.

"Where's Lisa?" Barbara asks again. I tell her. Then I answer Bischoff.

"I want immobilization. Help us roll her evenly." We use the board.

"Where's Lisa?" Barbara asks. That does it. She has asked the question once too often. Ben picks it up. We catch eyes. He knows.

"I'm going to call this in," he says. "I'll bring you what they say and the portable oxygen." The fire department has come; the road is closed. Bischoff helps but he's angry about the road closing. I call for more blankets and then we move her into the ambulance for the warmth. When we still don't go, Bischoff complains. The five minutes we have taken seem like five hours in this fog. "They want a second blood pressure," Ben says. I have already gotten it. It is holding, but her respirations have gone from twenty to thirty and her pulse is 104. I do a more careful abdominal exam. It is here.

"Right upper quadrant, and look—" The child has been brought in but Barbara doesn't seem to see or hear her. I start the oxygen and get out the I.V. equipment. Larry is being beautiful with the child. He tells her what is happening and why and that we will all ride in together. He straps her into the passenger seat and goes to get ready to pull out.

Ben comes back. "They want Ringer's." We start it. He does another blood pressure and there it is. Shock. The heart is beating 120 times a minute, the blood pressure is 90/80. We go.

Ben speaks continually, trying to enlist her help. I quicken the I.V. to replace the fluid that is draining away through some ruptured organ. We raise the bottom of the board and will her to hold, and we strap her in even more securely. A blood pressure every five minutes. A pulse. Ben does them quickly while I count respirations. It's working. She gains two points, four. Still low, but the heart is slowing a little. A heart pumping too fast can go into spasm, fibrillation, and at such a speed is pumping inefficiently when she most needs efficiency. The very mechanisms the body uses to combat early shock are destructive to it in deep shock. But Barbara is holding.

"They've moved the hospital again," Ben says. Then he remembers the child and tells her it's a kind of joke, that he really meant only that it seemed a long time.

"Is mommy dead?" the child asks. We tell her no. "Will she die?" Not so easy. I see Ben getting ready to say no, of course not, and I say, "We're working hard, hard to help her stay alive, and at the hospital they have even more things to help her." The child is silent for a moment or two, and then says in the same high, dry, level voice, "If mommy dies, can I stay with Aunt Kay and Uncle Henry?"

Ben is shocked. I am pleased. I am looking into the clear eyes of a survivor. Grief will come when it comes; life comes first. "I don't know," I say, "but maybe you can call your aunt and uncle when we get to the hospital. Where do they live?"

"In Russian Grove. It was where we were going when we got in the accident."

I tell her they will certainly be called. She sits back, almost pleased. Part of life is still possible.

Barbara gains and loses as the mechanisms of her body fight for control. The blood chemistry compensates and then decompensates. We are running the I.V. full open and I put in another line although the peripheral circulation is almost completely shut down and I have trouble getting a vein. All I know. All I can do. We talk about MAST pants but it would mean untying her and too much motion in the swaying of the ambulance. It is a decision that should have been made earlier, but I didn't know then, I only felt and there was no sign. She will not be roused now, although we talk to her often. Hearing is the last part of consciousness to go, and Ben wants her to throw her will into the unequal war. The hospital. It has been forever.

Thank God for radios. Everyone knows what we have. They help get Barbara in and begin to undress her. The nurses put in a tracheal tube and bring in the portable X-ray. Dr. Garson comes. I'm glad. Garson likes us and while he examines, he teaches. "Did you check pupils?"

"Yes, at first."

"Did you again?"

"No—"

"Well, look at 'em now. See—slight dilation, sluggishness. Look at this, here and here. She's had head trauma, too. You were wise to immobilize. I think we've got a c-spine. See the position she has her arms in. Look at this abdomen. I've got an operating room ready, but I want to put a tube in and see what's in the abdominal fluid."

It's all obvious now—the distension that wasn't there before, the change in the pupils that is a late sign—too late to have done me any good. I shiver.

Larry goes to be with the child. We look at the X-rays. "Aha," Garson says, "two cervical fractures. See—here and here, but I don't think the cord is involved. If you hadn't done what you did she might have bought it right then. Help us with the abdominal puncture. You'll have to hold her. It's going to hurt and we need to keep that neck exactly the way it is." Barbara moans and tries to fight us but she is too weak and disoriented. When the tube is pushed in, fresh blood shoots up into it. "That's all I wanted to know."

He turns for the head nurse. "Let's go," he says, then he turns to us. "I think this one's a clean save," he says. "If you hadn't immobilized and gotten lines in and oxygen on her when you did, she would have died on the way in. I think she'll make it now." The operating room people have come for her.

Ben and I go to the nurses' coffee room and suddenly I am almost too tired to stand. All the guessing and trying to read beneath flesh and past walls and lattices of bone have exhausted me. Ben is looking at me half-smiling. Then he smiles full, grins, laughs aloud. He can no longer contain the joy. He takes me in his arms—we take each other, hugging close, rocking back and forth. We are crooning to one another, laugh-crying, sing-moaning, humming something better to me than music. I smell Barbara's shocky-sweat on his coat or my own, our wet hair, and under it the sharp rousing smell of Ben's own body, sweat and maleness, his pheromone that has been calling me away from where I should be, to what I do not know. Then he kisses me gently, but fully, on the mouth.

Lights go off behind my eyes, as much warning as passion, and a knowledge wry and clear as any I have ever had. When he lets me go—when we each let go—he is brick red and I am no less deeply in love than I have ever been. "You look like a carbon monoxide victim," I say, and smile into his face, "and there's no need." Larry comes in, and before he can sit down, I have kissed him too, and Ben pounds him on the back.

"They think we might really have done it!" he cries. "Saved someone, actually saved someone! I wonder how long she'll be in the O.R. I mean, I wonder when we'll know for sure. Maybe we can come back and see her. There's no rule against that, is there?"

I laugh. "You love having done this, don't you? And you will want to tell her later, in as nice a way as possible, how glad you are—"

"Well—"

"I've had it happen a couple of times before, a big, dramatic save. We call them up later or go to the hospital for a visit and, of course, they don't remember—not a thing."

"But she was conscious when we first got there, answering questions, and later once or twice in the ambulance—"

"You can try if you like, but I don't think it'll work. You're not real to her—the whole thing is a blur—the fear of the fog, the sudden horror of the accident, pain perhaps, and terror. And of us, all the terrific immobilization we did, what we said or didn't say, nothing. It's a secret, this thing, that only the three of us know, and that Bischoff will know because we'll tell him. I've told victims who became frightened by my telling—they thought I wanted something from them. They didn't suspect for one minute what was behind my call or my visit. They resented the intrusion into their privacy; all those details I knew about their bodies and their accident, their time unguarded. No wonder they got defensive and suspected me of God knows what."

"How sad a commentary on the human condition," Ben says. He is smiling broadly.

"Our guilty secret," Larry says. He, too, is smiling.

"Our secret." I lift my Styrofoam cup. "To our very good health. To you, your magnificences, to me, my magnificence, to a clean save!"

And then we go home, Larry to school, Ben to his disturbed boys, and I to an irritated man, an unmessed bed, and a half-cleaned attic.

12

When I'm home, I watch the daytime talk shows. I've done it for years. When I was a young mother in the house for weeks on end, they represented one of my few contacts with the world outside. I would tell Saul when he came home what this or that movie star said about politics, morals, religion. Trends rose, loomed large, and died away. Even cataclysm can be comforting when it menaces with such regular variation. We had bomb shelters, open marriage, cryogenics, sex as a religious issue, sex as a political issue, sex as a racial issue, more sex, better sex. It is the daytime staple. We hang over the sink or push the mop or mend or peel or polish while we contemplate the thousand facets of that big diamond, or in some cases, rhinestone. Sometimes it isn't sex but something more interesting. This morning I'm wishing for something more interesting because I need to clean the oven and the range hood, and if I'm not taken out of myself, I will commit new infidelities with my unknowing lover in the birch groves, my green-spring wishes sun-shot with April tenderness but warm as June. When the wind blows, it will green-glimmer on our naked bodies. I notice that in these dreams I have moved backward, not forward, into the spring. I am not droopy in the breasts, not heavy in the thighs. The backs of my legs in these fantasies do not map the roads I have traveled. Only inside, where no one can see, am I my foxy middle-aged self, opened by a good husband and the babies that came teaching me as they broke free about the twined birth cord, love, and death. The smile could give it away and the eyes, but I can run a mile naked as a nymph and unwinded in the wind if only he will chase me, chase and catch me in the fox-copses, warm and then hot together. . . . The scouring pad is dripping in my hand. Who says there's no romance in housework?

When I put on the television, I see that I am not familiar with the guests by sight. That cheers me. We won't have a big star's humble origins today. Before burying my head in the oven, I look carefully at them. Two young men and two women well into middle age. Psychologists and their patients, perhaps? Ex-alcoholics or drug addicts? I look at the women for a clue.

There are two ways to take what happens to us. My way is the first way. I look my age because I do not fight it. These women look their ages because they do. They are whisper-thin, their hair dyed, their faces tightened and tightened again. The bodies may be the bodies of starveling girls but the eyes, the hands, the necks are those of fifty-year-old women. The host is talking about "alternative life-styles." The young men, it turns out, are married to the older women—not lovers but husbands.

They speak of the ways they met; in one case, the boy had been the date of the woman's daughter; in the other, a student in the woman's art class. The host wants to know all the de-tails—what's it like in bed? Wonderful, wonderful, everyone agrees. "Each of us should be free to express his true nature," says the woman under the bright red hair. "I have always felt young at heart." Mazel tov, I murmur into the oven. They are all liberated as hell back there in the daytime. I am deep in, stuck like a suicide, scouring the back wall. They speak of Kinsey's sex researches and numbers of climaxes possible in men of twenty-five as compared to women of forty-five who are at the peak of the female sex drive. What an error I have made! When I was twenty-three and ready to marry, I should have gone to a pregnant woman and contracted for her unborn son—our drives, you know. But I am being fanciful. They begin to tell me back there that I have thought of the whole marital arrangement in the wrong way. People marry to satisfy their needs. Needs change and so should partners. Every day is to be lived at its most exciting. No day will come again and that is why the Now is all we have and all we need. Good-bye, grandma, grandpa, all your wishes that I remember, Dead of the Camps whispering to me, grandchild who does not know me and no wonder: I am not Now enough; because I can remember my daughter's childhood. Drives are all. This moment is all we have. She's right, of course. Ben and I work well together. I should call him up and we should run away to Florida; I am at my sexual peak now and the beach is warmer than this ice-locked town. Saul needn't grieve. His drives are waning—he can get a girl of sixteen on her way up. But can she cook and sew and get along with Riva? More important, can she get along with Orval DeFrees, the plumber? No? Well, better cancel the whole thing, then, and finish the oven.

It's dim and still in here. The world is far away. Down the sides, resisting my razor blade, are crusts—the dripping and spatters of months of dinners—all now part of one unidentifiable and featureless existential cinder; the past is one with the Now. I begin to cry.

It's a good cry, one of the best I've ever had. In the close, acrid-smelling confines my sounds are saved, cherished, and echoed. They are loud enough to deafen me. I am Now, Now at last! I enjoy the simple release of it, but something catches and remains and makes me pull my head out of the oven to look back at the television. I want to look at those couples once more, to see something I missed, but they are gone. A quiz show is on instead.

In the weeping I had been thinking of Ben as a lover—not metaphorically, actually. We can be. We can grow slowly toward one another. I know he likes me well enough. Modern life is full of pains and losses. Why not take its advantages— freedom, the separation of morality from sex, a forgoing of some of the harder virtues.

Suddenly I am laughing. Who taught me such swift and subtle ways to justify plain old lust? I'm surprised at myself and a little in awe. The lies I tell myself when I eat desserts at parties are child's play compared with these. I laugh until I realize that it's noon and that I have spent an hour being hysterical in my oven. I spend the remainder of my oven time composing newspaper articles.

NEW "HIGH" IN SUBURBIA

National Institute of Health reports alarming statistics relating to a new psychedelic inhalant, available in most homes. Numbers of middle-aged women are spending up to two hours daily in their ovens inhaling a combination of carbon dioxide, oven cleaner, and burnt-on grease to achieve what they describe as illumination. The side effects of these fumes are giggling, weeping, changes in moral character, and a stiffness in the lower back. A $550,000 government project is being funded to ascertain whether the fumes are carcinogenic.

Having made the decision to consider sleeping with Ben in more than fantasy, a profound relaxation comes. Now, I have all the time in the world to let us move toward one another in the way of lovers. Romeo and Juliet were hot with teenage need—a three-day hurricane. I am going to play my old-lady trumps: time, patience, and love, all of which I have been learning for a generation. The hunger is the same. What is different is ripeness.

I am pondering all this when Geri calls. She wants to know if I will go Christmas shopping with her. I know we should take Riva; I've not yet gone out with her this month. She needs the exercise and the company—not only mine for once, but to be "one of the girls." But she is so slow now and full of complaints, the whole pace would be changed and there is getting her ready and talking her into it. Suddenly the word flashes before me. Adultery. I am going to be unfaithful to my husband. Since my life is not one of excess and riot, why not start now, think like a modern, go everywhere in the Now—no past, no future. "You're on!" I cry, and with no more thought than that, off we go. If an accident comes in, Rita and Ben will be there, Larry and Dorothy can back up if they are needed.

The wages of sin is a wonderful time. Instead of going to Midlothian, we take off to the new mall that has opened near Russian Grove. I've been hearing about it for months. The wealthier new developments are all gathered out that way, whether by design or coincidence, and the shopping center is brand new, lovely, and a bit pretentious.

The centers that came out here in the fifties brought to isolated new suburbs and old towns the bread and beans of ordinary living: Wards and Sears and Penney's. Curtain rods and bath mats, pretzels and pop. The gourmet department back in those days was a shelf with canned gravy, cider vinegar, and garlic salt. In the sixties, the centers enlarged and the choice got bigger, but always in a general way. Suddenly, mystically, in the seventies, a word was born, or rather kidnapped: boutique. It is Cosmos, the new center. Wood boutiques and gourmet boutiques and tiny "fun" clothing stores evoking a cleaned-up rural past we never experienced but wished we had. The Barn. The Attic. The Shed. The Tree. The Calico Tree. The Licorice Tree. The Weathervane. "I've got to bring Riva here someday soon. She'll see a peasant Europe gone sweetly genteel, a touched-up Shedletz."

Geri laughs. "You're a closet materialist."

"Closet nothing! Heaven for me will be a sewing, notions, yard goods, and hardware store one-acre square. No, cancel that."

"Why?"

"What if God answers prayers!" We laugh.

God. He has been tolerant of me; the way I keep Sabbaths and holidays is not what was ordained for my people; He has played fair with me in my part of our special unequal relationship. Will I be at war with my part of God, now that I am warming myself at illicit fires, burning the well-aged timber of my middle years? Because, Romeo and Juliet, Paolo and Francesca, Héloïse and Abelard, Tony and Cleo: The best fires are not made of green wood. Forcibly, I return myself to the contemplation of the problems at hand: Geri's gifts for Christmas, my Chanukah "things" sent to Kimberley and Miriam.

We start for home at five, sated, boutiqued-out. "If I see one more clever saying stenciled on an apron, I'll go into diabetic coma."

"Ah, the terminal cutes," Geri says. "I used to get them every Christmas. Brian would decide I should be at home making cookies and piecing quilts. Of course, I was working full time, too, at the insurance company, so I had to rush home and into a frilly apron while he stayed out filling himself with Christmas cheer."

"Where is he now?"

"In Chicago—married again. I hope she hits back at least."

I look at her unable to comfort. Since the night of the abuse call, she has begun to talk about some of the misery she's been through. It's all bitterness, rage, and fear, and too spendthrift of feeling to remember that there must have been other times, at least in the beginning, of love and fun. Geri needs the one-sided view now, but the one-sidedness makes it singularly hard to listen to. I know I'm there to listen only. "Why not stay for dinner. Saul will be home early."

"I've got to get back and wrap these presents. Besides there is a new man in radiology at Midlothian. Did you see him there on the last day-run? He's coming over to help me wrap."

"Geri, a date, how nice."

"Date," and she laughs, "how dated that sounds!"

"I can never see you as cringing and afraid. I know it's happened because you've told me, but—do circumstances alter everyone so terribly—are we all so little ourselves—?"

"That's part of the nightmare," she says slowly, "that I watched myself change, pull tighter and tighter, get weaker and weaker. I see it now happening with some of the people in the nursing home—illness, strokes, the loss of their old selves. Champion cooks lose their feel, deft carpenters become putterers—they've stopped believing in themselves, they shrink inside their own clothes, they don't cast their own shadows. That's why we get angry with them. In the nursing home sits Mrs. Blair. She managed the food services of a huge Chicago hospital for fifteen years, and that was when women managers were few and far between. Her daughter told me she had thirty people working under her—she hired and fired, did all the buying of everything from sides of beef to paper napkins. Now her whole day, her whole life, is spent complaining about another daughter who visits too little. I stopped believing long ago that she ever managed anything. So, apparently, did she."

I get, just for a second, a flash picture of Ben fighting shadow assailants in a dark alley, gouging and kicking. I can hear the grunting, the sound of the blows. I shiver. Geri looks at me, so I laugh and say, "I got a picture of us—two crabs in the nursing home, both adrenaline junkies. We get our kicks by short-circuiting the other patients' pacemakers so we can rush in and do the rescue bit." Geri laughs too. "Red lights and sirens on our wheelchairs."

"Geri, how can I help Riva?"

We have suddenly come full circle. "You're still feeling guilty about not taking her along?"

"I guess so."

"Well, we'll just have to do it again next week and bring her with us."

"Yes, and thanks for it. I have to stop wishing for the Riva who used to be here, the one for whom a sudden invitation was the making of her day. It's hard to face the fact that part of me wants to be free of her."

When Geri leaves I sit down for a while and rest. I am sad about Riva, but under it all there is a new sweet warmth—my secret. Where does it come from, this wish to say: I am more than what you see before you. A separate source of power and strength is warming me. Do members of the thousand secret cults and brotherhoods in this country bear this little hidden light to their initiates? I smile. I laugh aloud. Bring it all on, the mystical handshake, the secret smirk; were those your shoes I saw sticking out from under that cultist robe? I, too, belong to a secret organization. Secret lovers.

SECRET LOVERS OF BEARDED—

Never mind, making a banner was a bad idea anyway. And sooner or later, a day, two, three, I will see him again, be warmed again by his eyes, breathe in his laugh, touch him, move behind him in some work or another, touching the half-length of our bodies. In the meantime, he will lie in many beds here and in other places: in medieval France in the sweet summer of 1115, in Jerusalem and biblical Gilboa, and Gilboa,

138

Pennsylvania, in Violet Cleve's glade, sun-dappled green in the dead of winter the way I am now, and summer-warm, the way I am now.

He comes on the first night of Chanukah, light to light. He brings Riva a little present and tells stories about the kids at Longhill—funny-sad stories—their trouble makes the textures of the stories a little harsher than what goes on in junior high school, but his children are not psychotic so much as troubled by behavior they can't control. If I love this kind, dark-shining man for nothing else, it is for the possibilities he sees all around him. In his world, it's all still to be done, still well and easily done with goodwill and hard work. Children can grow whole and strong under his smile, old people can be protected, and still share in the spontaneous sudden wish, the kindling word. We light the lights and say the prayers—he's eager to learn the words and the meanings. In spite of myself, I am passingly annoyed at the unknown couple who denied Chanukah and Sabbath lights to his childhood. Who was she, that woman who let such a child grow up in a songless house? Never mind, my own children were bored by the songs I tried to teach them, and he is all for me to do now—mine. I have sworn never to think myself superior to any other mother—how soon I forget those vows I made under the lash. Did she sing you lullabies, that woman, even once?

I have made the traditional food—carrot tzimmes and beef brisket and potato pancakes with apple sauce. Saul laughs with Ben. "I'm glad you came tonight. When the kids left home, the 'special' food went with them. Thanks to you, it's back."

We dine splendidly. There is a nut torte waiting in the kitchen for its unveiling, and as I get up to cut it, I realize Saul is right. I've gone overboard. Duplicity should be more subtle. Guarding the word, the gesture, the look, I've been betrayed by my own mother, who taught me the equation of love and food.

Oh, graceless Grace, hunched over your sink, red of face and chapped of hands, you have flowers in your hair and they will not be hidden. At the door are your size nine combat boots, but at the lace ends there are little golden bells and they will sound whithersoever you go— The alarm. No. Yes. For a split second I want to break the box.

First aid at 313 Tulip. "Start on that cake," I cry. "We'll be back as soon as we can." We are out the door and civilization is behind us. "Hang on," I say and Ben and I jump into the car. "The snow has melted off this side of the hill and there's a shortcut that will get us to Amsterdam fast." I am thinking as we bump over the field toward a stand of trees at the end of Pine Street that the house is on the street where Dr. Mellinger lives. There's no snow here but the wind has littered the way and it's rougher than I remember. Still, in three hundred yards or so we are through the trees and on the back side of Pine Street. We take a quick right and put on the car horn. The way is clear.

It's Doc's house. The sheriff is outside. It must be a patient, I think, and then I realize I think so because I want it to be so. Doc Mellinger is one of the pillars of this town, not a decorative pillar, but a bearer of weight. I shake my head and run. The ambulance has just come.

Then I see Doc at the door. He motions like a phantom and says quickly, "Upstairs, front bedroom." We bound up. Why didn't he tell us what this is? Heart attack? Diabetic coma? I go to the doorway and look at the room. It's messy and the bed is unmade, so I don't see for a split second—then I feel Ben behind me; I move in and see her on the bed.

It's Faye Mellinger. "Faye?" No response. I come in close. "Faye!" I am shaking her shoulder. Nothing. I can see her breathing; it is dangerously slow. "Time me one minute," I tell Ben. The others have come in. "Tell Doc he'll have to get ready to put a tube in." From Faye's mouth comes the gassy barbiturate smell.

"Doc's in no shape—"

"Doc needs to answer these questions—how much and when, and to get a tube in! My airway won't do this job. Oxygen and a bag!" I cry behind me. Ben gives me the minute. Eight breaths, and not deep ones: I have to make her want to breathe. I press the flesh at the ridges of her eyes. She opens both eyes suddenly, glaring at me for the pain. "Faye!" I cry into her face. "Tell me what's happened!"

"Leave me alone," she murmurs, "I want to die."

"What?" I shout. "I can't understand you!" The next words are not clear. "Do plantar reflexes," I say to Ben, "up the bottoms of her feet heel to ball with your thumbnail."

"Why?"

"Because it's annoying and a good neuro-status indicator." The oxygen comes and we use the mask and a bag to force air into her lungs.

"Can we get the gurney up these narrow steps?" Geri asks.

"No chance."

"Then let's do a carry, quickly."

It's difficult going down the narrow stairs. Ben does her legs, Claude her arms and head. Ellie and I follow trying to get some oxygen bagging in as we go. At the bottom of the stairs, I see that we have come a little way with Faye herself. She is restless and her eyes are fluttering. Everything has picked up, pulse and color and blood pressure. We may be able to get by without the tube. Rita is talking to Doc. I look around and see what I think. The details are being dealt with. We'll need two in back just in case, and a driver. I look at Ben. He is obeying orders but doing no more. The intuitive, bright rescuer is not here with me, and there's only a minute to ask him quickly and softly, "What's up?"

"I'll load," he says, "but can you send someone else?"

"Can I call you when we get back?"

"I'll wait at the firehouse."

"It may take hours."

"I need to see you."

I nod. Like lovers planning, secret and desperate. Geri has started the I.V. and we load. Doc will go in with his son, who has been called. He has refused to ride with us, even with the possible need. He has fallen apart; professionals sometimes do with their own. His wife has attempted suicide and it's all he can think of. He is a husband now, and not a doctor at all. Amazement, rage, and shame. It's all he can handle and now she is well enough to cry aloud: "Let me die! I want to die!" I look at him and his face is set. He is struggling to put distance between himself and his pain.

We go. She's too near unconsciousness for us to induce vomiting. I suspect it's too late anyway. The drug's effects are well advanced. We torment her awake. Does she have children? Yes. What are their names? "Leave me alone." What are their names? "I don't remember." I shake her. What are their names? How can the gestapos of the world derive pleasure from this? The crafty human will do anything to escape his pain. He claws toward unconsciousness, but his body betrays him. It wants awareness even when awareness is my knuckle kneading the breastbone, my thumbnail pulled up his feet. The blood yearns toward the brain, the heart trembles to continue its endless work; the valves wink together and are flipped apart in a kind of joy even under the worst despairs we know. The King of the Universe has built the hunger in electrochemical codes—ion deficits, negative pressure in a million capillaries and alveoli, yearning imbalance at the walls of the membranes: I need, I seek, I want. Is it any wonder that far away on our surfaces contentment is so fleeting?

Together, Ellie and I fight with Faye. Pneumonias begin now, when the system slows. We need to get her breathing up and her heart quickened. We can't get joy, so we will do with anger. We force air into her lungs now and then, and let it come out in rage at us and the world. When we get to the hospital we are worn out. I'm glad Ellie is here. Because she works days at the school I seldom get to ride with her, but she's solid—I have forgotten how solid she is. The hospital is ready and Faye goes right in. When I can, I take a quick look out into the waiting room. Doc Mellinger has just arrived with his son. I see them sitting together among the survivors, as forlornly as anyone else. They need news, comfort, reasons—most important, they need something no doctor can tell them, that this pain will not be shared with the town. No details will come from us who are their neighbors and, in a place the size of Gilboa, often their judges. I wonder of the three of us, who would be best at delivering such a message. I decide to ask. In small towns, relationships are not always what they seem. I get a picture of C.A. as a child, watching Violet Cleve walking toward him, and I smile in spite of myself.

Claude and Ellie are in the coffee room writing up the run. I ask them. Ellie smiles and rises. "If no one minds, this one's mine," she says. " 'Fore I got the job cookin' up at the school, I done houses. In those days, you didn't get what they're asking now. Doc Mellinger, he carried us for months at a time, this and that. He knows I keep my word. Besides, us poor but honest types, we got cred-i-bility." She winks at me, gets up, and goes. Claude smiles up at me. "Your mouth is open," he says.

Then I want to get home to Ben, who's waiting. It comes to me that his being around the firehouse is going to look suspicious, that he's not geared to thinking self-protectively, and that if he were, it would lessen him somehow. We are not making love except in my mind, and there is no reason for Ben to creep around, hiding, except that if he doesn't, the town will feel something, register his differences and my subtle tremors on its seismograph.

When we pull up to the firehouse, there is no one there. I'm half relieved. He has thought better of it and gone home, but as we close the doors, Ellie says, "Here comes Mr. Ben with two of his kiddos."

They don't walk, although the night is cold. They saunter.

Had they had canes and hats, they would have come soft-shoe like Fred Astaire, the three of them. "Hi," he says. "We've been to the Famous."

"The saloon?"

"The bowling alley."

"You must be cold, walking all the way here—"

"We knew you had a run and we thought we might get a ride home."

"Hop in."

"One second," Ben says. He takes the boys over and introduces them carefully to Claude and Ellie, telling them what each one does on the squad and in his regular job. I am proud. He hasn't forgotten that he means to end the silence between the school and the town. The boys are shy—they're not our boys of the water fight—but they shake hands and smile when Ben says, "These are some of my better bowlers."

In the car, they're still shy. They smell of fresh air and sweat and French fries. "You fellows have had quite an evening," I say.

"Just a couple of hours," one of the boys answers.

"Fun, though?"

"Yeah."

As I drive to the school, we come up over the town and see the moon, perfectly round and glowing almost red. It's so perfect no one says anything; a breath might blow it away. All the roads are enchanted. We see no one and no one passes us. The grounds of Longhill are caught in the full light—literally moonstruck. When we pull in, Ben says, "Can you wait for me a minute? We have to check in." I nod and say good night to the moon-bowlers.

I know I can't stay long and it feels like an imprisonment. Saul doesn't demand an accounting of my time, but he knows when I left and how long an ordinary run takes. A long talk with Ben will mean lying, a thing I don't deserve to have to do,

Ben comes and slides in beside me. "It's good of you to take this time," he says, "and the dark makes it easier to talk . . ." We both look out at the moon-wonder for a while. I can't see his face, but I feel him close beside me.

"What happened on the run this evening? You froze up."

He says nothing for a moment and then, "How can you— how can you believe in freedom and then deny freedom to others?"

"What freedom do you mean?"

"I mean the freedom of that woman to take her own life!"

Again time moves between us. Miriam once said, "I have absolute right over my own body!" Ben is sitting close in the small car; our shoulders are touching. "Do you think we were wrong to intervene?"

"Yes; when she said, 'Let me die,' we should have let her."

"Which voice should we have listened to, her mind or her body?"

"What do you mean?"

"Didn't you see that struggle to breathe, that incredible effort her eyes made to focus?"

"Ultimately—"

"Yes, but is this the ultimate? Play this out: You have a victim with bilateral overriding femoral fractures—pain beyond description. He has a gun near him. If he asked you, would you give it to him?"

"No, of course not!"

"Why not?"

"Well, I know about the pain, but I'd tell him we were going to use traction—it would ease the pain dramatically and in a couple of hours things would be changed, he'd be—" He laughs a little. "I guess I see. Do you think the cases are the same?"

"I think she needs a chance to look over the borders of her present pain."

"But that excuses your—our—taking over her choices—"

"Yes, but not ultimately. Ultimately, as you said, the choices are hers."

"How, when you're going to pull her away—"

"I think the only clear message is success. *Sure* death is all around us. Why didn't she jump off the overpass at Exit 18? Why didn't she take Doc's gun and go six miles out Van Riper and shoot herself in the head? Don't you see how mixed her message was? I'm not sure what percentage of her wants to live, but this way, we'll be able to ask her three months from now. And she can still try the gun or the bridge."

"Do you believe the desire just hit her suddenly?"

"I believe she was angry at Doc. I think we sometimes use our lives for more than living them. When Geri tells me about herself and Brian—no, erase that, but think for a minute—no, don't think—feel. I leave you now and go home and immediately take forty sleeping pills and die. You hear about it late tomorrow. Now, tell me."

"I guess I'd . . . well, I would wonder if it was something I'd said. Yes, yes, it would haunt me."

"And you never *could* know, could you? I would have slapped you in the face and gone away beyond all your questions and protestations. The last word."

"How did you come to know that?"

"Something like it happened to me once many years ago."

"When?"

"When I was in college."

"You mean someone did that to you?"

"To himself, to me, to a lot of people. His name was Manny LeVine. God, I haven't thought of him in years. I think the family was newly wealthy and trying hard to forget it. Manny reflected all that and more. I was attracted by his brilliance and fascinated by his cynicism. He held me the way acrobats and wire walkers hold us, with wonder and terror." In the darkness beside me, Ben chuckles. I see what I hadn't seen before, the pose it must have been. "Old ploy?" I ask.

I feel his grin.

"The oldest. I'm sorry, go on."

"I wanted him to ask me out and was afraid he would. At last, he did ask me in his usual, offhand way, almost mockingly, like a dare."

"Aha," says Ben in the darkness.

"At first it was all right. Dinner and some good talk. We went to a movie. But on the way home, he began his little mocking witticisms—the Jews, their pretensions, their shallow compromises. He was brilliant and I laughed and agreed. I think he saw then that my laughter was at 'us,' not at 'them,' that for all my impatience with Jewish faults I was seeing myself as one of the group—a believer, faults and all. He became more savage. I told him so. We began to argue. He called me a hypocrite—we didn't use the term cop-out then, but there were other words. Defensively, I, too, got more extreme than I wanted. I told him he was more destructive to his people than a Christian anti-Semite could be. He left me standing in the middle of the street and went to his room and hanged himself. They didn't find him for two days."

"That sonofabitch!"

"Precisely, but I didn't come to that decision for a year. Now. Doc Mellinger."

"I see." He is silent, thinking. Then he says, "Are we naturally that cruel?"

"I think we are naturally that selfish."

He kisses me very gently on the cheek. I turn back and kiss him too. "Thanks," he says.

"Thank you." I know his kiss is gratitude; now he can stay on the squad without compromising his feelings or integrity.

"Thanks for the party," he says, remembering his manners. Early this evening was days ago. "It would have been a lovely evening."

"You're welcome. Good night."

The experience I tell Ben is true, but it has more than one

147

face and I see another view of it now. When Joshua left college and didn't let us know until he wrote all that time later from Nogales, Mexico, the letter spoke of strangling and stifling. In the year that followed, I had to live as best I could, to make no link in memory with college suicides or people who couldn't live with their own pasts. I still don't know why Josh left school, why he felt as he did, how Saul and I figured in his changes. Probably the LeVines didn't either; the mystery will be there forever at the core of their memorial. I shudder.

Ben gets out and walks toward his little house. I go home to Saul, already asleep. I've told this story only to Saul and now to Ben. Twenty-five years ago when I told it first it was a different story. I was young and not a parent and the experience had a different meaning for me. The main characters in it, the boy and girl, have, in the intervening years, been joined by parents and grandparents—the stage is no longer mine alone as it was then, but a busy place indeed, a father and mother, two sets of grandparents, brothers and sisters, aunts and uncles, the rabbi, and the rescuers.

I wanted at one time . . . I had thought to give this memory to Joshua and Miriam, to tell them what it had been like. When they were home, they were too young or too self-involved to hear it. My small store of experience lies next to the boxes of school clothes and remnants in the back bedroom. With Ben, the story has been reborn in its changed form, the new cast assembled. It's a shame to reduce once-living people to stories but there is no cure for it. In their new shape, they serve our purposes and not their own. In their new form, they are remembered.

I ride home. It's still early. I could tell Saul about Ben—that he was unable to make the run, that I had to talk with him, to hear him and then to try to help him, but I'm afraid. Lines in my face would change and he would see. My voice would testify against me, my hand, my body would tell a truth I don't want Saul to know. When I pull up to our house, I see the lights are still on. Most of the houses I passed were dark; here and there is the blue glow of a television. For the first time in years—I can't remember how many—I wish I didn't have to go in. We've had our arguments, and one or two terrible fights that drove one or the other of us out into rains, dark nights, or gray days. When it was I, I felt this way about coming back again, but the times were rare enough and here I am with no argument, no reasons, except a reason I can't speak of. Why can't I be like talk-show people—have my affair, go and come in guiltless joy, keep the knowledge from Saul not out of anguish but because it's easier, the way I spare him Riva's complaints and Lou Epstein's fussing. It's a nice choice, made by someone else. So, too, is the other choice, not to go home at all, but to slip into a small, elegant hotel somewhere and send my personal maid for a few days' necessaries. As it is, if I don't want to sleep in the car, I will have to go in and face him.

I'm shy. I feel like a stranger. The kitchen light is on. Saul has left some milk in a pan for me and the cocoa out. The dishes of our Chanukah celebration have not been washed, but are stacked neatly on the counter by the sink. I creep into the dining room. It's been cleared but the cloth is still on the table and full of crumbs. If I busy myself with all this, I won't have to go upstairs for another hour. I bring out the little portable television and set it up on the counter in the kitchen.

The movie has begun. It's good old Bette Davis: *Beyond the Forest*, a kind of sandlot *Madame Bovary*. I love watching what the early fifties saw as selfishness and depravity. I love Bette's passionate hates. Even her love is half hate—but the lover, David Brian, has no heart. Those days featured dedication in its men, not ambition. It seems to me we always praised the rugged, simple virtues in our heroes and took the rap for being materialists.

I am enjoying myself greatly. The work makes me feel natural in my house again. There is a deep satisfaction in cleaning up, "putting things to rights." When I go upstairs, there is cleanliness and order behind me and "selfish" Bette swept up in a mess of closing commercials. I am in command again. Saul has left the little light on in the bedroom. I creep in. He is asleep but for a long moment I don't recognize him.

Isn't Saul younger, much younger than this? This man's hair is white and his face is wrinkled and jowly. What's happened in so short a time? You leave them alone for a few hours and look what they do! I know that people get older, everyone gets older, but I didn't expect this in my own house, this awful betrayal! I get into bed and turn over toward sleep. Can one infidelity breed so many others? He's old enough to be my father!

13

After the first of January there's an unexpected truce from the demands of the alarm box. A heavy snow falls, but magically, the drivers get cannier and do not rush so fast. The drunken children go elsewhere or drink less. There are no calls for a week.

I've knitted sweaters for Joshua, Miriam, and Kimberley. I'll send them out into the silences, hoping they fit and are liked. Sanjit can wear his under his sacred garment that is sacred everywhere but warm enough only in India. Of such fine adjustments is exile made. I also begin to knit a set of dream-plans, secret acts in secret places, if and when Ben and I are ready to slip away small into hiding.

It's not easy. I'm known everywhere, seen coming and seen going in the subliminal, organic rhythm of the day, not watched, but noticed. In small towns there is no contingency planning for adultery; no secret tunnels make networks beneath the streets, no cellar rooms are served by hidden staircases. Suddenly, I feel limits and boundaries all around. We would have to go to Midlothian or Tarrant, something too calculated and impossible, really, for just an hour or two.

Then I know. Violet's house. The top floor of Violet's house. It comes to me in the middle of cleaning one day, that Violet Cleve's house, which she has willed to the Garden Club, is deserted but not abandoned. I still have the key she once gave me. The attic is dusty but dry. A mattress and a small heater are all we would need. To save the pipes, the electricity has not been turned off.

And there is a pleasant view from that attic window—the hills and woods to the south. An easy walk or ride from Longhill; one would need only to bypass the single row of houses on Cleve Road to be secret enough. I'm so pleased with my plan that I'm chipper all evening. All the good new words for women suddenly apply to me—masterful, self-determining. Miriam would be proud; she'd have to be whether she wanted to or not. The ideology would demand it. The evening rocks back and forth with suppressed glee.

Everywhere I'm careful. I don't follow Ben with my eyes, although I want to. When I pass behind him in the ambulance, I don't pause. When the group meets, I don't sit near him unless it falls naturally to do so. My passion has all the humorous reversals of the times. I am like nothing so much as a Victorian rake setting about the seduction of the lead soprano in the church choir. It has a single-mindedness to it that I don't like. While the meals are made and the rooms kept clean, while Saul's shirts get folded and Riva gets her shopping trips, the true focus of my life has narrowed smaller and smaller to the tug of war at meetings and training, to the accidents that now mean, in addition to the challenge and the work, a chance that Ben will be there, that we'll ride in the ambulance together and have the sweet intimacy of talk on the way back, to the question of whether he will ask me and when, whether I will ask him and when. I learn a man's lesson—that of the two, the seducer is the more seduced.

Trenkler's Law takes over. (Alf Trenkler was a history major back in my college days. He told me once that his proof of God's existence was that as soon as he became interested in a subject, the world hastened to oblige. Answers leaped out at him. Major articles suddenly appeared. Friends, not knowing of the new interest, began to mention obscure exhibits in out-of-the-way places, treasures surfaced.) I have marveled many times at Trenkler's Law. When one is pregnant, the world is pregnant; when a son is a devotee, the world erupts in garish blue gods, and I am approached at the shopping center by someone's once-Jewish child.

Now it's news of Ben. From Milo at the drugstore and C.A., Lou Epstein, and Orley Flett ("Beard 'n' that put me off at first, but that Ben's a sharp feller. Nice with them morons they got up to the school. I seen him with three or four of 'em on the way to Pinecrest. Picked 'em up in the truck. They didn't do nothin' simple, acted pretty normal, if you ask me"). I learn parts of his schedule by coincidence; I know when he goes to the bank and when to the laundromat ("I saw one of your rescue people down at the coin-op Wednesday morning—the bearded one . . . "). I begin to feel like one of those desert snakes waiting for prey. It's a combination of opposites that keeps that forked tongue flicking in and out of the almost closed mouth, a patient passion, a slow haste, a waiting at once active and passive. We watch our patients that way, simply sitting but completely intent. Because of his stillness, the predator passes unnoticed; because of his raptness, the predator doesn't notice anything but the prey.

Riva has turned down the last two trips to Midlothian. I'm only aware of what this means when the third trip comes up. Before that, to my shame, I was only relieved. The trips have been getting harder. Riva is fussier. Suddenly, I hear that she's gotten impatient with her readers, two lovely little girls from the junior high. I hear, too, that she's been asking them not to read but to shop for her and that except for Shabbos and Havdalah here, she's not left the house in weeks.

She must have gone much further into blindness without letting us know. I'm frightened and angry, almost as frightened and angry as she. I wait that evening for Saul to come home, and before dinner, because I haven't the patience or strength to wait longer, I tell him what I think—what I know. Predictably, he flies out at the target nearest to him. "How could you let this go on so long—"

"I suppose I've been denying it the way she does—"

"Why didn't you notice her condition—why was it left to the girls to tell you?"

"I don't go around checking up on her or them. One of their mothers called today and I found out almost by accident. Riva didn't want us to know. She made excuses every time our trips came up. Friday nights and Havdalahs she's been coming here without a word."

"Except last week—"

"For which she had an excuse. I can't corner her. She didn't want us to know; it's as simple as that. She's as much afraid of the dependence as we."

"But now she goes to the doctor—no more excuses and no more denial!" he shouts.

"As though I could force her. For how long have we pleaded with her? Saul, I'm not going to take blame for this or be the one who should have done something and didn't. Remember how we both asked, pleaded, offered, even made appointments—"

"There are ways of convincing people, knacks, subtle things—"

"What subtle things?"

"I don't know, but a little cajolery, a little wheedling—"

"Don't you know after all these years that I can't do that? I can't do it on the ambulance and I can't do it to you and I can't do it to her—"

"If you hadn't been so busy with that damn ambulance and everyone else's rescues, you might have found a way—"

It's unfair and he knows it and I do, too, and should discount it. He's afraid he's to blame for allowing his mother to go so long without medical care. What if this condition was preventable, some trouble that seen early could have been cleared up with treatment? It would be a kind of criminal negligence, a shame that would haunt him for the rest of his life. "I'm her daughter-in-law, not her daughter. I'm also me. I respect Riva and I hope she knows it. Cajolery—she'd know it was the end of any real feeling I had for her!"

But he is too angry and his anger rises against the rock that waits behind this one: Josh and Miriam. "All very independent and modern and it's not playing games, it's doing what has to be done."

"And what's that?"

"It's not letting—it's when the kids were young, not letting them—"

He has never come so far. Had I played a game, had I been the right kind of woman, he wants to say, yearns to say, the children might have been saved for us. Miriam would have married a nice Jewish man from Midlothian, Joshua would be in college now, pursuing an ordinary worldly goal. All because of me. "Good God, we give them our *lives* as an example—what else is there to do—for me to do?"

"You could have—I don't know, something. You let them off too easily; you weren't severe enough."

I should be furious at his blaming, deserved or undeserved, but his confusion, his inability even to make clear what the fault is, is so transparent, his own pain so awful, I haven't the spirit to answer him. I want to say something about these recent years, how the country has changed, truths I'm learning from Ben, but I know there has always been this kind of pain. Adam blamed Eve for Cain—if only you had—if only you hadn't— Somehow thinking of Eve makes me think of Lou Epstein. The innocence, no doubt. Lou Epstein is the Duppis of our congregation. She is shallow, unreasonable, tactless, and foolish. She has three children and she is as tactless and foolish with them as she is with everyone else and she is loved and honored by them in a way I have never been and never could be by mine. It makes me sad, not angry. "Saul, whatever you need to do, don't blame me for the person I am and the person you love."

"I know," he says, "I know it was my fault, too. I should have made her go, made the kids—"

This is even worse. The anger I had been looking at suddenly looks back at me. "No more! I can't wheedle and you can't foresee. We gave them what we had. Enough! Enough!"

He's as near to weeping as I have ever seen him, but with anger or anguish I can't tell. To my sorrow he conquers the tears. "It's beyond me," he says.

"That's not all that's beyond us. Good God, even the ruby rings you get in gum machines aren't made decently of glass anymore!"

"What the hell are you talking about?"

"That times change, but people—"

"People—"

"Years ago your own dear gray-haired mother went adventuring. She was always full of adventure. She'd hate it if we took over her life."

"You know a good eye doctor?"

"No, but I'll find one."

"Make an appointment and we'll both take her."

"Good idea. Very good."

"You want a ruby ring?"

"Not if you're going to get it out of the gum machine at Wood's."

"If she's blind, really blind, we'll have to bring her here—"

"Riva's eccentric but she's not crazy. There are choices to be made. She needs to be asked what *she* wants to do."

"We asked our kids and look."

"So why ruin a perfect record?"

God, said Albert Einstein, is subtle but not malicious. Riva argues and cries, refuses and rages, but submits at last. We go to Midlothian and she is examined by a doctor who tells us that the blindness is occlusion of the blood vessels that serve the retina. It is part of the general hypertension she has had for years, over which some control was achieved by the medication she took. The blindness was foreseeable but not preventable. Not our fault. The doctor is of the new school; he doesn't blame, he explains, and Riva's defenses part slightly to let him talk to her. He describes what has happened—the constriction and atrophy of these vessels happens in aging. "It's seldom total blindness—you can see shapes, light and dark, movement, and you do recognize people, don't you?" She nods. "I want to tell you this," he says, "even though it seems cruel. I'm doing it because when you know it, you will begin to work around it. It can get worse but it will never improve. What you see now is all you'll see."

Thank God, she weeps. I had expected anger directed at him, at us, at the Lord, but she weeps like an overtired child. He takes us aside. "Give her some time," he says. "Encourage her to be angry or sad or whatever. In a couple of weeks bring her back and we can begin to make some plans. There's training available for you and for her. Her general health is good but sitting around the house moping will soon destroy it. Get her to save and use her anger; anything but passivity. She'll need challenge, stimulation; you may have to fight her—"

"She's my mother," Saul says.

"Get tough," the doctor answers, "but not for a couple of weeks."

Nothing has changed but we feel better. On the way home, Riva cries and then sleeps. I, too, am tired, now that the truth is out. I start to dive into a Ben-dream, but then I look over at Saul. His face is tight and he is hunched up at the steering wheel as though he was climbing it. "You must be tired, and instead of relaxing, you're all over the wheel—"

He laughs. "I haven't felt this shaky since I came home from the hospital with you when Miriam was born."

"I remember that trip—you seemed happy."

"I was scared stiff; the weight suddenly—two other lives. I kept thinking, 'What if the store folds.'"

"But surely you knew you were good at merchandising, good with people, comfortable with the life here, good with Elia."

"Sometimes all that is beside the point. I saw it in Korea and later in college, people brighter than I, more original, more gifted in every way, who couldn't connect, or if they did, couldn't live with their successes. There was a kid at school with us—I think you knew him—Manny Something."

"LeVine."

"Yes, that's right. It was before Korea. I was a freshman. I didn't know you yet."

Saul has forgotten what I told him all those years ago about Manny LeVine. A form of denial—jealousy, maybe, over a suitor of any kind who could so affect my life. Now is not the time to remind him, but I can say something. "Manny LeVine killed himself—what did that have to do with you?"

"I guess the deaths I'd seen—the failures, the breakdowns—I blamed them on the war—a foreign country, fear, the army, boredom. I said to myself that what I was seeing wasn't 'normal'—wasn't 'real life.' Then the war was over and I went to college and a man—talented, free, American, rich, handsome, with a future I envied a little—committed suicide. It was my first peacetime jolt and that somehow made it worse than if it had happened in Korea. I guess it symbolized something for me so I've thought a lot about it then and since. And it was there the day I brought you home, you and Mirele."

"I didn't know that."

"I guess it was he more than anyone else who decided my career."

158

"How?"

"I thought: If someone as brilliant as he can't make it, how can I count on anything? I know—knew then, that I wasn't brilliant or special. Even doing everything I could do, all the study and all the training, I couldn't keep up with the top men. I got tired of fighting it, and the war made me realize that I didn't want the competition of big success. I guess you wondered why I came back so automatically to Gilboa, to the store—"

"No, never."

"You didn't wonder why I didn't at least *try* New York or Chicago?"

"Saul, we all thought then, and I still do, that you had the perfect thing waiting for you. It's a good store in a place you like. You live on a human scale with family and neighbors. When Elia got used to you being grown, he gave you plenty of room. I never dreamed you thought this could be second best to anything."

"I'm not a great brain, but I have an imagination like anyone else. If I hadn't settled for this, I think, we could be—well, richer. We'd live in a city, have cultural advantages, vacations, travel . . ."

"Listen, while you're imagining, why be a piker? Dump me and get someone who looks great in high-fashion couture and could further your career."

"You," he says matter-of-factly, "are one decision I never had misgivings about. When I found you, I wasn't settling for less."

Deftly and unknowingly, he has cut me in pieces. He has done it so suddenly there isn't time to catch my breath. All our years married. The kids, Elia and Riva, growing inward, growing older, all summarized, seen all in all, in spite of everything, judged that it was good. I want to hug him and at the same time cry. I can't do either, so I just sit and say nothing.

"Perk up," he says, "if we can get Riva trained to handle this, we won't have to pussyfoot around about it anymore. Could you live with her if she needs to come and stay with us? You wouldn't be tied to the house, we'd see to that."

"I think I could. If Riva likes me, she may want to come."

"But certainly she likes you."

I laugh and tell him some of the imperatives exerted on mothers-in-law, especially of sons. He is surprised, but I think also a little moved. These relationships he sees as part of woman's mystery, a part I am sharing with him.

"With so much depending on the wife, is it any wonder her mother-in-law treads carefully?"

"And my careless, unsubtle mother has done this?"

"I think she must have. Convention and propriety once saw to our relationships, but now it's all personal preference—no rules, no guarantee."

"Good Lord, it makes the vulnerable more vulnerable still."

"Yup, and all the weight's on love."

"Amazing—" He's relaxing a little now. "Absolutely amazing."

Riva stays with us overnight and the next day and the day after that. She weeps often and wanders around the house peering at what the doctor has told us are blurs of light and dark forms, moving or still. She has become blinder with being told that her condition is real and irreversible. A calculated cruelty, the doctor said. Without it, she will never begin the necessary training to come to terms with it.

I see Geri on a run and tell her. She offers me a leave of absence. I refuse. It's not dedication, it's that I won't be imprisoned by Riva without the need. "We've called her little readers back. Poor kids, they thought it was something they'd done. They're willing to come twice a week after school and read. Saul will be looking in at lunchtime if I'm not home."

"But what if she falls?"

"What if I fell, or you? Is it selfish what I'm doing, or sane?

I don't know, but I do know that I look terrible in martyr's robes."

"They do emphasize your hips."

"Always the truth from a friend."

"Can I help?"

"Yes. Don't stop coming over, you and Rita. Don't change what you say or do when you're there. Riva is still going to have to make her own world." Brave talk. Telling it to Geri, I tell it to myself.

At the squad meeting, I let Ben know that I need to see him. Can I give him a ride home? Yes, he has jogged to the firehouse from Longhill and was planning to jog back, but the cold— "Cold nothing. You realized it was all uphill." He laughs. It's all been done quietly but not secretly, and around us the squad gives no special glances. No signals are raised. Sometimes secrets are best kept by blabbing them.

When we're in the car, I start to turn up Federal and Ben puts his hand on my arm. "I want to talk to you, too, but not in the car in front of the school. I know a place we can go."

"Where?"

"Start out Marshaltown. Take the Monetan exit."

I look around. The others have left. We will not be seen, I hope, driving away from Longhill and not toward it. "Where are we going?"

"To a nice new dark saloon that's just opened one mile off Exit 19."

"More saloons, more drunks; more drunks, more work."

"Why do they make these places so dark? All this needs is bats."

"Easier to talk in the dark."

"Why here and not my car?"

"I'll go into that later. You seemed sad and tense at the meeting and I think you need something to eat and maybe something to drink."

"Not booze; do they have coffee?"

"They have to, it's the law."

When the waitress comes, I see her looking at Ben appreciatively. I do not exist for her. I am a noise in her ear. "Do you have sandwiches?"

"Yeah."

"I'd like a Swiss cheese on toast and coffee."

"Nothing to drink?" she asks.

"No, thank you," Ben says. "She's an alcoholic. I'll have a Scotch and water." When the waitress leaves, he says, "Now she won't hassle us about getting you to drink something. Your abstinence is costing them money." I'm dumbfounded. Both the problem and Ben's means of dealing with it are completely strange to me. Then he sits back and looks at me warmly and says, "Something's made you sad and worried. Tell me now."

I tell him about Riva; all of it; my own fears, selfish and unselfish, Riva's, too, and Saul's. It doesn't take long because he understands the meaning of what worries us. I am aware as I tell him that Saul would not approve, would think it disloyal somehow, to speak of such family matters. As I finish, the food comes. The waitress now sees me with sympathy, fighting my battle with alcoholism, while my handsome, callous escort purposely mocks me with the ultimate temptation. She bangs his drink down on the table with a look that could bend iron. When she leaves, we laugh, although for me there is some chagrin in it. We have lied twice for no reason but our own convenience.

"Do your kids know about Riva?" he asks. It surprises me that he would think of them as possible sources of help.

"They know generally, but they're not free to come, and that's what the need is—people. Riva needs to be jogged out of her rut now. Since Elia died, she's been coasting, but she can't afford to do that anymore."

"In your world, everything serves a purpose, doesn't it? Can't a thing or a person just be because he is?"

"Is that what you tell your disturbed kids?"

"We think everyone should be respected because of his humanity."

"Nice, in a theoretical way, but even in modern zoos they've learned they have to give the animals challenges—something to do. Love and work, Freud says. Ask your kids how the world feels about purposeless people, humanity and all. The appendix traps waste and gets infected."

Ben doesn't know it, but I see I have gainsaid myself. Whose fantasy is the eternal Sunday-afternoon picnic? Whose yearning is it to play on a thousand summer hills, loving and swimming? Eden. "Ben, Riva isn't a philosopher. She needs work and a purpose like anyone else. I don't want to send her down in the mines. I want her to be self-sufficient for as long as she can be. I want her to be able to afford choices."

"They'll teach her to cook and she hates that."

"It's not the cooking she hates, but what it represents. She may learn to like it since now it represents not bondage but freedom."

"Would she like to help up at the school?"

"When she's done her training—when she's ready to go out and try new things, will you ask her?"

"Yes, I will."

"She may turn you down. Mothering isn't something she jumps at either."

"It won't be mothering. I'm not sure what it will be."

"I think we should go now, it's getting late."

"Yes." We get up.

"Dutch treat," I say and go for my purse.

"Next time—"

"Please—" It shames me; he can't be making much at the school.

"I don't take money from drunks," he says.

163

I don't want to argue so I laugh. "You know, I'll never be able to come back here after that."

"You wouldn't anyway—it's not your kind of place."

"Is it yours?"

"Not anymore."

"Why did we come here then, instead of talking in the car?"

He helps me on with my coat and says matter-of-factly, "I wouldn't have been listening to you in the car. I would have been wanting to touch you and to kiss you, and then to make love to you."

I must have stopped dead in my tracks because he touches me gently on the shoulder. "Let's go."

It's hard to drive home; I am trembling. When I let Ben out of the car, he kisses me gently on the cheek. I say, "We are going to have to figure this out carefully."

"I know. I know what I want, but the decision is up to you." I turn the car around and ride home slowly, numbly. This is what I have been dreaming of, making wild, wide fantasies about, yearning for, and now that it's more than a dream, I'm shaken by it. Why didn't I throw my arms around him and let him take me to his bed? When I get home I stand for long minutes at the door of my house, wishing I was free of all of it, Saul and Riva, Joshua and Miriam, Gilboa, reality. I sigh and go in.

The lights are out. The house is dark. That's strange enough, but there are clumping noises at the back. I think to call out, loath to leave the doorway in case something is wrong. "What's happening?"

I turn the light on and Riva out in the kitchen cries, "Go back to bed, you don't have to watch me!" She is haunting the darkness. From the sound of it, she certainly hasn't developed any of the famous preternatural sharpness of the blind person's other senses, a sharpness I suspect is simply an increased attention. She has not heard the rattle of my keys or the door opening.

"It's not Saul," I answer. "It's Grace. I'm home." I go into the kitchen. Riva is standing by the table. Defenses go up and then her face softens again.

"I'm practicing how it will be."

"Oh, Riva!" I go and hug her, a thing I seldom do except ritually, on the Sabbath. "The doctor says it won't ever get pitch-dark like that!"

"He also said in a way it was a shame, because if it did get dark, I would have to learn how to live in it, and this way I bump along not blind and not seeing."

"You heard that? I didn't think you were listening."

"I wasn't but I heard it later. I heard it tonight."

"Will you let me call the agency now and see what they want us to do?"

"I'm so old, I'm afraid I'll fail—"

"The way you've failed all your life? The way you failed to come to Gilboa to a stranger and make a marriage? The way you failed to learn the language, failed to raise three good chil-dren, failed to make decisions about what to do when Elia died?"

"I was younger then—coming here. It was hard, but I was younger—"

"Listen, Riva, on Thanksgiving you told us about a fool of a girl who left Shedletz at the age of fifteen happy because no one there had ever *heard* of Gilboa. Now you're going to pay for your big mouth. I'm nuts about that girl. I won't let you sell her out, and make no mistake, she's still somewhere inside you. It's time to move on, to move to a new country and learn a new language. Do it, or that girl will hate you."

She stands in the middle of the floor like a deer caught in the headlights of a car. Her eyes are wide, one hand at her mouth. "I'll think," she says, "I'll make a plan."

"By Passover?"

"Yes, by Passover. Now let me do what I was doing. Go to sleep and let me be here." I hug her again. "Why do you hug me now—I never—we don't do that so much."

"I realized you can't see now when I'm looking lovingly at you, or smiling."

"Oh," she says, "then it isn't pity?"

"You're not the type."

I leave her and go back and turn out the hall light. In a moment the kitchen goes dark also. In another there is the scraping of a chair. I'm so tired. Trying to convince someone of something is the hardest work I know. I will lay it all down to sleep. When I sleep, it will sleep too, the trouble.

On summer nights this town is still close to the vast silences and wonders of the stars. Few lights are left on after midnight. The sky comes down, the hills move close. One can lie on the front lawn and fall into the sky weightlessly, wheeling and dancing, or be caught in the bed of leaves at the top of our maple or the Caetanos' willow and ride like a bird as the wind takes the branches. Ben and I are small birds nesting in one another's plumage, riding the leaves—

I snap awake. An alarm? No—what then? Something, something forgotten, done or not done—I can't remember what. It has awakened me without giving itself a name and now I can't get back to sleep. Turning in bed I find I have grown an extra arm. If I lie on my back, there is no place for me to put it comfortably and it weighs on my chest. I turn on my left side. That throws full weight on the left arm and the shoulder begins to ache. However I turn, there's no place to put the extra arm. What adds rage to discomfort is that I will face the morning gritty-eyed and dry-mouthed and have to patch the day together. There's nothing to do but wake up my ghosts and make them keep me company. "Take delight"—you said it yourselves. Why not? The best people tell us that the future is a nightmare, yet to be lived. No fuel, the ozone layer busted, nuclear war, nuclear death, total destruction of the environment or totalitarian gray. Worldwide starvation. I love Saul, but he and I are going to have to do all that grim futuristic stuff together. Why shouldn't I sing a little wilder melody than was allowed in my mother's day?

It's the young man who speaks this time, waving his hand in a gesture I have marvelously re-created from my childhood. "What do you know about your mother's day? You think we were victims only of our persecutors even then? What if, God forbid, the total world's end is delayed twenty years? There you'll be, adulterous for nothing!" The older man nudges him. "Don't ask what if it doesn't come—what if it does?" And there they leave me in the wilderness of the night.

On such nights I pray for accidents. Let me work at least at useful things. Let me peer into the dilated eyes of Old Man Bluyot, one of our resident drunks, fallen in the alley in back of the Famous or under his own porch as he did one night in April, I remember. . . .

14

We begin to plan for Passover. As a matter of form, I call Miriam and invite her, although I know she won't come. She's excited about her own plans. At the Center they're having a WomanSeder. Instead of commemorating Moses and the Children of Israel, this celebration will feature their own liberation from the Egypt of male domination. To my surprise, she asks after Riva. "Riva's through the worst part of the prebeginning of the worst part. If anyone needed a woman's support group now, she does. It's time for her to move, to gather her forces. What would you say if we did come out there, the two of us? Small-town domestic life doesn't give her the variety of experience that the women in your group might. I'd like to see her meet a group of women who are on a different edge than she."

There is a silence, and then, "Mother, you don't understand; these women have suffered all their lives. They're not middle-class women. Many of them have been in jail. They're tough-talking blacks and angry Chicanos, ex-addicts and prostitutes, some of them—"

"Riva wasn't always 'middle-class,' and would any of them change places with her, with old age and blindness?"

"She just wouldn't fit in."

"You're probably right."

She's probably right. The "sisterhood" of Miriam's part of the Movement is as fussy as a covenanted country club. Riva has been tipsy twice in her life, in jail never. The strongest drug she takes is aspirin, her vilest word is "hell." But somewhere, since the true sisterhood of family is so limited, are the artificial sisters of a group, a center. Not now, not here, but somewhere and sometime.

Miriam has forgotten or never learned to love our seders. How could my feelings not have communicated themselves? I love the songs and the reading, old words never changing, great words about great hope. And the four questions. For years, there has been no child. Kimberley—I ask. "Mother, Kimberley's only six. She's not ready for the culture shock of Gilboa. She's used to a much different life-style." Right again. A small child all alone, lost in our life-style, would definitely be a bummer, a drag. All my longings are impractical and unfashionable. I wish my daughter good yontiff and hang up. Life-style. I didn't name *my* kid after a diamond mine.

The guest list: How many we used to be, how noisy and festive. Elia, who filled any house, expanding into it through the door; Riva, a younger, less frightened Riva; one or the other of Saul's sisters, her husband, their kids; Miriam and Joshua; Saul and me. I don't want the silence on this night, even though it's companionable enough. I start calling around town. I call older couples like us whose kids are gone, the Levines, the Jacobses, and Mrs. Rifkin, whose husband died last year. One couple is going to the children, one is having the children come to them. Mrs. Rifkin will come and so will the Jacobses, but none of the younger couples I try. Some are making their own seder; the Pinecrest couple is figuring out if they want to be Jews at all.

I go to get Riva to come with me to the attic and help get the Passover dishes. That act, more than the seder, is Passover to me. I have years to remember—my own mother and my sisters in Chicago, when I was the girl, and here in Gilboa when I was the mother and Miriam was the girl. Year after year we brought down the glasses and the dishes in boxes and put them in the cabinets we had cleaned. Before the most pious father strokes his sacred beard and begins to contemplate the ceremony of the season, the mothers have already begun it.

One of the mothers, though, is fast asleep. I think to rouse her and then decide against it. She's been trying to learn the house by feel all morning and later she'll learn cabinets and cupboards, too. I go up alone singing "Eliahu Hanavi" to get into the spirit.

But once up, I find I'm not quick to get the dishes. I haven't been back here since the day Saul and I half-did the cleanup and the place where we stopped still waits for me; disapproval, light as slutswool, sits in the corners. The Passover things are on the other side of the attic, where there is more order. When I was up with Saul, I put the boxes of family pictures over near them. Before I know it, I'm looking in one of them, my own early pictures in a box I brought here as a bride and haven't looked at since.

Here I am, seven years old, seven or eight, and how much I look like Miriam at that age! The expression is a little haughty too, but oh, how well I remember the outfit. It was a birthday present; I loved that plaid skirt and the white blouse and green sweater I got with it! I wore them to school until they were ragged and outgrown.

What was she like, that girl? Very romantic, if I remember correctly, and a fairy-tale addict. "Snow White and Rose Red," the "Twelve Dancing Princesses." She didn't know then what fevers and torments sexual tension could evoke, so her princes and princesses coupled only in metaphor, riding together on fast

170

horses and dancing on palace balconies through starry nights. How would you see my life now, Gracie? Boring. Boring, Gracie? What about the rescues, the excitement of night runs, red light, and siren? Icky. I laugh aloud. Wait a minute. There is something she would have approved of—Saul and I went to Jamaica on our fifth anniversary. Iridescent hummingbirds flew around our heads. We saw the very underground lake crossed by the twelve princesses on their way to their vast diamond-lit cavern. We, too, danced under the stars. What would she think, I wonder, about what I now contemplate, a romance with a tall, dark, and mysterious stranger. Too old. Both of us too old.

This Grace would be for the whip and the wall. Seventeen and puritanical as a Hawthorne goody. Here she stands face front, "proving" something. I had forgotten how rigid she/I was, but the stance and expression proclaiming Don't Tread On Me are more than half fear. Ben is "the right age" for her but he wouldn't have looked twice at this freedom fighter and she would have seen him as utterly irredeemable, a drug fiend and war deserter. To the wall with both of us!

Oh, look, here's Mrs. Grace. Shyer, much shyer than her virgin self. Where was this taken? Chicago? Good God, I forgot we had gone there that time after we were married. How anguished my parents had been! That was the time we told them our decision to live in Gilboa when Saul finished school. What about it, married lady, wearing her wedding crown invisibly, secretly, wherever she went? Your future self rides fire engines and mourns for things and people you haven't yet seen. What about this yearning of mine? Why not? The man is kind and wise. Times have changed. In the picture the shy face stiffens: it is inconceivable. There's still enough of the seventeen-year-old Grace in this twenty-three-year-old wife to cringe at the words *adultery* and *infidelity*. What bothered her, that newly opened, well-opened woman? Oh, yes, I remember now—the move to Gilboa and into the house of her in-laws.

What a surprise that was, and so much happier than the conventional wisdom, including parents' advice. Riva was the secret. She had never liked homemaking and was glad to give it to me. Instead of seeing me as an interloper in her kitchen, she welcomed me with open arms; when I arranged things to suit myself, she hailed it as a blessing. She loved having me there—so did Elia. It was only Joshua's birth that caused them to leave and get the smaller place nearer the store.

Look at this one—a young mother, harried and hollow-eyed with lack of sleep. The whole world has dropped to its knees to button and unbutton, to wipe and wash. Saul is a mountain. The universe is this house and the block or two we travel on good days. She was too busy and too sleep-denied to think about loving somewhere else. I look back at my seven-year-old self again. How shamelessly we romanticize our children. How easily we teach them to romanticize themselves and their life. If my case were to be submitted to these judges and all the others before and after, how horrified they would be. No matter that all those people shaded into me. The wind of their disapproval comes cold across my face. In the meantime, it's Passover. Honor thy fathers and thy mothers and thy selves. So I heft the box of Passover dishes down the stairs. Gracie hates habits, young Grace fumes at the hypocrisy of ceremonies, yet the Passover begins with this drawing of women all over the world to cellars and attics. In Chicago, I know my mother is even now busy with plates and menus for my sister and my brother and his family. I think I'll give her a call.

"How are you, Mama?"

"Fine. How are you?"

"Fine—I just wanted to say hello."

"Well, don't talk long, your last call we gabbed so long, I felt guilty. It's freezing here. I feel like I haven't been out in weeks."

"It's cold here, too. Miriam isn't coming in and Joshua is still busy with his religious convictions. Since I'm lonely for them, I figured you must be lonely for me, so here I am."

"I'll tell you, Gracie, it doesn't hurt so bad after a while—their going away, I mean. I don't miss you for weeks at a time, and then I get a terrible bout of it—like pain. So I call or you call, and I still miss you. Then I sit down and figure: She's healthy, she's happy, she's where she belongs with her husband. And, to be truthful, I couldn't live with you running around in a fire truck at all hours. The pain fades away then."

"I only hope mine will."

"Oh, listen to this. You know the Silvers; Ruthie is in my canasta club. Her son is Kenny, a brilliant boy—you remember I told you when he got a scholarship to Yale. While he was there, he started taking drugs and then he went all around the country from one drug place to another. Three years. And then he joined the Moonies—"

"Mama—"

"Wait. The point is, he was in that for three years."

"That's six years lost."

"Yes, that's what I'm saying. Ruthie came in last week looking like she'd stood on her head for a month. The boy is twenty-five; she didn't think much would change for him. Now she tells us he has quit the Moonies and gotten himself a job and is going to night school—electronics or something."

"I'm glad for her, Mama, really."

"Yes, be glad, and listen, don't write Joshua off."

"Oh, Mama, he fought so hard against learning Hebrew. Now he's soaking up Sanskrit because it's the holy tongue—"

"The last word has not been said on him!"

"No wonder the Lord doesn't know what to make of us. We're all junkies—hope junkies."

She is serious now. "There are worse drugs in the world. You could die a worse death."

I fight a sudden desire to ask her—to tell her about Ben. What would she say? I don't want to risk hearing fear in her voice because she would think I meant to leave Saul, to do something wild. I suddenly wonder if among all her years, years I see as boring and unfulfilling, there wasn't more than the bridge talk and the supper table and the market and the synagogue. "Mama, would you say you had a happy life?"

"It's not over yet."

"So far . . ."

"So far, yes. You once told me my life was boring to you, the clubs and the groups, but in our group we always felt we were up in the front of things. We raised money to support dozens of good causes. We dressed well and got out. In our group, you didn't let yourself sit home and get fat, although our houses were always clean and our children neat."

"Yes, Mama."

"Don't laugh; your grandmother didn't even speak English!"

"Mama, do you remember that plaid skirt and the white blouse you got me for school when I was seven?"

"No . . ."

"Well, it was my favorite outfit. Thanks for getting it." I wonder if Miriam has an outfit she remembers.

There is a silence on the line and then, "You know, a few days ago I was remembering something I wore when I was a girl. It was a blouse. I was nine or ten and for my birthday my mother made it. She bought eyelet—a yard or so of eyelet—and she sewed it on the neck and sleeves like a little ruffle and she threaded a red ribbon through it. Oh, how I prized that blouse. We were so poor, the eyelet and the ribbon must have been the price of a meal for them. Funny that we should both think of those things."

The night before the seder, Ben calls. There is a Jewish boy at Longhill; may he come also? "Certainly!" I cry; "even though I know what's behind it, that it will get you out of asking the four questions as the youngest one here."

He laughs. "I don't think he knows the questions."

"Do you?"

"I said them once years ago at my grandmother's, but I've forgotten."

"Let me write them out in English and he can read them over so we won't be springing anything on him. I'll come by in about an hour and deliver them."

"I'll come out."

"No, it's cold today. Where will you be?"

"In the main building."

I haven't been at the school during the daytime since the new buildings were put up. There is nothing to remind me of the communes or the fire except the one or two old outbuildings now remodeled into tiny houses. On the foundation of the old main house, a new structure has been built, but it faces to the east now, not the north. I drive up and look all around. With the change of the house's direction, the entire form of the area has changed and so, also, its feeling. I no longer associate the place with burning, filth, and death. When I go in, I am smiling.

They have tried assiduously to keep it from looking like a school or an institution of any kind. There is no "office," in fact, no one about. I call "Hello." There is human noise coming from various places in the building, but I hesitate to go looking. I cry "Hello" again, and this time three voices answer "Just a minute" from various places. One voice is Ben's. Suddenly, there are more people than I need, a young woman and two kids and another man and Ben. He introduces them. I've caught them all in the middle of their day and they're working to be polite about it. Would I like to be shown around the school? "No thanks, not this time. I just came by to drop this off." Ben is uncomfortable. Perhaps he wants me to see into his life here, too, but it's the wrong time. "I want to visit," I say, "but not today, and I have to get home and get ready for the seder. Besides, I'd like to bring Riva." I give Ben the paper and go. As

I drive the short way home, I have, like an afterimage, a sight of the girl—woman—who was there with him. She was small and dark with the modern figure, almost boylike, but what arrests me now isn't her size but her—location. People distance themselves in proportion to their intimacy and liking. Saul and I stand near one another, and God knows the closeness of our bodies is one thing I have had to be careful about with Ben. The girl (I have forgotten her name) was standing very close to him. I look again. Yes, she was. The image of them is trapped there behind my eyes.

The boy's name is Jason Bloom. Ben brings him precisely on time, and stiffly they meet the other guests. Saul tries to put everyone at ease while I finish with the table. They are strangers to each other and have forgotten that "ceremonial" doesn't, in this case, mean formal. Jason is terrified. I see that his love for Ben has betrayed him into coming much farther than he felt was safe. Ah, Jason, you are not alone. If I could ease your fears I would, but I myself hang by a stalk like yours, in a wind you have not yet encountered. Saul brings the guests to the table. We begin the service. Following our family tradition, the reading goes around the table except where the leader's part is absolutely necessary. When we come to the four questions, Jason rises, quivering to begin.

He is embarked on a course between the shame of having the simple words taken away from him and read by someone else and the terror of having to go through them himself. To his credit, he chooses the terror. It takes forever, but he is finally done and gratified when we applaud him. We are suddenly exiles together. Saul stops the ceremony and tells the story of his first time asking the four questions in Hebrew. I give my story, Riva hers, the Jacobses theirs, which, it turns out, they have never told one another although they've been married for thirty-five years. Mrs. Rifkin speaks about seders, but not the ones of her youth. Her comment is about the voices of the questioners changing over the years, little by little, until they were deep and there were no children at the table.

We go on and then we sing. Ben doesn't know the songs and the Jacobses know tunes that are different from ours, but we limp along and where there are two versions, we let people sing theirs also. Then we eat the ritual meal and the actual one, and we tell more seder stories. Riva tells about the seders they had in Shedletz that were, she says, full of rules but no more pious than what we have now. She remembers the famous matzo balls of her grandmother that were made year after year with great pride and that the family ate for forty years without telling Grandma they tasted strongly of soda.

We finish the ceremony, then we sing some more. In the middle of a song, Ben sits bolt upright and when we come to the end he cries, "I got it—I know it!" It's broken, fragmented, full of mispronunciations and corruptions, but it is "Chad Gadyo." As he sings it, I tell Jason the words in English. It's a song children love—stick beats dog, fire burns stick, water puts out fire—it doesn't matter if they are taught the mystical and historical meanings behind these metaphors; they see the great circle of the world from the tiny deed to the universal mystery of God's orderings. Jason sees it. Ben must have, to have remembered all these years. We sing with him, clapping and stamping. Mr. Jacobs sings a version that includes little imitations of the animals—ga---d-yo bleated like a lamb, *chal van*! barked like a dog—and Saul, a seder leader again when he thought that time was over for him forever, raises his glass and says, "I would like to toast this holiday, the oldest continuously celebrated religious ceremony in recorded history." I know he is speaking to a son who cannot hear him, or at least in part to that son, over the miles and the landscapes that separate the generations. I am looking closer, here, where the remnant is gathered. I see Ben and Jason smiling at one another. Mr. Jacobs begins to sing

"Who Knows One," a counting song, clapping and stamping. Ben and Jason sit silent. "Come on," I cry, "sing the tune if you don't know the words!" Jason begins to clap halfheartedly. It's all too strange for him, too sudden, the foreign language, the strange rhythms and tunes. I look at the child who doesn't know any of the songs, and at Ben, who knows only in a mangled way. Remnants, shreds. Can such shreds ever remake the garment?

On Sunday, Geri and Rita come to kidnap me to Cosmos. Cinema Two has started to play old movies on Sunday afternoons and the center has several new shops we haven't seen. The towns are closed on Sunday and the malls make the most of it. I need the diversion; Saul tells me to go. He's glad to promote me in some feminine enterprise at last: shopping with the girls—so much more fitting than rescue with the girls. So much less dangerous. We banter it back and forth, and I realize it has been some time since we were lighthearted enough to do that.

I cannot share my preoccupations with Saul. Ben and I have been on five or six runs together, but never alone. He's waiting for me, wondering why I can't say what I yearn to say and do what I so hunger to do. I wonder, too. Why shouldn't I be liberated and modern and free? Two cheers. A cheer and a half. Only in daydreams have I been free, gloriously free, to laugh and make love. In common daylight, I look at him over the fences of his life and mine and yearn.

Elaborately "off duty," we pile into Rita's car and head for Russian Grove. We have until three, when Geri's friend will pick her up and take her to work. Years and years ago, I used to watch farm people coming into Gilboa on Saturday morning with hours to spare. Some of them had such eagerness, such eyes for everything, making the most of the day. We go to the new import store, where I see plans and wool for an Aran sweater. I buy two sets, although they are expensive. We eat lunch at what used to be called a tea room; we talk and laugh. Ghosts of my mother's luncheons rest lightly now. I, too, have changed. "If we hurry," Rita says, "we can make the movie."

"*The Vampire in the Girls' School?*"

"No, the golden oldie in Cinema One—*The Graduate*."

"Isn't that the one—"

I remember. Mrs. Robinson seducing a boy. She is a python, he a mole. She looked better at forty-six than I did at thirty-eight when I saw the thing, but she was ophidian, her eyes glittered lidlessly for him. It was all a good joke, the lovely young people fleeing, as they did in the fairy tale, from the witch. "You two go if you want—I'll meet you afterward."

"Oh, come with us, Grace, it's a good movie."

"*Good?* It panders to every young person's martyr-picture of himself, it's *mother* as an adjective. It's unliberated and mean-spirited. I will not see Mrs. Robinson cornering her furry little prey in bedroom after bedroom. I won't watch one more middle-aged-woman dirty joke. I—"

They are looking at me with startled eyes. I get a sudden picture of the time I was nine when a guest passed a plate of eggplant salad to me and I cried "Gaaaach!" and clutched my throat. My mother smiled a somewhat brittle smile and said, "A simple 'No, thank you' is sufficient." I have been sufficient. Far more than sufficient. "I'm sorry, really," I say, "you're treading on a cherished corn. It's Ruth in *The Pirates of Penzance* and Katisha in *The Mikado*, it's everyone's comic relief, but just because I'm sick of it is no reason why you shouldn't go. You kids go along and see it. I'll hang around and do some more of these stores and we can have coffee afterward before Geri has to leave."

They won't hear of it, and after arguing back and forth a bit, we all go to another group of stores where I feel duty-bound to buy a few more things. The spontaneity has evaporated from the day, thanks to me. I could have gone and kept my mouth shut. I could have begged off more gracefully. Too late now. At three we go with Geri to pick up her ride, and to make amends, I take Rita out for coffee. Cappuccino, whipped cream, and booze. Very elegant. Too late to flavor the afternoon. "I'm sorry," I say again. Rita shakes her head.

"Frankly, I'd forgotten the details of the damn thing. I remembered Dustin at that awful party and some of Mrs. Robinson. If I'd thought it out before, I never would have suggested—"

"Just that old bad parent joke . . ."

"Come on, Grace, I know you're in love with Ben Sloan."

Silence. I can hear the pulses trying. Death must feel like this when it begins—no blood to the brain to think with; I hang in the moment, impaled on nothing, thinking nothing, not breathing, not moving. Then, the body decides, chemically: air hunger, and the heart slams down on its treasure of blood and the valves cry, "No escape!" and the billion capillaries pull and the blood pours into my face and Rita goes black-red in front of me as sight is overwhelmed in all the blood I blush with. Rita, in front of me, smiles and shakes her head. "What a poker player you'd make, what an international spy! Drink up, Mata Hari, we're only signed out 'til five."

After a moment, I can speak. "How did you know? God, Rita, does it show so blatantly? Who else knows?"

"I don't think anyone does but me. Geri is so turned off men and so busy with her own man-woman problems that she doesn't see most of what goes on. I think the others on the squad think of you in a different way—they've already classified you as married, settled, and they no longer look that closely."

"I counted on that; it's what makes the universe dependable. What made you see it?"

"I'm single, remember. I looked at Ben for a while myself. He isn't my type, but I watched him and that meant watching you, too."

"Yes, I'm in love with him."

"Feels good, saying it out loud, doesn't it?"

"Yes."

"I don't mean this to offend you, but you know you're awfully cute. That blushing. I think it's sweet."

"Homemade vanilla ice cream. And as bland."

"You know he's got it on with Whatserface—the art teacher up at the school . . ." Another silence, and the picture of them together that day, close together, and one or two comments—someone seeing them hand in hand—

"I thought so, yes."

"Does it make you jealous?"

"No, sad."

"Sad?"

"I can't say why, I haven't thought it out yet."

"He hasn't, uh, made comparisons, has he?"

"We haven't slept together—not yet."

"Oh, I assumed you had."

"Not modern, as you said, not modern at all. Tell me, while you've been looking, what do you think his feelings are?"

"It makes me a little jealous to say this. He cherishes you. I think he cherishes you."

"Then what about Whatserface?"

"Why does one person have to satisfy all the needs of another person?"

"How do I love thee, let me count the people?"

"Grace, sex just isn't the commitment it once was, and actually, neither is love."

"Good God, I feel like Rip Van Winkle. Where have I been all the while this was going on around me?"

"Happily married."

"Touché."

"Oh, yes, need I tell you I'm a legal secretary—"

"Nice precise mind—"

"I know so many secrets about people in this town that they all blend together. Yours, too."

"It disgusts me that I've been wearing it on my face for you to see."

"Why think of it as your weakness? Why not think of it as my strength—that Rita is damn perceptive."

"O.K."

"And stop looking so miserable. Nothing's changed."

"Then you're not so perceptive after all."

Riva is ready. She has banged her shins too often playing blind. She has been through terrors waking and sleeping and has grieved in a thousand ways. I've not been wise or even clever, but I've kept before her a picture of the woman I knew when I was first married, a woman of curiosity and courage. Thank God for myths. She will dream herself into the picture that will sustain her—the courageous mother, the peasant survivor, the great lady. Sometimes it's all there is in the dark. I have lied her into a heroic image and she takes up the lie and consents to go on living. All I have to do is to be careful not to trap her in the lie, or bind her with it too tightly. Together, we make the call to the agency for the blind. The news is splendid. They will send a teacher, blind or sighted as Riva wishes, here to Gilboa to teach her the ways of survival and mobility. We won't have to go away to a school and live there. Riva has been silent on the extension phone during the early part of the discussion. Now she says, "You mean I'll be able to live on my own—all my own?" I feel a pang of hurt. She sounds so eager for it. Who is being stung by the myth now? Two minutes a bird and look at her flying!

"Oh, yes," the phone voice says, "if you have no other dis- abilities. Most of our clients prefer independence."

"Independence," Riva says. "Yes, I'll take that plan." They set a day and a time together.

It means that she will be going back soon to her own apart- ment and that I'll be free to indulge my passions, whatever they may be. I had dissembled to Rita, about the knowledge of Ben and the young woman. It was true that I had "seen them together," but "together" spares me too much. He's young and young people nowadays go easily into and out of sex relationships. It's a difference, one of many, between our generations. If I want to play in his green meadow, I will have to play by his rules.

It may not be so easy to leave my reality for his. I don't understand his rules or his limits. He lies too easily, he has sex too casually, he is the heir of a world far different from mine—tolerant, a little chilly with independence, but dependent in ways I never was. He expects not only survival but infinite possibilities and a freedom of choice almost an absolute, like freedom of speech. There are only legal limits, which he can break by choice, no social ones. Because nothing is forbidden, no one can break a rule. There are no tragedies, only "problems."

And then there is his gentleness, his generosity, his kindness and fairness, his ready laughter and hunger to learn, his wonderful body on which no compromises have yet begun to drag. I'm thinking all this with my face in a book, sitting beside Saul in bed reading. This is one of Saul's favorite times and of all the things he dislikes about Gilboa Fire and Rescue, the worst is the disruption of this quiet half hour of his day. Our movements together are familiar and matter-of-fact and we savor them. If—when—one of us dies, the other will have no more brutal moment to face than the nightly turning off of the light. Good night Saul, good night Ben, good night Mrs. Robinson cornering her prey, Katisha comically ruining her mascara with grief. Good night to the three Howards: Leslie, Shemp, and Catherine. Ben would not have heard of any of them.

15

I remember the Howards, especially Shemp and Catherine, to add to my collection of tables of bridge. On our honeymoon, Saul and I thought up that game, and every so often one of us thinks of a new set of partners to add. The idea is a bridge tournament played by couples. At one table, for example, are the Franklins, Ben and Aretha, playing the Browns, John and Molly. The point is to make the most improbable matches one can, and of course, male and female. I argued for months over my favorite pair, the Marxes, Karl and Groucho, but Saul would never allow it. It's easy to get prominent men—it's the women who are the problem. Shemp Howard was one of the Three Stooges, Catherine was a wife of Henry VIII—which reminds me—Catherine and Jack Paar.

There is a softening in the wind, the water of melted snow doesn't run in the channels; it seeps into the earth and the earth swells, and the heaped banks break open to reveal the softest of green shoots. Miracles begin. Storms of freezing sleet and blizzard wind beat at our borders and when they are past, our most fragile cherry branches still bear their clusters of blossoms translucent as the membrane in an eggshell. All the old people in town congratulate one another. In a month the knotted knuckles of arthritic hands will lie open in the warm sun, the bones will forgive their owners the insults of winter, doors will open and windows for the sweet breeze to run free in the house and chase the slutswool under the beds. It's a hunger as keen as pain. Every late freeze fills me with anguish for the freeing spring. Now when I can almost see it over the rim of next week, I yearn for it more than ever.

Riva has begun what she calls her "blind lessons"; Saul is busy with a new line of sport and jogging clothes. The fire department wants a new truck. Riva's little readers come in their delicate spring clothes and tell her they cannot read for her this summer; they are going to camp. I will have to search again.

And Ben. When the hills get green, we'll walk up over town and down the other side into groves that lovers stopped going to when the car came to Gilboa. Once or twice we've been alone but it's been weeks since our talk and I've looked longingly at him when no one else was looking and he's called me twice on small details and we've stayed talking about everything and nothing.

Geri and I are cleaning up the ambulance one afternoon, restocking after a run, when C.A. comes by. As fire chief, he's often at the station when we are, but this time I sense he has come because we are there. He's still not entirely easy with Geri and begins with me instead. "Hard run?"

"No; as a matter of fact, it was your nephew, Bob Ray. He was messing around on the little kids' playground at the school and got beaned with a swing. He was O.K. when we got there; we called Marice to come take him home. Then, of course, we got a bunch of complaints—toes, noses, fingers. They all wanted to come into the ambulance and have lights shone in their eyes, too." C.A. laughs but I can see he is uncomfortable. "Something you wanted to see us about? I hope it's not something bad."

"Depends on how you look at it. I was up at the town council meeting Wednesday and they got talking about the good job the groups was doin', fire and rescue both, and the end of it was they want to give us some kinda token of appreciation—"

"Money!" I clap my hands. "Oh, C.A., tell me they'll get behind a fund for some power equipment—"

"No, they want to give us a party."

"Oh, shit!" Geri cries. I can see C.A. wince delicately, but in principle he agrees. No one understands but our own people. There are no social differences at work; it's one of the charms of the job, but when we aren't working we fall into the same natural lines as the rest of town. The church choir is the same and so is the Garden Club. Friends find one another. C.A. admires Ben's skill at an accident, but they have nothing to say to one another at a party. Orley Flett has made his accommodation with Ben and his "morons" for the sake of the job, but he has strong feelings about Geri and in his private, honest moments, about me, too, a woman wearing a man's clothes and doing man's work. With this party, the council wants to give lip service to a myth about small towns, a peaceable kingdom myth that town people have heard on radio and television for so long they feel they owe it to themselves to try to believe. If the "party" was cake and coffee, pretzels and pop, beer and ale supplied after a meeting or a bad fire, we could sit up in the firehouse for an hour and tell one another war stories and feel honored by the town and the town council. Alas, such is not the plan. They want to give us an "evening" in the town hall, husbands and wives and kids, Saul and Riva, hose and heels, suits and ties. Ben and Orley. Geri and Orley. C.A.'s wife, Jeannie, who personifies my definition of the term *ninny*, and all of us dutifully "mixing" to please the town council and bear witness to the myth. Some myths are simply boring.

"Oh, C.A., did you plead for us—did you tell them?" He looks at me hopelessly like a shaven dog.

"I couldn't tell 'em straight out—I said there was things we needed. I asked 'em could we put it to a vote, a party or some-thin' practical, and they waved their hands like the Holy Father does when he blesses people, excuse the comparison." I love the comparison. I immediately put Mayor Blair in the papal purple and Tom Bisoglio in a cardinal's hat. It makes my day.

"When is this mistake to take place? Nothing personal, C.A., but as you well know, Saul isn't wild about my part in this business. I doubt I could get him to spend fifteen minutes at a party for it."

"Nothin' personal, Grace, but I see his point. I'd think twice about lettin' Jeannie go out all hours and me home diggin' sup-per out of the freezer."

Beside me, Geri stiffens. Doesn't she know by now that Jean-nie Bordereau never wanted anything but a big strong someone to admire her and order her every move? C.A. is unconscious of his gaffe. "The thing's to be Saturday week." He stands there looking so wounded and guileless that I want to hug him and then punch him in the nose. Saturday nights are his square dance nights, and but for fires and rescues, C.A. never misses one. Duty versus love.

I decide to boycott the event. I am the toy of passion, the slave of time, but I don't figure I owe all that much to the town council. Perhaps Saul will want to go for appearance's sake. Ben may see things another way. I need an excuse to be with him. I'm trying to think of one when he calls and asks if he can come over. "Yes, of course," before I know I have said it. This visit will be different; he always came in the late afternoon with Saul expected. This is the early afternoon. Last month, it might have made no difference. There was nothing to note about the time. Now, I feel it. We both do.

We can't stay here. We should get a couple of old quilts and go over to Violet's house. Weeks ago I dug up the key and put it aside. The day is warm. It reminds me of a woman early in pregnancy, breathless and somnolent, milky and a bit swollen and breast-tender. I putter around waiting for Ben. Here he comes up Bullwinkle Boulevard. Could anything be more innocent? He is jogging. Up the middle of the street he comes, thinking of nothing but his rhythm and his pace, intent as a marathon contender. I love and crave him beyond all reason. I ache to be with him in Violet's attic, but we need an alibi for the afternoon, so first, the firehouse.

"Hi," he says.

"Hi," I say.

We want to kiss but don't. "Walk to the firehouse with me and let us murmur sweetly as we work on the rescue truck that hasn't been restocked since the last big run. Then, I have someplace else to take you."

A quick look and he understands and says, "Good idea," and we walk slowly to the firehouse where the ancestral faces, proud and solemn, can look upon us. We talk desultorily about the school and the runs we've made, and he says, "Have you decided?"

I laugh. "Yes."

"But you have—uh—reservations?"

"Compunctions. I have feelings about infidelity and you don't understand that, do you?"

"I don't know much about infidelity. If you ask me what *fidelity* is, I think of loyalty. It's a word they use in wars a lot—loyalty to the corps. It means you have to swallow anything they give you."

"And in marriage?"

"I guess it means only one expression of love—"

"You would say 'experience everything,' but people who do seem to end with a terrible alienation. No one's ever managed to have community without fidelity."

"If there wasn't sexual jealousy—"

"The only way to be free of sexual jealousy is not to care enough. Make no investment and one draws no pain. That's too high a price."

"Are you thinking about Star?"

"Star . . . ?"

"The woman you met at the school . . . that I was with."

"Partly, yes."

"Comparing—are you thinking I would compare?"

"I'm not young anymore, not glowing with youth—"

He stops me. We've been putting clean blankets in the rescue truck and rolling up stretcher straps. I have a blanket in my arms. He has turned me to him, blanket and all, and he takes me by both shoulders. "I want to be with *you*, to make love to *you*. Don't ever, *ever* accuse me of being so young, so ignorant, so shallow, as to fall for the surface look of a thing and miss all there is beneath the surface. I did that when I was seventeen! Can you think of yourself that way, or me that way?"

"I didn't think—"

"You did think. You think too much, you weigh, consider, plan. *Be* for once, and trust our knowing each other."

These disguises my friends and I have put on—the crow's-feet and gray hair, the flesh, the drooping parts of us—for so long we have fooled so many people—I thought we had fooled everyone, and for odd moments even ourselves. He has seen through the disguise, seen past it to where, in the aging body, is a younger soul. Yes, but there's more. "There's more. Fidelity is a virtue to me, and the virtue a source of pride. I know I've been unfaithful already in my heart."

"Then the virtue is a myth."

"And the myth is the only way I can keep being the hero of my own life. The myth kept you from pimping and drug dealing. You said you were a good person basically, and good people live with 'honor,' 'honesty,' 'self-respect.' "

"I suppose they were loaded words—myths."

"Don't despair of them. How else could you force yourself toward what you should be?"

"And if you are so happy with that, why do you want to give it up?"

"Because I'm nuts about you."

"Oh." I see the intensity bothers him a little. I've never equated my myths—virtues of necessity—with passion or intensity. It surprises me.

"Some bad news." We walk through the drooping day and I tell him about the party. "I'm planning a subtle, very subtle, resistance: I'm not showing up. But if you want to come—"

"Not really. I know it's hard for C.A. and Orley and some of the others to take me. I like breaking down their objections but a party isn't the way."

"It wasn't our idea, it was His Eminence Mayor Blair and Cardinal Bisoglio."

"Where are we going?"

"On the back porch are two quilts in a plastic bag. Then we go to Violet Cleve's house."

"Who is she?"

"A friend who was. If this town has its sandlot Pope Leo and its bush-league Richelieu, it also had its Sainte Chantal."

"Where did you learn all that history?"

"College."

"Why didn't they teach it to us?"

"They were scared you wouldn't like it. They were afraid of you."

I hadn't been to Violet's house since the funeral. At first glance, it looks the same, but there's no lying death away. Some bushes have been broken down by kids and undermined by dogs. There's a side window out, over which a neighbor has put a board. We go in.

The ladies of the Garden Club are giving it their best. Someone has visited to dust and vacuum, but there are other forces at work—mice and rust and lovers and children. We go upstairs. There the rooms are formally arranged with the antiques there were in the house and evidences of Violet's sentimentality removed. I want to throw the quilts over her bed and be there with Ben, but when I pat the bed, a musty odor rises from it.

The whole room conspires against us—antimacassars and pillow shams. Ben shakes his head slowly and hefts the bag of quilts and we go up still farther to the attic.

It is narrower, darker than I remember it. Someone has eaten a package of Cheeze-its and the mice have gone mad over the crumbs. Bits of the bag are scattered on the floor. I look at Ben sheepishly. "It isn't as I had pictured it, and of course we'd have to get some more amenities—bring them in and take them out— I wouldn't want the whole town's lovers to troop over here; we'd have to reserve space months in advance."

He takes me in his arms. It's sympathy, not lust. We kiss and the feelings open. "Forget the house-hunting," he says. "You have no talent for it. Leave it to me."

"This is a small town—"

"If you want a place, I'll find one."

"Nothing at the school—" I could bite my tongue. We're standing facing one another, still holding, embarrassed. Then the sound comes loud and clear up through the main street. The fire alarm.

Sometime back, in the late thirties, a family named Sergeant lived for a while in Gilboa. They were very active socially. She was on the Altar Guild, of which church no one would ever say. He was a deacon and fair to be councilman. One night their furnace exploded. Flames burst through the roof, smoke poured through the windows and so did people. From the front, Mr. Sergeant, mother-naked as the saying goes, and a woman who was not Mrs. Sergeant, likewise. Out the back door came Mrs. Sergeant, bare except for long, black silk stockings, and with her the mayor of the moment wearing some kind of leather loincloth. It's a famous firehouse story, and now it lives again in reverse. Everyone knows we are both in town, and I didn't call myself out of service. We are dressed, thank God. We tear downstairs and out the back door, quilts and all. We've walked here and I curse the time wasted.

"You're the jogger!" I cry and throw Ben the keys. "Pick me up."

He's gone in a flash and by the time I'm at Federal I can see the car coming. Bonnie and Clyde. I get to the middle of the street and jump into the car. "I stopped in the house and got your turnout but I forgot the boots."

"What is it?"

"Factory," he says, "and working."

At the firehouse, we see that two trucks have already gone. There are extra coats and boots on the wall. We suit up and Jack and Lin Hoopes come and we climb into the big pumper and go. The fire is in the factory at the end of Tulip—the farthest building down where the western end of the town is cut by the freeway. As we come up, we look at what there is: It's all there to be seen, whole and all at once. No wonder men love contact sports; seen adversaries in an arena no larger than a factory or a ball field. C.A. is there already. The fire is in a little "L" addition built onto the body of the factory. This portion is showing flame all around; we will not save it. The problem will be to prevent the fire from spreading.

"It's the storage for their special chemicals," C.A. cries to us. "Protect the factory exposure!"

"Do you want us to use air packs?"

"Yes, but don't get close. Stuff's exploding and may shoot fire. Let's get it down first. We've got line backing you up. Lay your two-and-a-half!"

We lay heavy line. Even holding it is a two-man job and at the pressure we need to raise the stream two or three stories, three of us are working as hard as we can just to hold the hose steady. When the water is gone, we plug into the hydrant and go back up again. From time to time, explosions rip through the storage place, threatening our "side." We lower the stream and change pressure to hit the bottom floor of the factory portion.

Lots of smoke but now no flame. The place has been evacuated and the streets are full of spectators like waves flowing in too close and out again slowly. We move, gaining ground. By the time we have all the visible fire, I think exhaustion has dimmed my vision and then I realize that it's night coming on. Some of the men have put on safety suits and gone in. Heavy smoke in some places, they say, but no fire. We'll need to keep a truck on this all night because there may be a rekindle, and some of the chemicals are unstable. The factory superintendent tells us we are all lucky—a new shipment was due and the stock was depleted. C.A. is proud of us. The work was well done and the fire not arson. No deaths, no injuries. It is still hot in the storage "L" and, magically, some of the drums of chemicals have not exploded. The question now is how much effort should go into cooling them down. Too fast and they might explode. C.A. has called some chemical experts from Midlothian. The combination of gases liberated and formed in the fire and in the air could be lethal, and without the force of our water driving them away, they might resettle on us or someplace in town.

Ben follows the two men and asks questions as they test the air. I can only stare stupidly at them. I am too tired to stand. Wet and stinking, I begin to shiver as the night deepens. There are blankets under the seats on the fire truck and a supply of dry, packed, inch-and-one-half hose in the bed, and I lie down to rest for a while. The next thing I'm aware of is a strange voice, and of being shaken. "Who is it?"

"It's Orley—come get up." It is fully dark where I'm lying. All the truck lights are turned on the fire, but I see in the reflected light above me Orley grinning down. "Picnic's over, Miz Dowben, fireworks is done, and the chil-ren is gettin' ready to go home."

I sit up, still stinking. "I guess I slipped away."

He nods. "What's worse, them news media's taken some pictures of you up here."

I scramble up and stretch; Orley helps me down off the back

of the truck to go and help people load hose. A huge job is ahead of us. As close as we were, we have dirtied fifteen hundred feet of hose at least. It will all have to be broken down, cleaned, and hung, and clean hose repacked in the trucks, a crude house-wifery—it recalls the early months of motherhood when one learns to work in a haze of half-conscious exhaustion.

I'm surprised to learn that it's nine-thirty. We've been work-ing since three or so. Other trucks come in and we plan a schedule relieving one another at the factory. Ben and I to-gether, without thinking, raise our hands for the three to seven shift. I hope no one notices. We're standing on opposite sides of the room. I walk over. "Finish up here and I'll run you home," I say, "and pick you up at a quarter of." He makes a face. I do what self-protection needs to be done: "You look like the poster boy for a mine cave-in."

"Nothing personal, but have *you* looked in a mirror?"

"I'd give you a glove in the face for that, but I'm afraid it would stick. Come on."

I take him home. We're too tired to talk much and we stink too much to kiss. "I'll see you at a quarter of, clean and sweet-smelling."

"And fast asleep."

I smile at that. We'll meet in the dark and go down to the fire and take over the light truck from Claude and Orley. We won't touch one another and probably not talk much because we're still tired. Gracie, seven years old, is disgusted; Grace, seven-teen, incredulous; Mrs. Grace, saddened. Some lovers.

At seven o'clock we're off duty. Numb with tiredness and hun-ger, I ask Ben to come home for breakfast. He nods his head, unable to face the school.

Saul is cheerful over the eggs I have made. "I saw you people on television last night. It was pretty good coverage. They even had you sleeping in the back of the truck."

"Why didn't they have me pulling hose or show me on the line for four hours, I wonder?"

"Makes a cuter story the other way. More human interest. By the way, do you know who owns that factory?"

"No, who?"

"Will Burris—they used to live here in a house on Tulip. I went to school with him. He lives in Midlothian now, and about a year ago he bought the factory from Catlin. You must have seen him at the scene without knowing who he was. At seven or so he stopped by the store. I think he wanted to ask me about the competence of the department—he didn't know I had married into it. Anyway, I told him what I knew, and apparently his insurance company people said you all did a good job. We went out for a drink after I closed and we talked for a while. The upshot of it was that we are invited to a party he and his wife are giving in Midlothian on the fifteenth."

"The fifteenth—that's the evening of the town council's mess. Lovely. We won't have to hide under the couch with the lights off that night. We can go to Midlothian instead."

16

It's a large house in a section of the city I have never seen. All the houses are beautifully kept and substantial. We are suddenly conscious, as we drive down the block, of the clothes we are wearing, that they may not be right. My hands are clean but obviously work-roughened, like the lady in the dish-soap commercial. Even before we've found the place, I'm intimidated. There it is, huge, stone—lovely, really. Saul reminds me that we are here to enjoy an evening and nothing else. He went to school with Will and liked him then. Will had been in the Korean War and had been two years in a Korean prison. When he came back ("sick and rich"), he bought an abandoned shirt factory in Midlothian, which he converted to produce the then-new synthetics. About four years ago, he went into more specialized fabrics and got the plant in Gilboa to produce bonding chemicals of some kind. I'm curious about the chemistry because of the fire. Perhaps I'll get a chance to talk to him about it.

We go in and a maid takes our things. Ordinarily, I would be looking at such a room appreciatively but practically. It's a big room in a big house, a lot to manage; two in help, maybe three, but because I remember what Saul said about fear and failure, and taking second best in Gilboa, I see what I think he is seeing, a comparison from which, however inimical it is to his true wishes, he must be suffering, at least for the moment. So, I do not speak. Any word would be defense and any defense would be an admission of the reality of the comparison. So we stand until Elaine Burris comes forward and introduces herself and takes us in.

And there my comparisons begin. She has a svelte figure and her hair is coiffed stylishly. Her dress is lovely and flattering, the result of perfect fitting by a private dressmaker or of weeks of shopping. She walks beautifully. At our age, these attributes of form and style are not free gifts but hard-won virtues. Tennis, swimming, the gym. No home manicures, no greasy doughnuts at the firehouse. It will take everything I have not to fall into a Ma Joad parody because I, too, feel at the hard end of a comparison that, in so varied a culture as ours, shouldn't exist. Does exist.

We mingle, chatting, moving slowly, sampling the evening. The talk is party talk, but at a level well removed from my experience. Boats, trips, ski weekends. Guaymas and its hotels. Vegas, Acapulco. They don't discuss the features of these places, only the conditions. Sometimes I ask questions, sometimes I drift away. A man and his wife have just come from Turkey. She tells me where they stayed. Two men are talking about what they do to unwind. It's all vigorously physical and when asked about my husband, I mention that he does little more than walk home from the store. "Competition in my field is so stiff," the man on the left says, "that I have to get rid of the tension somehow." It allows me to ask him what his field is. "Specialized surgical dressings," he says. "Will and I are working on an idea." I ask him the name of his company. He tells me tolerantly that it is national, but so specialized that I'm not likely to know it. "Tell me anyway." When he does, I tell him I know his company well, but that since they changed their product we don't use it anymore. Now he looks at me, really interested. He asks me what I do and I tell him, and now he is very interested indeed and so am I. We are customer and merchant; no more party banter; we are into good, deep, animated shoptalk. We are enjoying one another thoroughly. He talks about price per thousand. I tell him the plastic backing on his dressings may be O.K. in a nice warm operating room, but it gets brittle in the cold, and his adhesives lose all their sticking power at temperatures below sixty. "Our new trauma dressing is meant to breathe and not to adhere."

"Yes, but it doesn't absorb either. By the way, *that* stuff does do well in the cold—"

"But it doesn't absorb."

"No."

"Whose product have you been using?"

"You won't like this . . ."

"Go on."

"When you switched to your new fiber, we bought up all the old stuff we could lay our hands on. We're still using the old stuff. God knows what we will do when it's all gone."

He asks me other questions; I ask him questions, too. He's excited about his new products. I beg him to make a line for street use. We're both sorry, I think, when dinner is announced. It means we will have to "mingle."

Now and then I look over at Saul and see him talking with someone. His lack of shyness with women stands him in good stead this evening. He has gone to the most attractive ones here. I'm happy, because except for my dressings man, the evening has been rather dull for me. He sees me and waves. Married message: She's charming but don't worry. I wave back and wander off to the buffet. The dinner food is very good but very rich. All of these women must be on diets, yet I see them eating here. Perhaps they starve for the week before and after; they're all so slender.

After the dinner, the rich dessert, the coffee with liqueur, Elaine Burris announces that we are to play a game. It's a party game they played somewhere else and it was a lot of fun. We're to separate—men on one side, women on the other. The things we are to do have all been written down, numbered, and put in a hat in the middle. The numbers are doubled so each man is paired with a woman and the "couple" will do what it says on the slip with the appropriate number. From across the room, Saul and I catch eyes again. He shrugs. I haven't played party games in years, but the group isn't ours—perhaps it's what people do here in Midlothian after dinner. I think back to the earlier conversations, and I begin to see the sense in it. We are not the only strangers; none of the people know one another—the men are business contacts of Will's, the poor wives probably know no one at all. It's a business-obligation evening and Elaine must have felt uncomfortable with our unsortedness and thought of this as a way to loosen us up a little and possibly to keep the man in the green vest away from the woman in orange and the big man in brown away from the bar. People are going up to get the numbers. Maybe it will be fun. Elaine is standing by the bowl encouraging us. "Don't be so lazy," she says, "you don't need any special skills." I go up and take a number. Sixteen. I hear a man call that number and I go over to him. He's a man I haven't met, a pleasant-looking man with a shock of salt-and-pepper hair. "Have you done this before?" I ask.

"I've played charades, but I don't think this is a charade crowd. I've never played this." We smile at one another. Our number says FREE ASSOCIATE. Elaine tells us that the words will be given to us when our turn comes. She goes to the center of the room and tells us to form a circle.

"Sit on the floor," she says. The men protest, the women don't, so we end with a combination of people sitting on chairs or leaning against the walls or on the floor.

The game begins. Couple number one answers its question:

What was your first job and how much did you get paid? I'm amused by the answers. The lady, coiffed like a movie star, was a pin-girl in a bowling alley in Coffeeville, Kansas. She got 75¢ an hour, raised to 85¢. He is Will's accountant, I hear someone say. His first paying job was as a soda jerk in New Britain, Connecticut, $1.25 an hour. The older men roar with outrage; $1.25 was prince's wages. Couple number two is asked what for each is his favorite time of day. For him, it's supper; for her, the hour after the kids have gone to school.

I'm having fun; the questions are personal but not intimate, and it's interesting to listen to people giving history and feelings they wouldn't ordinarily be telling a room full of strangers and to ponder, lightly, the incongruities of life. Number four is asked which was their toughest year. She says the fourth year, when the babies were small. He's my medical dressings man. He says the first year, getting work, and then about six years ago, moving out into his own company. Looking around, I think we must all be married couples with children. Number five's question is about their first "dwelling place," number nine's is about in-laws, and when they answer, Saul and I catch one another's eye. My wisdom about Riva and me was conventional and he remembers. Saul is half of number thirteen. They are asked about their happiest day so far. She says it was the day of the birth of her first child. Saul shrugs and says he remembers being very happy the day he came back from Korea alive and uninjured, his wedding day, his college graduation. But the day he is thinking of is not one of these, and not even a whole day but an afternoon and early evening last fall, walking with me over the fields in back of the town. We were remembering my time as a bride in Gilboa, mourning a friend, and then talking about the history of the hill on which we were walking, and there was later talk of some painful things in our lives, but even in the pain there was such a consciousness of—he pauses and then says, ". . . bounty; our health, our happiness, our gratitude. I guess that's it." It's a moving moment, and surprising to me because I remember the day well. It was the eve of Yom Kippur, the time of my Moonie, and a strange day of all days to feel bounty. I can't say any of this, but I think I want to save it for the ride back.

Before I know it, number sixteen is called. My partner reads the slip. "Oh, yes," Elaine says, "I have the words here. The whole point of this is that you don't edit. Just say what comes into your mind when you hear the word. O.K.?"

We nod, wondering, perhaps, if we should speak at the same time or one after another.

"*Whiskey*," Elaine says. My partner immediately says, "Relaxing." I say, "Drunk." We laugh.

"O.K., then, *poverty*." "Cold," I answer. "Packing boxes," my partner says. He looks surprised at himself.

"What does that mean?" someone asks. I start to defend us both. After all, we were asked to associate, not explain, but my partner shrugs and says, "We were very poor before my Dad died. We were always moving, packing up and getting out before the rent came due. When I heard the word, I got a picture of a cracked linoleum floor and packing boxes."

There's a cry from down the line. My partner's wife is pointing at him with a look of wonder on her face. "Oh God," she cries, "come to our new house and see if it isn't true. There's not a bare floor in it. I wanted cork in the kitchen, but he wouldn't let me—carpeting everywhere, even Astroturf on the back porch!"

We all laugh, kindly laughter, but I begin to wonder about this game. People's lives have hidden rooms, the doors to which may open more easily than they realize. I see Geri, shocked and almost destroyed by the sudden opening of a door in the too-neat house of a beaten wife. Years later she had forgotten the power of the nightmare behind that door, the power of a ghost still to harm. Is anyone so secure, even these confident and successful people? I look around. No one seems disturbed. My partner doesn't. Of course, *having been* poor is not *being* poor.

There is some cachet in having been poor and tonight his wife has learned something about her husband that she didn't know before. There are only two more words for us to do and only one more couple after us and everyone is interested, including me.

"You've done *poverty*," Elaine says, "what about the word *rich*."

"Lucky Lenore!" My partner's answer is immediate, and so is his change of mood. "Not a mistress, folks, sorry to disappoint you; it's our boat, our new ketch."

Elaine turns to me. I, too, am smiling. "I could say mink coat, but it wouldn't be true. The real picture I got was of a Sunday afternoon years ago when I was as rich as it is possible to be. I had four licorice rolls, the penny kind, a wax nose, a new Batman comic, and a long summer afternoon in which to enjoy it all." I look around. People are remembering. It's nice.

"One more," Elaine says, "I've saved the best for last: *love*." My partner says, "Family."

I imagine an arm flung out to keep someone from falling, only the arm is my arm. I say, without thinking, single words, one after the other. "Save . . . guard . . . protect . . . defend . . ."

There is silence. I seem to have been caught at something. At what? Someone titters and someone else says in a half-whisper, "That's so . . . so *military*." Oh no, lady, not military—maternal, atavistic, primitive, and for me, true. I could have said *sex* in this crowd and been applauded. My God, I could have said *Ben*! The thought makes me shiver. But I didn't say either of those things. What I said without thinking and now weigh in my mind is true for me, however unfashionable, however maternal, in a group that's trying to forget its age. Elaine passes on to the next couple.

On the way home, Saul laughs at me. "Protect, defend—my God, they'll never ask another fireman!"

17

It's 2:00 A.M. and we are home from the party. I'm sitting on the bed in a fog of feelings the names for which I don't know. I am an essential part of the happiest moment in Saul's life and wondering what Ben's happiest moment was, and knowing I'm not and never could be part of that, be our loving however wild and splendid, and there's my definition of love, which I just gave to a roomful of strangers. Saul is solicitous. He thinks I'm upset because I made some obscure social blunder. "Gracie, when people ask other people to reveal themselves, they have no one to blame if the revelations aren't what they wanted to hear."

"And you, were you surprised?"

"I can't say I was. You are a very tough broad, a survivor. You know what I remembered when you said that?"

"No, what?"

"Once when some older kid took a sock at Josh. He was about three then; the other kid was maybe five. You saw it and tore out of the house with a look on your face—you could have ripped that kid apart."

"They didn't understand that, did they?"

"I did."

"Sorry I didn't say 'Saul.' "

"At least you didn't say 'drunk punks on the highway.' "

"Good God, you're *jealous*!"

"Well, yes, in a way. Yes, I am. The thing I hate the most besides the danger is the Pavlovian quality of it all. The box goes off and wherever you are, whatever you're doing, you get that look, a sort of look, and bang, you're gone like a zombie. The worst weather, day or night, and there I am, left behind in some funny way, or some not-so-funny way, to pick up the dishes or go on with the party or make excuses to Mother. This is a time when we should be enjoying life, traveling, growing old gracefully."

"I want to do all that in twenty years. I don't want a make-work hobby. You're thinking of Violet now, aren't you—something nice like the Garden Club. But Violet's 'hobby' was integral to her life and the life of this town."

"I'm not telling you to stop this damn work of yours, I'm telling you I sometimes hate it and that I—" The alarm. The summoning tone, the piercing, edge-setting tone. Who says God has no sense of humor?

I look at Saul hard. "Do you want me to stay here and prove I love you?"

"No," he says. "No, no, no, go on the goddamn thing."

The call has come as "medical emergency," which could be anything. I wonder as I pound out to the car if the dispatchers do this to pique our interest. There is no way to think about a situation that is described in such words. All I know is that it is not a home address, but one mile out Cleve Road. That's long past where the blacktop ends. The road is washboard and a few farmsteads that will be lying somnolent under the moon. Has someone drunk himself into danger of some kind? A raped girl dumped on the side of the road? Maybe it's a baby to be born—

wouldn't that be nice! Looking, looking as I go, I finally see what it could be and I pull up behind a truck where a man stands waving. The truck's door is open and it's well off to the side of the road. The man comes over to the car, seeing my red light. "I 'uz comin' out my road there and seen this truck—I thought the guy was sleepin', pulled over like he is, but when I stopped, I heard the motor runnin'—" I get out of the car and begin to walk to the truck. The man follows. "I gone over to him and then I seen—I went and turned the thing off and left the door open and gone and called the sheriff."

The ambulance has pulled up behind my car. I call to Larry to bring the portable lights. I'm at the truck and touching the figure lying on its side on the seat. The touch is cold, even under the clothes. Our lights come on and suddenly the cab is lit up like a movie set. I tell Larry to stand the others down.

A movie set. A silent movie. The corpse is yellow, but the cherry-red carbon-monoxide-loaded blood is pooled in his dependent parts, the left side of his face, his left arm. I leave him and go to the back of the truck, a pickup, open in back, an old truck, dented and rust-pocked. I don't know why I'm going there—yes, I do, extenuating circumstances. There's the hose—it looks like a vacuum cleaner hose connected to the exhaust pipe. One wasn't long enough—he's gotten two and fitted them into one another. How neat it all is, how still, how carefully the circumference of the pipe has been measured. I can see him going down some list or other of replacement hoses. Look there, the boxes that the hoses came in are still in the back of the truck and so, I see, is the little glass cutter with the circle attachment he used, and my eye goes up to the window in back of the cab and a hole so neat and round that the hose fits it perfectly. How satisfied he must have been at such a perfect job. Rage is building in me, a cold, unfathomable rage, a rage so opaque and consuming that I cannot feel the night anymore, or hear my team around me. The rage is wordless; nothing explains it. People are moving here but I don't even see who they are. I am interested only in this satisfied soul. I go back to him and look again now that his stage is well lit, to see my fill of him.

Nothing has been left to chance. He's lying carefully, legs drawn up, gloved hands between his thighs. On his head is a knitted cap, a lovely cap, with a pompom; his jacket is well lined. It wouldn't do, after all, to get out here and be chilled. He's lying on a little pillow he has taken from home. It wouldn't do to get out here and be uncomfortable one's last time resting. He is not a day over twenty-two and so silent, so far beyond my hand, that I am conscious of nothing and no one but my own rage at him, now that I cannot heal him. I get up into the truck and look down at him and then I slam my hand down on him as hard as I can, once and then once again, and I scream into his dead, unlined, unmarked, unworried face: "You—savage! You selfish savage! The waste! The waste!"

In the world in back of me someone is calling. I want to ignore it, to pull this corpse down like so much scaffolding and tramp it to pieces, but I listen a little and I feel something behind me lifting me off the step. For a moment I think it might be Ben, but it's not, it's Claude. "Come on down from there," he says and literally carries me away.

It's forever, God knows how long, before I realize what I have done. For that time I don't hear or see, and the rage has its time with me. When I do come back, I'm walking with Claude outside the lighted wedge of the truck and the cars, the accident that was no accident.

"I shouldn't have slugged him."

"No."

"A rescuer shouldn't lose his temper at a victim."

"No."

"The EMT should treat a deceased victim with the care and consideration that he would show to a member of his own family."

"That's right."

"The book says that."

"The Yellow book says that. The old book. The new edition, the Orange one, doesn't say it."

Claude is still holding my arm. "Are you telling me that the Orange book approves of angry rescue workers beating up corpses that displease them?"

"I don't believe it's in the text. It must be in the appendix. The section on trauma says it's O.K. as long as you don't leave marks."

"I could get thrown off the squad."

"Possibly. Why don't you take a few cracks at me—no extra charge. I think you could use the release. Aim at my arms. All the books speak highly of that."

"I didn't do that, did I?"

"No, it's just an option."

"I feel sick."

"Want to throw up?"

"Almost."

"Listen, about leaving the squad. It would be O.K. with me, but then it'd mean that anyone with a weakness—anyone who suddenly finds himself going through swinging doors and meeting himself on the other side—any person who did that would have to get off the squad, too, and that would leave only Ellie and me and we're both busy during the day."

"What are they all doing back there—why don't they clear?"

"Waiting for the coroner and for you. They've been telling jokes about the victim because Bischoff noticed the hat and gloves he was wearing. They match. Hand knit. His mom, maybe."

Then I do throw up, suddenly, and afterward I laugh, bent over to avoid my own boots. "Lucky it wasn't a couple of hours earlier. We would have gotten a whole gourmet dinner, as the lady said, the white wine coming up with the fish."

Claude laughs. "You *are* a pistol—here's a Kleenex."

"How many people saw me?"

"I don't know. They all saw me pull you away. Most of them saw your face, that you were awfully mad."

"Claude, am I coming apart? This is so terrible."

He waits a long time before he says anything. He's a teacher, Claude is; he weighs his words. "I know what the bylaws say and the books too, but the coffee-room gossip is true, truer than the bylaws and the books. Everyone has something he steps back from. Not everyone takes a crack at a victim, but everyone has a weakness he trembles at. Your problem was that you didn't know what your weakness was. Now you do. Suicides. Successful ones."

But he's wrong, and I know it. This death is a metaphor, the way Geri's beaten wife was a metaphor to her and Faye Mellinger "trying to die" was a metaphor to Ben. The metaphor is not about death or freedom, it's about sons.

Now I'm trembling and cold. I've surprised myself twice in eight hours. Who would have known so set and settled a grandma could be capable of such surprises?

The coroner comes. Most of the squad has gone home. Tomorrow—today—is Sunday, and we'll all sleep late. Claude has seen that I'm all right and gone back to the ambulance to take it home. He's right about the joking we do—it's a crude truth, but true all the same. When there is a death and nothing we can do and no one to protect, kin or friends, we vent our helplessness on one another. A gallows-humor poster, *Last Aid*, has been hanging in the firehouse for months, as much a death-fetish as the desiccated claw the shaman waves. I tell myself a joke. Lucky this kid wasn't Jewish. I would have dragged him out of the truck and killed him again. Yentas of the world unite: you have no one to lose but your sons.

Look over there—it's morning. Time to go home. I get in my cold car in the cold dawn, quaking with cold. A person soon forgets how bad vomit tastes. It's always a surprise. I turn my head to pull out into the road and something brushes the side of my face. I put my hand up and find that I'm still wearing my pearl-and-diamond earrings from the party. A nice touch, with the red rescue coat and the face pale with nausea. I realize, too, that four words at a party of strangers last night and two slaps at a stranger's face this morning have decided my future with Ben. I have no words to give it a reason but it's there and the word is *no*, a "no" so dry and ordinary it could be any "no" at all.

I'm home by sunup. I take a bath to warm up and crawl dumbly into bed. How old I feel this moment and how truly one with the aged of Gilboa, for whom the winter is one long war against chills and drafts, winds and snows and bitter weather. I drift off.

Geri's calling. I've slept so long it's almost two. I've been speaking to her for a minute or two before I remember last night's shame, that there are sure to be repercussions and that they are sure to be soon. Is this why she's calling? It doesn't seem to be. She's talking about the town council's party. "About what you'd expect. C.A. and Rufus Ates brought along a little mixer for the punch. I was there with a man I met at Linda's. It was a real vintage party out of the fifties; the school combo played for dancing. You could see it was their idea of a geriatric dance program. Imagine their surprise, all of our surprise, when someone got up and did, actually did, those old dances the way they were supposed to be done? And you know who? *Orley Flett!* He danced with Janice Ates and Jeannie Bordereau. Orley is a gorgeous dancer—fox-trot, rhumba, tango, waltz. You should have seen him! Of course the food was very good—everyone's prize recipe. Eight kinds of pie. Jeannie Bordereau baked her peach whip-cream thing and didn't know how to cut it. That woman doesn't have the sense God gives bricks."

"I went to a party, too," I say. "I'll tell you about it when I see you. One of the guests was head of A.T.D., you know, the surgical dressing company—" We talk some more, desultorily. I want to tell Geri, but I'm not ready yet and the phone isn't easy for me. Later, when I see her. In an hour, she is calling again.

"Listen, Grace, the reason I called—it's about Rita. You were on this morning's run, weren't you?"

"Yes."

"I got the stand down and turned back, but Rita went. It was a suicide, wasn't it?"

"Yes."

"You didn't treat?"

"No, we didn't treat."

"Then what the hell happened?"

"You mean to me?"

"I mean to Rita. She called this morning quiet as you please and quit the squad."

I have been, this night into morning, angry, sad, ashamed, and resigned. I've felt nausea, betrayal, and the blind-deafness of rage. What is this terrible fear doing here? Who took the floor out of my house? "Geri—are you sure? What reason did she give?"

"No reason. Hello, how are you, I'm quitting the squad. I'll turn in my equipment, call box, and coat tomorrow. My reasons are personal. Good-bye."

"I want to stay here today; I need to be here at home," I say. "Can you come over?"

"No, I've got some people due any minute. Tell me."

I tell her, but not about Rita. I didn't even see Rita. I tell her about what I said and what I did and about Claude and his walking with me beyond the line of lights and cars.

"Could she have known the man, the suicide?"

"I don't know."

"I can't leave these people—will you call her?"

"Yes."

And we hang up. It takes fifteen minutes of circling the room glaring at the phone before I come around on it again and force myself to pick it up and use it. Leave the squad—how can she? Don't I know her work? Don't I work easily and comfortably with her? Don't I know her ways, her walk? Doesn't she have a place in the strange mixture of all of us that rounds us out and defines us?

I'm almost surprised when she answers and in an ordinary voice. At first we're shy with one another. "Geri told me you were leaving the squad."

"Yes, that's so."

"With no reason."

"Oh, yes, I have a reason—"

"I think I know what the reason is."

"I don't think you do."

"Can you come over and tell me—I need to be here today because of Saul and what happened this morning, but I need to know—we all do."

"I'm not sure I can talk about it—"

"Rita, we deserve, don't we, because of what we've done together all this time . . ."

"I suppose so."

"Then will you come?"

"You're not going to try to talk me out of this, are you?"

"I may—I have no morals, you know that, and my ethics are lying in pieces one and one-half miles out Cleve Road."

Rita laughs. "Lucretia McEvil."

"In a red rescue coat."

We sit over coffee. Outside Saul is working in the garden. We used to grow flowers, which gave us tremendous pleasure. Now, with the energy crunch and the money crunch and the environmental crunch we grow vegetables that are buggy, stringy, and tough, and cost more than the flowers did and give us no pleasure. I haven't told him about the run yet. He thinks my gray face is only sleeplessness.

"Rita, what happened?"

She looks at me out of her new eyes, sadder and wiser. "This isn't about you the way you think it is. I told you it would be hard. It's not a thing that has many facts, proofs, or witnesses; it's only real."

"Go on."

"My cousin, Angelo, was a combat photographer in Vietnam. He took pictures of men being shot and men walking in mine fields. It was because of his work that I realized that to show those soldiers doing those things, there had to be a photographer walking there too, standing up in the middle of it all, *taking* the pictures. I asked him how he could dare to do it, and he said, 'When I'm out there I get interested in the light, the angle, the timing, the composition. I'm not conscious of the danger because I'm not part of the war; I'm involved in my work.' That's how the squad is and how you have to be. It's how I used to be. Now comes the part that's hard to explain. Last month—do you remember the run with the couple, that nice couple who were sideswiped by the beer truck?"

"Yes, vaguely."

"Do you remember that when we were getting ready to load, another truck came by, out of control?"

"I was in the car with the woman. I didn't even see the truck go by."

"I was walking in the dark on shattered glass, smelling the wreck-stench. I had the gurney and I was coming back to you with it—it was hard to control because on that sharp downhill curve I had to be careful not to let it get away. I was walking near the side and I heard the truck and before I could do anything, and that's important—before I could think—it was coming down on me and pulling me into it, and there were handles, knobs, bolts that stuck out of the front edge and then the back that whipped past me, and I tried to pull back because what if I got caught on one of them, and then it was gone and the wind of it almost lifted me up to twist me and dump me down like so much wet wash. The power of it—the force—there was no choosing to step back or turn or run. When it was over I stood there for a second, shivering, and then I got busy loading. The cops had gone after the trucker and I heard later that they got him. I finished my job and we drove the people in and filled out the reports. I thought it was all over. I was happy and surprised at how well I had taken it. I went on runs after that without any panic—I thought there was no problem. Then, last night—"

"Me?"

"Yes—no—I'm not sure. It was dark and then we brought the lights and I saw you go up and then you screamed, or it was like a scream, and suddenly I started to shake and I was back again in the wind of that flapping awful thing, all the same thoughts and feelings again, that terrible panic. The ambulance was there, the police, but for me it was dark outside that little . . . island . . . of light the same way it had been before. Far away I could hear all of you buzzing like mosquitoes; I looked at all of you and you had all been shrunk up to tiny, tiny people running around in the tiny, tiny world you inhabited. It was a funny feeling to have outgrown you physically so that we could no longer even talk to one another."

"What about a leave of absence, time off, and then you could come back . . ."

"No, the trust is gone. Seeing other people's horror isn't like seeing your own. I don't have any . . . I'm not invulnerable like my cousin Angelo anymore, like all of you."

We talk about other things then, town gossip, the council's party. Rita asks me about Ben, and the sadness I have been holding at bay comes flooding in everywhere until I'm crying. When I look up at her to tell her that I know this is no way to comfort a friend, I see she is crying, too. So we sit and bawl for a while.

The next day I write a full description of what happened on the call and I mail it to Geri. The words are precise and dry. No explanation, facts only. Claude calls to tell me he is also writing his version of the event. The normal penalty for such an act is dismissal, but they know I know what I've done and would never do anything like it again, so they go to the next punishment down: suspension, sixty days. Saul is infuriated. How dare they judge me at all, after what I have done for them, the work, day and night, the sacrifices, the training! "Darling, what if it had been your son, helpless because he was dead, and a rescue worker hit him twice?" "The dead are beyond help, beyond being hurt." He lies in my defense. Part of his anger is at me and we both know it. If I didn't do this work he wouldn't have to answer such questions.

On Thursday, Geri calls me and tells me that I've been suspended for the maximum time, but since a sixty-day suspension would take me into late spring, our very busy season, and the Ochsners are on vacation and Ellie's mother is ill, we're too short of personnel for a sixty-day suspension and I'll have to take ten days instead. I accept it, knowing it's for longer than ten days, longer than sixty. People will watch me for years, perhaps, at suicides. They'll forget how many I've seen before this and that I acted "appropriately." On the first day of my suspension, I deliver my badge, rescue coat, key, call box, and light to the firehouse. Then I go to Longhill with a note for Ben. I ask him to give me the ten days of my suspension as time alone. I need silence and withdrawing for a while.

Ten days later, a Sunday morning, I find the key lying on my mat. Someone has rung the bell and run away. I take the key and go to the firehouse. There is no one there. Inside, on the captain's desk, are my coat, call box, and light laid out ceremonially. The badge is on the coat. There is a cake on the call box and a knife is stuck in it. Ellie—it has her touch. The cake says WELCOME HOME. People come by all morning.

18

Gilboa opens outward into the spring. The Garden Club gives a show and the high school graduates vote to hold ceremonies outside. Doors are open, curtains billow in the open windows. In the hills over town we fight the fires started by foolish campers. In the ditches and on the roads we look into the bleary eyes of boys on spring beer busts. Kneeling beside Ben on broken glass, I try to find a cure.

The love that dare not speak its name used to be homosexual; now it's maternal. We're supposed to "let our children go." I did. I am supposed to be content if I never see them or hear from them again. I am supposed to be content if they disdain my values and renounce my "life-style." I am to endure the loss of them out of my life, without a murmur. The popular wisdom says it's all for everyone's best. If this is to be so, then I salute you, Mrs. Robinson, tense as a basket-cobra, slender as a ferret. Go to your joys whatever, whoever. How many of your hungers are made of loneliness? You bore and raised a fashionable family, whom you were to love beyond your own life and from whom you were to expect nothing. No bargains in nature are so unequal. The inequality of it cries out for balancing in both of us, and in walks her little mole, and my glorious young man, bearded and handsome, smiling and warm, and ignorant of his weight to tip the balance back.

Is there any modern wisdom murmuring on the talk shows that says to us that the parental passions may be the ones displaced? I'm only now beginning to laugh when I think of the faces of the people to whom I said, "Save, guard, protect, defend." They were embarrassed. Better to have coupled love and lust. Better to have named six popular positions rapid-fire. Better to have had the affair before those words could come to stand before us, those wife-and-mother words, those knuckles at the breastbone, those virtues of necessity.

The squad and the fire department have a picnic on the hill in back of our house. It's a good-bye picnic for Rita, who at first didn't want to come. We want to tell her in our rough way that we understand and "forgive" her fear and want to say good-bye as we would for someone moving away. It's a lovely picnic; it represents us. Most of the firemen pitch horseshoes; someone has brought a volleyball net and there's a game. Some of us sun ourselves and read. We are separately together. I have brought some sewing and after a half hour of the volleyball, I subside gladly onto the sidelines. Ben comes and sits beside me. I tell him that Gilboa has a huge town picnic on the Fourth of July. "It's one month away so there's plenty of time to plan. Why not bring all the Longhill kids?"

"O.K., I'll see what we can do."

"We'll help. Rita said she would, too. I don't want us to forget her just because she isn't working with us."

"I think you decided to forget me," he says.

I look at him and smile. "Never. I will never forget you. But I've had some time to think—"

"Thinking is a mistake," he says. "Only feeling isn't."

"I am feeling, and what I feel is love. That's not forbidden to me, only its sexual expression is."

"You're talking like a Victorian heroine."

"I am no one's heroine, but I have the words of other generations written all over me—one hundred years of unerased graffiti. The words are faded, but clear enough to read."

"What's wrong with what we both want to do? Making love is an expression of love."

"So is this smile I'm smiling, so is my making you a Sabbath dinner. My shortest day, my dear, dearest one, is filled with love for you."

"But ultimately—"

"Are we at the ultimate yet—the world's last minute? Ultimately, we all die alone, but does that mean we all live alone?"

"Are you sure you're not just scared of convention, discovery, your own feelings?"

"Yes, and more, my own body, too, not a young girl's body, that you would see naked. Cowardice is civilization's good right arm, morality's major general. Do you complain of that?"

He thinks for a moment and then says, "No, I guess not, although that wouldn't stop me if I wanted someone." Then, "What made you decide this way?"

"You mean what changed my mind?"

"Was it Star?"

"Maybe a little."

"My relationship with her is entirely different from my relationship with you—"

"I know, but we missed one another by a generation and Star helped show me that. I also discovered that I was as much upset by her not being Jewish as by your relationship."

"*What?*"

"When I thought of you and Star together, I felt it as a metaphor."

"What metaphor?"

"Promise you won't laugh?"

"I promise."

"The physiological decompensation in traumatic hypovolemia."

"What?" He looks at me and laughs. "What are you talking about?"

"I knew you'd laugh. Tell me about hemorrhage—physiologically. Quote the Orange book to me."

"Well," and he shrugs, "if an artery is severed or an organ—a vascular organ—is ruptured, the patient loses blood—keeps losing it."

"Go on."

"The body tries to compensate by shutting down the peripheral circulation so that the blood is 'shunted,' in a sense, to the brain and vital organs. The heart pumps faster to get the available blood around the system faster. Are you serious about this?"

"Yes, go on."

"The pressure drops because there is less blood in the system. The patient breathes faster in an effort to get more oxygen to the lungs and so to the brain. These compensations are set off biochemically—you know all this, what's your point?"

"Your patient is still bleeding, Ben. You haven't treated but stood by and watched. Talk."

"Well, untreated he begins, sooner or later, to decompensate. He needs fluid but he sweats, losing further volume. He needs oxygen desperately, but his breathing becomes more shallow."

"You're doing fine. Keep it up."

"The part of the vascular bed that's open freezes wide open in neurogenic spasm, allowing more blood to escape. The acid-alkaline relationship goes way over into acidity and this renders the tissues and vessels permeable, and vital fluid seeps away all over the system. Your patient is dying. Beyond fifty percent of this fluid loss, no drug or transfusion can save him. What's this all about?"

"How many of our people died in the Holocaust?"

"Six million. I once heard that. It is the number, isn't it?"

"Plus the Jewish men from England and America who died in the war against the Nazis and in the Pacific."

"Yes."

"What percent of all our people?"

"I don't know."

"One-third. Upwards of one-third. And what degree of shock is a greater than one-third loss?"

"Moderate to deep shock."

"Decompensation?"

"Oh, yes, surely, if it's not stopped."

"The decompensation has set in. The loss continues through assimilation or the intermarriages where the Jewish partner leaves his faith, or to secular faiths, like humanism or ethical culture, or to other faiths—fluid loss through the now permeable membrane. We thought of Israel as a transfusion, but it won't save us. Its people are too embattled and there's no strong, moderate religious voice coming from them. There's orthodoxy, impossible for most of us, or socialist secularism. Well, Ben, what's your diagnosis?"

He watches me. "Emergency medical technicians are not allowed to diagnose."

"O.K., wise guy, your assessment."

"Deep shock—possibly irreversible."

"It wouldn't matter, I suppose, if the world was heading toward something better than the religions it has now, but there is no evidence of that. The humanists have tried again and again to invite the Jews sweetly to their Breakfasts of Conciliation. Remember the animals' breakfast? The chicken said to the pig, 'I'll supply the eggs if you supply the ham.'"

"What is this all about?"

"It's about the kind of love I have for you, which is as intense and deep as I have ever had or ever will have."

"But you don't want us to go to bed together."

"No."

"Why not?"

I don't tell him part of it would be incest; I can't. I don't tell him that I think God may be resigned to waste but I'm not, and not to the waste of the seed of an endangered species, literally or metaphorically. I only say, "Stereotypes are wonderful things. Mine is the nice middle-aged lady who is somebody's mother and takes soup to sick neighbors. It's not that I'm against adultery on principle, I'm just not the type." I am laughing for the sake of the ball players and the horseshoe pitchers who are near enough to see us.

"Do you want us to stop seeing one another?"

The day goes dark and my laughter stops. "Look," I say, "someone's dimmed the sun."

"I'd like to keep on being a Sabbath guest, a friend—"

I smile at him. "I have *arcus senilis* in one eye," I say. "It must effect radical changes in the vision because you look so beautiful to me."

"You're hiding behind your *arcus senilis*, your soup-to-sick-neighbor-old-lady-stereotype."

"You bet your ass I am."

The next day, Riva has the three of us over to watch her. It's supposed to be so that we will know and be comfortable with her new skills. It's really a performance, something to crown the slow, shin-barking, toe-stubbing, finger-burning work of weeks. It's heralded by a phone call she has dialed herself and includes a lunch, planned, shopped for, and prepared by her. She and the teacher pull out all the stops. They show us systems of marketing and organizing cabinets, food, and clothing—the message is always that a life without sight can be lived well with choice and independence. Nothing has been left out and Riva is careful for her public appearance now as she never was when she saw herself. The teacher stands aside as Riva serves her meal, then washes the dishes, and cleans the kitchen.

"So often blind people fear ridicule from the outside more deeply than an inability to survive in their own homes," the teacher says, "but as soon as we can show them that they can mark their clothing for color, and feel for the proper shoes, and not leave home with dirty faces or smudged lipstick, they fear going out less. Riva has a great deal to do yet, but she has mastered her home skills very well."

We are amazed, and say so. Ben is full of plans for her with his kids at school. Saul is happy, Riva herself triumphant. I am all that, too, and at the same time almost unbearably sad. Did I want Riva miserable and dependent? Never. Then what is it that makes me want to collapse on the floor in tears, to howl like a wounded animal, to tear my clothes and quench the household fires like a mourner? It's the loss of Ben and also something more.

It's spring. Look outside. The trees are in full green. Look around. The light in here is a spring light. Why do I feel funeral clothes flapping around me? I'm sitting with Ben and Saul on Riva's sofa. She and the teacher have taken chairs beside us. It's time to answer our questions. Saul asks some, Ben others. No matter that they are warm and comfortable in the airy room; I'm sitting perversely in the false November of a bleak interior landscape, and suddenly I know why. It has nothing to do with Riva's afternoon and everything. I want to tell someone but I don't know who would understand.

"Riva, let me ask you a question that's not about your training. When Miriam and then Joshua left, did you cry or grieve for them?" Everyone looks surprised. I know it's the wrong time for such a question, but why? Neither answer will shame her.

"Yes, some, I think," she says.

"Why didn't you tell me?"

"You would have thought it was criticizing you, that you were a bad mother."

"Yes, I suppose that's true."

"Did you?" Riva asks.

"I thought I did, but I guess not enough. They not only left me—us—they did it repudiating our values for those they said were truer and better and which did not include us."

"It was inevitable," Saul says. "We chose and they had to. Their worlds have wider possibilities than ours did."

"Maybe it won't be forever," Riva says, so that I must fight the impulse to kiss her, my Shedletz hope-junkie.

"Everyone has to find his own way," says Riva's teacher sweetly.

I look at Ben. He is looking at me. He is guessing part of it, only part. He is seeing me again as a mother, the mother of someone his own age. Now he understands who I slapped, into whose face I cried "Waste! Waste!" Now he sees why I will not change my mind in spite of all my love. I think he knows why there was an intensity in that love that seemed strange to him. For the shadow of an instant, I see incredulity in his face, and then it changes. He smiles a subtle, gentle smile and almost imperceptibly nods his head once.

"Don't be sad about them," Riva says.

"Then don't you be sad about being blind," I say, and we all laugh, the teacher, too, although for a second Saul glares at me. He's a perceptive man but he's unaware of his mother as a courageous woman. Because he's her son, he thinks of her as being less than she is.

And I know what's before me: the long, slow cure, the walk with Ben back into friendship, a slower way going than the way I've come. Drudgery of love. However kindly he forgives, it will give him pain that he has been, even subconsciously, confused with someone else, a metaphor. But he's not only that, not even mostly that, and I'll have to tell him without touching, without kissing, without running any rapids on tender afternoons. We return to Riva's lesson. Is June light really so flat, its sun so cold?

The Fourth of July. We are at the town picnic, drunk with exhaustion. All weekend we have been fighting the careless fires of little boys in backyards and high school kids in the hills. June was dry and the woods are dusted with moss spores and hazed with pollen. I have come to the picnic because the picnic is a tradition in Gilboa and because Riva, to my tremendous surprise, has asked Irene Savitt, her teacher, to come. I protested at first—the crowds, the confusion. "But the plan of it hasn't changed since 1950—" Riva said "—the food and the booths, the games and the people. I can still see enough not to bump into everyone, not to wave a cane around in the crowd." She and Irene have done it all, eaten the potato salad and the pies and the roasted corn, ridden on the fire engine, played games by the dozen, guessed the number of beans in the jar, been involved in the quilt raffle, sampled everything and talked to everyone. I am amazed, confounded. Sighted, she had never been so free or so unselfconscious. Where did this rebirth come from, this joy, like a tree broken from its roots in the hair-thin crack in a rock? God be praised! God, praise your Man! As the day goes on, I see firemen here and there dropping down like tired children. They lie curled up under the trees of the town square or in the fire trucks, cool in the firehouse, whose doors are open for the rest rooms, or warm on the courthouse grass where people have spread quilts and blankets to sleep off their lunches. Later, everyone plans to go to Midlothian for the fireworks, which are world-famous in Gilboa. Saul is taking Riva and Irene, hoping that Riva will be able to see some of it. I am "committed to the district" for the night's fires. In a blur of exhaustion, I seek my old pumper and hose bed and I am soon fast asleep.

Another Ben-dream. We are swimming in the underground lake in Jamaica, but the water, after the first cold shock, is warm. We soon become blind like the fish in that lake and more naked than the fish so that with all the lengths of our smooth bodies we may feel one another undulating through the blue gloom. The feeling is as funny as it is sensuous. Soon we are having a water fight, splashing one another. I wake up. Someone has put a fire coat over me. It is Rita, sitting beside me, smoking.

"What time is it?"

"About three," she says. "You were shivering so I put that coat over you. I didn't mean to wake you up."

"Is it a good picnic? I'm too tired to know."

"That's one thing I'm reclaiming now that I'm off the squad—unbroken sleeps; seven of them every week. I can plan days in advance and I don't have to prepare my dates for my not showing up."

"You miss us terribly, don't you?" I am laughing.

"I thought I would, but I don't. I never loved the work the way C.A. does, or Geri, or you, and when I almost got hit by that truck, the fear I had always had—it wasn't worth facing anymore."

"I've discovered that my truck wreck isn't worth facing either."

"You mean Ben?"

"Yes, Ben."

"I'm disappointed. I thought you were more liberated than that."

"What if this need I have isn't really a sexual 'need' at all, but a longing for which I have no definition? What if because I can't give it a name, I look around at the names that are available and give it one of those?"

"Grace, we all need love—"

"Yes, but a love so narrowly defined?"

"But we're all becoming more liberated—"

"Are we? Do you know in movies of the thirties men embraced one another and no one thought of homosexuality? In my mother's time, women friends linked arms when they walked and no one felt called upon to define the nature of that friendliness."

224

"You're denying—"

"Yes, yes and no. It's another paradox in a life full of them. For all our new sexual knowledge—" I've got my hands raised; all I need is a podium, when in come Ben and Star and two of the kids. He wants to show them the ambulance. We greet them, jumping down from the truck. Once again I try to look at him objectively, but am unable. Love isn't blind, it's astigmatic, blurring the edges, softening the outlines. As we kid and banter with each other, I am aware of his affection by how much my outlines are blurred to him. Then I look at Star looking at Ben looking at me. Because she's so young she sees me as even older than I am. Some of our kidding is faintly sexual and it confounds her. Ben sees me as ten pounds overweight; to Star, it's thirty. Ben sees me as having character in my face; to Star, it's lined. Ben sees me as regal; to Star, I'm old. I don't like her cold judgment and I would leave if I could, but it means sacrificing the warmth I have of him, in a summer that, just begun, is already flying fast, fast like twenty years of summers before it. Star is wearing tight shorts; her body is lithe and tan and compact and she is fashionably bustless and very proud of it all. I don't blame her, but I am reminded that youth is nothing in particular to be proud of; anyone who doesn't die before he's nineteen will live to be nineteen, and this helps me look back at her from eyes that do not reflect her scathing pity for me.

And Rita sees it all. Her organizing, evaluating mind is coolly gathering the exchanges, labeling and filing. Once I look at her and get a faint shrug-smile and know I should go, but Star, because she can't go either, is staying with a vengeance. She has begun to touch Ben, to run her hand down his arm, to hug his shoulder. I'm surprised that this causes me some pain. Love (guard, protect, defend) should be made of sterner stuff, but she obviously doesn't know that Ben and I have gone or are going carefully, cautiously together back into friendship. He hasn't told her. Gallantry. I could kiss him for it.

I walk over to the rack and hang up the fire coat. Nineteen is a

225

difficult age to be; she can't let pain enough alone. "Has Ben told you," she says, "that he's going back to school—in Chicago?"

Now I'm really angry at her. Whatever happened to all that sisterhood stuff the women's movement talks about? I feel as though I'm in a thirties movie with Jean Harlow. All I can do is play it straight. "Oh, Ben, really?"

"There's a new paramedic program up there; it's a career program. Working in the city, I'll be paid, and good money, too."

"When are you leaving?"

"I've been accepted for the fall. I'll leave in September."

"I'll miss you," I say quietly, "I've started already." He smiles at me and I have the additional delight of surprising Star. Honesty—ha, another old-lady trump. She imagines I should have more pride. There are so many other things I would wish for first.

Now, I'm free to leave. What was to have been done by Ben with a scalpel was done by Star with a hatchet and I'm free. The severing isn't over but it has begun.

When I tell Saul and Riva, they smile and are enthusiastic and we spend several minutes giving one another reasons why it's so good. Longhill isn't a career—the pay can't be much, and with his gift for children and his medical training, it's only reasonable that he should go as far as he can. You old hypocrites, you lie in your dentures! He'll take his laughing presence, his hopeful youth, his deft, gallant optimism out of your lives, too, but still you give lip service to the new conventions, you spout the new pieties. When he leaves, we will never see him again or hear about him. If and when he marries, no echo of it will ring in Gilboa. Touch and go, as they say.

Miriam's birthday. I call to wish her well. "What do you want this year? I send you sweaters, which you may not even need in California. You've never said, but you might want something else. I can't buy a film for you, but is there something?"

"Let me think. I don't use fancy clothes because it looks bad, coming in like queen of the Junior League when the people I work with all have so little. The film thing is over. We had something set up and we got ripped off. Our group's changed anyway—the interests are shifting. The whole constituency of the group, needs, all of it. Sometimes I yearn for dear old changeless Gilboa and a little of that peace. What's happening there with you and Dad?"

"Dad's fine; he hates my work as much as ever, your grandmother charmed everyone at the Fourth of July picnic—" Then, because I can't resist it, I answer what seems to me her unutterable smugness about our lives: "Back in June I was supposed to take a sixty-day suspension, but I did it in ten because even our part of 'society' is speeding up." There is a long silence on the other end, then, "You? Suspended? How come? I thought you were the backbone of that group, second in command and all that."

"Third."

"O.K., third."

"Things don't stay the same anywhere; they change. We change, even in Gilboa."

"I did sound a little superior, didn't I."

"Yes, you did."

"I'm sorry; people have been telling me I do that, and enough of them have told me so I guess it's true. Please, tell me what happened."

"I took a sock at a corpse."

"You *what*?"

"I hit a dead person. Twice. Claude had to pull me off."

There is another long silence. Her voice, when it comes, is quiet. "Was it someone you knew?"

"No, a total stranger."

"A man?"

"Yes."

Another pause. "Did you know anything about him?"

"Only that he was young and resourceful and well-coordinated and a good planner and that he was wearing a hand-knitted cap and gloves."

"Auto accident?"

"Suicide."

Another silence. "A runaway, wasn't it, a boy who looked like Josh."

This time the silence is on my side. She's done what none of them has done, not even Saul, who credited what I did to over-tiredness and some strangers at a party.

"Mother—?"

"I'm sorry—I'm just amazed and a little relieved. Way out there in California I forgot how bright you were."

"We've never talked about Josh—his running away, the religion, all that, and I'm sorry, I just never had the nerve. Did I tell you I visited him there in Illinois?"

"No, when?"

"Eight or nine months ago—no, it was longer than that, a year, I guess. I was at a workshop in Ohio and I dropped in on him."

"What was it like?"

"It was crazy, part of it, everybody dressing up, another art, another language, another diet—like the old-time monasteries in which every single outside tie and experience is purposely cut. Yet—I think he misses the tie a little—maybe more than a little. They're told never to talk about their pasts, but when we were alone, he did. The group has a business, you know—"

"No, I didn't—what is it?"

"They make a kind of apple candy. It's sold locally, but they do rather well."

"Is he part of it, the business, I mean?"

"Yes, and we talked about that some."

I laugh; a business means the world, the English language,

228

bookkeeping, the IRS, reality. "I'm glad you went to see him. It's so painful for us that it's hard to do any more than once a year. It's been about fourteen months since my last visit."

"Go again. You can meet in the candy place, which isn't quite so full of poster gods. Maybe if you could do that, you wouldn't—"

"I wouldn't have to beat up dead strangers—"

"It must have been awful for you—you so hate to lose your cool."

Again I am amazed but not with recognition. Is that the way she sees me? Is that the way the world sees me? Am I so stiff, so prim? I want to remind her in my defense that I weep my way through Yom Kippur, conjure ghosts, live with rebellious past selves, love. "I had no idea—I didn't know you had that picture of me, so rigidly controlled."

"People around here say that I'm the same way. Frankly, I don't know any other way to be when everything else changes with the speed of light."

I am humbled, amazed, stilled. Miriam has never said any of these things to me. I want to tell her that I understand and appreciate what she has said, that I'll respect her doubts, that I have my own, that on our separate thin ice, I want us to be able to reach across to one another and touch, where paradoxically, surer purchase would not have held us. I can say none of this, not yet.

She's going on. "I'm glad you called, Mother. I have a favor to ask."

"Ask away."

"I've got a chance to interview for a job in Chicago—a very good inner-city thing, and I'll need to look around at the whole area before I consider a move. I used to drop Kim off at a commune with friends when I had to spend a few days away, but that's broken up and now there's nowhere. Can I send her to you in Gilboa?"

"Darling, how long have we been asking to have her here?"

"Well, it won't be until fall."

"Why don't you come early and stay for a few days until she's easy here and then go on to your interview?"

"Let me think about it."

"Why did you tell her about your suspension, and that terrible thing? It happened months ago." We are in the kitchen. I am cleaning up after dinner.

"I couldn't stand her picture of us—dear dumb Gilboa full of bourgeois boobs."

"Don't you have any pride?"

"You've heard of the energy crunch—I'm in a pride crunch. I thought I had left that behind when I took up motherhood. Now I'm not so sure. Miriam saw my reasons all the way from California. I don't know why, but her knowledge comforted me. We had a good talk after that. She thinks I hit Joshua that night, stopped trying to understand and just slugged him in absentia. She's been to see him."

"Joshua? When?"

"Soon after we did. She thinks he's not the perfect automaton he's trying to be. She thinks he misses some of what he had here. She sees me as a very different person than I see myself as being. It makes me wonder."

"And Kim—you said she might let us have Kim for a visit—"

"We're second choice, who knows maybe tenth choice, but yes. Miriam always despised the rooted, married, settled part of us, but it's what's left after the communes fold and the Safe House closes. Funny; it was then I told her that way out here in Gilboa, people have passions, get angry, lose their cool, know despair."

"It's what I can't understand," he says, and raises his hands in a gesture Elia used to use. "That even after you were driven to that rage, striking out in the awful pressure of the awful work you do, and suspended, publicly humiliated, here you are still doing it even though you know people are going to wonder about you, wait for you to fall apart again. *Why*, Grace?"

"The pain came from outside the work. I like the work. It's housewife's work, bringing order out of chaos. I'm a good housewife. I learned it in your town, with your family, in your house. And what about you? Even after you fit Lou Epstein into the clothes she wants, all two sizes too small, you still sell clothes."

"Grace, why does Mirele hate us so?"

"I don't think she does. I don't think she ever did."

"Well, why is she indifferent, then?"

"Indifference would never distance itself so far or take so aggressive a stand. I don't know what she feels—I only know she sees us differently than we see ourselves."

"I could never have talked to her about—well, if something had happened to me, I could never have begged that way for her understanding and approval."

I tell him about Mrs. Teller and her two daughters and the pain I felt as I listened to them gabbing away about the commonest details of their lives as they waited to learn whether or not she would have a thumb on her right hand. He hears me out with a small smile on his face. I am washing the dishes as we talk. He is sitting at the kitchen table behind me but I feel his attention. He's very quiet. "Have you seen her since?" he says when I am finished.

"No, I called the hospital the day after, but I haven't run into her anywhere."

"I have. She comes in now and then. She lost the thumb."

"Oh, I'm sorry. What a shame!"

"Well, they took her index finger and moved it somehow and cut the top off and made *it* into a thumb. She says it's like losing a little finger, but she has the use of the hand. She showed me."

"A ride-with-the-punches message if ever I heard one."

"I don't know if I can ride with Miriam's punches."

"You have to go with loss of cool, man. In the modern, liberated world, it's every person for itself. Distinctions are out, parents, children, brothers, sisters, age, sex, gender. Shit's as good as chateaubriand, it's just that most people aren't into shit—"

"Stop talking like that, it scares me."

It scares me too. It's anger at Miriam, at Joshua, at Ben. It's corpse-punching. Why should I be angry at Ben, I wonder? He offered all he had. I was the one who ran after a son, and in the fogs we fought and the blizzards we endured, thought I saw a lover. What if that corpse had punched back? It did. It did. "I'm sorry," I say. "I've been commanded to live part of a people's unlived joy, and instead I'm terrified of possibilities. Miriam was talking about Chicago, *Chicago*, where my folks are, where my cousins are, and a chance for Kim to have family. I guess I was saying all that because I'm afraid it won't happen."

"Is there anything I can do to make you feel better?"

"No, but thank you. I'll need a good long cry at some hugely inopportune time—at the supermarket checkout, for example, touched off by the picture on a can of peas."

For the next few days, Saul walks gingerly, not coming too close, not touching, making no demands. People treat the maimed this way, and the dangerous. Which am I? I feel maimed and who knows the truths I could tell if I put my mind to it?

Slowly, inexorably, Ben goes about unbinding the few lines he has laid here. He has stopped going on most night runs and only when I am going also does he come to the hospital. On the way back we talk about Jewish history, Chelm tales, legends. I tell him the stories my grandfather told me, of the dybbuk and the golem, Bontsche Shweig and Lilith. I tell him about Masada and Baal Shem, but I, too, am casting off the stitches in our fabric and I don't touch at the patterns that underlie it all, the God-wrangle, the paradoxes, that make me celebrate this faith in however incomplete a way. Gilboa's not a town of Jews. Maybe what I say is only an echo—the memory of a vivid voice and not the voice itself. So we are gentle with one another, and gently, softly, we unbind.

A call. It's a heavy August afternoon. I'm in the hammock on the shady side of the house. I had intended to read a long article on fractures but the day overwhelms me. The clouds tower over the trees, the trees tower over my swinging bed. Cradled so, the words on the page soon carry no meaning. I'm half asleep when the tone comes. "Gilboa Fire and Rescue: you have a first aid four miles west on Van Riper. The Bluyot farm." The message repeats.

Bluyot is one of our staples, faithful to a narrowing cycle of accidents and emergencies. He is alcoholic, he has cirrhosis and heart trouble and diabetes and a survivor's wisdoms. Even as volunteers, we have to charge a fee for the support of the ambulance; Bluyot has never paid a single bill, because he knows we must support our indigent. In Gilboa, he's as free as an emperor who never needs cash. He steals from the shopping center because he resents that they won't give him food. In town, he goes from store to store getting day-old cake and stale bread, broken cookies, moldy cheese. He is rural poor, a natural. When sober, he's a tree surgeon, as undependable sober as drunk, but when he wishes, he works well enough to support himself and his numbed wife in those few things he cannot beg or steal. Their children, four boys and two girls, are grown and gone I think to prisons and madhouses the nation round; rooting, wronged and embittered, where they are blown. They resist all solutions. It is, perhaps, the message they were sent with.

Sometimes I wonder if any of us travels more slowly to a Bluyot call. I don't; it's a point of pride with me, vanity, perhaps, that I treat him with all the courtesy and care that I do anyone else. He has announced to the world that he is not like anyone else. He is above the ordinary, or beneath it, but not to be judged by its laws. Perhaps I am obscurely insulting him when I am "professional."

Past Vere the land goes barren. Even in summer the trees are scanty of leaf and spindly and there are gullies cut through the clothing topsoil showing their involved geology, the rock strata crushed and twisted, gaping, like wounds. Here and there, the skeleton of a dead farm lies with its barn-ribs open to the sun or caving in upon its spine. The farms date from the days before the car. They're close to the road, sometimes cut in half by it, house on one side, barn on the other. At the narrowest part of the road, unblessed by a single softening tree, I see Bluyot's house coming up on the left.

In most places in the world, poverty is expressed in barrenness; it is life bleached bare. When, on our golden tour of Jamaica, we passed slums, not even a frayed rag flapped from the wash lines between the houses. Everything available was in use. Bluyot's poverty is American poverty. It is glut. His shack has additions of painted doors stolen from wreckers, tile and brick in patches. There's tar paper covering some of it and the carapaces of old car bodies piled up here and there. In the front lies a field of broken machinery, like a crop, rusted and sprung. I pull up. Larry's here already, but I see him coming from around the house. "I can't raise anyone—where are they?" I go back to the car and sit in it and lean on the horn. Once, twice. Behind me the ambulance slides to a stop.

From an outbuilding, Molly Bluyot comes kicking her way through some sunning cats. "You took your time gettin' here."

"What's happened?" Larry asks.

"He fell," she says simply. She makes a vague gesture in our direction and we follow her into the house.

I almost gag. The oily smell of rats, spoiled food, sweat,

mildew, feet, and an anaerobic rot-smell I cannot place. He's lying half under the kitchen table on his face. We turn him and begin to examine, touching lightly here and there; there is no pulse at the wrist, no eye response, no blood pressure. In a while he opens his eyes himself. "What—"

"You fell, Mr. Bluyot," Larry says. "Tell us what happened."

Bluyot goes from one of us to the other, slowly, with his watery drunk's eyes, puzzled and vacant. If I looked into the blackness of his pupils with an ophthalmoscope, I would see the terrible injuries of his years of alcohol, his diabetes, his ruined heart.

"I can't move," he says; then, "It took me a long time."

"What?"

"Dyin'," he says, and he goes and does it.

For a split second we consider what we could do, the breathing and the I.V., the oxygen, the airway, chest compressions. There isn't enough left to bring him back; there hasn't been for years. In his sixties, he looks eighty. If we begin we are committed to do it all—I put my hands up as though in surrender, and make my statement: "There's no way—" Larry agrees. We check vitals again. Negative. In the instant of our decision I look at his wife. Does she want us to try it all? "Mrs. Bluyot . . ." She shrugs and walks away. Nothing we do either way will make a difference. We call the police for the coroner.

We cover Bluyot and there is a barely concealed rush to get out of the fetid house. I want to comfort the widow; it is what is done back there in civilization, but she has gone away into the maze of outbuildings. Ben has come and Ellie. We send the ambulance back and I tell everyone to go. I have the time.

After the ambulance leaves, I see that Ben has stayed behind. I sit beside him on the bleached and warping steps as though we were the owners of this shambles, taking our ease in the shaded overhang of the roof. For a long time we do not speak, preferring to lose ourselves in the summer pulse, crickets in the dry grass, bird chirps, the wars of insect armies fighting at the foundations of the house.

"I'll have been here almost a year," he says, "a long stay for me, the longest since college."

"A good year, I hope." We smile. I can't remember the last time I felt such keen gratitude. He's like the sunshine, warmth unearned, like a field of blackberries to a hot and tired hiker. I measure our moments the way happy people measure the days of their vacations—without greed.

"Something's changed in me," he says, "for the worse, I guess. When I was in college, all this would have meant something different to me; a man dead in there of poverty and despair—a social calamity really. I should be angry; in college, I would have been demanding the changes that would prevent this poverty."

"What is the price for preventing this and the drunken children on the highways?"

"I don't know. Gilboa's a nice town, a good town, and you couldn't keep Bluyot from being the way he is."

"In the ideal planned society, Bluyot's kids would have been taken by the state and you would not have been allowed to light in this town and strike lights in the Longhill kids and lights in me, and then to fly away again." What a joy it is to tell him all this without hesitation or fear.

"Only part of me wants to fly. Star is getting demanding and I see how little I can really do for those kids."

"I think you've done a great deal for them, and for the town. Tell the other teachers at Longhill to keep bringing the kids to our Christmas parties and our Fourths of July."

"O.K., and you don't have to sit so far away," Ben says; "you've made the decision and I'll honor it, but we can touch."

"What I am trying to do is to climb into objectivity."

"It is still an uphill climb?"

"Would you have it otherwise?" We grin at each other and

then I move close and we sit contented in the sun, wishing to be nowhere but where we are. Now and then we murmur something to one another. "The kids used to run after him and tease him. They called him Blue Yo-Yo."

"Why did you go into this work?"

"What do you do with mother love and mother wit when the babies are grown and gone away?"

"Most of the people in fire-rescue are men."

"What you did with the kids—was it fathering or mothering?" He smiles.

"I'll be sorry to leave here. Summer's almost over. That weed's turned red."

"Yes, it's always the first. Violet used to call it harbinger."

"How is Riva?"

"Her official training will soon be finished. In some ways she's never been so free, but the fine tunings of her relationships will all have to be done over."

"I suppose so."

"Remember our people."

Old neighbors, old friends, we sit on Bluyot's slanting, weather-warped steps, and wait for the coroner.

19

I'm at the Pinecrest shopping center weighting my cart with holiday food. Ben will be leaving the week after Rosh Hashanah. Then he will be gone. Last night, coming home from a run, I told him about the ghosts—not how I conjure them or about their commandment, but that I think of them now rather than during that day in May put aside for their memorial. It's now, when the first harvests come in and the summer's end weighs heavy in the bins and baskets at the supermarket, that a sifting of ash comes to drift on the sweet wind and blow through the shopping malls. The season of memory and memorial. The Days of Awe. He asked me then why I think of them so much—the Holocaust comes up often in my conversation and to him it's as antique as the time of Pharaoh. He fears what he interprets and what others have told him was the passivity, acquiescence of the victims in their own murder. In the darkness of the ambulance I didn't seem as old as someone who would remember the first pictures and the first names of the opened charnel houses, and before that tattooed escapees, knocking on doors all over the world crying out that there existed such places and not being believed. The nightmare has conditioned my thinking ever after; it's the metaphor of evil that separates my generation from others with other metaphors. I've judged other wars through the prisms of that one and mistaken those wars, it turns out. And the loss, the unutterable loss—the "hemorrhage, yes, you told me about that."

In the dark, I heard his voice go cold. He'd been assaulted by the crudity of my biochemical images. The biochemistry is insulting, I suppose, because it is so neutral. His feelings wage war against that neutrality, acid balances and synapses, pumps and tubes that fill and refill. Praising the miracle of will, personality, choice, freedom, self, he walks past the simpler one of his own body. What is "natural" is unthinking. He expects the faithful engines to move—secret and silent forever. What a generation gap that is!

I wonder how the camp people felt about their bodies. Did they curse them for living when their owners wanted to die? Did they see them working in spite of blows, exposure, and starvation with a kind of awe, or a rage at God for what He had made so well for survival, come what may? I read accounts of the Camps and I learned that many of the people there rose and fell in the small wheel of each day and in the great wheel of each year with as many of the blessings and activities of our busy faith as they could make. They said the prayer that welcomes the new day, with fringes made in secret and worn in secret; they gave the traditional thanks for the first new leaf of the first tree of spring, a spring even the tyrant could not withhold from them. I want to tell Ben that although I am as fortunate and free as they were starved and imprisoned, my need has come to be the same as theirs, it's a need that transcends theology. It's a need for form, a rhythm of holidays and observances that celebrates goodness in the minutest, most practical ways— the structure of the year in special foods and observances, the rhythm of cleaning and baking, a structure, however maimed and compromised, in which I live. For which, God help me, I have no words.

"Why did you laugh just then?" Ben had said.

"I was thinking of how little you liked my hemorrhage meta-phor and how hard it must be for you to understand my fears for our people."

"You've taught me a lot. Haven't I taught you to be less afraid?"

"Wouldn't that be nice!" We both laugh.

"I'd like to leave you with that," he says.

"I'd like you to get the things I remember—I would heap you with riches—I would give you Violet Cleve, if I could, and my father's father, and my cousin Terry, who died in the war—I wanted—I have so much—"

"You've given me so much already—"

"I'm telling you you're going to be missed; the keenest pain there is besides homesickness and loss by death. You want meaning—there it is."

"You wanted to make a better Jew of me—"

"God created everything including the minds that doubt His existence. Am I wiser than God?"

"You're more believable."

"But He's taller."

After Rosh Hashanah, on the first of the Days of Awe, I write a letter to Joshua.

My part of God is a God of Laws and of a universe of order. Your part of God is a God of Laws and of a universe of order. I had forgotten that. Jewish Law commands me during this week of Judgment to beg the forgiveness of anyone I have wronged in thought or deed during the year. I believe I have wronged you in a way I'm not even sure of. Perhaps last year or the year before but certainly this year, when you were following the dictates of your conscience. I am asking your forgiveness and am giving you, without any other condition or qualification, mine. If someday you will be able to visit us, we would be very happy to see you. If someday we may visit you, we will be very happy to make the trip.

I call Miriam to plan Kimberley's visit. The workshop is coming closer, excitement is building. Upper-class feminists won't be leading things this time, she says. The poor will have the floor and run the meeting and Third World representatives will be there. Then, right after that there's the interview—Chicago. In the middle of her conversation, she stops. "Mother, Kim is so small to be going across the country and changing planes—"

"You're right. Come to Philadelphia and we'll be waiting for you there," I say. I've never heard maternal worry from Miriam and it warms me.

"I'll be bringing some of her schoolwork with her. Please see that she does it. They're very particular at that school."

I am dumbfounded. I had imagined Kimberley—Kim—in a ghetto school with the deprived children of Miriam's women's group. I ask about the school.

"I wanted an integrated school. The only really integrated one here is the University experimental school. The standards are very high."

"Tell me one thing I need to know. Kimberley will be here around Succos time. I want to take her to a celebration and share it with her, but I don't want to do it like an anthropological expedition. Does she know she's Jewish?"

"Well, not 'til recently, but the Jewish children in her class have been inviting her to various things—"

"Oh," I say, "then it will be all right with you?"

"Yes, I suppose so. About what you told me—the squad—are things O.K.?"

"It'll take time. They'll have to see I'm all right—"

"That may take *years!*"

"Not really. In the work we do, time speeds up. One year, I think."

I say good-bye and hang up the phone and cry aloud to the Yom Kippur ghosts. "Do we have another generation in us? Can Saul and Riva and I stand together and see ahead into the fog, the outline of a generation that will remember us?"

Ben is gone. There's a hole in the night when the calls come, a place vacant where he should have been standing, a yawning lack in the squad that now has only what there was before he came. When the phone rings, it can only be one of them or someone from town or someone who isn't Ben. He haunts the streets where he jogged and the firehouse and the road between here and Longhill. Is love the less because it's understood? Is loss the less because the world is full of other people? Sometimes in the afternoons I sit up in Miriam's room, which has been made ready for Kimberley weeks in advance, and grieve there because the pain of Ben's leaving has no other outlet. Rita, who knew and would have understood, has gotten a job in Tarrant. She thinks of us and her three years with us as an illness from which she has been delivered, a hot, hectic illness full of fevered action and hallucination in which the lights flashed and the sirens screamed. I know that part of my aching loss of Ben is "light of the fire," the drama that makes death-house inmates the recipients of love letters. Larger than life we stood against the wreckage—I remember the little sports car chewed up under the tractor and the dead man impaled on the harrow; his first corpse. The wisdom of my time teaches no mother-need, no family beyond its babies. I needed something from the young that wasn't pain. I got a joy so keen it feels like pain. Now the joy and the pain have taken themselves away and only the auto wrecks and the literally broken hearts remain.

And on the third day after Rosh Hashanah, I see my ghosts

242